Further praise for Wealth Management Planning

"A comprehensive bang-up-to-date tour de force with practical examples to help and guide with all tax problems for the international client with UK connections. My copy is to be kept by my desk at all times."
Stephen Arthur, Barrister, Lincoln's Inn

"This book gives comprehensive coverage to the complicated subject of taxation for Financial Planners. Many clients increasingly have diverse and complex needs often spanning different fiscal regimes and to meet their goals and objectives need a greater level of support. This book will be very valuable to all those Financial Planners who wish to extend their learning and reference and desire to meet the needs of such clients."
Nick Cann, Chief Executive of the Institute of Financial Planning

"In this book, Malcolm Finney presents a comprehensive summary of the UK tax rules in straightforward language and with many practical examples. It is a notable achievement to put incomprehensible tax legislation into such readily understandable terms; anyone advising on wealth management will find this to be an invaluable guide to the subject."
Malcolm Gunn, Consultant, Squire, Sanders & Dempsey LLP

"The author demonstrates considerable skill in explaining complicated tax rules in a manner that makes them easy to assimilate and understand. The everyday, 'jargon free' language of this book, coupled with the lack of references to legislation, make it very easy to read and digest. The book contains chapter summaries, useful appendices and numerous worked examples, which provide a very clear, helpful explanation of some difficult tax rules. The book's contents cover wide areas of the tax system, and yet provide sufficient technical depth to be a valuable point of reference for those involved in wealth management and financial planning."
Mark McLaughlin, CTA, Mark McLaughlin Associates

"A valuable new text explaining the tax treatment applicable to financial planning products and strategies for UK domiciled persons (UK resident or expats) and non domiciled UK residents. This book will be of interest to a wide readership ranging from students of law and tax, the interested layman seeking in depth knowledge and professionals including solicitors, accountants, financial planners, private bankers and trustees. Although there are more detailed specialist textbooks on individual subjects covered in this volume such as trusts or non domiciliaries, the value of this book is it brings all elements of personal financial planning together in one volume and is written in a lucid clear style with practical examples included at every step to illustrate the points being made. Of particular interest is the updated coverage including the complex rules on inheritance tax and trusts in FA 2006 and non domiciliaries in FA 2008. Malcolm is to be commended on distilling a vast amount of detailed material into a logical and well ordered framework."
Andrew Penney, Managing Director, Rothschild Trust Corporation Ltd

"Malcolm Finney's book is stimulating, innovative and refreshingly practical. Anyone wanting either a high-level understanding of tax principles involved in wealth management or a deeper insight should read this book."
Jacob Rigg, Head of Policy, Society of Trust and Estate Practitioners, STEP Worldwide

Wealth Management Planning

The UK Tax Principles

Malcolm James Finney

WILEY

A John Wiley and Sons, Ltd, Publication

Copyright © 2008   John Wiley & Sons Ltd, The Atrium, Southern Gate, Chichester,
West Sussex PO19 8SQ, England

Telephone   (+44) 1243 779777

Email (for orders and customer service enquiries): cs-books@wiley.co.uk
Visit our Home Page on www.wiley.com

All Rights Reserved. No part of this publication may be reproduced, stored in a retrieval system or transmitted in any form or by any means, electronic, mechanical, photocopying, recording, scanning or otherwise, except under the terms of the Copyright, Designs and Patents Act 1988 or under the terms of a licence issued by the Copyright Licensing Agency Ltd, Saffron House, 6-10 Kirby Street, London, ECIN 8TS, UK, without the permission in writing of the Publisher. Requests to the Publisher should be addressed to the Permissions Department, John Wiley & Sons Ltd, The Atrium, Southern Gate, Chichester, West Sussex PO19 8SQ, England, or emailed to permreq@wiley.co.uk, or faxed to (+44) 1243 770620.

Designations used by companies to distinguish their products are often claimed as trademarks. All brand names and product names used in this book are trade names, service marks, trademarks or registered trademarks of their respective owners. The Publisher is not associated with any product or vendor mentioned in this book.

This publication is designed to provide accurate and authoritative information in regard to the subject matter covered. It is sold on the understanding that the Publisher is not engaged in rendering professional services. If professional advice or other expert assistance is required, the services of a competent professional should be sought.

Other Wiley Editorial Offices

John Wiley & Sons Inc., 111 River Street, Hoboken, NJ 07030, USA

Jossey-Bass, 989 Market Street, San Francisco, CA 94103-1741, USA

Wiley-VCH Verlag GmbH, Boschstr. 12, D-69469 Weinheim, Germany

John Wiley & Sons Australia Ltd, 42 McDougall Street, Milton, Queensland 4064, Australia

John Wiley & Sons (Asia) Pte Ltd, 2 Clementi Loop #02-01, Jin Xing Distripark, Singapore 129809

John Wiley & Sons Canada Ltd, 6045 Freemont Blvd, Mississauga, ONT, L5R 4J3, Canada

Wiley also publishes its books in a variety of electronic formats. Some content that appears in print may not be available in electronic books.

Library of Congress Cataloging-in-Publication Data

Finney, Malcolm.
  Wealth management planning : the UK tax principles / Malcolm Finney.
    p. cm.
  Includes bibliographical references and index.
  ISBN 978-0-470-72424-8 (cloth)
  1. Wealth tax—Law and legislation—Great Britain. 2. Income tax—Law and legislation—Great Britain.
  3. Capital gains tax—Law and legislation—Great Britain. 4. Inheritance and transfer tax—Law and legislation—Great Britain. 5. Tax planning—Great Britain. I. Title.
  KD5533.F56 2008
  343.4106'2—dc22
                                                                                                2008047073

British Library Cataloguing in Publication Data

A catalogue record for this book is available from the British Library

ISBN 978-0-470-72424-8 (H/B)

Typeset in 11/13pt Times by Integra Software Services Pvt. Ltd, Pondicherry, India
Printed and bound in Great Britain by CPI   Antony Rowe, Chippenham, Wiltshire

This book is dedicated to my late mother, Audrey Finney,
and my late father, Alfred James Finney

DISCLAIMER

The views expressed herein are exclusively those of the author. Neither the author nor the publisher can accept any responsibility for any loss occasioned as a result of any action taken by any person in reliance upon the contents hereof however such loss may arise. No comments made herein should be construed as offering advice. Independent professional advice should always be taken.

Contents

About the Author	xxvii
Preface	xxix
Abbreviations	xxxiii
PART ONE: THE BUILDING BLOCKS	**1**
1 Tax Systems and their Bases of Taxation	**3**
Background	3
Categories of Tax	4
Capital v. Income Distinction	5
Worldwide v. Territorial Tax Systems	5
(a) Income and Capital Gains Taxes	5
Worldwide Basis	6
Territorial Basis	6
Territorial Basis plus Remittances	6
Residency	6
Citizenship Test	6
Source Basis	7
(b) Inheritance Tax	8
Trailing Tax Imposition	9
Summary	9
2 UK Taxation: An Overview	**11**
Background	11
Domicile, Residence and Ordinary Residence	11
Domiciled Individual	11
Non-domiciled Individual	12
Persons Other Than Individuals	13
UK Taxes and Law	13

Capital v. Income Distinction	14
Rates of Tax (2008/09)	15
Income Tax	15
Capital Gains Tax	17
Inheritance Tax	18
Allowances	18
Tax Returns	19
Income and Capital Gains Tax	19
Inheritance Tax	19
Timing of Tax Payments	20
Income and Capital Gains Tax	20
Inheritance Tax	20
Summary	20
3 Domicile	**21**
Background	21
Concept of Private International Law Not Taxation	21
English/Welsh, Scottish or Northern Irish	23
Importance of Domicile for UK Tax Purposes	24
Categories of Domicile	25
Domicile of Origin	26
(i) Legitimate v. Illegitimate Child	26
(ii) Father Dead at Date of Birth	27
(iii) Parents Married but Separated	27
(iv) Legitimation	27
(v) Loss of Domicile of Origin	28
(vi) Resurrection of the Domicile of Origin	28
(vii) Adoption	29
Domicile of Dependence	30
(i) Children and Domicile of Dependence	31
(ii) Married Women and Domicile of Dependence	32
Domicile of Choice	35
(i) Misleading Nature of the Word "Choice"	36
(ii) Age Requirement	38
(iii) Two Basic Requirements	38
Non-UK Domiciled Individuals Spending Significant Time in the UK	51
UK Domiciled Individuals Failing to Acquire Non-UK Domiciles of Choice	55
UK Domiciled Individuals Successfully Acquiring Non-UK Domiciles of Choice	58
Abandonment of a Domicile of Choice	65
Special Categories of Individual and Domicile of Choice	67

	(i) Individuals of Ill Health	68
	(ii) Employees	68
	(iii) Member of the Armed Forces	69
	(iv) Diplomats	69
	Deemed UK Domicile	69
	(i) Three-year Rule	69
	(ii) 17 Out of 20 Tax Year Rule	70
	(iii) 15 Tax Years Plus Two-Day Trap	70
	(iv) Dealing with Deemed UK Domicile Status	71
	(a) Avoidance	72
	(b) Plan Accordingly	72
	(c) "Split" Domicile	72
	(d) International Dimension	73
	Summary	73
4	**Residence and Ordinary Residence**	**75**
	Background	75
	Lack of Definitions and IR20	75
	Dual Residence	76
	Split Tax Years	76
	Income Tax	77
	Capital Gains Tax	78
	Temporary Non-UK Residence	79
	Capital Gains Tax	79
	Income Tax	80
	Residence Rules and IR20	81
	Short Absences	81
	The 183-day Rule	81
	Arriving and Departing the UK	82
	Arriving in the UK	82
	Departing from the UK	87
	Summary	90
5	**Residence, Ordinary Residence and Domicile: Some Practical Points**	**91**
	Background	91
	The Tax Return	91
	Domicile	93
	Claim for the Remittance Basis to Apply	94
	IHT Return	95
	Domicile and Residence Rulings	95
	Domicile Ruling	96
	Residence Ruling	96
	Summary	98

6	**Income Source and Asset Situs**	**99**
	Background	99
	Income Source	99
	Rental Income	99
	Dividends	100
	Authorised and Unauthorised Unit Trusts	100
	Authorised	100
	Unauthorised	100
	Interest	101
	Mutual (Offshore) Funds	101
	Asset Situs	101
	Inheritance Tax	102
	Tangible Property	102
	Registered Shares	102
	Bearer Shares	102
	Intangible Property	102
	Ordinary Debts	102
	Speciality Debt	102
	Bank Accounts	102
	Unit Trusts	103
	Nominees	103
	Life Policies	104
	Capital Gains Tax	104
	Tangible Property	104
	Registered Shares	104
	Bearer Shares	104
	Ordinary Debts	105
	Unit Trusts	109
	Life Policies	109
	Summary	109
7	**The Principles and Implications of Joint Tenancy and Tenancy in Common Ownership for Spouses and Non-Spouses**	**111**
	Background	111
	Legal Title	111
	Beneficial Ownership	111
	Land	113
	Legal Title	113
	Equitable Interests	113
	Tax Issues	114
	Inheritance Tax	115
	Income Tax	116

Spouse Joint Ownership	116
Non-spouse Joint Ownership	117
Capital Gains Tax	118
Spouse Joint Ownership	118
Non-spouse Joint Ownership	118
Non-UK domiciled Individual	118
Spouses	119
Summary	121

PART TWO: THE MAJOR TAXES   123

8   Capital Gains Tax   125

Background	125
Basics	126
Inter-spouse Transfers	127
Calculating the Tax	129
Annual Exemption	129
Payment of the Tax	130
Year of Death	130
Pre FA 2008 Reliefs	131
Indexation Allowance	132
Taper Relief	134
Business Asset	136
Taper Relief and Share Sales	136
Gifts of Assets (not Inter-Spouse)	138
Non-resident Recipient	139
Precipitation of an Immediate Inheritance Tax Charge	139
Business Assets	142
Effect of Gift Relief	142
Non-UK Situs Assets	144
Impact of FA 2008	145
Introduction of New 18% Rate; Abolition of Indexation Allowance and Taper Relief	145
Higher Rate Taxpayer	146
Employees Owning Shares in the Employer Company	149
Sole Trader	149
Buy to Let	149
"Banking" the Indexation Allowance/Taper Relief	150
Capital Losses	152
UK Domiciled and UK Resident Individual Capital Loss Utilisation	152
(1) Connected Person Capital Losses	154
Non-UK Domiciled and UK Resident Individual Capital Loss Utilisation	154

(1) Overseas Capital Loss Utilisation for the Non-UK Domiciled but UK Resident Individual pre FA 2008	154
(2) Overseas Capital Loss Utilisation for the Non-UK Domiciled but UK Resident Individual post FA 2008	155
Entrepreneur Relief	162
Disposal of the Whole or Part of a Business	162
Disposal of One or More Assets in Use for the Purposes of the Business at the Time at Which the Business Ceases to be Carried on	163
Disposal of One or More Assets Consisting of Shares or Securities of a Company	163
Disposal Qualifying as an "Associated" Disposal	163
Relevant Business Assets	164
Claim for, and Amount of, Relief	164
Offshore Companies	165
Leaving/Arriving in the UK	167
Summary	168

9 Inheritance Tax: The Basics — 169

Background	169
Territorial	170
Domicile	170
Deemed UK Domicile	170
Rates of Inheritance Tax	171
Lifetime Gifts	172
Chargeable Lifetime Transfer (CLT)	172
Potentially Exempt Transfer (PET)	173
Quantum of a Transfer of Value	173
Taper Relief	175
PET	175
CLT	176
Seven-year Cumulation Period	177
Lifetime	177
CLTs Only	177
CLTs and PETs	179
Persons Responsible for Payment of Inheritance Tax and "Grossing up" on Lifetime Transfers	179
CLTs	179
Additional Inheritance Tax Liability	180
Grossing up	180
PETs	182
Death Estate	182
Assets	182

	Assets Beneficially Owned	182
	Gifts with Reservation	183
	Qualifying Interests in Possession	184
	Assets not Forming Part of the Death Estate	185
	Liabilities	185
	Reliefs	187
	Rate on Death and the NRB	187
	Death Estate	188
	Payment and the Bearing of Inheritance Tax on Death	188
	Payment of Inheritance Tax on Death	188
	Bearing of the Inheritance Tax Charge on Death	190
	Gifts with Reservation	190
	Qualifying Interests in Possession	190
	Beneficial Asset Entitlement	191
	Specific Gifts Bear Their Own Inheritance Tax on Death	193
	Inheritance Tax Liabilities on the Lifetime Transfers	194
	Inheritance Tax Liabilities on the Lifetime Transfers Due to Death	195
	Death Estate	196
	Planning Considerations: Initial Thoughts	197
	Summary	198
10	**Inheritance Tax: Exemptions and Reliefs**	**199**
	Background	199
	Exempt Transfers	199
	Lifetime only Exempt Transfers	200
	Annual Exemption	200
	Normal Expenditure Out of Income Exemption	201
	Gifts in Contemplation of Marriage Exemption	202
	Gifts for Family Maintenance Exemption	203
	Death only Exempt Transfers	203
	Transfers in Lifetime or on Death Exemptions	203
	Inter-spouse Transfers	203
	Inter-spouse Transferable NRB	204
	Miscellaneous Exemptions	209
	Ordering of Exemptions	209
	Reliefs	210
	BPR	211
	Relevant Business Property	211
	Businesses not Qualifying	212
	Pro-rata BPR	213
	Ownership Requirements	214
	Inter-spouse Transfers	216
	BPR and Death within Seven Years of a Transfer	217

	Order of Transfers	219
	Settled Business Property	220
	Pre 22 March 2006 Created Interest in Possession Trust	220
	Post 22 March 2006 Created Interest in Possession Trust	220
	Discretionary Trusts	221
	Agricultural Property Relief	221
	Ownership Requirements	222
	APR and Death within Seven Years of a Transfer	222
	Quick Succession Relief	222
	Summary	223
11	**Inheritance Tax: Gifts with Reservation**	**225**
	Background	225
	Exemptions	228
	Exemptions	228
	Inter-spouse Gifts	228
	Full Consideration	228
	Co-ownership	228
	Trusts	229
	Pre-Owned Assets	229
	Summary	231
12	**Inheritance Tax: Excluded Property**	**233**
	Background	233
	Non-settled Property	233
	Settled Property	233
	Excluded Property and the Non-UK Domiciled	234
	Non-UK Situs Property	235
	Minimum Length of Time to Hold Assets	236
	UK Situs Assets	236
	Authorised Unit Trusts (AUT) and Open Ended Investment Companies (OEIC)	236
	UK Government Securities or Gilts	236
	Foreign Currency UK Bank Accounts	238
	Channel Islands and the Isle of Man	238
	Settled Property	239
	UK Situs Trust Assets	241
	AUTs and OEICs	242
	UK Government Securities and Gilts	242
	Foreign Currency UK Bank Accounts	242
	Mixing UK Situs and Non-UK Situs Property in a Trust	242
	Excluded Property and Gifts with Reservation	243
	"Excluded Property Trusts" and FA 2006	244
	Summary	245

13	**Inheritance Tax Administration**	**247**
	Background	247
	Lifetime Transfers	247
	CLT	247
	PET	247
	Excepted Transfers	248
	Excepted Settlements	248
	Death Estate	249
	Excepted Estates	249
	Low Value Estates	249
	Exempt Estates	250
	Foreign Domiciliaries	251
	Transferable NRB	251
	"D" Forms	251
	Clearance Certificate	251
	Penalties	252
	Non-UK Resident Trusts	252
	Obtaining Information	252
	Summary	252
	PART THREE: TRUSTS	**253**
14	**Trusts: An Overview**	**255**
	Background	255
	The Trust	255
	Equity	257
	Trusts Today	257
	Protection of Minors	257
	Bankruptcy Protection	258
	Will Substitute	258
	Tax Aspects	258
	Discretionary Trust	258
	Interest in Possession Trust	259
	Lifetime and Will Trusts	259
	Summary	259
15	**Inheritance Tax: Trusts**	**261**
	Background	261
	Discretionary Trusts	261
	Exit Charge before the First 10-year Charge	262
	Ten-year Charge	263
	Interest in Possession Trusts	265
	Immediate Post Death Interest (IPDI)	266
	Transitional Serial Interest (TSI)	267

Accumulation and Maintenance Trusts (A & M)	268
Discretionary v. Interest in Possession Trust	268
Pre FA 2006	268
Post FA 2006	269
"Excluded Property" Trusts and Domicile	270
Summary	270

16 UK Resident Trusts: Income and Capital Gains Taxation   271

Background	271
UK Resident v. Non-UK Resident Trusts	272
Pre 6 April 2007	272
Capital Gains Tax	272
Income Tax	272
Post 5 April 2007	272
FA 2008 Impact	273
Income Tax	274
Capital Gains Tax	274
Income Tax	274
Discretionary (and Accumulation and Maintenance) Trusts	275
Interest in Possession Trusts	275
Beneficiaries	276
Discretionary Beneficiaries	276
UK Resident Beneficiary	276
Non-UK Resident Beneficiary	277
Interest in Possession Beneficiaries	278
UK Resident Beneficiary	278
Non-UK Resident Beneficiary	279
Capital v. Income	279
Capital Gains Tax	280
Pre FA 2008	280
Post FA 2008	280
Anti-avoidance Provisions	281
Income Tax	281
Settlor Interested Trusts	282
Discretionary Trust	283
Interest in Possession Trust	283
Income of Trust Paid to or for Benefit of Unmarried	
Minor	284
Bare Trusts for Unmarried Minors	285
Capital Payments to the Settlor	285
Capital Gains Tax	286
Settlor Interested Trusts post FA 2008	286
Settlor Interested Trusts pre FA 2008	286

UK Resident Trust for Non-UK Domiciled but UK Resident Individuals	287
Income Tax	287
Capital Gains Tax	288
Inheritance Tax	288
UK Resident Trust for UK Domiciled and UK Resident Individuals	288
Income Tax	288
Capital Gains Tax	289
Inheritance Tax	289
Summary	290

17 Non-UK Resident Trusts: Income and Capital Gains Taxation — 291

Background	291
FA 2008 Impact	291
Income Tax	292
Capital Gains Tax	292
Income Tax	293
Discretionary Trusts	293
Interest in Possession Trusts	294
Beneficiaries of the Non-UK Resident Discretionary Trust	295
Anti-avoidance Provisions	296
Settlor Interested Rules: Income Tax	297
Sections 720 and 731 ITA 2007	297
Settlor Interested Rules: Capital Gains Tax	301
Section 87 TCGA 1992 (Charge on Beneficiaries)	303
Transitional Provisions	308
"Washing out"	310
Offshore Income Gains	311
Interaction of the Various Apportionment Rules with Respect to "Capital Payments"	314
Non-UK Resident Trusts for Non-UK Domiciled but UK Resident Individuals	314
Income Tax	314
Capital Gains Tax	315
Inheritance Tax	316
Non-UK Resident Trusts for UK Domiciled and UK Resident Individuals	316
Income Tax	316
Capital Gains Tax	318
Inheritance Tax	319
Summary	319

PART FOUR: INVESTMENTS AND PROPERTY — 321

18 Investments — 323

Background — 323
Deposit-based Investments — 323
Money Market Accounts — 324
Fixed Interest Securities — 325
Shares (Including AIM Shares)/Options — 325
  Ordinary Shares — 325
  Zero Coupon Preference Shares — 327
  Alternative Investment Market (AIM) Shares — 327
Individual Savings Accounts (ISAs) — 327
  Post FA 2008 — 328
    Self-select ISAs — 328
  Pre April 2008 — 329
    Maxi ISA — 329
    Mini ISA — 329
Packaged/Insurance Investments — 329
  Term and Whole of Life Assurance Policies — 329
    Term Assurance — 329
  Whole of Life Assurance — 330
    Husband and Wife — 330
  Single Premium Bonds — 330
Venture Capital Trusts (VCTs) and Enterprise Investment Schemes (EISs) — 336
  Enterprise Investment Scheme — 336
    Income Tax Relief — 337
    Capital Gains Tax Relief — 337
  Venture Capital Trust — 338
    Income Tax Relief — 338
    Capital Gains Tax Relief — 338
  Chargeable Gains Deferment Possibilities (EIS only) — 338
Collective Investments — 339
Offshore Funds — 339
  Tax Treatment — 340
    Distributor/Reporting Status Offshore Fund — 340
    Non-distributor Status Offshore Fund — 341
  Irish Offshore Funds — 342
Structured Products — 342
Limited Partnerships — 343
  Private Equity Funds — 343
  Property Funds — 344
Limited Liability Partnerships (LLPs) — 344

	Real Estate Investment Trusts (REITs)	344
	Self-invested Personal Pensions (SIPPs)	344
	Summary	344

19 Main Residence or Home — 347
Background — 347
Capital Gains Tax — 348
   Overview — 348
      Two or More Residences of the Individual — 348
      Non-UK Property — 348
      Married Couple and Cohabitees — 349
      Total v. Partial Capital Gains Tax Exemption — 349
      Profit Motive — 351
Residence — 351
Deemed Periods of Residence — 351
More Than One Residence — 352
   Electing Main Residence — 353
   Planning and the Election — 354
Married Couples — 355
Inter-spouse Transfers — 356
Lettings Relief — 357
Trusts and Sole or Main Residence — 358
Death and Sole or Main Residence — 359
Inheritance Tax — 360
   Lifetime Planning — 361
      Joint Ownership Arrangements — 361
      Cash Gift — 362
      Sale — 363
      Gift plus Rent Payable — 363
      General Comments — 364
   Death Planning — 364
Summary — 366

20 Non-UK Domiciliaries and UK Homes — 367
Background — 367
Ownership — 367
   Individual — 367
   Non-UK Resident Trust — 368
   Non-UK Registered Company — 369
Financing the Acquisition — 370
Preliminary Conclusions — 370
Summary — 371

21	**Stamp Duty and Stamp Duty Land Tax**	**373**
	Background	373
	Stamp Duty/Stamp Duty Reserve Tax	373
	Stamp Duty Land Tax	374
	Matrimonial Home	374
	Purchase of House plus Chattels	375
	No Consideration	375
	Linked Transactions	376
	Matrimonial Breakdown	376
	Trusts	377
	Interest of Beneficiaries	377
	Appointments	377
	Non-UK Resident Trusts	377
	Bare Trusts	378
	Death	378
	Instruments of Variation	378
	Life Policies	378
	Summary	379
	PART FIVE: THE INTERNATIONAL DIMENSION	**381**
22	**Non-UK Resident Taxation**	**383**
	Background	383
	General Rules	383
	Income Tax	383
	Capital Gains Tax	384
	Inheritance Tax	384
	Types of UK Source Income	384
	Trading Income	385
	Property Income	385
	Employment Income	385
	Savings Income: Interest and Dividends	385
	Interest	386
	Dividends	386
	Some Points to Note	387
	Summary	387
23	**Accessing Offshore Monies: The Non-UK Domiciled Perspective**	**389**
	Background	389
	Categories of Non-UK Domiciled Individual	390
	Consequences of A Claim	393
	£30 000 Charge	395

Nomination	395
Where no Claim is Necessary	401
Remittances to the UK	401
Alienation of Income and Gains and Asset Purchase	403
Conditions A/B	403
Condition C	404
Condition D	404
Extensions of the Definition of "Remittance to the UK" for Each of Conditions A/B, C and D	404
Conditions A/B	405
Condition C	407
Condition D	408
Transitional Provisions (pre 6 April 2008 Income/Gains)	408
Income or Gains (Other than RFI) Arising pre 6 April 2008	408
RFI Arising pre 6 April 2008	409
Pre 12 March 2008 Condition	410
Pre 6 April 2008 Condition	410
General Transitional Rule	412
"Relevant Debt" and "UK Services"	413
Exempt Property	415
Clothing, etc. and the "Personal Use Rule"	415
Property Below £1000 Rule	416
Temporary Importation Rule	416
Repair Rule	417
Property and Public Access Rule	417
Exempt to non-Exempt Property	417
Offshore Income Gains	418
Mixed Funds	419
(i) Arising Basis and Remittance Basis Mixed Income	420
(ii) Income and Capital Gains Taxable on Remittance	420
(iii) Tax-free Capital and Remittance of Taxable Income	420
(iv) Tax-free Capital and Taxable Chargeable Gains	420
Segregation of Income and Capital Gains	422
Gifts of Assets Precipitating Foreign Chargeable Gains	424
Cessation of Source	425
Offshore Mortgages	426
Grandfathering Provisions	427
Loans Secured on Property: IHT Impact	428
Loans Secured on Property: Capital Gains Tax Impact	428
Temporary Non-UK Residents	428
Income Tax	428
Capital Gains Tax	430
Summary	431

24	**The Offshore Dimension**	**433**
	Background	433
	The Offshore Financial Centre	434
	Offshore Financial Centre Vehicles	438
	Companies	438
	Trusts	439
	Offshore Financial Centre Uses	442
	Tax Planning	442
	Probate Mitigation/Will Substitute	442
	Asset Protection	443
	Choosing an Offshore Financial Centre	443
	UK Tax and Information Disclosure Requirements	445
	Tax Exposure of Trust Settlor	446
	Relocation to an OFC	447
	Summary	448
25	**International Taxation**	**449**
	Background	449
	Double Taxation	449
	Double Tax Agreements	450
	Income and Capital Gains Tax Agreements	450
	Inheritance Tax Agreements	452
	Pre 1975 Agreements	453
	Post 1975 Agreements	454
	European Union/Community	456
	EU Savings Directive	456
	Background	456
	Savings Income	457
	"Interest" only	457
	Information Exchange	457
	Withholding Tax	458
	Withholding Tax v. Information Supply	458
	Non-Member States and TIEAs	459
	Switzerland and the USA	459
	Savings Directive and Directive 77/799/EEC	460
	Implications of the Savings Directive	460
	Human Rights	462
	Summary	463
	PART SIX: WILLS, PROBATE AND TAX ISSUES	**465**
26	**Wills**	**467**
	Background	467
	Requirements for Valid Will	467

Types of Will	468
Marriage	469
Separation/Divorce	469
Revocation	469
Intestacy	470
Types of Gift	470
Failure of Gift	470
Survivorship Clause	471
Witnessing the Will	474
Capacity to Inherit	474
UK "Forced Heirship"	474
Foreign Aspects	475
Succession	476
Capacity	477
Formal Validity	477
Material Validity	477
Construction	477
Revocation	478
Miscellaneous Matters	479
"Forced Heirship"	479
Probate	480
Inheritance Tax	480
Excepted Estates	481
Assets not Requiring Probate	481
Jointly Held Assets	482
Life Policies	482
Pension Death Benefits	482
Chattels	483
Bare Trusts	483
Small Payments	483
General Tax Issues	483
Inheritance Tax	483
Capital Gains Tax	483
Income Tax	484
Inheritance Tax Planning: Some Thoughts	484
Married Couples	487
Cohabitees	488
Single Persons	488
Charitable Giving	488
Foreign Aspects	489
Post Death Issues	490
Deeds of Variation and Discretionary Will Trusts	490
Deeds of Variation	490

	Capital Gains Tax	494
	Discretionary Will Trusts	495
	Capital Gains Tax	496
Intestacy		496
Some Points to Note		496
Summary		497

Appendices — 499

Bibliography — 539

Index — 543

About the Author

Malcolm Finney, B.Sc. M.Sc. (Bus Admin) M.Sc. (Org Psy) MCMI C Maths MIMA, runs his own tax consultancy and training firm, Pythagoras Training.

Malcolm's previous experience has included working for the international finance and international tax consultancy J.F. Chown & Company Ltd (now Chown Dewhurst LLP); as partner and head of international tax at the international accountancy firm Grant Thornton LLP; and as head of tax at the London-based law firm Nabarro Nathanson.

Malcolm has written extensively on tax matters, has spoken at tax seminars both in the UK and abroad and has been a visiting lecturer at the University of Greenwich Business School.

Preface

Wealth management, personal financial planning, estate planning and private client planning are just a few of the terms used to describe the structuring of an individual's affairs, be that personal and/or business, in a tax efficient manner.

Various professionals are involved in providing advice concerning such structuring including private bankers, financial planners, investment advisors, lawyers, accountants and others. No one advisor is able to deal effectively with all aspects of an individual's affairs. However, the need for more than one advisor can cause communication breakdown and the neglect of those aspects with which the particular advisor is unfamiliar.

Whatever the nature of the role that any particular advisor fulfils, an understanding of the basic tax principles and concepts which impact upon an individual's personal wealth is a necessity. Without such a basic understanding, competent and proactive advice is not possible.

The primary emphasis of this book is on the UK tax implications for effective wealth management advice including consideration of the three main UK taxes, namely, income tax, capital gains tax and inheritance tax. However, the possible international tax implications cannot be ignored and where appropriate these are also addressed.

The approach taken in the book has been to try to ensure each chapter is as self-contained as possible to enable readers to "dip in and out" as needed. However, this has not always been easy to achieve. Where necessary, cross-reference to other chapters is made to help track related issues. Numerous practical examples throughout the book are used to illustrate the text.

It is common in tax texts to litter each chapter with cross-references to statutes and tax cases. This approach has not been taken in this book (for better or worse) as it is not primarily intended for the tax specialist but for those who require knowledge of the tax issues relevant to wealth planning without the need for supporting "chapter and verse". Having said this, the Appendices do contain some material of a statutory nature which it is felt may be of help to the reader without, hopefully, being overwhelming at the same time.

Tax changes both in the UK and in the wider world continue and in view of the major changes introduced in the Finance Acts 2006 and 2008, in particular, it seems timely to reassess the underlying UK tax principles applicable to wealth management planning.

The UK for many years has been a "tax haven" for those individuals categorised as non-UK domiciled (in simple terms, albeit not very accurately, those of foreign nationality). Such individuals have for many years been granted significant tax breaks. The Finance Act 2008 (FA 2008) has dramatically changed the UK tax landscape for the non-UK domiciled individual forever. The changes, their impact and implications are addressed in detail in the book.

FA 2008 has not only affected the non-UK domiciled individual but also those of UK domicile status (basically, English, Northern Irish, Scottish and Welsh nationals) in particular with respect to capital gains tax. This has significant consequences for individual investment planning.

Although the number of measures in the FA 2008 affecting inheritance tax are minimal one major change has been introduced, the so-called "transferable nil rate band" which has affected the historic approach to inter-spouse inheritance tax planning on death.

However, two years earlier the FA 2006 made fundamental changes to the inheritance tax treatment of trusts which has caused the need for a rethink as to how and under what circumstances trusts may still be viable in any inheritance tax planning exercise.

At the international level little has been done over recent years to expand the UK's network of double taxation conventions applicable to inheritance tax, of which there are few in number. The major emphasis appears to have been to expand the already large number of double taxation agreements which deal with income and capital gains taxes and to try to conclude so-called Tax Information and Exchange Agreements with a number of offshore financial centres. Indeed, only in April this year the Treasury Committee announced yet another new inquiry into offshore financial centres.

The decisions of the European courts (namely, the European Court of Human Rights and the European Court of Justice) continue to affect the tax position of the individual including, for example, the decisions in *De Lasteyrie v. Ministere de L'Economie (2004)*, *Heirs of van Hilten-van Heijden v. Inspecteur van de Belastingdienst/Particulieren/Ondernemingen buitland te Heerlen (2006)* and *Burden and another v. United Kingdom (2008)*.

The EU Savings Directive is currently under review, three years after its introduction in 2005, as the view appears to be held that it has not been as effective as intended as its provisions are being readily and easily circumnavigated by taxpayers.

Money laundering regulations continue at a pace; however, for the legitimate they should present little conceptual problem though undoubtedly will increase the administrative burden of carrying out or implementing any financial plan.

It should be assumed that references in the text to spouses also applies to registered civil partnerships.

While perhaps somewhat self-evident, tax law does not stand still and therefore it is important to check the up-to-date position whenever tax issues are relevant.

Every attempt has been made to try to ensure that this book reflects the law as at 31 July 2008 but any errors are exclusively my own.

A companion website to the book contains additional material and will also include quaterly updates. Go to www.wiley.com/go/wealth management planning.

I would like to offer my thanks to the staff of John Wiley & Sons Ltd. including Kerry Batcock, Sam Hartley, Jenny McCall, Amy Webster and Viv Wickham without whose joint efforts the book would never have seen the light of day.

Finally, I would like to extend my grateful thanks to my partner, Karen Donnelly. She has not only borne the brunt of the typing of numerous drafts but has for many months been forced to live a hermit-like existence due to the extended spells I seem to have spent locked away trying to get to grips with all the new changes, in particular Schedule 7 Finance Act 2008.

Malcolm Finney
West Sussex
July 2008

malcfinney@aol.com

Abbreviations

AIM	Alternative Investment Market
APR	Agricultural property relief
APT	Asset protection trust
BPR	Business property relief
CLT	Chargeable lifetime transfer
DMPA 1973	Domicile and Matrimonial Proceedings Act 1973
EC	European Community
ECHR	European Court of Human Rights
EEC	European Economic Community
FA	Finance Act
FSA	Financial Services Authority
HMRC	Her Majesty's Revenue and Customs
IBC	International business company
ICTA 1988	Income and Corporation Taxes Act 1988
IPFDA 1975	Inheritance (Provision for Family and Dependants) Act 1975
IHT 1984	Inheritance Tax Act 1984
IMF	International Monetary Fund
ISA	Individual savings account
ITA 2007	Income Tax Act 2007
NRB	Nil rate band
OECD	Organisation for Economic Cooperation and Development
OFC	Offshore financial centre
OFD	Offshore disclosure facility
PET	Potentially exempt transfer
SD	Stamp duty
SDLT	Stamp duty land tax
SDRT	Stamp duty reserve tax
TCGA	Taxation of Chargeable Gains Act 1992
VAT	Value added tax

Part One
The Building Blocks

1
Tax Systems and their Bases of Taxation

BACKGROUND

Every country has its own rules which determine the extent of an individual's tax liabilities. Such liabilities may be those relating to an individual's income, capital gains and/or assets.

Typically, income is subject to some form of income tax; capital gains (often but not always) to some form of capital gains tax; and assets to some form of wealth and/or inheritance tax on death and/or lifetime gifts.

It may be that not all types of income are subject to income tax and/or that not all gains are subject to some form of capital gains tax. It may also be that certain categories of asset are excluded from any inheritance tax whether on death and/or lifetime gifts.

Rates of a particular tax will inevitably vary often depending upon the quantum of income/gains and often also depending upon the status of the individual taxpayer.

No two countries' tax systems are identical and great care is thus needed, in particular, whenever a taxable event (e.g. sale of an asset; death of an individual) occurs which may be subject to tax in more than one country; where this occurs double taxation is said to arise (see Chapter 25). Almost certainly, for example, the tax rules which apply in France will be different from those applicable in the UK which in turn will no doubt be different from those of the USA.

As a consequence, in seeking to ascertain the tax implications of a particular transaction it becomes necessary to identify which countries' tax systems are in point, the status of the person concerned, the type of income/assets involved and the nature of the transaction.

Two simple examples may serve to illustrate the point.

Example 1.1
Henry Marlowe lives in England with his wife Mary and their two young children Joanne and James. Henry's father has died but his aged mother continues to live alone in her own home.

Henry wishes to ensure that in the event of his death his wife, children and mother will be provided for in a tax efficient manner.

It thus becomes necessary first of all to identify which countries' tax systems are in point. Rather obviously it would appear that only that of the UK is involved as all the parties involved live in the UK and, prima facie, all income arises, and all assets are located, within the UK.

In principle, therefore Henry's primary issue is to ensure that on his death any UK tax liabilities which may arise are minimised. Prima facie, this would involve considering and mitigating the impact of any UK inheritance tax liability which will in principle arise on Henry's death.

However, in practice it is by no means unusual to find that the tax issues are far more complex than those of Henry's in the above Example 1.1 involving more than one country's tax regime.

Example 1.2
Raymond Brown married Claudia Schmidt and they now both work in the UK where they have done so for 20 years. They own properties in the USA, the UK and Germany and have share investments in companies located in Hong Kong, Canada and South Africa. One of their two adult children, Samantha, now lives in Italy and the other, George, lives in Cyprus.

If Raymond had a similar objective to Henry above (i.e. mitigating tax arising on his death to ensure all family members are adequately provided for) the tax issues would be far more complex. It is necessary to examine the tax implications of Raymond's death in all of the countries listed in order to ascertain the ramifications of each of the tax systems and to seek to resolve any possible double tax which may arise.

Optimal tax planning for Raymond would thus not, for example, be achieved by simply mitigating any UK inheritance tax liability if, in so doing, the tax ramifications in the USA, for example, were made substantially worse.

A truly international approach is necessary.

CATEGORIES OF TAX

The main categories of tax (albeit not exhaustive) are those which apply to:

- income (income taxes);
- capital gains (capital gains taxes);
- inheritance (inheritance taxes);
- death (estate taxes); and
- wealth (wealth taxes).

Not all countries levy all these types of tax and, as will be seen below, sometimes the nomenclature adopted by a particular country may differ from that of another country when in fact the taxes being levied are basically the same.

For example, in some countries (e.g. the UK) the term "inheritance tax" is used to refer not only to the tax levied on an individual's death but also to the tax levied on any lifetime gifts made by such individual. In other countries, the term "inheritance tax" may be used to apply only to lifetime gifts (the term "estate tax" being used to describe the tax levied on the individual's death).

CAPITAL v. INCOME DISTINCTION

For some countries no distinction is made between income and capital gains (e.g. Belgium, Denmark, Italy, Japan, Spain and Sweden) with both being taxed at the same rates; in other countries income and capital gains are taxed at different rates (e.g. in the USA the marginal income tax rate is 35%; whereas *capital gains* are subject to tax at the marginal rate of 15%); indeed, some countries not only tax income and capital gains at different rates but distinguish between short- and long-term gains (e.g. short-term gains refer to gains arising within two years in the case of France; Italy three years; and the USA 12 months); and in some countries (e.g. Barbados, Gibraltar, Guernsey and the Isle of Man) capital gains are simply not taxed at all.

Which approach a country adopts may be extremely critical. In particular, where a country's tax system *does* distinguish between income and capital gains (as does the UK) it is often the case that capital transactions are usually taxed more favourably (as in the UK). This usually arises either because the rates applicable to capital gains are lower than those applicable to income and/or the bases of computation are more favourable.

In the UK, for example, before the recent changes introduced in FA 2008 although the marginal (i.e. highest) rates of income and capital gains taxes were the same, i.e. 40%, the bases of computation were very different with the more favourable treatment being accorded to capital gains (this was primarily due to the application of taper relief which exempted a percentage of any indexed capital gain from capital gains tax; taper relief did not apply in computing income tax liabilities; see Chapter 8). Following FA 2008 changes, the marginal rate of income tax remains at 40% but the rate of capital gains tax is 18% (see Chapter 8).

It is because of this difference in treatment that in some countries investment returns are often structured to provide the investor with capital gains not income benefits in order to produce an overall lower tax liability. To combat such approaches it is not unusual to find tax legislation which is designed to deem any, de facto, capital gain as an income benefit thus nullifying any tax advantage of structuring for capital as opposed to income treatment (e.g. the UK tax system's treatment of non-distributor offshore fund "profits" and the "profits" of offshore single premium bonds; see Chapter 18).

WORLDWIDE v. TERRITORIAL TAX SYSTEMS

(a) Income and Capital Gains Taxes

Most countries' tax systems can be conveniently, albeit loosely, categorised as either a *worldwide*- or a *territorial*-based system of taxation (although within a particular country the method of levying tax on individuals may be different from that applying to companies or other forms of taxpayer).

Worldwide Basis

Under the worldwide system of taxation, generally speaking, *residents* of a country are taxed on their worldwide income and capital gains. In other words, irrespective of where any income or gains arise (whether within the country of residence or elsewhere) they will be subject to tax as appropriate by the country in which the individual entitled to the income or gains is resident.

The UK has adopted a worldwide-based system as has, for example, Australia, Germany, Italy, Japan and the USA.

Territorial Basis

Under the territorial system of taxation *residents* are taxed only on income and capital gains arising within that country's borders; income and capital gains arising outside thereof are not subject to tax.

Countries adopting this approach include Bolivia, Ecuador, Ghana, Israel, Malaysia, Panama, Singapore, Venezuela and Zambia.

Territorial Basis plus Remittances

Some countries which adopt the territorial system, however, extend the tax base of *residents* to include overseas income and/or capital gains but only if such income or gains are remitted (i.e. brought back) to the country of residence.

Countries adopting this approach include Ghana, Israel, Malaysia, Mauritius, Singapore and Thailand.

While there are, of course, variants of the above three tax systems, in principle, most countries' tax systems fall into one of the three categories.

Residency

Irrespective of the variant of tax system adopted it is usual for the taxes levied on any income and gains to be levied on *residents* (basically, individuals who live in the country) of the particular country (see Chapter 4 for a more detailed consideration of the term "resident").

However, there are one or two notable exceptions which, while adopting a "residence"-based tax system, also utilise additional criteria.

Citizenship Test

The adoption of a citizenship criterion to determine the taxability of income and gains, while very unusual, is in fact utilised by some countries including the USA.

The USA adopts a worldwide basis of taxation, as does the UK, but unlike the UK and most other countries, the USA extends its tax system to tax the income and gains of its citizens wherever they are resident. Thus, while in many cases an individual can avoid a particular country's tax system by no longer residing in that country, a *citizen* of the USA does *not* escape US income and capital gains taxes simply by losing US residency by, for example, moving to live elsewhere (e.g. in the UK or Bermuda).

Thus, a citizen of the USA who does not live in the USA (i.e. is not resident therein) but resides in, say, the UK is still in principle liable to USA income and capital gains taxes on worldwide income and gains (as well as in this case being liable to UK income and capital gains taxes).

Other countries which also tax on the basis of citizenship include Ecuador, Liberia and South Korea.

Levying tax on the basis of citizenship is, however, very unusual. By far the most common system is for a country to simply levy its income and capital gains taxes only on its residents (as applies in the UK).

Source Basis

Whether a country's tax system is a worldwide- or territorial-based system typically a country will also levy its taxes on *non-residents* but only with respect to income and/or capital gains arising within the country's borders. In other words, if the source of the income arises within the country or the capital gain arises on an asset situated within the country then that country will tax the non-resident (see Chapters 6 and 22).

For example, invariably any real estate income (e.g. rents) arising from real estate in any country will be subject to income tax in that country (i.e. where the real estate is located) even if the owner of the real estate is not a resident of the country.

Example 1.3
A German resident who owns UK real estate will be subject to UK income tax on any rental income arising from the real estate even though the individual is not a resident of the UK (such individual may also be subject to German tax on the income as a resident of Germany).

Example 1.4
Henry Bone is a resident of the Cayman Islands and has invested in US equities. Henry will be liable to US taxation on any dividend income arising on his investment.

In the case of the UK, although UK source income of a non-UK resident is liable to UK income tax, certain types of UK source income in such cases may not in fact be so liable (see discussion of "exempt" income in Chapter 22).

Although non-residents of a country are invariably subject to some form of tax in that country on income arising within that country the position with respect to capital gains may vary. Thus, some countries *do* levy their capital gains tax on disposals of assets situated within their country by non-residents while other countries do not.

In the case of the UK, for example, a non-UK resident is *not* subject to capital gains tax on the disposal of UK situs assets (unless the asset(s) form part of a UK-based trade or business).

Example 1.5

Joe America Junior, a US resident, has sold a number of his UK equity investments. Even though the assets sold are UK situs no UK capital gains tax charge arises on the sales.

(b) Inheritance Tax

Most countries levy some form of tax on the death of an individual. In addition, many countries will levy some form of tax on gifts made by an individual during their lifetime.

Terminology varies widely between countries as do the bases and underlying methodology upon which such taxes are levied.

As to terminology, common terms include *death tax, inheritance tax, estate tax/duty* and *gift tax*.

Unlike income and capital gains taxes which generally apply to *residents* of a country, taxes levied on death and/or lifetime gifts are often based upon an individual's *domicile or nationality* status. However, residence is also used by a number of countries to determine liability.

The person liable for such tax (i.e. death tax; gift tax, etc.) also varies among countries. Sometimes (as in the UK) on death the amount of the individual's death estate (assets owned at date of death less liabilities) is ascertained and tax is then levied on the estate, i.e. the tax payable on death is in fact paid out of the deceased's death estate before any assets of the estate can be transferred to the deceased's beneficiaries under the deceased's will.

However, it is not unusual for some countries to levy their tax arising on death, not on the death estate itself (as in the UK), but on those individuals who actually inherit a part of the deceased's estate, i.e. the heirs (see below).

Sometimes a country may impose a tax on death *and* a different tax which applies to lifetime gifts. This is the case with the USA which imposes both an *estate tax*, applying only on death, *and* a separate tax on lifetime gifts, namely, a *gift tax*; two separate taxes. In the UK the same tax, i.e. inheritance tax, applies both on death and to lifetime gifts (see Chapter 9).

Examples of differences among countries concerning death and related taxes include:

- *in the UK* the liability on death is that of the deceased's estate and the extent of the liability depends upon the *deceased's domicile status at the date of death*;
- *in Spain* the liability is that of the heirs with the liability depending upon the *principal residence* status of the *heirs*;
- *in South Africa* the liability is that of the deceased's estate and depends upon the *ordinary residence* status of the *deceased*; and
- *in Germany* liability is dependent upon the *domicile status* of the deceased and the heirs and is a liability of the heirs, the amount of liability depending upon the relationship of the heir to the deceased.

Trailing Tax Imposition

The term "trailing tax" usually refers to the levying of a country's taxes on an individual even when, prima facie, the individual is no longer within that country's tax regime for tax purposes.

In the UK, for example, a UK domiciled individual is liable to inheritance tax on worldwide assets. However, even where such individual loses the UK domicile status (e.g. by acquiring a non-UK domicile of choice; see Chapter 3) the individual still remains within the charge to UK inheritance tax on worldwide assets for a further period of three years (see Chapter 3).

Similarly, a Dutch national is still within the Dutch death tax net for a further 10 years after losing Dutch residency; a German national continues to be caught in the German death tax net for a further five years; and a US citizen or "long-term" permanent resident who has renounced either status but is caught under the trailing income/capital gains tax rules is automatically also deemed to still be within the death/gift tax net for a 10-year period.

The concept of trailing taxes is often overlooked when considering an individual's tax affairs. It is most likely to apply where the individual has moved from one country to another (possibly with the sole or main objective of mitigating taxes).

SUMMARY

It is important to recognise that each country's tax system may vary significantly from that of other countries.

The rules applicable in the UK are thus not necessarily reflected elsewhere.

Typically, the taxes levied by a country will include some form of income tax on income; capital gains tax on capital gains; and death tax and/or gift tax arising on death and/or lifetime gifts.

Nomenclature adopted often varies among countries and the same term may be used in a different sense in different countries.

Optimal tax planning may involve a consideration of the impact of different countries' tax systems and in particular their interaction if double taxation is to be avoided.

2
UK Taxation: An Overview

BACKGROUND

Since the mid-1990s the UK has adopted a self-assessment system of taxation.

Thus, the taxpayer is personally responsible for not only completing a Tax Return for a tax year but also working out any tax liabilities arising for the tax year and then ensuring that payment of any outstanding tax is made by the relevant dates.

Any taxpayer who is chargeable to income tax or capital gains tax and who has not received a Tax Return to complete is under an obligation to notify HMRC within six months of the end of the tax year in which any taxable income and/or chargeable gains arise. Failure to notify within the prescribed time limit will result in a penalty.

DOMICILE, RESIDENCE AND ORDINARY RESIDENCE

As discussed in Chapter 1 the UK's tax system is a worldwide-based system and thus residents of the UK are taxable on their worldwide income and capital gains.

However, the *domicile* status of the resident individual also impacts upon the extent of the individual's tax liability.

Domiciled Individual

A UK *domiciled, resident and ordinarily resident* individual is exposed to all forms of UK taxation (income tax, capital gains tax and inheritance tax) on all income, capital gains and assets wherever such income and gains arise and wherever such assets may be located (i.e. the worldwide basis of taxation).

An income tax liability thus arises when the relevant income arises and a capital gains tax liability arises when an asset is disposed of, e.g. sold. This basis of taxation is referred to as the *arising* (as opposed to the *remittance*; see below) basis, i.e. income and/or capital gains are taxed when such income or gains arise irrespective of where the monies are located or banked.

Example 2.1
An individual who is UK domiciled, resident and ordinarily resident is subject to UK income tax on any interest which arises on a Swiss bank account even if the interest monies are retained in Switzerland; similarly, any capital gain arising on the sale of USA equities is subject to UK capital gains tax even if the sale proceeds are banked in the USA.

With respect to inheritance tax, a UK domiciled (whether resident or ordinary resident in the UK or not) individual is liable to inheritance tax on worldwide assets on death and on any lifetime gifts.

Example 2.2

A UK domiciled, resident and ordinarily resident individual at the time of death owned UK equities, a Spanish villa and a bank account in the USA.

UK inheritance tax will arise on all the assets.

Although unusual, a UK domiciled individual who is resident but not ordinarily resident is subject to income and capital gains tax on the same basis as a non-UK domiciled individual (see below).

Non-domiciled Individual

For the *non-UK domiciled* individual, however, slightly different rules apply.

A *non-UK domiciled but resident and ordinarily resident* individual is subject to income and capital gains taxes on the *remittance basis* with respect to *non-UK source* income and *non-UK source capital gains*. *UK source* income and capital gains are, however, subject to UK income and capital gains taxes in the same manner as applies to the UK domiciled individual, i.e. the arising basis.

Example 2.3

A non-UK domiciled but resident and ordinary resident individual receives interest on a bank deposit in the UK; interest on a bank deposit in Luxembourg; rental income on a house in Spain; and dividends on UK equities.

The individual's non-UK domicile status means that a liability to income tax arises on the UK source bank interest and the dividends on the UK equities on the arising basis.

However, the interest on the Luxembourg bank deposit and the rental income from the Spanish property are only subject to income tax if and when the monies are remitted (i.e. brought to) the UK. So long as the interest and rental income remain outside the UK no income tax liabilities arise thereon.

However, there was (i.e. pre FA 2008) one exception to the remittance rule for non-UK domiciled but UK resident individuals which concerned the Republic of Ireland. Income (technically "relevant foreign income") which comprises dividend income, interest income, property income and trading income arising in Ireland and "employment income" from employment with an employer resident in Ireland were not subject to the remittance basis but the arising basis. This treatment, however, was relatively recently (early 2007) found to be in breach of European Community rules. As a consequence, action was taken in FA 2008 to correct what had been for many years an anomaly and thus income arising on or after 6 April 2008 within the Republic of Ireland will be subject to remittance basis treatment for the non-UK domiciled but UK resident individual.

Thus, pre FA 2008, investments (e.g. bank deposits) in the Republic of Ireland by a non-UK domiciled but UK resident and ordinarily resident individual, generally speaking, were not tax efficient. Post FA 2008, however, this is no longer the case.

Thus, investments by non-UK domiciled but UK resident individuals in Republic of Ireland mutual funds (primarily so-called "distributor" funds) which were tax inefficient pre FA 2008 are no longer tax inefficient in this regard (see Chapter 18).

It is worth noting, however, that the remittance basis did, pre FA 2008, apply to the non-UK domiciled but UK resident individual with respect to capital gains arising on the disposal of Republic of Ireland situs assets for UK capital gains tax purposes; this continues to apply post FA 2008.

With respect to inheritance tax, the non-UK domiciled individual is liable to inheritance tax on UK situs assets only; non-UK situs assets are not subject to inheritance tax (see Chapter 6 for determinations as to what is, and is not, UK and non-UK situs income and assets). The residence and ordinary residence status of an individual is in principle irrelevant to an individual's inheritance tax liabilities (but see Chapter 9).

Example 2.4

An individual who is non-UK domiciled but UK resident and ordinarily resident at death owned a UK house; a house in Florida, USA; UK equities; Canadian equities; a bank deposit in Switzerland; a bank deposit in the UK; and a farm in South Africa.

The UK inheritance tax liability arising on death applies to UK situs assets only, namely, the UK house, UK equities and the UK bank deposit.

All the other assets fall outside any charge to UK inheritance tax (although, of course, there may be liabilities arising due to death in the other countries).

In short, if a non-UK domiciled but resident and ordinary resident individual does not remit any non-UK source income or non-UK source capital gains to the UK any liability to income and capital gains tax is restricted to UK source income and UK source capital gains. On death, inheritance tax is also restricted to a charge on UK situs assets only.

PERSONS OTHER THAN INDIVIDUALS

UK tax is payable not only by individuals but also by:

- companies (corporation tax);
- trustees (income, capital gains and inheritance tax);
- personal representatives (income and capital gains tax).

UK TAXES AND LAW

HMRC, Her Majesty's Revenue and Customs (effective 2005 and now a single body), formerly Inland Revenue and Her Majesty's Customs and Excise (two separate bodies), is the body now responsible for tax assessment and collection.

The UK taxes for which HMRC are responsible include:

- income tax;
- capital gains tax;
- corporation tax;

- inheritance tax;
- stamp duty and stamp duty land tax;
- VAT.

The main legislation which deals with UK taxation is contained in various Acts of Parliament and includes:

- Taxes Management Act 1970;
- Inheritance Act 1984;
- Income and Corporation Taxes Act 1988;
- Taxation of Chargeable Gains Act 1992;
- Income Tax (Earnings and Pensions) Act 2003;
- Income Tax (Trading and Other Income) Act 2005;
- Income Tax Act 2007;
- Miscellaneous Finance Acts (e.g. Finance Acts 2006 and 2008).

Unfortunately, no single Act contains all the legislation relating to a particular tax and therefore to determine taxability at any point in time requires, typically, that a number of different Acts be examined (e.g. an inheritance tax liability would require, inter alia, an examination of, in particular, the Inheritance Tax Act 1984, Finance Act 1986 and Finance Act 2006).

CAPITAL v. INCOME DISTINCTION

The UK's tax system distinguishes between transactions which give rise to income and those which give rise to capital gains. The former is subject to income tax and the latter subject to capital gains tax; two totally separate taxes.

As a very broad general rule, capital rather than income treatment was pre FA 2008 more "tax" favourable (primarily due to the availability of taper relief which only applies to capital gains and not income; see Chapter 8). Hence, many investments were structured to provide the individual investor with a capital gain on sale/maturity of the investment rather than an income return. For the higher rate income taxpayer any income arising on an investment would be charged at 40% whereas any capital gain while in this case also subject to a nominal rate of 40% would in effect in many cases be much lower where taper relief applied (a reduction to a possible effective rate of as low as 10% or 24% depending on the investment; see Chapter 8).

Post FA 2008 the distinction between income and capital continues. However, while the higher rate taxpayer continues to be exposed to income tax at 40% on income a new capital gains tax rate of 18% has been introduced (possibly reduced further to 10% due to the newly introduced entrepreneur relief; see Chapter 8). Taper relief and indexation have both been abolished.

The tax effect of any transaction cannot thus be ascertained until a determination has been made as to whether it is one of capital or one of income. Even when a determination has been made it may be that specific legislation will re-characterise its nature (e.g. by deeming what would normally be a capital gain to in fact be an income gain; see Chapter 18 where the tax treatment of offshore funds illustrates this re-characterisation).

RATES OF TAX (2008/09)

Tax rates are fixed in advance for a "tax year" (or "year of assessment" as it is also known) which runs from 6 April in any year to the following 5 April inclusive. The 2008/09 tax year runs from 6 April 2008 to 5 April 2009 (however, for companies the rates are fixed for a financial year, i.e. 1 April 2008 to 31 March 2009).

Income Tax

Income tax is levied on, inter alia, the income of individuals and on the income of trustees. More specifically income tax is levied on *taxable income* which is an individual's total income for a tax year from all sources less certain allowances, reliefs and deductions (e.g. relief for certain interest payments; personal allowance; charitable payments, etc.; see Appendix 1).

From 6 April 2008 FA 2008 has reduced the basic rate of income tax from its former 22% to 20% and has abolished both the former "starting rate" (i.e. 10%) and the "savings rate" (i.e. 20%). In their place is a new "starting rate for savings" to be levied at 10% on the first £2320 of savings income. However, as its name suggests, the new "starting rate for savings" only applies to savings income (i.e. it does not apply to, inter alia, employment income; self-employed income; rental income or dividend income). The 10% "starting rate for savings", applicable for the tax year 2008/09, should not be confused with the 10% "starting rate", applicable to earlier tax years.

For tax years prior to 2008/09 the basic rate of income tax had been 22% and the previous "starting rate" of 10% applied to both savings and non-savings income (but not dividend income).

Dividend income post 5 April 2008 continues to be subject to income tax in the same manner as before this date. Thus, dividend income is subject to the "dividend ordinary" rate of 10% or the 32.5% "dividend upper rate".

The rates of income tax applicable to individuals for the tax year 2008/09 are:

Basic rate	(20%) on taxable income between	£0 and £34 800
Higher rate	(40%) on taxable income over	£34 800

The rates of income tax applicable to individuals for the tax year 2007/08 were:

Starting rate	(10%) on taxable income between	£0 and £2230
Basic rate	(22%) on taxable income between	£2231 and £34 600
Higher rate	(40%) on taxable income over	£34 600

Although a "new starting rate for savings" of 10% applies for the tax year 2008/09 the legislation requires that non-savings income is to be subject to tax before savings income which is itself to be subject to tax before dividend income. As a consequence, if an individual's taxable non-savings income equals or exceeds the limit of £2320 the 10% rate will simply not be applicable. In other words, if the individual's non-savings taxable income is, for example, £2320 this will be subject to income tax at the new basic rate (i.e. 20%) and any savings income of such individual will also be subject to income tax at the 20% basic rate.

Example 2.5
Joseph Turner for the tax year 2008/09 anticipates receiving the following income:

Non-savings income (e.g. salary)	£8355
Savings income (e.g. bank interest)	£5320

His personal allowance is £6035.

	Non-savings £	Savings £
Salary	8355	
Bank interest		5320
Less personal allowance	(6035)	—
Taxable income	2320	5320
Income tax liability = 2320 × 20% + 5320 × 20% = £1528		

Example 2.6
Joseph Turner's brother, Barry, for the tax year 2008/09 anticipates receiving the following income:

Non-savings income (e.g. salary)	Nil
Savings income (e.g. bank interest)	£13 675
His personal allowance is £6035.	

	Non-savings £	Savings £
Salary	Nil	
Bank interest		13 675
Less personal allowance	—	(6035)
Taxable income	Nil	7640
Income tax liability = 2320 × 10% + 5320 × 20% = £1296		

In Examples 2.5 and 2.6 above although the gross (i.e. pre-tax) income and "taxable income" of each of Joseph and Barry are identical in amount, because Barry has no non-savings income he is able to utilise the newly introduced 10% "starting rate for savings". However, as Joseph's non-savings taxable income exceeds £2320 none of his savings income is able to be taxed at the 10% rate. Thus, Barry's tax liability is 10% of £2320 (i.e. £232) less than Joseph's liability.

The new starting rate for savings of 10% will thus only in fact apply to any savings income if the individual's non-savings taxable income is below £2320.

Prior to 2008/09 the 10% "starting rate" applied to both non-savings and savings income and thus either an element of non-savings income and/or an element of savings income would always be taxed at the 10% rate.

Taxable income may consist of three types of income, namely, non-savings income, savings income and dividend income each of which are liable to tax at different rates. For the tax year 2008/09 the rates are as follows:

Non-savings income (NSI) taxed at	20%/40%
Savings income (SI) taxed at	10%/20%/40%
Dividend income taxed at	10%/32.5%

"Savings income" includes "relevant foreign income" (e.g. foreign interest and dividend income), and thus the above rates of income tax applicable to savings income and dividend income are equally applicable to relevant foreign income. For the non-UK domiciled but UK resident individual, however, relevant foreign income is subject to rates of 20% and 40% for 2008/09.

Capital Gains Tax

Capital gains tax is levied on the chargeable gains of individuals and on the chargeable gains of trustees. Chargeable gains are gains which arise on the disposal (e.g. whether sale or gift) of certain assets (e.g. shares; real estate). Basically, the gain is the difference between sale proceeds and original cost less the relevant annual exemption (£9600 for the tax year 2008/09; £9200 for the tax year 2007/08).

For tax years prior to the tax year 2008/09 such gains were treated as the highest part of an individual's income, i.e. the capital gains tax liability of an individual was calculated assuming that the capital gains were taxed after the non-savings income, savings income and dividend income had each been taxed.

Thus, the rate of capital gains tax applicable to chargeable gains of an individual depended upon that individual's level of taxable income. For example, a taxpayer who was subject to income tax at 40% on taxable income would then be subject to capital gains tax at the same rate, i.e. 40%.

The rates of capital gains tax applicable to individuals for the tax year 2007/08 were 10%, 20% or 40%.

However, FA 2008 has fundamentally changed the basis of subjecting chargeable gains to capital gains tax (including the abolition of the indexation allowance and taper relief).

For disposals effected on or after 6 April 2008 a flat rate of 18% (possibly 10% where entrepreneur relief may be available; see Chapter 8) will apply to chargeable gains. The level of an individual's taxable income will thus be irrelevant in determining the rate of capital gains tax on or after 6 April 2008.

The 18% rate of capital gains tax introduced by FA 2008 applies equally to both UK domiciled and non-UK domiciled individuals.

Inheritance Tax

As indicated above, FA 2008 has introduced major changes to the taxation of chargeable gains; reduced the rate of basic income tax (to 20%); and abolished the 10% rate for non-savings income.

However, the changes to inheritance tax introduced by FA 2008 are by comparison relatively insignificant. It had been two years earlier that the provisions of the FA 2006 radically altered the manner in which inheritance tax is to be levied on trusts and transfers into and out of trusts (see Chapters 9 and 15).

Inheritance tax is levied on lifetime gifts made by an individual and on the death estate on an individual's death.

In lifetime, gifts are in principle subject to a 20% rate of inheritance tax. The death estate of an individual is subject to a 40% rate of inheritance tax.

For the tax year 2008/09, a so-called "nil rate band" (i.e. a rate of 0%) applies to the first £312 000 of lifetime gifts and/or the death estate. For the tax years 2009/10 and 2010/11 the corresponding figures for the nil rate band are £325 000 and £350 000, respectively. For the tax year 2007/08, the equivalent figure was £300 000.

Trustees may also be liable to inheritance tax. In the case of a discretionary trust inheritance tax liabilities may arise on each successive 10-year anniversary of the date the trust was created and on any distributions made out of the trust by the trustees (the so-called "exit charge"). Other types of trust (e.g. interest in possession) may, depending upon the date of creation and other factors, be subject to a different regime (see Chapters 9 and 15).

ALLOWANCES

Every individual *resident* in the UK is entitled to various allowances which may be used in calculating taxable income or chargeable gains.

In the case of income tax, one example is the personal allowance which for the tax year 2008/09 is £6035 (£5225 for tax year 2007/08). Higher rates of personal allowance apply to those aged 65 and over (or 75 and over).

In certain cases personal allowances are also available to non-residents of the UK including citizens of the EEA or the Commonwealth, residents of the Isle of Man and the Channel Islands and residents of countries with which the UK has a double tax agreement.

In the case of capital gains tax individuals are entitled to an annual exemption which for the tax year 2008/09 is £9600 (£9200 for tax year 2007/08).

Trustees are not individuals for tax purposes and thus they are not entitled to the above personal allowances for income tax purposes.

Trustees are nevertheless entitled to an annual exemption for capital gains tax purposes for the tax year 2008/09 of £4800 (£4600 for tax year 2007/08) which is, however, reduced (i.e. pro-rated) if the individual who created the trust (i.e. the settlor) has also created additional trusts (in any event a minimum of £960 applies to each trust for the tax year 2008/09).

Non-UK domiciled but UK resident individuals are in principle also entitled to personal allowances for income tax purposes and the annual exemptions for capital gains tax purposes. However, FA 2008 may affect such entitlements (see Chapter 23).

TAX RETURNS

Income and Capital Gains Tax

Prior to the tax year 2007/08 a Tax Return (see Appendix 3) covering income tax and capital gains tax needed to be filed on or before 31 January following the end of the relevant tax year (e.g. 31 January 2008 for tax year 2006/07).

However, for the tax year 2007/08 and subsequent tax years two separate filing dates have been introduced (these amendments were introduced in FA 2007). For *paper* Tax Returns the new filing date is brought forward to 31 October after the tax year concerned (e.g. 31 October 2008 for the tax year 2007/08). For Tax Returns filed *online* the filing date will remain at 31 January following the tax year concerned (e.g. 31 January 2009 for the tax year 2007/08).

Thus, for the tax year 2008/09 the *online* filing date will remain at 31 January 2010 but the paper filing date is brought forward to 31 October 2009.

The effect of the change is that the filing of Tax Returns in paper format (i.e. not filed online) will henceforth need to be filed some three months earlier than in the past (i.e. 31 October rather than 31 January).

Failure to file a Tax Return by the deadline results in an automatic penalty of £100; continuing failure to file attracts additional penalties.

Inheritance Tax

With respect to inheritance tax there are no regular returns required. Unlike the Tax Return applicable for income and capital gains taxes which in principle requires filing every year, returns associated with inheritance tax tend to be event driven (e.g. death or making of lifetime gift) rather than tax year/time driven (see Chapter 13).

The relevant Tax Returns may be different for individuals and trustees (see Appendix 3).

TIMING OF TAX PAYMENTS

Income and Capital Gains Tax

Income tax and capital gains tax liabilities arising in respect of a tax year must be paid on or before 31 January following the relevant tax year. Thus, for example, for the tax year 2007/08 such taxes need to be paid on or before 31 January 2009. Failure to pay by the deadline will result in interest charges on late payment.

Payments on account may need to be made during the tax year and before the 31 January deadline. Such payments are made on account of the ultimate tax liability for the tax year. They are based upon the income tax payable of the previous tax year and each payment on account is equal to 50% thereof. They are payable on 31 January within the tax year and on 31 July after the end of the tax year (e.g. on 31 January 2008 and 31 July 2008 in respect of the tax year 2007/08). The need for such payments may arise where the individual is, for example, a sole trader or a partner in a partnership or if significant untaxed investment income is received. The 31 January payment after the end of the relevant tax year (i.e. 31 January 2009 in the above example) represents any balancing payment due for the tax year 2007/08 after taking into account the payments on account already made.

Payments on account are only made in respect of an individual's income tax liability for a tax year but not in respect of any capital gains tax liability.

Inheritance Tax

Unlike income and capital gains tax payments, inheritance tax payments are made, in general, six months after the end of the month in which any charge arises (be it a charge on a lifetime gift or on death), i.e. inheritance tax is payable according to the timing of a chargeable event rather than at set times as for income tax and capital gains tax (see Chapter 13).

SUMMARY

The main UK taxes are income tax, capital gains tax and inheritance tax.

The extent of an individual's tax liabilities depends upon the domicile, residence and ordinary residence status of the individual.

Each of the above three taxes are entirely separate and each have their own set of rules.

FA 2008 has made few material changes with respect to inheritance tax but significant changes with respect to income and, in particular, capital gains tax.

The tax treatment of UK domiciled and non-UK domiciled individuals is significantly different.

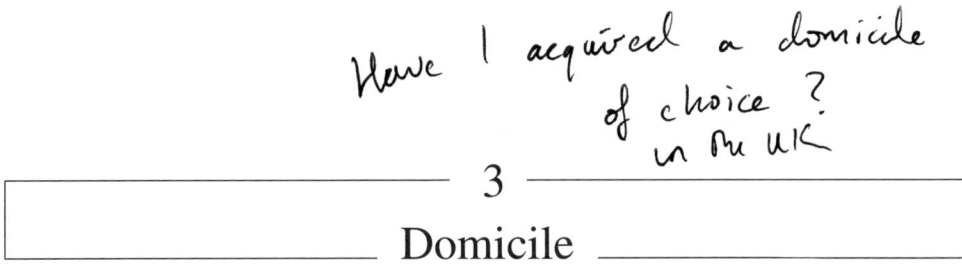

3
Domicile

BACKGROUND

The domicile, residence and ordinary residence status of the individual are critical to a determination of the individual's potential exposure to income, capital gains and inheritance tax. Any combination of these three attributes is possible; for example:

- domicile, resident and ordinary resident;
- domicile, resident but not ordinary resident;
- non-domicile, resident and ordinary resident;
- non-domicile, non-resident and non-ordinary resident.

It is therefore of the utmost importance that before any advice and/or wealth management planning is commenced the status of the individual with respect to each of these three attributes is clarified.

This chapter and Chapter 4 will examine in some detail the concepts of domicile, residence and ordinary residence.

CONCEPT OF PRIVATE INTERNATIONAL LAW NOT TAXATION

Domicile is a concept of private international law not taxation and the rules are laid down by common law (and statute). It is an artificial legal construct and has been imported for use in issues of taxation from the law of family relations and family property.

The general importance of the concept of domicile is that it is used to connect an individual to a place and thus in turn permits the law governing that place to apply to the individual. Thus, for example, an individual who possesses an English domicile will find that it is English law which will govern his personal relationships including issues such as the validity of marriage; jurisdiction in divorce; legitimacy and adoption; wills and the devolution of movable property on an intestacy (i.e. the distribution of property on death where no will exists).

Not all countries, however, adopt domicile as the relevant concept to determine which personal law is to apply to an individual. Many European countries (e.g. France, Germany) with a civil law-based system have tended to adopt the concept of nationality as the relevant personal law rather than that of domicile. Furthermore, the term domicile when used in other countries is not always used in its UK context. The French Civil Code (Article 102) states:

> the domicile of any French person, as to the exercise of his/her civil rights, is the place where he/she is principally established.

Where other countries whose legal system is based on common law (e.g. Australia, USA) have in principle adopted the UK's concept of domicile, local legislation has often amended its meaning (e.g., in Australia the automatic reversion to the domicile of origin has been abolished). It cannot therefore be assumed that the implications of domicile under UK law will be exactly reflected under those laws of such foreign common law countries.

An example outside of taxation of the importance of domicile is the Inheritance (Provision for Family and Dependants) Act 1975 which applies only to the estates of persons who die domiciled in England and Wales. The rules of private international law apply in determining the person's domicile.

The 1975 Act came into force in respect of deaths after 31 March 1976 but has no application to Scotland or Northern Ireland (Scotland has a system of fixed inheritance tax rights and Northern Ireland has a statutory order similar to the 1975 Act).

Broadly speaking, the Act (as subsequently amended) permits certain categories of individual (e.g. surviving spouse; children; cohabitee) to lodge a claim against the estate of a deceased person for provision. However, where the deceased's domicile status is unclear the claimant has first to satisfy the court that the deceased died domiciled in England (or Wales).

It is therefore not unusual for cases heard by the courts to determine domicile of a deceased to emanate from claims under the 1975 Act as was the situation in the cases of *Agulian v. Cyganik (2005)* and *Morgan v. Cilento (2005)* (see below). Thus, not all domicile cases are exclusively tax driven.

In *Henderson v. Henderson (1965)* it was said that:

> Domicile is that legal relationship between a person ... and a territory which invokes the system as [his] personal law ....

Domicile is normally identified with an individual's permanent home. Lord Cranworth in *Whicker v. Hume (1858)* said:

> By domicile we mean home, the permanent home.

In *Winans v. AG (1904)* it was said:

> A person may be said to have his home in a country if he resides in it without any intention of at present removing from it permanently or for an indefinite period.

However, domicile cannot automatically be equated with home. An individual's domicile status may not in fact be related to the country of location of the individual's permanent home and indeed may be determined to be a country which the individual has never visited and in which no permanent home exists or has ever existed (e.g. the determination of an individual's domicile of origin).

Domicile is not the same as nationality or citizenship. An individual may be a British citizen yet still possess a non-UK domicile. Similarly, the acquisition of British citizenship (i.e. the acquisition of a British passport) does not automatically result in the acquisition of a UK domicile.

In *IRC v. Bullock (1976)* it was stated:

[handwritten: Citizenship comes before Domicile]

> Domicile is distinct from citizenship... and not to acquire UK citizenship would not be inconsistent with... having acquired a domicile in the UK....

In the case of *Al Fayed v. Advocate General (2002)* HMRC appeared to accept that the acquisition of UK citizenship would not necessarily result in the acquisition of a UK domicile:

> The matter was taken further at the end of 1985 when the first petitioner's [Al Fayed] advisers raised the question of his acquiring United Kingdom citizenship. On 23 December 1985 Mr Sargent of PMM [Al Fayed's advisors] telephoned Mr Stribblehill [HMRC] to say that the brothers had it in mind to take out United Kingdom citizenship and that he had advised them that that was unlikely to affect their domicile status. Mr Stribblehill took the matter up with Mrs Winder of the Claims Branch [HMRC]. *She advised him that United Kingdom citizenship would have no effect on the first petitioner's domicile.* Mr Stribblehill then conveyed this advice to Mr Sargent and that particular matter came to an end.

ENGLISH/WELSH, SCOTTISH OR NORTHERN IRISH

When used in a statute the term "United Kingdom" has the meaning provided by the Interpretation Act 1978, namely, Great Britain (i.e. including England, Scotland and Wales) and Northern Ireland.

Domicile is, strictly speaking, linked to a particular system of law which may be that of a country or it may be that of a subdivision thereof.

Thus, while it is common practice to refer to an individual's "UK domicile" status, strictly speaking, an individual cannot possess such a UK domicile. In this case the individual's domicile status is that of England/Wales (the same legal system applying in England and Wales) *or* Scotland *or* Northern Ireland (these countries comprising the UK).

Similarly, it is not possible for an individual to possess, for example, a Canadian, American or Australian domicile (i.e. a domicile in the federation). In such cases it is

[handwritten: Domicile is Eng/Wales or NI or Scotland — but tax is same]

necessary to determine in which particular province or state the individual is domiciled (e.g. Alberta, British Columbia re Canada or California, Texas re the USA).

This may give rise to unexpected problems. For example, an individual possessing an English domicile of origin may move to, say, Alberta in Canada successfully acquiring a domicile of choice in Alberta. The individual, at a later date, then decides to leave Alberta for good and move to British Columbia but is not sure of his future intention at that time (i.e. the individual is not sure if he intends to remain indefinitely in British Columbia). The consequence of the move and the lack of clarity of intention is that the individual's English domicile of origin would automatically resurrect even though the individual is simply moving from one province in Canada to another. Great care is thus needed when an individual moves from one province/state within a federation to another province/state within the same federation as there is a real risk of a resurrection of the individual's domicile of origin at that time (which may prove extremely problematic for UK tax purposes if that domiciliary has a UK domicile of origin).

On the other hand, in the case of many other countries a single system of law applies throughout and an individual may then be said to possess that country's domicile (e.g. Norway, Sweden and Turkey).

For general legal purposes it is thus necessary to determine whether an individual is English/Welsh, Scottish or Northern Irish domiciled. However, for UK tax purposes this is not strictly necessary because the same tax laws apply to each of these countries. Accordingly, the term "UK domicile" (and where appropriate non-UK domicile) will be adopted to apply whether, technically speaking, the actual domicile of the individual is English/Welsh, Scottish or Northern Irish.

For UK tax purposes it is thus generally only necessary to identify whether an individual is UK domiciled or non-UK domiciled.

IMPORTANCE OF DOMICILE FOR UK TAX PURPOSES

The concept of domicile has been imported for UK tax purposes and its importance for an individual in the context of taxation (as was seen in Chapter 2) is that:

- it is the primary determinant of the extent of an individual's inheritance tax liabilities;
- it determines if the "remittance" as opposed to the "arising" basis applies to non-UK source income and non-UK source capital gains for the non-UK domiciled (and resident) individual.

Domicile is also relevant to trustees/trusts. Although unclear, the proper law of the trust (i.e. the law under which the trust is to be governed) is likely to determine its domicile status.

It is important to note that the term *domicile* is being used as it is used in its traditional sense in English law. In other countries the term may mean something different.

Thus, it may be that English law determines that an individual is held to be domiciled in a country other than the UK (e.g. Italy) despite the fact that the laws of Italy (in this example) would treat the individual as domiciled outside of Italy.

CATEGORIES OF DOMICILE

There are three primary categories of domicile (the concept of "deemed" domicile is treated separately as it only applies specifically for inheritance tax purposes) applicable to individuals:

- domicile of origin;
- domicile of dependence;
- domicile of choice.

An individual can never be without a domicile (i.e. one of the above). Lord Westbury in *Udny v. Udny (1869)* stated:

> It is a settled principle that no man shall be without a domicile, and to secure this result the law attributes to every individual as soon as he is born [a] domicile ... This has been called the domicile of origin, and is involuntary ....

As a consequence, at birth, an individual automatically acquires a domicile of origin.

The case of *Udny v. Udny (1869)* concerned the question of the legitimacy of a child born out of wedlock but whose parents subsequently married. Prior to the Legitimation Act 1926, English law did not know the concept of legitimation whereas Scottish law did. The case thus turned on the domicile status of Colonel Udny, who had fathered a son out of wedlock (but subsequently married the mother). Legitimation of the child required the father to be domiciled in Scotland at both the date of birth and date of marriage. The court decided that Udny had possessed a Scottish domicile at the relevant times and thus the child was legitimated.

At any point in time for any one purpose an individual may possess only one domicile status (*IRC v. Bullock (1976)*).

An individual's domicile status may change through life either due to the operation of law (e.g. the imposition on a child of a domicile of dependence) *or* due to the individual's own choice (i.e. choosing a different domicile). Where an individual's domicile status changes at any point in time, for whatever reason, the individual's former domicile status is said to be *displaced* by the new domicile status.

There is, however, a presumption that an existing domicile status of an individual continues until it is proved that a new domicile has been acquired. The burden of proof of a change in domicile lies with the person who asserts it (*Winans v. AG (1904)*).

Example 3.1

John Smith was born with a UK domicile of origin.

When John was 30 years old he decided to emigrate to Indonesia where he ultimately died at age 75 and was buried.

It is likely that John would have acquired an Indonesian domicile of choice subsequent to emigrating from the UK and this domicile of choice would have displaced his original UK domicile of origin.

John would therefore have died with a non-UK domicile (i.e. an Indonesian domicile of choice) for UK tax purposes (inter alia, meaning any inheritance tax liability on his estate would arise only on UK situs assets).

If HMRC challenged John's change of domicile status it would be for John (or his executors in the event of his death) to prove the change.

While the domicile status of an individual may thus be displaced by another domicile status, this latter status may itself also be subsequently displaced.

Over the years a number of cases have come before the courts which have involved domicile determinations. Such determinations, however, have not always been driven by taxation factors.

Each of the above three categories of domicile will now be examined in turn.

Domicile of Origin

As indicated above, an individual's domicile is generally equated to the location of his permanent home (basically the place which the individual regards as his main home which usually means the country with which his ties are closest).

However, with respect to an individual's domicile of origin this is a concept of law and is determined at birth by law and may have no direct connection with the location of a permanent home. Accordingly, an individual's domicile of origin may be that of a country where the individual has never visited and in which no permanent home exists.

(i) Legitimate v. Illegitimate Child

The domicile of origin of a child is determined at birth by the domicile of the *father* if the child is legitimate *or* that of the *mother* if illegitimate (*Udny v. Udny (1869)*; *Henderson v. Henderson (1967)*). Per Lord Westbury in *Udny v. Udny (1869)*:

> It is a settled principle that no man shall be without a domicile, and to secure this result the law attributes to every individual as soon as he is born the domicile of his father, if the child be legitimate, and the domicile of the mother if illegitimate.

A child is legitimate if born in wedlock (i.e. born of a marriage valid under English law) which requires that the parents are married to one another at the time of the child's birth.

An illegitimate child is thus one born to parents who are not married to each other (or whose marriage has been declared void).

Example 3.2
John and Mary Smith are *married*. They are each UK domiciled. Their son Bob at birth acquires a domicile of origin which is determined by his father and thus is UK.

Example 3.3
Henry Brown and Karen Smith are *co-habiting* but are not married. They are each UK domiciled. Their daughter Barbara at birth acquires a domicile of origin which is determined by her mother and thus is UK.

Example 3.4
Charles Johnston is *cohabiting* with Helga Schmidt. Charles is UK domiciled and Helga is German domiciled. Their son Adolf at birth acquires a domicile of origin which is determined by his mother and thus is German.

Example 3.5
Charles Johnston is *married* to Helga Schmidt. Charles is UK domiciled and Helga is German domiciled. Their son Adolf at birth acquires a domicile of origin which is determined by his father and thus is UK (compare Example 3.4).

However, the position in Scotland has recently changed following the Family Law (Scotland) Act 2006. Under this Act the status of illegitimacy is abolished and thus the child's domicile status is now determined in the same manner irrespective of whether the child is legitimate or not (section 21). In addition, rules are now provided (see section 22) to determine the domicile status of a child under age 16 (irrespective of whether the child is legitimate or illegitimate).

Further complications may, however, arise in determining an individual's domicile of origin at birth.

(ii) Father Dead at Date of Birth

If the child is legitimate but not born during the father's lifetime (i.e. the father is dead at the actual date of the child's birth) then the child's domicile of origin is determined by the *mother's* domicile at the date of birth.

(iii) Parents Married but Separated

If the child is legitimate but the parents are separated (i.e. not living together), but not divorced at the date of birth, the child's acquires a domicile of *origin* which is that of his *father* but a domicile of *dependence* determined by that of his *mother* (assuming the child has no home with the father).

(iv) Legitimation

An illegitimate child's domicile of origin may be changed (i.e. displaced) on legitimation (i.e. the marriage of the child's natural mother and father; *Re Spence deceased, Spence v. Dennis & Another (1990)*).

On legitimation, while retaining the domicile of origin derived from the mother (as the child was illegitimate at birth) the domicile of origin is displaced by a domicile of dependence which will be that of his father (during his father's lifetime). In the event of the father's death, however, the child's domicile of dependence would revert to that of the mother.

Example 3.6 (using facts from Example 3.4)
Charles Johnston is cohabiting with Helga Schmidt. Charles is UK domiciled and Helga is German domiciled. Their son Adolf at birth acquires a domicile of origin which is determined by his mother (as Adolf is illegitimate) and thus is German.

Subsequently, Charles and Helga get married thus legitimating Adolf.

As a consequence, while Adolf's domicile of origin remains unchanged (i.e. German) it is, however, now displaced by a domicile of dependence which is that of his father, i.e. UK.

(v) Loss of Domicile of Origin

A domicile of origin is fixed for life and cannot be lost by *mere* abandonment; it needs to be positively displaced. It is very cohesive in nature but it can be displaced by the individual acquiring a domicile of choice, or if the individual is a child, by the child acquiring a domicile of dependence (see below).

A domicile of origin will not, however, be lost even if the individual has in fact left the country of this domicile and has no intention of returning to it *until* a domicile of choice in another country has been acquired (*Somerville v. Somerville (1801)*).

Example 3.7
In Example 3.6 above Adolf's German domicile of origin was that of his mother's domicile at the date of his birth (as Adolf was illegitimate).

If Adolf's mother and father do *not* subsequently marry Adolf's domicile of dependence would depend upon the domicile status of his mother and thus would change if and when his mother's domicile status changed.

However, on his subsequent legitimation (i.e. the marriage of his natural mother and father) his German domicile of origin is displaced by a UK domicile of dependence (namely, that of his father).

(vi) Resurrection of the Domicile of Origin

Even where a domicile of choice has displaced a domicile of origin (e.g. if the individual emigrates from the UK acquiring a domicile of choice in a new country) the individual's UK domicile of origin may be resurrected at any time in the future. For it to resurrect would require that the domicile of choice be abandoned without, at the same time, a new domicile of choice having immediately been acquired.

Thus, the lack of abandonment of an acquired domicile of choice precludes the domicile of origin resurrecting.

Example 3.8
Susan Poole possessed a UK domicile of origin. She decided to emigrate to Japan and in so doing acquired a Japanese domicile of choice which displaced her UK domicile of origin. After 15 years she changed her mind and decided it was time for a change and moved to Thailand. She had no intention any longer of residing in Japan permanently.

However, she was not sure at the time of the move to Thailand that she intended to reside there indefinitely.

Her UK domicile of origin would automatically resurrect.

In essence, a domicile of origin may thus be displaced but it remains, as it were, in the background in abeyance waiting for resurrection if the facts support such resurrection.

Lord Westbury in *Udny v. Udny (1869)* stated:

> As the domicile of origin is a creature of law, and independent of the will of the party, it would be inconsistent to suppose ... that it is capable of being by the mere act of the party, entirely obliterated and extinguished. It revives and exists whenever there is no other domicile ....

However, in one circumstance only a domicile of origin can actually be *replaced* and not just *displaced*. In this case the individual's domicile of origin (i.e. the domicile acquired at birth) is literally no longer deemed to exist having been totally replaced by a replacement domicile of origin status.

This occurs where a child is adopted.

(vii) Adoption

Adoption extinguishes the parental responsibility of the child's birth parents and vests it in the adopters. Adoption is the complete legal transference of parental responsibility and makes the child a full legal member of the "new family".

The Adoption & Children Act 2002 is the relevant current statute which came into force on 30 December 2005 replacing the Adoption Act 1976.

A child must be under 18 to be adopted.

An adopted person is treated in law as if the person is the legitimate child of the adopter(s) (i.e. the adopted child is treated in law as born to the adopter(s) in wedlock; section 67(1)).

Thus, an adopted child's "original" domicile of origin (i.e. the domicile acquired at birth) is *replaced* by a "new" replacement domicile of origin.

The adopted child's "new" domicile of origin is generally accepted as being determined at the time of the child's birth not at the date of adoption (although there are arguments that the relevant date is in fact the date of adoption).

This "new" domicile of origin is determined as if the child had been the legitimate child of the adopter(s). Thus, a fiction is created.

The child's "new" domicile of origin is that of the adopting father (as it is assumed that the adopted child is the legitimate child of the adopters).

The effect of adoption is thus that the child's domicile of origin as originally determined by the child's natural parents (legitimate or not) is overridden by that determined by the domicile(s) of the adopter(s).

Adoption is the only occasion when an individual's domicile of origin may literally be *replaced* (not just displaced) by a replacement domicile of origin.

Example 3.9

Henri Jacques and his wife Marie Jacques, both French domiciled, had a legitimate child François who thus acquired a French domicile of origin from his father. François was born in 2004.

François in 2007 was adopted by John and Mary Smith a married couple each UK domiciled.

François' original French domicile of origin is replaced by that which would have arisen if François had been born legitimately to John and Mary.

Assuming therefore François had been born legitimately in 2004 to John and Mary he would at that time have acquired a domicile of origin of his father (i.e. John), namely, the UK.

François' original French domicile of origin will be *replaced* forever by a UK domicile of origin. It will be this UK replacement domicile of origin that will be capable of resurrection.

Example 3.10

Fred Gamble, who is UK domiciled, is cohabiting with Inga Sweden who is Swedish domiciled. Inga has a child, Jacob, who is illegitimate from a former relationship.

Fred and Inga decide to marry and Fred agrees to adopt Jacob.

At birth Jacob acquired, as a domicile of origin, the domicile of his mother (as he is illegitimate), namely, Swedish.

No domicile consequences arise for any of the individuals on Fred and Inga's marriage (including that of Jacob as he is not legitimated on the marriage as Fred is not his natural father).

However, if following the marriage Fred decides to adopt Jacob, Jacob's original domicile of origin (Swedish) is replaced by that of Fred determined at the date of Jacob's birth (it being assumed that Jacob was born legitimately to Fred and Inga).

Jacob's domicile of origin is now that of the UK (i.e. that of Fred) which replaces forever his original Swedish domicile of origin.

Domicile of Dependence

An individual's domicile of dependence, as the name suggests, is a domicile which is dependent or determined according to the circumstances of someone else (usually that of the father or mother). The domicile of dependence of an individual is the same as and changes (if at all) with the domicile of the person on whom the individual is legally dependent.

A domicile of dependence is imposed.

The concept is potentially applicable in two circumstances:

- children;
- married women.

The Domicile and Matrimonial Proceedings Act 1973 (DMPA 1973) (which came into force in 1 January 1974) provides that a child can only acquire a domicile of choice from age 16 onwards or below 16 if validly married (under English law a marriage is, however, void if one of the parties is under age 16; the person under age 16 need not be the English domiciled individual for the marriage to be void; section 2 of the Marriage Act 1949). However, this part of the 1973 Act (namely, section 3(1)) only in fact extends to England, Wales and Northern Ireland.

Before this date, at common law, a child ceased to be a dependent person on reaching the age of majority. Pre 1 January 1974 and post 1 January 1970 (when the Family Law Reform Act 1969 came into force) the age of majority was 18. Before 1 January 1970 the age of majority was 21.

In the case of Scotland, pre 25 September 1991, a child was able to acquire a domicile of choice on reaching age 12, if a girl, or 14, if a boy (*Arnott v. Groom (1846)*). However, the Age of Legal Capacity (Scotland) Act 1991 provides that the acquisition of a domicile of choice requires the individual to be at least age 16 (thus bringing Scotland in line with England, Wales and Northern Ireland).

It should be noted that a child under age 16 *may* be validly married under a foreign law if each of the individual's law of domicile at that time permits it (thus, for example, a non-UK domiciled individual under age 16 could possibly validly marry in Las Vegas, USA, an individual who was also non-UK domiciled if their respective laws of domicile permit this).

In the case of married women, the 1973 Act abolished the automatic acquisition of a domicile of dependence on marriage for marriages on or after 1 January 1974.

(i) Children and Domicile of Dependence

(a) Legitimate
The domicile of dependence of an unmarried legitimate child under age 16 is determined by, and changes with, the domicile of the father during the father's lifetime. On the death of the father the child's domicile depends upon the mother's.

(b) Illegitimate
The domicile of dependence of an unmarried illegitimate child under age 16 is determined by, and changes with, the domicile of the mother.

(c) Legitimation
On legitimation, the domicile of dependence of the child is that of the father.

A parent's domicile may change by, for example, the parent acquiring a domicile of choice different from their domicile of origin. This would cause the child's domicile of origin to change to that of the parent's new domicile of choice but for the child would be a domicile of dependence. The child's domicile of origin would thus be displaced with the newly acquired domicile of dependence.

Example 3.11
Tom and Susan Smith are married, each possessing a UK domicile of origin, and have a legitimate daughter Jane who possesses a UK domicile of origin.

Tom and Susan decide to emigrate and settle in Spain and in so doing each acquire a Spanish domicile of choice which now displaces their UK domicile of origin.

The emigration occurs when Jane is 5.

Jane acquires a Spanish domicile of dependence as her father's domicile, on whom Jane's domicile depends, has itself changed to Spanish.

Assuming at age 16 Jane is still living in Spain with her parents, her Spanish domicile of dependency is re-categorised as a Spanish domicile of choice.

A child's domicile of dependence may change more than once if the parent's domicile, on whom the child's domicile depends, also changes.

Example 3.12
Following from the facts of Example 3.11 Tom and Susan after a number of years in Spain change their minds about residing in Spain indefinitely and decide to leave Spain and settle permanently in Italy, thus each acquiring Italian domiciles of choice.

Jane's Spanish domicile of dependence would now be displaced with an Italian domicile of dependence (assuming that the move to Italy and the parents' change in domiciles occurred while Jane was under 16).

(d) Parents live apart
Where a legitimate or legitimated child's parents live apart the child's domicile of dependence is that of the mother if the child has a home with her but not with the father (if the child, however, also has a home with the father the child's domicile of dependence is that of the father). In the event of the mother's death the child retains the dead mother's domicile of dependence unless subsequently the child has a home with the father in which case the child's domicile of dependence is that of the father.

(e) Conversion to choice
A child's domicile of dependence remains as such until the child becomes aged 16 and thus ceases to be dependent. The child's domicile of dependence at age 16 continues, albeit re-categorised, as a domicile of choice under DMPA 1973 (see also *Gulbenkian v. Gulbenkian (1937)* and *Harrison v. Harrison (1953)*).

(ii) Married Women and Domicile of Dependence

(a) Pre-1 January 1974 marriage
Prior to 1 January 1974, on marriage, a woman automatically under common law acquired a domicile of dependence which was the domicile of her husband at that time (*Lord Advocate v. Jaffrey (1921)*). This would displace her domicile of origin and

her domicile status thereafter would change with that of her husband's domicile status irrespective of her own wishes or intentions and irrespective of whether she lived with her husband or not.

The rule under which a woman *automatically* acquired her husband's domicile on marriage as a domicile of dependence was abolished effective 1 January 1974 by DMPA 1973. However, the Act is not retrospective and, thus, for marriages taking place *before* this date the "old" rules continue to apply, i.e. on marriage the woman automatically acquired a domicile of dependence which would be that of her husband.

Section 1 of the Act, however, provides:

> Where immediately before [1 January 1974] a woman was married and then had her husband's domicile by dependence, she is treated as retaining that domicile (as a domicile of choice, if it is not also her domicile of origin) unless and until it is changed by acquisition or revival of another domicile on or after [1 January 1974].

Thus for a pre 1 January 1974 married woman, on 1 January 1974 her domicile of dependence is re-categorised as a domicile of choice. On or after this date she is capable of acquiring a different domicile of choice (or she may cause her domicile of origin to resurrect) by doing whatever the law requires for a new domicile of choice to be acquired, whether she remains married or not. In practice, where the woman remains married and living with her husband this may prove difficult.

Interestingly, only one case has come before the courts (post 1 January 1974) concerning the domicile status of a woman who married prior to 1 January 1974. This was the case of *IRC v. Duchess of Portland (1982)* in which the Duchess of Portland failed to convince the courts that she had acquired a domicile of choice in Quebec (which in fact was her domicile of origin) after 1 January 1974 following her marriage (pre 1 January 1974) to a UK domiciled male.

Example 3.13
Christina Athens possessed a Greek domicile of origin.

In May 1970 she married Herbert Spencer who possessed a UK domicile of origin.

On marriage, Christina would have acquired her husband's domicile (i.e. UK) as a domicile of dependence.

On 1 January 1974 her UK domicile of dependence would be treated as a UK domicile of choice.

Example 3.14
Barbara Tree, a UK domicile individual, married Fergus O'Leary, a Republic of Ireland domiciled individual, on 30 May 1972.

On marriage Barbara would have acquired her husband's domicile (i.e. Republic of Ireland) as a domicile of dependence.

On 1 January 1974 her Republic of Ireland domicile of dependence would be treated as a Republic of Ireland domicile of choice.

The case of *Re Scullard (1956)* concerned a woman who had married a UK domiciled male in 1893 thus acquiring a UK domicile of dependence. Despite the marriage she left her husband in 1908 and never returned to him but remained married to him. In 1947 she went to live in Guernsey and expressed the intention of spending the rest of her days there.

She died in 1955 six weeks after her husband who died possessing a UK domicile, and between his and her death she had been too ill to evince any intention in respect of her domicile.

As she remained married she was unable in law to acquire a domicile different from that of her husband. The court, however, found that in her lifetime she had clearly expressed her intention to make her permanent home in Guernsey and there was no reason why this would not become effective in law once her husband had died; no overt act on her part being required after her husband's death.

Note in the *Re Scullard* case all relevant acts were pre 1 January 1974 and thus the Domicile and Matrimonial Proceedings Act 1973 was not in point.

(b) Exception to automatic domicile of dependence on marriage
Interestingly, there is, however, one exception to the automatic domicile of dependence arising on a pre 1 January 1974 marriage, namely, in the case of a female US citizen. This exception does not arise under common law but specifically due to the terms of the bilateral double taxation agreement between the UK and the USA.

Article 4(6) of the UK/US double taxation agreement provides:

A marriage before 1st January 1974 between a woman who is a USA national and a man domiciled within the UK shall be deemed to have taken place on 1st January 1974 for the purpose of determining her domicile on or after 6th April 1976 for UK tax [*i.e. income tax and capital gains tax; not inheritance tax*] purposes.

Thus, a female US citizen marrying a UK domiciled male before 1 January 1974 is *not* treated as automatically acquiring her husband's domicile (i.e. UK) as a domicile of dependence. Her domicile status is determined under the normal rules. This position, however, applies only for UK income tax and capital gains tax purposes (it does not apply for UK inheritance tax purposes in which case the above domicile of dependence rule will be in point).

Example 3.15
Joan Texas, a US female citizen, married Peter Joseph, a UK domiciled individual, prior to 1 January 1974.

In determining Joan's liabilities to UK income tax or capital gains tax her domicile status will be determined on normal principles. She will thus not have acquired automatically a UK domicile of dependence on her marriage to Peter.

Other things being equal, she will retain her US domicile of origin and so be liable to UK income tax and capital gains tax only on UK source income and UK source gains; non-UK situs income and non-UK situs gains only falling to be taxed in the UK if remitted to the UK.

However, for inheritance tax purposes she will be deemed to have acquired a UK domicile of dependence (thus, in principle, being liable to UK inheritance tax on her worldwide assets).

(c) Post 31 December 1973 marriage

For marriages on or after 1 January 1974 the woman's domicile is determined under the normal rules and no domicile of dependence is automatically assigned to her on marriage.

Thus a marriage on or after 1 January 1974 has, per se, no impact on the woman's domicile status at the time of marriage although if on marriage she lives with her husband in the country of his domicile (whether choice or origin) it may be the case that at some point her husband's country of domicile becomes that of his wife as a domicile of choice.

Domicile of Choice

The acquisition of a domicile of choice is no easy matter. However, where it does occur it does so at a particular point in time.

Mr Justice Lewison in *Gaines-Cooper v. RCC (2007)* in this regard stated:

> ... It follows, therefore, that there will ... be a particular moment in time at which his domicile changes if he acquires a domicile of choice which replaces his domicile of origin. Before that moment, his domicile will have been his domicile of origin. After that moment it will be his domicile of choice. Locating the moment may be a difficult question of fact.

Determining this point in time in practice can be very difficult. The reasoning in a number of court decisions in this regard does at times appear to be contradictory.

However, Scarman J. in *Re Fuld's Estate (No. 3) (1968)* stated:

> ... that the difficulty of reconciling the numerous statements arises not from a lack of judicial thought, but from the nature of the subject. The cases involve a detailed examination of the facts and it is not surprising that different judicial minds concerned with different factual situations have chosen different language to describe the law.

Nevertheless, it is by no means unusual for a higher court (e.g. Court of Appeal) to conclude with findings completely different from those of the lower court (e.g. High Court); examples include the classic case of *Winans v. AG (1904)* and *Agulian v. Cyganik (2006)*.

In determining whether a new domicile of choice has been acquired the courts have commented and/or found, inter alia, as follows:

- a special motive for residing in a country (father's dying wishes) does not preclude domicile of choice arising (*Somerville v. Somerville (1801)*);
- actual residence *and* an intention to reside in the new country must be present although the length of actual residence, per se, is not important (*Bell v. Kennedy (1868)*);
- proof of a change of domicile is "on a balance of probabilities" basis (*Re Fuld's Estate (No. 3) (1968)*);
- acquisition of nationality and a passport in a new country is not conclusive evidence of the acquisition of a new domicile of choice in that country. Conversely, acquisition of British citizenship which includes the need to sign a declaration that the individual intends to reside in the UK does not, per se, mean that a UK domicile of choice arises (*Wahl v. IRC (1932); Fayed v. AG (2002)*);
- registering on the electoral roll as an overseas elector is also ignored in determining UK domicile status (IR20).

Some of the factors which have been considered in deciding whether changes of domicile have occurred include:

- membership of clubs;
- churches attended;
- naturalisation;
- lifestyle;
- wife and/or children accompaniment;
- burial arrangements;
- health;
- wills;
- bank accounts;
- statements made in autobiographies;
- statements made orally to relations and third parties;
- relationships with the local vicar;
- location of dwellings;
- length of time in country;
- business interests;
- allocation of time.

As stated in *Casdagli v. Casdagli (1919)*:

> Nothing must be neglected that can possibly indicate the bent of the resident's mind...His aspirations, whims, amours, prejudices, health, religion, financial expectation – all are taken into account.

(i) Misleading Nature of the Word "Choice"

It should be noted that the term "choice" in the phrase "domicile of choice" is perhaps a little misleading.

First, in two situations domiciles of choice are provided by law and do not arise as a consequence of a *choice* made by the individual; namely, the law specifically provides for a domicile of choice to apply where a child's domicile of origin has been displaced by a domicile of dependence and the child attains age 16 and in the case of a pre 1 January 1974 married woman effective 1 January 1974.

Second, it may be that an individual who, for example, possesses a *non-UK* domicile of origin acquires a UK domicile of choice inadvertently. This situation could arise where the individual resides in the UK and where, on the facts, the courts conclude that it was the individual's intention to reside there permanently or indefinitely. This the court may conclude on the factual evidence before it even if the individual had not explicitly stated this to be the case or indeed wanted it to be the case.

Can be forced to have UK Dom.

Thus, in *Douglas v. Douglas (1871)* it was stated:

> If the [requisite] intention exists and if it is sufficiently carried into effect certain legal consequences follow from it, whether such consequences are intended or not and perhaps even though the person in question may have intended the exact opposite.

This was, in fact, the situation in *Re Steer (1858)* where Mr Steer was held to have died domiciled in Germany despite an explicit declaration in his will that he had no intention of renouncing his English domicile of origin.

There are, of course, many examples where HMRC may wish to argue that an individual who possesses a non-UK domicile of origin has in fact acquired a UK domicile of choice. HMRC may want to so argue because:

- the individual owns significant non-UK situs assets and has died while living in the UK: and/or
- the individual has significant non-UK source income and/or non-UK realised capital gains.

In each of the above two situations the consequence of the individual being treated as having acquired a UK domicile of choice is that on death (or lifetime gifts) the individual's worldwide assets (i.e. including non-UK situs assets) would be subject to inheritance tax and with respect to income and/or capital gains arising outside the UK both income tax and capital gains tax would apply on the arising (not remittance) basis.

However, a *domicile of choice* (as the name suggests) may be acquired *voluntarily* by an individual. In other words, it is possible for an individual to explicitly attempt to acquire a domicile of choice different from that person's domicile of origin or indeed different from an already acquired domicile of choice. The newly acquired domicile of choice would then displace either the domicile of origin or an earlier acquired domicile of choice.

Thus at its simplest, for example, a domicile of choice would, in principle, arise if an individual effectively made a permanent home in a country different to the country of the individual's domicile of origin. Such individual may emigrate from the UK (the domicile of origin) to Canada thus acquiring a domicile of choice in Canada which would displace the individual's UK domicile of origin; technically, the domicile of choice would need to be within one of the Canadian Provinces not Canada per se.

(ii) Age Requirement

To acquire a domicile of choice an individual must be aged 16 or over (in the case of England/Wales and Northern Ireland; however, in Scotland pre-25 September 1991 a child was able to acquire a domicile of choice at the end of pupillarity, namely, 14 for a boy and 12 for a girl).

(iii) Two Basic Requirements

IR20 (see Appendix 3) provides:

> You have the capacity to acquire a new domicile (a domicile of choice) when you reach age 16. To do so, you must broadly leave your country of domicile and settle in another country. You need to provide strong evidence that you intend to live there permanently or indefinitely. Living in another country for a long time, although an important factor, is not enough in itself to prove you have acquired a new domicile.

Lord Chelmsford in *Bell v. Kennedy (1868)* stated:

> A new domicile is not acquired until there is not only a fixed intention of establishing a permanent residence in a new country, but until also this intention has been carried out by actual residence there.

Thus, for an individual to acquire a domicile of choice requires positive action and two conditions need to be satisfied:

- the individual must actually take up residence in another country; *and*
- the individual must have the fixed intention of residing permanently or indefinitely in the new country of residence.

Thus, *residence* in a country without the requisite *intention*, however strong, without actual *residence* will *not* result in the acquisition of a domicile of choice; *both* conditions must be satisfied.

It does not matter which of the two aspects occurs first. An individual may thus form an intention to reside followed by the actual residence or, alternatively, the individual may acquire actual residency with the requisite intention arising thereafter.

Example 3.16
Michael Furlow possesses a UK domicile of origin.

He emigrates to Italy, at age 25, where he has since resided and has stated that he intends to reside there indefinitely.

Michael will have acquired an Italian domicile of choice which will displace his UK domicile of origin.

Example 3.17

Tom Furlow, Michael's brother (see Example 3.16 above), also possesses a UK domicile of origin and also left the UK to live in Italy.

However, unlike his brother Michael, Tom wasn't sure whether he wanted to remain in Italy indefinitely.

Tom's UK domicile of origin will continue to subsist and he, unlike his brother, will not have acquired an Italian domicile of choice.

If in due course Tom does decide to remain in Italy indefinitely then at that point in time he will acquire an Italian domicile of choice.

The issue of an individual's "intention" is perhaps one of the most difficult and contentious areas of domicile. It is often made even more difficult by the fact that the death of an individual may be the trigger for a domicile determination to be made at which time, of course, the individual is no longer around to comment.

Perhaps a classic example of this difficulty is illustrated by the different conclusions reached in the various courts which heard the case of *Winans v. AG (1904)*.

The case concerned an eccentric American millionaire who was born in the USA in 1823 living there until 1850. He then moved to Russia thereafter spending time in Russia and the UK (in particular to avoid the Russian winters; Winans was paranoid about his health) between 1860 and 1893. From 1893 until his death four years later in 1897 he lived entirely in England. After leaving the USA he never returned.

He dreamed of one day returning to the USA and of building a fleet of cigar-shaped ships which he said would allow the USA to gain superiority over the British fleets. The ships were to be docked in Maryland, USA.

The case was heard by the High Court, the Court of Appeal and was finally decided by the House of Lords.

The House of Lords decided by a majority of two to one in favour of Winans, i.e. that he had retained his domicile of origin (which was either New Jersey or Maryland in the USA) and had thus not acquired a UK domicile of choice.

On the other hand, the High Court and the Court of Appeal, comprising in total five judges, had unanimously found against Winans holding that he had acquired a UK domicile of choice.

Statements made in the House of Lords by each of the Lords included the following:

> When he came to this country [UK], he was a sojourner and a stranger, and he was I think a sojourner and a stranger in it [UK] when he died. (per Lord Macnaghten)

> He had one and only one home, and that was in this country [UK]. (per Lord Lindley)

The third Lord, Lord Halsbury, was simply unable to make up his mind and thus the presumption of continuance applied (i.e. no change in Winans' domicile status had been clearly shown to have occurred).

This case admirably illustrates the difficulties in deciding whether an individual has or has not formed an intention to reside permanently/indefinitely in a particular country.

Each of the two legs (residence and intention) of the test will now be considered.

(a) Residence
(i) Meaning   The term "residence" when used in the context of domicile is not the same as when the term is used for general UK taxation purposes.

For the purposes of the law of domicile the term *residence* in a country refers to:

> physical presence in that country as an inhabitant of it.
> (per Nourse J. in *IRC v. Duchess of Portland (1982)*)

In this regard, residence must be more than casual residence or residence as a visitor however often and however extensive those visits may be.

It is possible for an individual to reside in more than one country at the same time. Nourse J. in the *Duchess of Portland* stated:

> ... a case where the domiciliary divides his physical presence between two countries at the same time ... it is necessary to look at all the facts in order to decide which of the two countries is the one he inhabits.

(ii) Duration of residence   Length of residence in a particular country may be indicative of the acquisition of a domicile of choice therein but, per se, is not conclusive. IR20 under the heading "Domicile of Choice" states:

> Living in another country for a long time, although an important factor, is not enough in itself to prove you have acquired a new domicile.

In *Ramsay v. Liverpool Royal Infirmary (1930)* it was stated:

> ... mere length of residence by itself is insufficient evidence from which to infer the animus [intention]; but the quality of the residence may afford the necessary inference.

Ramsay v. Liverpool Royal Infirmary (1930) concerned a Mr George Bowie who was born in 1845 in Glasgow, with a Scottish domicile of origin, and who died in 1927 in England and was buried in England. The issue at stake was the validity if his will which would have been valid if he had died in Scotland but invalid if he had died in England. At age 37, in 1882, he gave up working for a living and for the rest of his life lived off his mother, sisters and brothers. In 1892 he moved to Liverpool, again living with his family, and left England after this time only twice, never, however, returning to Scotland. He expressed to others that he never intended to return to Scotland (desiring to be buried in Liverpool). His mother died while he was alive but he refused to attend her funeral which was held in Scotland. His will provided for the residue of his estate to be left equally between three Glasgow- and one Liverpool-based charities. The House of Lords on appeal from the decision of two lower Scottish courts held (confirming the earlier decisions) that he had died domiciled in Scotland.

In various cases the courts have held that residence, for the purposes of the law of domicile, may only need to be for a few days or even for part of a day. Thus, an immigrant may acquire a domicile of choice immediately upon arrival in the country in which the immigrant intends to permanently settle. Ownership or the renting of a house/flat is not necessary for residence to arise; for example, a room in a hotel or a friend's house (*Stone v. Stone (1958)*) is sufficient. Length of residence in effect is, per se, irrelevant. What is important is that residence must be residence in the pursuance of an intention to settle permanently or indefinitely.

In *Bell v. Kennedy (1868)* Lord Chelmsford stated that:

> If the intention of permanently residing in a place exists then residence in pursuance of that intention, *however short*, will establish a domicile.

Bell v. Kennedy (1968) concerned a determination of the domicile status of Mr Bell whose wife had died and at the time of her death possessed a domicile of dependency upon him; thus a determination of her domicile status could be determined only once that of Mr Bell had been determined.

Mr Bell had a Jamaican domicile of origin having been born in Jamaica of Scottish parents. He had been educated in Scotland but then returned to Jamaica. He left Jamaica in 1837 for good arriving with his wife in Scotland to look for an estate to buy and to settle in Scotland. While in Scotland he resided with his mother-in-law. In the event, for various reasons (including the weather), Mr Bell could not decide whether he wanted to settle in Scotland, England or the south of France. At this point in 1838 his wife died. The court held that:

> The question is, had he any settled fixed intention of being permanently resident in Scotland on 28th September 1938 [date of wife's death]...he was resident in Scotland [at the date of his wife's death], but without the animus manendi [the intention to remain], and therefore he still retained his [Jamaican] domicile of origin.

This was held despite very clear evidence that he was determined never to return to Jamaica.

Nourse J. in *Re Clore (No. 2) (1982)* in a similar vein stated:

> ... if the evidence of intention is there, particularly where the motive is the avoidance of taxes, the necessary intention will not be held to be missing merely because the period of actual residence is a short one.

The adequacy of even a very short period of residency to acquire a domicile of choice if intention of permanent residency is present was ably demonstrated in the American case of *White v. Tennant (1888)* where it was held that residence in the new domicile (the State of Pennsylvania) *of one afternoon* (i.e. literally a few hours) was sufficient for Mr White to have acquired a new domicile of choice in the State of Pennsylvania.

Mr White had previously possessed a domicile of origin in West Virginia and had returned there after one afternoon at the new house in Pennsylvania, as Mrs White, due to the poor condition of the house, had refused to spend a night in the house until its state had been improved. Mr White died before he could return to Pennsylvania. The court (Supreme Court of Appeals West Virginia) held:

> He [Mr White] had taken the decision to move to Pennsylvania; arrived in Pennsylvania in order to become an inhabitant of it; and had the intention of residing there indefinitely. Mr White had simply returned to West Virginia on a temporary basis, with no intention of moving back their again permanently. This was sufficient to satisfy the requirements.

(iii) Illegal residence Until recently, illegality was perceived as precluding the possibility of the acquisition of a domicile of choice. However, it is now accepted that a domicile of choice may be acquired even if the individual is resident in a country illegally. Thus, in *Mark v. Mark (2005)* (a matrimonial case involving the jurisdiction of the court to entertain a divorce petition within section 5 DMPA 1973) the House of Lords decided that the legality of a wife's presence in the UK (i.e. even if presence in the UK was a criminal offence under the Immigration Act 1971) was irrelevant to a determination of her domicile of choice (overriding *Puttick v. A-G (1980)*).

Nevertheless, the illegality may (perhaps not surprisingly) cast doubt on the individual's intention to remain in the country indefinitely.

(iv) Dual residence It is perfectly possible for an individual to spend time in more than one country in which case a domicile determination becomes more complex.

In particular, it becomes necessary to ascertain, where two residences exist, which takes precedence. However, it is to be appreciated that a determination as to which residence takes precedence leads to satisfaction of the requirement of actual residence; nevertheless, intention to reside there permanently/indefinitely also needs to be demonstrated.

In *IRC v. Duchess of Portland (1982)* Nourse J. stated:

> ...where a domiciliary divides his physical presence between two countries at a time...In that kind of case it is necessary to look at all the facts in order to decide which of the two countries is the one he inhabits.

In the earlier case of *IRC v. Bullock (1976)* Buckley L.J. noted:

> A man may have homes in more than one country at one time. In such a case, for the purposes of determining his domicile, a further enquiry may have to be made to decide which, if any, should be regarded as his *principal home*.

In *Plummer v. IRC (1987)* Hoffmann J. stated that in cases of dual or multiple residence (as was the situation in *Plummer*) guidance can usefully be obtained from the comments of Lord Westbury in *Udny v. Udny (1869)*:

> Domicile of choice is a conclusion or inference which the law derives from the fact of a man fixing voluntarily his sole or *chief residence* in a particular place, with an intention of continuing to reside there for an unlimited time.

Continuing, Hoffman J. stated:

> ...loss of a domicile of origin or choice is not inconsistent with retention of a place of residence in that country if the chief residence has been established elsewhere.

Unfortunately, neither of the phrases "principal home" or "chief residence" used in the above cases were explained or discussed. However, in the recent case of *Gaines-Cooper v. RCC (2006)* the Commissioners, commenting upon these two phrases, stated:

> ...but a country which is of most importance to an individual, or the centre of his interest, is likely to be the place of his *chief or principal residence.*

The case of *Gaines-Cooper v. RCC (2006)* had to consider specifically the issue of dual residence.

Mr Gaines-Cooper, currently aged 69, possessed an English domicile of origin but had tried to argue that for the period 1992/93 to 2003/04 he had in fact acquired a domicile of choice in the Seychelles. The Commissioners disagreed holding that he had never abandoned his domicile of origin and thus remained for this period English domiciled, i.e. a Seychelles domicile of choice had never been acquired.

This decision was subsequently confirmed by the High Court in 2007.

Prima facie, Mr Gaines-Cooper appeared to do "all the right things". He bought a house in the Seychelles; he expressed the wish that his ashes be scattered there; he married a Seychellois woman; *and in his wills he stated that he lived there and his domicile status was that of the Seychelles.*

Unfortunately, this, according to the Commissioners, was not enough to have resulted in a domicile of choice in the Seychelles having been acquired.

The strong connections which Mr Gaines-Cooper retained with the UK were perceived by the Commissioners as continuing and arguably fatal to his claim of the acquisition of a domicile of choice in the Seychelles. In particular, and of decisive impact was the acquisition and retention of significant properties in the UK in which he and his family lived albeit that for certain periods the properties were rented out to third parties. In this regard the Commissioners said that:

> We regard as significant the fact that nearly all of the Appellant's connections with the UK were located in a comparatively small area of the contiguous counties of Berkshire and Oxfordshire... born there... went to school... mother lived there... married twice... purchased two houses... business offices... attended Royal Ascot... son went to school... We also regard the 1999 will... to be of significance. It was prepared by English solicitors; it is to be construed and take effect according to English law; and the... guardians of [the son] live in the UK... retained his British citizenship and did not apply for citizenship in the Seychelles....

Mr Gaines-Cooper was resident (for the law of domicile purposes) in two places, namely, the UK and the Seychelles, and as a consequence it was necessary for the Commissioners to determine which of these two residences was in fact Mr Gaines-Cooper's chief or principal residence.

The Commissioners not only felt that Mr Gaines-Cooper's chief residence remained that of the UK and not the Seychelles but also were of the view that he lacked the "intention" to reside in the Seychelles indefinitely. He thus failed to satisfy either of the two legs of the test used to ascertain whether a domicile of choice has been acquired.

The case of *IRC v. Duchess of Portland (1982)* involved the issue post 1 January 1974 of a pre 1 January 1974 marriage and a degree of dual residence. The court held that the Duchess of Portland, at the time of her death, had not lost her domicile of dependence acquired automatically on her marriage (pre 1 January 1974) to the Duke (her non-UK domicile of origin having been displaced). The Duchess had been dually resident in the UK and Canada.

Pre 1 January 1974 (i.e. in 1948), a lady with a domicile of origin in Quebec married the Duke of Portland (thus becoming the Duchess of Portland) who possessed a UK domicile of origin. The Duchess visited Quebec regularly; maintained a home there; stated that she intended to return there if her husband should pre-decease her; and he had agreed to retire to Quebec. The Duchess argued that she had acquired a domicile of choice in Quebec during the summer of 1974 whereas HMRC argued that she had a UK domicile of choice.

The court held that she was UK domiciled. It stated that this domicile could only be abandoned by her ceasing to reside in the UK *and* also by intending to cease to reside there. The Duchess had not in fact ceased to reside in the UK and had been a visitor to Quebec *but had not become an inhabitant thereof.*

More specifically, Nourse J. said:

> Her physical presence in Quebec has been for periods of limited duration... to which [i.e. Quebec] it is her intention to ultimately return. That is not enough to have made her an inhabitant of Quebec.

On marriage the Duchess had acquired a UK domicile of dependence on her husband which, on 1 January 1974, was treated (under DMPA 1973) as a UK domicile of choice.

Had she married the Duke *after* this date she would not have automatically acquired his domicile as a domicile of dependence. On marriage, prima facie, her domicile of origin in Quebec would have continued to subsist. As she always intended to return to Quebec then it is highly likely she would not have acquired a UK domicile of choice, remaining Quebec domiciled throughout.

This case arguably illustrates that, other things being equal, a pre 1 January 1974 married woman is treated less favourably than a woman married on or after this date.

(b) Intention

(i) Evidentiary issue The establishment of a non-UK domicile of choice by an individual, originally possessing a UK domicile of origin or an earlier acquired domicile of choice, to the satisfaction of the courts (or HMRC) is basically an evidentiary issue.

Thus, the primary need is to be able to prove that not only has a residence in a foreign country been established as the sole (or principal/chief residence if more than one residence is maintained) residence but also that a clear intention to reside there indefinitely or permanently subsists.

It seems clear from a number of the decided cases (e.g. *Re Clore (1984)*) that statements an individual may make in lifetime, whether in writing (e.g. in an autobiography or memoir) and/or verbally to close friends and others, can often be crucial in the determination of domicile. This may be because the courts view such utterances as representing the "real" truth and intentions of the individual rather than what such individual may say to, for example, the authorities, e.g. HMRC, in response to questions on forms (DOM1/P86), applications or by way of what are sometimes referred to as declarations be they statutory declarations or otherwise.

(ii) Hearsay evidence An individual may, of course, testify as to his intentions (as was the case in the *Gaines-Cooper* case) but as is evident from a number of the cases discussed above, and below, domicile determinations are quite often made after the individual has died, at which time, of course, the individual concerned cannot speak for himself/herself.

Hearsay is defined (section 1 Civil Evidence Act 1995) for civil proceedings as:

> a statement made otherwise than by a person while giving oral evidence in the proceedings which is tendered as evidence of the matters stated.

At common law the definition is:

> an assertion other than one made by a person while giving oral evidence in the proceedings . . . as evidence of any fact asserted.

Hearsay evidence was in the past generally inadmissible but now in civil proceedings this is no longer the case and thus declarations of intention by an individual to others made out of court may be given in evidence (*Bryce v. Bryce (1933)*).

The 1995 Act obliges a judge to take into account:

> any circumstances from which any inference can reasonably be drawn as to the reliability or otherwise of the evidence when estimating the weight (if any) to be attached to an item of hearsay evidence.

Thus, inter alia, no doubt any judge would form a view as to the reliability of a witness and consequently the reliability of his/her hearsay evidence. An example, albeit not concerned with either taxation or domicile, is the case of *Brownsville Holdings v. Adamjee Insurance (2002)*. The case concerned the loss of a yacht.

A witness, called by the insurers, confirmed that the owner of the lost yacht had made an informal admission to the witness that he (the owner) had ordered the yacht to be scuttled so as to be able to recover the insurance proceeds. The court gave no weight to this testimony on account of the witness's evident motive not to tell the truth, her unreliability in other respects and the inherent probability that the owner of the yacht would have confessed to her in the circumstances existing at the time.

Indeed, in the *Gaines-Cooper* case where Gaines-Cooper testified on his own behalf and oral evidence was also given by various other individuals, the commissioners said:

> Before finding the facts we comment on the evidence of [Gaines-Cooper] . . . gave evidence for four and a half days of the ten day hearing. *As many of our findings depend upon his oral evidence* we have to say how we found him as a witness . . . did his best to be truthful and honest but . . . he made mistakes . . . we looked for corroborating evidence . . . but much of his oral evidence was digressive and discursive and unsupported by any documents. Some of the evidence related to events as far back as 1971 which is now thirty five years ago. [Gaines-Cooper] had an impressive memory but was not always certain about dates . . . .
> . . . [Gaines-Cooper] . . . sometimes appeared [confused] . . . full supporting documentation was not produced . . . we are not confident that all the dates and names given in oral evidence were accurate . . . .

> ...For these reasons we <u>approach the oral evidence of</u> [Gaines-Cooper] with some caution. We bear in <u>mind that the burden of proof in these appeals is on</u> [Gaines-Cooper].

With respect to the oral evidence of a number of the third party witnesses the Commissioners commented:

> ...we bear in mind that the witnesses admitted that they knew very little of the Appellant's life outside the Seychelles...We regard the evidence of these witnesses, therefore, as of relevance to the Appellant's attachment to the Seychelles rather than establishing the place of his principal attachment.

In the High Court, on appeal, Mr Justice Lewison stated:

> Clearly they [the Commissioners] did not accept his [Gaines-Cooper's] evidence...In my judgement the Special Commissioners' evaluation of Mr Gaines-Cooper as a witness demonstrates no error of law.

Again, in *Re Clore (1984)* (see below) it is patently clear that the judge had given great weight to the hearsay evidence of Clore's friends and family which, it would seem, outweighed the other factors considered in the case.

(iii) Declaration of intention   Declarations of intention may be made in writing and/or in testimony by the individual concerned and/or verbally to a third party who may testify in court accordingly under the hearsay rule exception.

When in the form of writing such declarations, typically, are either "free-standing" documents or included as part of the individual's will.

In determining an individual's domicile status, in *Devon v. Devon (1834)* Kindersley V.-C. stated:

> There is no act, no circumstances in a man's life, however, trivial it may be in itself, which ought to be left out of consideration in trying the question whether there was an intention to change domicile. A trivial act might possibly be of more weight with regard to determining this question than an act which was of more importance to a man in his lifetime.

In *Casdagli v. Casdagli (1919)* Lord Atkinson referring to the case of *Winans v. AG (1904)* said:

> ...the tastes, habits, conduct, actions, ambitions, health, hopes, and projects of Mr Winans deceased were all considered as keys to his intention to make a home in England.

Nevertheless, despite statements such as these made in the various decided cases the issue of "declarations of intent" has been in virtually all decided cases *at best noted and at worst completely ignored.*

All forms of declarations of intention whether made informally (albeit in writing) or by way of a statutory declaration (i.e. a written statement of facts which the person making it (the declarant) signs and solemnly declares to be true before a commissioner for oaths; Statutory Declarations Act 1835) or in testimony whether by the individual concerned or a third party have, perhaps, not surprisingly been *viewed by the courts with extreme suspicion.*

The courts have indicated that declarations of intention which specifically refer to the word "domicile" are unlikely to be of any real value as the individual making the declaration is generally unlikely to fully appreciate or understand the significance or meaning of the word. Thus, Romer L.J. in *AG v. Yule and Mercantile Bank of India (1931)* stated:

> I am not prepared to attach any importance to a declaration by a man as to his domicile unless there is some evidence to show that the man knew what "domicile" means... Domicile is... a legal concept on which the views of a layman are not of much assistance.

Even where the courts could be persuaded that the individual did demonstrate an understanding of the concept of domicile, the courts, in any event, view such declarations with, it seems, a high degree of scepticism. In *Bell v. Kennedy (1868)* the Lord Chancellor stated:

> An Appellant [Bell, who had testified on his own behalf in the case] has, naturally, on an issue like the present [i.e. domicile] a very strong bias calculated to influence his mind, and he [i.e. Bell] is, moreover, speaking of what was his intention some twenty five years ago [i.e. at the date of his wife's death in 1838].

Similarly, in *Re Craignish (1892)* the court viewed with scepticism the husband's testimony that he and his wife (who had died) considered her to be domiciled in Scotland at her death, noting that the consequence was that he (the husband) became entitled to one half of her property.

According to *Crookenden v. Fuller (1859)*:

> ... [declarations as to domicile are] ... the lowest species of evidence ....

As indicated above, with respect to testimony made by an individual to whom an oral statement as to intention has been made, the courts are particularly concerned with credibility of the witness giving the testimony. In *Hodgson v. De Beauchesne (1858)* it was stated:

... the court must be satisfied not only of the veracity of the witness who depose to such declarations, but of the accuracy of their memory, and that the declarations contain a real expression of the intention of the deceased.

It is not uncommon for declarations as to domicile status to be made by individuals in their wills along the following lines:

Inasmuch as I am a British subject having my original domicile in England (which domicile I have never relinquished or abandoned) it is my wish and intention that this my will ... shall be construed and operate so far as the case admits as if I were now and remained until my death domiciled in England.
(made by Frank Lawton in his will; see *Re Lawton (1958)*)

In *Re Lawton (1958)*, despite Lawton's declaration in his will, the courts held that he had in fact died domiciled in France where he had died having been living there for the best part of 63 years of his life. Interestingly, the use of the phrase "... domicile I have never abandoned" by Mr Lawton in his will perhaps lends some support to the comments made by Romer L.J. in *AG v. Yule and Mercantile Bank of India (1931)*; note, a domicile of origin cannot simply be abandoned.

Similarly, in *Re Steer (1858)*, Mr Steer was held to have died domiciled in Germany despite an explicit declaration in his will that he had no intention of renouncing his English domicile of origin.

See also *Re Liddell-Grainger's Will Trusts (1936)* where, again, declarations in a will were basically disregarded.

While apparently viewed with suspicion and scepticism, irrespective of the form the declarations may take, the courts accept that in principle they are a factor to be considered. Thus, in *Ross v. Ross (1930)* (a case concerning a choice of law rule (Italy v. UK) applicable to a will of a female British citizen who had died domiciled in Italy and who had cut her son out of her will) the court stated:

Declarations as to intention are rightly regarded in determining the question of a change of domicile, but they must be examined by considering the persons to whom, the purposes for which, and the circumstances in which they are made, *and they must be further fortified and carried into effect by conduct and action consistent with the declared intention.*

Thus it would seem that declarations of intention are in principle, per se, acceptable as evidence of intention but of very limited, if any, value in practice. It is the reality and facts which ultimately decide issues of domicile status.

In other words, the court will examine whether the individual's declarations of intention were carried through in practice. In this regard the conduct of the individual after the point in time at which a change of domicile may have occurred may also be taken into consideration.

[margin note: Deeds, not Words, matter]

In *Re Grove (1888)* Lopes J. said:

> ... in order to determine a person's intention at a given time, you may regard not only conduct and acts before and at the time, but also conduct and acts after the time, assigning to such conduct and acts their relative and proper weight and cogency.

(See also *Bremer v. Freeman (1857)*.)

(iv) Acquisition of citizenship It is not decisive as a matter of law that the acquisition by an individual of citizenship of a particular country confirms an intention to remain in that country indefinitely or permanently (*Al Fayed v. AG (2002)*). Thus, it does not follow that the acquisition of citizenship means the automatic acquisition of a domicile of choice or indeed vice versa.

In *F v. IRC (2000)* an Iranian exile, who died in the UK in 1992 and had spent the bulk of his life in England, was held not to have acquired a UK domicile of choice. At the time of the Iranian revolution F had sent his wife and children to live in the UK. He had been placed on an exit bar list in Iran due to alleged non-payment of certain tax liabilities which up to the date of his death he had attempted to get removed. He regarded Iran as his home. He owned a UK home and in 1980 obtained indefinite leave to remain in the UK. In 1982 he acquired British citizenship in order to acquire a British passport to ease his international travel in the course of his business. In applying for British citizenship he had falsely claimed that he had left Iran to escape religious persecution. Despite this lie the Commissioners held that he had always intended to return to Iran when it was safe to do so and thus he retained his Iranian domicile of origin. In effect the Commissioners were of the view that the statement made on the application for citizenship did not in fact represent F's true intentions. The Commissioners commented:

> He disliked the English weather, English fruit and the English class system and he thought that England and its economy were on a downward spiral ... his house adjoined the local church but his relationship with the local vicar was poor and he took no part in village life.

In an earlier case (*Wahl v. AG (1932)*), some 70 years earlier, a not dissimilar conclusion had also been reached on not dissimilar facts. In that case Wahl made statements in the course of applying for British citizenship which did not prejudice his non-UK domicile status. In the course of applying for British citizenship Wahl (a German citizen and possessing a German domicile of origin) had made a statutory declaration to the effect that he intended to continue to reside in the UK indefinitely and had no intention of leaving the UK. Despite the statement the courts held that it was not sufficient to outweigh the other evidence to the contrary.

Similar issues arose in the case of *Buswell v. IRC (1974)*. Buswell possessed a Transvaal domicile of origin, married an English woman, acquired South African nationality and acquired a property in South Africa visiting there on average three months per year. In 1952, however, he had completed Form P86 and in so doing had answered the question thereon "Do you propose to remain permanently in the UK?" in the affirmative; answering the follow-up question "If not, how long do you expect to remain in this country" by simply inserting a "dash".

The High Court agreed with the finding of the Commissioners (the lower court) that Buswell had acquired a UK domicile of choice; in so doing they attached great weight to the answers given on the P86.

However, the Court of Appeal disagreed. They found that Buswell had not acquired a UK domicile of origin stating:

> ... that in attributing a decisive importance to ... answers on the Form P86, given at a time when he had been back in this country less than five months after an absence of ten years and against the background to which I have referred, the Commissioners acted upon a view which could not reasonably be entertained.

Thus, while statements made on Form P86 (or indeed Form DOM1; see *Surveyor v. IRC (2002)* below) are of course extremely important and need to be made with great care they are not automatically decisive if all other facts point to a contradictory conclusion.

NON-UK DOMICILED INDIVIDUALS SPENDING SIGNIFICANT TIME IN THE UK

There are many cases where individuals, each possessing non-UK domiciles of origin, but who have spent significant amounts of time in the UK, have found themselves (or their executors) seeking to argue that despite the length of time spent in the UK and their lifestyles they have not, de facto, acquired UK domiciles of choice.

Such cases do not, in general, auger well *vis-à-vis* the UK domiciled individual seeking to assert non-UK domicile status on the grounds of having acquired a domicile of choice overseas. This is particularly so if one of the main arguments is premised upon length of residence in the overseas country concerned.

Typically, such cases have turned on the issue of "intention".

Two leading cases, namely, *IRC v. Group Captain Bullock (1976)* and *Re Furse (1980)*, both involve individuals possessing non-UK domiciles of origin and each of whom spent significant time in the UK and indeed each of whom died in the UK. Despite apparent similarities between the two cases and the decision in *Re Furse* coming within four years of the *Bullock* case the courts reached different conclusions as to their respective domicile status.

In *IRC v. Group Captain Bullock (1976)* the Court of Appeal (*reversing* the decision of the High Court) held that an individual who had lived in the UK for more than 40 years who had a domicile of origin in Nova Scotia, Canada, had *not* acquired a UK domicile of choice on the ground that he always intended to return to Canada after the death of his wife who was English. The court held that this contingency was of sufficient substance to represent a real determination to return home; it was not simply a vague hope or aspiration. This, however, had the perhaps unintended consequence that his wife (because of the marriage in 1946 to an English male before 1 January 1974) also was domiciled in Canada despite the fact that she apparently hated the place (see also *Buswell v. IRC (1974)*).

Factors considered by the court included aspects of Captain Bullock's lifestyle:

- the fact that he retained his Canadian nationality and passport;
- no British passport was ever acquired;
- he was an avid reader of the local Toronto newspaper;
- he never voted in any UK elections;
- his will was drawn up under Nova Scotia law and contained a statement of his intention to return to Nova Scotia should his wife pre-decease him.

Buckley L.J. in the Court of Appeal decision in *Bullock*, commenting upon "intention", said:

> I do not think it is necessary to show that the intention to make a home in a new country is irrevocable . . . or that . . . he will have no opportunity to change his mind. In my judgement the true test is whether he intends to make his home in the new country until the end of his days unless and until something happens to make him change his mind

Furthermore, Buckley L.J. also commented:

> The question can perhaps be formulated in this way where the contingency is not itself of a doubtful or indefinite character: is there a sufficiently substantial possibility of the contingency happening to justify regarding the intention to return as a real determination to do so upon the contingency occurring rather than a vague hope or aspiration.

Four years later in *Re Furse (1980)* a different conclusion to that in the *Bullock* case was reached, arguably on not dissimilar facts.

In *Re Furse (1980)* the last 39 years of an American's (domiciled in Rhode Island, USA) life had been spent farming a farm which he and his wife had purchased in England. He was married with children, originally coming to England at the age of 4.

He died aged 80 in England but had expressed an intention to return to the USA if he became unable to operate his wife's farm due to incapacity. The High Court held that his intention was too vague and indefinite and that on the balance of probabilities he really wanted to remain in the UK until his death and held that he died having acquired a domicile of choice in England.

Fox J. commented upon the *Bullock* case as follows:

> In *IRC v. Bullock (1976)* both the requirements referred to by Buckley L.J. were satisfied. The contingency was a wholly clear and well-defined contingency, namely whether the propositus survived his wife; and there was a substantial possibility that the contingency might occur, having regard to the respective ages of the propositus and his wife.

He then contrasted the two cases:

> The present case, it seems to me, is very different. The fundamental difference in outlook between Group Captain Bullock and the testator [Mr Furse] was that, while Group Captain Bullock had every wish to leave England, the testator was entirely happy here.

It would appear that the different decisions in the above two cases to a great extent centred around what constituted an "acceptable" contingency (as defined by Buckley J. in *Bullock*). In *Bullock* the contingency was "acceptable" whereas it was not in *Furse*.

The case of *Re Fuld's Estate (No. 3) (1968)* concerned the validity of a will and a number of subsequent codicils executed by Peter Fuld. Fuld had been born in 1921 in Germany with a German domicile of origin. He died in England in 1961 following serious illness. He spent his time between the UK and Germany and had married a German lady. The court held that he had died possessing his German domicile of origin as at no time had he indicated any intention of remaining in the UK permanently. As a result, his will and the first of the four codicils were held valid; the remaining three codicils were thus invalid. Commenting upon "intention", Scarman J. stated that:

> If a man intends to return to the land of his birth upon a clearly foreseen and reasonably anticipated contingency ... the "intention" required by law [i.e. the intention to reside in the new territory indefinitely] is lacking ... but, if he has in mind only a vague possibility, ... such a state of mind is consistent with the intention required by law.

He went on to say that the ultimate decision in each case is one of fact which would need to take into account:

> the weight to be attached to the various factors and future contingencies in the contemplation of the propositus, their importance to him, and the probability, in his assessment, of the contingencies he has in contemplation being transformed into actualities.

By way of example, Scarman J. in *Re Fuld's Estate (No. 3) (1968)* stated that a clearly forseen and reasonably anticipated contingency upon which a return to the country of the individual's domicile of origin might be the end of a job but a return premised upon making a fortune (or some sentiment about dying in the land of his father's) would be unacceptable.

In *Re Furse (1980)* the court did not accept that returning to the USA if and when some ill-defined deterioration in health occurred was, in Scarman J.'s language, "a clearly foreseen and reasonably anticipated contingency.

The case of *The Executors of Robert Moore Deceased v. CIR (2002)* involved ascertaining whether a US citizen who died in the UK had acquired a UK domicile of choice. Unlike the cases above, however, the time spent in the UK was not, relatively speaking, excessive.

Robert Moore had a domicile of origin in Missouri; was a US citizen; and travelled on a US passport. He died in March 1997 in London where his funeral took place but his ashes were scattered in Ireland. He had properties in both the UK and USA. In 1991 Mr Moore was granted leave to enter the UK for the limited purposes of his employment as an artist and in answer to a question raised by the immigration officer said: "I am planning to use the UK as a base to travel to the continent regularly". The leave to enter the UK expired in March 1995 and although it was not renewed he remained in the UK. He travelled on a US passport and filed US tax returns (but no UK tax returns were filed).

Two wills were made, one of which (the US prepared will) dealt with his US assets and the other (the UK prepared will) dealt with all non-US assets. His New York connections remained including the fact that his investments were managed from New York.

Two witness statements stated that the witnesses regarded Mr Moore as an American and one of them stated that he did not wear British clothes or eat British food. One of them also stated that they thought he wanted to go to the USA for medical treatment but died before actually doing so.

The Commissioners held that Mr Moore had not acquired a UK domicile of choice at the date of his death as there was no clear evidence that he had intended to acquire a domicile of choice in the UK but there was a lot of evidence that demonstrated that he had kept up his connections with New York. The Commissioners also referred to the statement to the immigration officer which they suggested did not indicate that Mr Moore wanted to make England his permanent home.

A more recent case involving a long-stay in the UK followed by death therein is that of *Agulian & Anr v. Cyganik (C/A 2006)*.

The case considered the domicile status of a Cypriot national, not in fact for tax purposes but for the purposes of the Inheritance (Provision for Family and Dependants) Act 1975 (broadly, an Act under which certain categories of person who feel aggrieved as to their inheritance under someone's will may seek a greater share of the deceased's estate from the courts).

Mr Andreas Nathanial died in the UK in 2003 aged 63, having been born in Cyprus in 1939. He had come to England aged 18 for safety reasons. He had lived in England for approximately 43 years although he had returned to Cyprus for a brief period in 1972; had a significant UK business (UK assets worth circa £6.5 million); and had made a will in 1995 under which his fiancée Renata Cyganik, with whom he had lived as man and wife (who was in fact in the UK illegally) and to whom he became engaged in 1999 and intended to marry in 2003, was to inherit £50 000.

Ms Cyganik brought a claim under section 2 of the 1975 Act against Agulian's estate for financial provision. This required that she was able to establish that the deceased had died domiciled in England (i.e. he had acquired a domicile of choice in England displacing his Cypriot domicile of origin).

The C/A, reversing the High Court (which had held that he had acquired a UK domicile of choice at some point between making his will in 1995 and his engagement in 1999), held that he had not acquired an English domicile of choice in the UK but his Cypriot domicile of origin had subsisted as he had maintained significant connections with Cyprus throughout his life (e.g. he had sent one of his daughters to be educated in Cyprus where she remained; watched Cypriot TV as well as speaking Greek while in the UK; sent significant sums of money to Cyprus; and bought two flats in Cyprus). It was accepted that he had become deemed domiciled for inheritance tax purposes.

The *Agulian v. Cyganik* case is yet another example of an individual who, despite having spent a significant amount of his lifetime living in the UK, was held not to have acquired a UK domicile of choice; his original non-UK domicile of origin persisting.

Prima facie, this seems to indicate an approach by the courts which suggests that long-term UK residency as an indicator of the acquisition of a UK domicile of choice is not of the utmost importance but just one, and not necessarily a powerful, indicator. The approach also seems to confirm that an individual's domicile of origin is extremely adhesive.

UK DOMICILED INDIVIDUALS FAILING TO ACQUIRE NON-UK DOMICILES OF CHOICE

While there are cases where individuals have successfully acquired domiciles of choice (see below), for many this has proved difficult.

In *Jopp v. Wood (1865)* the courts held that an individual who had possessed a UK (in fact Scottish) domicile of origin had not subsequently acquired an Indian domicile of choice.

John Smith went to India in 1805, when a minor, acquiring his majority in 1807. His father died in 1814 and Smith wrote a letter to his mother indicating strongly his intention ultimately to return to Scotland. In 1819 he returned to Scotland taking an active part in the management of the family estate. He then returned to India but kept up constant correspondence with the agents of the estate. In this correspondence he constantly referred to his return to Scotland; directed that different parts of the estate be planted; and mentioned his intention of building upon it. He also purchased an adjoining property and sent money back to Scotland to discharge charges against the estate. At the date of his death John Smith had lived in India for some 25 years.

On these facts the court held that John Smith, far from having acquired a domicile of choice in India, had shown a desire at all times to retain his Scottish domicile of origin.

In *Re Clore (1984)* Sir Charles Clore (possessing a UK domicile of origin) had also not been so lucky. He had emigrated to Monaco and had become a Monégasque resident. He had left the UK solely to avoid UK death tax by acquiring a Monégasque domicile of choice. On his death it was held that he had never acquired such a domicile and his English domicile of origin had subsisted.

This case admirably illustrates the importance and significance of utterances, whether in writing or by word of mouth, made by an individual to others in determining the individual's domicile status.

The court considered that there was evidence to support the acquisition of a domicile of choice in Monaco. This evidence included the fact that Sir Charles Clore had severed various important connections with the UK; had established connections with Monaco including residing there; and the fact that he had received professional advice as to the need to acquire a non-UK domicile if UK estate duty was to be avoided. With respect to this last point Nourse J. stated:

> ... the professional advice which Sir Charles received was given not solely with the immediate object of his acquiring a non-resident status for income and capital gains tax purposes, but with the long term objective of his acquiring a foreign domicile....

Indeed, Nourse J. also stated:

> ... if the evidence of intention is there, particularly perhaps where the motive is the avoidance of taxes, the necessary intention will not be held to be missing merely because the period of actual residence is a short one.

However, the court decided that other factors overrode the above.

In particular, a number of his closest friends testified as to parol (anything done by word of mouth) declarations which had been made by Sir Charles late in his life which confirmed that Sir Charles had never been happy in Monaco; that he continued to be interested in buying properties in Israel and/or France; and that in his "heart of hearts" he had never truly abandoned England – he often referred to England as "home" and right up to his death in London certain of his actions were tentative in nature.

Accordingly, Nourse J. held that he had died domiciled in England.

Four years later in *Plummer v. IRC (1988)* yet another individual (female in this case) possessing a UK domicile of origin failed to convince the court of her acquisition of a domicile of choice in Guernsey. Unlike *Re Clore (1984)* and *Jopp v. Wood (1865)*, however, Elizabeth Plummer was alive at the court date and thus able to testify. The case involved issues of UK income tax (not death tax).

Plummer was born of UK domiciled parents in 1965. In 1980 her mother and sister moved to Guernsey but her father only spent weekends and holidays there (he remained in the UK). Plummer continued to remain in the UK for her education but spent weekends and holidays in Guernsey at her mother's house. She had acquired, inter alia, a Guernsey passport, bank account and driving licence. She stated an intention to settle permanently in Guernsey once her education in the UK had finished.

The court considered that Plummer was in fact a resident of both the UK and Guernsey and thus the court needed to identify her chief residence. The court were of the view that Plummer had not in fact settled in Guernsey as an inhabitant of it and the reasons why she had not (namely, due to her need to finish her education in the UK) were, the court said, irrelevant. It was inappropriate to consider that her mother's house was Plummer's chief residence.

Interestingly, the court said:

> If the taxpayer had in 1980 broken altogether with England and settled in Guernsey like her mother and sister and then, even after a relatively short interval, returned to England for study, the quality of her presence here [UK] might have been such as to prevent a revival of her domicile of origin.

In *Civil Engineer v. IRC (2002)* an individual had spent 30 years living and working in Hong Kong. The Commissioners, however, found no evidence to support his argument that he had acquired a domicile of choice in Hong Kong (even if so held, his UK domicile of origin had resurrected as, following his return to the UK, he appeared to have no intention of a return to Hong Kong; in effect, holding that even if a domicile of choice had been acquired he no longer resided there and had by his actions demonstrated an intention no longer to reside there permanently).

(See also *Gaines-Cooper v. RCC (2007)* and *IRC v. Duchess of Portland (1982)*.)

Example 3.18
Felipe Sanchez possesses a Spanish domicile of origin.

He met a UK domiciled woman and married her in 1975. Since that time they have both lived in the UK.

In 1980 they had two children who were educated in the UK and continue to live in the UK (now adults).

Felipe owns no property in Spain and has visited Spain only once since 1975.

Felipe died in 2007 and was buried in the UK having previously made a will governed by UK law and drawn up by a UK firm of solicitors.

On these facts it is highly likely, whether Felipe intended or not, that he will have died possessing a UK domicile of choice which will have displaced his Spanish domicile of origin. Whether this is in fact the case will depend upon all the relevant surrounding issues.

However, prima facie, Felipe appears to have behaved in a manner which suggests he intended to remain in the UK indefinitely and showed no indication of any serious intention to return to Spain.

Example 3.19
Manuel Sanchez, Felipe's brother (see Example 3.18 above), possesses a Spanish domicile of origin.

He met a UK domiciled woman and married her in 1975. Since that time they have both lived in the UK.

In 1980 they had two children who were educated in the UK and continue to live in the UK (now adults).

Here the resemblance to Felipe's life changes.

Manuel has maintained his villa in Spain and has, since arriving in the UK, returned to Spain for visits on a regular basis. He has always stated to everyone in his family that as soon as the children have finished full time education in the UK that he (with his wife) intends to return to live indefinitely in Spain.

He has been advised to make two wills, one under Spanish law and one under UK law, which he has done.

Compared to his brother, Felipe, Manuel's Spanish domicile of origin is likely to have remained intact. It is highly unlikely that Manuel has acquired a UK domicile of choice.

UK DOMICILED INDIVIDUALS SUCCESSFULLY ACQUIRING NON-UK DOMICILES OF CHOICE

It is important to appreciate that in common law systems the concept of "domicile" is central to many issues of law not just issues of taxation. A change in an individual's domicile status may thus have implications beyond taxation.

The general importance of the concept of domicile is that it is used to connect an individual to a place and thus in turn permits the law governing that place to apply to the individual. Thus, for example, an individual who possesses an English domicile will find that it is English law which will govern his personal relationships including issues such as the validity of marriage; jurisdiction in divorce; legitimacy and adoption; wills and the devolution of movable property on an intestacy (i.e. the distribution of property on death where no will exists).

There is a presumption that an individual's domicile status at any point in time persists (*AG v. Rowe (1862)*) until it can be shown that it has changed due to action taken by the individual concerned, whether intended or not.

For an individual to acquire a domicile of choice requires positive action and two conditions need to be satisfied (in any order):

- the individual must actually take up residence in another country; *and*
- the individual must have the intention of residing permanently or indefinitely in the new country of residence.

This does, however, raise two questions, namely:

- on whom is the onus placed to demonstrate a change in an individual's domicile status? and
- on whoever the onus of proof is placed, what is the standard of proof?

Irrespective of on whom the burden is placed and irrespective of the standard of proof required, the burden is an extremely heavy one as is evidenced in the statement by Lord Macnaghten in *Winans v. AG (1904)*:

> How heavy is the burden cast upon those who seek to show that the domicile of origin has been superseded by a domicile of choice!

It is clear that the onus of proving a change in domicile lies fairly and squarely with the person so asserting, as is clear from statements made in *Winans v. AG (1904)* and in *Re Fuld's Estate (No. 3) (1968)*. In *Winans v. AG (1904)* it was stated:

> The onus of proving that a domicile has been chosen in substitution for the domicile of origin lies upon those who assert that the domicile of origin has been lost.

Similarly, in *Re Fuld's Estate (No. 3) (1968)* it was stated:

> It is beyond doubt that the burden of proving the abandonment of a domicile of origin and the acquisition of a domicile of choice is upon the party asserting the change.

This is, of course, a double-edged sword.

For the UK domiciled individual wishing to argue the acquisition of a new non-UK domicile of choice then the onus of proof lies with the individual. On the other hand, where such an individual has been successful in so arguing, any attempt by HMRC at a subsequent date to argue that the individual's UK domicile of origin has resurrected lies with HMRC.

With respect to the standard of proof, two decided cases appear to differ. Both cases were heard in the Probate Division; one case concerned a petition for divorce (*Henderson v. Henderson (1965)*) and the other, *Re Fuld's Estate (No. 3) (1968)*, concerned challenges to the validity of a will and codicils thereto.

In *Henderson v. Henderson (1965)* Sir Jocelyn Simon stated:

> ...clear evidence is required to establish a change of domicile. In particular, to displace the domicile of origin in favour of a domicile of choice, *the standard of proof goes beyond a mere balance of probabilities.*

However, around the same time, Scarman J. in *Re Fuld's Estate (No. 3) (1968)* when considering the issue of changes in the domicile status of an individual stated:

> It is beyond doubt that the burden of proving the abandonment of a domicile of origin and the acquisition of a domicile of choice is upon the part asserting the change ... but ....
> is it to be proved beyond reasonable doubt or upon a balance of probabilities?... *The formula of proof beyond reasonable doubt is not frequently used in probate cases, and I do not propose to give it currency*... Two things are clear; first, that unless

the judicial conscience is satisfied by evidence of change, the domicile of origin persists; and secondly, the acquisition of a domicile of choice is a serious matter not to be lightly inferred from slight indications or casual words....

In *Buswell v. IRC (1974)* Orr L.J. commenting upon Scarman J.'s comments in *Re Fuld's Estate (No. 3) (1968)* stated:

I am satisfied that Scarman J. was not recognising the existence of some general standard of proof intermediate between criminal and civil standards but was merely emphasising that in the application of the civil standard the degree of proof required will vary with the subject-matter of the case.

It is thus now generally accepted that the proof required is the civil law's standard, i.e. on a balance of probabilities.

One of the most recently decided cases, where an individual possessing a UK domicile of origin successfully acquired a non-UK domicile of choice, was that of a Mr Anthony Shaffer in the case *Re Shaffer, Morgan v. Cilento (2004)*. The case, as in *Agulian v. Cyganik (2006)*, concerned the possible application of the provisions of the Inheritance (Provision for Family and Dependants) Act 1975; in particular, whether Mr Shaffer's original UK domicile of origin had resurrected at the time of his death.

The *Shaffer* case was decided by the High Court and revolved around a claim made by a Ms Minutolo who had had a relationship with Mr Shaffer during the latter part of his life (during which time Shaffer was still married to Diane Cilento) and sought to claim under the Inheritance (Provision for Family and Dependants) Act 1975. For the courts to entertain such a claim Mr Shaffer would have had to have died domiciled in England (or Wales).

Mr Anthony Shaffer, the playwright, possessed an English domicile of origin. He died aged 75 in late 2001 in England having spent a significant amount of time in Australia having acquired a visa in March 1985 entitling him to stay indefinitely; the visa was periodically renewed (last occasion 11 June 1999 valid until 23 October 2002). He never applied for Australian citizenship (due apparently to his dislike of "pomp and circumstance" as stated by Diane Cilento, his wife).

He was held to have acquired a domicile of choice in Queensland, Australia, and his UK domicile of origin had not revived before his death (despite returning to the UK and dying there) as he had not abandoned his non-UK domicile.

In concluding that Shaffer had acquired a domicile of choice in Queensland, Australia, the judge said:

The particular factors to which I have given weight... are:

- ...[marriage] in Queensland and... matrimonial home there
- ...most of his personal possessions were [shipped] to Queensland where they remain

- it was the place where he was most creative, and creation was perhaps the most important thing in [his] life
- by 1985 [left UK March 1985] he had sold almost all his assets in England and for the best part of a decade owned no home there either directly or indirectly
- he had deliberately acquired residence in Australia for tax purposes, and part of his desire to do so was the abolition of death duties in Queensland
- his bank account and credit card were Australian
- when the Studio [a flat in the UK] was acquired [1995] it was an Australian company which acquired it not Anthony
- in September 1997 he stated in an official form that he intended to live permanently or indefinitely in Australia
- he exercised the right to vote in Queensland
- ...
- until the mid-1990s he spent the majority of his time in Australia
- in 1999 he made a will in Queensland
- ...
- he never stopped talking about Karnak as his home
- on the day [fifth] before he died [6 November 2001], he stated that he lived in England for only half the year; and answered the questions applicable "if you are from abroad" [these answers were given in a questionnaire for the purpose of registering with an NHS doctor].

With respect to whether Shaffer's UK domicile of origin had resurrected (i.e. had Shaffer abandoned his domicile of choice) the judge said:

> I have not taken it [i.e. a memoir written by Shaffer in his last year of his life and published on the day of his death] as evidence of historical facts, but it has helped me in forming a view about Mr Shaffer's state of mind during its composition... the memoir seems to me to show that Anthony still regarded Karnak as his home in the early summer of 2001 [the year of death] and that he was not contemplating a return to England full time... may be [by the date of death] his return to Queensland was withering. But I do not consider it died before Anthony did.

This was so held despite the fact that Shaffer had:

- retained his memberships of London clubs but he was an overseas member or absent member of each;
- he was registered on the electoral role at the studio;
- joined the Conservative party in his local constituency;
- subscribed to a residents' association;
- visited the UK; and
- died while in the UK.

His visits to the UK were motivated by:

> ... his need for cultural stimulation over and above what Australia could give him. Part of it was also ... to see his two daughters ... [and] his mother ... But part of it was also his need for medical treatment ... Yet London also grated. Sir Peter [Shaffer's twin brother] told me that Anthony deplored the changes that had taken place in England during his lifetime and that he felt that London was "no longer his place".

The contrast between the *Gaines-Cooper* and the *Shaffer* cases could not perhaps be much greater and the different conclusions reached by the courts seem hardly surprising. Interestingly, while the judge in the former case commented upon the witnesses and their testimony, this did not occur in the latter case.

In another relatively recent case, *Surveyor v. IRC (2002)*, an individual who possessed a UK domicile of origin was also held to have acquired a Hong Kong domicile of choice. To some degree this case seems, on its facts, to lie somewhere between *Gaines-Cooper* and *Shaffer*.

The individual in 1986 took up an employment opportunity in Hong Kong which had been offered by his UK employer. In 1990 he married a UK national who was living in Hong Kong but the marriage took place in the UK. All three children were born in Hong Kong. In 1997 the individual (plus wife) applied for permanent residence status in Hong Kong (which was granted) which enabled him to live and work in Hong Kong without the need for a work permit; to travel in and out of Hong Kong without requiring a passport or visa; and, an entitlement to vote in elections. The individual rented accommodation due to the high cost of purchase but did purchase an apartment in 1994 which in the event was too small for a family home; it was sold and a move back into rented accommodation occurred.

In 2000 the individual was transferred to the employer's Singapore business where accommodation was provided by the employer. Regular visits were made back to Hong Kong and strong links were maintained there. Two years later the individual resigned and returned to Hong Kong purchasing an apartment as a family home.

In 1998 a 30-year lease of a plot of land was acquired in Thailand and in 1999 building commenced on what was to be a holiday home.

In February 1999 Form DOM1 was completed and a ruling sought from HMRC as to the individual's domicile status. No immediate ruling was forthcoming and following a transfer of approximately £250 000 into a Jersey discretionary trust in August 1999 HMRC refused to accept that the individual had acquired a Hong Kong domicile of choice.

On the DOM1 the individual stated that he had acquired a Hong Kong domicile of choice; that his general intention was to remain in the Far East (not explicitly Hong Kong) as was evidenced by the building of the home in Thailand.

The Commissioners found that in August 1999 (the date of the £250 000 transfer) the individual had the intention of residing permanently in Hong Kong until the end of his days unless something happened to make him change his mind. The individual had the intention of leaving the UK and not returning. The Commissioners also found no problem with the building of the house in Thailand or the statement on the DOM1. The Commissioners were of the view that the existence of the Thai house did not alter the intention to make Hong Kong a permanent home nor did it suggest the individual intended to reside in more than one country. The move to Singapore was held not to have affected the intention to reside permanently in Hong Kong or to have resulted in the resurrection of the UK domicile of origin.

Further, evidence concerning the individual's family, social, business and financial ties all supported the Hong Kong connection and there was no evidence in this regard to suggest the individual's residence in Hong Kong was purely for commercial reasons.

The case of *Allen and Hateley (executors of Johnson deceased) v. RCC (2005)* involved an elderly lady who had returned to the UK for medical reasons and had then died in the UK having lived with her family for the last six years of her life. She had possessed a UK domicile of origin but had subsequently acquired a Spanish domicile of choice.

She maintained a house in Spain and had said that she wanted to return there and would have done so if her family had agreed to have looked after her in Spain.

Despite her expressed intention to want to return to Spain she had not long before her death bought a house in the UK. Nevertheless, the Commissioners held that she had died domiciled in Spain (i.e. she had not abandoned her Spanish domicile of choice) appearing to have accepted that she would have returned to Spain if she could have done so. Weight also seems to have been attached to the fact that she had spent very little of her adult life in the UK.

In the light of the purchase of a UK property it is perhaps surprising that the lady in question was not held to have died with her UK domicile of origin resurrected; the purchase, prima facie, suggesting an intention to return and remain in the UK.

The impact of health issues on domicile status are complex.

In the cases of *Shaffer* and *Allen* despite a return to the UK in part driven by illness and the fact of dying in the UK it would seem that other factors were perceived by the courts to be overriding and the foreign domiciles of choice subsisted.

On the issue of health and domicile in the case of *Moorhouse v. Lord (1863)* Lord Kingsdown stated:

> Take the case of a man labouring under a mortal disease. He is informed by his physicians that his life may be prolonged for a few months by a change to a warmer climate and that at all events his sufferings may be mitigated by such a change. Is it to be said that if he goes to Madeira he cannot do so without losing his character as an English subject, without losing his right to the intervention of the English laws as the transmission of property after his death, and the construction of his testamentary instruments. My Lords, I apprehend that such a proposition is revolting to common sense and common feelings of humanity.

The comments and inference from *Moorhouse v. Lord (1863)*, however, contrast with the earlier decision in *Hoskins v. Matthews (1856)*.

In this case, a Mr Matthews, who possessed a UK domicile of origin, moved to Florence, Tuscany, at the age of 60. The move was motivated by a spinal injury which he thought would benefit from the warm climate. He died there 12 years later and was held to have acquired a domicile of choice in Tuscany. Turner L.J. stated:

> [Mr Matthews on moving to Tuscany was not at the time of the move] in any immediate danger or apprehension. He was, no doubt, out of health, and he went abroad for the purpose of trying to effect other remedies and other climates... but I think he was not driven to settle in Italy by any cogent necessity. I think that in settling there he was exercising a preference, and not acting upon a necessity, and I cannot venture to hold that in such a case the domicile cannot be changed.

A more recent case involving health issues, to a degree, is that of *Reddington v. MacInnes (2002)* which was a case of testamentary succession.

A Mr John Grant Riach possessed a Scottish domicile of origin. He died in Bournemouth, England, age 95 in December 1999. The issue arose as to whether he died domiciled in England or Scotland.

Mr Riach had contracted emphysema during the latter part of his working life and on his retirement returned to Falkirk with his wife in 1966. His emphysema deteriorated and he experienced difficulty in breathing. He and his wife had spent holidays in Bournemouth in the past and he enjoyed the climate which he thought was good for his health. The family purchased a house in Bournemouth and moved there in 1976.

It was said that on moving to Bournemouth he had on a number of occasions said "I'm not making another move" and when asked "would you ever move back to Scotland" he had always replied in the negative. The judge commented as follows:

> ... the question of what the deceased's motive had been in moving to Bournemouth in 1976, I am not satisfied, that ultimately, in this case, much turns on that factor... I suspect that the choice of Bournemouth may well have been motivated by both considerations [to enable his wife to be closer to her family and his wish to live in a more temperate climate].
>
> I have reached the clear conclusion that, by the date of his death, the deceased had acquired a domicile of choice in England. The evidence:
>
> - his repeated remarks that his move to England was to be his last move;
> - the length of his residence in England;
> - the fact that he remained in England after his wife died; and
> - lastly and perhaps, most tellingly, his directions, in his will, that his remains should be buried in Bournemouth,
>
> taken together, in my judgement, establish that the deceased had made England his permanent home where he intended to end his days.

It is arguable that the above three cases suggest that no change of domicile will occur where the move to the other country is to receive medical treatment or to alleviate suffering even where death is likely to occur in the country and the individual knows he will never return to the home country. Thus, even in the case of an individual with a UK domicile of origin who has subsequently acquired a non-UK domicile of choice, a return to the UK in these circumstances should not automatically cause the resurrection of the UK domicile of origin.

However, where although the move may be due to health reasons it is not perceived as a move motivated by one of necessity, but of preference; the individual may well be held to have either acquired a new domicile of choice or, more likely in practice, to have resurrected the domicile of origin.

On the other hand, the consequences for domicile status of a move motivated by, or involving, health considerations may be determined on factors perceived to be of more weight than the issues associated with the individual's health.

(See also *Re Steer (1858)* and *Re Lawton (1958)*.)

ABANDONMENT OF A DOMICILE OF CHOICE

A domicile of choice (unlike a domicile of origin) having been acquired (whether by design or otherwise) may subsequently be lost by abandonment. In practice, this requires:

- the ceasing of residence in the country; *and*
- the ceasing to intend to reside permanently in the country concerned.

It is not necessary for the individual to have acquired another domicile of choice; the act of giving up residence *and* the intention to remain permanently is sufficient; although one without the other is insufficient.

Thus, in *Udny v. Udny* Lord Westbury said:

> ... expressions are found ... that the first or existing domicile remains until another is acquired. This is true ... [for] the domicile of origin, but cannot be true ... [for a] domicile of choice ....

It is thus not necessary to acquire a new residence; the act of ceasing to reside in a country is sufficient. However, the need to cease actual residence is admirably demonstrated in the case of *In the Goods of Raffenel (1863)*.

A woman (Madam Raffenel) with a domicile of origin in England had married pre 1 January 1974 a Frenchman thus acquiring a French domicile of dependence. They both lived in France. The husband died. The wife decided to leave France to return to live permanently in England which would mean the loss of her French domicile of dependence and the resurrection of her UK domicile of origin. She boarded the ship (a paddle steamer) in Calais but became seriously ill before it left and so she disembarked and returned to Dunkirk where she died.

The court held that she had not abandoned her French domicile of dependence because although her intention was to return and live permanently in England she had not in fact actually lost her French residency. It was stated:

> ... the French domicile was [not] abandoned so long as the deceased remained in the territory of France ... she never left France, and intention alone is not sufficient ....

Similarly, the case of *Zanelli v. Zanelli (1948)* concerned a petition for divorce by an English woman from her Italian husband who had acquired an English domicile of choice but who had deserted her and had subsequently returned to Italy. The issue to be decided was whether the husband at the time of desertion was domiciled in England; if he was then the English courts could hear the petition and grant the divorce if appropriate (which they did in fact do). Lord Parq commented:

> ... he cannot be said to have lost his domicile of choice even at the moment when he stepped into the train with his ticket in his pocket. Having regard to what was decided ... *In the Goods of Raffenel* ... I do not think that, when he stepped on board the ship which was to carry him to the Continent, he had yet lost his domicile of choice ... although the husband may have given up an intention to reside here [UK at the time of desertion], he certainly had not given up residence here [UK] ....

In effect, residence will cease not when arrival elsewhere occurs, but when it is given up, i.e. when the individual has left that country's boundaries or legal jurisdiction.

However, it is now strongly arguable that, strictly speaking, it is not even necessary to cease to reside in the country of the domicile of choice if the individual's chief residence is in fact established elsewhere (*Plummer v. IRC (1988)*). This might be the case where, for example, an individual possessing a UK domicile of origin successfully acquires a non-UK domicile of choice. Subsequent thereto, whether by design or otherwise, the individual acquires de facto a "second" domicile of choice which is decided to be the individual's chief residence and thus new domicile of choice (even though residence in the country in which a domicile of choice was initially established has not ceased).

For the UK domiciled individual who acquires a non-UK domicile of choice this latter domicile would thus be lost if the individual ceased to reside in the country concerned *and* expressed the intention of no longer wishing to reside there indefinitely. The danger for such individual is that unless another domicile of choice is immediately acquired the original UK domicile of origin would automatically resurrect (*Udny v. Udny (1869)*).

In the case of the non-UK domiciled individual who acquires a UK domicile of choice this latter domicile would be lost if the individual ceased to reside in the UK and expressed the intention of no longer wishing to reside there indefinitely.

It is this aspect of the concept of domicile of origin (namely, its ability to automatically resurrect) that causes it to be regarded as extremely adhesive.

Example 3.20

Mario Milan and his wife arrived in the UK in the mid-1950s. Both possessed Italian domiciles of origin.

In 1970 they both expressed an intention to remain in the UK indefinitely thus each acquiring UK domiciles of choice.

In 2007, however, on retirement they decided that as they no longer worked in the UK and the fact that the majority of their family were in Italy they would leave the UK for good and return to Italy.

The consequence of this decision is that their previously acquired UK domiciles of choice would be abandoned and their original Italian domiciles of origin would be automatically resurrected.

Example 3.21

Henry and Joyce Hodges, both possessing UK domiciles of origin, emigrated to France in 1990 and in so doing each acquired a French domicile of choice.

In 2005 they decided that perhaps, on reflection, Spain might have been a better choice of country in which to retire and so moved there with the immediate intention of remaining in Spain indefinitely.

Henry and Joyce would have lost their French domiciles of choice on the move to Spain but would then have immediately acquired domiciles of choice in Spain.

In this case their respective UK domiciles of origin would not have been resurrected following the abandonment of their French domiciles of choice as Spanish domiciles of choice were immediately acquired.

In practice, the Hodges may have found their Spanish domiciles of choice subject to attack by HMRC had one or both of them died within a short period of taking up residence in Spain; probably, HMRC would seek to argue that their UK domiciles had at that point resurrected as the requisite intention to reside in Spain indefinitely had not in fact been formed.

SPECIAL CATEGORIES OF INDIVIDUAL AND DOMICILE OF CHOICE

[handwritten note: If forced to move (e.g. for illness) domicile doesn't change]

Lord Westbury in *Udny v. Udny (1869)* stated:

> Domicile of choice ... which the law derives from the fact of a man fixing voluntarily his sole or chief residence in a particular place ... There must be a residence freely chosen, and not prescribed or dictated by external necessity, such as the duties of office, the demand of creditors, or the relief from illness ....

The reference to "freely chosen" should not, however, be taken literally. Where perfect freedom to make a choice does not exist then residence, per se, should not be utilised on its own to infer "intention"; other factors supporting "intention" should be sought.

In a variety of cases domiciles of choice have arisen in such circumstances including, for example, where an individual resided in a country in deference to his father's dying injunction (*Somerville v. Somerville (1801)*); where an individual resided in a country in deference to his wife's wishes (*Aitchison v. Dixon (1870)*); and, in order to marry (*Fasbender v. AG (1922)*) even though perfect freedom of choice did not exist.

This issue of "freely chosen" is of particular relevance in the following cases:

- individuals of ill health;
- employees;
- members of the armed forces;
- diplomats.

(i) Individuals of Ill Health

There appears to be no clear authority on the issue of whether a domicile of choice is acquired by an individual residing in a country due to ill health.

It thus may be the position that an individual residing in a particular country due to ill health may, as a result, acquire a domicile of choice in that country to displace the domicile of origin although on balance this would seem to be the exception rather than the rule.

An individual who travels to a country for medical treatment with no intention of staying thereafter would not have acquired a domicile of choice therein. Indeed, arguably even if such individual travels to a country purely for medical treatment knowing that the illness cannot be cured and that death in the country where the medical treatment is being carried out is inevitable will not cause domicile status to become that of this country; assuming that no intention to remain there has been formed. Similarly, an individual who is taken ill in a country and cannot for the time being travel is, again, unlikely to have acquired a domicile of choice therein.

On the other hand, an individual who is advised that a move to another country is likely to lengthen life may make the move with the intention of remaining there indefinitely (i.e. until death) thus acquiring a domicile of choice therein.

(ii) Employees

Generally speaking, an employee who is sent to work in a country other than the employee's domicile of origin will not acquire a domicile of choice there.

Whether the employee is a public servant or of a private employer the rules applying to determine domicile status are the same in each case. Indeed, there are no special considerations in determining the domicile status of such an employee.

The mere fact of working in such a country, per se, does not result in an automatic acquisition of a domicile of choice. Intention to reside their indefinitely or permanently would need to be shown by the person asserting it.

(iii) Member of the Armed Forces

Generally speaking, as in the case of an employee, a member of the armed forces sent on active service to another country will not acquire a domicile of choice there.

However, this does not preclude such a domicile being acquired if the conditions as to residence and intention exist (*Donaldson v. Donaldson (1949)*).

(iv) Diplomats

Diplomatic and consular immunity has existed for centuries under common law. Much of the common law practices are now enshrined in various Vienna Conventions.

However, both diplomats and consular officials are public servants (as indicated above) and no special rules apply in determining domicile status.

Thus, as under the normal rules, residence and intention with respect to the country concerned must subsist for a domicile of choice to arise.

Issues normally associated with diplomats, including possible immunity from local courts, etc. are of no consequence in determining domicile status.

DEEMED UK DOMICILE

Domiciles of origin, dependence and choice are determined according to the UK's common law rules.

Unlike any of these three categories of domicile the concept of *deemed UK domicile* is a creature purely of tax statute and specifically only applies for inheritance tax purposes and for no other purpose (i.e. it is of no relevance for income and/or capital gains tax purposes).

It is thus quite possible for an individual to possess a non-UK domicile for general law purposes (e.g. a non-UK domicile of origin) yet still be deemed UK domiciled for inheritance tax purposes only.

The concept of deemed domicile was only introduced in 1974 when capital transfer tax was introduced.

An individual may be deemed UK domiciled in one of two circumstances:

- a UK domiciled individual (determined under general law) is deemed UK domiciled for a further three-year period following the acquisition of a new domicile of choice;
- a non-UK domiciled individual (determined under general law) is deemed UK domiciled if the individual has been resident in the UK for at least 17 out of the 20 tax years ending in the relevant year (i.e. the tax year in which a determination needs to be made).

Great care is needed in applying either of these two deeming provisions.

(i) Three-year Rule

For the UK domiciled individual either of the above two provisions may be in point and both provisions would need to be considered. For example, an individual who ceases to be UK domiciled on, say, 1 May 2002 (i.e. because of the acquisition of a non-UK domicile of choice) will, under the first of the above provisions, be deemed to continue to be UK domiciled until 30 April 2005 (i.e. for a three-year period).

(ii) 17 Out of 20 Tax Year Rule

However, if such individual had been resident in the UK for the past 20 tax years (the 20th being the tax year 2002/03, the tax year of departure) then the individual will, under the second of the above two provisions, continue to be deemed UK domiciled in the tax year 2005/06 (in 2005/06 the individual would still have been UK resident for 17 out of the last 20 tax years). Therefore, the individual would remain UK deemed domiciled until 5 April 2006.

(iii) 15 Tax Years Plus Two-Day Trap

It must also be appreciated that residence for part of any tax year counts as residence for that tax year in ascertaining whether the 17 tax years out of 20 has been breached. The effect may possibly be that residency for 15 tax years plus an additional one day of residency in each of two additional tax years may lead to breaching the test.

For example, an individual arrives in the UK on 5 April 1991 becoming resident (and indeed ordinarily resident) from this day of arrival. He remains in the UK for the next 15 tax years finally leaving the UK on 6 April 2006. He has thus been resident for 15 (complete) tax years, i.e. 1991/92 to 2005/06 inclusive, plus he has also been resident in each of the tax years 1990/91 and 2006/07 although only in fact residing in these two tax years for one day in each; a total of 17 tax years. Nevertheless, the impact is that deemed UK domicile status will continue to apply through to 5 April 2007 inclusive, after which as the individual has left the UK (thus becoming non-UK resident) he will no longer breach the 17 tax years out of 20 rule.

However, an individual who is under general law non-UK domiciled but who is caught under the deemed UK domicile rule because of the satisfaction of the 17 out 20 tax years rule does not continue to be deemed UK domiciled for a further three years after leaving the UK (the three-year rule only applying where the UK domicile status for inheritance tax purposes was that determined by the common law rules).

Example 3.22
Sarah Tobin possessed a UK domicile of origin but has not resided in the UK for the past 17 out of the last 20 tax years.

On 1 May 1998 she left for Italy but was unsure of her long-term intentions.

On 1 July 2005 she decided that she wished to remain in Italy indefinitely.

From 1 July 2005 under the normal common law rules she would have acquired an Italian domicile of choice.

However, for inheritance tax purposes only, she would remain deemed UK domiciled for three more years, i.e. until 30 June 2008.

Example 3.23
Chuck Timber possessed a Canadian domicile of origin.

He arrived in the UK on 1 September 1980 intending to return to Canada when he retired.

However, he died in the UK in August 1996 prior to retiring.

He thus died in the tax year 1996/97. In that year Chuck had been resident in the UK for 17 tax years out of 17 tax years.

He thus died deemed UK domiciled for inheritance tax purposes even though he would have probably retained his Canadian domicile of origin for other UK tax purposes.

As indicated earlier a child's domicile of dependence follows that of the parent on whom the child's domicile legally depends. However, where this parent becomes deemed UK domiciled for UK inheritance tax purposes this deemed domicile status of the parent has no effect on the child's domicile of dependence.

Example 3.24
Johan and Magya Kupp each possessed Danish domiciles of origin. They decided to spend some time in the UK but had no intention of remaining in the UK indefinitely. Their intention was always to return to Denmark.

They each became deemed UK domiciled for inheritance tax purposes after having resided in the UK for 17 tax years.

Despite their deemed UK domicile status for inheritance tax purposes their daughter, Ursula, aged 10 continued to possess her Danish domicile of origin (i.e. that of her father).

Note, however, that even where an individual becomes deemed UK domiciled for UK inheritance tax purposes, exempt gilts continue to qualify as excluded property (see Chapter 12).

It should also be noted that the double tax agreements concerning inheritance tax with France, India, Italy and Pakistan (all pre 1975) do not import the deemed domicile concept (nor in fact do these agreements affect lifetime gifts; they apply on death only) (see Chapter 25).

(iv) Dealing with Deemed UK Domicile Status

In principle, it should not be difficult for an individual who is non-UK domiciled to ensure that this domicile status is retained.

However, for inheritance tax (and only inheritance tax) purposes it is possible for a non-UK domiciled individual to become deemed UK domiciled simply due to the passage of time (i.e. falling to be treated as UK resident for 17 out of the past 20 tax years). The acquisition of deemed UK domicile status, albeit only for inheritance tax, is generally speaking probably better avoided.

The two basic options where the issue of deemed UK domiciled status may be, or is, in point are:

- to try to avoid deemed domicile status arising ab initio; or
- to accept that it will occur and plan accordingly.

(a) Avoidance

Thus if, for example, an individual had been resident in the UK for the last 20 tax years then prior to 5 April of the 20 tax year the individual would need to take steps to become non-UK resident. The individual would need to be non-UK resident for the next four successive tax years in order that the 17 tax year "clock" could be restarted.

After a four tax year absence, on reacquiring UK residency thereafter the individual would only then have been UK resident for 16 out of the previous 20 tax years. This status would subsist for the next 17 tax years before the individual would fall foul of these rules again.

This option may, however, not always be a practical option.

(b) Plan Accordingly

For the individual possessing a non-UK domicile of origin the adverse inheritance tax impact of becoming deemed UK domiciled (i.e. worldwide assets falling subject to inheritance tax) may be mitigated by ensuring that any overseas assets continue to remain excluded property for inheritance tax purposes after deemed UK domicile status arises.

Excluded property includes any non-UK situs assets owned by a non-UK domiciled individual. Thus excluded property status is lost once deemed UK domicile status arises.

However, if such assets are settled prior to the individual becoming deemed UK domiciled in an appropriate (e.g. discretionary) offshore (i.e. non-UK resident) trust, then the assets would continue to constitute excluded property even after the settlor has become deemed UK domiciled (see Chapter 12).

With respect to any UK situs assets, if these can be relocated outside the UK then they could also be settled as above; thus turning otherwise taxable assets into excluded property.

For the UK domiciled individual who acquires a non-UK domicile of choice but remains deemed UK domiciled for three more years any potential inheritance tax exposure may be mitigated during this period by the purchase of UK gilts which rank as excluded property for the non-ordinarily resident individual (see Chapter 12).

(c) "Split" Domicile

Following the change in law contained in the Domicile and Matrimonial Proceedings Act 1973 (which became effective from 1 January 1974), inter alia, a woman who marries on or after this date does not automatically acquire the domicile status of her husband at the date of marriage (see above). The woman simply retains her domicile status at the date of marriage; her future domicile status is determined under the normal rules.

One consequence of this change in law is that it is no longer unusual for a husband and wife to possess different domiciles, so-called "split domiciles". There are thus four possible permutations for a married couple:

1. both UK domiciled;
2. both non-UK domiciled;
3. UK domiciled husband/non-UK domiciled wife;
4. UK domiciled wife/non-UK domiciled husband.

As a general rule, any transfer of assets between spouses can be effected without precipitating any capital gains tax or inheritance tax consequences. However, regarding inheritance tax, only the first £55 000 of transfers is actually exempt from inheritance tax where the transfers are *from* a *UK* domiciled spouse *to* a *non-UK* domiciled spouse (i.e. points 3 and 4 above). Transfers in excess of this amount are treated as potentially exempt transfers and thus may be subject to inheritance tax should the transferor spouse die within seven years thereof.

In the case of all other transfers between spouses unlimited transfers may be made without limit and without precipitating any inheritance tax liability.

In the case of capital gains tax there is no equivalent provision and thus, in principle, all inter-spouse transfers may be made without precipitating any capital gains tax liability (see Chapter 8).

(d) International Dimension

There are few inheritance tax-based double tax conventions. In total there are 10 of which four, namely those with France, India, Italy and Pakistan, are pre 1975 agreements and thus dealt with estate duty but are deemed to have been extended to cover inheritance tax (section 158 IHTA 1984).

These agreements, however, have no application to lifetime transfers but do preclude the UK's deemed domicile rules from applying (see Chapter 25).

The other agreements are not so limited.

SUMMARY

Domicile is probably the most important characteristic of an individual which determines the individual's liabilities with respect to income, capital gains and inheritance taxes. Until a determinant of the individual's domicile status is made it is not possible to implement a wealth planning strategy which will be tax efficient.

The three main categories of domicile are domicile of origin, dependence and choice.

Every individual must at all times possess a domicile and only one domicile can apply at any one point in time for any specific purpose.

A domicile of origin is acquired at birth but later in life a domicile of choice may be acquired which would supersede the individual's domicile of origin.

Deemed UK domicile is a status applicable only for inheritance tax purposes.

An individual may be deemed UK domiciled for UK inheritance tax purposes while being non-UK domiciled under common law.

4
Residence and Ordinary Residence

BACKGROUND

The terms "residence" and "ordinary residence" are similar but not identical. The difference can be very important. Thus, whether an individual is UK resident *and* ordinarily resident *or* is UK resident *but not* ordinarily resident may be critical to the individual's tax liabilities. If an individual is UK domiciled, UK resident but *not* ordinarily resident in the UK the remittance basis of taxation would apply to the individual's non-UK source income and non-UK source capital gains in the same manner as applies in the case of a non-UK domiciled but UK resident individual.

Example 4.1
John Smith is UK domiciled and UK resident but is *not* ordinarily resident in the UK.

John has a bank account in Belgium which earns interest; the interest is directly credited to the account. John also receives dividends on a holding of Hong Kong equities which are credited to his bank account in Jersey.

Although John is UK domiciled and UK resident because he is *not* ordinarily UK resident the interest and dividend income are not liable to UK income tax unless remitted to the UK.

It is also the case that certain of the UK's anti-avoidance provisions do not apply to individuals who are not ordinarily resident in the UK.

LACK OF DEFINITIONS AND IR20 *[new version early '09]*

Although reference is made in certain statutory provisions (e.g. section 831 ITA 2007) to the term "residence" such references are for specific purposes only and there is in fact no general definition of the term for all purposes.

For a general approach to residence (and ordinary residence) and the closest to what might be termed a definition are the comments made in the booklet produced by HMRC (when previously called Inland Revenue) referred to as IR20 entitled "Residents and non-residents: Liability to tax in the UK" the current edition of which was issued in May 2008 and is a slightly updated version of the earlier edition dated December 1999 (see Appendix 3). The latest version is only available "online" as it takes no account of the significant changes (albeit not directly with reference to residence, per se) introduced in FA 2008. HMRC have confirmed that a completely updated version of the booklet will be released in early 2009 following a period of consultation. The booklet despite its title also refers to domicile.

The booklet sets out HMRC's views as to what constitutes residence and ordinary residence (and indeed domicile) which have been extrapolated from a variety of decided tax cases over time. The booklet also attempts to provide pragmatic solutions where the strict application of the law would produce inequitable consequences. Perhaps the classic example is that IR20 permits, in certain restricted circumstances, the tax year to be split in terms of a period of residency and a period of non-residency (or vice versa). Under the law there is no provision for such a split.

Nevertheless it is to be appreciated that IR20, as such, is not a statement of the law (but HMRC's views thereof) and thus can be challenged although, other things being equal, in practice any such challenge is likely to meet with great resistance.

In view of the importance of IR20 much of what is said below is based on the booklet's content (see Appendix 3).

DUAL RESIDENCE

The individual may be resident in more than one country at the same time (a so-called "dual resident"). This can arise, for example, due to different countries adopting different rules used to determine residence. For example, in the UK (see below) residence is typically determined according to the number of days an individual physically spends in the UK in a tax year, whereas in Belgium the individual's residence status may be determined according to the location of that individual's centre of vital interests (broadly, where his economic, social and family ties are closest).

It may therefore be that the individual's centre of vital interests is located in Belgium but in one particular tax year the individual also spends in excess of 183 days in the UK. Such individual may thus fall to be treated as UK resident under the UK rules but at the same time be treated as Belgian resident under the Belgian rules, i.e. dual resident.

It is thus *not* possible for the individual to argue that he is *not* UK resident simply because he is resident somewhere else.

Where dual residency does arise resort can often be had to the terms of an appropriate double taxation agreement (see Chapter 25) which will typically resolve the issue so as to prevent double taxation arising (i.e. tax in more than one country on the same income and gains). Even in the absence of an appropriate double taxation agreement a country's domestic tax law will, in any event, often enable relief from double taxation to be obtained (as is the case in the UK).

SPLIT TAX YEARS

An individual is resident and/or ordinarily resident for a complete tax year; as a matter of law a tax year *cannot* be split for this purpose and an individual by law cannot thus be resident for part of a tax year but non-resident for the other part of the tax year (*Gubay v. Kington (1984)*).

However, *by concession* HMRC accept that in certain circumstances a tax year can be split both for income tax and capital gains tax purposes. In general, this splitting of the tax year is available to an individual *arriving* in the UK to take up residence part way through a tax year *or* an individual *departing* from the UK part way through a tax year (see below).

Where a tax year is split into a period of residency and a period of non-residency the issue arises as to how an individual's income and capital gains tax liabilities are to be computed for such a tax year. Two specific concessions, namely, ESC A11 and ESC D2 (see Appendix 3), detail how the individual's income and capital gains tax liabilities in split year circumstances are to be calculated.

It is vitally important, however, to appreciate that HMRC concessions are not the law. In principle they are designed to alleviate aspects of the law where perceived unfairness arises. It is not therefore surprising to find that HMRC may well seek to challenge the use of a concession if it is being used for what HMRC perceive as an abuse. Every concession is thus qualified by the words:

> A concession will not be given in any case where an attempt is made to use it for tax avoidance.

An example of the refusal to apply a concession concerning split tax years is the case of *R v. IRC, ex parte Fulford-Dobson* (1987).

In this case a wife gave her husband an asset just prior to his taking up full-time employment abroad which he then sold, albeit before the following 6 April. HMRC refused to apply any concessional treatment (i.e. refused to accept that from the day following Mr Fulford-Dobson leaving the UK he had lost his UK residency) and, as a consequence of denying Mr Fulford-Dobson non-UK residence status, levied capital gains tax on the gain he had made from the sale. The court upheld HMRC's treatment and a subsequent judicial review of HMRC's approach by the taxpayer was also unsuccessful.

In short, Mr Fulford-Dobson's attempt to split the tax year of his departure from the UK (see below) so that when he sold the asset he thought he would be regarded as not UK resident (and thus outside the scope of capital gains tax) failed and he was held to have still been UK resident when the asset was sold. HMRC took this approach, denying the split tax year concession, because they perceived that Mr Fulford-Dobson was seeking to abuse the concession.

Income Tax

The first circumstance dealt with in ESC A11 applies where the individual *arrives* in the UK to take up permanent residence *or* intends to stay for at least two tax years.

The second circumstance applies where the individual *leaves* the UK for permanent residence abroad *or* leaves to work full time abroad under a contract of employment which spans at least one complete tax year.

Under Concession A11 where its conditions are satisfied an individual's income tax liability will be ascertained only by reference to the period of residency during that tax year (whether the individual is arriving in, or departing from, the UK). The precise calculation of the amount of taxable income, however, is slightly different in each of the two cases (and not discussed here).

Capital Gains Tax

Concession ESC D2 allows the tax year to be split so that the individual who arrives in the UK part way through a tax year will be subject to capital gains tax only on disposals made on or after the date of arrival.

Similarly, ESC D2 provides that the individual who departs from the UK part way through a tax year will be subject to capital gains tax only on disposals made to the date of departure.

However, in the former case (i.e. arrival in the UK) the Concession will apply only where the individual has not been UK resident or ordinary resident in any of the five tax years prior to the tax year of arrival.

In the latter case (i.e. departure from the UK) the Concession will apply only where the individual has not been UK resident or ordinary resident for at least four out of the seven tax years immediately preceding the tax year of departure.

Where the Concession does not apply the individual will be liable to capital gains tax for the complete tax year of arrival or departure.

Example 4.2

An individual arrives in the UK on 4 August 2007 and is treated as resident and ordinarily resident from that date. He has not been resident or ordinarily resident in the UK during the five prior tax years.

In May 2007 he had sold his holding of UK equities in XYZ Ltd making a capital gain of £200 000 and in October 2007 sold his holding of UK equities in ABC Ltd making a capital gain of £150 000.

Under Concession D2 he will *not* be liable to capital gains tax on the sale of the XYZ Ltd shares but *will* be subject to capital gains tax on the sale of the ABC Ltd shares.

However, if the individual prior to arriving in the UK on 4 August 2007 (i.e. in the tax year 2007/08) had been, say, resident in the UK in the tax year 2002/03, i.e. within the five previous tax years (prior to tax year 2007/08), then capital gains tax would have been leviable on both of the above share sales (even though one of the sales had in fact occurred prior to the acquisition of residency in the UK).

In the above Example 4.2 (i.e. where only the capital gain on the ABC Ltd shares was taxable) if the sale of XYZ Ltd shares had precipitated a capital loss and the sale of the ABC Ltd shares had precipitated a capital gain the capital loss could not be utilised (e.g. offset against the gain) and the full amount of the capital gain would be taxable. In such a case, if possible, the sale of the ABC Ltd shares should have been made prior to the date of arrival in the UK and the sale of the XYZ Ltd shares should have been made after the date of arrival (ensuring that the capital gain would then not have been taxed while the capital loss could have been utilised, e.g. by carrying it forward for offset against future capital gains). Where both sales were subject to capital gains tax (i.e. the latter part of Example 4.2) then the capital loss could be offset against the capital gain (see Chapter 8).

TEMPORARY NON-UK RESIDENCE

Individuals who leave the UK for a period of non-UK residency would normally expect to fall outside the charge to UK income tax (other than on UK source income) and capital gains tax.

However, anti-avoidance provisions may apply to deny such exemption thus continuing to levy tax even though the individual has acquired non-UK residency. These provisions apply in principle for periods of non-UK residency of less than five complete tax years (see below).

Although pre FA 2008 capital gains tax might arise in the above circumstance whether the individual was UK or non-UK domiciled, FA 2008 has in fact broadened the provision which applied pre FA 2008.

In the case of income tax, pre FA 2008, there was no equivalent provision to that applicable for capital gains tax purposes. However, post FA 2008 a new provision has been introduced but only applies to non-UK domiciled individuals.

Capital Gains Tax

Where the individual has been resident in the UK for at least four of the immediately preceding seven tax years prior to the tax year of departure and becomes non-UK resident for less than five complete tax years any capital gains arising on assets owned prior to departure will be subject to capital gains tax (and any capital losses allowable).

The charge, however, will be levied in the tax year of return.

The above applies to both UK and non-UK domiciled individuals.

If the five tax year period of absence condition is met then any capital gains (or capital losses) arising in any of these five tax years (on assets owned at the time of departure) are not subject to capital gains tax (or allowable).

Similarly, if the individual is not resident for the four out of seven tax year period prior to the tax year of departure, a non-UK residence period of five tax years is not required in order to dispose of assets owned on departure without a capital gains tax charge arising.

Assets acquired and sold during a five complete tax year period of absence are not subject to capital gains tax under the above rule; thus, neither gains nor losses arising on such assets are chargeable/allowable.

Example 4.3

An individual leaves the UK on 6 November 2007 for five subsequent complete tax years. The individual has been resident and ordinarily resident in the UK for at least four out of the seven tax years prior to the tax year of departure, i.e. prior to 2007/08.

In February 2008 (having left the UK) the individual sold a piece of UK real estate (owned prior to departure) making a capital gain and also sold UK equities (owned prior to departure) making a capital gain in June 2008.

Although at both dates of sale the individual had left the UK, and indeed lost his UK residency and ordinary residence status, Concession ESC D2 would not apply to relieve the capital gain arising on the real estate sale from capital gains tax. Capital gains tax would therefore be chargeable on the gain made on the sale and would be chargeable in the tax year 2007/08.

However, the capital gains on the sale of the equities which occurred in the tax year of departure would not be subject to a capital gains tax charge.

For the non-UK domiciled individual, pre FA 2008, while the above rules applied it was still possible for remittances to the UK of non-UK source capital gains effected by the non-UK domiciled individual while non-UK resident to be made without precipitating a capital gains tax charge. Post FA 2008 this is no longer possible in certain circumstances (see Chapter 8).

Income Tax

Under the new rules contained in FA 2008 relevant foreign income (broadly, interest and dividends arising outside the UK) of a non-UK domiciled individual remitted to the UK while the individual is non-UK resident may fall subject to income tax on the individual's return to the UK.

This will arise where the individual has been resident in the UK or ordinarily resident therein for at least four tax years out of the immediately preceding seven tax years prior to the tax year of departure *and* the individual is not non-UK resident for at least five full tax years between the tax year of departure and the tax year of return. In this case any relevant foreign income which is remitted to the UK after the tax year of departure and before the tax year of return will be treated as remitted in the tax year of return and subject to income tax in that tax year of return.

The relevant foreign income so caught is that which has arisen in the tax year of departure (thus, including relevant foreign income which arose in the tax year of departure but after actual departure) or an earlier tax year including such income which arose before the tax year 2008/09, i.e. there is no transitional relief for pre 2008/09 relevant foreign income.

Example 4.4

A non-UK domiciled individual leaves the UK on 6 November 2008 returning on 6 April 2012 i.e. within five complete tax years. The individual has been resident and ordinarily resident in the UK for at least four out of the seven tax years prior to the tax year of departure, i.e. prior to 2008/09.

In October 2009 (having left the UK) the individual remitted relevant foreign income to the UK which he had received in tax years prior to the tax year of departure.

This relevant foreign income will be subject to income tax in the tax year 2012/13 (i.e. the tax year of retrun).

RESIDENCE RULES AND IR20

The rules determining an individual's residence and/or ordinary residence status (based on IR20) may be broken down into the following four categories:

- short absences;
- the 183-day test;
- arrivals in the UK;
- departures from the UK.

Each will now be considered in turn.

Short Absences

An individual will continue to be resident and ordinarily resident in the UK if the individual normally lives in the UK and only leaves the UK for short breaks/trips.

Example 4.5

Henry Lodge lives in the UK but every Christmas travels to the USA for a three-week holiday with his uncle. He also usually spends two weeks in Spain during the summer on holiday.

Henry will simply continue to be resident and ordinarily resident in the UK throughout the tax year despite the overseas trips.

The 183-day rule

There are no exceptions to this rule.

Any individual who is physically present in the UK in any tax year for at least 183 days in aggregate will be treated as resident for that tax year (but not automatically ordinarily resident; this will depend upon other factors; see below). The number of days is arrived at by simply adding up days spent in the UK. It is not necessary for the 183 days to arise on the same visit; they may thus arise over a number of visits to the UK in the tax year.

Generally speaking, pre FA 2008, days of arrival and days of departure from the UK were ignored when ascertaining the number of days spent in the UK for any particular tax year (or where averaging calculations are performed; see below).

Example 4.6

Alberto Ginnini was a frequent visitor to the UK. Each visit, however, usually lasted for just a few days at a time.

In the tax year 2007/08 Alberto visited the UK as follows: for the whole of May (31); June (30); and July (31).

He returned later in the year spending: the whole of October (31); November (30); and December (31) in the UK.

He also spent 10 days in March in the UK.

Days of arrival and departure have been ignored.

In total the number of days Alberto spent in the UK was: 30 + 30 + 30 + 30 + 30 + 30 + 8 = 188 days.

Alberto will thus be treated as UK resident for the whole of the tax year 2007/08 (i.e. from 6 April 2007 to 5 April 2008 inclusive).

However, from 6 April 2008 following FA 2008, days of arrival are no longer ignored when ascertaining the number of days the individual spends in the UK in a tax year. A day in the UK is now (effective 6 April 2008) determined according to whether the individual is in the UK at midnight.

Example 4.7
Gerard Black arrived in the UK on 7 May 2008 and left on 20 May 2008.

The number of days spent in the UK is 13 days.

Pre FA 2008 this number would have been 12 days.

However, there is also an exemption for passengers who are in transit between two places outside the UK. This exemption caters for people who have to change airports or terminals when transiting through the UK. It allows people to switch between modes of transport, so they could fly in but leave by ferry or train, for example. Days spent in transit, which could involve being in the UK at midnight, will not be counted as days of presence in the UK for residence test purposes so long as during transit the individual does not engage in activities that are to a substantial extent unrelated to their passage through the UK.

Arriving and Departing the UK

Even where the individual fails to meet the 183-day test referred to above, the individual may still fall to be treated as resident in the UK under one or more of the alternative tests of residence.

In applying these other tests the approach of HMRC is to consider two categories of individual:

- individuals *arriving* in the UK;
- individuals *departing* from the UK.

Arriving in the UK

Individuals arriving in the UK are divided into three categories:

(i) the three-year rule/permanent;
(ii) short-term visitors split into:

(a) short-term visitors with *unclear* intentions;
(b) short-term visitors with *fixed* intentions;

(iii) long-term visitors.

These are arbitrary categories determined by HMRC designed to offer a practical solution to residency determination.

(i) Three-year rule/permanent rule
The individual coming to live in the UK permanently *or* coming to the UK in order to remain for three years (not tax years; just normal years) or more is treated as resident *and* ordinarily resident from the date of arrival.

The reference to "remain" refers to arriving in the UK and staying there for a continuous period, except perhaps for short business trips abroad and/or holidays.

It should be noted that even if in these circumstances the individual is not in fact in the UK in the tax year of arrival for at least 183 days (see above) this makes no difference to the individual's status. He is still treated as resident *and* ordinarily resident from the date of arrival.

Example 4.8
Helen Schmidt has always lived in Germany. She arrives in the UK on 1 January 2007 intending to remain in the UK for at least three years. She will be classified as resident *and* ordinary resident from 1 January 2007.

Note that this applies even though in the tax year 2006/07 (the tax year of her arrival) she will in fact be in the UK for significantly less than 183 days.

Any other visitor (i.e. one who does not intend to stay here indefinitely or for at least three years) is classified as either a short- or long-term visitor (see below).

(ii) Short-term visitors
A short-term visitor is the individual who arrives in the UK but does not at that time intend to remain in the UK either indefinitely or for at least three years (i.e. will not satisfy point (i) above).

In order to determine the individual's status HMRC seeks to classify the individual into either one of two categories.

(a) Unclear intentioned short term visitors   The individual who on arrival in the UK is unclear about his future intentions will fall to be regarded as resident and ordinarily resident from the commencement of the fifth tax year after arrival if over the preceding four tax years the number of days spent in the UK per tax year on average equals 91 days or more (in ascertaining this average, days of arrival and departure were ignored pre 6 April 2008. On or after this date, however, the "midnight" test referred to above will apply.)

The calculation to work out the average is:

$$\frac{\text{Total visits to the UK}}{\text{Relevant tax years}} \times 365 = \text{Annual average visits}$$

Example 4.9

Inga Johanson arrived in the UK for the first time on 1 October 1999. She was uncertain of her likely future intentions.

In the event, her visits to the UK over the first four tax years were as follows:

1999/00	100 days
2000/01	90 days
2001/02	80 days
2002/03	170 days

Over the first four tax years, including her tax year of arrival, the average number of days spent in the UK per tax year was 110 days (i.e. $[[100 + 90 + 80 + 170]/[365 + 365 + 365 + 365]] \times 365$).

As a consequence of breaching the 91-day per tax year average over her first four tax years of visits Inga would be classified as resident *and* ordinarily resident from 6 April 2003 (i.e. commencement of the fifth tax year after arrival).

Thus, despite spending time in the UK in the previous four tax years (albeit never breaching the 183-day test in any particular tax year) Inga became neither resident nor ordinarily resident in any of them.

Example 4.10

Inga Johanson is contemplating returning to the UK sometime in the tax year 2008/09. She indicates that on current plans she will make three separate visits as follows:

(i) arrive 10 November 2008; leave 15 November 2008;
(ii) arrive 20 December 2008; leave 3 January 2009;
(iii) arrive 6 March 2009; leave 31 March 2009.

She calculates that she will be in the UK for 41 days in 2008/09.

However, in the light of FA 2008 changes she will in fact be spending 44 days in the UK.

It may be that although initially an individual is unclear about likely future visits to the UK, prior to the commencement of the fifth tax year the individual decides that intentions have become clear and that visits (over the first four tax years) will breach the 91-day test. In this case the individual will be treated as resident and ordinarily resident from the commencement of the tax year in which the decision is taken.

Example 4.11

Henri Jacques arrived in the UK on 10 December 2000 with unclear intentions as to his future visits.

He is in fact in the UK for 80 days in the first tax year 2000/01. In the tax year 2001/02 he is in the UK for 120 days.

In the third tax year 2002/03 his intentions become clear such that over the first four tax years his visits will average at least 91 days in each tax year (i.e. on average over the four tax years 2000/01, 2001/02, 2002/3 and 2003/04).

He will, as a consequence, be treated as resident *and* ordinarily resident from 6 April 2002, i.e. the commencement of the tax year of his intentions becoming clear.

From the tax perspective, other things being equal, for the short-term visitor it is preferable to remain non-UK resident and non-UK ordinarily resident for as long as possible (this, of course, would reduce the quantum of any UK tax liabilities and would probably avoid the need to file a UK Tax Return). It is thus preferable to defer any real decision (if at all possible) to remain in the UK until as late as possible with a view to becoming resident (and ordinarily resident) only after four complete tax years. The facts will, however, determine if this is feasible.

(b) Fixed intentioned short-term visitors If on arrival in the UK the individual is clear that average visits in the following four tax years will equal or exceed 91 days per tax year (and in fact the intention is carried out) then the individual will be treated as resident *and* ordinarily resident not from the date of arrival (as normal) but from 6 April of the tax year of his first visit (i.e. an element of backdating occurs).

Example 4.12
Taking the facts of Example 4.9 above but in this case assuming Inga, on arrival in the UK, indicates that her intention will be to average at least 91 days per tax year over the ensuing four tax years means that she will be treated as resident *and* ordinarily resident from the beginning of the tax year of her arrival, i.e. 6 April 1999 (not the date of her arrival in the UK, i.e. 1 October 1999).

Compare this with Example 4.9 where residency and ordinary residency for Inga started from 6 April 2003, some four years later.

As indicated above, delaying the acquisition of UK residency (and ordinary residency) is generally preferable. In Inga's case (see Examples 4.9 and 4.12 above) the consequences in Example 4.9 would thus be preferable to those in Example 4.12. However, it is important to appreciate that an individual on arriving in the UK cannot necessarily simply choose which of the two options is "better". In other words, if on the facts an individual on arriving in the UK knows that the 91-day test will be breached then such individual cannot "pretend" to fall into the category of "unclear intentioned short-term visitor" thus attempting to achieve a deferral of the date of commencement of residency.

Example 4.13
Sammy Smith Jnr is self-employed in the USA.

He is offered an assignment in the UK which will involve him spending approximately at least three to four months in each of the next four tax years.

In this case Sammy knows that although he will be classified as a short-term visitor his intentions, ab initio, are clear.

He will thus be treated as resident and ordinary resident from 6 April of the tax year of his arrival.

(iii) Averaging: the computational rules (arrivals)

As indicated above, in determining the number of days spent in the UK on average per tax year by short-term visitors, days of arrival and departure for periods prior to 6 April 2008 were ignored. Furthermore, any days (i.e. not days of arrival or departure) spent in the UK because of exceptional circumstances (e.g. illness of individual or immediate family) were also *normally* ignored (this practice continues post 6 April 2008).

Similarly, such "illness" days are also ignored in applying the 183-day test (see above).

Post FA 2008 the "midnight" test will be adopted for averaging computations.

(iv) Long-term visitors

If the individual comes to the UK for a specific purpose (e.g. to work) for at least two years but less than three years (if three years or more the above "three-year rule" would apply; see above) then such individual will be resident (but not ordinarily resident) from the date of arrival to the date of departure (as for the above "three-year rule" this would apply even if in the tax year of arrival the 183-day test was not itself satisfied).

Ordinary residence, however, commences from the beginning of the tax year after the third anniversary of the date of arrival (assuming that no accommodation in the interim has been bought (or acquired on a lease of three years or more) or that no property was already owned prior to arrival in the UK).

Example 4.14

Tom Cobber arrived in the UK on 15 July 2007 from Australia to work for the UK subsidiary of an Australian bank. His secondment was for a period of two years. No UK property was owned by Tom prior to his arrival.

Tom will be treated as resident from 15 July 2007, his date of arrival, and will not become ordinarily resident unless he is still in the UK three years later, i.e. on 15 July 2010; in which case, he will become ordinarily resident from 6 April 2011.

However, in the case of a long-term visitor ordinary residence will commence from the date of arrival (in line with residency) if accommodation is already owned prior to arrival *or* accommodation is bought in the tax year of arrival *or* accommodation is/has been acquired in the tax year of arrival on a lease of three years or more. Alternatively, ordinary residence commences from 6 April of the tax year in which such accommodation becomes available if this is after the tax year of arrival.

Example 4.15

Assume the same facts as in Example 4.14 above but in the tax year of his arrival (i.e. 2007/08) Tom buys a UK property (or enters into a three-year lease on a property).

Tom's ordinary residency will now commence from his date of arrival, i.e. 15 July 2007.

It should, however, be noted that the ownership of accommodation, per se, does not trigger ordinary residence. If, for example, an individual owned UK property and decided simply to make a two-month short-term trip to the UK (e.g. for a holiday) the existence of the accommodation will not result in the individual becoming resident and/or ordinary resident of itself. Satisfaction of one of the above tests would also need to be met (the strict accommodation rule was abolished in 1993).

Departing from the UK

For the individual leaving the UK a determination of residence and ordinary residence status is dependent upon which of two categories the individual is regarded as satisfying. The two categories are:

(i) full time working abroad;
(ii) the three years abroad/permanently.

(i) Working abroad
If the individual leaves the UK to work abroad and satisfies the following conditions then such individual is not resident and not ordinarily resident from the day following the date of departure to the day before the return to the UK at the end of the period of the contract. The conditions to be satisfied are:

- the individual must work full time abroad;
- under a contract of employment spanning a complete tax year; and
- any visits to the UK during the period of absence must amount to less than 183 days in any tax year and less than 91 days per tax year on average.

On returning to the UK the individual is treated as coming to the UK permanently (see above) and is thus resident and ordinarily resident from the date of arrival in the UK.

Example 4.16
Brian Brown has managed to secure for himself a contract of employment with a company based in Bahrain.

The contract is for the period 1 March 2007 to 30 June 2008 (and thus spans a complete tax year, namely, 2007/08) and the contract also requires him to work full time (thus two of the three conditions above are satisfied).

Brian left the UK to take up his contract on 25 February 2007 and returned to the UK on 7 July 2008. He made no return visits to the UK during his period of absence (thus satisfying the third condition above).

Brian will be treated as neither resident nor ordinarily resident from 26 February (i.e. the day after his departure from the UK) to 6 July (the day before his return to the UK) inclusive as he satisfies the conditions set out above.

Had Brian's contract of employment run from 1 March 2007 to, say, 31 January 2008 then Brain would be treated as remaining resident and ordinarily resident in the UK throughout this period as all the conditions above are not satisfied, namely, the contract of employment does not span a complete tax year.

It is important that during the period abroad any return visits to the UK should be kept to a minimum and, in any event, under no circumstances should any visits aggregate

183 days or more in any tax year *or* average 91 days or more over any four tax year period. If in fact any individual did during his period of absence visit the UK for anything like any of the above periods of time it is highly likely that HMRC would in any event challenge the fact that the contract was full time.

The above rules also apply to an individual who leaves the UK to work full time in a trade, profession or vocation (i.e. not necessary to be an employee; self-employed is acceptable).

A helpful concession is to regard any accompanying spouse as also becoming non-resident and non-ordinarily resident for the relevant period even where the spouse is not in fact working abroad, but simply accompanying the other spouse.

Example 4.17
In Example 4.16 above if Brian is accompanied by his wife, Mary, even though Mary will not be working abroad she would similarly be treated as neither resident nor ordinarily resident during her period of absence. It would be important, however, that she does not breach either the 183-day or 91-day tests.

(ii) Three-year/permanent rule
An individual will be treated as neither resident nor ordinarily resident from the day following the day of departure if the individual leaves the UK for at least three years *or* permanently. The reference to the word "permanently" in essence refers to emigration. Any return visits during the period of absence must not amount to either 183 days or more in any tax year *or* 91 days or more on average per tax year measured over a four tax year period.

The three years refers to a normal period of three years (i.e. it does not have to be three tax years).

Example 4.18
Karen Green left the UK on 21 August 2007 to live for at least three years in Spain in a flat she had purchased some years ago and where in the past she has spent her summer holidays.

She has let out her house in the UK on a three-year lease.

Karen will be treated as neither resident nor ordinarily resident in the UK from 22 August 2007 until the day before her return to the UK.

(iii) Averaging: the computational rules (departures)
The averaging rules used to determine whether the 91-day test has been breached by an individual who is leaving the UK after being resident and/or ordinarily resident are computed in a slightly different manner to the computation applied to determine the position for short-term visitors. The denominator in the two formulae is different.

In the present case the formula used is:

$$\frac{\text{Total visits to the UK}}{\text{Total period since leaving}} \times 365 = \text{Annual average visits}$$

Note that days spent in the UK in the tax year before the date of departure are excluded.

Example 4.19

An individual who has been living in the UK decides to leave the UK permanently on 5 October 1997. Between leaving and the following 5 April 1998 the individual returns for 30 days. As a consequence, the individual will become neither resident nor ordinarily resident from the day following the date of departure.

However, intermittent return visits to the UK are likely to occur. The 91-day average test will thus be used to ascertain if in fact despite leaving the UK, residency and/or ordinary residency is reacquired. The average number of days in the tax year thus needs to be computed.

For the tax years 1998/99, 1999/00 and 2000/01 visits are as follows:

1998/99	100 days
1999/00	60 days
2000/01	70 days

$$\text{Average per tax year} = \frac{30 + 100 + 60 + 70}{182 + 365 + 365 + 365} \times 365 = 74 \text{ days}$$

Thus the 91-day test has not been breached.

The next test would be at the end of the next tax year 2001/02 and would cover the tax years 1998/99, 1999/00, 2000/01 and 2001/02 (i.e. the first tax year 1997/98 would now drop out of the computation); in effect a rolling four-year period would be constantly reviewed.

While great emphasis is put on counting days spent in the UK in determining the residency and ordinary residency status of the individual, any attempt to abuse the rules is likely to be met with challenge from HMRC.

Two recent cases graphically illustrate this issue.

In *Shepherd v. R&CC (2006)* an airline pilot spent half the year flying outside the UK. He rented a flat in Cyprus from October 1998 and sought to argue that for the tax year 1999/00 he was not UK resident on the grounds that he was in the UK for less than 91 days. Excluding days of arrival and departure the total days actually spent in the UK was 80 days.

He still maintained and used his UK residence while in the UK which occurred as he was required to spend time in the UK before and after each flight.

Special Commissioners held that he remained UK resident for the tax year (while possibly also qualifying to be Cypriot resident). They argued that there had been no distinct break in the pattern of his lifestyle in October 1998 and thus he remained UK resident for 1999/00. The High Court then refused to interfere with the findings.

In the case of *Robert Gaines-Cooper v. HMRC (2006)* (see Appendix 5) for a more detailed discussion of the case) the Special Commissioners held that it was not necessary to consider the 91-day test as Robert Gaines-Cooper had never in fact left the UK which was a prerequisite. The conclusion that he had never left the UK was arrived at by considering his lifestyle, habits, etc. including the number of days spent in and out of the UK.

In looking at the days spent in and out of the UK, given his pattern of visits, the Commissioners felt that it would be misleading to wholly disregard days of arrival and departure.

It thus seems quite clear that any attempt to lose UK residency (and ordinary residency) requires that a clearly identifiable break with the UK occurs. Only if such a clean break with the UK can be identified is it then possible to claim the treatment set out above and, in particular, be in a position to make return visits to the UK without in principle affecting any non-residence (and non-ordinary residence) status; subject, of course, to not breaching either the 183-day or 91-day tests.

In the event that a clean break from the UK cannot be identified the individual will simply remain resident and ordinarily resident during his period of absence.

SUMMARY

Determination of the individual's residence and ordinary residence status for a tax year is important. While the law is to a degree somewhat vague in this regard, IR20 adopts a very practical approach and is worthy of study (see Appendix 3).

The rules contained in IR20 are divided into providing guidance as to a determination of residence and ordinary residence status with respect to individuals arriving in the UK and individuals departing from the UK.

Any individual spending at least 183 days in the UK in any tax year will automatically be resident.

However, other tests may also cause the individual to become resident and ordinarily resident even if the 183-day test is not breached.

FA 2008 has introduced a statutory definition of when an individual is regarded as spending a day in the UK. If the individual is in the UK at midnight, then that day counts as a day in the UK. This new statutory rule applies from 6 April 2008. Pre 6 April 2008 days of arrival and departure were normally ignored.

5
Residence, Ordinary Residence and Domicile: Some Practical Points

BACKGROUND

[handwritten annotations: "Arriving in UK P86" pointing to "completion"; "left or leaving UK" pointing to "P85"]

Information about an individual is primarily gathered from the completion of the Tax Return (which relates to income and capital gains taxes). In addition, various forms may also have been completed including forms DOM1, P86 and P85 (see Appendix 3). It is important to ensure that any information supplied to HMRC is accurate. While errors can be subsequently corrected this may prove problematic and/or embarrassing.

THE TAX RETURN

The UK's tax system is now one of self assessment which means that an individual is responsible for, inter alia, filing a Tax Return and settling any tax liabilities within specific time limits. In so doing the individual is required to determine domicile, residence and ordinary residence status for the particular tax year under review. HMRC may, or may not, then challenge this determination. Unless these statuses are determined the individual will be unable to ascertain the relevant tax liabilities (e.g. income and capital gains tax liabilities).

For example, a non-UK domiciled but UK resident and ordinary resident individual is not liable to income tax or capital gains tax on non-UK source income or non-UK source capital gains unless such income/gains are remitted to the UK whereas a UK domiciled and UK resident individual would be so liable.

HMRC are currently in the course of redesigning the Tax Return which will apply for the tax year 2008/09 and subsequent tax years. The commentary below, however, relates to the Tax Return as it currently stands (i.e. for the tax year 2007/08) although it is also perhaps worth noting that the 2006/07 Tax Return itself has also been slightly amended from prior tax years, in particular with respect to the "Non-Residence, etc." Supplementary Pages.

"Question 8" on page TR2 of the main part of the Tax Return specifically asks:

> Were you, for all or part of the year to 5th April 2008, one or more of the following – not resident, not ordinarily resident, not domiciled, in the UK or were you dual resident in the UK and another country?

("Question 9" on page 2 of the main part of the Tax Return for 2006/07 asked:

> Do you consider that you were, for all or part of the year, (a) not resident in the UK and/or (b) not ordinarily resident in the UK and/or (c) not domiciled in the UK *and this was relevant to your income tax or capital gains tax liabilities* or (d) dual resident in the UK and another country?)

"Question 5" on page TR2 of the main part of the Tax Return specifically asks:

> Did you receive any foreign income or income gains (other than from employment or self employment)?
> ...
> Do you want to claim relief for foreign tax paid?
> ...
> You may not need the Foreign Pages if ... you are claiming the remittance basis ....

If to either of Questions 5 or 8 the answer "yes" is provided then it becomes necessary for the individual to complete what are referred to as "Supplementary Pages".

With respect to Question 8 the relevant Supplementary Pages are headed "Non-Residence, etc." and extend to two pages NR1 and NR2.

Pages NR1/NR2 are subdivided into six sections as follows:

- Residence status;
- Time spent in the UK (if you were not resident or not ordinarily resident in the UK);
- Personal allowances;
- Residence in other countries and double taxation relief;
- Domicile;
- Any other information.

(Pages NR1/NR2 of the Tax Return 2006/2007 are subdivided into six sections as follows:

- Residence status;
- Time spent in the UK (if you were not resident or not ordinarily resident in the UK);
- Personal allowances;
- Overseas residence and double tax relief;
- Domicile;
- Additional information.)

Consider now the Domicile section in the supplementary "Non-Residence, etc." pages NR1/NR2 for the 2007/08 Tax Return.

Domicile

Five boxes within this section require answering.
The five questions are as follows:

- Box 22. If you are domiciled outside the UK and it is relevant to your Income Tax or Capital Gains Tax liability, put "X" in the box.
- Box 23. If 2007/08 is the first tax year that you have said that your domicile is outside the UK, put "X" in the box.
- Box 24. If you have put "X" in box 22 and have a domicile of origin within the UK, enter the date on which your domicile changed.
- Box 25. If you were born in the UK but have never been domiciled here, put "X" in the box.
- Box 26. If you have put "X" in box 22 and you were born outside the UK, enter the date you came to live in the UK.

For many individuals identifying a date of any change in domicile status from UK to non-UK (Box 24) is likely to prove extremely difficult. The "Notes" to pages NR1/NR2 HMRC suggest that *if* the precise date is not known then 5 April at the end of the tax year of change be inserted (implicitly assuming that the tax year of change will clearly be identifiable). The "Notes" add that if the tax year identified is itself an approximation then this should be drawn to HMRC's attention by commenting accordingly in the section on page NR2 "Any other information", Box 27.

An alternative answer, and perhaps better option, with respect to Box 24 may be to insert the precise date of arrival in the new country of domicile as the date when the new domicile was acquired. Certainly, if a UK domiciled (of origin) individual decided to emigrate from the UK to country "X" with the firm intention of remaining indefinitely in country "X" then the date of arrival would be the date of the acquisition of the new domicile of (in this case) choice in country "X". It would then be advisable to enter into Box 27 this information as justification for the date entered in Box 24.

[Margin note: Only for those looking to lose UK domicile]

In Box 22 the statement "relevant to Income Tax or Capital Gains Tax liability", according to the "Notes", will be the case for the non-domiciled individual if, inter alia, the individual answers "yes" to the following question:

> Did you have, or could you have benefited from, any income arising abroad or gains on assets situated outside of the UK for the year ended 5th April 2008 that will not be wholly remitted to the UK?

It is usual for individuals who first arive in the UK to be asked by HMRC to complete and file Forms DOM1 and P86 (see Appendix 3.)

Strictly speaking, neither of these forms (i.e. the DOM1, P86 or the P85) has to be completed (unlike the Tax Return and NR1/NR2) as they are not statutory forms, although most practitioners tend to do so on behalf of their clients. It would, however, be perfectly legitimate to supply all relevant information instead by way of letter. One advantage of this latter approach is that only directly pertinent information needs to be disclosed. Certainly, some of the information requested on the forms arguably does not have a direct bearing on a determination as to the individual's residence or domicile status.

For example, if an individual has never acquired UK residency in the past then the question on Form P86 asking "where and for whom did you work during the five years before your arrival in the UK?" (question 7a) is arguably of no relevance and any answer represents the supply to HMRC of gratuitous information; similarly the follow-up question, 7b (relating to employment dates), is equally of no relevance. This is certainly the position if none of the duties under the employment were performed in the UK (question 7c).

In a similar vein, arguably some of the questions on Form DOM1 are irrelevant to a domicile determination. Questions 1 to 4 on the Form, while of relevance once a determination has been made (as the information extracted relates to details of non-UK source income and gains) are not relevant to a domicile determination ab initio.

Nevertheless, when any of these forms is completed great care should be taken and such forms should only be completed under professional advice. Once information has been supplied to HMRC any attempt to subsequently amend or change it is likely to be viewed with some scepticism.

However, it will be recalled that in the case of *Buswell v. IRC (1974)* (see Chapter 3) HMRC drew the court's attention to answers the taxpayer had supplied on the Form P86 in attempting to show the taxpayer's intention re taking up residence in the UK as was also the case in *Surveyor v. IRC (2002);* nevertheless the courts in both cases overlooked the, prima facie, "counterproductive" answers given by the taxpayers.

While an individual's domicile status tends to apply for a number (many) of years, and does not change on a year to year basis, it is now necessary in principle for a non-UK domiciled individual to claim this status every tax year on the Tax Return (effectively by "ticking" Box 22 on NR2 of the Supplementary Pages).

Claim for the Remittance Basis to Apply

Box 1 of page F1 of the Supplementary Pages headed "Foreign" asks:

If you are making a claim for the remittance basis, put "X" in the box.

The "Notes" to page F1 state:

If you did not bring in or transfer any overseas income to the UK during the year you do not have to complete the "Foreign" pages just to claim the remittance basis. Put a note in the "Any other information" box on your Tax Return to say you are claiming the remittance basis, but had no remittances during the year.

IHT RETURN

For inheritance tax purposes, claims following death that the deceased was non-UK domiciled results in the need for completion of Form D2 (see Appendix 3). Inter alia, information requested on the form which presumably according to HMRC is relevant in this regard includes:

- nationality of the deceased;
- where the deceased was born;
- outline of educational and employment history;
- date of leaving UK to set up their main residence abroad;
- dates of return to the UK;
- length of stay in the UK;
- purpose of stay in the UK.

In addition, the Notes to the Form state:

> You should also say why the deceased did not intend to remain in, or return to, the UK at the date of death and give details of the evidence you have used to arrive at this conclusion.

This statement in effect derives from the various cases decided by the courts in seeking to determine whether individuals have acquired a non-UK domicile of choice (if originally UK domiciled) or a UK domicile of choice (if originally non-UK domiciled).

It should be appreciated that while such information is requested on the individual's death HMRC may already have on file information concerning the individual obtained from the individual's Tax Return (plus Supplementary Pages) and Forms DOM1, P86 and P85.

DOMICILE AND RESIDENCE RULINGS

For many individuals a confirmation of their residence and/or domicile status by HMRC is not only comforting but permits a degree of tax planning to be undertaken with some certainty.

Historically (i.e. before the introduction of self assessment) it was not necessary to make annual claims with respect to either residence or domicile status. It was possible to obtain from HMRC a ruling as to an individual's residence and domicile status. This ruling would then apply for the foreseeable future (not just for one tax year) subject, of course, to any material change of circumstance on the part of the individual concerned.

However, today such rulings are now the exception rather than the norm.

Below is an extract from HMRC's *Tax Bulletin* 29 (June 1997):

Domicile Ruling

Initial non-domicile claims may be made on form DOM 1, form P86 or in the SA tax return. We will continue to deal with initial non-domicile claims which are made before we have received the return for the year in which the claim is made. And we will let claimants know how their claim to be non-domiciled in the UK has been treated. But we may ask questions to check the validity of the claim as part of a formal Schedule 1A TMA 1970 enquiry into the claim or as part of a Section 9A TMA 1970 enquiry into the SA tax return.

...

But where, for example, an individual:

- has a domicile of origin outside the UK; and
- has come to the UK only for the purpose of employment; and
- intends to resume residence abroad when the employment ceases; and
- has given such information on a Form P86

we are unlikely to issue an enquiry into the domicile position.

A similar statement was made re residence:

Residence Ruling

Because individuals will, in appropriate cases, self-certify their residence status on their SA return, there is no need for the Inland Revenue to give a prior "ruling" on an individual's residence status. And so we have changed our procedures regarding such residence "rulings". We will continue to ask individuals for information about their residence or ordinary residence status. *But neither tax offices nor Financial Intermediaries and Claims Office (FICO) intend to provide residence "rulings" as we have done in the past.*

Given that individuals will decide what they regard their residence status to be, we propose to end our existing practice of advising an individual in the fourth year of the consequences of continuing to make regular visits to the UK exceeding an average of 90 days per year.

In a more recent pronouncement in one of HMRC's IHT Newsletters, commenting specifically on inheritance tax and domicile, HMRC commented:

Domicile is an important factor for Inheritance Tax; on death, the deceased's domicile determines the succession to personal property, so it may affect the amount of spouse or civil partner exemption available. For both the transfer on death and for lifetime transfers, the deceased/transferor's domicile determines the territorial scope of IHT. And for transfers between spouses or civil partners, the amount of exemption is limited to £55 000 if the deceased/transferor is domiciled in the UK but the spouse or civil partner is not.

We sometimes receive calls to our Helpline asking for assistance to establish the deceased/transferor's domicile. Our agents can help with filling in form D2/D31 and can talk in general terms about the impact of domicile for IHT. But they are not able to provide a definitive answer about a taxpayer's domicile over the phone. That decision can only be made once an account for the chargeable event concerned has been delivered. When delivering the account, please make sure that you complete form D2/D31 as fully as practicable, as this allows us to resolve the question of domicile as efficiently as possible.

Naturally, we are unable to comment about a person's domicile unless an event which gives rise to an IHT charge occurs.

One of HMRC's manuals (namely, EIM at 1635) states:

> An individual's domicile is of concern to the Revenue only where it is relevant to the computation of liability. The instruction at EIM 42804 [which deals with domicile status of employees in the UK] should be followed for cases wholly within Schedule E. In other cases domicile will only be relevant where the taxpayer has income arising abroad, or gains arising on assets situated outside the UK, which will not be wholly remitted to the UK.
>
> If an individual claims to be not domiciled within the UK, and the case is not wholly within Schedule E (see EIM 42804), issue form DOM1. If the completed form DOM1 shows that domicile is immediately relevant submit it together with the file to The Centre for Non-Residents Bootle for a ruling. If form DOM1 shows that domicile is not relevant, decline to examine the claim to be not domiciled.

In view of the fact that, in general, a domicile ruling may not be forthcoming if the individual wishes to have some clarity it is often suggested that an event be triggered by the individual precipitating a potential tax liability which thus attempts to force HMRC to consider the matter. Where this ploy is adopted the question arises as to the amount of the potential UK tax liability which is to be precipitated. If this amount is de minimis then HMRC would probably simply refuse to be withdrawn at that point. However, what is and is not de minimis is a subjective judgement.

Various amounts are bandied about by tax professionals; thus potential tax liabilities which have been suggested range from £5000 to £50 000. Perhaps a half-way house of circa £15 000 to £25 000 may be appropriate.

One such possibility in this regard is for the individual to create a settlement on which, say, one or more non-UK situs assets are settled. For example, cash in a non-UK bank account of, say, £350 000 (i.e. an amount in excess of the nil rate band; £312 000 for the tax year 2008/09) might be settled. If the individual *is* non-UK domiciled no inheritance liability arises (as the non-UK property is excluded property for inheritance tax purposes) whereas if the individual possesses a UK domicile the transfer would be subject to an inheritance tax charge (as the transfer in this case would constitute a chargeable lifetime transfer).

Alternatively, such individual could arrange to receive material non-UK source income (e.g. interest on non-UK situs bank account; dividends on non-UK situs shares) and/or realise non-UK source chargeable gains (e.g. sale of non-UK situs shares, real estate). The individual's domicile status is of direct relevance to a determination of the resultant tax liability.

However, there is no guarantee that HMRC will choose to examine the transaction consequent to which a domicile ruling may still not be forthcoming.

The better option is for an opinion to be sought from an appropriately qualified professional as to the individual's domicile status. On the basis of this opinion suitable wealth planning may then be carried out.

SUMMARY

Under self assessment the individual is required to determine the residence, ordinary residence and domicile status for a tax year. HMRC may then choose to investigate whether the individual's determinations are, in HMRC's view, correct.

Generally speaking, HMRC will not issue, in advance, rulings as to the individual's domicile or residence status. It may be possible to cause HMRC to examine a particular transaction so as to "force" HMRC to form a view of the individual's domicile status, although this approach is generally not to be recommended.

The completion of the Tax Return (and Supplementary Pages) requires careful thought with respect to any answers/information given. Similarly, the same careful thought also needs to be given with respect to information provided on completion of forms DOM1, P86 and P85.

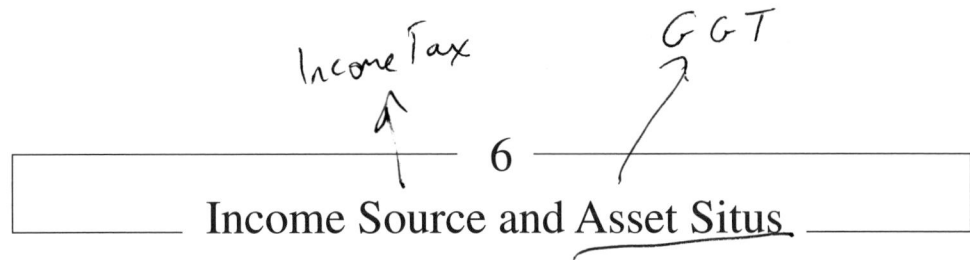

6
Income Source and Asset Situs

BACKGROUND

The need to identify the location and/or type of a source of income and the situs and/or type of an asset is necessary in order to determine if, and the extent to which, a liability to tax (whether income, capital gains or inheritance) arises.

As discussed in Chapter 9, for example, a non-UK domiciled individual is subject to inheritance tax on *UK situs* assets only. Such individual, if UK resident, is subject to capital gains tax on capital gains arising from disposals of non-UK situs assets only if the gains in respect thereof are remitted to the UK and subject to income tax on non-UK source income only if such income is remitted to the UK.

An individual who is not resident in the UK (irrespective of domicile status) is subject to income tax on *UK source* income only.

For the UK domiciled and UK resident individual the importance of income source and asset situs would also extend to the need to ascertain whether, for example, any foreign tax liabilities arising on such income or gains may be offset against the UK tax charges thereon (see Chapter 25).

Thus, in principle, income source identification is important for income tax purposes and asset situs is important for capital gains tax and inheritance tax purposes.

It should be noted that the rules set out in this chapter are those applicable under UK domestic law. In certain cases these rules may be modified by the terms of a double taxation agreement to which the UK is a party.

INCOME SOURCE

Generally, UK common law applies to determine the source of income for income tax purposes, i.e. the income tax legislation does not have its own set of rules to determine source.

The location of a source of income is, perhaps surprisingly, not always the same as the location of the asset from which the income arises (e.g. dividend income arising on registered shares may have a source location different from the situs of the shares; see below) although often the two will be the same.

The source identification rules for the main types of income are set out below.

Rental Income

The source of rental income is the location of the real estate giving rise to the income.

Example 6.1

Harry Redditch receives rental income from:

- a property he owns in the UK; and
- his holiday home located in France.

For UK tax purposes the rental income from the UK house would possess a UK source and that from the French property a non-UK source.

If Harry is UK domiciled and UK resident the rental income from both properties will be subject to income tax on the arising basis.

If Harry is non-UK domiciled but UK resident an income tax liability would be precipitated on the UK source income (on the arising basis) but no such liability would arise on the French source income unless and until it was remitted to the UK.

Dividends

The source of dividend income arising on shares in a company is the location of the company's residence which will usually (but not always) be the place of incorporation of the company.

Under UK tax law a company is UK resident if it is incorporated in the UK *or* its "central management and control" is exercised from within the UK (broadly applicable if the company's board of directors meet and take key strategic decisions in the UK). Thus, a UK incorporated company is automatically UK resident and thus any dividends arising from its shares are UK source income.

Open ended investment companies (commonly referred to as OEICs) are still companies and thus the above rule applies to them in the same manner, i.e. any income from the shares in an OEIC will possess a UK source if the OEIC is UK resident.

Authorised and Unauthorised Unit Trusts

Authorised

Authorised unit trusts (AUTs) for the purposes of income tax are treated as companies and the rights of the unit holders as shares in the company.

Thus, any income arising on an individual's investment in the units of an AUT is UK source income.

Unauthorised

Unauthorised unit trusts (UAUTS), unlike AUTs, are not treated as companies for income tax purposes. Generally speaking, UAUTS are set up outside the UK.

UAUTS (generally, but not necessarily, trusts with foreign trustees, i.e. non-UK resident) may be opaque or transparent. Any determination as to the source of income arising on the units will depend upon the precise constitution of the trust and the law under which the trust has been created.

Broadly, where the trust is transparent an individual's investment in the units of the trust will give rise to income which does not have its source in the situs of the units themselves but in the underlying investments of the trust which, of course, may be different.

On the other hand, where the trust is opaque (i.e. not transparent) an individual's investment in the units of the trust will give rise to income whose source will be the situs of the units (not the underlying investments of the trust). The situs of the units is the place where the register of units is located, which is invariably the country under whose law the trust has been created.

Interest

There appears to be no single factor which determines the source of interest income. Factors which are important include:

- the debtor's residence status;
- the place where the debt is enforceable; and
- the place at which payment of the interest on the debt is made.

Other things being equal, it is likely that interest credited on a deposit account with either a UK incorporated bank/building society or the UK branch of an overseas incorporated bank/building society will possess a UK source as it is in the UK that the debt is likely to be enforceable and any interest is likely to be credited.

Similarly, interested credited on a deposit account with a foreign incorporated bank or the overseas branch of a UK incorporated bank will possess a non-UK source.

The above would apply whether the deposit was in sterling or a foreign currency.

Mutual (Offshore) Funds

See the above discussion re OEICs, AUTs and UAUTs as, typically, offshore funds are structured in one of these forms.

ASSET SITUS

As indicated above, the situs of assets is primarily relevant for capital gains tax and inheritance tax purposes. However, perhaps surprisingly, different rules apply for each of these two taxes.

As there are no specific rules laid down in the inheritance tax legislation which govern the situs of particular assets it is the common law rules which will apply.

For capital gains tax purposes, however, the capital gains tax legislation does provide a set of rules which governs asset situs for capital gains tax purposes (subject to the common law rules applying where the capital gains tax rules do not provide a determination).

Despite this difference in approach between the two taxes in many cases (but not always) the situs of an asset is in fact found to be the same for capital gains tax and inheritance tax purposes.

Inheritance Tax

Tangible Property

Tangible property (e.g. real estate; paintings; antique furniture; jewellery) is located where the asset is physically situate at the time.

Registered Shares

The registered shares of a company are situated where the principal share register of the company is maintained (i.e. not where the company is resident which applies in income source identification; see above).

Bearer Shares

Bearer shares are located where the bearer share certificates are physically situate at the time (treated basically the same as tangible property; see above). Thus, their location is not dependent upon any share register (as applies for registered shares).

Intangible Property

Choses in action are generally situate in the country where they are properly recoverable or can be enforced. Examples of choses in action are debts, shares, interests in trusts, etc.

Ordinary Debts

The situs of a debt is basically where the debtor resides (i.e. where the debt is normally recoverable). Whether the debt is secured or not makes no difference.

Speciality Debt

A speciality debt is an obligation under seal securing a debt. Such a debt is located where the deed is physically located (similar to the situs of bearer shares; see above).
  A deed is a written document which must be signed, witnessed and delivered and it must be made clear that it is intended to be a deed (sealing is no longer required; Law of Property (Misc. Provisions) Act 1989 post 1 August 1990).

Bank Accounts

Bank accounts are, generally speaking, ordinary debts and are thus situate at the place of residence of the debtor, i.e. the location of the branch of the bank where the account is kept, i.e. that is where the customer can withdraw his money (note, however, that a foreign currency bank account in a UK incorporated bank or the UK branch of a foreign incorporated bank, despite being UK situs, is treated as excluded property for inheritance tax purposes for the non-UK domiciled, non-UK resident and non-UK ordinarily resident individual; however, this excluded property treatment only applies on death, not gifts inter vivos; see Chapter 12).

Unit Trusts

[handwritten: Different from Income Source]

The situs of units in AUTs and UAUTs is determined by the law governing the AUT or UAUT. The situs of the underlying assets of the trust is thus, arguably, not relevant.

Nominees

The location of assets held by nominees is determined according to the rules applicable to the category of the asset held by the nominee not where the nominee itself may be situated (i.e. nomineeship is effectively transparent for asset situs location purposes). *[handwritten: look-through]*

This rule is often either forgotten or misunderstood as it is not unusual to find advice to the effect that the use of a nominee can change the situs of the underlying asset. The implication that then follows is that nominees are a useful tool in mitigating both inheritance tax and capital gains tax. However, this is not the case. *[handwritten: Nominee cant change situs]*

Thus, it is often suggested, for example, that the use of an overseas situs nominee is effective to remove an otherwise UK situs asset from the UK; it is not.

Example 6.2

Michelle Paris is a non-UK domiciled individual and owns a 25% shareholding in a listed UK incorporated company. Her investment in the shares is thus UK situs.

The shareholding is extremely valuable and in the event of her death will be subject to UK inheritance tax.

Her local advisor has advised that she should have the shares held not in her name but in the name of a Swiss-based corporate nominee which would cause the shares to be no longer UK situs.

Unfortunately, this is not the case and the shares would remain UK situs.

There is thus no UK inheritance tax advantage to be gained by a non-UK domiciled individual holding any UK situs asset via an offshore nominee. However, if the offshore vehicle utilised is a non-UK registered company owned by the individual which is the beneficial owner (i.e. is not a nominee) of the UK situs asset then the situs of the asset now held by the individual is non-UK (i.e. the shares of the non-UK registered company). *[handwritten: eg for Property ??]*

The corollary of the above is that the use of a UK-based corporate nominee to hold non-UK situs assets for a non-UK domiciled individual will not cause the otherwise non-UK situs assets to become UK situs (i.e. the underlying asset situs remains offshore). *[handwritten: eg Shareholdings]*

[handwritten: Don't think it works ✓]

Hence, the use by a non-UK domiciled individual of the nominee services of, for example, a UK-based stockbroker (or bank) to hold non-UK situs shares and securities (the underlying shares/securities will still qualify as excluded property for inheritance tax purposes) will not create UK situs assets for inheritance tax purposes.

Example 6.3

Friedrich Berlin, a non-UK domiciled individual, owns significant US equities and UK equities.

His UK stockbroker has suggested that for convenience all Friedrich's share portfolio should be held by the stockbroker's UK nominee company.

This would not cause Friedrich's holding of USA equities to become UK situs.

Life Policies

For inheritance tax purposes life policies are treated as debts and thus the residence of the debtor rule (see above) applies.

Thus, a policy under hand as opposed to a policy under seal (i.e. a deed) is situate where the debtor company (i.e. life insurance company) is resident.

A policy under seal (i.e. a speciality debt) is located where the instrument (i.e. policy) is located.

Capital Gains Tax

As indicated above the capital gains tax legislation has its own rules which determine the situs of a number of assets for capital gains tax purposes. Where these rules do not determine a particular asset's situs the normal common law rules will apply.

Tangible Property

No rule is provide in the capital gains tax legislation and thus the normal common law rule applies, i.e. tangible property (e.g. real estate; paintings; antique furniture; jewellery) is located where the asset is physically situate at the time.

Registered Shares

Registered shares are generally situate where the principal share register of the company concerned is located; usually, the company's place of incorporation/registration.

Bearer Shares

No rule is provide in the capital gains tax legislation and thus the normal common law rule applies, i.e. the situs is wherever the bearer share certificates are physically situate at the time.

Ordinary Debts

It is with respect to debts that the biggest difference between the capital gains tax situs rules and those of the common law (which apply for inheritance tax purposes) arises.

For capital gains tax purposes a debt is located where the *creditor* (not debtor as applies for inheritance tax) is resident. Thus, in principle, a UK resident individual creditor causes all debts due to such individual to be UK situs.

However, the legislation modifies this rule with respect to foreign currency debts.

In the case of a foreign currency bank account which is owned by a non-UK domiciled but UK resident individual such an account is *only UK situs if the bank/branch where the account is held is in the UK*. Thus, foreign currency bank accounts held by such an individual with overseas banks outside the UK are *not* UK situs.

Sterling bank accounts, however, are subject to the resident creditor rule.

These rules have significant impact for the non-UK domiciled but UK resident individual.

Foreign currency itself is a chargeable asset for the purpose of capital gains tax. Thus disposals of the currency are in principle chargeable to capital gains tax. A deposit of foreign currency into a bank account is thus a disposal of the foreign currency for capital gains tax purposes. However, where the foreign currency has been acquired for an individual's (or his dependant's) personal expenditure outside the UK it is exempt from capital gains tax.

This let-out will not, generally speaking, apply to the non-UK domiciled individual who will typically acquire foreign currency not specifically for personal expenditure outside the UK but simply as a consequence of personal activities, e.g. foreign currency generated from overseas earnings or investments; gifts of foreign currency from family members; asset sales; etc.

A foreign currency bank account is also a chargeable asset for the purpose of capital gains tax. As noted above, a foreign currency bank account is located where the creditor is resident unless the creditor is a non-UK domiciled but UK resident individual. In this latter case the foreign currency bank account is located in the UK if and only if the bank/branch where the account is maintained is located in the UK.

To the extent that the foreign currency bank account is located in the UK then for the non-UK domiciled but UK resident individual potential capital gains tax liabilities are likely to arise.

Any withdrawal from the account is a disposal for capital gains tax purposes. This is because the withdrawal leads to the bank satisfying its debt obligation to the depositor and the depositor is thus deemed to have made a disposal of a chargeable asset, i.e. a disposal of the debt due from the bank (which is a chargeable asset).

The "withdrawal" may be effected either by literally withdrawing the funds in person or having the monies moved inter-bank from one account to another.

It is *not* necessary for a capital gains tax charge to arise for the foreign currency to be converted into sterling at any point; all that is required is that a chargeable disposal is made.

The quantum of any capital gains tax liability is based upon the difference between the sterling value of the withdrawal at the date of the withdrawal and the sterling value of that foreign currency amount at the date it was deposited into that account. A *capital gain* will thus arise where sterling has *depreciated* against the particular currency over the relevant time period; similarly, a *capital loss* arises where sterling has *appreciated*.

Example 6.4

Tom Bellinger Jnr, a non-UK domiciled but UK resident individual, opened a dollar denominated bank account in the UK with $100 000 which at that time had a sterling equivalent of £75 000.

Three years later he withdrew the whole amount which at the date of withdrawal had a sterling equivalent of £85 000 due to the depreciation of the sterling/dollar rate.

Tom Bellinger Jnr will thus have made a taxable chargeable gain of £10 000.

As indicated above, the withdrawal by Tom Bellinger Jnr in the above Example 6.4 could have been made either literally by making a cash withdrawal or, alternatively, by arranging for the dollars to be transferred to, say, his dollar account back in the USA. Irrespective of which of these two routes is adopted a disposal of the debt due from the bank in the UK has arisen (i.e. the UK bank has satisfied its debt due to him) and a possible capital gains tax liability arises.

In the above Example 6.4 if sterling had appreciated against the dollar (i.e. at the date of withdrawal the sterling equivalent was, say, £70 000) then a sterling loss (£5000) would arise which would be available for relief (by offsetting the capital loss against any capital gains of the same or future tax years; see Chapter 8).

A non-UK domiciled but UK resident individual is liable to capital gains tax on non-UK situs assets if any part of the sale proceeds is remitted to the UK, otherwise no such liability arises.

Consider therefore the following scenario.

Assume a non-UK domiciled but UK resident individual maintains a number of US dollar accounts with various overseas banks (e.g. OB1 and OB2). If the individual effects a transfer between the accounts in each of the two banks (i.e. a simple transfer of dollars from the account with OB1 to the account with OB2) a chargeable gain will arise if sterling has depreciated against the dollar between the time of the original deposit with OB1 and the time of the transfer from OB1 to OB2. As the individual is non-UK domiciled but UK resident any such gain is not subject to UK capital gains tax unless some part of the foreign currency transferred between the accounts is remitted at some point in time (not necessarily immediately) to the UK.

In effect therefore, whenever such transactions occur outside the UK effected by non-UK domiciled but UK resident individuals capital gains and/or capital losses are thus being precipitated albeit at the time without UK tax consequence if no reimittance to the UK occurs.

It also needs to be noted that any transfer of foreign currency from an overseas foreign currency bank account to a UK foreign currency bank account may precipitate a chargeable gain in the same way. The withdrawal from the overseas bank account is a chargeable disposal albeit one made outside the UK. However, if the monies that are being withdrawn are being immediately transmitted to the UK bank account the overseas gain has now been remitted and a capital gains tax charge arises.

Example 6.5

Bob Wind, a non-UK domiciled but UK resident individual, has three dollar bank accounts. Two, OB1 and OB2, are with banks in the USA and one, UKB, is with a UK-based bank in the UK.

Bob's father, on Bob's birthday, gave him a present of $700 000 by transferring the monies into Bob's account, OB1. At that time the rate of exchange was $2/£1.

For UK capital gains tax purposes no taxable event has occurred other than the fact that Bob has now acquired a chargeable asset (i.e. a debt due from OB1) worth in sterling £350 000.

A couple of months later Bob transfers the whole amount to OB2. At that time the exchange rate was $1.75/£1. The sterling equivalent of the withdrawal from OB1 is thus £400 000.

For capital gains tax purposes at that time Bob has made a chargeable gain of £50 000. It is not immediately subject to capital gains tax as Bob has not remitted the monies to the UK (as a non-UK domiciled but UK resident individual the remittance basis applies to non-UK source chargeable gains).

Three months later Bob transfers the monies to his UK bank account, UKB. At that time the exchange rate was $1/£1. The sterling equivalent of the withdrawal from OB2 is thus £700 000.

The remittance of the $700 000 from OB2 to UKB has unfortunate tax consequences for Bob.

First, the £50 000 gain arising on the transfer from OB1 to OB2 is now subject to capital gains tax as the monies (i.e. the $700 000) have now been transferred to the UK.

Second, the £300 000 gain arising on the transfer from OB2 to UKB is subject to capital gains tax as the monies (i.e. the $700 000) have now been transferred to the UK.

Bob thus faces a capital gains tax charge on two chargeable gains (i.e. the £50 000 and the £300 000) even though all that has really happened is that he transferred the monies (namely, $700 000) from bank account to bank account.

Perhaps worse is to come, as a further such charge may arise as and when he transfers the monies from UKB to another account whether in the UK or overseas (depending upon the movement in the $/£ rate of exchange).

It might be thought that perhaps on balance any sterling movements will tend to be both up and down against a particular foreign currency and thus over time any gains which might arise are simply offset by any losses which might arise. While this may be the case "in the real world" unfortunately pre FA 2008 any such loss which does arise is *not* an allowable loss for capital gains tax purposes if the loss arises on a non-UK bank account and therefore cannot be offset against any gains. For the non-UK domiciled but UK resident individual inequity of treatment with respect to non-UK foreign currency bank account gains and losses thus arises (i.e. gains are taxable but losses are not offsettable).

FA 2008 has, however, modified the capital gains tax position with respect to capital losses arising from disposals of non-UK situs assets (including non-UK situs foreign currency bank accounts). Any capital loss arising on a disposal of a non-UK situs asset on or after 6 April 2008 is now an allowable loss (i.e. the loss may be off-set against capital gains). This is a much improved position compared to that pre 6 April 2008.

However, FA 2008 also details specific rules as to when and how any such capital losses may in fact be so utilised which is not perhaps as advantageous as might be thought at first sight (see Chapter 8).

Example 6.6
Kalari Sahara, a non-UK domiciled but UK resident individual, has opened dollar accounts with banks OB1, OB2 and OB3 all situated outside the UK. In OB1 she has deposited $500 000, a gift from her father. In OB3 she has deposited $400 000, a gift from her mother. OB2 has a nil balance.

In the tax year 2008/09 she transfers the $500 000 dollars from OB1 to OB2 precipitating a capital gain of £100 000. Later in the tax year she transfers $400 000 dollars from OB3 to OB1 precipitating a loss of £75 000. No remittances to the UK are made in the tax year 2008/09.

As no remittances are made to the UK, under the new FA 2008 rules the capital loss is offset against any non-remitted capital gains. Thus Kalari is able to offset the capital loss against the capital gain giving rise to a net gain of £25 000.

Should Kalari in Example 6.6 above decide to remit any of the $ to the UK she has two options. If she remits the $500 000 from OB2 she will trigger a capital gains tax charge on the net capital gain of £25 000. However, should she remit the $400 000 from OB1 no capital gains tax charge will arise as the transfer of this amount precipitated a capital loss. This amount can therefore be remitted without tax charge.

If she had transferred both amounts into OB2 and then remitted from OB2 to the UK this remittance would trigger a capital gains tax charge on the £25 000 net gain.

Inevitably, the typical non-UK domiciled but UK resident individual may often be involved in transactions which involve more than one foreign currency and where deposits and withdrawals are occurring with frequent regularity.

The ability to keep track of such withdrawals and deposits and the consequent potential capital gains and/or capital losses, in practice, may be somewhat difficult if not impossible. Nevertheless, these difficulties do not remove the tax charge and in practice it may be necessary to carry out some sort of averaging over time to arrive at a representative amount of chargeable gain/loss.

The following summary is perhaps worth noting:

first, non-UK domiciled but UK resident individuals should *not* maintain foreign currency bank accounts with banks in the UK;
second, transfers, even between overseas foreign currency bank accounts, may precipitate chargeable gains which will be subject to a capital gains tax charge if the monies are ever remitted to the UK;
third, conversion into sterling is *not* a prerequisite to a capital gains tax charge arising;
fourth, capital losses arising on movements on foreign currency bank accounts located outside the UK are offsettable only with respect to disposals on or after 6 April 2008;
fifth, UK-based foreign currency bank accounts are also in principle within the charge to UK inheritance tax (another reason for keeping all foreign currency bank accounts outside the UK; see Chapter 9).

For the non-UK domiciled and non-UK resident individual, however, none of the above issues with respect to capital gains tax arise. Capital gains tax only applies if an individual is either UK resident or UK ordinarily resident (see Chapter 8).

Unit Trusts

The situs of units in AUTs and UAUTs is determined by the law governing the AUT and UAUT.

Life Policies

A life policy is not regarded as a debt for capital gains tax purposes and thus the creditor rule (referred to above) does not apply.

A life policy issued subject to UK law will be UK situs. A life policy issued under non-UK law will be situate as determined for inheritance tax purposes.

SUMMARY

The rules relating to the determination of the source of income or the situs of assets tend to be taken for granted and are thus often overlooked.

The two issues are extremely important and go to the heart of the taxability of the non-UK domiciled individual. They are, however, also of importance to the UK domiciled and UK resident individual as well as the non-UK resident individual.

Unless specific provision is made in the tax legislation with respect to income source or asset situs the normal common law rules apply.

The capital gains tax issues arising out of foreign currency bank accounts should in particular be noted with respect to the non-UK domiciled but UK resident individual. However, FA 2008 has to some degree ameliorated the adverse capital gains tax position which subsisted pre FA 2008 in this regard.

7
The Principles and Implications of Joint Tenancy and Tenancy in Common Ownership for Spouses and Non-Spouses

BACKGROUND

Of crucial importance with respect to property ownership is the need to understand that English law recognises two forms of ownership, namely, *legal* ownership and *beneficial* ownership. This possible split of ownership is understood in common law jurisdictions but is a concept not readily understood or permitted under civil law jurisdictions.

For UK tax purposes it is the beneficial title which is important. Thus, if an individual "X" is shown as the registered owner of shares in company "C" (in the share register of company "C") then, prima facie, dividends paid on those shares belongs to "X". However, if "X" has executed a declaration of trust in favour of individual "Y" then for tax purposes it is "Y" who is the beneficial owner of the shares and thus any dividends paid belong to "Y" not "X", and the income tax liability thereon is that of "Y" not "X".

"X", in this example, is said to be the legal owner while "Y" is the beneficial owner.

In many cases the legal and beneficial owner of property is the same.

LEGAL TITLE

If property is owned by two or more individuals then the legal title to the property can only be held as *joint tenants*.

On the death of one of the legal joint tenants the legal title will then vest automatically in the survivors.

As indicated above, the holders of the legal title will in many cases also be the holders of the beneficial title.

BENEFICIAL OWNERSHIP

Beneficial ownership of property, on the other hand, may be held either as *joint tenants* or as *tenants in common*.

In the case of beneficial joint tenants each co-owner's interest in the asset is not only equal but identical in every respect. In the case of beneficial ownership as tenants in common each tenant in common may own equal or unequal shares in the property.

The effect of beneficial ownership as joint tenants is that:

- on the death of one of the joint tenants that joint tenant's interest in the property passes automatically by survivorship to the remaining joint tenants irrespective of any will the individual may have made.

The effect of beneficial ownership as tenants in common is that:

- on the death of one of the tenants in common that tenant in common's interest in the property passes according to that tenant's will (or intestacy in the event of no will). The above survivorship rule does not apply.

Strictly speaking, on the death of a beneficial joint tenant that tenant's interest in the property ceases with the consequence that the interests of the other joint tenants in the property proportionately increase.

Of the two forms of beneficial ownership, in general, that of tenants in common offers greater flexibility from a tax planning perspective. This is because if the matrimonial home, for example, is owned beneficially as joint tenants, then on death (e.g. of the husband) the wife will automatically inherit, offering no flexibility for any tax planning. If, on the other hand, the ownership had been beneficially as tenants in common the testator could have decided to leave his (in the above example) interest to, say, the children in his will if this was likely to be more tax effective.

Thus, ownership as tenants in common permits interests in property to be left by will (to whoever may be appropriate) whereas ownership as joint tenants offers no such choice (i.e. the survivorship rule automatically applies).

On the other hand, beneficial ownership as joint tenants does mean that on the death of one of the co-owners that co-owner's interest in the property passes automatically to the surviving joint tenants and probate is not required (see Chapter 26). This is because in essence the joint tenant's interest in the asset is not regarded as part of the individual's estate on death for probate purposes (although, of course, it is included as part of the deceased's estate for inheritance tax purposes). The lack of the need for probate arguably eases the administration and other matters at an emotional time for the survivors.

In determining whether an asset is held beneficially as joint tenants or tenants in common the intentions of the parties at the time of acquisition of the property would need to be examined. Should two purchasers purchase the property with each providing different levels of contribution the presumption is that each owns an interest corresponding to their respective contributions (i.e. ownership will be assumed to be as beneficial tenants in common). However, to remove doubt, where the intention of the parties is that the respective beneficial interests should reflect the precise contributions by the parties then the ownership should be structured as beneficial tenants in common ab initio.

However, even though the respective contributions to the purchase price of the property may be unequal if the parties agree that each should own the same proportion of the property the ownership may be structured as beneficial joint tenants (as under this form of ownership 50/50 is assumed). Alternatively, ownership could be structured as beneficial tenants in common but showing ownership 50/50. In either case it should be noted that the individual providing the greater contribution to the purchase price will be regarded as having made a gift (or transfer of value) to the other purchaser with possible inheritance tax consequences (e.g. if two brothers purchase a property for £1 million and one contributes £600 000 and the other £400 000 with an agreement that each should own 50% of the property the former will have made a PET of £100 000) (see Chapter 9).

LAND

The above discussion applies to all forms of property including land (e.g. the matrimonial home).

However, in view of the importance of the matrimonial home (and real estate in general) the issues of ownership of land will be examined in a little more detail.

Legal Title

The acquisition of the legal title to land by a purchaser involves the conveyance of the title to the purchaser followed by registration as the registered proprietor. Where more than one purchaser effects the purchase the legal title is registered in their respective names as co-owners in the form of a joint tenancy. It is not possible for the legal title to be held as tenants in common. To hold legal title requires that the individual be of full age (i.e. age 18 or over).

The law dictates that no more than four persons can hold the legal title to land (i.e. only four joint tenants can hold the legal title). [handwritten: 74 use a company]

As the joint legal tenants may be different from those owning the equitable/beneficial interests in the land the joint legal tenants are under a statutory duty to consult the beneficiaries (i.e. the individuals owning the equitable or beneficial interest in the land) and give effect to their instructions/wishes.

Equitable Interests

Co-owners of equitable (i.e. beneficial) interests in land may hold their interests in the form of a joint tenancy or tenancy in common.

The main differences between the two forms of ownership have been highlighted above.

It should be noted that the ownership structure of land which is owned as beneficial joint tenants may be changed by the simple act of "severance". If land is held beneficially by two joint tenants either can sever the joint tenancy by, for example, writing to the other joint tenant. The land will then be held as tenants in common. Inter alia, the principle of survivorship will then no longer apply.

If the land is held by a number of joint tenants any one joint tenant can sever their joint tenancy by writing to all the other joint tenants. The consequence would then be that the individual effecting the severance would own as tenant in common but the others would continue to hold their respective interests as joint tenants.

Perhaps, interestingly, severance by any joint tenant does not require the consent of the other joint tenants, merely notification to them of the severance.

If therefore beneficial ownership has initially been structured in the form of joint tenants such structure is not fixed for all time. Conversion to tenants in common is relatively straightforward and precipitates no tax consequences.

Severance under a will, however, is not possible, i.e. severance needs to be effected in lifetime. Nevertheless, for inheritance tax purposes a fictional world is in fact created under which a beneficial joint tenancy may be severed after the death of one of the joint tenants enabling a redirection of the deceased's interest in the property from the surviving beneficial joint tenants to any other beneficiary or beneficiaries. This fiction involves the use of a deed of variation (see Chapter 26).

↳ a beneficiary can redirect a gift to a more tax efficient beneficiary

TAX ISSUES

As indicated above the concepts of beneficial joint tenancy and beneficial tenancy in common have primary importance vis-à-vis real estate/land, in particular the matrimonial home. However, the concepts are in principle of equal application to other forms of asset (e.g. bank accounts; shareholdings; etc.). To a degree, the choice between the two forms of ownership may well be driven by factors other than taxation as outlined above (e.g. a desire to avoid probate).

Irrespective of the form of the asset the major attraction of assets being held as beneficial joint tenants is the application of the survivorship rule and the consequent lack of the need for a grant of representation (i.e. probate). The surviving beneficial joint tenant simply has immediate access to the whole of the asset (assuming two joint tenants, e.g. husband and wife). This may be particularly important with respect to cash. A bank account held by husband and wife as beneficial joint tenants may be accessed immediately following the death of one of the tenants; no probate is required and no "freezing" of the account occurs.

Although very unusual, bank account ownership may be by way of tenants in common. However, there appears to be no particular advantages as invariably the whole point of a joint bank account is that the holders intend any monies therein to be available to both parties at all times. If the account is structured as tenants in common, separate records of each of the parties' contributions and withdrawals must be kept which in practice is somewhat cumbersome and unduly administrative. In such cases it would be much simpler to open two separate accounts for each of the parties.

Another example is life insurance. If, for example, the husband effected a life policy on his own life without any further action on his part then on his death the policy proceeds will be paid into his estate (i.e. to the executors) and will as a result be subject to inheritance tax. Neither his wife nor children will be able to access such monies until probate has been granted and the estate administered. However, if the husband had settled the policy in trust for his wife and/or children then on his death (following production of the death certificate to the life office) the policy proceeds could be paid directly to the trustees of the trust and then by the trustees to the wife and/or children, as appropriate, without the need to wait for probate (in addition, this approach would also result in savings of inheritance tax; see Chapters 18 and 26).

Inheritance Tax

Prior to 9 October 2007 (i.e. the date of the Chancellor's Pre-Budget Report) for inheritance purposes ownership of assets by way of beneficial tenants in common was often preferred particularly in connection with the matrimonial home.

By owning the home in this manner allowed each spouse to leave their particular share (normally 50%) in the home under their will to a discretionary trust (set up under their will) for the benefit of their surviving spouse and/or children. This had the effect of ensuring that the first spouse to die did not wasted their nil rate band (see Chapters 9 and 26).

If the matrimonial home had been owned as beneficial joint tenants then the respective interest of the spouses in the home would pass on death by survivorship and could thus not be left by will. The effect for inheritance tax would be that the inter-spouse exemption would apply to the share of the deceased spouse on passing to the surviving spouse but with the attendant possibility that the deceased's nil rate band would remain unutilised.

However, following the Pre-Budget Report (now FA 2008) the concept of the transferable nil rate band between spouses (not cohabitees) has to a degree removed the need for the use of the discretionary will trust and, in turn, the need for ownership as beneficial tenants in common (see Chapter 9 and 26).

However, there may still be other reasons why matrimonial ownership as beneficial tenants in common is preferable to ownership as beneficial joint tenants (see Chapter 26). (Wills Chap.)

Whether property is owned as beneficial joint tenants or as tenants in common, per se, makes no difference to the valuation of the deceased's interest. In arriving at a valuation (under either ownership structure) the value of the deceased's share would be affected by the fact of the joint ownership (i.e. any person inheriting the deceased's share would still in principle only own 50%, say, not 100% of the property concerned). As a consequence, it is not unusual for the deceased's share to be valued with a 10 to 15% discount.

This discount does not, however, apply to property held by husband and wife (whether held as beneficial joint tenants or tenants in common).

Income Tax

Spouse Joint Ownership

Special rules apply to the income tax treatment of property (of any description) held by spouses in their joint names.

In such cases, any income arising from the property held in joint names is treated as income to which the husband and wife are entitled equally. They are thus treated as each being entitled to 50% of the income arising from the property. Thus rule applies even if in fact the spouses contributed to the property in unequal proportions. For example, if a husband and wife open a joint bank account with the husband contributing £10 000 cash to the account and the wife contributing £5000 cash to the account, for income tax purposes each spouse will be treated as entitled to one half of any interest credited to the account.

It is, however, possible for this rule to be displaced. Where the spouses are not beneficially entitled to the income from the property in equal shares the spouses can make a declaration of their respective beneficial interests in the income and the property from which the income arises, provided that the beneficial interest of the spouses in the property correspond to their beneficial interest in the income. Thus, in the above example the spouses could make a declaration under which the capital and interest are to be split two thirds/one third in line with their respective contributions.

It is thus not possible for the property itself to be shared between the spouses in a different proportion to that of the income (for example, the declaration cannot specify a property split of, say, 80/20 with an income split of, say, 60/40).

To be effective for income tax purposes notice of the declaration must be given to HMRC within a period of 60 days from the date of the declaration and must be on the prescribed form, Form 17 (see Appendix 3). The declaration then has effect for income arising on or after the date of the declaration.

On the other hand, it may be that the automatic assumption of equal split of income between spouses can in fact be used as part of tax planning.

For example, if a husband and wife open a bank account in joint names where the husband contributes £10 000 cash to the account and the wife contributes £5000 cash to the account, without any declaration being signed, then any interest arising on the account (say £1500) will be allocated for income tax purposes as to £750 to the husband and £750 to the wife. If the husband is a higher rate taxpayer (i.e. 40%), whereas the wife is a basic rate taxpayer (20% for tax year 2008/09; 22% for tax year 2007/08), there will be an income tax saving on the "extra" £250 interest allocated to the wife even though, strictly speaking, her entitlement should only be one third of the £1500 interest income (i.e. £5000/£15 000).

In this particular example it is probably even better (for income tax purposes) for the spouses to enter into a subsequent declaration of trust under which the husband possesses, say, a 10% beneficial interest in the account and the wife the balancing 90%. Assuming the relevant Form 17 is then duly lodged with HMRC the husband will be subject to income tax on interest (using the figures above) of £150 (i.e. 10% of £1500) and the wife on interest of £1850 (i.e. 90% of £1500). Income tax will be saved due to the wife receiving the bulk of the interest as she is a basic rate taxpayer. The declaration of trust by the husband in effect constitutes a transfer to his wife of 57% of his initial interest of 67% (i.e. two thirds) leaving him with 10%. His wife's interest correspondingly increases from the initial 33% (i.e. one third) to 90%. Although this is a gift for inheritance tax purposes as it is inter-spouse it is exempt (unless the transfer is from a UK domiciled to a non-UK domiciled spouse; see below).

Another example might be where, for example, the husband owns a valuable piece of income producing real estate. As a 40% taxpayer he is exposed to this rate of tax on the rental income. His wife has no income. The husband, however, may not wish to transfer any significant part of the real estate to his wife but would like to reduce his income tax liability.

The husband could therefore enter into a declaration of trust under which he transfers a 1% beneficial interest in the property to his wife; he thus retains 99% beneficially of the property. No declaration is made (i.e. no Form 17 is lodged with HMRC). As a consequence, under the above rule, each spouse will now be subject to income tax on 50% of the rental income. The husband will have effectively reduced his income tax liability on the rental income (as 50% is allocated to his wife) while he still retains the bulk (99%) of the property.

→ assumed income split is 50/50

Doesn't work for "earned income"

Non-spouse Joint Ownership

In the case of property ownership in joint names where the individuals concerned are not spouses, the rules are slightly different.

There is no rule under which income from property in joint names is automatically split 50/50.

The beneficial entitlements to both the underlying property and any income therefrom are determined according to the facts and agreement between the parties.

Thus, it is quite feasible for property to be owned beneficially in proportions which do not reflect the respective beneficial entitlements to income (which is not possible for spouses). (except 50/50 of course)

Hence, for example, two brothers open a bank account in their joint names. Brother 1 contributes £10 000 and Brother 2 £30 000. Despite their respective contributions the brothers could agree that Brother 1 is to be beneficially entitled to 40% of the asset yet Brother 2 is to be beneficially entitled to, say, 90% of the interest income arising on the deposit.

Implicit in the agreement with respect to the property ownership in the above example is that Brother 2, for inheritance tax purposes, will have made a PET (see Chapter 9) of £6000.

Such an agreement could not be made had the two individuals been spouses. Form 17 referred to above is irrelevant as it only applies to spouses.

Capital Gains Tax

Spouse Joint Ownership

Property in the joint names of husband and wife will be assumed (in the absence of other evidence) for capital gains tax purposes to be held equally beneficially. Any gain arising on a disposal of the property (e.g. gift or sale) will be apportioned equally.

However, property may be held in unequal proportions if this refelects the true facts. Thus, for example, property may be purchased with the husband contributing 80% of the purchase price and the wife the balancing 20%. Beneficial ownership for capital gains tax purposes will accordingly be 80/20 (even though in the absence of a completed Form 17 (see above) any income arising from the property will be split 50//50) and any gain arising on a disposal of the property (e.g. gift or sale) will be apportioned correspondingly (i.e. 80/20).

Non-spouse Joint Ownership

There is no equivalent assumption, as outlined above, with respect to non-spouse joint ownership.

Thus, the purchase of property with unequal contributions by non-spouses will be owned beneficially in proportion to the contributions of the contributors. Any gain arising on a disposal of the property (e.g. gift or sale) will be apportioned correspondingly.

NON-UK DOMICILED INDIVIDUAL

Care is required in particular when considering the form of property ownership where one spouse is UK domiciled whereas the other is non-UK domiciled. The issue is one of inheritance tax.

Transfers from the UK to the non-UK domiciled spouse are exempt for inheritance tax purposes only up to the first £55 000; over and above £55 000 the nil rate applies with respect to the next £312 000 and subject to a rate of 20% or 40% above £367 000 depending upon whether the transfer is a lifetime transfer or a transfer on death (see Chapter 9).

Thus, unlike inter-spouse transfers between two UK domiciled spouses or two non-UK domiciled spouses or transfers from a non-UK domiciled to a UK domiciled spouse all of which are exempt from inheritance tax, transfers from a UK domiciled to a non-UK domiciled spouse may precipitate inheritance tax consequences.

It is important therefore that transfers from a UK to a non-UK domiciled spouse are controlled and do not arise by accident. This may arise where an asset is held as beneficial joint tenants. On the death of the UK domiciled spouse the surviving non-UK domiciled spouse would inherit automatically.

By way of example, if the matrimonial home was owned as beneficial joint tenants and worth, say, £2 million if the UK domiciled spouse was the first to die, £1 million less £367 000 (see above) would fall subject to inheritance tax at 40% on passing to the surviving non-UK domiciled spouse.

Unfortunately, the same inheritance consequence would arise even if the ownership was structured as beneficial tenants in common; the only difference being that ownership as tenants in common permits the UK domiciled spouse to decide to whom their interest was to be left under their will. This could be important.

For example, using the above figures, if the UK domiciled spouse by way of will left their interest to the children (i.e. not to the surviving spouse) and the surviving non-UK domiciled spouse left their interest on death to the children the aggregate inheritance tax on the £2 million estate would be reduced as compared to where the ownership structure was by way of beneficial joint tenants.

The position is similar where joint bank accounts are held by such spouses. Such accounts are invariably held as beneficial joint tenants and thus the survivorship principle applies on death. Thus, if the UK domiciled spouse is the first to die all the above inheritance tax issues just discussed arise again.

The answer in principle with respect to bank accounts is to arrange for them to be held as beneficial tenants in common (which is, however, somewhat difficult in practice as discussed above) but certainly for no beneficial joint bank accounts to be held. Each spouse should ideally open their own account in their sole name. This then enables the cash in the account to be left by way of will, as appropriate, allowing inheritance tax to be minimised.

In any event, the non-UK domiciled spouse ought as a matter of principle to maintain the minimum of amounts of cash in UK bank accounts, such accounts being "fed" by transfers from non-UK situs bank accounts as and when needed. In this regard it should be remembered that non-UK bank accounts are excluded property for inheritance tax purposes for the non-UK domiciled individual (see Chapter 12).

SPOUSES

As indicated above, considering the structuring of property ownership is important as it may impact on the tax consequences should a transfer of an interest in the property be effected. While beneficial ownership by way of a joint tenancy may offer conveniency it does not offer the same flexibility as ownership as tenants in common.

Effecting changes to interests in property as part of a reorganisation of family owned property is often necessary to mitigate future tax consequences. In the UK, greater flexibility with respect to the reorganisation of family owned property is permitted compared to that in many other countries where "forced heirship" rules may prohibit uninhibited transfers (see Chapter 26). In addition, in England there is no concept of community property as exists in many civil law jurisdictions (see Chapter 26). However, it is important that any transfer is executed correctly. The law lays down the rules which must be observed if transfers of interests in property are to be valid.

As a general strategy, for all UK taxes, the "best" principle to follow is that of estate equalisation; in other words, each spouse's income and assets should be of such amounts as allow advantage to be taken of all forms of relief and exemptions applicable under each of the three major taxes, i.e. income tax, capital gains tax and inheritance tax.

For example, each spouse needs a net estate of at least £312 000 (for 2008/09) for inheritance tax purposes so as to be in a position to utilise their nil rate band.

It may be, however, that this need for equalisation for inheritance tax purposes has to some extent been made less relevant following the introduction of the transferable nil rate band (see Chapter 9).

It may also be less relevant where one spouse is UK domiciled and the other spouse is non-UK domiciled. In such a case it may be arguable that the UK domiciled spouse's income and assets should be extremely small in order that full use of the non-UK domiciled's status may be taken. However, in practice this may be undesirable for various reasons and thus a degree of equalisation would still seem to be appropriate.

Despite the fact that spouses are subject to the various taxes as two individuals a key advantage which spouses have over cohabitees, two sisters, two brothers, etc. is the general ability to transfer income and assets between themselves without limit (subject to transfers for inheritance tax purposes from a UK domiciled to a non-UK domiciled spouse) and without any tax charges arising (however, although historically HMRC has not challenged inter-spouse transfers, recently HMRC have tried to use the settlement provisions to challenge such transfers where HMRC perceived that the transfers were being used for tax avoidance purposes; the most recent example is the so-called Arctic Systems case (*Jones v. Garnett (2007)*). This case concerned income transfers between spouses and was thus a case concerned with income tax.) Provisions to prevent abuse in this area are likely to be introduced from 6 April 2009.

It is this ability to effect tax-free transfers between spouses that enables a degree of tax efficient planning to be carried out relatively easily.

It is important to appreciate that any transfers inter-spouse need to be legally effective (i.e. the rules applicable to the particular form of property need to be observed) and for tax purposes must in principle be made without any attaching conditions. Otherwise the settlement legislation (basically, the provisions that deal with trusts) will be applied and thus, for example, any income arising from the asset transferred will simply continue to be subject to income tax on the part of the transferor, not transferee, spouse.

In short, therefore, the gift must literally be unconditional and irrevocable with the transferee spouse being unfettered as to how the gift may then be used; basically, no strings should be attached to the gift.

This was particularly important pre FA 2008 where non-UK source income of one spouse was transferred to the other spouse enabling the latter spouse to remit the monies to the UK without any tax charge arising. Any imperfections in effecting the gift would invalidate the otherwise favourable tax consequences. Post FA 2008, however, inter-spouse transfers of this nature are no longer tax effective (see Chapter 23).

SUMMARY

Ownership of property under English law may take the form of legal and beneficial ownership.

The latter is important for all UK tax purposes.

The two forms of beneficial ownership are the joint tenancy and tenancy in common. Under the former, interests in the property on death pass automatically to the survivor. Under the latter, the interest of the deceased may be left by will.

While there are pros and cons of each form of beneficial ownership, probably, on balance, tenants in common offer the greater flexibility from the tax planning perspective.

Part Two
The Major Taxes

8
Capital Gains Tax

BACKGROUND

FA 2008 has made significant amendments to the rules applicable to capital gains tax. These amendments and their implication are examined in detail below. The new rules introduced by FA 2008 apply to any disposal on or after 6 April 2008 irrespective of the date of acquisition of the asset.

The changes affect both UK and non-UK domiciled individuals albeit in different ways and in different degrees.

The key changes introduced by FA 2008 were the:

1. introduction of a single rate of capital gains tax, i.e. 18%;
2. introduction of a new form of relief, "entrepreneur relief";
3. amendments to the offshore "settlor interested" trust provisions;
4. amendments to the offshore "capital payments" trust regime;
5. amendments to the rules with respect to "remittances" of offshore capital gains;
6. amendments to the rules with respect to offshore capital losses;
7. abolition of the indexation allowance;
8. abolition of taper relief;
9. abolition of the UK resident "settlor interested" trust provisions.

All these changes became effective with respect to any form of disposal effected on or after 6 April 2008 whether the asset was purchased on or before or after this date.

Of the above nine key changes those that affect the UK domiciled individual are, in particular, (1), (2), (7), (8) and (9).

Of the above nine key changes those that affect the non-UK domiciled individual are, in particular, (3), (4), (5) and (6).

Nevertheless, any consideration of the capital gains tax position of either UK or non-UK domiciled individuals, post FA 2008, should take account of all of the above changes.

This chapter will concentrate on the capital gains tax position post FA 2008. However, in view of the fact that Tax Returns for the tax year 2007/08 need to be filed, on or before 31 October 2008 (for "paper" returns) or on or before 31 January 2009 (for "online" returns), the capital gains tax position for the tax year 2007/08 (and in effect prior tax years) will also be addressed (the FA 2008 changes will not impact on the content of the 2007/08 Tax Return which will need to be based on pre FA 2008 law).

It is also important to understand the pre FA 2008 position in order to put the FA 2008 changes into perspective.

Unless otherwise stated all comments below apply to both the pre and post FA 2008 position.

BASICS

Capital gains tax is payable by individuals, trustees and personal representatives (but not by companies) on capital gains made by persons who are either resident and/or ordinarily resident in the UK.

For UK domiciled and UK resident individuals capital gains tax is chargeable on disposals of worldwide assets. For non-UK domiciled but UK resident individuals capital gains tax is levied on disposals of UK situs assets but only on non-UK situs assets if any chargeable gain is remitted to the UK.

Capital gains tax is not levied on UK situs assets of non-UK residents (unless such non-residents are trading in the UK).

Chargeable gains are those gains arising on, inter alia, disposals of chargeable assets. Such assets include paintings; jewellery; shares; options; etc. and thus include both tangible and intangible assets.

Some assets are, however, exempt from capital gains tax including:

- an individual's main residence;
- national savings certificates and premium bonds;
- motor vehicles suitable for private use;
- most government securities (i.e. gilts);
- life assurance policies when held by the original beneficial owner;
- investments held within Individual Savings Accounts (i.e. ISAs);
- foreign currency for an individual's private use;
- pension rights;
- prizes and betting winnings.

A potential charge to capital gains tax arises whenever there is a "disposal" of a chargeable asset. A disposal may be a straightforward sale or it may be a gift (it may also include, for example, the loss or destruction of an asset or the creation of one asset out of another, e.g. the grant of a lease out of a freehold).

A disposal occurs at the date of an unconditional contract (e.g. the date of disposal of land is typically the date of the "exchange" of contracts not "completion") or the date when the condition is satisfied if the contract is conditional.

At its simplest, a chargeable gain arising on an asset disposal is the difference between the sale proceeds (or market value in the case of a gift; see below) and original cost. However, certain other costs may also be deductible including the incidental costs of acquisition and disposal (e.g. fees for professional services; advertising costs); enhancement costs so long as they are reflected in the nature of the asset at the date of disposal (e.g. an extension on a property); and the costs of defending title to the asset (e.g. legal costs in defending the owner's title to the asset; not normally deductible for capital gains tax purposes as such costs are often deductible in computing income tax liabilities).

Example 8.1
Gordon Green bought some shares for £150 000 selling the shares two years later for £500 000.
  Gordon's chargeable gain is £350 000.

Gifts constitute disposals (and thus may give rise to chargeable gains) and are assumed to have occurred at market value.

Example 8.2
Gordon Green bought some shares for £150 000 and two years later gave them to an old friend. At the time of the gift the shares were worth £500 000.
  Gordon's chargeable gain is £350 000 as it is based on the market value of the shares (even though Gordon received no monies from the gift).

Where a transaction occurs between "connected persons" it is also assumed that the transaction is effected at market value irrespective of the actual price (if any) paid. For this purpose a person is connected with:

- his spouse;
- his relatives (brothers, sisters, ancestors and lineal descendants);
- the relatives of his spouse;
- the spouses of his and his spouse's relatives.

However, the significance of disposals to connected persons is that any capital loss which may arise on a disposal to a particular connected person may only be offset against capital gains arising on disposals to the same connected person.

Example 8.3
Gordon Green bought some shares for £150 000 and two years later his sister purchased the shares from Gordon for £200 000 at a time when the shares were worth £500 000.
  Gordon's chargeable gain is £350 000 as it is based on the market value of the shares as Gordon's sister is a "connected person". Had Gordon gifted the shares to his sister his capital gains tax position would be the same.

INTER-SPOUSE TRANSFERS

While spouses are "connected", the above market value rule does *not* apply to inter-spouse transfers.
  Disposals between spouses, irrespective of domicile status, living together do *not* give rise to chargeable gains or allowable losses. Any such transfers are treated as if the transfer gave rise to neither gain nor loss.

Post-FA 2008, an inter-spouse gift of an asset is treated as if the asset had been transferred at its original cost.

Example 8.4
Jon Smith purchased shares worth £55 000 in 2003 and after 5 April 2008 transferred the shares to his wife, Barbara, when the shares were worth £100 000.

Jon would be assumed to have transferred them for £55 000 (i.e. original cost) irrespective of their market value at the date of transfer. This would then give rise, on Jon's part, to neither a loss nor a gain.

Barbara is assumed to have paid £55 000 for the shares acquired from her husband (irrespective of what she may or may not have in fact paid).

If Barbara later sold the shares when they were worth £165 000 she would make a chargeable gain of £110 000.

Inter-spouse transfers offer potential planning opportunities in particular where one spouse is non-UK domiciled (even if UK resident). A UK domiciled and resident spouse could gift (or sell thus avoiding any potential inheritance tax liability) a non-UK situs to a non-UK domiciled but resident spouse. As an inter-spouse transfer no capital gains tax liability arises on the gift.

The non-UK domiciled but UK resident spouse could then subsequently sell the asset capital gains tax free if the capital gain arising on the sale is not remitted to the UK (see Chapter 23). Alternatively, the recipient spouse could settle the asset on a non-UK resident trust which would not precipitate a capital gains tax charge at that time; a subsequent capital gains tax charge would arise, if, for example, the trust appointed the asset out to a UK beneficiary at some point in the future (see Chapter 17). In addition, the trust would be an excluded property trust for inheritance tax purposes thus protecting the donor's estate against a future inheritance tax charge should the donor become UK domiciled (see Chapter 12).

Pre FA 2008, an interspouse gift of an asset was treated as if the asset had been transferred at its original cost *plus* the amount of any indexation allowance, if any, arising between the date of acquisition by the transferring spouse and the date of the transfer.

Example 8.5
Jon Smith had purchased shares worth £25 000 in 1995 and in February 2008 (i.e. pre FA 2208) transferred the shares to his wife, Barbara, when the shares were worth £100 000.

Indexation allowance amounts to £35 000.

Jon would be assumed to have transferred the shares for £55 000 (i.e. original cost) plus the indexation allowance (£35 000) irrespective of their market value at the date of transfer. This would then give rise, on Jon's part, to neither a loss nor a gain.

Barbara is assumed to have paid £55 000 plus £35 000, i.e. £90 000, for the shares acquired from her husband (irrespective of what she may or may not have in fact paid).

If Barbara later sold the shares when they were worth £165 000 she would make a chargeable gain of £75 000.

It will be noted in Example 8.4 above that as the shares had been purchased after 5 April 1998 no indexation allowance was available as the indexation allowance only applied from date of purchase to 5 April 1998 (see below). However, even if the shares had been purchased pre 6 April 1998, any indexation allowance is now lost were a disposal of the shares to occur on or after 6 April 2008 (see below).

CALCULATING THE TAX

Appendix 2A sets out the pro forma which may be used to calculate an individual's chargeable gains (or losses) on or after 6 April 2008 and also the pro forma where the disposal occurred before 6 April 2008 (Appendix 2B). It will be noted that there is a specific order in which certain deductions need to be made. For example, the annual exemption (see below) is the last deduction made; any indexation allowance is deducted before taking into account taper relief (see below); etc.

Pre FA 2008, a capital gain was treated as the highest part of the individual's taxable income. It was treated as if it was savings income and thus was subject to tax at the 10%, 20% or 40% rates as appropriate. However, post FA 2008 the capital gains tax rate is no longer linked to the rate of income tax applicable to the individual. For disposals on or after 6 April 2008 a single rate of 18% applies (subject to the application of entrepreneurial relief, see below).

Annual Exemption

Personal allowances (those available to reduce income subject to income tax) cannot be deducted in arriving at the amount of chargeable gain. However, an individual is entitled to an annual exemption (£9200 for 2007/08 and £9600 for 2008/09). This exemption represents the amount of chargeable gains which can be made in a tax year without precipitating a capital gains tax charge.

If, in any tax year, the annual exemption is not fully utilised (or utilised at all) any unused element cannot be carried forward (or backward) for use in other tax years, i.e. it is simply lost.

In the case of trustees, however, their entitlement to an annual exemption is restricted to 50% of the amount available to an individual (i.e. £4800 for 2008/09).

In the case of personal representatives the annual exemption is the same as for individuals in the tax year of death of the individual and for the following two tax years. Thereafter no annual exemption is available to personal representatives.

Following changes introduced in FA 2008 for certain non-UK domiciled but UK resident individuals, however, entitlement to the annual exemption is denied. A non-UK domiciled but UK resident individual who claims remittance basis treatment for a tax year will be denied the annual exemption (and in addition any entitlement to any of the personal allowances) (see Chapter 23).

PAYMENT OF THE TAX

Capital gains tax is payable on or before 31 January following the tax year in which the chargeable gains arises. There are no interim or payments on account as is the case for income tax.

Example 8.6
Herbert Jones sold a number of his personal chattels (antique paintings; jewellery; and shares) during the tax year 2008/09 realising aggregate chargeable gains of £55 000 (pre annual exemption).

The capital gains tax liability arising on the £45 400 (i.e. 18% thereof) is payable on or before 31 January 2010.

There are, however, provisions providing for the capital gains tax liability for a tax year to be discharged by instalments as opposed to one lump sum. Instalment payments may be used where:

(a) the consideration received from the disposal is itself payable in instalments over a period exceeding 18 months;
(b) there is a gift of assets (not subject to gift relief; see below) which comprise unquoted shares;
(c) there is a gift of quoted shares where the donor has "control" (broadly, owns at least 51% of the voting capital); or
(d) there is a gift of land.

Under (a) above, the tax payment instalments may be spread over a maximum period of eight years (although the last tax instalment may not be made later than the date of the last instalment of the consideration arising from the disposal). No interest is charged under this option unless any of the tax instalment payments are made after the due dates.

Under (b), (c) and (d), the tax instalments may be made over a period of 10 years by 10 equal annual instalments. Unlike the position under (a) above, interest is charged on the outstanding instalments and should the asset be subsequently sold (after the initial gifting) any outstanding tax payments (plus interest) become payable.

However, with respect to gifts it is not possible to utilise the instalment basis where a gift relief claim could have been lodged (see below). Whether in fact the claim was lodged is irrelevant.

YEAR OF DEATH

On the death of an individual there is no assumed deemed disposal of the deceased's assets. Thus, no capital gains tax liability arises on an individual's death.

All assets beneficially owned by the deceased at death are revalued to their market values at the date of death (i.e. probate value). The consequence is that there is an

b'cos there's IHT to pay instead

Capital Gains Tax 131

automatic uplift in the values of the assets owned at death. Any latent gains in the assets owned at death are thus "wiped out".

Beneficiaries under the deceased's will (or intestacy; see Chapter 26) are deemed to inherit the assets at their market values at the date of death (i.e. their probate value).

Example 8.7
George Kay died on 6 July 2008.
At the date of his death his estate comprised:

- cash at bank £300 000;
- quoted shares with a market value at death £400 000;
- antique paintings with a market value at death £150 000.

George had originally purchased the shares for £50 000 and the painting for £110 000.
No capital gains tax liability arises on George's death.
All his estate was left to his daughter Georgina.
Georgina thus inherits the assets at their value at the date of George's death.
If a week later Georgina sold the shares for £410 000 her chargeable gain would be £10 000 (i.e. £410 000 less £400 000) not £360 000 (i.e. £410 000 less £50 000).
The latent gain on the shares of £350 000 at the date of death is "wiped out". *but have to pay IHT*

In the tax year of death, any capital losses on assets sold/gifted prior to death (unlike the usage of other capital losses; see below) may be utilised not only against capital gains made prior to death in the tax year of death but may also then be carried back to the three immediately preceding tax years and offset against capital gains assessable in those tax years (at no other time can capital losses be carried back to prior tax years).

However, any losses in the tax year of death must be offset against gains of that tax year to the fullest extent possible (even if for that tax year part or all of the annual exemption is lost/wasted) before any surplus unused capital losses can be carried back to prior tax years.

PRE FA 2008 RELIEFS

As indicated above, a chargeable gain arising on the disposal of an asset, at its most simplest, is the difference between sale proceeds and original cost.

However, pre FA 2008, two major forms of relief were available to reduce this chargeable gain further. These reliefs were, namely:

- indexation allowance;
- taper relief.

Neither of these reliefs applies to disposals on or after 6 April 2008.

Indexation Allowance

An indexation allowance was an attempt to levy capital gains tax only on the "real" gain as opposed to the "monetary" gain arising from an asset's disposal. In other words, it was an attempt to adjust any monetary capital gains due to the change in value of money over time; in effect attempting to take inflation into account.

The indexation allowance could reduce a capital gain, ultimately to nil. It could not, however, turn a gain into a loss nor increase the size of any loss.

An "indexed gain" was thus the amount of the chargeable gain arising on an asset disposal after reduction by any indexation allowance.

The indexation allowance was, however, abolished for individuals (and trusts) on 5 April 1998. From 6 April 1998 taper relief replaced the indexation allowance (see below). Despite its abolition, any disposal of an asset on or after 6 April 1998 which was acquired before 6 April 1998 still qualified for an indexation allowance from the date of the acquisition of the asset to 5 April 1998 but not beyond.

The acquisition of an asset on or after 6 April 1998 (i.e. after the indexation allowance was abolished) meant that no indexation allowance was available on a future disposal (although taper relief would in principle apply).

The indexation allowance was arrived at by applying an "indexation factor" to the relevant items of expenditure utilised in purchasing the asset.

The indexation factor was equal to:

$$\frac{\text{RPI for month of disposal (or April 1998 if earlier)} - \text{RPI for month of purchase (or March 1982 if later)}}{\text{RPI for month of purchase (or March 1982 if later)}}$$

The "index factor" was normally found as a decimal and rounded to three decimal places.

RPI refers to the Retail Price Index; a series of indices produced by HMRC.

Example 8.8

John Suez purchased an asset in June 1990 for £100 000.
He sold the asset in:

(a) January 1996 for £150 000;
(b) March 2006 for £200 000.

The RPIs for June 1990, January 1996 and April 1998 were, respectively, 126.70, 150.20 and 162.60.

Re (a), the indexation allowance is: [[150.20 − 126.70]/[126.70]] × £100 000 = £18 500

Re (b), the indexation allowance is: [[162.60 − £126.70]/[126.70]] × £100 000 = £28 300

Thus, under (a), the indexed gain will be: £150 000−£100 000−£18 500 = £31 500
Thus, under (b), the indexed gain will be: £200 000 − £100 000 − £31 500 = £68 500

If, however, John had purchased the asset in August 1998 (i.e. after 5 April 1998) no indexation allowance would have been applicable.

Example 8.9
Brian bought shares in March 1995 for £120 000 and sold them in July 1998 for £100 000.

Brian's gain will be £100 000 less £120 000, in fact a capital loss of £20 000.

Although in principle an indexation allowance was applicable it cannot be used to increase the size of any capital loss.

Thus, Brian's capital loss remains at £20 000.

Example 8.10
Brian bought shares in March 1995 for £120 000 and sold them in July 1998 for £125 000.

Brian's gain will be £125 000 less £120 000, i.e. £5000. However, an indexation allowance was applicable equal to: 0.102 × £120,000, i.e. £12 240.

Brian's indexed gain thus, prima facie, equals £5000 less £12 240, i.e. a capital loss of £7240.

The indexation allowance could not turn a capital gain into a capital loss.

Thus, the indexation allowance of £12 240 simply reduces the capital gain of £5000 to nil.

Inter-spouse transfers are deemed to occur at no gain/no loss to the transferor spouse (see above). This has the effect that such transfers are assumed to have occurred for a consideration equal to original purchase cost plus the indexation allowance to the date of the transfer.

Example 8.11
Joan and Dick Garden are married.

Joan decided to transfer to Dick a factory she owned.

Joan had purchased the factory for £250 000 and at the date of transfer to Dick she was entitled to an indexation allowance of £14 000.

The transfer will be assumed to have occurred for a consideration of £264 000.

On a future sale by Dick the cost of the asset to Dick will be assumed to have been the £264 000.

Dick may himself also be entitled to an indexation allowance on a future disposal measured from the date he received the asset from Joan to the date of sale (or 5 April 1998 if earlier).

Following FA 2008 no indexation allowance will apply to the disposal of an asset which occurs on or after 6 April 2008 irrespective of the date of purchase of the asset.

Thus, any asset purchased pre 6 April 1998 (and thus entitled to an indexation allowance up to 5 April 1998) and still held (i.e. not disposed of) on 6 April 2008 will on a future disposal lose any accrued indexation allowance. A disposal prior to 6 April

2008 to realise and thus utilise the indexation allowance might have been appropriate (see below "Banking indexation allowance").

Taper Relief

The indexation allowance was abolished for disposals of assets by individuals effective 6 April 1998 but was replaced by taper relief.

Taper relief applied to disposals on or after 6 April 1998.

Thus on the disposal of an asset, acquired pre 6 April 1998, on or after 6 April 1998 (but pre 6 April 2008; see above) both an indexation allowance *and* taper relief might apply.

Taper relief reduced the *indexed gain* by a percentage determined by both the type of asset sold and the length of time for which the asset had been held.

The maximum taper relief percentage was 75% which applied on the disposal of a *business* asset held for *at least two years*. The maximum taper relief percentage which applied on the disposal of a *non-business* asset was 40% which applied only when the asset had been held for *at least 10 years*.

Example 8.12

Gertrude Smithers sold an asset making an indexed gain of £100 000.

If the asset qualified as a *business* asset which she had held for at least two years then the taper relief would be [75% of £100 000, i.e. £75 000]. The gain thus taxable would be £25 000.

If the asset qualified as a *non-business* asset which she had held for at least 10 years then the taper relief would be [40% of £100 000, i.e. £40 000]. The gain thus taxable would be £60 000.

The length of time an asset was held was measured in complete years (effectively being rounded down for part year ownership) and was measured from the later of the date of acquisition and 6 April 1998. The timing of an asset sale could thus dramatically affect the percentage of taper relief due. For example, a business asset held for one year and 11 months would be entitled to 50% taper relief; had the asset been held for one more month, i.e. two years, 75% taper relief would have applied (see tables below).

Example 8.13

Bob Foot purchased a non-business asset in January 1996 and sold it in 13 November 2006.

Bob would be entitled to an indexation allowance measured from January 1996 to 5 April 1998 plus taper relief from 6 April 1998 (not from January 1996) to 13 November 2006.

Taper relief would thus be based upon a period of ownership of nine complete years (it will be noted that 6 April 1998 to 13 November 2006 amounts to eight complete years. However, a "bonus" year is also available as the asset was owned on 17 March 1998 (see below) making nine years in total).

Where an asset is transferred inter-spouse, on a future disposal by the recipient spouse the transferor spouse's period of ownership is deemed to be a period of ownership by the recipient spouse for taper relief purposes. In effect, the recipient spouse is deemed to have held the asset from the date it was originally acquired (but only for taper relief purposes).

Example 8.14

Tom and Myrtle Bishop are married and in December 2005 Tom transferred to Myrtle a non-business asset he had acquired in September 1994.

Myrtle sold the asset in January 2008.

For taper relief purposes Myrtle is deemed to have owned the asset from September 1994 to January 2008. In terms of complete years this amounts to nine years plus one "bonus" year making a total of 10 years (as taper relief only applies from 6 April 1998; indexation allowance applying before this date).

Inter-spouse transfers could, in certain circumstances, give rise to a loss of taper relief on a subsequent sale by the transferee spouse and thus caution needed to be exercised when such transfers were made (see below).

As indicated above the percentage of taper relief applicable on a disposal depended upon the type of asset and the time period for which the asset was held (post 6 April 1998). The tables below set out the various percentages applicable:

Non-business assets:		
Qualifying period of ownership in complete years (after 5.4.98)	*Percentage reduction*	*Percentage chargeable*
1	Nil	Nil
2	Nil	Nil
3	5%	95%
4	10%	90%
5	15%	85%
6	20%	80%
7	25%	75%
8	30%	70%
9	35%	65%
10 or more	40%	60%
Business assets:		
1	50%	50%
2 or more	75%	25%

In the case of a *non-business* asset only, which was held on 17 March 1998, one "bonus" year of taper relief is normally granted on a disposal of the asset (this did not apply to business assets).

Business Asset

A "business" asset was defined (for periods post 6 April 2000) as:

- an asset owned by an individual, partnership, trustee or PRs and used in a trade carried on by the owner of the asset *or* by a qualifying company or by a third person; *or*
- an asset held by an individual for the purpose of an employment (full time or not) with a person (individual or company) carrying on a trade; *or*
- a shareholding held by an individual in a *qualifying* company (*whether UK or foreign*).

A *qualifying company* was a *trading company* where *one or more* of the following apply:

- the shares of the company were not listed (e.g. an AIM company) on a recognised stock exchange (NASDAQ is a recognised stock exchange); *or*
- an individual held at least 5% of the voting rights (if listed) in the company; *or*
- the individual was an employee or officer of the company; *or*
- a *non-trading* company if the individual was an employee/director of the company and held (together with connected persons) $\leqslant$ 10% of shares or voting rights (thus, an employee of an investment company may receive business asset treatment re the shares; *effective for disposals on or after 6 April 2000*).
("Shares" includes "securities".)

Trading company included, for example, the trade of furnished holiday lettings and property development but *not* share investment or property investment (e.g. activities of commercial or residential landlord).

It is important to note that the legislation applying to taper relief changed over time. For example, the definition of a business asset did not remain constant in particular in relation to shares. As a consequence, the nature of an asset held by the same individual might change through time for taper relief purposes (see below).

Taper Relief and Share Sales

With respect to taper relief two important points are worth noting:

1. the definition of "business asset" changed materially on 6 April 2000; and
2. the possible loss of taper relief on the sale of a business asset, e.g. (possibly shares) following a previous inter-spouse transfer.

(1) Shares in trading companies pre 6 April 2000
For periods of ownership up to 5 April 2000 for a shareholding to qualify as a business asset required satisfaction of either of the two following conditions:

(a) ownership of $\geqslant$ 25% of the voting rights in the trading company; *or*
(b) ownership of $\geqslant$ 5% of the voting rights in the trading company exercisable by the taxpayer who was a *full time* employee of the company (or full time officer).

Pre 6 April 2000 (unlike the position post 5 April 2000) there was no distinction between listed or unlisted companies.

However, with effect from 6 April 2000 these rules were changed and a distinction was introduced between listed and non-listed companies (see above).

One major impact of the changes was that many shareholdings pre 6 April 2000 qualified as non-business assets but qualified as business assets thereafter. For example, a pre 6 April 2000 shareholding of, say, 2% in a non-listed company would before this date qualify only as a non-business asset whereas from that date it would qualify as a business asset. The effect in such cases was that an apportionment of any gain arising on a disposal was required.

Example 8.15
George Smith owned 5% of an unlisted company. He was not an employee of the company.

He acquired the shares in February 1996 and sold them in October 2005.

Up to 6 April 2000 the shares qualified only as a non-business asset becoming a business asset thereafter.

For taper relief purposes the shares were held from 6 April 1998 through to October 2005, i.e. seven complete years. However, from 6 April 1998 to 5 April 2000 the shares qualified for non-business asset treatment (i.e. two years).

From 6 April 2000 to October 2005 the shares qualified for business asset treatment (i.e. five complete years).

Thus, 2/7ths of the indexed gain would qualify for non-business asset taper relief and 5/7ths for business asset taper relief. (Indexation to 5 April 1998 would of course also apply.)

The taper relief percentages applied to each apportioned indexed gain would be based on eight years giving non-business taper of 30% (because of the "bonus year" making eight not seven years; see above) and business taper of 75%.

(2) Inter-spouse share transfer and subsequent sale
An inter-spouse transfer of a shareholding followed by a disposal by the transferee spouse could lead to a loss of business asset treatment on the disposal.

On a disposal by the transferee spouse following an inter-spouse transfer, for taper relief purposes it was assumed that the transferee spouse owned the asset from the date it was acquired by the transferor spouse (see above). For business asset treatment on the disposal the shares must have qualified as a business asset in the ownership of the transferee spouse (i.e. from the date of acquisition by the transferor spouse). This may not always have been the case.

Example 8.16
Robert Swatch was an employee of XYZ Ltd, a listed company.

Robert acquired 1000 shares in XYZ Ltd in January 1992 which represented a shareholding interest in XYZ Ltd of <5%.

Robert gave these shares to his wife, Mary, on 1 April 2001.

She sold the shares on 10 April 2005 never having worked for XYZ Ltd.

For the period 1 April 2001 to 10 April 2005 the shares did not qualify as business assets on the part of Mary as she was not an employee of XYZ Ltd nor did she own at least 5%.

For the period 6 April 1998 to 1 April 2001 (a period of deemed ownership by Mary) the shares would not have qualified as business assets on her part.

As a consequence, for the whole period 6 April 1998 to 10 April 2005 the shares did not qualify as business assets on the part of Mary. Therefore non-business asset relief applied.

Mary is deemed to have owned the shares for the period 6.4.98 to 10.4.05 (seven complete tax years plus a bonus year, i.e. eight years), i.e. 30% taper relief based on eight years, ownership as a non-business asset.

It should be noted that had Robert retained ownership of the shares for the whole period and then sold them he would have been entitled to non-business asset treatment for the period 6 April 1998 to 5 April 2000 and business asset treatment from 6 April 2000 to 10 April 2005, i.e. non-business asset taper of 30% (applied to 2/7ths of the indexed gain) and business taper of 75% (applied to 5/7ths of the indexed gain).

The above example demonstrates that transfer of shares inter-spouse may not always have been tax effective.

It was, and is, not unusual in tax planning for families for assets to be transferred inter-spouse. This may be effected in order to mitigate inheritance tax, for example. It is also quite common for such transfers to be effected to ensure each spouse can utilise their respective reliefs and exemptions including their capital gains tax annual exemption (£9600 for tax year 2008/09).

The above Example 8.16 illustrates, however, that while such transfers may enable efficient utilisation of a spouse's annual exemption for capital gains tax purposes the overall position may have been worsened due to a net loss of taper relief.

Following FA 2008 no taper relief will apply to the disposal of an asset which occurs on or after 6 April 2008 irrespective of the date of purchase of the asset.

Thus, any asset whether purchased on or after or before 6 April 1998 (and thus entitled to taper relief) and still held (i.e. not disposed of) on 6 April 2008 will on a future disposal lose any accrued taper relief. A disposal prior to 6 April 2008 to realise and thus utilise the accrued taper relief might have been appropriate (see below "Banking indexation allowance").

GIFTS OF ASSETS (NOT INTER-SPOUSE)

As indicated above, all inter-spouse transfers do not precipitate a capital gains tax liability. They are assumed to have taken place at no gain/no loss. With one exception (i.e. transfers from a UK to a non-UK domiciled spouse) all inter-spouse transfers do not precipitate a liability to inheritance tax.

Capital Gains Tax 139

The position with respect to non-inter-spouse transfers is different, typically giving rise to a charge to capital gains tax.

Tax planning for families often involves the transfer of assets between family members. It is not unusual to effect such transfers in the form of gifts whether the gifts are from one individual to another or are gifts into trust or are gifts out of trusts.

The gift of an asset (or indeed sale at undervalue) potentially precipitates both capital gains and inheritance tax consequences. An outright sale at market value, however, only precipitates a capital gains tax liability.

The gift of an asset for capital gains tax purposes is deemed to have given rise to a disposal at market value; a liability to capital gains tax may thus arise even though no cash or other form of consideration is given for the asset (see Example 8.2 above).

Where a capital gains tax liability does arise on a gift the main problem for the donor (be that the individual or the trust) making the gift is the immediate lack of sales proceeds from which to discharge any capital gains tax liability. Accordingly, in certain cases "gift relief" may be available to the person (i.e. individual or trust) making the disposal pursuant to which no immediate capital gains tax becomes payable. In effect, a deferral of the capital gains tax liability occurs and in some cases this deferral may become complete avoidance if, for example, the individual recipient of the gift dies while still owning the asset gifted.

In order for gift relief to apply *all* of the following conditions must be satisfied:

- the recipient (i.e. transferee) of the gift must be either UK resident or UK ordinarily resident;
- the donor *and* donee must jointly elect for gift relief to apply;
- the gift must either be of a business asset *or* it must precipitate an immediate charge to inheritance tax.

Non-resident Recipient *rules out gift relief*

Thus, a gift of any situs asset (i.e. whether UK or non-UK stitus) by a UK domiciled and UK resident individual to another individual who is not UK resident or a non-UK resident trust will not be eligible for gift relief. The gift by a non-UK domiciled but UK resident individual of a UK situs asset will also not be eligible for gift relief if made to such persons.

Precipitation of an Immediate Inheritance Tax Charge

Gifts into UK resident trusts may in principle qualify for gift relief. Post FA 2006 as all gifts into trusts on or after 22 March 2006 are now chargeable transfers (thus precipitating an immediate inheritance tax charge) gift relief will apply to such gifts.

Gifts to another individual, however, will not precipitate an immediate inheritance tax charge (as such gifts constitute potentially exempt transfers; see Chapter 9) and thus gift relief is not available on such gifts (i.e. under this condition; see below where the gift qualifies as a "business asset" in which case gift relief may be available).

Gift Relief ctd.

It should also be noted that no actual inheritance tax on the gift actually needs to be payable "for an immediate inheritance tax charge to occur". For example, a gift into a discretionary trust is a chargeable lifetime transfer and an immediate inheritance tax charge arises. However, if the amount of the gift falls within the nil rate band the liability is at the nil rate and thus will not result in any inheritance tax actually being payable (see Chapter 9). Nevertheless, gift relief is available to the donor.

FA 2006 has had the effect of widening the scope of those gifts into trusts which may qualify for gift relief. Pre FA 2006, only gifts into discretionary trusts were chargeable lifetime transfers thus precipitating an immediate inheritance tax charge. Gifts into interest in possession or accumulation and maintenance trusts, however, constituted potentially exempt transfers (with no immediate inheritance tax charge arising) and thus in respect of which no gift relief would be available (see Chapters 9 and 15).

However, on or after 22 March 2006, gifts into any of the above three types of trust are now treated as chargeable transfers, thus qualifying for gift relief.

No gift relief

While gifts *into* UK resident trusts may qualify for gift relief this is not the case if the trust is "settlor interested" and the gifts are made on or after 10 December 2003. A trust is settlor interested for this purpose if either the settlor or spouse can possibly benefit from the trust. However, under the provisions of FA 2006, where on or after 6 April 2006, a dependent child (see Chapter 16) of the settlor could possibly benefit under the trust it is to be also treated as "settlor interested" whether the trust was set up on or after 6 April 2006 or before this date; in effect, effective 6 April 2006 the definition of a "settlor interested" trust for hold-over relief purposes has been widened.

The effect of the above FA 2006 change together with the other inheritance tax changes to trusts introduced by FA 2006 (see Chapter 15) is to increase the possibility that a transfer by a settlor into a settlor interested trust could precipitate both a charge to capital gains tax (as no gift relief is available as the trust is settlor interested) and a charge to inheritance tax (as the transfer is, post 6 April 2006, a chargeable transfer). The issue is that no relief for any inheritance tax charged on the transfer is available for offset against any capital gains tax charged thereon.

While typically gifts into trust now qualify for gift relief it may also be the case that gifts *out* of a trust may also qualify. The appointment of an asset out of, for example, a discretionary trust precipitates a disposal of the asset for capital gains tax purposes; similarly, in the case of interest in possession trusts termination of the interest in possession (whether on death or in lifetime) may precipitate a disposal either actual or deemed.

In the case of discretionary trusts appointments of trust assets out to beneficiaries precipitate an immediate inheritance tax charge (whether the transfer of the assets is pre or post FA 2006); the "exit charge" (see Chapter 15). Gift relief thus applies in such cases. Indeed, gift relief also applies where the appointment is made out of a non-UK resident trust to a UK resident individual (although such non-UK resident trusts are not in principle within the charge to capital gains tax, this is not the case if the trust is carrying on some form of trade within the UK).

With respect to qualifying interest in possession trusts the position is a little more complex but in principle gift relief may be available. The termination of a qualifying interest in possession trust may arise on the death of the interest in possession beneficiary or a termination in lifetime. Following a termination the trust may come to an end or another successive interest in possession may arise.

Where the qualifying interest in possession terminates due to the death of the beneficiary and the trust then terminates the trust is deemed to have disposed of the trust assets for market value albeit without a capital gains tax charge arising; a simple rebasing of the trust assets thus occurs. The trustees now effectively hold the trust assets as bare trustees for the beneficiary entitled thereto. However, where the trust assets which are deemed to have been disposed of were subject to an earlier gift-relief claim, then any held-over capital gain does fall subject to capital gains tax. Nevertheless, the held-over capital gain may itself then be subject to a further gift-relief claim whether the trust assets are business assets or not.

Where the interest in possession terminates due to the death of the beneficiary but the trust does not then terminate but a successive interest in possession then arises, basically the same consequences arise as above (although note that the trustees after the deemed disposal do not then hold the trust assets as bare trustee for the new interest in possession beneficiary). The successive interest in possession will not, however, be a qualifying interest in possession if it arises on or after 22 March 2006 (unless it qualifies as a transitional serial interest or an immediate post death interest arising under a will; see Chapter 15). As above, if the trust assets deemed disposed of were subject to an earlier gift relief claim a further claim for hold-over relief may be made whether the trust assets are business assets or not.

Where the qualifying interest in possession terminates in the lifetime of the beneficiary and on or after 22 March 2006 and the trust terminates the trustees are subject to capital gains tax on a deemed disposal of the trust assets. Thus, unlike the positions outlined above an actual charge to capital gains tax arises. This charge extends to including any previously held-over capital gain. However, if the assets concerned qualify as business assets the whole of the deemed capital gain may be held over under a gift relief claim.

Where the trust does not terminate as above on the lifetime termination of the qualifying interest in possession (i.e. the trust assets remain in the trust) no capital gains tax consequences occur (i.e. the trust assets simply remain in the trust at their original costs).

With respect to terminations of non-qualifying interests in possession (e.g. an interest in possession which arises on or after 22 March 2006 (but is not a transitional serial interest or an immediate post-death interest)), whether on death or in lifetime, no capital gains tax consequences arise where no beneficiary then becomes absolutely entitled to the trust assets. Where absolute entitlement does arise then a charge to capital gains tax arises on the deemed disposal although hold-over relief may be available on the whole capital gain.

Gift Relief ctd.

It should also be noted that transfers out of (but not into; see above) settlor interested trusts may qualify for gift relief.

Although one of the general conditions referred to above for gift relief to apply is that *both* the donor and donee must jointly so claim, in the case of transfers *into* trusts only the donor need elect for the gift relief to apply (i.e. the consent of the trustees is not required).

Business Assets

If the gift does not precipitate an immediate inheritance tax charge it may still qualify for gift relief. This will be the case where the asset gifted qualifies as a business asset, namely:

(a) any asset used by the donor for the purposes of a trade, profession or vocation carried on by the donor or his/her personal company;
(b) shares or securities held in the donor's *personal trading company*;
(c) shares or securities of a trading company which are not listed on a recognised stock exchange.

A *personal company* is one in which the donor controls at least 5% of the voting rights and can be either quoted or unquoted.

Note that, unlike the position with respect to taper relief (see above), there is no "employee" test for gift relief.

e.g. Giving you biz to your son

Thus, as gifts between individuals are potentially exempt transfers for inheritance tax (not precipitating an immediate inheritance tax charge) such gifts may qualify for gift relief only if the asset gifted is a business asset.

No gift relief, however, is available on a transfer of shares/securities *to a company* (although transfers of land, for example, to a company would qualify for gift relief).

Effect of Gift Relief

The effect of the application of gift relief pre FA 2008 was that the *indexed gain* (i.e. the gain before taper relief) of the donor is "rolled over" against the deemed cost of the asset to the donee. Post FA 2008 (as the indexation allowance has been abolished), the gain that is "rolled over" is simply the difference between the market value at the date of the gift and original cost.

The term "rolled over" refers to the mechanics of computation. The capital gain arising on the gift is deducted from the market value of the asset gifted at the date of the gift so that "market value less capital gain" is then the base cost for the recipient of the gift. This means that the donor completely avoids a capital gains tax liability which arises on the gift. However, the donee, on a subsequent sale of the asset, effectively becomes liable to capital gains tax on any gain which may have arisen during the donee's ownership period *plus* the gain which was "rolled over".

Gift Relief ctd.

The donee thus pays capital gains tax on the original donor's gain plus the gain arising since acquiring the asset. Nevertheless, a measure of capital gains tax deferral is achieved.

Example 8.17
Neil Bonnet gave his shareholding of unquoted shares in a trading company worth £1 million to his son Mike in July 2008. Neil had originally purchased the shares for £700 000 in March 2005.

Mike sold the shares exactly one year after receiving them (i.e. in July 2009) from his father for £2.75 million.

Neil and Mike elect to claim gift relief on the gift from Neil to Mike.
The consequences are that:

- Neil avoids a capital gains tax charge arising on the gift; and
- Mike is deemed to have acquired the shares for £1 million less £300 000, i.e. £700 000 (i.e. the deemed cost to Mike is the market value of the gift less the gain arising on the gift).

On the subsequent sale by Mike, for £2.75 million, Mike will be liable to capital gains tax on £2.75 million less £700 000, i.e. £2 050 000.

While any "rolled-over" gain is subject to capital gains tax on a subsequent disposal by the transferee this will also be the case if the transferee emigrates within six years of the end of the tax year of acquisition of the gift still owning the asset at the time of emigration (in this case the "rolled-over" gain is deemed to have been precipitated, precipitating a capital gains tax charge on the "rolled-over" gain, even though no actual disposal will have occurred).

However, if the transferee dies not having disposed of the asset, no capital gains tax charge arises on any rolled-over gain (on death no disposal of assets arises; all assets held on death are simply revalued at their market values at that time; see above).

Using the facts from Example 8.17 above, assume that no gift relief is claimed (even though this is possible). The consequence is that the donor (i.e. Neil) precipitates a capital gains tax liability at the date of the gift (see Example 8.2).

Example 8.18
Using the facts from Example 8.17 above, assume Neil and Mike do not claim gift relief on the gift from Neil to Mike.

Neil's chargeable gain on the gift to Mike would thus be £300 000.

On the subsequent sale by Mike his chargeable gain will be £2.75 million less £1 million, i.e. £1.75 million.

Together, Neil and Mike's chargeable gains total £2 050 000.

This aggregate figure is the same as the figure in Example 8.17.

Although the capital gains tax liabilities in Examples 8.17 and 8.18 are the same, no account has been taken of the timing of the liabilities.

Gift Relief is just a timing thing (Also good if value falls)

Capital gains tax is payable on or before 31 January of the tax year following the tax year of the disposal. By not claiming gift relief, the timing of the payment of the liability of the donor (i.e. Neil) is brought forward to 31 January 2010 from 31 January 2011. As gift relief could be claimed it is not possible for Neil to make use of the instalment basis (see above). Timing of the payment of tax liabilities should always be taken into account.

Pre FA 2008, however, the position was different. One possible downside of claiming gift relief was that any taper relief which may have accrued to the donor was lost (i.e. the donee's period of ownership did not include that of the donor as applied to inter-spouse transfers). This meant that the overall capital gains tax position of both donor and donee could have been worse than it would have been if no gift relief had been claimed.

There is in fact no restriction as to how many times capital gains may be "rolled over" by way of gift relief. Thus, for example, a father could give his shares to his son, both claiming gift relief. The son may subsequently gift the same shares to his brother, again both claiming gift relief, etc. It is, of course, important that all the gift relief conditions are satisfied at the dates of the various gifts.

In the event that after a number of such gifts the ultimate donee dies, not having disposed of the shares, all gains of all the parties are simply wiped out as, on death, the shares would be simply revalued at their then market values (death does not give rise to disposals for capital gains tax purposes).

Non-UK Situs Assets

Pre FA 2008 the gift of an overseas situs asset (see Chapter 6) by a non-UK domiciled but UK resident individual did not precipitate a capital gains tax liability. Thus, for example, no capital gains tax liability arose where such an individual transferred a non-UK situs asset into a non-UK resident trust or made a gift of the non-UK situs asset to another individual. The reason why no capital gains tax liability arose was that the remittance basis applied but as no consideration was actually received a remittance of the non-UK situs capital gain was not possible.

Nevertheless, the gift still constituted a disposal and the donee, whether a trust or an individual, was deemed to have acquired the asset at its then market value (i.e. any capital gain on a future disposal by the recipient trust or individual will be calculated using this market value as the base cost).

Gift relief in such circumstances was not necessary.

While this was the position for gifts effected prior to 6 April 2008, for such gifts effected on or after 6 April 2008 a potential capital gains tax charge now arises. This is because the definition of what constitues a "remittance" has been broadened by FA 2008. Thus, should the asset gifted (or any property deriving therefrom) be remitted to the UK at some point in the future then the capital gain arising on the gift will be treated as having been remitted (see Chapter 23).

IMPACT OF FA 2008

Introduction of New 18% Rate; Abolition of Indexation Allowance and Taper Relief

For disposals effected pre 6 April 2008 the rate of capital gains tax (10%, 20% and/or 40%) depended upon the income tax position of the individual. If the individual was, for example, a 40% taxpayer on income then the 40% rate would apply to any capital gains.

Following FA 2008 the rate of capital gains tax is 18% irrespective of the income tax position of the individual. Thus, for a higher rate income tax payer, prima facie, the capital gains tax position on a post 5 April 2008 disposal produces a lower quantum of capital gains tax than a disposal pre 6 April 2008 as the rate is reduced from 40% to 18%.

For a basic rate income tax payer, prima facie, the capital gains tax position on a post 5 April 2008 disposal produces a lower quantum of capital gains tax than a disposal pre 6 April 2008 as the rate is reduced from 20% to 18%.

It would thus appear that all post 5 April 2008 disposals will precipitate lower amounts of capital gains tax.

This, however, is not necessarily the case because the above figures are the nominal rates of capital gains tax and ignore the possible implication of the indexation allowance and taper relief; both of which (applied with respect to disposals pre 6 April 2008) may reduce the nominal rate to an effective rate lower than the new 18% rate.

In other words a pre 6 April 2008 disposal had the advantage of possible claims to both an indexation allowance (if the asset had been purchased on or before 5 April 1998) plus taper relief (for assets owned on 6 April 1998 or acquired later) which might well reduce the rate of capital gains tax to an effective rate lower than the new 18%.

As a consequence, before the introduction of the new 18% rate, it was advisable to ascertain whether a disposal pre 6 April 2008, rather than post this date, should be effected.

As the "effective" rate depended upon the particular facts it was difficult to lay down a simple rule applicable to all situations. It was necessary to take into account not only possible claims to indexation allowance and taper relief but also the income tax position of the individual (as this would dictate the nominal rate of capital gains tax applicable).

In short, there are "winners" and "losers".

The following examines the comparative position for the individual pre and post FA 2008 on different categories of asset and assumes, for comparison purposes, that the new "entrepreneur" relief (under which the rate of capital gains tax is 10%) would not apply to a post FA 2008 disposal (see below).

If this new rate did apply then this might, depending upon the facts, affect the conclusions below (i.e. may make a disposal post FA 2008 more capital gains tax efficient than a pre FA 2008 disposal).

It is to be noted in this regard, however, that assets which qualified as business assets for taper relief may not necessarily qualify for the new entrepreneur relief. A particular example is that of a holding of listed shares by an employee in the employer company which qualified as business assets for taper relief but is unlikely to qualify for the new entrepreneur relief (see below).

Higher Rate Taxpayer

Non-business asset, no indexation allowance but taper relief
For the higher rate (i.e. 40%) income taxpayer the disposal of a non-business asset (i.e. as defined for taper relief purposes) in respect of which no indexation allowance was available the better option is to effect the disposal on or after 6 April 2008.

Even assuming a maximum claim to taper relief of 40% (applicable after a 10 complete year period of ownership) the effective rate of capital gains tax on a pre 6 April 2008 disposal would have been 24% (i.e. 60% of 40%).

For lesser taper relief claims the position for a post 5 April 2008 disposal becomes even stronger.

Non-business asset, indexation allowance and taper relief
Where an indexation allowance could be claimed (because the asset had been purchased pre 5 April 1998) *and* taper relief could also be claimed the conclusions in this case varied.

The original proposal to introduce an 18% rate of capital gains tax was made at the time of the Pre-Budget Report on 9 October 2007. Any non-business (or indeed business) asset held at this date in respect of which an indexation allowance could have been claimed meant that the asset had been held for at least nine complete years for taper relief purposes increasing to 10 complete years with the so-called "bonus" year (i.e. re "non-business" asset assuming asset held on 17 March 1998). This produced a 40% taper relief percentage.

Mathematically, if the difference between the sale proceeds and original cost of the asset was less than four times the indexation allowance then a pre 6 April 2008 disposal would have produced a lower capital gains tax liability; otherwise a post 5 April 2008 is preferable.

Example 8.19

Harry Orange purchased listed shares in ABC Ltd in May 1990 at a cost of £45 000.
Their market value on 5 April 2008 was £155 000.
The shares qualified for non-business asset taper relief, which after 10 years was 40%.
Harry's indexation allowance amounted to £12 960.

Sales price minus original cost = £155 000 − £45 000 = £110 000
Four times the indexation allowance = 4 × £12 960 = £51 840

Thus, the better option would be for Harry to sell *post* 5 April 1998.

Assume therefore Harry sold on 5 April 2008 versus 6 April 2008:

5 April sale:
[[£155 000 − £45 000 − £12 960] × [1 − 0.40]] × 40% = £23 290

6 April sale:
[£155 000 − £45 000] × 0.18 = £19 800

Example 8.20
Using facts as in Example 8.19 above but changing the acquisition date by Harry to March 1982, i.e. Harry Orange purchased listed shares in ABC Ltd in March 1982 at a cost of £45 000, then this will affect the amount of the indexation allowance.

Their market value on 5 April 2008 was £155 000.

The shares qualified for non-business asset taper relief, which after 10 years was 40%.

Harry's indexation allowance amounted to £47 115
Sales price minus original cost = £155 000 − £45 000 = £110 000
Four times the indexation allowance = 4 × £47 115 = £188 460

Thus, better option would be for Harry to have sold *pre* 5 April 1998.
Assume therefore Harry sold on 5 April 2008 versus 6 April 2008:

5 April sale:
[[£155 000 − £45 000 − £47 115] × [1 − 0.40]] × 40% = £15 092

6 April sale:
[£155 000 − £45 000] × 0.18 = £19 800

It is therefore clear that for a higher rate income taxpayer in relation to a non-business asset (for taper relief purposes) the impact of the indexation allowance was extremely important as to the decision whether a pre or post 6 April 2008 disposal should be effected. The greater the indexation allowance, other things being equal, the more likely that a pre 6 April 2008 sale should have been effected (see "Banking the indexation allowance/taper relief" below).

Business asset, no indexation allowance but taper relief
For the higher rate (i.e. 40%) income taxpayer the disposal of a business asset (as defined for taper relief purposes) in respect of which no indexation allowance was available, the better option depended upon the amount of taper relief available (this was not the position for a non-business asset; see above).

Assuming a maximum claim to taper relief of 75% (applicable after a two complete year period of ownership) the effective rate of capital gains tax on a pre 6 April 2008 disposal would have been 10% (i.e. 25% of 40%). This demonstrates that a pre 6 April 2008 disposal (at 10%) should have been effected.

Assuming a claim to taper relief of 50% (applicable after a one-year but less than two-year period of ownership) the effective rate of capital gains tax on a pre 6 April 2008 disposal would have been 20% (i.e. 50% of 40%). This demonstrates that a post 5 April 2008 disposal (at 18%) should have been effected.

Assuming a claim to taper relief of 0% (applicable to an asset held for less than one complete year) the effective rate of capital gains tax on a pre 6 April 2008 disposal would have been 40%. This demonstrates that a post 5 April 2008 disposal (at 18%) should have been effected.

Business asset, indexation allowance and taper relief

The original proposal to introduce an 18% rate of capital gains tax was made at the time of the Pre-Budget Report on 9 October 2007. Any business asset held at this date in respect of which an indexation allowance could have been claimed meant that the asset had been held for at least two complete years for taper relief purposes. This produced a 75% taper relief percentage.

Even without an indexation allowance if taper relief of 75% applied then a pre 6 April 2008 disposal mitigated any capital gains tax liability (see above). Thus, where, in addition, an indexation allowance was available it must necessarily follow that a pre 6 April 2008 disposal will again mitigate any capital gains tax liability.

Example 8.21

Harry Orange purchased listed shares in ABC Ltd in May 1990 at a cost of £45 000.
 Their market value on 5 April 2008 was £155 000.
 The shares qualified for business asset taper relief, which after two years was 75%.
 Harry's indexation allowance amounted to £12,960.
 The better option would be for Harry to have sold *pre* 5 April 1998.
 Assume therefore Harry sold on 5 April 2008 versus 6 April 2008:

5 April sale:

$[[£155\,000 - £45\,000 - £12\,960] \times [1 - 0.75]] \times 40\% = £9704$

6 April sale:

$[£155\,000 - £45\,000] \times 0.18 = £19\,800$

Example 8.22

Using facts as in Example 8.21 above but changing the acquisition date by Harry to March 1982, i.e. Harry Orange purchased listed shares in ABC Ltd in March 1982 at a cost of £45 000, then this will affect the amount of the indexation allowance.
 Their market value on 5 April 2008 was £155 000.
 The shares qualified for business asset taper relief, which after two years was 75%.
 Harry's indexation allowance amounted to £47 115.
 The better option would be for Harry to have sold *pre* 5 April 1998.

Assume therefore Harry sold on 5 April 2008 versus 6 April 2008:

5 April sale:

[[£155 000 − £45 000 − £47 115] × [1 − 0.75]] × 40% = £6289

6 April sale:

[£155 000 − £45 000] × 0.18 = £19 800

As demonstrated above, for the higher rate taxpayer a disposal of a business asset which on or before 5 April 2008 would have qualified for 75% taper relief should have been effected pre 6 April 2008 to mitigate any capital gains tax charge. However, where no indexation allowance was available the amount of taper relief determined the better option.

Three examples of the "winners" and "losers" are considered below.

Employees Owning Shares in the Employer Company

As the 75% taper relief accrued after only a minimum holding period of two years many high rate taxpayers on 5 April 2008 did in fact hold business assets which if not sold pre 6 April 2008 would result in a higher capital gains tax charge on a sale on or thereafter. Thus, for example, the employee who held shares in his/her employer company, whether listed or not (such shares qualifying for taper relief purposes as business assets) for the two-year minimum period as at 5 April 2008, would find that they are worse off if they have held on to their shares for sale post 5 April 2008.

A sale pre 5 April 2008, however, was less capital gains tax efficient if the taper relief was 0% or 50%.

Sole Trader

The above was also the case for the sole trader or partner who decided to sell their business (which qualified as business assets).

Buy to Let *sell after Apr 08*

On the other hand, for the higher rate taxpayer who had, for example, a number of so-called "buy to let" properties (buy to let properties qualifying as non-business assets for taper relief purposes) the effect of the introduction of the 18% rate meant that a sale post 5 April 2008 would decrease their charge to capital gains tax (unless the properties had been acquired pre 5 April 1998 and a significant indexation allowance had accrued).

As a consequence of the perceived inequality in the above (and other) situations a new relief, namely, entrepreneur relief, was introduced in FA 2008 designed in principle to resolve this perceived inequality (see below). However, not all the perceived inequalities have, as a consequence, been removed.

[handwritten at top: Transfer to spouse pre Apr '08]

"Banking" the Indexation Allowance/Taper Relief

The outright abolition of both the indexation allowance and taper relief led to consideration by individuals as to whether a pre or post 6 April 2008 disposal should be effected (as discussed above).

However, in a number of cases a sale of an asset pre 5 April 2008 was not ideally desired (and in some cases was not possible) for various reasons. The issue therefore arose as to whether, even without an outright sale pre 6 April 2008, the indexation allowance and/or the taper relief which may have accrued on the asset could somehow be preserved (given that a disposal on or after 6 April 2008 is not entitled to either the indexation allowance or taper relief).

Such preservation was in principle only possible if a pre 6 April 2008 disposal occurred. While the preservation of accrued taper relief was a little more complex, preservation was possible. In addition, a preservation of accrued indexation allowance could also be effected.

The preservation of accrued indexation involved a simple inter-spouse transfer. Such a transfer results in no gain/no loss to the transferor spouse. In short the transferor spouse is assumed to have transferred the asset to the transferee spouse at original cost plus indexation up to the date of the transfer. This had the effect that the transferee spouse owned an asset with a base cost of original cost plus indexation and thus on a future sale, even after 5 April 2008, the accrued indexation allowance would be implicitly taken into account in calculating any resultant gain.

In effect the "best of both worlds" is achieved. Not only is any accrued indexation not lost but any sale on or after 6 April 2008 is subject to capital gains tax at 18%.

However, any taper relief which had accrued to the transferor spouse at the date of the transfer to the transferee spouse was not, as such, so transferred. While the transferee spouse (for taper relief purposes) is assumed to have acquired the asset at the same time it had been acquired by the transferor spouse (giving rise to deemed taper relief available to the transferee spouse) it would only be available for use as and when the transferee spouse made a disposal (which, if after 5 April 2008, would mean no taper relief due to its abolition).

Example 8.23

Suzanne and Fred Groves are married. Both Fred and Suzanne are higher rate taxpayers.

Fred had inherited some listed shares many years ago on his father's death. Fred's father had died in January 1983 and at that time the shares were worth £35 000.

Fred had held onto the shares, mainly for sentimental reasons and was not particularly disposed to sell them but did appreciate that as at March 2008 accrued indexation amounted to £33 880, a not insignificant sum.

At March 2008 the shares were worth £100 000.

His advisor pointed out to Fred that a sale after 5 April 2008 for £100 000 would precipitate a capital gains tax liability of 18% of [£100 000 − £35 000], i.e. £11 700.

A sale by Fred in March 2008 (i.e. pre 6 April 2008) would precipitate a capital gains tax liability based on an indexation allowance of £33 880 plus taper relief of 40% (the shares were not business assets for taper relief purposes) of

$$40\% \times 60\% \times [£100\,000 - £35\,000 - £33\,880] = £7\,468$$

A third option was for Fred to make an inter-spouse transfer to Suzanne pre 6 April 2008. This would precipitate no capital gains tax charge (as it was inter-spouse) and would mean Suzanne acquired the shares at a base cost of [£35 000 + £33 880], i.e. £68 880.

Assuming Suzanne then sold the shares on or after 6 April 2008 for £100 000 her capital gains tax liability would be

$$18\% \times [£100\,000 - £68\,880] = £5602$$

Had the shares inherited by Fred on his father's death constituted a business asset (e.g. unquoted shares) the position would be a little different.

While, as above, a sale by Fred after 5 April 2008 or an inter-spouse transfer followed by a sale after 5 April 2008 would produce the same figures of £11 700 and £5602, respectively, a sale by Fred pre 6 April 2008 would have produced a capital gains tax liability of [£100 000 − £35 000 − £33 880] × 25% × 40%, i.e. £3112 (the lowest of all the three figures).

The possibility of "banking" the indexation allowance was therefore a serious consideration if the individual did not ideally wish to effect a third party sale pre 6 April 2008. The decision, as illustrated in Example 8.23 above, was not necessarily clear cut and depended in part on whether the asset was a business or non-business asset for taper relief purposes.

While the inter-spouse option would not have preserved any accrued taper relief, a transfer into trust would have enabled such preservation while at the same time also preserving any indexation allowance.

The transfer into trust would be a disposal for capital gains tax purposes and if the trust was "settlor interested" (which would be highly likely) a capital gains tax charge would arise at that time on the individual transferring the asset into trust (i.e. the settlor). Gift relief on the transfer would not be available due to the trust being "settlor interested" (see Chapter 16).

The trust would then effect any future sale with any gain being taxed at the rate of 18% on the part of the trust (the trust could then distribute the proceeds to the beneficiaries).

The overall effect would be that a lower overall capital gains tax charge would arise.

Example 8.24

Bert Scroggins, a higher rate tax payer, had acquired for £50 000 a shareholding of listed shares in VWX Ltd in May 1984. The shares did not qualify as business assets for taper relief purposes.

As at March 2008 Bert's shareholding had accrued an indexation allowance of £41 400 and taper relief of 40%. The value of the shares was £150 000.

A sale by Bert after 5 April 2008 would precipitate a capital gains tax liability of 18% of [£150 000 − £50 000], i.e. £18 000.

If Bert, pre 6 April 2008, settled the shares on trust a capital gains tax liability of 40% × 60% × [£150 000 − £50 000 − £41 400], i.e. £14 604 would have been precipitated.

The trust would have a base cost of the shares of £150 000 and so a subsequent sale at £150 000 would produce a nil capital gains tax liability.

By utilising the trust route the aggregate capital gains tax charge would be £14 604 compared to £18 000 if the trust route was not used.

Thus, utilising the trust produced a capital gains tax saving.

Greater savings would have been possible utilising the trust option if the asset concerned was a business asset with accrued taper relief of 75%.

CAPITAL LOSSES

FA 2008 has modified the position for the non-UK domiciled but UK resident individual on the utilisation of capital losses against capital gains.

The key difference is that following FA 2008, the non-UK domiciled but UK resident individual may now utilise capital losses arising on the disposal of non-UK situs assets (prior to FA 2008, capital losses arising on the disposal of non-UK situs assets by the non-UK domiciled but UK resident individual could not under any circumstances be utilised to offset the capital gains of such individuals).

The changes apply to disposals on or after 6 April 2008 and thus any capital losses on non-UK situs assets which arose prior to this date cannot under any circumstances be utilised under the new rules.

Although the non-UK domiciled but UK resident individual may, post FA 2008, utilise non-UK situs capital losses, the manner in which they may be used is laid down in FA 2008. In addition, the manner in which such individuals may use UK situs asset capital losses (post FA 2008) has been affected.

FA 2008, however, has not changed the position for the UK domiciled and UK resident individual who both pre and post FA 2008 has been, and continues to be, able to utilise capital losses on non-UK situs assets.

UK Domiciled and UK Resident Individual Capital Loss Utilisation

As indicated above, the pre and post FA 2008 position with respect to the utilisation of capital losses has not changed.

Any capital losses which arise in a tax year must be offset against any chargeable gains for that tax year; this is compulsory. As a consequence, this may mean that an individual's annual exemption for that tax year may be lost.

Current tax year capital losses are offset before any capital losses brought forward may be used.

If the amount of capital losses exceeds the amount of chargeable gains for the tax year the excess may be carried forward to future tax years for offset against future chargeable gains. Such capital losses can be carried forward indefinitely. Such an excess cannot, however, be carried back for use in earlier tax years (except for capital losses arising in the tax year of death between the previous 6 April and the date of death).

Any capital losses carried forward are offsettable against any net chargeable gains for the tax year concerned (i.e. available for offset after any capital losses of that tax year have been offset against any chargeable gains of that tax year). However, any such losses brought forward are only offset against the net gains of the tax year so as to reduce the net gains to no less than the annual exemption amount for that tax year (thus preventing the loss of the annual exempt amount unnecessarily for that tax year). Any still unused capital losses may then be carried forward to the next and succeeding tax years until fully utilised.

There is no differentiation between capital losses arising on UK situs assets and those arising on non-UK situs assets. There is therefore no requirement to keep the amounts of each separate.

Example 8.25

Eric Fitch, a UK domiciled and UK resident individual, has made capital gains and capital losses as follows:

	2006/07	2007/08	2008/09
Capital gains (UK situs assets)	20 000	24 000	22 000
Capital losses (UK situs assets)	5000	10 000	7000
Capital gains (non-UK situs assets)	15 000	7000	17 000
Capita losses (non-UK situs assets)	36 000	11 000	13 000
Annual exemptions	8500	9200	9600

2006/07

The utilisable capital losses for 2006/07 are £41 000. These must be offset against the aggregate chargeable gains for the tax year of £35 000 leaving unused capital losses for carry forward of £6000. The annual exemption of £8500 has effectively been wasted.

2007/08

The utilisable capital losses for 2007/08 are £21 000. These must be offset against the aggregate chargeable gains for the tax year of £31 000 leaving net gains of £10 000.

However, there is £6 000 of capital losses brought forward from 2006/07.

Under the rules, however, it is not possible to utilise capital losses brought forward to the extent that the net gains after their use fall below the annual exemption, i.e. if the £6000 of capital losses were offset in full aginst the £10 000 of net gains the resulting figure would be £4000 which is less than the £9200 annual exemption.

Thus, only £800 of the capital losses brought forward may be used leaving net gains of £9200 which are then reduced to nil by the annual exemption

This leaves capital losses available for carry forward of £5200.

2008/09

The utilisable capital losses for 2008/09 are £20 000. These must be offset against the aggregate chargeable gains for the tax year of £39 000 leaving net gains of £19 000.

However, there is £5200 of capital losses brought forward from 2007/08 which reduce the £19 000 net gain figure to £13 800.

The annual exemption of £9600 reduces this figure to a final net chargeable gain figure for 2008/09 of £4200.

(1) Connected Person Capital Losses

Where a capital loss arises on a disposal between connected persons (e.g. disposals between brother and sister; settlor and trust) the loss can only be relieved against any capital gains arising in the same or future tax years on disposals to the same connected person, i.e. any capital loss arising in such circumstances cannot be used in general to offset any other capital gains.

Non-UK Domiciled and UK Resident Individual Capital Loss Utilisation

For the non-UK domiciled but UK resident individual, however, the position pre FA 2008 was different with respect to the usage of capital losses compared to that for the UK domiciled and UK resident individual.

While capital gains arising on the disposal of non-UK situs assets were (and post FA 2008 continue to be) within the charge to capital gains tax if and when such gains were/are remitted to the UK, capital losses arising on such disposals (i.e. disposals of non-UK situs assets) could not be used for offset against any gains (whether arising on UK or non-UK situs assets) of the individual under any circumstances.

In short, capital losses arising on the disposal of non-UK situs assets were completely unusable.

Post FA 2008, however, capital losses whether arising on UK or non-UK situs assets can now be offset against capital gains which arise on UK or non-UK situs assets.

(1) Overseas Capital Loss Utilisation for the Non-UK Domiciled but UK Resident Individual pre FA 2008

Where a non-UK domiciled but UK resident individual owned a non-UK situs asset which if sold would have realised a capital loss, two options were open to the individual.

The simplest solution was for the individual to effect a gift of the asset outside the UK (to avoid any possible income tax remittance issues; see Chapter 23) to the UK domiciled spouse (assuming, of course, the spouse was UK domiciled). As the gift was an inter-spouse gift it was regarded as taking place such that neither gain nor loss arose. The recipient UK domiciled spouse could then effect the sale precipitating a capital loss which such spouse could then use to offset against any current or future chargeable gains of the spouse.

Example 8.26
Henry Blue is married to Frida. Henry is UK domiciled but his wife is Swedish domiciled.

Frida purchased some Swedish quoted shares some years ago for £100 000. The shares are now worth £20 000.

Should Frida sell the shares, the capital loss of £80 000 could not be used by Frida (for example, for offset against any non-UK capital gains she may make).

Frida decides to gift the shares to Henry. The gift is assumed to have taken place at no gain and no loss to Frida, i.e. Henry is assumed to have acquired the shares for £100 000 (the original purchase price paid by Frida).

Henry subsequently sells the shares for £20 000 realising a capital loss of £80 000 which he can use to offset against any capital gains he may make in the same tax year (or he can carry any surplus unused part of the loss forward to future tax years).

Pre FA 08

Alternatively, the asset's situs might have been capable of importation by the non-UK domiciled individual into the UK, if possible, prior to sale (although this may give rise to remittance problems for income tax purposes; see Chapter 23). The asset could then be sold and it would then have been the sale of a UK situs asset and thus any capital loss arising (even if to a non-UK domiciled individual) would have been available for offset against the individual's capital gains of the same and future tax years.

Example 8.27
Agneta Schmidt, a non-UK domiciled but UK resident individual, bought an item of jewellery for £75 000 at an auction in Switzerland. She has kept the jewellery at her villa in Switzerland.

She has discovered that the jewellery is in fact now only worth £55 000 and so she decides to sell it.

In order for the capital loss to be utilised against any of her capital gains, the situs of the asset must be UK. She accordingly brings the jewellery into the UK and then sells it producing a capital loss of £20 000 which she can then utilise.

Pre FA '08

Which of the above two basic courses of action should have been taken would, of course, have depended upon the surrounding facts at the relevant time.

(2) Overseas Capital Loss Utilisation for the Non-UK Domiciled but UK Resident Individual post FA 2008

Whilst for the non-UK domiciled but UK resident individual the two options just discussed are still viable (post FA 2008), capital losses arising on the disposal of non-UK situs assets (now referred to as "foreign capital losses") on or after 6 April 2008 can now be used to offset such individual's capital gains.

For the non-UK domiciled but UK resident individual who is not required to claim the remittance basis (but who can still use this basis; see Chapter 23 categories (a), (b) and (c)) or where a claim needs to be made but is not made (i.e. the arising and not remittance basis then applies) capital losses on non-UK situs assets may be automatically offset against the chargeable gains in the same manner as applies to the UK domiciled and resident individual. As categories (b) and (c) comprise non-UK domiciled but UK resident individuals who have no UK source income or capital gains and who have not remitted any non-UK source capital gains, any capital losses arising on non-UK situs assets will thus automatically be offset against any non-UK situs unremitted capital gains.

For such individuals falling within category (a) (which requires unremitted income/gains of less than £2000) capital losses arising on non-UK situs assets will effectively be offsettable against remitted capital gains (and any UK source asset capital gains).

Example 8.28

Lorida Melbourne, a non-UK domiciled but UK resident individual, remitted £10 000 (i.e. all) of her non-UK situs capital gains for 2008/09 to the UK. She has also made non-UK situs capital losses of £17 000 in 2008/09.

Her UK situs asset capital gains are £11 000.

She has not remitted £1750 of interest which has arisen on her Isle of Man bank account in 2008/09.

Lorida will fall into category (a) and thus the remittance basis will apply automatically for 2008/09.

She is able to offset her capital losses on the same basis as a UK domiciled individual.

Thus, £17 000 of capital losses may be offset against the £21 000 of capital gains.

For those individuals falling within categories (a), (b) and (c) above the annual capital gains tax exemption is available to use against net capital gains for a tax year.

Where, however, the remittance basis needs to be claimed by the non-UK domiciled but UK resident individual (i.e. where the remittance basis does not apply automatically; see Chapter 23 categories (1), (2) and (3)) and is so claimed the rules are more complex.

In such cases the new rules do not simply allow aggregate capital losses, whether arising on the disposal of non-UK or UK situs assets, to be offset against aggregate capital gains, whether arising on non-UK or UK situs assets. Any capital losses arising on non-UK situs assets pre FA 2008 cannot in any event be used.

Consider first the position pre FA 2008.

Example 8.29

Heinz Berlin is a non-UK domiciled but UK resident individual who in the tax year 2007/08 had the following chargeable gains and capital losses:

UK situs asset capital gains	£25 000
UK situs asset capital losses	£5000
Non-UK situs asset capital losses	£20 000
Non-UK situs asset capital gains	£12 000 (unremitted)

Heinz is able to offset the £5000 capital losses against his £25 000 capital gains producing net capital gains of £20 000.

The £20 000 capital losses are simply not available for use.

The £12 000 capital gains are subject to tax only when remitted to the UK.

The first tax year in respect of which a claim to the remittance basis is made requires the individual to also make an election if the individual is to be able to offset non-UK situs capital losses arising post FA 2008. A failure to make the election precludes the individual utilising any post 5 April 2008 non-UK situs capital losses forever. It is therefore of crucial importance that active consideration be given to the need for an election as soon as possible.

The election referred to above is irrevocable and thus once made cannot be revoked at any time. It is a "one-off" lifetime election.

For many non-UK domiciled individuals the first tax year in respect of which a claim for remittance basis treatment is likely to be made is the tax year 2008/09 (i.e. the first tax year that the provisions of FA 2008 apply). This may, however, not apply in every case. For example, in the tax year 2008/09 the individual may not have any or only de minimis non-UK situs income and/or capital gains and thus a claim to the remittance basis may not be worthwhile (this is particularly so where the £30 000 may be potentially payable). In such cases the election could be made in a later tax year (i.e. in the tax year when the remittance basis is claimed).

Once the individual makes the election the following ordering rules also apply for all future tax years including those where the individual for a particular tax year is automatically entitled to remittance basis treatment (i.e. the individual satisfies (a), (b) or (c) above).

The provisions of FA 2008 lay down the order in which utilisable capital losses *must* be offset; in other words the order laid down is mandatory and the individual does not have complete freedom on the manner of utilisation of the capital losses.

"Utilisable capital losses" refers not only to foreign capital losses but also capital losses arising on disposals of UK situs assets and may include capital losses brought forward from prior tax years. The capital losses which may be carried forward (on or after 6 April 2008) are pre 6 April 2008 unutilised capital losses arising on UK situs asset disposals; plus unutilised foreign capital losses arising on or after 6 April 2008; plus unutilised capital losses arising on or after 6 April 2008 on disposals of UK situs assets. In effect, therefore, a "pool" of carry forward capital losses may arise in which there is no distinction between foreign capital losses and capital losses arising on disposals of UK situs assets.

Capital losses of the tax year (i.e. capital losses arising on UK situs assets and foreign capital losses) in which capital gains also arise are to be offset against such capital gains before any capital losses brought forward from prior tax years may be utilised. This merely continues the principle of capital offset which applied pre FA 2008.

The mandatory order of utilisable capital losses for the tax year is as follows:

(a) the losses are offset against gains arising from non-UK situs asset disposals which are remitted to the UK in the same tax year in which the disposals occur;
(b) any surplus of losses still remaining must be offset against gains arising on the disposals of non-UK situs assets arising in the tax year but not remitted to the UK;
(c) and again to the extent that a surplus of losses still remains, such surplus must be offset against any other chargeable gains arising in that tax year (other than gains arising on non-UK situs assets arising in earlier tax years but then subsequently remitted in the tax year concerned; section 87 gains (i.e. those gains apportioned to UK resident but non-UK domiciled individuals from non-UK resident trusts) are also unavailable to be offset by utilisable capital losses); basically gains arising from UK situs asset disposals.

Where capital gains arising from the disposal of non-UK situs assets are not remitted until a later tax year, following the tax year of disposal, such remitted gains in that tax year of remittance are not eligible for reduction by any utilisable capital losses. It may be, however, that such gains were reduced in the tax year of the disposal by an offset of utilisable capital losses available for that tax year (i.e. it is in effect a net gain which is subject to capital gains tax in the tax year of remittance).

Example 8.30

Mate Sydney is a non-UK domiciled but UK resident individual.

He made an election in 2008/09 re non-UK situs capital losses as he is claiming remittance basis treatment for the tax year.

In the tax year 2009/10 he had the following chargeable gains and capital losses:

UK situs asset capital gains	£5000
UK situs asset capital losses	£15 000

Non-UK situs asset capital gains of £12 000 which arose in the tax year 2008/09 were remitted to the UK in 2009/10.

The non-UK situs asset capital gains of £12 000 arising in the tax year 2008/09 but remitted and subject to capital gains tax in the tax year of remittance, i.e. 2009/10, cannot be reduced by the surplus unused capital losses of £10 000 (i.e. £15 000 less £5000) arising in the tax year 2009/10.

Thus, only capital gains arising in a particular tax year can be reduced by the offset of capital losses which are available for offset in that tax year (which may include capital losses from previous tax years brought forward).

Capital Gains Tax

It is also to be noted that non-UK domiciled individuals covered by these rules (i.e. those non-UK domiciled individuals who are UK resident and who have claimed remittance basis treatment) are denied the annual exemption (£9600 for tax year 2008/09) or indeed any form of personal allowance (for income tax purposes).

Once capital losses on UK situs assets for the tax year and foreign capital losses arising in the tax year have been offset as above, utilisable capital losses brought forward may then be used to the extent that there are still capital gains against which these losses may be offset.

Example 8.31

This example is Example 8.29 above but the tax year 2007/08 is changed to 2008/09.

Heinz Berlin is a non-UK domiciled but UK resident individual who in the tax year 2008/09 had the following chargeable gains and capital losses:

UK situs asset capital gains	£25 000
UK situs asset capital losses	£5000
Non-UK situs asset capital losses	£20 000
Non-UK situs asset capital gains	£12 000 (unremitted)

Heinz has £25 000 of capital losses available for utilisation (this compares to a figure of £5 000 for 2007/08 in Example 8.29).

First, these capital losses must be offset gainst any non-UK situs capital gains arising in 2008/09 and remitted to the UK. In this case there are no such capital gains.

Second, these capital losses must be offset gainst any non-UK situs capital gains arising in 2008/09 and not remitted to the UK, i.e. £12 000. Thus, the £25 000 reduces the £12 000 to nil leaving capital losses of £13 000.

The £13 000 of capital losses can now be used to reduce the capital gains arising from the UK situs assets (i.e. £25 000) to £12 000.

No further reduction is available as Heinz is not entitled to the annual exemption.

Comparing Examples 8.29 and 8.31 shows quite different capital gains tax consequences for Heinz.

Example 8.32

Benito Italy, a non-UK domiciled but UK resident individual, had the following capital gains and capital losses. Any gains remitted were remitted in the same tax year as the gains arose. Appropriate claims and election were lodged.

Tax years:	2008/09	2009/10	2010/11
Capital gains (UK assets)	(1) 10 000	4000	15 000
Capital losses (UK assets)	(2) 7000	15, 000	15 000
Capital gains (non-UK assets) unremitted	(3) 25 000	nil	9000
Capital gains (non-UK assets) remitted	(4) 5000	10 000	7000
Capital losses (non-UK assets)	(5) 9000	8000	6000

(Continued)

Offset as follows:

	2008/09	2009/10	2010/11
Capital loss pool	16 000	23 000	[21 000 & 9000]
Offset against (4)	(5000)	(10 000)	(7000)
Offset against (3)	(11 000)	nil	(9000)
Offset against (1)	nil	(4000)	(5000)
Capital loss pool c/f	nil	9000	9000

Net taxable position:

Tax years:	2008/09	2009/10	2010/11
Capital gains (UK assets)	(1) 10 000	nil	1000
Capital gains (non-UK assets) unremitted	(3) 14 000	nil	nil
Capital gains (non-UK assets) remitted	(4) nil	nil	nil
Taxable capital gains	10 000	nil	1000
Potentially taxable when remitted	14 000	nil	nil

Note: For the tax year 2008/09 the aggregate capital losses are £16 000 and the aggregate chargeable gains are £15 000 (£10 000 plus £5 000). Nevertheless, a capital gains tax charge still arises for this tax year as some £11 000 of the capital losses were absorbed by unremitted non-UK asset capital gains leaving none of the capital losses available to reduce the UK asset capital gains of £10 000.

Where eligible capital losses have been offset as set out above then the gains against which the losses have been offset are correspondingly reduced. Thus, inter alia, the offset of utilisable capital losses against non-UK source gains which are not remitted in the tax year in which the disposal is made still effects a reduction in those gains and it is thus the net gains which, if remitted in a future tax year, are then subject to capital gains tax (albeit that no capital losses can be offset against such remitted capital gains in the tax year of remittance).

In the case of the utilisation of capital losses against capital gains which have arisen in the tax year on the disposal of non-UK situs assets but have not been remitted to the UK in that tax year (i.e. (b) above) and where such losses are insufficient in amount to reduce such gains to zero FA 2008 lays down the ordering of such offset. The order of offset is as follows:

First, capital losses are offset against the gains on the non-UK situs assets in the order in which the gains accrued but offsetting the losses against the later accrued gains first (effectively, a LIFO basis);

Second, to the extent that certain gains accrued on the same day, the losses are pro-rated against each gain.

Perhaps surprisingly FA 2008, while now permitting the utilisation of foreign capital losses for non-UK domiciled but UK resident individuals, no attempt has been made to segregate foreign capital losses from UK situs capital losses for the purpose of utilisation. As indicated above, a simple pool of all capital losses is created.

Not surprisingly, FA 2008 does require the pool of losses to be utilised against non-UK situs capital gains (remitted and then unremitted) in the first instance. Thus, no offset against UK situs capital gains is possible unless the pool of losses is sufficiently large to absorb in the tax year the quantum of non-UK situs asset capital gains arising in that tax year whether such gains are remitted or not. Where the quantum of the capital loss pool arising from capital losses of the tax year is insufficient it may still, however, be possible for an offset against UK situs capital gains if, for example, there are sufficient capital losses that have been brought forward from prior tax years.

It can thus be seen that whereas pre FA 2008 capital losses arising on UK situs asset disposals were immediately offsettable against gains arising on UK situs asset disposals, post FA 2008 this is not the case. Until such losses (aggregated with any non-UK situs losses of the same tax year plus any losses brought forward) have been offset against non-UK situs asset gains first they cannot be offset against the UK situs asset gains.

A touch of "swings and roundabouts" it seems.

Example 8.33

Norris Manilla, a non-UK domiciled but UK resident individual, anticipated making the same quantum of capital gains and capital losses for the tax year 2008/09 as he had in the prior tax year 2007/08. He assumed that because of the FA 2008 changes under which non-UK asset capital losses could be used to offset capital gains that his net capital gains (after capital loss offset) would be less for the tax year 2008/09 and thus his capital gains tax liability would be smaller.

He does not remit the capital gains arising on non-UK assets.
His capital gains and capital losses were:

Tax year:	2007/08	2008/09
Capital gains (UK assets)	35 000	35 000
Capital losses (UK assets)	5 000	5 000
Capital gains (non-UK assets)	17 000	17 000
Capital losses (non-UK assets)	10 000	10 000
Net taxable capital gains	30 000	30 000

Although the capital losses of £10 000 on the non-UK assets for tax year 2008/09 are usable (whereas this was not the case for tax year 2007/08) they are first offset against the capital gains of £17 000 arising on the non-UK assets thus not impacting on Norris's capital gains tax liability for 2008/09.

If Norris remitted the capital gains arising on the non-UK situs assets each tax year then the position would be:

	2007/08	2008/09
Net chargeable gains	47 000	37 000

Assuming these were Norris's only capital gains, the £47 000 2007/08 figure would be reduced by the then annual exemption of £9 200 giving a net figure of £37 800.

For 2008/09 the figure of £37 000 remains as Norris is not entitled to the annual exemption for 2008/09.

The provisions of FA 2008 have improved the capital gains tax position of the non-UK domiciled but UK resident individual albeit at the cost of some complexity. huh!

It does, however, mean that the remittance of foreign capital gains to the UK is reduced to the extent that foreign capital losses are available for offset. Indeed, with appropriate planning it is possible to make use of foreign capital losses to reduce foreign capital gains yet only remit from the sale proceeds of assets in respect of which capital losses arose (see "Segregation of income and capital gains" in Chapter 23).

See Chapter 6 for a discussion on the capital gains implications of non-UK source foreign currency bank accounts which post FA 2008 is now more favourable.

Entrepreneur Relief

This new relief in principle applies to gains arising on disposals of businesses on or after 6 April 2008. It also extends to certain disposals effected before this date (see below).

Entrepreneur relief is available to individuals, trusts and personal representatives.

In principle it is designed to replace business asset taper relief but in many ways it is modelled on the former relief referred to as retirement relief (which was phased out between 1998 and 2003). However, unlike the former retirement relief, where the individual concerned needed to be at least 50 years old, there is no age requirement for entrepreneur relief.

Entrepreneur relief provides relief from capital gains tax in respect of "qualifying business disposals".

Qualifying business disposals comprise material disposals made by an individual which comprise:

(a) a disposal of the whole or part of a business;
(b) a disposal of one or more assets in use for the purposes of the business at the time at which the business ceases to be carried on;
(c) a disposal of one or more assets consisting of shares or securities of a company;
(d) a disposal qualifying as an "associated" disposal.

However, the conditions attached to each of the above categories are different (see below).

Disposal of the Whole or Part of a Business

The business disposed of must have been owned by the individual throughout the period of one year ending with the date of the disposal.

Disposal of One or More Assets in Use for the Purposes of the Business at the Time at Which the Business Ceases to be Carried on

The business must have been owned by the individual throughout the period of one year ending on the date on which the business ceases to be carried on and that date (i.e. the date of cessation) must be within three years of the date of the asset disposals.

Disposal of One or More Assets Consisting of Shares or Securities of a Company

Throughout the period of one year ending with the date of disposal of the shares or securities the following conditions must have been satisfied:

- the company concerned must have been a trading company;
- the individual must have owned at least 5% of the ordinary share capital and 5% of the voting rights;
- the individual must have been an officer or employee of the company.

Alternatively, all of the above conditions are satisfied throughout the period of one year ending with the date on which the company ceases to be a trading company and that date (i.e. the date the company ceases to be a trading company) is within the period of three years ending with the date of the disposal.

The term "trading company" referred to above does not include a letting business other than furnished holiday lettings.

Disposal Qualifying as an "Associated" Disposal

An "associated" disposal does not stand alone but is reliant on an attachment to one of the above three categories of material disposal.

Three conditions need to be satisfied. The first is that a material disposal of business assets is made by the individual which consists of either the disposal of the whole or part of the individual's interest in the assets of the partnership or is the disposal of shares or securities of a company.

The second is that the disposal by the individual is made as part of the individual's withdrawal from participation in the business carried on by the partnership or by the company.

The third is that throughout the period of one year ending with the earlier of the date of disposal of the material disposal of business assets and the cessation of the business of the partnership or the company the assets disposed of are in use for the purposes of the business.

It is the individual's withdrawal from participation in the business carried on by the partnership or by the company (the second condition above) which constitutes the disposal associated with a relevant material disposal.

Relevant Business Assets

Not all business assets necessarily qualify for entrepreneur relief.

Where the qualifying disposal does not consist of a disposal of shares or securities in a company (i.e. the disposal must fall within (a), (b) or (d) above) entrepreneur relief only applies to disposals of relevant business assets (including goodwill) which are:

- assets used for the purposes of a business carried on by the individual or a partnership of which the individual is a member (for (a) and (b) above);
- assets used for the purposes of a business carried on by the partnership or company (for (d) above).

However, assets that do not qualify (i.e. excluded assets) are shares and securities and any other assets that are held as investments.

As the above only applies where the qualifying disposal does not consist of a disposal of shares or securities in a company there is no need to distinguish assets owned within the company on a sale of shares or securities in a company.

Claim for, and Amount of, Relief

Unlike the position with respect to business asset taper relief and the former retirement relief where no formal claim to these reliefs was necessary entrepreneur relief does need to be formally claimed.

The claim must be made by the individual on or before the first anniversary of the 31 January following the tax year in which the qualifying disposal was made (broadly, 22 months after the end of the relevant tax year).

A claim may only be made, however, where the result of the qualifying disposal is a "net gain" (see below).

The "net gain" is the amount of capital gains arising on the disposals of any relevant business assets (see above) less any capital losses arising thereon.

The net gain figure is then reduced by 4/9ths giving rise to a net amount of 5/9ths of the net gain which is then subject to 18% (i.e. an effective rate of 5/9ths of 18%, namely, 10%).

However, account also needs to be taken of the possible restriction of the lifetime allowance of £1 million (see above). If the net gain figure arising from a qualifying disposal in a tax year when added to the aggregate net gains from earlier qualifying disposals exceeds £1 million, only that amount of net gain which causes the aggregate of net gains to fall within the £1 million qualifies for entrepreneur relief. The excess is subject to capital gains tax at the normal 18% rate.

The £1 million lifetime allowance refers to aggregate net gains which refer to the amounts before the 4/9ths reduction is applied.

Where on a qualifying disposal the net figure is a net loss, no claim to entrepreneur relief on such a disposal can be made. It thus follows that such a net loss cannot be utilised to reduce the aggregate of net gains arising on previously made qualifying disposals thus reducing the amount of utilised lifetime allowance. Any gain or loss taken into account in arriving at a net gain figure on a qualifying disposal is not treated as a chargeable gain or an allowable loss for capital gains tax purposes.

In the case of a disposal associated with a relevant material disposal (but only in such cases) special provisions exist. These provisions provide that only a proportion of any gain or loss may be eligible for inclusion in the calculation of the net gain/loss figure.

The extent of such inclusion depends upon, inter alia, whether the asset disposed of was in use for the purposes of the business throughout the period of ownership by the individual; whether the whole or only a part of the asset was used in the business; whether the individual is concerned in carrying on the business for only a part of the period during which the asset is used for the purposes of the business; and/or whether any rent was paid by the business for their use.

The balance of any amount which does not fall to be eligible for entrepreneur relief is, however, treated as a chargeable gain (and thus subject to 18% without any entrepreneur relief) for capital gains tax purposes (thus, for example, other capital losses of the individual brought forward may be offset against such gains).

Although entrepreneur relief applies to disposals on or after 6 April 2008, as indicated above, certain pre 6 April 2008 disposals may still qualify for the relief.

For example, an individual may have sold shares in a company in exchange for shares in an acquiring company or a mixture of cash and loan notes. Where such transactions occurred it may be that the capital gain on the transaction is not deemed to arise until the new shares acquired are sold or the loan notes are redeemed. If the sale or redemption takes place on or after 6 April 2008 the original gain (in whole or in part) is attributable to the post 6 April 2008 disposal. If the individual at the time of the original pre 6 April 2008 disposal would have been entitled to entrepreneur relief (i.e. at that time would have satisfied the relevant conditions on the assumption entrepreneur relief was in point on that date) then such relief will be available to reduce the extent of any capital gains deemed to have arisen post 6 April 2008. Thus, advantage of the 10% effective rate can be taken.

It needs to be noted, however, that the post 6 April 2008 deemed gain does utilise a part of the £1 million lifetime allowance.

OFFSHORE COMPANIES

Capital gains tax is inapplicable to companies whether UK resident or not. UK resident companies are subject to corporation tax on their profits as are non-UK resident companies who carry on a trade within the UK. Non-UK resident companies not carrying on a trade within the UK are subject to income tax on UK source income albeit at the basic rate only.

However, in the case of non-UK resident companies any capital gains which are made by such companies may fall subject to capital gains tax on the part of the companies' shareholders. This applies if the company (were it to in fact be UK resident) would qualify as a close company. A close company is broadly defined as a company which is under the control (basically, more than 50% of the voting power of the company) of five or fewer shareholders.

Thus, where the non-UK resident company would be a close company if it was UK resident its capital gains are apportioned to its shareholders in proportion to their shareholdings. The shareholders are then liable to capital gains tax on the apportioned capital gains. A shareholder must own more than 10% of the company to be subject to an apportionment (i.e. a 10% or less shareholding cannot result in an apportionment).

Pre FA 2008, the shareholders subject to an apportionment are those shareholders who are UK domiciled and UK resident individuals or UK resident trusts (see below for position re non-UK resident trusts).

The apportionment to UK domiciled and UK resident individual shareholders precipitates a capital gains tax charge on their part as does the apportionment to UK resident trusts.

As indicated above pre FA 2008 an apportionment could not be made to non-UK domiciled but UK resident individual shareholders. However, with respect to capital gains made on or after 6 April 2008 apportionments can now be made on such individuals. Nevertheless, in such cases the remittance basis is in point unless the capital gains arise on the disposal of UK situs assets of the company; in this latter case the remittance basis will not apply and a capital gains tax charge will arise on such individuals in the same manner as applies to UK domiciled individuals. Where the remittance basis applies the individual will be subject to capital gains tax should the company, for example, remit the sale proceeds to the UK (the company qualifying as a "relevant person").

The apportionment process applies to capital gains arising on disposals on an asset by asset basis as opposed to simply apportioning the aggregate capital gains of the company over its accounting period/tax year. Thus, whoever the shareholders are at the time the company makes a capital gain are then subject to the apportionment.

Any such apportioned capital gains may be offset by the shareholder's own capital losses subject to below.

Where the company makes a capital loss on an asset disposal such loss is apportionable to the shareholders at that time although its utilisation by the shareholders is restricted. The capital loss apportioned to the shareholder may only be utilised against capital gains apportioned to the shareholder in the same tax year whether from the company making the capital loss or other companies in which the shareholder is also a shareholder and which would also be close companies if UK resident. Such apportioned capital losses must be offset against apportioned capital gains before the shareholder's own capital losses may then be offset against any remaining surplus capital gains so apportioned. However, a surplus of apportioned capital losses cannot be utilised and are thus simply lost.

Post FA 2008, where non-UK domiciled but UK resident individuals are now also subject to the apportionment process, capital losses of the company which are apportioned to such individuals can only be offset against apportioned capital gains remitted in the tax year in which the capital gains are made by the company. Thus, apportioned capital gains remitted in tax years after the capital gain is made cannot be offset by any capital losses (apportioned or otherwise).

Non-UK resident trust shareholders in non-UK resident companies are also subject to apportionment as indicated above although no capital gains tax charge arises as the trusts are non-UK resident. Nevertheless, the apportioned capital gains do fall within the potential charges under sections 86 and/or 87 TCGA 1992 (see Chapter 17). The above rules relating to capital losses for the individual also apply to trustees.

Broadly, the capital gains of the non-UK resident company apportioned to its non-UK resident trust shareholder may be subject to capital gains tax on the UK domiciled and UK resident settlor of the trust under section 86 or on UK domiciled and UK resident beneficiaries who receive capital payments from the trust.

Post FA 2008 such apportioned capital gains may also be subject to capital gains tax on non-UK domiciled but UK resident individuals who receive capital payments in the UK under section 87 (section 86 is inapplicable to non-UK domiciled individuals).

The above discussion with respect to capital gains made by non-UK resident companies also applies to offshore income gains made by such companies.

LEAVING/ARRIVING IN THE UK

An individual is liable to capital gains tax in a tax year if such individual is either resident *or* ordinarily resident in the tax year concerned.

It is thus in principle possible for an individual to leave the UK, become neither resident nor ordinarily resident and sell any assets owned without precipitating a capital gains tax liability followed by a return to the UK. The absence from the UK need only extend to one complete tax year if the absence involves working outside the UK full time under a contract of employment which spans at least one complete tax year (see Chapter 4). This is because by concession such individual would be regarded as neither resident nor ordinarily resident from the day following departure to the day prior to return to the UK.

Alternatively, absence from the UK for at least three years for whatever reason (work or otherwise) would also result in the acquisition of non-UK residency and ordinary residency.

However, effective 18 March 1998, the rules were amended pursuant to which the length of time during which an individual had to become neither resident nor ordinarily resident to avoid a capital gains tax charge on sales of assets owned prior to departure was increased (basically, to five complete tax years).

Under the new rule, if an individual has been resident in the UK or ordinarily resident therein for at least four tax years out of the immediately preceding seven tax years prior to the tax year of departure the individual is required to become and remain non-UK resident for at least five full tax years after the tax year of departure if a capital gains tax charge is to be avoided on the disposal of assets held prior to the date of departure. In this case, any capital gain then arising on a disposal of assets within this five tax year period (of assets held prior to departing the UK) can be effected without a capital gains tax charge. Assets acquired and sold during the five tax year absence are not subject to capital gains tax; thus neither gains nor losses are chargeable/allowable.

FA 2008 has also introduced provisions affecting the non-UK domiciled but UK resident individual in this regard.

Under FA 2008 provisions where such an individual makes a disposal of a non-UK situs asset owned prior to departure and the proceeds are remitted to the UK during a less than five tax year period of absence such remittances will be deemed to have been made in the tax year of return and thus subject to capital gains tax in that tax year. Prior to FA 2008 such remittances would not have fallen subject to capital gains tax.

SUMMARY

The rate of capital gains tax following FA 2008 is 18% and is no longer linked to the rate of income tax payable by the individual. If the relevant conditions are satisfied the 18% rate may be reduced to an effective 10% under the newly introduced entrepreneur relief.

The new rules apply to disposals effected on or after 6 April 2008 irrespective of when the asset was acquired.

As a consequence of the above changes some individuals are "worse off" post FA 2008 whereas others are "better off".

Notable changes are the abolition of the indexation allowance and taper relief; the former which applied to assets owned prior to 6 April 1998 and the latter which applied to assets owned on or after 6 April 2008.

For non-UK domiciled individuals one of the changes introduced which is in principle favourable is the ability to utilise non-UK capital losses against chargeable gains; this was not possible pre FA 2008. Only capital losses arising on or after 6 April 2008 will be potentially offsettable.

On the other hand, the change under which gifts of non-UK situs assets may precipitate chargeable gains capable of remittance is less favourable for non-UK domiciled individuals.

Certain non-UK domiciled but UK resident individuals are denied the annual exemption (£9600 for the tax year 2008/09).

Furthermore, non-UK domiciled but UK resident individuals who leave the UK temporarily are now "caught" under an extension to the anti-avoidance provision which pre FA 2008 primarily only impacted on UK domiciled individuals.

9
Inheritance Tax: The Basics

Major changes to the inheritance tax treatment of trusts were made in FA 2006. These changes affected not only trusts created on or after 22 March 2006 but also trusts set up before that date. Transitional provisions were also introduced allowing steps to be taken, generally on or before 5 April 2008 (now post FA 2008 extended to 5 October 2008), with respect to trusts set up prior to the 22 March 2006.

This chapter concentrates on the post 22 March 2006 position. Where appropriate, reference will be made to the pre 22 March 2006 position.

Chapter 15 looks at trusts in more detail.

BACKGROUND

Inheritance tax is levied on lifetime *gifts* made by *individuals* and it is also levied on an individual's estate on death.

Thus, any *sales* made by an individual of assets owned for their fair market value cannot give rise to an inheritance tax liability as there is no gift element involved (i.e. there is no gratuitous intent or element of bounty).

Trustees are brought within the scope of the tax and participators (basically shareholders) in *close companies* are also within the ambit of the tax.

Certain transactions are *deemed* to be gifts and are thus also brought within the charge.

However, as will be seen in this chapter, not all gifts are subject to inheritance tax (e.g. some are exempt) and even where a charge in principle arises the rate applicable may be the 0% (nil) rate producing a nil amount of the tax to be paid.

Inheritance tax replaced capital transfer tax for events occurring after 17 March 1986. Technically, the change of name only occurred from 25 July 1986 when the Finance Act 1986 (which introduced inheritance tax) received the Royal Assent.

Most of the capital transfer tax legislation was retained and the Capital Transfer Tax Act 1984 was renamed the Inheritance Tax Act 1984.

On the introduction of inheritance tax opportunity was taken to make some changes of principle to those which had applied with respect to capital transfer tax. For example, the so-called gifts with reservation provisions (previously contained in the estate duty provisions) were reintroduced; inheritance tax would not be charged on transfers of value (basically gifts) made seven years or more before death; and the cumulation period applicable to chargeable transfers (transfers which are chargeable as opposed to exempt) was reduced from ten to seven years.

It is to be appreciated that while a gift may be subject to inheritance tax this does not preclude a capital gains tax charge also arising on the same gift (see Chapter 8).

[margin note: Stung twice]

TERRITORIAL

Domicile

Inheritance tax is levied on the worldwide assets of an individual who is UK domiciled. An individual's domicile status is, very broadly, the country which the individual regards as "home" (see Chapter 3).

Thus, an individual who regards the UK as "home" will, generally speaking, be UK domiciled.

A non-UK domiciled individual (i.e. someone who does not regard the UK as "home") is subject to inheritance tax only on UK situs assets. All non-UK situs assets of such an individual are thus completely outside the scope of inheritance tax and constitute "excluded property" (see Chapter 12).

An individual's domicile status, while of crucial importance in ascertaining an individual's exposure to inheritance tax (and indeed income and capital gains tax), is nevertheless not determined by tax legislation. Such status is determined according to common law (see Chapter 3).

However, the inheritance tax legislation has introduced the concept of the "deemed UK" domiciled individual which has application only for inheritance tax purposes.

Deemed UK Domicile

An individual who is non-UK domiciled at common law (i.e. as determined by the common law rules applicable to domicile) may nevertheless be categorised as "deemed UK" domiciled for inheritance tax purposes. This would apply to such an individual who had resided in the UK for at least 17 out of the last 20 tax years (see Chapter 3).

A UK domiciled individual (determined under common law) who acquires a non-UK domicile of choice is also "deemed UK" domiciled for three more years for inheritance tax purposes.

An individual who is deemed UK domiciled for inheritance tax purposes (but non-UK domiciled under common law) is treated in the same manner as an individual who is UK domiciled under common law; thus, inheritance tax will apply to the worldwide assets of such individual subject to certain exceptions.

The "deemed UK" domiciled rule does not, however, apply in the following situations:

- certain UK gilts are excluded property if owned beneficially by an individual who is non-UK domiciled under common law even if such individual is deemed UK domiciled under the inheritance tax legislation;

- certain UK savings are excluded property if held beneficially by an individual domiciled in the Channel Islands or the Isle of Man even if such individual is deemed UK domiciled.

RATES OF INHERITANCE TAX

The rates of inheritance tax are fixed for a tax year (i.e. 6 April to following 5 April).

For the tax year 2008/09 the rates of inheritance tax applicable to transfers on *death* (i.e. the death estate) are 0% for the first £312 000 of chargeable transfers and 40% on the excess amount over this figure.

The rates applicable on *lifetime* chargeable transfers are one half of those applicable on death, i.e. 0% up to £312 000 and 20% on the excess amount over this figure.

The £312 000 amount is referred to as the nil rate band (NRB). The NRB varies each tax year. For the tax years 2009/10 and 2010/11 the NRBs will be £325 000 and £350 000, respectively (for the tax years 2006/07 and 2007/08 the NRBs were £285 000 and £300 000, respectively).

Any lifetime gifts which fall within the NRB are chargeable albeit at the nil (i.e. 0%) rate thus in fact producing no actual liability. Similarly, on death the first portion of the death estate may fall within the NRB thus being chargeable at the nil (i.e. 0%) rate but producing no actual liability.

Example 9.1
Bernard Coke dies with a death estate valued at £512 000.
He had made no lifetime gifts.
The inheritance tax liability will be:

$$0\% \times £312\,000 + 40\% \times [£512\,000 - £312\,000] = £80\,000$$

Example 9.2
Henry Coke makes a chargeable lifetime transfer of £512 000.
The inheritance tax liability will be:

$$0\% \times £312\,000 + 20\% \times [£512\,000 - £312\,000] = £40\,000$$

As will be seen below, in order to work out the actual inheritance tax liability on a lifetime gift or on death involves a consideration of chargeable gifts which may have been made in the immediately preceding seven years. The purpose of such consideration is to ascertain the amount of the NRB which has already been utilised (by the earlier gifts) and thus how much of it is left unused to be used against the current lifetime gift or the individual's estate on death.

As the NRB in effect continually replenishes itself over time the individual may during their lifetime make chargeable transfers in excess of £312 000 yet still precipitate no actual inheritance tax charge on such transfers.

Following FA 2008 the NRB is now potentially transferable between spouses (see Chapters 10 and 26).

LIFETIME GIFTS

Although colloquially the term "gift" is used, the legislation refers to inheritance tax being levied on the value transferred by a chargeable lifetime transfer made by an individual.

The term "chargeable lifetime transfer" is rather unhelpfully defined in the legislation as any transfer of value which is not an exempt transfer.

Chargeable Lifetime Transfer (CLT)

An individual makes a chargeable lifetime transfer (commonly referred to as a CLT) when making a lifetime gift *to a trust* of whatever type (e.g. discretionary trust; interest in possession trust; accumulation and maintenance trust; note, however, transfers into a disabled trust are not CLTs but potentially exempt transfers (see below)).

An immediate inheritance tax liability arises at the date of making the chargeable transfer into the trust at the lifetime rate then in force (i.e. 20%).

If the individual, having made a CLT, dies within (i.e. in less than) seven years of the date of the transfer an *additional* inheritance tax liability also arises on transfer. The amount of this additional liability is based upon the quantum of the transfer of value *when originally effected* and on the time span between the date of the gift and the death of the donor (i.e. a relief referred to as taper relief may apply; see below). The rate of inheritance tax is that applicable on death (i.e. 40%).

Example 9.3

Brian Harris gave a cash gift of £700 000 to his discretionary trust on 10 April 2008.
No earlier lifetime gifts had been made.
This gift is a CLT and an inheritance tax liability arises at the date of the gift.
The quantum of the charge is:

$$0\% \times £312\,000 + 20\% \times [£712\,000 - £312\,000] = £80\,000$$

Example 9.4

Using the facts of Example 9.3, Brian subsequently died on 15 October 2008.
An additional inheritance tax charge now arises on the CLT based on the amount of the gift and the death rate at the time of death, i.e. 40%.
The additional inheritance tax charge is:

$$0\% \times £312\,000 + 40\% \times [£712\,000 - £312\,000] = £160\,000$$

For simplicity at this stage, Example 9.4 above ignores the impact of possible taper relief and the possibility of any reduction in any additional inheritance tax charge on death by any inheritance tax paid on the lifetime transfer (see Example 9.10 below).

(While all lifetime transfers made by an individual into all forms of trust are now (i.e. on or after 22 March 2006) chargeable transfers, prior to 22 March 2006 the only transfers into trust which were chargeable transfers were those transfers into a discretionary trust. Transfers into an interest in possession trust or an accumulation and

maintenance trust were, pre 22 March 2006, not chargeable transfers but potentially exempt transfers (see below)).

Potentially Exempt Transfer (PET)

A gift from one individual *to another individual* is a potentially exempt transfer (commonly referred to as a PET).

No inheritance tax liability arises at the date of making the PET. Indeed, if the individual then survives for seven years or more from the date of the gift no inheritance tax liability arises and the gift is made inheritance tax free.

An inheritance tax liability only arises *if* the individual dies within (i.e. less than) seven years of the date of making the gift. The amount of the liability is based on the quantum of the transfer *when originally effected*, the time span between the date of the gift and the death of the donor (i.e. a relief referred to as taper relief may apply; see below), and the rates in force in the tax year of death. However, where the value of the property transferred has fallen between the date of the gift and the date of the donor's death the lower value may be substituted.

Where the PET becomes chargeable, due to the death of the individual within seven years of the date of making the transfer, the inheritance tax liability is calculated using the rates applicable at the date of death. Currently (i.e. 2008/09), the rate in force on death is 40%.

Example 9.5
Brian Harris gave a cash gift of £712 000 to his son, Herbert, on 6 February 2001. In the following year on 14 August 2002 Brian gave a cash gift of £800 000 to his daughter, Samantha.

Each of these gifts qualifies as a PET and no inheritance tax charge arises at the dates the gifts are made.

Example 9.6
Using the facts of Example 9.5, Brian subsequently died on 15 October 2008.

The gift to his son made on 6 February 2001 was made more than seven years prior to Brian's death. No inheritance tax charge thus arises and the gift becomes totally exempt.

However, the gift to his daughter on 14 August 2002 was made within seven years of Brain's death and as a consequence becomes liable to inheritance tax.

The amount of the liability is:

$$0\% \times £312\,000 + 40\% \times [£800\,000 - £312\,000] = £195\,200$$

(taper relief has been ignored).

Quantum of a Transfer of Value

The amount of the transfer of value when a gift is made will normally equal the value of the gift. However, this may not always be the case (see Example 9.8 below).

Inheritance tax is actually charged on the amount of diminution in the individual's estate which arises due to the transfer. This, in turn, is the difference between the value of the estate before and after the transfer has been effected.

Example 9.7
Keith's estate amounts to £700 000.

He makes a lifetime cash gift of £200 000 to his discretionary trust. This is a CLT and thus an immediate inheritance tax liability arises.

After the gift his estate is worth £500 000.

The CLT is thus £700 000 − £500 000 = £200 000.

A slightly more complex example concerning the quantum of a transfer of value would be the following:

Example 9.8
Henry Tomb owns 51% of the ordinary share in his company XYZ Ltd.

He decides to gift 2% of his shareholding to his discretionary trust. This is a CLT and thus an immediate inheritance tax liability arises.

After the gift his shareholding is, of course, 49%.

The consequence of making the gift is that the reduction in Henry's estate is in fact much greater than the amount of the gift itself. This occurs due to the loss of control of the company (i.e. a 49% versus 51% shareholding).

The 2% shareholding (in isolation) may be worth, say, £10 000.

However, a 51% shareholding may be worth, say, £100 000 and a 49% shareholding worth, say, £75 000.

The transfer of value for inheritance tax purposes is (as indicated above) measured by the diminution of the donor's estate due to the gift (not the amount of the gift).

For Keith, his inheritance tax charge will thus be based on £25 000 (i.e. £100 000 less £75 000) not £10 000.

A similar issue to that raised in Example 9.8 above would also apply in situations where, for example, a gift is made of an item which breaks up a "set". An individual may own four valuable antique chairs which form a set. If one chair only was to be gifted then this would destroy the set. The difference between the value of the set of four chairs and that of just three chairs (after a gift of just one chair) is likely to be much greater than the value of the single chair gifted.

One final comment relates to CLTs (but not PETs).

In the case of a CLT (as will be seen below) the primary responsibility for payment of any inheritance tax liability is that of the donor. In such a case the quantum of any CLT is not only the amount of the gift itself but, in addition, any associated inheritance tax liability thereon as it is the sum of these two amounts by which the donor's estate is diminished.

This involves what is referred to as "grossing up" which is necessary to ascertain the quantum by which the donor's estate is in fact diminished (see below).

It is, however, possible for the donor and donee to agree that any inheritance tax liability arising will be that of the donee. In this case the donor's estate will diminish, as normal, by the quantum of the gift itself (ignoring the associated inheritance tax liability). No "grossing up" in this case will be necessary.

TAPER RELIEF

PET

In the case of a PET an inheritance tax liability only arises if the donor dies within seven years of the date of the gift.

Depending upon the time span between the date of the gift and the date of death taper relief may be available. The longer the time between the date of the gift and the date of death the greater the available taper relief and the smaller the resultant inheritance tax liability.

Taper relief reduces the quantum of inheritance charged on the gift not the quantum of the gift itself (in the case of business property relief, on the other hand (see Chapter 10), the relief reduces the quantum of the gift/transfer not the inheritance tax charged thereon).

The inheritance tax charged, before taper relief, is calculated on the value of the transfer at the date of the gift (not the value at the date of death) albeit at the rate of inheritance tax in force at the date of death. The amount of inheritance so calculated may then be reduced by taper relief.

The taper relief percentages are as follows:

Years between transfer and death	% of taper relief
Not more than 3 years	0%
More than 3 but not more than 4	20%
More than 4 but not more than 5	40%
More than 5 but not more than 6	60%
More than 6 but not more than 7	80%

Thus, for example, in the event of death not more than three years of the date of the gift no taper relief applies (i.e. there is no reduction in the charge).

In the event of death, say, more than six but less than seven years of the date of the gift any inheritance tax charge is levied at the then death rate (i.e. 40%) but then reduced by the relevant taper relief percentage, i.e. in this case 80%. This would produce an inheritance tax charge based on an effective rate of 20% of 40%, i.e. 8%.

Example 9.9

Tom Smith died on 18 September 2008 after he had made a gift to his daughter on 5 July 2003 of £812 000 (i.e. a PET).

Tom had made no other lifetime gifts.

Tom's death causes an inheritance tax liability to arise on the gift as he died within seven years of the date of the gift (more than five years but less than six years).

The rate of inheritance tax will be that applying on death (i.e. 40%) and the taper relief percentage will be 60%.

The inheritance tax charged is thus $0\% \times £312\,000 + 40\% \times 40\% \times [£812\,000 - £312\,000] = £80\,000$.

Without taper relief the charge on death would have been $40\% \times £500\,000$, i.e. £200 000. Taking into account the 60% taper relief leaves the £200 000 to be reduced by £120 000 leaving a net chargeable amount of £80 000.

CLT

As indicated above, although a CLT (unlike a PET) is chargeable at the date of the gift, if the donor dies within seven years of the date of the gift an additional inheritance tax charge also arises.

As in the case of a PET (see above), taper relief applies in the same manner.

With respect to a CLT, however, the possibility of a double charge to inheritance tax arises (i.e. a charge at the date of the gift *and* an additional charge if the donor dies within seven years). To ameliorate this possibility, in computing the additional inheritance tax charge credit is in principle given for any inheritance tax charged when the gift was originally made.

This tax credit is in addition to any taper relief which may also be available.

Computationally, taper relief is applied to reduce any additional inheritance tax charge *before* any offsetting of the inheritance tax charged at the date of the gift.

The additional inheritance tax charged, before taper relief, is calculated on the value of the transfer at the date of the gift (not the value at the date of death) albeit at the rate of inheritance tax in force at the date of death.

Example 9.10

Peter Rabbit made a gift into his discretionary trust of cash of £600 000 on 9 June 2005.

Peter died on 22 December 2008. He had made no other lifetime gifts.

The gift (i.e. in lifetime) was a CLT and an immediate liability to inheritance tax charge arises at the date of the gift equal to (assuming a NRB of £312 000)

$$0\% \times £312\,000 + 20\% \text{ of } [£600\,000 - £312\,000] = £57\,600$$

Peter died within four years (but more than three years) of the date of the gift. Additional inheritance tax liability thus arises and taper relief of 20% applies.

The rate of inheritance tax will be that in force at his date of death (i.e. 40%).

Additional inheritance tax charged is:

$$[0\% \times £312\,000 + 80\% \times 40\% \times [£600\,000 - £312\,000]] - £57\,600 = £34\,560$$

It may be observed, however, that the additional amount of inheritance charged after taper relief may in fact be less than that already paid in lifetime. In Example 9.10

above this would happen, for example, if Peter had died more than five but less than six years after the date of the gift. In this case taper relief would be available at the rate of 60% producing an additional inheritance tax liability of 40% × 40% × [£600 000 − £312 000}, i.e. £46 080. This is less than the £57 600 inheritance tax charged at the date of the gift in lifetime.

As a consequence, no additional inheritance tax would be payable but the excess (i.e. the £57 600 over the £46 080) cannot be reclaimed.

SEVEN-YEAR CUMULATION PERIOD

Lifetime

As mentioned above the amount of inheritance tax levied on a particular CLT (or on a PET if death occurs within seven years of the date of the gift) is dependent upon the donor's history with respect to the making of gifts over the immediately preceding seven years.

The necessity of reviewing the prior seven-year period occurs every time a CLT is made.

The purpose of the review is to ascertain whether the NRB (i.e. £312 000 for 2008/09) is available for use against the transfer under consideration which in turn will affect the amount of inheritance tax to be charged on the transfer.

When considering the availability of the NRB on lifetime transfers only CLTs within the previous seven years are considered. PETs are ignored because at the date of making a PET no actual inheritance tax liability arises and thus no part of the NRB is used by the PET at that time.

The position on death is different (see below).

CLTs Only

Example 9.11

Sharon Michaels has been advised to give away as much of her estate as she can in her lifetime in order to mitigate any inheritance tax charge which will arise on her estate should she di.e. prematurely. She decides that the best way to do this would be to set up a discretionary trust for various family members and to make regular transfers to it.

She makes transfers to the discretionary trust as follows:

1 June 1999	£92 000
5 August 2000	£200 000
10 December 2003	£100 000
23 October 2004	£150 000

All the gifts are CLTs.

Assume, for simplicity, that the NRB in each of the above tax years is £312 000. Strictly speaking the NRB applicable is that for the tax year in which the CLT is made.

The inheritance tax liabilities on each gift would then be as follows:

1 June 1999 (£92 000)
£92 000 @ 0% = £nil
i.e. the whole of the gift falls within the NRB.

5 August 2000 (£200 000)
In the previous seven years a CLT of £92 000 was made.
Thus, only [£312 000 − £92 000] = £220 000 of the NRB is left to use.

£200 000 @ 0% = £nil
i.e. the whole of the gift falls within the NRB.

10 December 2003 (£100 000)
In the previous seven years CLTs of £92 000 and £200 000 were made.
Thus, only [£312 000 − £292 000] = £20 000 of the NRB is left to use.

£20 000 @ 0% + £80 000 @ 20% = £16 000
i.e. of the £100 000 gift only £20 000 of it falls within the NRB; the balance (i.e. £80 000) is taxed at the lifetime rate of 20%.

23 October 2004 (£150 000)
In the previous seven years CLTs of £92 000, £200 000 and £100 000 were made.
Thus, the whole of the NRB has now been used up by gifts made within the previous seven years.

£150 000 @ 20% = £30 000
i.e. the whole of the gift of £150 000 is taxed at the lifetime rate of 20%.

In Example 9.11 above, by making all her gifts within a seven-year period, Sharon utilised all her NRB thus precipitating inheritance tax liabilities on some of the gifts.

Example 9.12
Using the facts from Example 9.11 above, Sharon is contemplating making a further transfer into the trust of £70 000 on 10 October 2008 (i.e. a CLT).

The only gifts made in the previous seven years were those made on 10 December 2003 (£100 000) and 23 October 2004 (£150 000).

The two earlier gifts on 1 June 1999 and 5 August 2000 were made seven years or more before the proposed gift. As a consequence, they are ignored when ascertaining the available NRB; it is as if they had never taken place.

Thus, only £250 000 (i.e. £100 000 + £150 000) of the NRB is regarded as having been utilised. £62 000 of the NRB (i.e. £312 000 − £250 000) thus remains unused.

The inheritance tax charge on the gift is:

$$£62 000 @ 0\% + £8000 @ 20\% = £1600$$

The effect of the cumulation period of seven years (which in effect is a moving period) is that when ascertaining the NRB availability at any time, gifts made seven years or more before this time can be ignored. The result is that the NRB in effect replenishes itself through time.

At its simplest, an individual could make a gift into trust of £312 000; seven years later make another gift of £312 000; etc. Each gift would be covered by the NRB and no inheritance tax liabilities would arise on any of the gifts.

CLTs and PETs

As indicated above, when ascertaining the lifetime inheritance tax charge on a CLT, PETs are ignored because PETs do not utilise any of the NRB.

Example 9.13
Using the facts of Example 9.11 above, assume that in addition to the CLTs made by Sharon that she also made a PET of £40 000 on 6 May 2004.

The PET will not change the lifetime inheritance tax liabilities arising on the CLTs shown in Example 9.11. The PET is simply ignored at this stage.

When an individual dies, however, the position discussed above is modified.

Suffice it at this stage to point out that on death any PETs made within seven years prior to the date of death will then become chargeable and any CLTs also made within this seven-year period will become subject to an additional charge to inheritance tax (see above).

The effect of this is twofold: first, such PETs will now utilise part of the NRB; and second, the amount of NRB previously utilised by the CLTs in lifetime will change due to the usage of some of it by the PETs.

This issue is discussed below when the inheritance tax liabilities arising on death and the death estate are considered further.

PERSONS RESPONSIBLE FOR PAYMENT OF INHERITANCE TAX AND "GROSSING UP" ON LIFETIME TRANSFERS

An exempt transfer (see Chapter 10) does not precipitate any inheritance tax liabilities whatsoever and thus the issue of who pays the liability is irrelevant.

However, the matter is relevant with respect to both CLTs and PETs.

In some cases more than one person may be potentially liable for any inheritance tax due.

CLTs

The primary liability for any inheritance due on a CLT is the transferor.

Should the liability not be discharged within the appropriate time limit (see below) the transferee may be liable.

In the case of spouses where one spouse has made a CLT and has also made a separate transfer to the spouse, the transferee spouse is also liable for any inheritance tax due on the CLT which is not discharged by the transferor spouse.

Additional Inheritance Tax Liability

Should the donor die within seven years of making the CLT an additional liability to inheritance tax may arise (see above).

The liability for this additional tax is that of the donee.

Should the liability not be discharged within the appropriate time limit the personal representatives of the deceased may be liable.

Grossing up

As indicated above, the inheritance tax liability (not the additional inheritance tax liability) arising on a lifetime CLT is primarily that of the donor.

The effect of this liability falling on the part of the donor is to increase the actual amount of the transfer of value made by the donor. The donor is no longer simply transferring, say, £50 000 cash but is also having to discharge any inheritance tax charge thereon with the consequence that the donor's estate in fact diminishes by the size of the transfer *plus* the inheritance tax payable. In essence the transfer is a *net* transfer; the *gross* transfer equalling the net transfer plus the accompanying inheritance tax charge.

It is the *gross* (not net) transfer figure which is used when reviewing the cumulation period (see above) to ascertain the amount of the NRB available.

The extent of the grossing up will in part depend upon how much of the NRB is available for offset against the transfer (which of course will be affected by CLTs made by the donor in the previous seven years). Where the value of the transfer (pre gross up) is below the available NRB then no gross up will in fact be necessary.

Example 9.14

Edward Comings transfers £400 000 into his discretionary trust. This is a CLT.

As the donor, Edward has the primary liability to discharge the inheritance tax arising on the transfer.

Assume that none of the NRB is available to offset against the transfer which would occur, for example, if in the previous seven years Edward had made other CLTs totalling in excess of the NRB.

The actual transfer of value made by Edward is then:

$$£400\,000/0.8 = £500\,000$$

This £500 000 is referred to as the *gross* transfer.
The inheritance tax liability is 20% × £500 000 = £100 000.
Thus:

- the gross transfer of value is actually £500 000 (not £400 000);
- the discretionary trust receives £400 000;
- the inheritance tax charge is £100 000.

Edward's estate diminished by £500 000 (albeit that £100 000 of it was to pay the inheritance tax charge).

Example 9.15

Using the facts from Example 9.14, but assuming that the whole of the NRB was available against the transfer into the discretionary trust which would occur, for example, if Edward had not made any earlier CLTs (or if Edward's earlier CLTs in the previous seven years were below the NRB). Of the £400 000 transfer the first £312 000 is charged at the nil rate giving an inheritance tax liability of nil.

The balance of £88 000 is then chargeable at 20%.

However, as Edward is liable for the inheritance tax charge this amount needs to be grossed up:

The amount which is chargeable at 20% is thus:

$$£88\,000/0.8 = £110\,000$$

The inheritance tax liability is 20% × £110 000 = £22 000.

The *gross* transfer of value is thus £422 000 (i.e. £400 000 + £22 000).

Thus:

- the discretionary trust receives £400 000;
- the inheritance tax charge is £22 000.

Edward's estate is diminished by £422 000 (albeit that £22 000 of it was to pay the inheritance tax charge).

Example 9.16

Toby Brewin transfers £250 000 into his discretionary trust.

He has made no earlier lifetime transfers. The whole of the NRB of £312 000 is thus available for offset against the transfer.

The inheritance tax liability on the transfer is nil and no grossing up is necessary.

In this case the *gross* and *net* transfer are the same, i.e. £250 000.

A comparison of Examples 9.14, 9.15 and 9.16 above shows the, perhaps not unsurprising, result that the greater the availability of the NRB the smaller the extent of the grossing up and a consequent smaller overall gross transfer. This, in turn, lowers the cost to the donor of effecting the CLT.

In the case of CLTs the parties to the transfer (the individual donor and the trustee donees) may agree that the donee (i.e. the trustees) will pay the inheritance tax liability, if any, which arises on the transfer. In this case the donor's estate will diminish only by the value of the gift and thus no grossing up will be necessary. This will produce a lesser cost for the donor but, on the other hand, the trustees will be left with less than the amount transferred due to the need for them to discharge the inheritance tax liability out of the transfer.

Example 9.17

Using the facts in Example 9.14, if the trustees agreed to discharge any inheritance tax charge on the transfer then the inheritance tax liability arising would simply be:

$$20\% \times £400\,000 = £80\,000$$

The donor, Edward, would gift £400 000 to the trust out of which the trust would discharge £80 000 of inheritance tax leaving the trust with net £320 000.

The decision as to who should pay the inheritance tax on a transfer into trust will thus usually be dependent upon the outcome of discussions between the donor and the donee (i.e. trustees) and the intention behind the gift.

The concept of grossing up has no relevance to the calculation of an inheritance tax liability on PETs although may apply on calculating inheritance tax on death.

PETs

An inheritance tax liability only arises on a PET if the donor dies within seven years of making the transfer. Should this occur the primary liability is that of the donee (not the donor as applies in the case of a CLT).

Should the liability not be discharged within the appropriate time limit (see below) the personal representatives of the deceased may be liable.

DEATH ESTATE

Inheritance tax is charged not only in lifetime on CLTs at the date of the gifts but also on the death of an individual. The inheritance tax charge is levied on the individual's death estate (i.e. assets owned at death less liabilities).

In effect, the individual is treated as making a transfer of value immediately before death of a value transferred equal to the value of the individual's estate (i.e. assets less liabilities) immediately after death.

Assets

The assets comprised in the death estate of the deceased comprise three categories:

- assets to which the deceased was beneficially entitled at death;
- "gifts with reservation" made by the deceased in lifetime;
- "qualifying interest in possession trusts".

The aggregate of the value of assets to which the deceased was beneficially entitled at death is referred to as the individual's "free estate".

However, not all assets to which the deceased was entitled beneficially on death are included. Perhaps the main category of asset which does not form part of the individual's death estate is that of excluded property (see Chapter 12).

Assets Beneficially Owned

Typically, the main part of a deceased's estate will comprise assets to which the individual is beneficially entitled (i.e. owns personally). Such assets may include, for example, cash at bank; shareholdings whether in listed or unquoted companies; premium bonds; chattels including paintings, jewellery, antique furniture; etc.

As a general rule such assets would typically pass under the deceased's will or under the intestacy rules if the deceased left no will.

The matrimonial home would also be included in the individual's death estate. The extent of the inclusion will depend upon how the property was owned. If the property was owned as to 100% by the one individual then, of course, the full value of the property will be included as part of the individual's death estate.

If, on the other hand, the individual owned the property as beneficial joint tenants with his/her spouse only 50% of the property's value would be included as part of the deceased's estate. If the property was owned with the spouse as beneficial tenants in common the appropriate proportion would be included which would generally depend upon the relative contributions to the purchase price by the respective spouse. Thus, for example, husband and wife may have purchased the property 70/30. On death the deceased spouse would include the relevant proportion which in this example would be the 70% or 30% as appropriate.

Assets (including the matrimonial home) which are owned as beneficial joint tenants pass on death by survivorship not under the deceased's will. Assets (including the matrimonial home) which are owned as beneficial tenants in common, however, do pass under the will of the deceased (i.e. not by survivorship).

Chapter 7 discusses these two types of property ownership in more detail.

However, irrespective of the manner of ownership of the asset the inheritance consequences are the same.

Gifts with Reservation

Also included in the individual's death estate are gifts which the individual may have made yet which the individual continues to benefit from.

Such gifts are referred to as "gifts with reservations". A typical example would be where a parent gifts the family home to one of the children but continues thereafter to live in it.

Another example of a gift with reservation would be if the deceased in lifetime had set up a discretionary trust of which he was a potential beneficiary, i.e. the deceased in lifetime, as a discretionary beneficiary, could have possibly benefited from the trust. Whether in fact the deceased in lifetime did or did not so benefit is irrelevant; the mere possibility is enough to cause the gift made by the individual into trust to be treated as a gift with reservation.

If the individual could not personally benefit under the relevant trust but, for example, the individual's spouse could so benefit, this would not cause the gift to be treated as a gift with reservation. The gift would then not form part of the deceased's death estate.

The consequence of the gift with reservation provisions is that even though in the real world the asset gifted no longer belongs to the individual making the gift, for inheritance tax purposes the asset is nevertheless deemed to be included as part of the individual's death estate on death.

The value of the gift included as part of the individual's death estate is the value of the gift at the date of death (not when made as applies to a CLT or PET). This means that no saving of inheritance tax arises by making the gifts with reservation.

Gifts with reservation are discussed in greater detail in Chapter 11.

Qualifying Interest in Possession

One category of trust is the so-called "interest in possession" trust (see Chapters 14 and 15).

An interest in possession trust is a trust under which one (or possibly more) individual is entitled to the whole (or part) of the income which arises to the trust. Such an individual is commonly referred to as the life tenant.

For inheritance tax purposes the life tenant is treated as owning the trust assets in respect of which the individual is entitled to the income which are then included as part of the individual's death estate. This is, again, a fiction as the individual while being entitled to the income from such assets does not in fact own the assets.

This treatment only applies, however, if the interest in possession is a "qualifying" interest.

"Qualifying interests in possession" include:

- interests in possession in trusts created in lifetime before 22 March 2006;
- interests in possession in trusts created by will whether before, on or after 22 March 2006.

Thus, interests in possession in trusts created in lifetime on or after 22 March 2006 do not qualify as qualifying interests in possession (and as a consequence the assets of the trust are not included as part of the death estate of the life tenant; see Chapter 15).

The value of the assets included as part of the individual's death estate (in the case of a qualifying interest) is the value at death not the value when the assets were settled in the trust.

Example 9.18
Albert Brown died on 5 June 2007. At his death he owned a house worth £600 000; cash at bank of £25 000; and quoted equities worth £75 000.

He was the beneficiary of an interest in possession trust which had been set up in lifetime in 2004 (at death the trust assets were worth £225 000) and was also the beneficiary of a second interest in possession trust which had been set up in lifetime by Albert's uncle in November 2006.

He was also one of the beneficiaries of a discretionary trust which he had set up a few years ago (at death the trust assets were worth £150 000).

On his death the proceeds of a life assurance policy which he had taken out some years ago on his own life were paid out to the executors of his will, a sum assured of £750 000.

Albert's death estate comprises:

Assets to which deceased was beneficially entitled		
House	£600 000	
Cash at bank of	£25 000	
Quoted equities worth	£75 000	
Life policy	£750 000	
		£1 450 000
Gift with reservation		
Gift with reservation		£150 000
Settled property		
Interest in possession		£225 000
Total death estate		£1 825 000

Although Albert was the beneficiary of an interest in possession trust set up by his uncle, as the trust was set up in lifetime after 21 March 2006 Albert's interest is not classified as a "qualifying" interest in possession and thus the trust assets do not form part of Albert's death estate.

The proceeds of the life policy fall subject to inheritance tax on Albert's death as on his death the policy proceeds were paid to his executors and formed part of his death estate. Typically, this is not usually the case. An individual will often take out a life policy on his/her own life but settle the policy in trust for, say, the spouse and children with the consequence that on the individual's death the policy proceeds are paid to the trustees of the trust and do not thus form part of the deceased's death estate thus saving an inheritance tax charge of 40% of the sum assured (see Chapter 18).

Assets not Forming Part of the Death Estate

Not *all* assets to which the deceased is beneficially entitled at death are included as part of the death estate. Such assets include primarily excluded property (generally speaking, *non-UK* situs property which is owned by non-UK domiciled individuals and certain *UK* situs property owned by such individuals; see Chapter 12).

Liabilities

Once having ascertained the aggregate of the assets comprised in the death estate certain liabilities of the deceased at death may be deducted therefrom to arrive at the deceased's *net* chargeable death estate.

The liabilities which are allowed to be deducted are those which have been incurred for a consideration in money or money's worth (e.g. a simple borrowing of money; a credit card debt) *or* are liabilities imposed by law (e.g. any outstanding income or capital gains tax liabilities of the individual; also included are any inheritance tax liabilities arising from a previous lifetime transfer if paid out of the deceased's estate).

Other deductible liabilities include reasonable funeral expenses; the term "reasonable" reflecting the deceased's standard of living and thus will vary from one individual to another. Such expenses also include a reasonable amount for the mourning of the family and servants and the cost of a gravestone.

The legal costs of administering the will are not, however, deductible.

Generally, where a liability is secured on property it will be deducted from the value of that property (e.g. a mortgage on a property will be deducted from the value of that property). Any excess unrelieved part of the borrowing may then be deducted from the balance of the individual's free estate (note that such excess is not, however, permitted to be deducted from any settled property in which the individual has an interest in possession).

Example 9.19
Using the facts in Example 9.18, Albert at his death had also incurred the following liabilities:

- a credit card unpaid bill of £3000;
- an outstanding income tax liability of £14 000;
- a mortgage on his house of £200 000.

Albert's death estate would thus be as follows:

Assets to which deceased was beneficially entitled:		
House	£600 000	
Less: mortgage	(£200 000)	
		£400 000
Cash at bank of	£25 000	
Quoted equities worth	£75 000	
Life policy	£750 000	
		£850 000
Less liabilities:		
Income tax liability	(£14 000)	
Credit card bill	(£3000)	
		(£17 000)
		£1 233 000
Gift with reservation		
Gift with reservation		£150 000
Free estate		£1 383 000
Settled property		
Interest in possession		£225 000
Total net chargeable death estate		£1 608 000

Reliefs

While assets are included at their respective market values at the date of death certain categories of asset may qualify for a measure of relief. In such cases the value of the asset is reduced for inclusion in the death estate.

One such example is business property relief (so-called BPR; see Chapter 10) which, depending upon the type of property, is either 50% or 100% of the value of the asset. Effectively, therefore, if 100% relief applies the business property will be included albeit at a "nil" value.

BPR applies to the *net* value of the business qualifying for BPR; thus any liabilities incurred for the purposes of the business are deducted from the asset values to arrive at the net value of the business. Assuming 100% relief, the deductibility of the liabilities is effectively wasted. Ideally, therefore, if possible, liabilities of the business should be charged against other property of the individual concerned in respect of which neither BPR nor any other similar relief is available. The effect would thus be to maximise the effect of any BPR and at the same time maximise the use of any liabilities of the deceased when calculating the death estate.

Rate on Death and the NRB

The rate of inheritance tax applying to the death estate is 40% (twice the lifetime rate of 20%).

However, it may be that some part, or all, of the death estate may be chargeable at the nil (0%) rate due to the availability of the NRB; the balance being charged at 40%.

It is thus necessary to ascertain whether any of the NRB is available at the date of death of the individual. To do this requires consideration of any lifetime gifts (whether PETs or CLTs) made by the deceased within the seven years prior to death as such gifts may have utilised a part or all of the NRB.

PETs as well as CLTs need to be considered. Although at the date of making a PET no inheritance tax liability arises and thus no part of the NRB is in fact utilised (see above) at that time, any PET made within seven years of death falls to be chargeable and at that time a part, or all, of the NRB will be utilised by the PET.

Example 9.20
Tom Collins made the following lifetime gifts:

1 January 2006	PET	£150 000
5 February 2007	CLT	£180 000

Assume Tom had made no earlier gifts.

Tom died on 13 July 2008 with a death estate of £600 000.

Assume that the trustees agreed to bear any inheritance tax charge on the CLT (this avoids the need to consider grossing up thus simplifying the example).

As Tom died within seven years of each of the lifetime gifts the PET becomes chargeable and additional inheritance tax arises on the CLT.

On Tom's death the position will be as follows:

PET (£150 000)

The whole of the NRB is available as no earlier gifts have been made.

Thus the inheritance tax charge on the PET due to Tom's death is nil.

£312 000 less £150 000, i.e. £162 000 of the NRB remains.

CLT (£180 000)

In the previous seven years Tom had made a PET of £150 000.

Thus only £162 000 of the NRB remains.

The additional inheritance tax charge on the CLT is:

$$£162\,000 \times 0\% + £18\,000 \times 40\% = £7200$$

(subject to any taper relief, if any, and offset of any lifetime inheritance tax paid ignored for present purposes; see Example 9.10 above).

Death Estate

In the previous seven years a PET and a CLT have been made.
Together the two gifts have utilised, in full, the NRB.
The inheritance tax charge on the death estate is:

$$40\% \times £600\,000 = £240\,000$$

PAYMENT AND THE BEARING OF INHERITANCE TAX ON DEATH

On death, inheritance tax is charged on the death estate. Two issues arise.

First, who is responsible for the actual *payment* of any such liability. Second, who ultimately bears the tax so charged. The person who simply discharges the inheritance tax liability arising on death may not be the same person(s) who ultimately bears the liability.

Payment of Inheritance Tax on Death

The death of the donor may result in an:

- inheritance tax charge on any PETs made within seven years of death;
- additional inheritance tax liability on any CLTs made within seven years of death;
- inheritance tax charge on the death estate.

The person primarily responsible for the discharge of any inheritance tax charge arising in the first two instances (i.e. PETs and CLTs) is in fact the same person who also bears the liability (i.e. the donee of the PET and/or CLT has the responsibility of discharging the inheritance tax arising on the gift due to the donor's death and in fact also bears the burden thereof).

The "death estate" comprises assets to which the deceased was beneficially entitled at the date of his death; gifts made by the deceased in lifetime which comprise gifts with reservation; and certain categories of settled property (i.e. such property in which the deceased possessed a qualifying interest in possession).

The responsibility for discharging the inheritance tax liability arising on the death estate is thus divided between three categories of person.

The *personal representatives* of the deceased are responsible for the inheritance tax liability in relation to the assets to which the deceased was beneficially entitled.

The *person in whom the property is vested (with respect to the gift with reservation)* is responsible for the inheritance tax liability in relation to the gift.

The *trustees* of the trust, in which the deceased at death had a qualifying interest in possession, are responsible for the inheritance tax liability in relation to the trust assets.

Example 9.21
Using the facts in Examples 9.18 and 9.19, Albert's death estate was as follows:

Assets to which deceased was beneficially entitled:		
House	£600 000	
Less: mortgage	(£200 000)	
		£400 000
Cash at bank of	£25 000	
Quoted equities worth	£75 000	
Life policy	£750 000	
		£850 000
Less liabilities:		
Income tax liability	(£14 000)	
Credit card bill	(£3000)	
		(£17 000)
		£1 233 000
Gift with reservation		
Gift with reservation		£150 000
Free estate		£1 383 000
Settled property		
Interest in possession		£225 000
Total net chargeable death estate		£1 608 000

The inheritance tax liability on the net chargeable death estate is equal to:

$$0\% \times £312\,000 + 40\% \times £1\,296\,000 = £518\,400$$

To determine the liabilities of the various persons the aggregate inheritance tax liability (£518 400) arising on the death estate (£1 608 000) is simply pro-rated according to the amounts comprised in the three categories.

Thus, the persons responsible for discharging this aggregate liability and the associated amounts are as follows:

Personal representatives:

$$[£1\,233\,000/£1\,608\,000] \times £518\,400 = £397\,504$$

Person possessing the gift which was subject to the gift with reservation rules:

$$[£150\,000/£1\,608\,000] \times £518\,400 = £48\,358$$

Trustees of settled property in which the donor at death had an interest in possession:

$$[£225\,000/£1\,608\,000] \times £518\,400 = £72\,538$$

An alternative way of calculating these respective liabilities is to ascertain the average rate of inheritance tax applicable on death and apply this rate to the respective figures. Thus:

$$\text{Average rate} = [£518\,400/£1\,608\,000] \times 100 = 32.24\%$$

Personal representatives:

$$32.24\% \times £1\,633\,000 = £397\,519$$

Person possessing the gift which was subject to the gift with reservation rules:

$$32.24\% \times £150\,000 = £48\,360$$

Trustees of settled property in which the donor at death had an interest in possession:

$$32.24\% \times £225\,000 = £72\,540$$

(The slightly different figures are due to rounding error re the 32.24% figure.)

Bearing of the Inheritance Tax Charge on Death

Example 9.21 illustrates the mechanics of calculation of the inheritance tax charge arising on the death estate and its division among those persons responsible for its discharge either in whole or in part. It does not, per se, identify who ultimately bears the burden of the liability.

Gifts with Reservation

With respect to any gifts with reservation effected by the deceased in lifetime, the person in possession of the property comprised in the gift not only has the responsibility of discharging the inheritance tax applicable to the property but also bears the liability (i.e. the tax is paid out of the assets of the recipient).

Qualifying Interests in Possession

With respect to any qualifying interests in possession of the deceased at the date of death the trustees thereof not only have the responsibility of discharging the inheritance tax applicable to the interests but also bear the liability (i.e. the tax is paid out of trust assets).

Beneficial Asset Entitlement

The discharge of the inheritance tax liability attributable to the assets (less liabilities) beneficially owned by the deceased at death is the responsibility of the personal representatives of the deceased. However, the personal representatives personally, of course, do not bear this liability. It is the beneficiaries who ultimately bear the liability.

The *general rule* (i.e. where the deceased's will makes no references to the discharge of any inheritance tax charges arising on death; see below and Chapter 26) is that this liability is regarded as part of the general testamentary and administrative expenses of the deceased's estate. This means that the inheritance tax liability is paid out of, and thus borne by, the residue of the estate (i.e. that part of the estate which is left over after the various specific legacies, etc. have been made (see Chapter 26). It is thus the beneficiary(ies) entitled to the residue (the so-called residuary beneficiary(ies)) who in this case bear the liability (and thus to this extent are worse off).

Where the inheritance tax liability is to be treated as a testamentary expense of the death estate the quantum of inheritance tax charged will vary according to how the testator's will is worded vis-à-vis which heirs are to receive, for example, specific gifts and which are to take the residue.

Example 9.22

Sally Holmes died having made no lifetime gifts.

Her death estate comprised £912 000 cash.

In her will she left cash of £500 000 to her husband with the residue being left to her two children to be split equally between them. Her will made no reference to inheritance tax.

As the will made no reference to inheritance tax the liability on her death is paid out of residue.

As will be seen in Chapter 10 gifts to spouses are exempt from inheritance tax. The £500 000 left to Sally's husband is thus not subject to inheritance tax on her death.

The balancing £412 000 left to her two children is subject to inheritance tax but part of this will be covered by the NRB as no part of this was used within the seven years prior to Sally's death.

$$\text{Inheritance tax liability} = £312\,000 \times 0\% + £100\,000 \times 40\% = £40\,000$$

This £40 000 is paid out of the residue (i.e. the children's inheritance). The children thus receive

$$[£412\,000 - £40\,000]/2, \text{ i.e. } £186\,000 \text{ each}$$

Her husband receives the full £500 000.

The children's gifts are received out of residue and thus after the inheritance tax liability arising on the whole of the death estate.

Example 9.23
This is similar to Example 9.22 above but in this case Sally slightly alters her will.

Sally Holmes died having made no lifetime gifts.

Her death estate comprised £912 000 cash.

In her will she left £412 000 to be split equally between her two children and the residue (i.e. £500 000) was left to her husband. As in Example 9.22 her will made no reference to inheritance tax.

As the will made no reference to inheritance tax then the liability on her death estate is paid out of residue.

However, in this case (unlike Example 9.22 above) the specific gifts to the children are treated as gifts *net* of inheritance tax and it becomes necessary to "gross up" these gifts to ascertain the inheritance tax liability.

Thus:

Grossed up gifts = [£412 000 − £312 000/0.6] = £166 667
Inheritance tax liability = [£166 667] × 40% = £66 667
The children received [£412 000]/2 = £206 000 each
Her husband received [£500 000 − £66 667] = £433 333

The children's gifts are received by them inheritance tax free as far as they are concerned.

The husband was anticipating receiving £500 000 but as this was the residue of his wife's estate this had to bear the inheritance tax charge on her estate; he accordingly received the £500 000 less the charge of £66 667.

A comparison of Examples 9.22 and 9.23 above shows the difference in the amount of inheritance tax payable on death and the differences in the net inheritances by the beneficiaries according to how the will has been drafted. The actual difference in the amount of inheritance payable is £66 667 less £40 000, i.e. £26 667, a not insignificant amount.

In Example 9.23 the wording of the will is such that the gifts to the children need to be "grossed up" which inflates the inheritance tax chargeable and thus reduces the net amount received by the residuary beneficiary as it is the residue that bears the inheritance tax chargeable.

The lesser amount of inheritance tax on Sally's estate is payable where Sally's husband inherits £500 000 as a specific gift (Example 9.22). However, each of Sally's two children then inherit only £186 000 each. If Sally in fact wants her two children each to receive £206 000 (as in Example 9.23) there would be nothing to stop her husband (under Example 9.22), having inherited £500 000, then to gift (albeit as a PET) the shortfall (i.e. £20 000) to each of the two children.

The children would have now received £206 000 (as Sally really wanted) and her husband would be left with £460 000 (£500 000 less £40 000 gift to children), still £26 667 more (i.e. £460 000 less £433 333) than under Example 9.23.

Specific Gifts Bear Their Own Inheritance Tax on Death

Examples 9.22 and 9.23 above highlight the different inheritance tax liabilities and thus net inheritances by the beneficiaries which arise as a consequence of the different manner in which specific gifts and the residue are left to the various beneficiaries. Despite the different wordings, however, the inheritance tax charge on the death estate is borne by the residue of the estate as a general testamentary expense of the estate.

The will, however, may specifically provide for some (not necessarily all) specific gifts to "bear their own tax". In such cases the inheritance tax liability arising on the aggregate assets less liabilities beneficially owned by the deceased at death is allocated as appropriate and is borne in part by one or more specific beneficiaries (in relation to their specific inheritance) and in part by the residue.

It is worth noting at this stage that irrespective of the deceased's will any assets located *outside the UK* bear their own tax and any property owned as beneficial joint tenants (under which the survivor automatically inherits) also bears its own tax.

Example 9.24

Using the facts from Example 9.23 above, Sally this time provides for the specific gifts to the two children each to bear their own tax.

Sally Holmes died having made no lifetime gifts.

Her death estate comprised £912 000 cash.

In her will she left £412 000 to be split equally between her two children each gift to bear its own tax and the residue (i.e. £500 000) was left to her husband.

The inheritance tax on the death estate is

$$0\% \times £312\,000 + 40\% \times [£412\,000 - £312\,000] = £40\,000$$

Thus:

Inheritance tax liability = £40 000
The children received [£412 000 − £40 000]/2 = £186 000 each
Her husband received £500 000

Comparing the consequences in Examples 23 and 24 shows that less inheritance tax is payable if the specific gifts bear their own tax; this is because in such cases no grossing up is necessary (as applies in Example 9.23).

From the above examples it is clear that the inheritance tax charge arising on the death estate of an individual depends upon the quantum of lifetime gifts which may have been made within the immediately preceding seven years (as this will impact upon the amount of NRB available to offset against the death estate); whether the will is silent or specifically provides for some or all of the specific gifts to bear their own inheritance tax liabilities; and the manner in which the will provides for the beneficiaries to inherit (e.g. specific gifts versus residue to surviving spouse or to other beneficiaries).

A further discussion on this aspect (i.e. wills) is in Chapter 26.

It is now proposed to provide a slightly more comprehensive example, albeit lengthy, which addresses the inheritance issues discussed so far. It will consider:

- the inheritance tax liabilities arising on lifetime transfers;
- the inheritance tax liabilities arising on lifetime transfers due to death;
- the inheritance tax liability on the death estate.

Example 9.25
David Dough made the following lifetime transfers:

1.1.00	CLT1	£80 000
5.6.01	PET1	£120 000
2.7.02	CLT2	£240 000
4.10.07	PET2	£300 000

David died on 2 May 2008 with assets beneficially owned less liabilities of £800 000.

At the date of his death David had a qualifying interest in possession in a trust which had been set up by his uncle in July 1999. At the date of David's death the assets of the trust in which his interest subsisted were £125 000.

David had agreed to pay any inheritance tax charge arising on the CLTs; thus, grossing up may be necessary.

It is assumed that the NRB throughout is £312 000.

Taper relief is ignored as is the offset of lifetime inheritance tax against any additional tax on a CLT.

In order to calculate the inheritance tax liabilities it is necessary to:

- calculate the liabilities on the lifetime transfers at the dates they were made;
- then calculate the liabilities on the lifetime transfers due to death;
- then calculate the liabilities on the death estate.

Taking each of these in turn:

Inheritance Tax Liabilities on the Lifetime Transfers

    1.1.00   CLT1   £80 000

No transfers have been made in the previous seven years and thus the whole of the NRB is available.

$$\text{Inheritance tax liability} = 0\% \times £80\,000 = \text{nil}$$

5.6.01   PET1   £120 000

As this transfer is a PET no inheritance tax charge arises at this date.

2.7.02   CLT2   £240 000

In the previous seven years the only transfer is CLT1 (PETs are ignored as they utilise no part of the NRB). CLT1 used £80 000 of the NRB leaving £232 000 of the NRB.

Thus, £232 000 of CLT2 will be subject to inheritance tax at the nil rate (i.e. 0%) but the balancing element of £8000 will be subject to tax. As David agreed to pay any inheritance tax on the CLTs this amount (i.e. £8000) will need to be grossed up.

Inheritance tax liability = 0% × £232 000 + [£8000/0.8] × 20% = £2000

The *gross* transfer is thus £242 000 (i.e. the net transfer of £240 000 plus the inheritance tax liability £2000 thereon).

4.10.07   PET2   £300 000
As this transfer is a PET no inheritance tax charge arises at this date.

Inheritance Tax Liabilities on the Lifetime Transfers Due to Death

Any PET or CLT made within seven years of death (i.e. on or after 3 May 2001) will be subject to an inheritance tax charge due to death.

1.1.00   CLT1   £80 000
CLT1 was made more than seven years before death.
Thus no additional inheritance tax charge arises on CLT1.

5.6.01   PET1   £120 000
Although this transfer is a PET, death occurred within seven years of the date it was made and thus an inheritance tax charge arises due to the death.
To ascertain the amount of the charge it is necessary to identify any transfers within the previous seven years which may have used some of the NRB.
CLT1 was made within this seven year period. CLT1 used £80 000 of the NRB leaving £232 000 unused.
Thus the inheritance tax charge on PET1 is

0% × £120 000 = nil

2.7.02   CLT2   £242 000 (note it is the *gross* figure used here not the net figure)
As CLT2 was made within seven years of death an additional inheritance tax charge arises on CLT2 due to the death.
To ascertain the amount of the charge it is necessary to identify any transfers within the previous seven years which will have used some of the NRB.
CLT1 and PET1 were each made within this seven year period. CLT1 used £80 000 of the NRB and PET1 used £120 000 leaving £112 000 of the NRB unused.
Thus the inheritance tax charge on CLT2 is

0% × £112 000 + 40% × £130 000 = £52 000

4.10.07   PET2   £300 000
As this transfer was made within seven years of death an inheritance tax liability arises due to death.
To ascertain the amount of the charge it is necessary to identify any transfers within the previous seven years which will have used some of the NRB.
PET1 and CLT2 were each made within this seven year period. CLT1 was made more than seven years before PET2 and thus is now completely ignored in calculating

the amount of the NRB available to PET2 (it is as if CLT1 never took place as far as ascertaining the NRB available is concerned).

In this case PET1 and CLT2 each used £120 000 and £242 000, respectively (the amounts of NRB arrived at here are not necessarily the same as those used when looking at PET1 and CLT2 discussed above).

There is thus no part of the NRB available for utilisation by PET2.

The inheritance tax charge on PET2 is thus

$$40\% \times £300\,000 = £120\,000$$

Death Estate

David died on the 2 May 2008 with assets less liabilities of £800 000 and a qualifying interest in possession worth £125 000.

To ascertain the NRB available it is necessary to look at any gifts which were made within the seven years preceding death, i.e. gifts made on or after 3 May 2001.

These gifts included PET1 of £120 000; CLT2 of £242 000; and PET2 of £300 000. Thus, all the NRB has been used by these three gifts.

The inheritance tax liability on death is thus

$$40\% \times [£800\,000 + £125\,000] = £370\,000$$

Of this amount:

[£800 000/£925 000] × £370 000 = £320 000 is payable by David's personal representatives

[£125 000/£925 000] × £370 000 = £50 000 is payable by the trustees of the trust in which David had his qualifying interest in possession

A number of comments on some of the principles contained in Example 9.25 above may be useful:

- to work out any inheritance tax liability on a transfer of value involves ascertaining the amount of NRB available for use by that transfer. To do this *always* requires a consideration of the immediately preceding seven years;
- in lifetime, PETs do not utilise any part of the NRB. However, on death any PET made within seven years of death will then utilise some part of the NRB;
- as time moves forward certain transfers of value "fall out of account" and thus are treated as no longer utilising any part of the NRB; in effect the NRB replenishes itself through time;
- transfers made within seven years of death utilise the NRB thus reducing the amount of the NRB available for utilisation by the "death estate"; and
- in the case of lifetime CLTs the amount of the CLT which is used in ascertaining the amount of NRB available for use by later CLTs is the *gross* not *net* amount.

PLANNING CONSIDERATIONS: INITIAL THOUGHTS

Theoretically, optimal inheritance tax mitigation occurs where assets are given away in lifetime directly to, for example, members of the donor's family with the donor subsequently surviving for seven years and dying without any (or minimal) death estate. The gifts constitute PETs and no inheritance tax liabilities arise.

For many, however, such a simple strategy is not feasible as, typically, any assets owned are needed during lifetime and are not available for gifting. The major asset is usually the home. In the past, schemes were developed which allowed the giving away of the family home yet still permitting the donors to continue living there but removing the home from their death estate. Such schemes, generally speaking, are no longer inheritance tax effective although some options in this regard do still exist (see Chapter 11).

Nevertheless, to the extent possible, gifts should be made as soon as practicable. As will be seen in the next chapter certain gifts are in any event completely exempt from inheritance tax and thus can be given away without even the requirement to survive seven years thereafter. Use of such exemptions should be maximised.

If the gift is a PET it may be possible to insure against the risk of an inheritance tax liability arising due to the death of the donor within the seven-year period (see Chapters 18 and 26). Typically, cost effective term assurance policies are utilised; use of a seven-year decreasing term policy will reduce premium levels. Writing such polices in trust for the beneficiaries makes the arrangements inheritance tax effective.

Where an individual is in a position to make lifetime gifts to family members it may be preferable, for a variety of reasons (e.g. recipients are minor children), for use to be made of trusts rather than making the gifts directly to the individual(s) concerned. Pre 22 March 2006 gifts into certain trusts (e.g. interest in possession and accumulation and maintenance trusts; not discretionary trusts) were PETs and if the settlor survived seven years no inheritance tax charge arose on the gifts. In many cases the NRB had not been utilised and thus even were death of the donor to occur within seven years of setting up the trust(s) the resultant inheritance tax charge was nil (NRB discretionary trusts were commonly set up by will rather than in lifetime).

However, for gifts into trusts on or after 22 March 2006 all such gifts are CLTs thus potentially precipitating an immediate inheritance tax charge at 20% of the gift (with the possibility of an additional charge if death occurs within seven years) subject to the availability of the NRB.

To this extent, the changes introduced in FA 2006 (effective 22 March 2006) have made trusts less inheritance tax effective.

Nevertheless, trusts continue to have a major role in tax planning (see Chapters 15, 16 and 17).

Effective drafting of wills is also an important element in any inheritance tax planning. In particular, careful thought should be given as to who should bear any inheritance tax charge which may arise.

SUMMARY

Inheritance tax is levied on gratuitous transfers made in lifetime and on death.

Both individuals and trusts are liable to inheritance tax.

Inheritance tax is levied according to the domicile status of the individual. A UK domiciled individual is liable on worldwide assets whereas a non-UK domiciled individual is liable only on UK situs assets. However, in certain cases, an individual non-UK domiciled under UK common law may be "deemed" UK domiciled for inheritance tax purposes. Similarly, an individual may be "deemed" UK domiciled for a period of time following the acquisition of a non-UK domicile.

Lifetime gifts are classified as potentially exempt transfers (i.e. PETs) or chargeable lifetime transfers (i.e. CLTs). The former fall subject to inheritance tax but only if the donor of the transfer dies within seven years, whereas the latter are in principle subject to inheritance tax at the date of the transfer.

The lifetime rate of inheritance tax is 20% and the rate applicable on death is 40% (these rates applying for the tax year 2008/09).

The nil rate band (NRB) is £312 000 (for the tax year 2008/09). Transfers falling within the NRB are subject to inheritance tax at the nil (i.e. 0%) rate. FA 2008 has introduced for the first time the concept of the transferable NRB. Transferability applies where one or both spouses die. on or after 9 October 2007. It does not apply where both deaths occurred prior to this date. The concept only applies to spouses.

The responsibility for discharging an inheritance tax liability may vary as between donor and donee; sometimes the primary liability is that of the donor whereas on other occasions it is that of the donee. However, irrespective of where the primary liability may fall provisions exist under which HMRC may seek to collect any inheritance due from other individuals/trustees.

10
Inheritance Tax: Exemptions and Reliefs

BACKGROUND

Chapter 9 provided an overall view of some of the basic principles underlying the charge to inheritance tax both on lifetime transfers and on death. The NRB was identified (£312 000 for the tax year 2008/09).

While lifetime transfers of value may precipitate an inheritance tax charge (e.g. CLTs) it is possible that such transfers may qualify for some form of relief or exemption. In the former case (i.e. relief) the transfer is in principle chargeable but its quantum is reduced due to the relief whereas in the latter case (i.e. exemption) the transfer is simply exempt (i.e. outside the scope of any such charge).

It may also be that on death, the death estate will be reduced in amount due to some form of relief and/or exemption.

This chapter will examine both reliefs and exemptions available in lifetime and on death.

EXEMPT TRANSFERS

A lifetime transfer of value may be a CLT or PET. However, a transfer of value may be an exempt transfer of value.

An exempt transfer is a transfer which does not give rise to an inheritance tax liability under any circumstances. Unlike the PET, survival for seven years thereafter is not a prerequisite for the exemption to apply.

A transfer of value may fall to be treated as exempt under more than one exemption category and thus it is possible for part of a transfer of value to be partially exempt under one category and part of it to be partially exempt under another.

Most exempt transfers are applicable only to lifetime transfers but certain transfers qualify as exempt but only on death. On the other hand, some transfers qualify as exempt whether effected in lifetime or on death.

Inheritance tax mitigation dictates that wherever possible full advantage should be taken of exempt transfers and any form of relief. Exempt transfers, in particular, represent a highly inheritance tax efficient manner of transferring wealth, in particular among family members.

Some of the exemptions are event specific (e.g. gifts in contemplation of marriage) and thus are "one-off" in nature. Others are recurrent (e.g. the annual exemption) although if not used in a particular tax year may be lost forever.

Perhaps the most underutilised, yet most tax efficient, exempt transfer for the affluent individual is the "normal expenditure out of income" exemption.

Perhaps the most common and highly effective exemption is the inter-spouse exemption (available in lifetime and on death). This exemption permits a high degree of movement of wealth, inheritance tax efficiently, in a family planning context. This option is subject to one caveat, namely, where the relevant spouses are comprised of one UK domiciled and one non-UK domiciled individual and transfers are made from the former to the latter (see Chapter 9).

Lifetime only Exempt Transfers

The main exempt transfers that *apply only to lifetime transfers* are as follows:

- annual exemption;
- normal expenditure out of income exemption;
- gifts in contemplation of marriage exemption;
- gifts for family maintenance exemption.

Each of these exempt gifts will now be considered in turn.

Annual Exemption

An individual may make gifts each tax year up to £3000 without precipitating an inheritance tax liability. If any part of the £3000 remains unused at the end of the tax year the unused part may be carried forward one tax year only for use in the next tax year.

Thus, on the first occasion when the individual first makes a lifetime gift the annual exemption will be £3000 (for the tax year in which the gift is made) plus £3000 carried forward from the previous tax year.

The exemption applies irrespective of the status of the donee (i.e. the person receiving the gift) and thus applies to gifts into trust as well as gifts to other individuals. Unlike the PET, no period of survival by the donor is necessary for the exemption to apply.

The £3000 exemption may apply to a larger gift, i.e. the first £3000 of a larger gift may be exempt under this exemption.

Where more than one gift is made in any tax year the annual exemption is applied in time order; thus, the earlier gift(s) possibly absorbing the whole exemption, i.e. no pro rating of the exemption over all the gifts.

However, where more than one gift is made on the same day pro rating applies across the gifts.

The annual exemption also applies on the lifetime termination of a qualifying interest in possession (see Chapters 14 and 15).

The annual exemption is available in addition to any of the other exemptions and thus tends to be applied to the gift after all other exemptions have been applied.

Example 10.1
Eric Beetle makes a gift of £53 000 cash to a discretionary trust on 3 June 2008.

He has made no other gifts in the tax year or indeed in any prior tax year.

The gift is a CLT (irrespective of whether the gift was on or after 22 March 2006 or before) but the first £6000 is exempt, i.e. £47 000 is the amount of the CLT.

£3000 represented the annual exemption for 2008/09 and £3000 was carried forward from 2007/08.

Chapter 9 explained the method of calculating the amount of the NRB available to offset against a particular gift. Inter alia, this involved identifying gifts (i.e. CLTs) made in the immediately preceding seven years. For simplicity, no account was taken in that chapter of any exemptions (and/or reliefs) which might apply. However, account of such exemptions (and/or reliefs) does need to be taken when ascertaining inheritance tax liabilities.

Example 10.2
Tom Sock made lifetime gifts of £500 000 to his discretionary trust in the tax year 2007/08 and £400 000 in the tax year 2008/09.

Tom had made no earlier lifetime gifts.

The CLT in 2007/08 is £494 000 (i.e. £500 000 − £6000) and in 2008/09 £397 000 (i.e. £400 000 − £3000).

The inheritance tax liability on the 2007/08 CLT (assuming NRB of £312 000) is 0% × £312 000 + 20% × (£494 000 − £312 000) = £36 400.

The NRB available for the CLT in 2008/09 is zero as the CLT in 2007/08 utilised all of it.

The inheritance tax liability is therefore 20% × £397 000 = £79 400.

It is assumed that the trustees agreed to pay the inheritance tax charges on the gifts.

Where in any tax year an individual makes more than one gift, one or more of which rank as CLTs and one or more of which rank as PETs, it is preferable to make the CLTs before the PETs. This is so that the £3000 annual exemption is applied against the earlier CLTs and not against the PETs. This is more likely to ensure that the exemption is used most effectively, i.e. should the donor survive seven years after making the gifts, the PETs will become exempt in any event and had the £3000 been offset against the PETs it would have been wasted.

Normal Expenditure Out of Income Exemption

This exemption is probably one of the most underutilised yet highly effective exemptions.

It applies if three conditions are satisfied:

- it is made as part of the normal (i.e. habitual) expenditure of the donor;
- it is made out of income taking one year with another; and
- after allowing for such transfers the donor is left with sufficient income to maintain his usual standard of living.

There is no monetary ceiling to the exemption and the amount of any gifts which may qualify under this exemption will vary from individual to individual depending upon individual circumstances, i.e. what may be "normal" expenditure for one individual may not be so for another. In essence, the greater the level of annual income of an individual the greater the potential, other things being equal, for larger annual gifts to be made which would fall under this exemption.

"One-off" payments will not qualify; a pattern of giving needs to be established although the exact amount given need not be fixed (e.g. could be arrived at by formula, e.g. x% of net income). The exemption does not require that the recipient be the same.

The term "income" means income after the payment of any income tax (i.e. net income) and is that arrived at using normal accountancy principles (not the tax rules). It has been suggested that gifts amounting to no more than one third of net income is generally acceptable.

Payment of premiums each year on a life insurance policy for the benefit of another may typically qualify under this exemption, the policy being used to fund any inheritance tax liabilities which might arise on lifetime transfers or on death. While such premium payments, if less than £3000 p.a., usually qualify in any event under the annual exemption discussed above, larger amounts may qualify under the normal expenditure out of income exemption.

However, for the purpose of this exemption (i.e. where calculating the quantum of income) the 5% p.a. withdrawals under the single premium bond form of investment (see Chapter 18) are not regarded as income; the 5% withdrawals are partial surrenders representing a return of capital (i.e. a partial return of the original single premium). Similarly, the capital element of a purchased life annuity is not accepted as income for the purposes of the exemption.

So long as the three conditions listed above can be satisfied this exemption offers the wealthy individual an excellent inheritance tax-free route to reduce their estate by gifting potentially significantly large sums of cash each year.

However, an individual who possesses large tracts of real estate but with limited income is unlikely to find this exemption of much use as the exemption only applies to expenditure out of *income* not capital.

Gifts in Contemplation of Marriage Exemption

Gifts made by one individual in respect of any one marriage may be exempt if given in contemplation of marriage. This generally means that the gift needs to be made ideally before the marriage or, possibly, contemporaneously with it. The gift should ideally be evidenced in some form; an accompanying letter confirming the fact that it is being made conditional on marriage is sufficient.

Technically speaking, if the marriage does not proceed the donor should recover the gift. Should the gift in these circumstances, however, not be recovered then it would constitute a PET.

Limits are set on the amounts of the gift and depend upon the relationship of the donor to donee as follows:

- the first £5000 by a parent of either party to the marriage;
- the first £2500 by one party to the marriage to the other or by a grandparent or remoter ancestor;
- the first £1000 in any other case (e.g. a gift by a sibling).

These limits are per marriage not per donor. Thus, for example, a parent of one of the parties to the marriage may give their son (or daughter) up to £5000 which will qualify as exempt.

If more than one gift is made by the same individual in respect of the same marriage the exemption is applied pro rata to each gift according to their respective values.

The exemptions apply not only to outright gifts from one individual to another individual (who is a party to the marriage) but also to gifts into certain trusts (but not all trusts). The trust must, inter alia, be primarily for the parties to the marriage, their issue and the spouses of their issue.

Gifts for Family Maintenance Exemption

This exemption covers gifts made as follows:

- by one party to a marriage in favour of the other for maintenance purposes;
- by one party to the marriage in favour of a child of either party for the maintenance, education or training of the child and made up to the later of the child attaining age 18 or ceasing full time education;
- in favour of a dependent relative (relative of the donor or donor's spouse who is incapacitated by old age or infirmity from maintaining himself/herself) which constitutes reasonable provision for care or maintenance.

This exemption is particularly important as it permits, for example, the parent of a child to educate the child by way of exempt expenditure. Note that the exemption does not cover transfers for the maintenance of other persons' children.

Death only Exempt Transfers

The exempt transfers that may be made *only on death* are very few. The main such exempt transfer is an inter-spouse transfer (see below).

Other transfers include certain *foreign currency* (this exemption does not apply to sterling accounts) bank or Post Office accounts which are held by non-UK domiciled and non-UK resident or ordinary resident individuals (such accounts are, however, not exempt if such individual makes a *lifetime* gift of the monies in the account).

Transfers in Lifetime or on Death Exemptions

Inter-spouse Transfers

This category of transfer is probably one of the most important and most used in family estate planning and applies to transfers whether effected in lifetime or death.

All inter-spouse transfers are exempt irrespective of timing and/or amount. All that is required is that the spouses are married; it is not necessary (as is required for inter-spouse capital gains tax purposes; see Chapter 8) for the spouses to be living together (i.e. they could thus be separated albeit not divorced).

The one limit to the exemption is where a *UK domiciled* spouse effects transfers to a *non-UK domiciled* spouse. In this case there is a £55 000 cumulative exemption limit. Thus, only transfers up to £55 000 in total throughout life can be transferred as exempt transfers where the donor spouse is UK domiciled and the donee spouse is non-UK domiciled. Once this amount has been exhausted any additional transfers would constitute PETs.

Thus, for the tax year 2008/09 up to £367 000 (i.e. £55 000 plus £312 000) could be transferred from the UK to the non-UK domiciled spouse without precipitating an actual charge to inheritance tax (even if the donor spouse died within seven years of the transfers). Any transfers above this £367 000 figure would fall to be treated as PETs precipitating no inheritance tax charge unless the donor spouse dies within seven years of the date of the gift.

The above £55 000 exemption applies to all inter-spouse transfers where the transfers are from a UK domiciled spouse to a non-UK domiciled spouse unless the transfers are effected pursuant to a court order following a divorce or judicial separation (an order which frees the parties to the marriage of their marital obligations; it does not, however, terminate the marriage) in which case all such transfers are exempt transfers.

Inter-spouse transfers between two UK or two non-UK domiciled spouses or from the non-UK domiciled spouse to the UK domiciled spouse are not subject to the £55 000 limit.

Inter-spouse Transferable NRB

The Pre-Budget Report of 9 October 2007 contained proposals (now contained in FA 2008) under which the unutilised part of the NRB on the death of the first spouse could be transferred to the surviving spouse. The transfer of the NRB in this manner is possible where one or both spouse deaths occur on or after 9 October 2007. Thus, no transfer is possible where both spouse deaths occurred prior to 9 October 2007.

One consequence of this transferability is that the need for spouses to equalise their estates may be less important but perhaps still wise (see below).

Pre 9 October 2007
The NRB is currently (i.e. for the tax year 2008/09) £312 000. This means that in any seven-year period the first £312 000 of chargeable lifetime transfers is liable to inheritance tax at the nil rate. To mitigate inheritance tax liabilities when the children of the spouses are to ultimately benefit from their parents' estates required equalisation of estates; equalisation of estates refers to the need for each spouse to possess an estate worth at least the NRB rate (i.e. £312 000). Where one spouse owns the majority of the joint estate then lifetime inter-spouse transfers should be effected to ensure that the

spouse with the lesser estate possesses a net (i.e. after liabilities) estate of at least £312 000.

Example 10.3
Bob and Jackie Fraser are married with three children. Bob and Jackie are each UK domiciled.

Bob's estate is worth £600 000. Jackie's estate is worth £24 000. They want their children to benefit from their joint estates.

Option 1
Bob and Jackie's wills leave everything to each other and the surviving spouse leaves everything to their children.

Assuming Bob dies first his £600 000 estate passes to Jackie under his will inheritance free due to the inter-spouse exemption (which applies in lifetime and on death).

On Jackie's death the £624 000 estate passes to the children.

Of this amount the first £312 000 is subject to inheritance tax at 0% and the balance (i.e. £312 000) is liable at the 40% rate giving a liability of £124 800.

Even if Jackie was to die first the consequences would be the same.

Option 2
Bob and Jackie's wills each provide that on their respective deaths their estate will be left to the children.

However, due to the imbalance of the respective estates Bob transfers in lifetime by way of exempt inter-spouse transfer £288 000. Bob and Jackie's estates are now each worth £312 000, i.e. the estates have been literally equalised.

Assuming Bob dies first his estate passes to the children. The inheritance tax liability is 0% on £312 000, i.e. nil.

On Jackie's death her estate passes to the children. The inheritance tax liability is 0% on £312 000, i.e. nil.

Compare Options 1 and 2
A comparison of the two options shows that under Option 2 there is a saving of £124 800 of inheritance tax. This is 40% of £312 000.

In effect Option 2 ensures that each of Bob and Jackie take advantage of their NRBs. Under Option 1, only Jackie (as the second to die) utilised her NRB as on Bob's death he left everything to Jackie and as it was an inter-spouse transfer it was exempt and the NRB was wasted. The effect is that both spouse estates are subject to inheritance tax on the second death with only one NRB available.

Under Option 2 the transfer to the children does not have to be directly to them beneficially. On the first death it would be possible to leave the assets in, say, a discretionary trust under which the beneficiaries would be the children and the surviving spouse. This would ensure that the surviving spouse would not be deprived of benefiting from the assets/income of the deceased's spouse estate should this prove necessary.

"Equalisation" is not, however, meant to mean that the estate of each spouse must be exactly equal but that each spouse's estate must be at least the size of the current NRB.

The other consequence of estate equalisation is that it enables each spouse to take advantage of the various lifetime exemptions referred to above. For example, as indicated above, the annual exemption of £3000 per annum is available to all individuals. It is thus important that each spouse is in a position each tax year to effect such transfers to, typically, other members of the family. Similar comments apply to the other exemptions.

In addition to the availability of the exemptions, various "reliefs" are available which reduce the quantum of inheritance tax charged on certain transfers (e.g. business asset property relief; see below). Equalisation of estates again permits maximum use by both spouses.

Post 8 October 2007

The transferable NRB operates by permitting the unused part of the NRB occurring on the death of the first spouse to die to be transferred and used by the second spouse on death.

It is necessary for a claim to transfer the NRB to be made by the executors of the will on the death of the surviving spouse. The claim must be lodged within two years of the end of month in which the surviving spouse dies.

Prior to the changes no such transference was permitted. Thus, as was illustrated in Example 10.2 Option 1 above, Bob's lack of utilisation of his NRB on his death did not allow his wife to utilise it on her subsequent death.

The change applies, as indicated above, where one or both spouses die on or after 9 October 2007. Thus, where both spouses died prior to this date the change does not apply.

The amount of the NRB of the first spouse to die which may be transferred is not an absolute amount but a percentage equal to the proportion of the amount of the NRB which has not been used. On the death of the second spouse the then NRB may be uplifted by applying this percentage to it.

Example 10.4

Using the facts of Example 10.3 above where each spouse leaves their respective estate to their surviving spouse.

Assuming Bob dies first his £600 000 estate passes to Jackie under his will inheritance free due to the inter-spouse exemption (which applies in lifetime and on death).

Thus, none of Bob's NRB has been utilised, i.e. 100% of his NRB has not been utilised.

On Jackie's death the £624 000 estate passes to the children.

However, at the date of Jackie's death she is entitled to her own NRB (£312 000) *plus* that fraction of it which was not utilised by her husband on his death (i.e. 100%).

Jackie's NRB is thus equal to:

$$£312\,000 + 100\% \times £312\,000 = £624\,000$$

(in essence Jackie becomes entitled to twice her own NRB).

On leaving the £624 000 estate to her children under her will no inheritance tax charge arises (compare Option 1 in Example 10.2 above).

Despite the fact that there was no equalisation of estates the transferability of the NRB overcomes this problem.

Example 10.5
Mary died on 15 May 2007 and her husband, Dick, died on 9 May 2008.

The NRB in the tax year Mary died was £300 000 (not £312 000). In the tax year Dick died the NRB was £312 000.

On Mary's death 25% of her estate went to her children and 75% to Dick. Thus, 75% of her NRB was not utilised.

On Dick's death his NRB will thus equal:

$$£312\,000 + 75\% \times £312\,000 = £546\,000$$

As will be seen from Examples 10.4 and 10.5 above, not only is the NRB of the first spouse to die transferrable but the extent of the transference is actually a function of the size of the NRB on the death of the surviving spouse. As historically NRBs have increased tax year on tax year this is quite an attractive change to the position prior to 9 October 2007.

Although the unused proportion of the NRB of the first spouse to die can be transferred to the surviving spouse on the latter's death the calculation must take into account any gifts made by the first spouse to die within seven years before death. Such gifts may each in part utilise some of the NRB applicable on death and thus reduce the unused element of the NRB.

Example 10.6
Mary died on 15 May 2007 and her husband, Dick, died on 9 May 2008. Mary left everything to Dick.

The NRB in the tax year Mary died was £300 000. In the tax year Dick died the NRB was £312 000.

Mary's death estate amounted to £250 000 and within the seven years prior to her death Mary had made a PET of £35 000 and a CLT of £65 000. The PET would, because of Mary' death, fall to be chargeable and the CLT would be subject to the additional charge. Both of these gifts would thus utilise £100 000 of the £300 000 NRB available on Mary's death.

On Mary's death, of the NRB of £300 000 one third of it was utilised by the two lifetime gifts totalling £100 000. Thus, two thirds of the NRB remains unutilised.

On Dick's death his NRB will equal:

$$£312\,000 + 2/3 \times £312\,000 = £520\,000$$

The introduction of the transferable NRB is also likely to bring about a reduction in the use of NRB discretionary trusts in the wills of spouses which were (and continue to be) utilised to ensure that on the death of each spouse their respective NRB was fully utilised, (see Example 10.3 Option 2), although there may still be advantages to retaining their use even post 9 October 2007 (see Chapter 26). For example, where an individual is married more than once the use of discretionary will trusts may prove advantageous.

It may be, for example, that one spouse survives two successive spouses and may thus be entitled to the whole or a part of the unused NRB of each spouse.

There is, however, a limit as to the amount a surviving spouse's NRB can be increased. The maximum increase is limited to the amount of the NRB on the surviving spouse's death, i.e. the maximum NRB on a surviving spouse's death is twice the amount of the NRB on death.

Example 10.7
Cindy Purple is married to Jack Purple.

Jack Purple died on 4 February 2008 leaving his whole estate to Cindy (i.e. utilising none of his NRB).

Cindy subsequently married Nicholas Green on 7 July 2008.

Nicholas died on 10 September 2008 leaving his whole estate to Cindy (i.e. utilising none of his NRB).

Cindy died on 11 July 2008 (when the NRB was £312 000).

Subject to the making of the relevant claims on Cindy's death a transfer of 100% of Jack's unused NRB plus 100% of Nicholas's NRB would in principle be available.

However, this would give Cindy three times the NRB (i.e. her own NRB plus that of each of Jack and Nicholas). The legislation accordingly limits the NRB available on Cindy's death, in such circumstances, to twice the NRB, i.e. £624 000.

It will be noted in the above Example 10.7 that despite three deaths only two NRBs are actually utilised, i.e. one NRB appears to be wasted. There is a possible solution to this.

Example 10.8
Using the facts from Example 10.7 above, Cindy Purple is married to Jack Purple.

Jack Purple died on 4 February 2008. Instead of leaving his whole estate to Cindy (i.e. utilising none of his NRB) it would be better if he left the amount of his NRB to a discretionary trust set up under his will thus utilising his NRB in full.

Cindy married Nicholas Green on 7 July 2008.

Nicholas died on 10 September 2008 leaving his whole estate to Cindy (i.e. utilising none of his NRB).

Cindy died on 11 July 2008 (when the NRB was £312 000).

Subject to the making of the relevant claim Cindy is able in principle to transfer 100% of Nicholas's NRB.

This would give Cindy twice the NRB (i.e. her own NRB plus that of Nicholas), i.e. £624 000.

In total three NRBs have been used.

It is to be noted that the transferability of the NRB is restricted to spouses only and thus has no application to cohabitees, even if living as husband and wife (contrast the applicability of the new "remittance" rules which do apply to such cohabitees; see Chapter 23); to single individuals; and former spouses or divorcees (although it does apply to married but separated spouses).

Miscellaneous Exemptions

In addition to the above exemptions transfers falling within any of the categories below will also be exempt whether effected in lifetime or on death.

These categories include gifts:

- to charities (UK-based charities only);
- for national purposes (e.g. gifts to the National Gallery; British Museum; certain libraries);
- to political parties (the party must be a "qualifying" party).

Ordering of Exemptions

More than one exemption may apply to a transfer.

The "normal expenditure out of income" exemption should be applied first and the "annual exemption" should be applied last.

Where more than one transfer has been made in a tax year the exemptions should be applied to the earlier transfers first. If more than one transfer has been made on the same day then the relevant exemption(s) should be pro-rated.

Example 10.9

Charles Royal makes CLTs on 5 July, 10 September and 17 December in the tax year 2008/09 of £10 000, £20 000 and £30 000, respectively.

The annual exemption of £3000 for 2008/09 is applied against the earliest transfer first, i.e. that of 5 July and thus of the £10 000 only £7000 is chargeable.

Had Charles not utilised the annual exemption for the prior tax year 2007/08 this could have been carried forward to the tax year 2008/09 making a total of £6000 of potential exemption.

In this case the £6000 of exemption would have been offset against the £10 000 causing the chargeable element thereof to be £4000.

In neither of the above cases would the later gifts of £20 000 and £30 000 benefit from any annual exemption.

Example 10.10

Betty Noon has a high net annual income and has for a number of tax years made significant transfers each tax year, amounting to £65 000, to one of her discretionary trusts.

In the tax year 2008/09 HMRC accept that only £62 000 of the £65 000 for the tax year should qualify under the "normal expenditure out of income" exemption.

Betty will be able to utilise her £3000 annual exemption for 2008/09 to offset against the balancing £3000 of the £65 000 thus reducing the chargeable amount to nil.

RELIEFS

Two of the most important reliefs available to mitigate inheritance tax charges are, namely:

- business property relief; and
- agricultural property relief.

These reliefs are commonly referred to as BPR and APR, respectively.
Another relief which is also available is:

- quick succession relief (commonly referred to as QSR).

Both BPR and APR apply to lifetime gifts and on death.

The main difference between APR and BPR is that BPR applies irrespective of the location of the property (i.e. BPR applies to property wherever located) whereas APR only applies to property situated in the UK, Channel Islands or the Isle of Man.

On a transfer of property it is possible that APR applies to part of the transfer with BPR applying where APR was inapplicable; APR applying in priority to BPR.

The importance of BPR and APR lies in the quantum of the reliefs.

In the case of BPR the percentage of relief is either 50% or 100% (depending upon the type of property) *of the value of the business property* transferred; in the case of APR, the percentage of relief is 100% *of the value of the agricultural property* transferred.

If the level of relief (whether BPR or APR) applying is 100% then effectively the transfer is not subject to inheritance tax (more specifically the transfer of value *is* subject to inheritance tax but with the amount of the transfer being reduced by 100%, i.e. to nil).

Example 10.11
Simon Grass died and at the date of his death he owned beneficially:

• cash at bank	£100 000
• listed UK equities in ABC Plc	£50 000
• unquoted shares in XYZ Ltd	£75 000
• house	£600 000

He did not "control" ABC Plc and thus the shares in the company do not qualify for BPR (see below). The shares in XYZ Ltd, however, do qualify for BPR.

Simon's death estate is thus:

Cash at bank		£100 000
Listed UK equities in ABC Plc		£50 000
Unquoted shares in XYZ Ltd	£75 000	
less: BPR (100%; see below)	(£75 000)	
		Nil
House		£600 000
Death estate		£750 000

If instead of the shareholding in XYZ Ltd, Simon had owned a factory worth £75 000 which was being used wholly for business purposes by a company over which Simon had control then on his death BPR would be available on the factory but at the rate of 50% and thus £37 500 would have been included in his death estate.

Not surprisingly, in view of the benefits arising from the reliefs each involve a number of conditions which need to be satisfied.

BPR

The term "business" is not explicitly defined in the legislation but is said to include "a business carried on in the exercise of a profession or vocation but does not include a business carried on otherwise than for gain". Thus, most profit-oriented business will in principle qualify as will the professions of doctor, accountant, lawyer, etc.

Nevertheless, as will be seen below, not all profit-oriented businesses are permitted to qualify.

Relevant Business Property

BPR applies to various types of property, referred to as relevant business property and, depending upon the type of property, the percentage of BPR is either 50% or 100% as follows:

- property consisting of a business or interest in a business (e.g. sole trader, share in a partnership): 100%;
- any unquoted shares in a company which is not listed on a recognised stock exchange (shares dealt in on the Alternative Investment Market (AIM), USM or OFFEX are all regarded as unquoted): 100%;
- unquoted securities in a company owned by the transferor which give the transferor "control" of the company ("control", broadly, meaning voting control) in determining if the transferor has control certain holdings of other persons (e.g. spouse) are also taken into account: 100%;
- shares (or securities) giving "control" of a quoted company: 50%;
- land, buildings, machinery or plant used wholly or mainly for the purposes of a business carried on by a company controlled by the transferor or by a partnership of which the transferor is a partner: 50%.

In the case of property consisting of a business or an interest in a business it is the *net* value of the business which is important. The net value is the total value of *business* assets less liabilities of the business (it may be that an asset of the business is not in fact a "business" asset and thus will not be eligible for BPR; such an asset is referred to as an "excepted asset"; see below). With respect to liabilities, such are deductible only if they have been *incurred for the purposes of the business*. If this is the case the liabilities are deductible whether they are secured against the business assets or not.

Example 10.12

Gerry Tincan owns all the shares in the family company which is unquoted.

The aggregate value of the business assets of the company is £1.5 million. With borrowings used for the purpose of the business of £500 000.

For BPR purposes the value of Gerry's shareholding is the net value of the company, i.e. £1.5 million less £500 000, i.e. £1 million.

It is irrelevant whether the borrowing is secured or not and whether it is secured against assets of the business.

Thus, even if the company had incurred the borrowing but it had been secured against Gerry's home (i.e. not the company's assets) the debt would still be deductible in arriving at the company's net value for BPR purposes.

However, a liability incurred to *acquire* a business (rather than for the purposes of the business itself) would *not* reduce the value of the business.

Example 10.13

Katie Small has decided that she would like to set up in business selling women's clothes.

She is told of a business which is for sale and decides to buy it.

She has insufficient funds from her own resources and so proposes to borrow the shortfall from her local bank and secure the borrowing against her home.

The borrowing from the bank is not a deductible liability for ascertaining the net value of Katie's business for BPR purposes once she has acquired it.

The borrowing was used to acquire her business and thus has not been incurred for the purposes of the business.

Businesses not Qualifying

However, not all types of business qualify for BPR.

Thus, a business or an interest in a business which consists *wholly or mainly* of one or more of the following, namely, dealing in securities, stocks or shares, land or buildings or the making or holding of investments (e.g. a buy to let business) *cannot* qualify as relevant business property (dealing in land or buildings does not encompass trades involving building construction or land development which may thus in principle qualify).

It also follows that shares or securities held in a company whose business consists wholly or mainly of one or more of these activities cannot qualify as relevant business property.

It is important to note that these activities, per se, do not prevent BPR from being available. The issue is whether the activity(ies) is that which is "wholly or mainly" being carried on or not. So, for example, the fact that a company may own an investment property from which rental income (i.e. investment income) is derived does not automatically disqualify the shares in the company from qualifying for BPR if the company's primary activity is that of a company trading in, for example, the purchase and sale of tractors.

Various factors determine what constitutes "wholly or mainly" including, for example, capital employed, turnover, profit and time spent by the owners and employees.

Pro-rata BPR

It may be that not all the assets of the business are in fact assets used for the purposes of the business (whether wholly or mainly) nor are in fact likely to be needed for use in the business in the future.

Such assets are referred to as *excepted assets*.

Where a business comprises in part excepted assets these assets are excluded from benefiting from BPR.

An example of an excepted asset would be the surplus cash of a trading company which has remained as a cash balance at the company's bank for a number of years and where it appears that there is no serious likelihood that it will be used in the company's business in the foreseeable future. Another example would be the ownership by a company of, say, a holiday villa or luxury yacht or other similar asset which is used almost exclusively by the family shareholders for private purposes.

In the above two examples the extent of any BPR would thus be reduced pro rata to take into account the excepted assets. It is important, however, that the extent of any excepted assets is not such as to jeopardise the claim to BPR in its entirety which could happen where the "wholly or mainly" test referred to above is not met.

Where the relevant business property is shares, the proportion of the value of the shares which qualifies for BPR where excepted assets are within the company is determined as follows:

$$\text{Value of shares} \times \frac{\text{Company's eligibile business property}}{\text{Company's total assets (before deducting liabilities)}}$$

It will be noted that liabilities of the company are ignored in determining the extent of BPR, thus reducing the value of the relevant business property qualifying for BPR.

Example 10.14

Natalie Shoe died leaving a death estate of £500 000. Comprised in the estate was a shareholding of 100% in an unquoted trading company, DEF Ltd, worth £150 000.

All the conditions for BPR were satisfied with respect to the shareholding in DEF Ltd.

However, the assets of DEF Ltd totalling £360 000 included a property valued at £60 000 which DEF Ltd let out to a third party. This property would constitute an excepted asset and would thus reduce the extent of any BPR on Natalie's shareholding as follows:

$$\text{BPR} = £150\,000 \times \frac{£300\,000}{£360\,000} \times 100\%$$
$$= £125\,000$$

Thus, £25 000 of the value of Natalie's shareholding in DEF Ltd would be included as part of her death estate (i.e. £150 000 − £125 000).

Ownership Requirements

The key point to note here is that the test involves "ownership" of property.

The legislation requires that for BPR to apply the relevant business property at the date of transfer (be that in lifetime or on death) has to have been owned for a minimum period of time by the transferor, namely, a minimum period of two years (also see below for the alternative "two years out of five years" test).

However, this does not mean that a particular asset has to itself have qualified as a business asset for a minimum period of two years. The important point is that at the date of the transfer the asset constitutes relevant business property (irrespective of whether this was the case prior to the date of transfer).

Example 10.15
Bert Blue has owned a shop for many years and has during this period let it out to Greg Green who has carried on his trade as a confectioner from the shop. The shop does not thus qualify as a relevant business property for Bert as it is an investment property.

Greg is about to retire and so Bert acquires his business.

Unfortunately, Bert dies one year later.

BPR will be available on the shop as it has been in Bert's ownership for the minimum two-year period and qualifies as relevant business property at the date of Bert's death.

Thus, even though the asset (i.e. the shop) was not relevant business property throughout the whole of Bert's ownership is not a problem.

It also should be noted that with respect to relevant business property which comprises a shareholding in a listed company that BPR applies only if the transferor has "control" (broadly, more than 50% of the voting capital) of the company. However, while the ownership requirement demands that the transferor has owned the relevant business property being transferred for a minimum period of two years, it is not necessary for the transferor to have had "control" for this two-year period. "Control" at the date of transfer is sufficient.

Example 10.16
Jane Smythe has owned 48% of the shares in ABC Ltd, a listed company, for six years.

She has just died and six months before she died she managed to acquire an additional 5% of the shares in ABC Ltd, making her total shareholding at death 53% (i.e. control).

BPR will be available on her death at the rate of 50% on the 48% shareholding (which had been owned for at least two years) because she had "control" of ABC Ltd at the date of her death.

The balancing 5%, which had not been owned at her death for the two year minimum period, will not be subject to any BPR.

Example 10.17
Tom and Dick each own 40% of a listed company XYZ Plc. They have each owned their shares for in excess of 10 years.

The balancing 20% is owned by members of the public.

Following a buy-back of shares four years ago (which results in the shares being bought back being cancelled with the consequence that the issued share capital of the company is accordingly reduced) Tom found that he owned 55% of the company's reduced issued share capital.

Should Tom die or make a lifetime transfer of the whole or any part of his shareholding BPR at 50% will apply.

There is no taper relief-type adjustment to BPR for periods of ownership less than two years; it is thus in this sense an all or nothing relief.

Example 10.18
At her death, Helen Brass had owned 50% of the shares in the family unquoted company for one year and 11 months exactly.

No BPR will be available to reduce the value of the shares on her death.

Example 10.19
At her death Sheila Brass, Helen's sister (from Example 10.18 above), had owned the other 50% of the family company for just a little over two years.

BPR will be available to reduce the value of the shares on her death.

A somewhat mild relaxation of the two-year ownership requirement applies to replacement business property. Thus, if the relevant business property owned has replaced other relevant business property the ownership requirement is treated as having been satisfied if the periods of ownership together equal at least two years out of the five years immediately preceding the transfer.

Example 10.20
Trevor Thatch is a cobbler and has been in practice as a sole trader for 10 years.

Following advice from his accountant he incorporates his business (i.e. transfers his sole trader business to the company in exchange for an issue of shares) and now owns all the shares in the company (which is unquoted).

Unfortunately, one year later Tom dies thus having held the shares for only one year.

In ascertaining if BPR is available on the shares the period of ownership of the shares may take into account the period of ownership of the sole tradership.

As Tom therefore held the shares and the sole tradership for at least two out of the previous five years BPR is in principle available on his death.

In view of the importance of BPR it is important than when carrying out any inheritance tax planning that it is not wasted whether by accident or otherwise. Inter alia, this involves making sure that the *appropriate* beneficiary inherits the property.

Example 10.21
On Susan Billings' death her death estate comprised £500 000 of which £300 000 related to her shareholding in an unlisted company. This qualified for BPR.

In her will she had left the shares to her husband.

The shares are not subject to inheritance tax as they have been left to her husband which is an inter-spouse transfer and therefore BPR is wasted.

If instead Susan had left the shares to her son BPR will not be wasted and the balance of her estate will be exempt due to the inter-spouse exemption.

In the above Example 10.21 by leaving the qualifying shareholding to her husband Susan had wasted the 100% BPR available thereon.

It is therefore important where possible for business property qualifying for BPR to be left by will (or gifted in lifetime) to chargeable beneficiaries (i.e. where an inheritance tax charge arises in principle) and not to be the subject of inter-spouse transfers.

Inter-spouse Transfers

Usually inter-spouse transfers tend to be treated the same for inheritance tax purposes whether the transfers are effected in lifetime or on death; and usually no adverse tax consequences arise due to inter-spouse relief.

With respect to BPR this is not always the case.

The transfer on *death* of relevant business property from one spouse to the other permits the surviving spouse to aggregate the period of ownership of the deceased with that of the surviving spouse with respect to future transfers.

This aggregation of periods of ownership is *not*, however, applicable in the case of *lifetime* inter-spouse transfers of relevant business property.

Note also that the ability to aggregate periods of ownership only applies to *inter-spouse* transfers on death not other transfers on death (e.g. from brother to brother or father to son).

Example 10.22
Hector Revenue and his wife Abigail have been married for many years and have a son, Harold, aged 32.

After leaving the service of HMRC, Hector decided to set himself up as a sole trader manufacturing and selling curtains.

After five years the business had grown significantly in value and Hector introduced his wife into the business as a full partner (50/50); henceforth the business operating as a partnership.

Abigail died 15 months after becoming a partner leaving her interest in the partnership to their son, Harold.

No BPR would be available on Abigail's death as she owned the interest in the partnership (albeit relevant business property) for less than two years; she was not able to include as part of her ownership period that of her husband Hector.

Example 10.23
Using the facts in the above Example 10.22, assume that on Hector's death he left the business to Abigail (i.e. no lifetime transfer to Abigail).

Abigail, however, died 15 months after Hector's death leaving the business to their son Harold.

BPR would be available on Abigail's death as she will be assumed to have owned the business for the actual period of ownership by her of 15 months *plus* the five-year period of ownership by Hector.

While almost invariably inter-spouse transfers do not make the overall tax position of the married couple "worse" this is not always literally the case.

Example 10.22 above highlights the very real dangers which can occur as a consequence of inter-spouse transfers. While such transfers may be effected in order to mitigate inheritance tax liabilities on future deaths it is crucial at least to be aware of possible adverse consequences accidentally arising which result in a worse position; not better.

A common situation in this regard is that of a father who owns 100% of the shares in the family company (an unquoted company) which he has built up over many years. In an attempt to "enfranchise" his son and daughter, who work full time in the business, their father transfers 50% of his shares to the two children (25% to each).

By transferring 50% of his shareholding in this way there is the perhaps very real risk that should either of the children die within two years of receiving their shares BPR will be lost on their respective shareholding.

On the other hand, if the father had simply kept 100% of the company and then left the relevant shareholdings to the children on his death, BPR at 100% would have applied to the whole shareholding (in addition, this would have been advantageous for capital gains tax purposes due to the tax-free uplift on death; see Chapter 8).

BPR and Death within Seven Years of a Transfer

A lifetime transfer of relevant business property is either a PET or a CLT.

If the former (i.e. a PET) and the transferor survives for seven years no inheritance tax liability arises and whether BPR applied or not becomes academic (effectively, the BPR is wasted).

If the latter (i.e. a CLT) then an immediate inheritance tax liability arises at 20% of the value transferred (assuming that the transferor's NRB has been exhausted). If BPR applies to the transfer at that time then the value transferred will be reduced to nil (if BPR is 100%) or reduced by 50% (if BPR at 50% applies).

Should the transferor die within seven years of the transfer, be it a PET or CLT, then the availability of BPR needs to be re-examined because in such circumstances *additional* conditions to those discussed earlier in the chapter need to be satisfied (recall that a PET becomes chargeable for the first time if the transferor dies within seven years of making it and a CLT becomes subject to *additional* inheritance tax in these circumstances having already been charged in lifetime; see Chapter 9).

The additional conditions which need to be satisfied at death are two-fold:

- the property transferred must continue to be in the ownership of the transferee (or until the transferee's death if the transferee dies before the transferor) *or* the original property transferred may be sold by the transferee but within three years thereof the transferee must have reinvested the sale proceeds in other relevant business property; *and*
- if hypothetically the property had been transferred by the transferee at the transferor's date of death it would at that time have qualified for BPR (ignoring the two-year minimum ownership requirement).

Both conditions must be satisfied.

If both conditions *are* satisfied at the date of death then the transfer of value at the date of the original lifetime transfer is reduced by the appropriate level of BPR thus reducing or removing completely any inheritance tax charge on the PET or additional charge on the CLT arising because of the death.

If this is not the case (i.e. both conditions are not satisfied at the date of death) any PET will simply be subject to inheritance tax without the applicability of any BPR. In the case of the CLT the lifetime charge remains unchanged (i.e. BPR having been applied to determine the inheritance charge in lifetime) but the additional inheritance tax charge arising due to death is calculated without the benefit of any BPR.

It is thus not correct (as commentators frequently state) that BPR on a CLT is "withdrawn" if the additional conditions at death are not satisfied. As stated above, no changes are made to the charge already levied on the lifetime transfer (i.e. it has been correctly computed on the basis that at that time BPR was applicable) but the additional charge arising on death is simply calculated without BPR being in point.

Example 10.24
Terry Ramsay owns all the ordinary shares in his unquoted trading company, Hardcore Steels Ltd, and has done so since he formed the company 10 years ago.

On 2 January 2006 he transferred 10% of the shares to his son valued at £100 000.

On 5 March 2006 he settled a further 30% of the shares on a discretionary trust, the beneficiaries of which are his son, daughter and brother valued at £350 000.

On 16 July 2008 Terry died.

Assume all of Terry's NRB had been utilised.

The gift on 2 January 2006 is a PET and thus no inheritance tax charge arises at that time.

The gift on 5 March 2006 is a CLT and in principle an inheritance tax charge arises at that time. However, BPR of 100% applies and thus the CLT in fact equals [£350 000−£350 000], i.e. nil (due to 100% BPR).

Terry's death causes the PET to become chargeable and the CLT to become subject to the additional tax charge.

The chargeable amounts are:

PET
Chargeable amount = £100 000−£100 000 [BPR 100%] = nil

CLT
Chargeable amount = £350 000−£350 000 [BPR 100%] = nil

Thus, no inheritance tax arises due to Terry's death. This does, however, assume that on Terry's death both the additional conditions (referred to in the text above) were satisfied.

Suppose, however, that at the date of Terry's death both his son and the trust had each sold their shares without purchasing replacement relevant business property.

As a consequence no BPR would be available on Terry's death. In this case the chargeable amounts would be as follows:

PET
Chargeable amount = £100 000
Inheritance tax charge = £100 000 × 40% = £40 000

A liability to inheritance tax charge arises because of a lack of BPR which in fact is no longer available as the conditions on death are not satisfied.

CLT
Chargeable amount = £350 000
Inheritance tax charge = £350 000 × 40% = £140 000

Again the conditions for BPR are not satisfied at the date of death.

However, the position in lifetime on the CLT (when at that time BPR was available) remains unchanged.

Order of Transfers

It is not unusual for land and buildings, in particular, to be held beneficially by a major shareholder of an unquoted family company and then let to the company for use in its trade. This approach avoids a possible double capital gains tax charge on a future sale of the shares in the company and/or its liquidation.

From the perspective of BPR, prima facie, no problems arise. The shares in principle qualify for 100% BPR and the land and buildings qualify for 50% BPR.

Suppose, however, that the father who owns, say, 100% of the company's shares decides to transfer his shareholding as a lifetime transfer to his daughter and son (50/50). He, however, feels that he would like to retain the land and buildings but is happy to continue to let the company use them for its trade as in the past.

Six months later the father unexpectedly dies.

The share transfers to his son and daughter are PETs which now fall chargeable to inheritance tax due to the father's death within seven years of the date of the transfers. At the date of making the PETs BPR was applicable. On the father's death the two conditions to be satisfied on death are satisfied, thus 100% BPR is applicable and, as a consequence, no inheritance tax charge arises on the PETs due to the father's death.

The land and buildings form part of the father's estate. Under his will the father left the land and buildings equally to his daughter and son. Unfortunately, BPR is not applicable.

BPR on the father's death requires that the property (i.e. land and buildings) has been owned by the father for a two-year minimum period (which is satisfied) *and* the property must at the time of death also have been used for the purposes of a business carried on by a company (which it was) *which the transferor (i.e. the father) "controlled"* (which he did not). At the date of death the father owned no shares in the company (having given them away in lifetime).

The land and buildings would thus be subject to inheritance tax on the father's death at 40% of their then value.

This charge could, however, have been easily avoided by ensuring that the father simply left both the shares *and* the land and buildings in his will at death.

It is therefore important that where lifetime transfers of relevant business property occur, which at that time would qualify for BPR, the donees (i.e. the son and the trustees in the above Example 10.24) are made aware of the conditions which need to be satisfied if BPR is to continue to be available on the subsequent death of the donor. In particular, that any sale of the property by the donee (without replacement qualifying property being purchased) will preclude BPR being available on the donor's death (or donee's death if earlier).

It should be remembered in this regard that any inheritance tax liability which might arise whether on a PET or CLT due to the death of the donor (within the seven-year period) is the liability of the *donee*, not the donor (see Chapter 13).

SETTLED BUSINESS PROPERTY

BPR (and APR) is still in principle available if the relevant business property is settled property, i.e. comprised in a trust.

Pre 22 March 2006 Created Interest in Possession Trust

Where any transfer of value is deemed to be made by the beneficiary with the interest in possession it is this beneficiary who needs to satisfy the conditions for BPR if it is to apply on such a transfer.

Post 22 March 2006 Created Interest in Possession Trust

Any transfer of value is no longer deemed to be made by the beneficiary with the interest in possession. Such a trust is now treated as a relevant property trust (i.e. the same as a discretionary trust; see Chapter 15) and thus the availability of BPR is determined according to the ownership by the trustees (not the beneficiary).

Certain interest in possession trusts set up on or after 22 March 2006 are still, however, treated the same as those created before this date. Primarily, this arises where the interest in possession trust is set up under a will (lifetime interest in possession trusts can no longer be set up on or after 22 March 2006 and be treated as a pre 22 March 2006 such trust).

Discretionary Trusts

Irrespective of the date such a trust is set up (whether pre or post 22 March 2006) it is the trustees' ownership which determines if the conditions for BPR on any transfers of value apply. Discretionary trusts are taxable entities in their own right and, unlike interest in possession trusts, no beneficiary has any automatic rights to the income (or indeed capital) of the trust.

BPR is relevant in the case of such trusts in ascertaining the amount of inheritance tax charged on the trust's 10 yearly anniversaries and on any exit charges (see Chapter 15).

AGRICULTURAL PROPERTY RELIEF

APR is available on transfers of agricultural property.

Agricultural property comprises agricultural land or pasture and any farm buildings, farmhouses and cottages that are occupied with the agricultural land as are of a character appropriate to the property. Effectively, occupation of such buildings must be ancillary to the agricultural land.

APR may also be available on transfers of shares in a farming company. This applies where the transferor had "control" of the company immediately prior to the transfer and the agricultural property forms part of the assets of the company. However, APR only applies to the value of the shares which reflects the agricultural value of the property in the company; nevertheless BPR may also be available on that part of the value of the shares which reflects any non-agricultural value.

As with BPR the form of the relief is a reduction in the transfer value of the agricultural land qualifying for the relief. The amount of the relief is 100%.

APR applies where the transferor had the right to vacant possession immediately before the transfer or the right to obtain such possession within the next 12 months (possibly 24 months) *or* where the agricultural property is let on a tenancy granted on or after 1 September 1995.

It may be that BPR also applies in addition to APR. APR applies to the agricultural value of the property which is the value on the assumption that the property was subject to a perpetual covenant prohibiting its use otherwise than as agricultural property. It is highly likely that the market value of the property will be greater than its value on this "agricultural" basis and, if so, BPR may be available on this excess amount (assuming the conditions applicable to BPR are satisfied; see above).

Ownership Requirements

At the time of the transfer of the agricultural property the property must have been occupied by the transferor for the purposes of agriculture throughout the period of two years ending on the date of the transfer or have replaced agricultural property which together with the replacement property was occupied for agricultural purposes for at least two years out of the last five years ending with the date of transfer.

Alternatively, the agricultural property must have been owned by the transferor throughout the period of seven years ending with the date of the transfer and occupied for the purposes of agriculture by the transferor or another throughout the period.

Agricultural property acquired on the death of a spouse permits aggregation of periods of ownership.

APR and Death within Seven Years of a Transfer

APR is available on death and on lifetime transfers (i.e. whether PETs or CLTs).

For APR to apply on a failed PET (i.e. where the donor dies within seven years of the date of the gift) or where additional inheritance tax arises on a CLT due to death within seven years of the date of the lifetime CLT the following conditions need to be satisfied:

- the original property must have been owned by the transferee throughout the period from the date of the lifetime transfer until the death of the donor; and
- immediately before the death of the donor the original property must qualify for APR on the part of the transferee.

Replacement property may not invalidate the above.

QUICK SUCCESSION RELIEF

QSR is a relief only available on death (for unsettled property).

Its purpose is to alleviate a double charge to inheritance tax which would otherwise arise as the same property would be taxed twice in a short period of time.

More specifically, QSR applies on death where the value of the deceased's estate has been increased by a chargeable transfer to the deceased which was made within the previous five years. It is irrelevant whether this earlier chargeable transfer was a lifetime transfer or a transfer on death.

The relief operates by reducing the amount of inheritance tax charged on the second chargeable occasion (i.e. on the death). The relief is a percentage of the amount of inheritance tax charged on the earlier transfer. The percentage varies according to the length of time between the earlier transfer and the date of death (in a sense a form of taper relief) as follows:

- 100% if previous transfer one year or less before death;
- 80% if previous transfer more than one year but not more than two years before death;
- 60% if previous transfer more than two years but not more than three years before death;
- 40% if previous transfer more than three years but not more than four years before death;
- 20% if previous transfer more than four years but not more than five years before death.

Thus, no QSR is available if the death following receipt of an earlier chargeable transfer more than five years thereafter.

Example 10.25
Elisabeth Terry died, having made no lifetime transfers, but with a death estate of £612 000.

In her will she left her daughter, Samantha, £306 000.

Unfortunately, Samantha died three and a half years later with a death estate of £512 000.

As Samantha died within five years of her mother from whom she had received a chargeable transfer, on Samantha's death a measure of QSR is available. If no such relief was available in such circumstances then effectively inheritance tax on £306 000 would be charged twice (once on Elisabeth's death and a second time on the death of Samantha).

Elisabeth's death
Inheritance tax liability = [£612 000 − £312 000] × 40% = £120 000
  Of this £120 000 some 50% thereof, i.e. £60 000, was paid in respect of the legacy to Samantha
  QSR = £60 000 × 40% = £24 000 (40% QSR is because Samantha died more than three but not more than four years after her mother)

Samantha's death
Inheritance tax liability = [£512 000 − £312 000] × 40% = £80 000
  Less: QSR of £24 000
  Net inheritance tax payable on Elisabeth's death = £56 000

SUMMARY

Transfers whether in lifetime or on death may qualify as exempt transfers or, alternatively, may be subject to some form of relief.

Most (but not all) exempt transfers apply only on lifetime transfers. However, the inter-spouse exemption (perhaps one of the most important of the exemptions) applies to transfers whether in lifetime or on death. For the particularly wealthy individual the "normal expenditure out of income" exemption should certainly not be overlooked.

One of the most important reliefs, available on lifetime transfers and on death, is BPR. Its importance lies in the extent of the relief which in a number of cases is 100%. However, it is important in order not to lose the relief that the donees of any transfers in lifetime are made aware of the conditions which need to be satisfied up to the date of death of the donor (or death of the donee if earlier).

APR is also an important and similar relief to BPR.

QSR is a relief only applicable on death. It is, however, useful as it prevents double taxation due to two deaths occurring within five years of each other.

11
Inheritance Tax: Gifts with Reservation

BACKGROUND

The concept of "gifts with reservation" (GWR) is a fiction of relevance only to inheritance tax. The concept thus has no implication for income or capital gains tax.

The GWR rules are intended to prevent an individual giving an asset away yet still thereafter continuing to enjoy the benefit of the asset and, at the same time, avoiding an inheritance tax charge on the asset on death on the grounds that the asset no longer forms part of the transferor's death estate.

Example 11.1
Henry Fosset has a number of valuable antique paintings hung up in his house.

He transfers the ownership of the paintings to his daughter but continues to leave the paintings hung up in his house.

The gift to his daughter would be treated as a GWR.

As a consequence, on Henry's death the value of the paintings at the date of death would form part of Henry's death estate.

Example 11.2
Sharon and Keith Smith own an unmortgaged and valuable home.

They transfer ownership of their home to their son and daughter but Sharon and Keith continue to live in the home as before.

The gifts to the son and daughter are treated as GWR.

The GWR rules were introduced to prevent the avoidance of inheritance tax on death by the use of devices such as illustrated in Examples 11.1 and 11.2 above.

The rules apply to lifetime gifts made on or after 18 March 1986.

It is not possible for a gift made by will to constitute a GWR.

While a GWR is treated as any other form of gift at the time it is made, on the death of the donor the value of the gift is treated as part of the donor's death estate and thus falls subject to inheritance tax as part of the deceased's death estate (almost as if the property/asset had never been given away in the first instance).

It is the value of the gifted property at the date of death (not the actual date of the gift) which forms part of the donor's estate. Thus, no so-called "asset freezing" occurs (i.e. that future growth in the value of an asset after making the gift remains outside the donor's estate).

The GWR rules thus create a fiction as on the donor's death the asset gifted by the donor in lifetime does not in fact belong to the donor but the donee.

Despite being included as part of the death estate on the death of the donor the initial gift is still treated as a PET (or CLT) and thus the death of the donor within seven years precipitates an inheritance tax charge on the PET/CLT (or additional tax on the CLT).

In this case a double charge to inheritance tax may arise (i.e. once on the PET and again on the asset as it is deemed to form part of the death estate of the donor). Provisions exist to ameliorate this potential double tax charge.

It is, however, to be appreciated that although for inheritance tax purposes there is this "deeming" of the asset to be part of the donor's estate on death the reality is that the ownership of the asset rests with the donee. Thus, were the donee to die the asset would form part of the donee's estate as normal.

Example 11.3
Nelly Foot owns £150 000 worth of UK listed equities.

She gifts the equities to her daughter, Karen, on condition that she (i.e. Nelly) retains all rights to future dividends on the shares until death.

The gift is a GWR.

Nelly dies on 13 June 2008. The value of the equities on 13 June 2008 are included as part of Nelly's death estate.

Two years later her daughter dies still owning the shares. The value of the shares is included as part of Karen's death estate.

The donee is also the owner for capital gains tax purposes. The base cost of the asset to the donee is the market value of the asset at the date of the gift (not at the date of the donor's death).

Example 11.4
Tom purchased listed shares in XYZ Plc for £100 000.

He transferred the legal ownership to his brother, Sam, when the shares were worth £300 000 but Tom retained the rights to all dividends arising on the shares.

The gift would thus be treated as a GWR.

Tom dies in June 2008 and the shares at that time are worth £650 000. For inheritance tax purposes the shares are included as part of Tom's estate at this value (not the £300 000 value).

Sam sells the shares in October 2008, after his brother's death, for £700 000.

For capital gains tax purposes Sam will have made a capital gain of £400 000 (i.e. £700 000 less £300 000).

Although the GWR forms part of the donor's estate on death any inheritance tax liability arising thereon is that of the donee not that of the estate (see Chapter 13).

Example 11.5
Geoff gifts his vintage car (worth £250 000) to his son, John, but keeps the car in his own garage and continues to use the car as if it still belonged to him.

The gift is a GWR.

Geoff dies with a chargeable death estate of £612 000; of this £262 000 represents the value of the car of the date of his death.

Geoff leaves his estate to his daughter, Isabella.

The inheritance tax liability on Geoff's estate is

$$40\% \times (£612\,000 - £312\,000) = £120\,000$$

The average rate of inheritance tax on death is

$$[£120\,000/£612\,000] \times 100 = 19.6\%$$

Thus, John is liable for inheritance tax of 19.6% of £262 000, i.e. £51 352.

The executors of Geoff's will are responsible for payment of £68 648 (i.e. £120 000 less £51 352).

For the GWR rules not to apply the donor must be excluded from all benefit during the "relevant period" *or* the donee must have full possession and enjoyment of the property either at or before the beginning of the relevant period. The "relevant period" is the period beginning seven years before death of the donor or, the date of the gift, if later.

Even if a GWR is made, if the donor subsequently releases the reservation the release itself constitutes a PET (assuming the gift is to another individual and not to a trust). If the death of the donor (i.e. the individual effecting the release) occurs within seven years thereof an inheritance tax liability will arise on the failed PET. In addition, at the date of the donor's death if the donee did not have full possession and enjoyment of the gift for the seven years prior to the donor's death the gift will also fall to be included as part of the donor's death estate. In effect a double charge to inheritance tax will have arisen; there is, however, rules to ameliorate this double charge.

If, however, the donor survives for seven years from the date of releasing the reservation no inheritance tax charge will arise on the PET and the GWR rules will not apply to the donor's death estate.

Example 11.6

Samantha Uptight has a piece of valuable jewellery which she gifted to her daughter, Cynthia, in March 1997.

However, Samantha continues to retain the jewellery in her own home and continues to wear it as and when she chooses. However, in June 2000 Samantha hands over the jewellery to Cynthia and Samantha no longer wears or has access to the jewellery from this date.

Samantha dies in September 2008.

As Cynthia (the donee) gained full possession and enjoyment of the jewellery more than seven years before Samantha's death the PET made by Samantha (i.e. the release of the reservation in June 2000) is no longer chargeable and the GWR rules do not apply on Samantha's death.

EXEMPTIONS

The GWR rules do not, however, apply in all cases where, prima facie, the rules might otherwise be expected to apply (see Chapter 12 for the interaction between the GWR rules and excluded property).

Exemptions

A gift which falls to be treated as an exempt transfer (see Chapter 10) is not caught by the GWR rules if the exempt transfer falls within, inter alia, the following exemptions, namely, small gifts; gifts in contemplation of marriage; or gifts to charities. However, gifts within the annual exemption or normal expenditure out of income exemption may be caught under the GWR rules.

Inter-spouse Gifts

The GWR rules do not apply to inter-spouse transfers.

Full Consideration

This exemption only applies in the cases of land or chattels.

If the donor's enjoyment of the asset is in return for full (i.e. market) consideration the GWR rules do not apply. It is critical, however, that full consideration is paid throughout the period of enjoyment of the asset if the GWR rules are not to apply.

Example 11.7
Bob and Myrtle Orange own their own home, which is mortgage free, and worth £850 000. They decide to gift it to their two sons, Harry and Tony, but remain in occupation.

Bob and Myrtle are aware of the GWR rules and agree with their sons to pay a market rent in return for continuing to live there.

The gift will not as a consequence be treated as a GWR.

It should be noted that the donees (i.e. the two sons in Example 11.7 above) will be subject to income tax on the rental income received from the donor (i.e. the parents in Example 11.7 above).

Co-ownership

Where a gift of an undivided share or an interest in land occurs the GWR rules are not in point if both the donor and donee occupy the land and the donor does not receive any further benefit at the donee's expense in connection with the gift. Thus, the GWR rules will not apply if the donee does not pay more than his/her fair share of the outgoings associated with the property.

No GWR issues arise even if the donor "overpays" his/her share of the relevant expenses.

It should be noted that the gift must be of an undivided share which means that a gift of the whole of the property would not satisfy the above condition.

TRUSTS

The GWR rules also apply to gifts into trusts.

Thus, if a discretionary trust is created by one spouse (the settlor) who does, or may fall within the class of beneficiaries, then the GWR rules will apply, i.e. the whole of the trust fund is included as part of the settlor's death estate.

On the other hand, if the settlor is excluded from the potential class of beneficiaries, the GWR rules do not apply. This is the case even if the settlor's spouse may benefit under the trust.

There is no GWR where the settlor, following the gift into trust, possesses a "qualifying interest in possession" in the trust. A "qualifying interest in possession" is one created in lifetime where the trust was created before 22 March 2006 (or created by will where the trust is created on or after or before 22 March 2006; see Chapter 15).

Following FA 2006, the termination of all interests in possession created prior to 22 March 2006 (and not terminated by this date) and the termination of all interests in possession created by will on or after this date are treated as gifts at that time by the individual possessing the interest. The gift is treated as a gift of the property in the trust in which the interest subsists.

If the individual, however, after termination of the interest in possession continues to be able to benefit under the trust a GWR will be deemed to have been made on the termination. Where, however, the individual's interest in possession is terminated in favour of, for example, the spouse who takes a qualifying interest in possession the GWR rules will not apply (because the property is not treated as settled by the gift; it is already settled).

Example 11.8
Brian Blue under his will left the residue of his estate on trust for his spouse under which she acquired an interest in possession.

No inheritance tax arose due to the inter-spouse exemption.

The trustees subsequently terminated the spouse's interest in possession so that she simply becomes a beneficiary of a discretionary trust.

The spouse is treated as having made a GWR. The gift was of the property in the trust in which her interest in possession subsisted and as she continues to be able to benefit under the trust, as a discretionary beneficiary, her gift is a GWR.

PRE-OWNED ASSETS

The pre-owned asset legislation was introduced to combat situations where an asset is given to another person but the donor still enjoys the benefit of the asset but the transaction is structured such that the GWR provisions discussed above are circumnavigated (i.e. do not apply). Where the legislation applies the donor is subject to an annual income tax charge on the "benefit" which the legislation defines.

The charge applies to:

- land;
- chattels (i.e. movable tangible property);
- "intangible property" in trust where the settlor retains an interest.

Chattels include valuable paintings, antique furniture, vintage wines, etc. and intangible property includes life policies and shares.

For the purpose of intangible property a settlor retains an interest in the settlement if the settlor is taxable on the income of the trust (if the spouse can benefit under the settlement this is ignored).

Various additional conditions need to be satisfied for the charge to apply but, where the charge does apply, in the case of land income tax is levied on the appropriate rental value of the property less any payments made by the individual to the owner (i.e. donee) of the property (e.g. payments of rent).

In the case of chattels, the income tax charge is levied on a figure arrived at by calculating a nominal interest charge on the value of the chattels less any contributions paid by the individual to the owner (i.e. donee).

In the case of "intangibles" the same approach as applies to chattels is followed.

Although introduced in the Finance Act 2004 the legislation potentially applies to any gifts made on or after 18 March 1986. However, an actual charge to income tax may apply only from 6 April 2005.

The individual can avoid the charge if an election is made under which the property is brought back within the GWR provisions, i.e. the property will then form part of the individual's estate on death as normal under the GWR provisions. If such an election is made the pre-owned asset rules are no longer in point.

There is a time limit in which the election must be made which is 31 January following the *first* tax year in which the pre-owned asset legislation would otherwise apply. For those individuals caught by the legislation when it first became applicable (i.e. 6 April 2005) the requisite deadline was 31 January 2007 which, of course, has already past. The election, however, only applies with respect to land and chattels.

For the individual originally caught (i.e. on 6 April 2005) or an individual who may be caught at some time in the future the decision whether to make the election involves a comparison of the respective tax charges. Thus, if no election is to be made then on death no inheritance tax will apply to the property gifted. On the other hand, for every tax year up to and including death an income tax charge will apply.

If, however, an election is made on death inheritance tax will apply to the property gifted. On the other hand, for every tax year up to and including death an income tax charge will have been avoided.

Prima facie, if the donor of the gift is, relatively speaking, "old" then it would seem that, other things being equal, no election should be made as the number of tax years in which an income tax charge will arise may be limited. If the donor is, relatively speaking, "young" then the reverse (i.e. an election) would seem appropriate.

SUMMARY

The GWR and pre-owned asset rules are extremely complex and it is easy for the individual to fall foul of them. Falling foul of them may prove costly in inheritance tax terms.

The GWR rules in essence catch what might loosely be termed "conditional gifts", i.e. the donor makes a gift conditional on retaining enjoyment rights over the property gifted. The GWR rules prevent attempts by the individual to gift property (so that it no longer forms part of the donor's estate) but still continue to enjoy the property thereafter. It does this by including the value of the property in the donor's estate on death.

Where the GWR rules fail to "catch" gifts intended to be "caught" it is more than likely that the pre-owned asset legislation will apply.

12
Inheritance Tax: Excluded Property

BACKGROUND

Chapter 10 examined the exemptions and reliefs available under the inheritance tax legislation. This chapter will examine the concept of "excluded property".

Excluded property is of primary importance to the non-UK domiciled individual but it does also have some (albeit lesser) importance for the UK domiciled individual.

Excluded property is property which is simply outside the scope of inheritance tax.

In other words, excluded property is generally ignored when ascertaining an individual's inheritance tax liability whether on a lifetime gift and/or on death.

Excluded property may comprise both settled and non-settled property.

NON-SETTLED PROPERTY

Property which is not settled property (i.e. property not in a trust) is excluded property if it is beneficially owned by a non-UK domiciled individual (see Chapter 3) *and* the property is not situate in the UK (see Chapter 6).

Thus, two conditions need to be satisfied if property is to qualify as excluded property, namely:

- the individual must be non-UK domiciled under common law *and* not deemed UK domiciled under the inheritance tax legislation; *and*
- the property must be non-UK situs.

Thus, any UK situs property cannot qualify as excluded property irrespective of the domicile status of the beneficial owner (subject to one or two exceptions; see below).

Similarly, any UK or non-UK situs property owned beneficially by either a UK domiciled individual (under common law) or a deemed UK domiciled individual (under the inheritance tax legislation) cannot so qualify.

The situs of property for this purpose is determined by the common law rules (see Chapter 6).

SETTLED PROPERTY

Despite the wide-ranging changes introduced in FA 2006 concerning the inheritance tax treatment of trusts (see Chapter 15) no changes were made explicitly to the excluded property rules vis-à-vis trusts. The position pre and post March 2006 re excluded property trusts (see below) is thus in essence the same (however, because of some of the changes introduced by FA 2006 an excluded property trust may lose this status in some, albeit, limited circumstances and account must be taken of this risk, however small; see below).

With respect to settled property (i.e. property in trust) such property is excluded property if the settlor was non-UK domiciled when the settlement was created *and* the property (at the relevant time, i.e. when the charge to inheritance tax needs to be considered) is *not* situate in the UK.

Trusts set up by non-UK domiciled settlors in which some of the property is non-UK situs are often referred to as "excluded property trusts". Strictly speaking, however, it is the non-UK situs property comprised in the trust which qualifies as excluded property. The trust, as such, is simply a trust and therefore to a degree the term "exluded property trust" may be misleading.

In the case of a discretionary trust excluded property is not part of the trust's relevant property (and thus is not subject to the ten yearly or exit charges which apply to discretionary trusts; and indeed most other trusts set up on or after 22 March 2006; see Chapter 15).

In the case of an interest in possession trust (set up pre 22 March 2006) the beneficiary with the interest in possession is not subject to inheritance tax on the death with respect to their interest in the excluded property of the trust (see Chapter 15).

A reversionary interest in a trust is excluded property irrespective of the domicile status of the settlor and the domicile status of the holder of the interest. A reversionary interest is defined as a future interest under a settlement whether vested or contingent. Thus, for example, an interest which is dependent on the termination of an interest in possession is a reversionary interest.

An interest under a discretionary trust cannot, however, constitute a reversionary interest.

The excluded property rules apply to settled property whether the trust is UK or non-UK resident (see Chapter 16). Thus, although from the excluded property perspective it does not matter if the trust is UK resident such a trust does have income and capital gains tax disadvantages for the non-UK domiciled but UK resident individual (see Chapters 16 and 17).

EXCLUDED PROPERTY AND THE NON-UK DOMICILED

Excluded property is central to most inheritance tax planning for the non-UK domiciled individual. For the UK domiciled individual excluded property has in reality very little role to play (with perhaps one exception concerning UK gilts; see below).

Example 12.1
Conswella Gomez, a non-UK domiciled individual, died in 2008.

Her death estate comprised £600 000 of UK listed equities; a UK house worth £1.5 million; US listed equities worth £200 000 and a Spanish house worth £1 million.

Inheritance tax on her death estate would be based on £2.1 million (i.e. the value of the UK situs assets).

The non-UK situs assets (i.e. the US listed equities and the Spanish villa) qualify as excluded property.

Example 12.2
Helmut Brazil on his death owned £100 000 of UK real estate; £75 000 of Brazilian real estate; $100 000 of cash in a bank account in a Swiss bank; and was the interest in possession beneficiary of a trust set up by his non-UK domiciled father which, at Helmut's death, comprised exclusively US equities worth £1 million.

Inheritance tax on his death estate would be based on £100 000 only (i.e. the value of the UK situs assets).

If at Helmut's death the trust had comprised of £1 million of UK equities, Helmut's death estate would be £1.1 million (as the property in which Helmut's interest in possession subsisted is not excluded property).

NON-UK SITUS PROPERTY

The situs of property is determined by the common law rules (see Chapter 6); where the property is non-UK situs and is beneficially owned by the non-UK domiciled individual it is excluded property.

However, if the non-UK domiciled individual who owns the non-UK situs property subsequently becomes deemed UK domiciled under the inheritance tax deemed domicile rule and/or under the common law (e.g. acquires a UK domicile of choice; see Chapter 3) any non-UK situs property held by such individual would no longer rank as excluded property.

Example 12.3
Zizzi Schoneberg, a German (i.e. non-UK) domiciled individual, lives in the UK.

She owns various US equities; a house in Spain; cash held in a bank in Liechtenstein; and various UK equities.

Apart from her holding of UK equities (which are UK situs) all the other property ranks as excluded property.

Should Zizzi die, inheritance tax would only be chargeable on the value of the UK equities.

Example 12.4
Using the facts in Example 12.3 above, Zizzi likes the UK very much but she does eventually intend to return home to Germany (thus retaining her German domicile of origin).

In the tax year 2008/09 she discovers that she has been UK resident for 17 tax years out of the previous 20 tax years and thus is now deemed UK domiciled for inheritance tax purposes (albeit still retaining her German domicile of origin under common law).

All her assets (both UK and non-UK situs) detailed in Example 12.3 above are now subject to inheritance tax on her death (or if any lifetime gifts are made) as none of them any longer qualify as excluded property.

Minimum Length of Time to Hold Assets

It is worth noting that a non-UK situs asset does not need to be held by a non-UK domiciled individual for any minimum time period for it to be treated as excluded property. Thus, if, for example, just prior to death a non-UK domiciled but UK resident individual who held a large sterling (or foreign currency) deposit with a UK bank (a UK situs asset) transferred the monies to an account with an overseas-based bank (i.e. a non-UK situs asset) and then died, say, one week later, the overseas sterling (foreign currency) account would rank as excluded property.

UK SITUS ASSETS

While it is primarily with non-UK situs assets that the concept of excluded property is concerned certain UK situs assets are specifically designated as excluded property. Such assets include the following.

Authorised Unit Trusts (AUT) and Open Ended Investment Companies (OEIC)

Despite being UK situs assets for inheritance tax purposes (see Chapter 6) units of an AUT or shares in an OEIC (incorporated in the UK) are excluded property if held beneficially by a non-UK domiciled individual.

However, should the non-UK domiciled individual who owns units in an AUT and/or shares in an OEIC become deemed UK domiciled for inheritance tax purposes the assets will no longer rank as excluded property.

UK Government Securities or Gilts

Despite being UK situs assets for inheritance tax purposes (see Chapter 6) UK Government securities or gilts are excluded property if they have been issued on or after 29 April 1996 and are held beneficially by an individual who is *non-ordinarily resident* in the UK; the domicile status of such individual is irrelevant to excluded property status (this is unusual).

The condition of non-UK ordinary residence (rather than the usual non-UK domicile requirement) means that even a *UK* domiciled individual may take advantage of excluded property status vis-à-vis UK gilts. Such advantage could be taken by the individual in the following scenario.

The UK domiciled and UK resident individual chooses to emigrate from the UK and in so doing hopes to acquire a non-UK domicile of choice (under common law). However, even where the non-UK domicile of choice is in fact acquired, under the deemed UK domicile rules (see Chapters 3 and 9) the individual remains deemed UK domiciled for inheritance tax purposes for three more years. During this three-year period the individual thus remains within the inheritance tax charge on worldwide situs assets.

One option open to such individual to minimise this exposure to inheritance tax is to liquidate various (otherwise inheritance taxable) investments and use the sale proceeds to purchase UK gilts which could be held during this three-year period. The gilts would rank as excluded property because, following emigration from the UK, the individual would become both non-UK resident and (more importantly for present purposes) non-UK ordinarily resident (see Chapter 4).

Example 12.5

Albert Gross, aged 46, who possesses a UK domicile of origin, has decided to emigrate from the UK to Spain.

On 1 July 2008 HMRC accepts that he has acquired a Spanish domicile of choice from this date.

However, he remains UK deemed domiciled for inheritance tax purposes for three more years, i.e. until 30 June 2011.

His total estate comprises £512 000 of UK listed equities.

To avoid a potential inheritance tax charge (which, assuming the availability of the NRB, would be £312 000 @ 0% plus £200 000 @ 40%, i.e. £80 000) on the UK listed equities should Albert die within the three-year deemed UK domicile period, Albert could sell the equities reinvesting the proceeds in UK gilts to be held for the requisite three-year period.

Due to his non-residence and non-ordinary residence status no capital gains tax arises on any capital gains.

Alternatively, Albert could choose not to liquidate his holding of the UK equities but to borrow, say, £200 000 secured against the equities. The £200 000 could then be invested in UK gilts.

Should Albert die within the three-year period of deemed UK domicile status his inheritance tax liability would be levied on his death estate which comprises assets beneficially owned less any liabilities, i.e. [£512 000 less £200 000], i.e. £312 000 @ 0%, i.e. nil.

The £200 000 of UK gilts rank as excluded property.

A potential saving of £80 000 of inheritance tax is thus achieved.

It may be noted that in the above Example 12.5 if Albert had lived all of his life in the UK he would in fact remain deemed UK domiciled up to and including 5 April 2012 (i.e. beyond the date of 30 June 2011 referred to in the example). It will be recalled that a UK domiciled individual remains deemed UK domiciled for up to three years from the date of the acquisition of a new non-UK domicile of choice *or* if in the relevant tax year (20011/12) the individual has been UK resident for at least 17 tax years out of the last 20 tax years (see Chapter 9).

Foreign Currency UK Bank Accounts

A bank account in a currency other than sterling is excluded property if held beneficially by an individual who is non-UK domiciled *and* non-UK resident *and* non-UK ordinarily resident.

Thus, even a foreign currency bank account held in the UK in a UK incorporated bank or the UK branch of an overseas incorporated bank could so qualify.

It must be observed, however, that the excluded property treatment only extends to the position on death. If a lifetime transfer was made of the foreign currency out of the UK-based account (i.e. UK situs) a potential inheritance tax charge would arise; in this case the account is not treated as excluded property.

Example 12.6

Abdul Mustapha is a non-UK domiciled individual who is also neither UK resident nor ordinarily resident. He has opened a dollar bank account with a UK bank in London in which he keeps approximately $1 million at any one time.

On his death the account would not be subject to inheritance tax as it is excluded property.

However, his daughter and her husband live in the UK and would like to buy a house. To help them, Abdul transfers $750 000 from his UK bank account to his daughter and her husband's joint dollar bank account in the same bank.

This would constitute a lifetime transfer of a UK situs asset on the part of Abdul and would not constitute a transfer of excluded property. It is a PET and should Abdul die within seven years of making the transfer inheritance tax will be charged (subject to the NRB). The charge, if this occurs, will be the responsibility of the donees, i.e. his daughter and her husband.

In Example 12.6 above, the exposure to inheritance tax on the lifetime transfer could have been easily eliminated. If Abdul had first transferred the monies to a non-UK bank account of his and then transferred the monies to the UK (or non-UK) bank account of his daughter and her husband, the transfer would have been of non-UK situs property (i.e. the non-UK bank account) by a non-UK domiciled individual, i.e. excluded property.

CHANNEL ISLANDS AND THE ISLE OF MAN

For a particular category of individual, namely, individuals domiciled in either the Channel Islands or the Isle of Man, certain types of savings are categorised as excluded property despite their UK situs.

These savings comprise:

- National Savings and Investment (NSI) premium bonds;
- NSI National savings certificates;
- NSI deposits with the National Savings Bank (or trustee savings bank);
- war savings certificates;
- any certified contractual savings scheme (e.g. SAYE schemes).

Even if an individual domiciled in the Channel Islands or the Isle of Man becomes deemed UK domiciled for inheritance tax purposes the above types of property remain excluded property.

Apart from the above, an individual domiciled in either the Channel Islands or the Isle of Man is treated in exactly the same manner as all other non-UK domiciled individuals.

SETTLED PROPERTY

As indicated above settled property, as well as property owned beneficially by an individual, may also qualify as excluded property if the relevant conditions are satisfied. These conditions are a little more complex than the situation where property is owned beneficially by an individual. Settled property will qualify as excluded property if the following conditions are satisfied:

- the settlor was non-UK domiciled *at the time of making the settlement*; *and*
- the settled property is not UK situs property at the relevant time.

Subsequent changes in the settlor's domicile status are ignored and thus, once set up, the non-UK situs property of the trust remains excluded property (see below, however, for one exception to this). In other words, if the individual settlor is non-UK domiciled when the trust is set up even if the individual subsequently becomes deemed UK domiciled the non-UK situs property in the trust remains excluded property.

A UK domiciled individual or a deemed UK domiciled individual cannot set up an excluded property trust as non-UK domicile status is required at the time of set up of the trust. Where a trust is set up by such an individual even if the individual subsequently becomes non-UK domiciled the property of the trust does not become excluded property.

In view of the definition of an excluded property trust various aspects of the trust are in fact irrelevant in making a determination as to whether a trust is an excluded property trust or not. Thus, the following aspects are *irrelevant* in this regard:

- the domicile status of the settlor at any other time (i.e. other than at the time of set up of the trust);
- the domicile status of the beneficiaries;
- the residence status of the trustees;
- the type of trust (e.g. discretionary or interest in possession);
- the residence status of the trust.

Excluded property trusts are of immense use and benefit for the non-UK domiciled individual for inheritance tax purposes. Technically, such a trust may itself be UK resident and although this may be efficient for inheritance tax purposes such a trust will have income and capital gains tax drawbacks (see Chapter 16). As a consequence, such trusts are almost without exception non-UK resident trusts.

The FA 2008 does not appear to have affected this conclusion, i.e. for the non-UK domiciled but UK resident individual non-UK resident trusts are to be preferred over UK resident trusts (see Chapters 16 and 17).

The two key advantages of an excluded property trust are that:

- the 10 yearly and exit charges applicable to relevant property trusts (i.e. basically all forms of trust set up on or after 22 March 2006; before that date only discretionary trusts were relevant property trusts) do not apply to excluded property trusts (this is not the case if UK situs property is part of the trust property; in this case 10 yearly and exit charges may apply with respect to the UK situs property);
- the death estate of a qualifying interest in possession beneficiary (i.e. an interest in possession arising under a trust set up pre 22 March 2006 or an interest arising under a will trust on or after 22 March 2006) does not include the non-UK situs property of the trust.

Example 12.7
A non-UK domiciled individual settled shares held in a Liberian registered company (i.e. non-UK situs) in a non-UK resident trust.

The trust is a discretionary trust whose beneficiaries comprise his two sons and one daughter.

The trust property (i.e. the shares) is excluded property, irrespective of the status of any of the beneficiaries, and neither the ten yearly nor exit charges apply to the trust. Any appointments out to the beneficiaries will thus not precipitate an exit inheritance tax charge even where the beneficiaries are UK domiciled.

Example 12.8
A non-UK domiciled individual settled shares in a Liberian registered company (i.e. non-UK situs) in a non-UK resident trust pre 22 March 2006.

The trust is a qualifying interest in possession trust for his brother (i.e. the brother is entitled to the income for life of the trust).

On the termination of the brother's life interest, for whatever reason, no inheritance tax charge would arise.

Example 12.9
A non-UK domiciled individual, Christina, settled shares in a Liberian registered company (i.e. a non-UK situs asset) in a non-UK resident trust pre 22 March 2006.

The trust property is excluded property.

The trustees decided after a period of time that it would be preferable to hold shares in a UK registered company rather than one registered in Liberia. They therefore sold the shares in the Liberian company, subsequently purchasing shares in a UK registered company.

The trust is a qualifying interest in possession trust for her brother (i.e. the brother is entitled to the income for life of the trust).

The brother unexpectedly dies.

An inheritance tax charge will arise on the brother's death because the property in the trust at the time of his death comprised UK situs property (i.e. UK registered company shares) and thus no longer ranked as excluded property. This is the case despite the fact that the trust was created by a non-UK domiciled settlor and for a time the trust assets were non-UK situs.

It is therefore very important to appreciate that even where a trust may at a point in time comprise excluded property should that property change and comprise in part UK situs property, that UK situs property would no longer rank as excluded property (as in Example 12.9 above).

The key point to note is that the property needs to be non-UK situs at the time at which a possible inheritance tax charge might arise, e.g. on the termination of a qualifying interest in possession (i.e. one arising in a pre 22 March 2006 trust); at the time of a ten yearly anniversary charge or at the time of an exit charge in the case of a discretionary trust.

As indicated above, there is no minimum time period for which assets need to be held to qualify as excluded property. This may offer the individual tax planning options. For example, the trustees of a non-UK resident discretionary trust (set up by a non-UK domiciled settlor) may at some point have decided that the greatest investment returns were obtainable on UK situs investments and thus so invested. As a ten yearly anniversary approaches (i.e. a time at which the ten yearly inheritance tax charge arises on the trust) the trustees could avoid such a charge by swapping the UK situs investments for non-UK situs investments held at the ten-year anniversary. No ten-year inheritance tax charge would then arise.

Consider also the position where a lifetime qualifying interest in possession trust has been set up (i.e. must be a pre 22 March 2006 trust) by a non-UK domiciled settlor with a non-UK domiciled life tenant (i.e. the individual with the interest in possession). Assume that the trust assets primarily consist of UK situs assets. It transpires that the life tenant has a terminal disease and is expected to die within the next six months. On the death of the life tenant an inheritance tax charge would arise on the UK situs assets which the life tenant is deemed to own and would thus form part of his death estate (see Chapter 9).

However, by disposing of the UK situs assets, in which the interest in possession subsists, and acquiring non-UK situs assets the property in which the interest subsists is then non-UK situs and thus excluded property; in which case on the life tenant's death no inheritance tax liability arises.

UK Situs Trust Assets

Certain UK situs assets if owned beneficially by a non-UK domiciled individual may still qualify as excluded property (see above). Such UK situs assets may also qualify as excluded property where comprised in a trust.

The assets concerned are:

- AUTs and UK incorporated OEICs;
- UK Government securities and gilts;
- foreign currency UK bank accounts.

AUTs and OEICs

AUTs and OEICs comprised in a trust qualify as excluded property if at the time the trust was created the settlor was non-UK domiciled.

No other factors are relevant.

UK Government Securities and Gilts

The rules here are relatively complex. The following are some of the key points to note.

In the case of a discretionary trust none of the beneficiaries of the trust must be ordinarily resident in the UK.

In the case of a qualifying interest in possession trust the individual with the interest in possession must be non-ordinarily resident in the UK.

Interestingly, with both types of trust, inter alia, the domicile of the settlor is not relevant and could thus be UK domiciled.

Foreign Currency UK Bank Accounts

Three conditions need to be satisfied for such an account to qualify as excluded property if comprised in a trust:

- the settlor must not have been UK domiciled when the trust was created;
- the trustees must be non-UK resident; and
- a qualifying interest in possession must subsist in the trust where the individual so entitled is neither UK domiciled nor UK resident.

Apart from AUTs and OEICs the various conditions which need to be satisfied with respect to the other types of property are less straightforward and on balance, other things being equal, such investments should perhaps be avoided as trust assets.

MIXING UK SITUS AND NON-UK SITUS PROPERTY IN A TRUST

As a general rule, trusts set up by the non-UK domiciled individual designed to hold property which will qualify as excluded property should avoid the trust comprising both UK and non-UK situs assets. It is preferable to segregate such assets into different trusts so as not to give rise to any issues or problems concerning the excluded property elements.

Two reasons for this are as follows.

First, if the trust is a discretionary trust, the inclusion of excluded property in addition to UK situs property has the effect of increasing the potential inheritance tax charge levied (on the UK situs property) on the ten yearly anniversaries of creation of the trust and also on property leaving the trust (i.e. the exit charge) even though the excluded property itself is not subject to such charges.

Second, HMRC appear to be of the view that property which is non-UK situs but which is added to a trust at a time when the settlor is UK domiciled is not excluded property (even though at the date of creation of the trust, as required by the legislation, the settlor was non-UK domiciled). HMRC, however, appear to accept that the non-UK situs property added at a time when the settlor was non-UK domiciled remains excluded property (but see the next point below).

In short, keeping UK and non-UK situs assets in separate trusts is advisable where excluded property status is unambiguously required.

EXCLUDED PROPERTY AND GIFTS WITH RESERVATION

The gifts with reservation rules are discussed in Chapter 11 and it may be preferable to read that chapter prior to reading this section. Suffice it to say for present purposes that a gift with reservation is a gift which after having made it the donor continues to benefit from it. Where such a gift is made the donor is still required to include the value of the gift (at the date of death) in the donor's death estate on which inheritance tax will then be levied.

In the context of trusts, the gift with reservation rules are overridden with respect to excluded property. Thus, where an individual makes a gift into trust which ranks as excluded property but also qualifies as a gift with reservation, at the date of the individual's death no part of the excluded property in the trust is included as part of the donor's death estate.

This conclusion is not changed should the settlor's domicile status become that of the UK by the time of death.

Example 12.10
A non-UK domiciled individual, Milano, settled non-UK situs assets on a non-UK resident discretionary trust.

Milano is also one of the potential beneficiaries under the trust.

The settlement of the assets on trust would thus constitute a gift with reservation by Milano as he may still possibly enjoy some benefit from the assets as he is one of the potential beneficiaries under the trust.

However, as the excluded property rules override the gift with reservation rules, on Milano's death none of the excluded property assets will fall to be treated as part of his death estate.

On the other hand, if prior to Milano's death the trustees were to sell the non-UK situs assets replacing them with UK situs assets the position would be different. In this case, on Milano's death the gift with reservation rules would apply and thus the

UK situs assets would be included as a part of Milano's death estate and thus subject to inheritance tax.

"EXCLUDED PROPERTY TRUSTS" AND FA 2006

It is commonly understood that once an excluded property trust has been created that it will remain so thereafter. While this is almost universally the position it may not always be so.

The excluded property trusts which may be caught in this regard are those set up prior to 22 March 2006.

Trusts set up on or thereafter are, generally speaking, not affected unless an immediate post death interest (an IPDI; see Chapter 15) in favour of the spouse arises. Such an interest might arise under a trust set up by will where the deceased died on or after 22 March 2006.

The problem arises where an excluded property trust has been set up (e.g. pre 22 March 2006) and the settlor (or spouse) is the initial interest in possession beneficiary (or they have successive interests in possession). In such cases the foreign settled property remains excluded property only if the settlor is non-UK domiciled at the date of creation of the settlement *and* the individual with the initial qualifying interest in possession is non-UK domiciled on termination of the interest in possession (or the individual with the successive qualifying interest in possession is non-UK domiciled when the interest terminates).

Thus, if the initial qualifying interest in possession terminates and at that time the life tenant is then UK or deemed UK domiciled (even though at the date of creation the settlor was non-UK domiciled) the foreign situs property in the trust ceases at that time to qualify as excluded property and it becomes subject to the relevant property regime (i.e. subject to ten yearly and exit charges). If, however, on termination of the initial qualifying interest in possession a successive qualifying interest in possession then arises, excluded property treatment will be determined as and when the successive interest terminates.

If the pre 22 March 2006 trust has been set up as an excluded property *discretionary* trust (i.e. no interests in possession) then no problems arise and the trust remains excluded.

Example 12.11
John Desantis, a non-UK domiciled individual, set up an excluded property trust in 1999 in which he had an initial life interest (i.e. a qualifying interest in possession). His wife, Sienna, also non-UK domiciled, had a successive life interest in her husband's trust.

John died three years later in 2002 and his wife died in late 2005. Each died deemed UK domiciled as they had each resided in the UK for 20 successive tax years.

At the dates of their deaths even though they each had a qualifying interest in possession no part of the trust assets are included as part of their death estates as the trust qualified as an excluded property trust.

However, on the death of Sienna, as she was deemed UK domiciled, the property in the trust will fall within the relevant property regime. Ten yearly and exit charges will henceforth arise as the trust property no longer qualifies as excluded property.

On or after 6 April 2008 at some point no further qualifying interests in possession will be capable of creation on the termination of an earlier such interest due to the FA 2006 changes. To avoid the trust then falling within the relevant property regime due to the loss of excluded property treatment will require the trust to terminate.

In the above Example 12.11, had Sienna died (UK domiciled or deemed UK domiciled) on or after 6 April 2008 and on her death their children acquired interests in possession, such interests would not be qualifying interests and thus if the trust did not terminate on her death it would then fall within the relevant property regime.

It is perhaps worth reiterating that the above potential problem (i.e. an excluded property trust falling at some point within the relevant property regime) only needs to be considered if the settlor or spouse (who possesses qualifying interest in possession) may die domiciled or deemed domiciled in the UK. If this is not likely to be the case the excluded property trust will continue to qualify as such.

SUMMARY

The term "Excluded property trusts" refers to trusts comprised of non-UK situs assets set up by a non-UK domiciled settlor. The term is slightly misleading as it is the non-UK situs property within any trust that may qualify as excluded property, not the trust itself. Thus, all the property of a UK resident trust may qualify as excluded property.

Excluded property is property which is not subject to inheritance tax; it is simply outside the ambit of inheritance tax.

Excluded property also comprises non-UK situs property beneficially owned by the non-UK domiciled. Certain limited categories of UK situs assets also qualify as excluded property. Excluded property is very important for the non-UK domiciled individual but of much less significance for the UK domiciled individual.

As a general rule, non-UK and UK situs assets should not be settled by the non-UK domiciled individual in the same trust.

It is possible that although non-UK situs property once settled by the non-UK domiciled individual is likely to remain excluded property forever there are limited circumstances under which this may not be the case.

13
Inheritance Tax Administration

BACKGROUND

Unlike the position with respect to income and capital gains taxes there is no annual return (e.g. Tax Return) which needs to be made by any person with respect to inheritance tax. Inheritance tax information typically needs to be disclosed when an event occurs (e.g. a lifetime transfer; death).

The information which needs to be provided to HMRC relates to lifetime PETs and CLTs made by individuals, transactions effected by trustees (e.g. appointment of trust property to beneficiaries) and on the individual's death.

The two main types of information provided to HMRC are referred to as "an account" and "a return".

The former details the transaction which may be subject to inheritance tax and is normally completed by the donor/transferor. The latter is normally completed by someone other than the donor/transferor detailing transactions which affect other persons.

LIFETIME TRANSFERS

The main transfers of value made in lifetime are CLTs and PETs (see Chapter 9). In the case of the former a liability to inheritance tax arises at the date the CLT is made (although it may be at the nil rate) whereas in the case of the PET a liability only arises if the donor dies within seven years of making the gift.

CLT

In the case of a CLT the transferor must deliver an account detailing the property comprised in the transfer including its value. The time limit for submission is twelve months after the end of the month in which the transfer took place.

PET

In the case of a PET no return is necessary when the gift is made. However, should the donor die within seven years of making the gift the donee is liable to deliver an account. The time limit for submission is twelve months after the end of the month in which the donor died.

The relevant form to be used is Form IHT 100 (see Appendix 3).

Excepted Transfers

In certain cases no account is required to be delivered. This applies to "excepted transfers". Following the major changes to inheritance tax contained in FA 2006 the rules re excepted transfers have been amended. The new rules apply to lifetime transfers on or after 6 April 2007.

An excepted transfer arises in one of two circumstances and refers to an actual not a deemed chargeable transfer.

The first is where the value transferred is attributable to either cash or quoted securities or shares and that value, together with the transferor's chargeable transfers in the previous seven years, does not exceed the threshold for payment of inheritance tax (£312 000 for tax year 2008/09) for the tax year in which the transfer is made.

The second circumstance is where the value of the transfer, together with the transferor's chargeable transfers in the previous seven years, does not exceed 80% of the inheritance tax threshold, and the value of the transfer does not exceed that threshold less the value of the transferor's chargeable transfers in the previous seven years.

In addition, no account need be completed where the transfer is excluded property (see Chapter 12) or where the transfer is exempt. An example of an exempt transfer is a transfer falling within the annual exemption (£3000 for tax year 2008/09); an inter-spouse transfer (subject to the £55 000 limit for transfers from a UK to a non-UK domiciled spouse; see Chapter 9).

Excepted Settlements

New rules also apply to "excepted settlements" where the chargeable event takes place on or after 6 April 2007.

Five categories of excepted settlement arise all requiring there to be no qualifying interest in possession (see Chapter 15) subsisting in the settled property (i.e. the settlement must be discretionary in nature).

The first category is a settlement where the settled property can comprise only cash, the trustees must be resident in the UK, the settlor must not have provided any additions to the settled property following the commencement of the settlement or have created any other settlements on the same day and the value of the settled property at the time of the chargeable event must not exceed £1000.

In relation to the other four categories there are general requirements applying to all categories and a specific requirement ("the condition").

The general requirements are that the settlor is UK domiciled at the commencement of the settlement and thereafter until the chargeable event (or his death, if earlier), the trustees must be resident in the UK throughout the existence of the settlement and there must be no related settlements. The specific requirement is that the value transferred by the relevant notional chargeable transfer does not exceed 80% of the inheritance tax threshold for the year in which the chargeable event occurs, ignoring for the purpose of determining the value any liabilities, exemptions or reliefs that would otherwise be deductible. These other categories are as follows.

The second category is a settlement where there is a chargeable event on or after 6 April 2007 which is a charge arising at the 10-year anniversary of the settlement.

The third category is a settlement where there is a chargeable event on or after 6 April 2007 at other times preceding the first 10-year anniversary of the settlement.

The fourth category is a settlement where there is a chargeable event on or after 6 April 2007 at other times following one or more 10-year anniversaries of the settlement.

The fifth category is a settlement where there is a chargeable event on or after 6 April 2007 where the charge to tax is on property in an age 18-to-25 trust by reason of an exit charge on the ending of the trust.

DEATH ESTATE

The executors of the deceased must deliver an account detailing all of the property which formed part of the deceased's estate immediately before death (excluding gifts with reservation) including property in trust in which the deceased had a qualifying interest in possession (e.g. an interest in possession under a pre 22 March 2006 trust; see Chapter 15). In addition, the executors are required to disclose details of any CLTs or PETs made by the deceased within seven years of death.

The account needs to be submitted within 12 months of the end of the month in which death occurred.

The relevant form to be used is Form IHT 200 together with the various "D" forms (see below and Appendix 3); all shortly to be replaced with a new Form IHT 400.

With respect to gifts with reservation the onus of submitting an account resides with the person who is liable for the inheritance tax thereon (i.e. the donee of the gift). The account needs to be submitted within 12 months of the end of the month in which death (giving rise to the charge) occurred.

Form IHT 100 should be used with respect to the account concerning gifts with reservation (see Appendix 3).

Excepted Estates

Where the deceased's estate qualifies as an "excepted estate" no account is required to be submitted.

An excepted estate is an estate where no inheritance tax is due and a full inheritance tax account is thus not required. From 6 April 2004 there are three types of excepted estate.

For deaths on or after 1 September 2006 to qualify as an excepted estate the following conditions must be satisfied.

Low Value Estates

These are estates where there can be no liability to inheritance tax because the gross value of the estate does not exceed the inheritance tax threshold (£312 000 for tax year 2008/09). The conditions for these estates are that

- the deceased died domiciled in the UK;
- the gross value of the estate does not exceed the inheritance tax threshold;
- if the estate includes any assets in trust, they are held in a single trust and the gross value does not exceed £150 000;
- if the estate includes foreign assets, their gross value does not exceed £100 000;
- if there are any specified transfers, their chargeable value does not exceed £150 000;
- the deceased had not made a gift with a reservation of benefit;
- the deceased did not have an alternatively secured pension fund, either as the original scheme member or as the dependant or relevant dependant of the original scheme member.

Exempt Estates

These are estates where there can be no liability to inheritance tax because the gross value of the estate does not exceed £1 000 000 *and* there is no tax to pay because one or both of the following exemptions apply:

- spouse exemption;
- charity exemption.

No other exemption or relief can be taken into account. The spouse exemption can only be deducted if both spouses have always been domiciled in the UK, and the charity exemption can only be deducted if the gift is an absolute gift to the organisation concerned.

The conditions for these estates are that:

- the deceased died domiciled in the UK;
- the gross value of the estate, does not exceed £1 000 000 *and*;
- the net chargeable value of the estate after deduction of liabilities and spouse exemption and/or charity exemption only does not exceed the inheritance tax threshold;
- if the estate includes any assets in trust, they are held in a single trust and the gross value does not exceed £150 000 (unless the settle property passes to a spouse or to a charity when the limit is waived);
- if the estate includes foreign assets, their gross value does not exceed £100 000;
- if there are any specified transfers, their chargeable value does not exceed £150 000 and;
- the deceased had not made a gift with reservation of benefit;
- the deceased did not have an alternatively secured pension fund, either as the original scheme member or as the dependant or relevant dependant of the original scheme member.

The appropriate form in each of the above two cases is Form IHT 205 (see Appendix 3).

Foreign Domiciliaries

These are the estates where there can be no liability to inheritance tax because the gross value of the estate in the UK does not exceed £150 000. The conditions for these estates are that:

- the deceased died domiciled outside the UK;
- the deceased was never domiciled in the UK or treated as domiciled in the UK for inheritance tax purposes;
- the deceased's UK estate consisted only of cash or quoted shares and securities passing under a will or intestacy or by survivorship;
- the gross value of the estate did not exceed £150 000;
- the deceased did not have an alternatively secured pension fund, either as the original scheme member or as the dependant or relevant dependant of the original scheme member.

The appropriate form is Form IHT 207 (see Appendix 3).

Although no account need be filed in the above cases a return must be completed (on one of the above forms) in order for probate to be obtained (see Chapter 26).

Transferable NRB

FA 2008 introduced the concept of the transferable NRB. To effect such a transfer requires a specific claim on Form IHT 216 (see Appendix 3). This form is to shortly be incorporated into the new Form IHT 400 (see above).

"D" Forms

When Form IHT 200 (referred to above) is submitted various additional forms must also be completed. These are the so-called "D" forms of which there are twenty two, namely, D1 to D22. Broadly, these forms provide back-up information which relates to the information disclosed on Form IHT 200.

Form D18, headed "Probate Summary", is stamped by HMRC once the inheritance tax due on the deceased's estate has been paid by the executors and is returned to them. The form is then submitted along with the application for probate (which cannot be granted until any inheritance due has been settled). Note that this is not a "clearance certificate" (see below).

Form D19, headed "Confirmation that no inheritance tax is payable", is stamped by HMRC and as with the Form D18 returned to the executors.

Clearance Certificate

Where inheritance tax is payable by the executors has been paid the executors may request that a clearance certificate be issued. Such an application should be made on Form IHT 30 (this is different from the stamped Form D18 which in a sense is only a receipt).

PENALTIES

Failure to deliver an account/return and/or discharge any inheritance tax liability in a timely manner may result in the levying of penalties and/or interest charges.

The penalty for failing to deliver an account is £100 (or, if less, the inheritance tax due) unless there is a reasonable excuse for the delay and a further £100 penalty may be charged if the account is more than six months late. Daily penalties of up to £60 per day may in some circumstances be levied.

Where fraud or negligence is involved the penalties may be much higher (e.g. up to £3000 for lodgement of a fraudulent or negligent account concerning a CLT).

Knowingly participating in the delivery of incorrect information attracts a penalty of up to £3000.

The level of any actual penalty will, according to HMRC, depend upon the gravity of the offence; the degree of cooperation by the taxpayer; and the degree of disclosure.

NON-UK RESIDENT TRUSTS

With respect to non-UK resident trustees where a person (other than a barrister) has been concerned with the making of a settlement which is not UK resident and the settlor is UK domiciled that person must make a return to HMRC. The return must be made within three months of the making of the settlement and must state the names and addresses of the settlor and trustees (no additional information needs to be disclosed).

However, no such return is required if a return has already been made by another person (which may be the trustees) or if the settlement is created by will.

OBTAINING INFORMATION

HMRC have extensive powers to require information and/or documents to be produced which is relevant to an inheritance tax charge.

SUMMARY

The making of a transfer by the individual or trustees of a trust and the death of the individual are all occasions that in principle require the disclosure of information to HMRC. Statutory forms are provided for this purpose including, in particular, Forms IHT 200 and IHT 205. Shortly a replacement Form IHT 400 is to be issued.

Time limits apply to the lodgement of any information, often a six-month period.

Penalties and/or interest charges may be levied if information provided is incorrect and/or late.

Non-UK domiciled individuals are not exempt from the need to provide information.

Part Three
Trusts

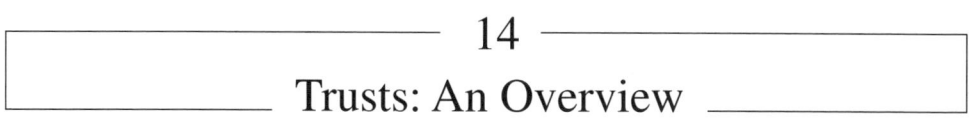

14
Trusts: An Overview

BACKGROUND

The concept of "the trust" is not one necessarily easily understood. The concept is alien to many civil law jurisdictions. Nevertheless, trusts are in practice widely used in family wealth planning often even by those individuals who are in fact nationals of civil law jurisdictions. Typically, in the latter case, the trusts will inevitably have to be located in jurisdictions which recognise the trust concept; often in an offshore financial centre (see Chapter 24).

The following three chapters concentrate on, and examine, the tax issues associated with trusts. It is important therefore that a basic grasp of the trust concept is obtained before reading the next three chapters.

This chapter attempts to explain the basics underlying the trust concept.

THE TRUST

Believe it or not there is no one universally recognised definition of the trust.

As a consequence, most text books tend to explain what a trust *is* rather than seeking to define it.

For present purposes a trust may be thought of as comprising an arrangement where one party gives an asset or assets to another party for the benefit of a third party or parties.

Example 14.1
John Smith who owns 100 ordinary shares in XYZ Ltd might give the shares to his brother Bill Smith for Bill to hold the shares for the benefit of his (i.e. John's) two children, Henry and Mary.

One reason why John in Example 14.1 above might do this is because his children are only aged nine and ten and are thus not really in a position to decide how to handle the shares and/or any dividend income which might be generated. Nevertheless, John would like them to benefit from any growth in the value of the shares and any income which may arise by way of dividends.

When John gave the shares to his brother Bill he would have told Bill that the shares were not for his personal benefit, i.e. Bill's personal use and benefit, but for the benefit of John's two children.

What John has therefore done is to create a trust of the shares.

However, Bill will also need to be told by John how he is to deal with the shares. For example, what should Bill do when any dividends are received; is he allowed to sell the shares and reinvest into different shares or other types of asset; how should Henry and Mary share in the trust income and/or trust assets, e.g. equally or in some other ratio; etc.

In practice, John may tell Bill that what he would like is for Bill to use the dividends and any other income the trust might receive to pay for the two children's education until the children reach the age of, say, 21. Bill is to then sell the shares or whatever assets are at that time then held in the trust and share out the sale proceeds between the children equally. Trusts of this type were very common (pre FA 2006) and were usually referred to as accumulation and maintenance trusts (see Chapter 9).

The trust language which is used to describe the above Example 14.1 is as follows:

- John is referred to as the *settlor* of the trust (i.e. he settled/transferred the shares to Bill);
- Bill is referred to as the *trustee* of the trust (i.e. he is trusted to look after the shares);
- Mary and Henry are the *beneficiaries* of the trust (i.e. they get the benefit of the shares);
- the shares comprise the *trust property/assets/fund* (i.e. the shares are comprised in the trust);
- the instructions which John gives to Bill as to what John would like Bill to do with the shares are normally in written form in a document referred to as the *trust deed*.

One of the key effects of a trust is that ownership of the trust fund is split between legal and beneficial ownership; the trustees take the legal title to the trust assets and the beneficiaries the beneficial title.

Thus, in the above Example 14.1, Bill would have the *legal* ownership of the shares (i.e. the shares will be registered with XYZ Ltd in Bill's own name) whereas Mary and Henry will have the *beneficial* ownership of the shares (i.e. they will get the benefit of the shares as if they in fact owned them in their own names).

Given that in Example 14.1 Bill has legal title to the shares it may be thought that he is in a position to deal with the shares as he so chooses including for his own benefit. However, if, for example, Bill sold the shares and kept the sale proceeds for himself Bill will have committed a *breach of trust*. As a consequence, Mary and Henry (the beneficiaries who are supposed to have benefited from the trust) would then have certain rights which would enable them to seek redress, e.g. they could require Bill to make good the loss they have suffered due to Bill's actions.

The ability to split asset ownership (into legal and beneficial) is unique to common law jurisdictions and is not readily understood in civil law systems (i.e. most countries in mainland Europe) but is at the very heart of the concept of the trust. While as indicated above civil law jurisdictions' own legal systems do not recognise trusts, as such, a number of these countries are signatories to the Hague Convention on the Law Applicable to Trusts and on their Recognition of January 1986. In the UK the Convention is given effect by the Recognition of Trust Act 1987.

Under the Convention the signatory territories agree in principle to recognise the trust concept.

EQUITY

The trust is a creature of equity.

Equity is now a body of rules which have evolved over time and originally emerged due to the perceived unfairness of the system of common law. Where it was perceived that the consequences of applying the common law could be said to be unfair equity then sought to take a more perceived just and fair approach.

As part of these attempts to ensure fairness and just consequences for all parties involved in a dispute the trust concept emerged. It was used at the time to resolve a number of issues. For example, the trust concept enabled a landowner to leave his land under his will which common law did not permit; under common law a married woman was not entitled to her own separate property such property being under the control of her husband; the trust effectively permitted a married woman to own her own property.

Trust law generally classifies trusts into various categories although for tax purposes (see below) these categories are not the ones generally adopted. Thus, trust law typically categorises trusts as follows:

- express trusts;
- implied trusts;
- resulting trusts;
- constructive trusts.

The development over the centuries of the trust concept has led to a body of equitable principles applicable to trusts and, in addition, various statutes have been passed which impinge on the operation of trusts (e.g. Trustee Act 2000; Trusts of Land and Appointments of Trustees Act 1996).

TRUSTS TODAY

Today the use of trusts is extremely wide ranging. For example, trusts are used for:

- charitable purposes;
- pension schemes;
- to protect minors, spendthrifts and persons of unsound mind;
- tax liability mitigation for families;
- protection from creditors;
- to provide anonymity in business dealings.

Protection of Minors

A discretionary trust (see below) enables a settlor to benefit his minor children while at the same time preventing them from gaining direct access to the trust assets and possibly squandering them unwisely or foolishly.

Bankruptcy Protection

A discretionary trust (see below) may also be used to protect the individual's assets from creditors in the event of the individual's bankruptcy. On the other hand, if a beneficiary possesses a fixed interest in the trust (e.g. a life interest in the trust income for life; see below) then in the event of bankruptcy of the individual the fixed interest will effectively become available to the creditors. The trust under which a life interest subsists (see below) is not classed as a discretionary trust (see below).

Will Substitute

A trust can also be used as a substitute will. An individual might transfer, for example, the major portion of his assets to a trust during his lifetime. The trust will then simply continue after his death on the terms set out in the trust deed; the trust assets having been settled on trust no longer forming part of the settlor's estate at death and thus will not form part of the distribution of assets under the will (for inheritance tax purposes, however, this may not always be the case; see Chapters 9 and 15). The balance of the individual's estate might then be disposed of by will.

A trust document (unlike a will) is a confidential document between trustees and beneficiaries and does not need to be filed with any authority and is thus not available for inspection by the public (as applies to wills).

TAX ASPECTS

For tax purposes the tax treatment of the various parties involved (i.e. trustees, settlor and beneficiaries) depends upon many factors (see Chapters 15, 16 and 17) including whether the trust is classified as:

- a "discretionary" trust; or
- an "interest in possession" trust.

Discretionary Trust

The key difference between these two types of trust is that in the case of a discretionary trust the beneficiaries have no *right* to obtain any current or future benefit from the trust; such beneficiaries can only *hope* that the trustees will exercise their (i.e. the trustees') discretion (hence the term discretionary) in their favour.

Using Example 14.1 above, if John Smith (settlor) transfers assets to a trust and under the trust deed the trustees (e.g. John's brother Bill and sister Barbara) are required to allocate the income and capital of the trust among the trust's beneficiaries (e.g. John's children Harry and Mary) as the trustees may determine, then this will be a discretionary trust.

Thus, one year the trustees may allocate, say, 50% of the income of the year to Mary and 25% to Harry with the remaining 25% of the income remaining in the trust. The following year, perhaps, the trustees may allocate, say, 30% of the income to Mary and 30% to Harry; the remaining 40% of income again remaining in the trust; etc.

The key point to note is that the beneficiaries can only benefit from the trust as and when the trustees exercise their (i.e. the trustees') discretion in their (i.e. the beneficiaries') favour.

Interest in Possession Trust

On the other hand, with an interest in possession trust the beneficiaries possessing the interest have a current fixed entitlement to the income of the trust as it arises. The trustees, with this type of trust, cannot deny the beneficiaries their rights to the trust income as it arises and thus the beneficiaries are not dependent upon the trustees exercising their discretion.

Using Example 14.1 above, if John Smith (settlor) transfers assets to a trust and under the trust deed the trustees (e.g. John's brother Bill and sister Barbara) are required to distribute the whole of the trust's income as it arises to the two beneficiaries (e.g. John's children Harry and Mary) equally, then this will be a trust with an (in fact two) interest in possession.

More than one beneficiary may possess an interest in possession as is the case in Example 14.1 above where both Harry and Mary each have an interest in possession. Normally, a beneficiary possessing the interest is often referred to as a "principal beneficiary".

It is also quite common for the interest to subsist for the individual's lifetime and in this case the beneficiary may also be referred to as a "life tenant". Alternatively, the interest may subsist for less than the lifetime of the beneficiary.

Lifetime and Will Trusts

Irrespective of the type of trust, whether discretionary or interest in possession, creation either during the settlor's lifetime or by will on death is possible.

Trusts created by will are, not surprisingly, referred to as "will trusts" and those created during lifetime "inter vivos trusts".

SUMMARY

Trusts may be created in lifetime or on death under a will.

The essence of the trust is the splitting of legal and beneficial ownership. The former resides with the trustees and the latter with the beneficiaries. The trustees' duties are governed by the trust deed and general trust law.

For tax purposes the two main types of trust are the discretionary trust and the interest in possession trust. The beneficiaries of the discretionary trust benefit under the trust as and when the trustees decide to make appointments to them whereas the beneficiary with the interest in possession has an automatic entitlement to the income (not capital) of the trust.

Although useful for wealth tax planning purposes trusts also may be used for non-tax reasons including the making of provision for minor children should the parents die while the children are minors; asset protection in the event of bankruptcy; and charitable purposes.

The trust, unlike a will, is confidential and may to some degree be used as a form of substitute will.

15
Inheritance Tax: Trusts

BACKGROUND

As indicated in Chapter 9 inheritance tax applies not only to individuals but also to trustees. FA 2006 made significant changes to the inheritance tax treatment of trusts (FA 2008 made virtually no changes). The changes brought in by FA 2006 apply not only to trusts set up on or after 22 March 2006 but also to trusts set up before this date subject to transitional provisions.

Inheritance tax in principle applies to transfers into and out of trusts and to the trust vehicle itself. The precise treatment depends upon the nature of the trust (e.g. whether discretionary or otherwise) although, post FA 2006, similarity of treatment prevails among the different types of trust which was not so pre FA 2006.

The basic thrust of the changes introduced by FA 2006 is to charge all trusts to inheritance tax in the same manner as applied to discretionary trusts pre FA 2006.

In short, the "relevant property regime" which applies (and always did apply) to discretionary trusts now, post FA 2006, applies to all trusts set up on or after 22 March 2006 (except for trusts for bereaved minors, trusts for the disabled and trusts with an immediate post death interest). The term "relevant property regime" refers to trust property in which no "qualifying" interest in possession subsists.

One of the main consequences of the FA 2006 changes is that transfers into trusts are now CLTs (and not PETs) and thus a possible 20% lifetime charge may arise (subject to the availability of the NRB). Other things being equal, this has made the setting up of trusts more inheritance tax expensive.

"Qualifying interest in possession" trusts which may have been set up pre or post FA 2006 (i.e. a trust in which one or more beneficiaries is/are entitled to the trust income as it arises) are not subject to the relevant property regime and thus the inheritance tax treatment of such trusts is different. What constitutes such a trust is examined below.

FA 2006 changes apply whether the trust is set up in lifetime or on death.

DISCRETIONARY TRUSTS

The relevant property regime applies to discretionary trusts. Both pre and post FA 2006 discretionary trusts are separate persons subject to inheritance tax in their own right. The charges on such trusts take the form of a 10 yearly/decennial (or principal) charge and an exit charge.

The 10-yearly charge (as its name suggests) is levied every 10 years commencing with the date the trust is created (i.e. the date of death for trusts created under a will).

The maximum charge is 6% and is levied on the value of the trust assets at that time. Any liability is payable by the trustees.

The exit charge applies as and when the trustees appoint trust capital to one or more beneficiaries or where under the terms of the trust a beneficiary becomes absolutely entitled to trust capital. The rate applicable depends upon the length of time between the date the exit charge arises and the date of the immediately preceding 10-year charge; broadly, the charge is 0.6% per year measured from the immediately preceding 10-year charge (subject to the maximum 6%). Any liability arising from the exit charge is payable by the trustees or the beneficiary; if the trustees discharge the liability then "grossing up" becomes necessary to ascertain the liability.

In addition to the above, inheritance tax is also chargeable on transfers into trust (e.g. on set-up) whether in lifetime or on death. Post FA 2006, all lifetime transfers into trust are CLTs (not PETs) and a consequent charge arises at that time (possibly at the nil or 20% rate).

The death of any beneficiary of a discretionary trust has no inheritance tax consequences for either the individual vis-à-vis the trust or for the trust itself.

Exit Charge before the First 10-year Charge

It may be that prior to the first 10-year anniversary following the setting up of the trust that an exit charge arises due to, for example, an appointment of trust capital to one of the beneficiaries absolutely. The charge is, in principle, based upon the value of the trust assets leaving the trust.

To ascertain the rate to be used in computing the exit charge involves the following: the calculation of the amount of inheritance tax on a "hypothetical transfer" is first calculated and the average rate of inheritance tax thereon then determined (the initial rate); 30% of this rate is then used to calculate the exit charge. The "hypothetical transfer" referred to above is based upon, inter alia, the value of the property comprised in the trust immediately after commencement and (if any) the value of any subsequently added property (the value of property in any related trust also needs to be taken into account). The availability of the NRB needs to be ascertained which involves identifying the CLTs made within seven years prior to the setting up of the trust.

The longer the time period between the date the exit charge arises and the previous 10-year anniversary the greater the applicable percentage rate.

Example 15.1
Peter Purple created a discretionary trust by settling £500 000 cash. The trust was set up on 18 June 2000.

Within the seven years prior to setting up the trust Peter had made a total of £134 000 CLTs.

On 20 July 2005 the trustees appointed £120 000 to one of the trust beneficiaries. The NRB for the tax year 2000/01 is £234 000.

Trust creation

On creation of the trust the inheritance liability is 20% of £400 000 (i.e. £500 000 less the remainder of the NRB (NRB in tax year 2000/01 is £234 000 of which the CLTs utilised £134 000) i.e. £100 000), i.e. £80 000.

The liability is paid by the trustees and thus of the £500 000 only £420 000 cash remains in the trust.

Exit charge

To ascertain the exit charge arising on the appointment on 20 July 2005 (i.e. in the tax year 2005/06) involves the following calculations.

Inheritance tax (calculated using the NRB for tax year 2005/06 on the initial value of the trust, i.e. £420 000; NRB was £275 000 for 2005/06) on the "hypothetical transfer" of £420 000 is

$$20\% \text{ of } [£420\,000 - [£275\,000 - £134\,000]] = £55\,800$$

$$\text{Initial rate} = £55\,800/£420\,000 = 13.2857\%$$

The rate of inheritance tax actually payable in calculating the exit charge is 30% of the above initial rate multiplied by the number of complete quarters between 18 June 2000 and 20 July 2005 divided by 40, i.e.

$$30\% \times 13.2857\% \times 20/40 = 1.9929\%$$

Therefore the exit inheritance tax charge is

$$1.9929\% \times £120,000 = £2391$$

It may thus be observed that if no CLTs have been made within the seven years prior to setting up the discretionary trust and the amount settled equals the then NRB, no exit charge can arise on any appointments out of the trust in its first 10 years. This is because the initial rate is 0% due to the applicability of a full NRB.

Ten-year Charge

This charge, unlike the exit charge, arises simply due to the passage of time.

The charge is based upon the value of the trust assets at the date of the 10-year anniversary. It takes into account the aggregate of CLTs made within the seven years prior to the creation of the trust and any appointments made out of the trust in the 10 years preceding the 10-year anniversary.

Example 15.2

Belinda York created a discretionary trust on 5 October 1998 with various assets the aggregate value of which was £365 000. In the immediately preceding seven years she had made CLTs of £55 000.

On 18 November 2003 and 23 March 2004 appointments totalling £155 000 were made to beneficiaries of the trust.

On the 10-year anniversary, i.e. 5 October 2008, the value of the trust assets was £500 000.

The inheritance tax charge on the value of the trust property (£500 000) at the 10-year anniversary is (taking into account the available NRB of £312 000 less the amount already utilised, i.e. £210 000):

$$0\% \times [£312\,000 - [£55\,000 + £155\,000]] +$$
$$20\% \times [£500\,000 - [£312\,000 - [£55\,000 + £155\,000]]] = £79\,600$$

The average rate = £79 600/£500 000 = 15.92%

Rate actually charged = 30% × 15.92% = 4.7760%

Inheritance tax charge on 10-year anniversary is 4.7760% × £500 000 = £23 880

It may thus be observed that if no CLTs have been made within the seven years prior to setting up the discretionary trust and no appointments are made out of the trust prior to the first 10-year anniversary and the amount initially settled equals the then NRB and assuming the growth in value of the trust assets is exactly in line with the increase over this 10 years of the NRB, no inheritance tax charge arises on the 10-year anniversary.

Even where the growth over the 10 years of the trust assets is in excess of the corresponding growth in the NRB, the inheritance tax payable on the 10-year anniversary may still be relatively small.

Example 15.3
Belinda York created a discretionary trust on 5 October 1998 with various assets the aggregate value of which equalled the then NRB of £223 000. In the immediately preceding seven years she had made no CLTs.

No appointments were made to beneficiaries of the trust.

On the 10-year anniversary, i.e. 5 October 2008, the value of the trust assets was £412 000.

The inheritance tax charge on the value of the trust property (£412 000) at the 10-year anniversary is:

$$20\% \times [£412\,000 - £312\,000] = £20\,000$$

The average rate = £20 000/£412 000 = 4.8544%

Rate actually charged = 30% × 4.8544% = 1.4563%

Inheritance tax charge on 10-year anniversary is 1.4563% × £412 000 = £6000

After the first 10-year anniversary subsequent exit and 10 yearly charges will continue to be levied.

The above illustrates that where a NRB discretionary trust is set up, whether in lifetime or on death, even though an inheritance tax charge in principle arises every 10 years the aggregate amounts of inheritance tax payable over time is still likely to be significantly less than had the individual died beneficially owning the assets (when the rate would be 40%).

INTEREST IN POSSESSION TRUSTS

Pre FA 2006 all interest in possession trusts contained, by definition, "qualifying interests in possession". However, post FA 2008 this is no longer necessarily the case.

Post FA 2006, qualifying interest in possession trusts comprise any of the following:

- interest in possession trusts created pre 22 March 2006 (whether in lifetime or on death);
- interest in possession trusts created on or after 22 March 2006 by will which contain an immediate post death interest (IPDI);
- interest in possession trusts created pre 22 March 2006 where a successive interest in possession arises on or after 22 March 2006 (a "transitional interest" (TSI)).

Thus, not all trusts which contain an interest in possession will be "qualifying" interest in possession trusts. In particular, all lifetime trusts created on or after 22 March 2006 which contain an interest in possession will *not* be qualifying interest in possession trusts and such trusts are subject to the relevant property regime applicable to discretionary trusts (see above).

Trusts for disabled beneficiaries and for bereaved minors create qualifying interests in possession (neither trust is discussed here).

Example 15.4

Hubert Grey having discussed matters with his wife, Mildred, decided to set up a lifetime trust under which Mildred was to have a life interest.

Hubert had been thinking about setting up the trust in early 2006. However, it was not until June 2006 that the trust was set up.

The consequences for Hubert are that:

- the gift of assets he makes into the trust is a CLT on which an inheritance tax charge arises if the value of the gift exceeds £312 000;
- the trust is governed by the relevant property regime and thus 10 yearly and exit charges may arise;
- however, on Mildred's death, no part of the trust assets in which her interest subsists will form part of her death estate.

Had Hubert set up the trust pre 22 March 2006 the consequences would have been that:

- the gift of assets he made into the trust would have qualified as a PET;
- the trust would not be governed by the relevant property regime and thus 10 yearly and exit charges would not arise;
- however, on Mildred's death, the trust assets in which her interest subsisted would form part of her death estate.

The main attributes of a qualifying interest in possession are two-fold. First, the interest in possession beneficiary is treated as beneficially entitled to the property contained in the trust in which the interest subsists. Thus, inter alia, on death the trust assets in which the interest subsists are treated as part of the interest in beneficiary's death estate. This contrasts sharply with the inheritance tax position of a beneficiary under a discretionary trust. Second, transfers into such trusts qualify as PETs (however, as post FA 2006 qualifying interest in possession trusts cannot be set up in lifetime this point is somewhat academic).

In addition, if the qualifying interest in possession terminates in lifetime and the trust ends at that time the beneficiary will have made a PET. If, on the other hand, the trust continues following the lifetime termination no PET will have been made (unless a transitional serial interest arises at that time; see below) as the beneficiary will have made a CLT and the continuing trust will fall within the relevant property regime.

The termination in future of *non-qualifying* interests in possession will, in principle, precipitate no inheritance tax consequences (the beneficiary not being treated as the beneficial owner of the trust assets). However, should the trust terminate at this point an exit charge (see above) may arise (non-qualifying interest in possession trusts being subject to the relevant property regime; see above).

Immediate Post Death Interest (IPDI)

The IPDI arises as a consequence of FA 2006.

An IPDI is an interest in possession trust which is created by will (i.e. on death) and the person entitled to the interest in possession must have become beneficially entitled to it on the testator's death. If the interest arises at a later point in time (i.e. not immediately on the death of the testator) it will not qualify as an IPDI.

As the IPDI is a qualifying interest in possession, on the death of the beneficiary with the IPDI the trust assets in which the IPDI subsists are included as part of the beneficiary's death estate.

The termination in lifetime of the IPDI is a CLT and the trust at that time falls into the relevant property regime.

Any further interest in possession which arises on the termination of the IPDI will not qualify as an IPDI.

An IPDI for a surviving spouse under the testator's will constitutes an inter-spouse transfer and thus is exempt from inheritance tax.

The execution of instruments of variation, post death, is relatively common as part of inheritance tax planning (see Chapter 26). It is possible for an IPDI to be created by instrument of variation.

Example 15.5
Cary Grunt died in July 2008 and his will provided for an interest in possession trust with his son, Egbert, as life tenant with remainder to his three sisters.

Egbert's interest would qualify as an IPDI.

If Egbert's interest was terminated by the trustees in his lifetime in favour of one of Cary's sisters causes Egbert to have made a CLT. Cary's sister's interest, however, does not qualify as an IPDI (as it did not arise immediately on Cary's death).

Example 15.6
Harvey Moon's will left his total estate to his wife, Ursula.

Following Harvey's death Ursula feels that her daughter, Tabatha, should have inherited some part of Harvey's estate.

Tabatha, however, is a bit of a spendthrift and so Ursula is advised to execute a deed of variation in favour of Ursula under which Ursula is given an interest in possession under a trust created by the deed of variation.

Ursula's interest in possession will qualify as an IPDI.

Transitional Serial Interest (TSI)

The concept of the TSI was introduced as a transitional measure due to the FA 2006 changes under which the termination of a qualifying interest in possession on or after 22 March 2006 was no longer automatically treated as a PET (i.e. on lifetime termination where the trust continues) which had been the position prior to this date.

Under FA 2006 the transitional period was set to expire on 5 April 2008, but FA 2008 extended the deadline to 6 October 2008.

A TSI arises where a pre 22 March 2006 interest in possession terminates on or after 22 March 2006 but before 6 October 2008 and on the termination another person immediately becomes entitled to an interest in possession; the latter interest in possession is the TSI. On the subsequent termination of the TSI in lifetime a CLT will arise and the trust will fall into the relevant property regime.

In the case of spouses the position is slightly different. Where on the death of a spouse the surviving spouse becomes entitled to an interest in possession, even if this occurs on or after 6 October 2008, the surviving spouse's interest qualifies as a TSI.

Under the transitional provisions it may make sense where the pre 22 March 2006 interest in possession beneficiary is relatively speaking "old" to terminate the interest (before 6 October 2008) and replace it with a TSI for a much younger beneficiary thus extending the time period in respect of which the pre FA 2006 rules apply.

The replacement of a TSI by a subsequent interest in possession will not itself qualify as a TSI (even if the subsequent interest in possession arises before 6 October 2008).

Example 15.7
Joshua Tree set up a trust in 2000 under which his son, Gerard, was entitled to an interest in possession which qualifies as a qualifying interest in possession.

Should Gerard die his daughter, Cynthia, will then acquire an interest in possession.

Gerard's death before 6 October 2008 will cause Cynthia's interest to qualify as a TSI but his death on or after 6 October 2008 will cause Cynthia's interest no longer to qualify as a TSI.

On Gerard's death the trust assets in which his interest subsisted will form part of his death estate.

The death of the beneficiary with a TSI, as it is a qualifying interest in possession, will cause the trust assets in which the TSI subsists to form part of the beneficiary's death estate.

ACCUMULATION AND MAINTENANCE TRUSTS (A & M)

A & M trusts are a form of discretionary trust. However, such trusts receive favourable inheritance tax treatment. This favourable treatment precludes 10 yearly and exit charges arising and transfers into such trusts are PETs not CLTs.

However, it is no longer possible to set up on or after 22 March 2006 the "old" A & M-type trust.

For A & M trusts already in existence the "old" (very favourable) rules will continue to apply if on or before 5 April 2008 the terms of the trust are amended so that the capital of the trust will vest in the beneficiary at age 18 (almost universally most A & M trusts provide for vesting of such capital at age 25; often even then the beneficiary instead is given an interest in possession and not the capital).

If the terms are not amended within this time frame to provide for capital entitlement at age 18 the A & M trust henceforth becomes subject to the relevant property regime (i.e. 10 yearly and exit charges). The first 10 yearly charge arises 10 years from the date of creation of the trust, not 10 years from 6 April 2008.

The concept of the "18 to 25" A & M trust has, as a consequence, been introduced as a "halfway house-type measure". For A & M trusts in existence on 22 March 2006 if the terms provide, or are changed to provide, for capital to vest at age 25 the relevant property regime will not apply until the beneficiaries reach age 18 and then will only apply to the settled property for the period from age 18 to 25.

The decision whether to amend the terms of the A & M trust (if necessary) was for many individuals not an "inheritance tax" decision but a decision based upon whether age 18 is an appropriate age for an individual to inherit significant assets from the trust; age 25 is generally felt to be more appropriate.

DISCRETIONARY v. INTEREST IN POSSESSION TRUST

Pre FA 2006

One of the major distinctions between the two types of trust was that on set-up in lifetime, transfers into discretionary trusts were CLTs thus precipitating the 20% tax charges (unless the NRB was available). On the other hand, transfers into interest in possession trusts were PETs and no inheritance tax liability occurred if the transferor survived seven years. In principle, the interest in possession trust was therefore less costly on set-up in lifetime.

Indeed, on death (subject to the NRB) the creation of a discretionary will trust precipitated the 40% inheritance tax charge even if the surviving spouse was a beneficiary. The creation by will of an interest in possession trust for the surviving spouse created no inheritance tax charge as the inter-spouse exemption applied.

On the other hand, on the death of the beneficiary with the interest in possession the trust assets in which the interest subsisted formed part of the beneficiary's death estate and thus were liable to inheritance tax of 40%. The use of the interest in possession trust may therefore remove assets from the individual's death estate (i.e. that of the transferor) but simply causes it to form part of the death estate of the relevant interest in possession beneficiary. The death of the beneficiary of a discretionary trust precipitates no such charge.

The discretionary trust is, however, subject to 10 yearly and exit charges which are inapplicable to the interest in possession trust, although the maximum rate applicable is 6% (which compares extremely favourably with the 40% rate applicable to the death estate of the individual).

Post FA 2006

For the discretionary trust nothing has changed post FA 2006. All the comments made above with respect to discretionary trusts thus continue to apply.

However, for the interest in possession trust created in lifetime post FA 2006, the regime applicable to that of the discretionary trust now applies. The cost of set-up in inheritance tax terms has thus increased as transfers into such trusts are now CLTs precipitating a 20% charge (subject to the NRB) as opposed to PETs which applied pre FA 2006. Nevertheless, on the death of the interest in possession beneficiary no part of the trust assets now form part of the beneficiary's death estate.

The decision over the creation of a lifetime discretionary trust or interest in possession trust post FA 2006 is thus inheritance tax "neutral".

For the interest in possession trusts created pre FA 2006 the pre FA 2006 rules continue to apply to the trust; thus nothing changes. The termination of the interest in possession (subsisting before 22 March 2006) before 6 October 2008 and the substitution of a new such interest (creating a TSI) may defer the time at which the trust falls into the relevant property regime. This could be achieved by the replacement interest in possession beneficiary being of a younger age and/or healthier. Whether this is appropriate will depend upon the relevant facts.

In the case of will trusts the inter-spouse exemption applies if the trust created by the will gives rise to an IPDI for the surviving spouse. On the surviving spouse's death the trust assets in which the IPDI subsists will form part of the death estate. However, on termination of the IPDI in the surviving spouse's lifetime the surviving spouse will have made a CLT and the trust will at that time fall within the relevant property regime.

"EXCLUDED PROPERTY" TRUSTS AND DOMICILE

"Excluded property" trusts were not affected by FA 2006. Thus, non-UK situs property settled by an individual who at that time is non-UK domiciled (nor deemed UK domiciled) will continue to fall outside any inheritance tax charge. This applies irrespective of whether the trust is a discretionary, interest in possession or A & M trust (see Chapter 12).

SUMMARY

Trusts are an important weapon in the armoury of the wealth advisor even though the tax treatment of trusts is complex.

For the non-UK domiciled individual the non-UK resident "exempt property trust" is a "must" due to its extreme inheritance tax efficiency. However, care is required to ensure that adverse income and capital gains tax consequences do not arise.

While FA 2006 has changed the inheritance tax treatment of trusts quite markedly they still offer potential inheritance tax advantages.

Even without major tax (of whatever kind) advantages trusts offer flexibility of planning and where married couples have small children, for example, trusts may offer comfort that the children have been provided for in all eventualities.

The creation of the inheritance tax efficient A & M trust is no longer possible on or after 22 March 2006. To ensure such tax advantages are maintained on or after 22 March 2006 (with respect to pre 22 March 2006 A & M set-up trusts) amendment to the terms of the trust need to have been made before 6 April 2008.

Lifetime interest in possession trusts which are created on or after 22 March 2006 automatically fall within the relevant property regime. Such trusts created before this date, however, continue to be subject to the rules applicable before 22 March 2006.

The concepts of the IPDI and TSI effectively extend the applicability of the pre 22 March 2006 rules to interest in possession trusts created pre 22 March 2006 (subject to possible action pre 6 October 2008) or by will on or after this date.

16

UK Resident Trusts: Income and Capital Gains Taxation

BACKGROUND

Chapter 14 provided a brief overview of the trust concept and Chapter 15 discussed the inheritance tax implications of the different types of trust.

This chapter will look at the income and capital gains taxation of trusts which is a highly complex subject. It is important therefore to bear in mind that this chapter, perhaps more than the other chapters in the book, will contain many generalisations to which there may be many exceptions.

The taxation of a trust depends upon the following factors:

- residence of the trust (i.e. UK resident or non-UK resident);
- type of trust (e.g. discretionary versus interest in possession);
- residence status of the settlor;
- domicile status of the settlor;
- residence status of the beneficiaries;
- domicile status of the beneficiaries.

While the trust, as will be seen below, is a separate taxable entity from both the settlor and the beneficiaries, certain anti-avoidance provisions may apply, the consequences of which may be that it is the settlor, and not the trust, who is subject to tax on the trust's income and/or capital gains.

The approach adopted in this chapter is first to consider the tax treatment of UK resident trusts ignoring the possible application of these various anti-avoidance provisions which may override this tax treatment. The impact of these anti-avoidance provisions is examined thereafter.

Strictly speaking, it is the trustees of the trust (not the trust, per se) who are liable to any income and/or capital gains tax charges. Trustees are treated as a single person, or single body, distinct from the persons who are in fact the trustees (companies and individuals may be trustees).

This chapter will first examine the tax treatment of *UK resident* trusts. The following chapter will then examine the tax position of *non-UK resident* trusts.

UK RESIDENT v. NON-UK RESIDENT TRUSTS

Pre 6 April 2007

Capital Gains Tax

FA 2006 changed the rules used to determine the residence of a trust for capital gains tax purposes. The new rules are effective from 6 April 2007 and their introduction in FA 2006 allowed action to be taken to avoid, for example, non-UK resident trusts falling to be treated as UK resident on or after 6 April 2007 (see below).

Previously, a trust was non-UK resident if:

- all or a majority of the trustees were neither resident nor ordinarily resident in the UK; *and*
- the general administration of the trust was ordinarily carried on outside the UK.

A UK resident professional trustee (broadly, a person carrying on the business of trust management) was, however, deemed to be resident outside the UK if the whole of the settled property consisted of property provided by someone who at that time was neither UK domiciled, resident nor ordinarily resident. The general administration of the trust was regarded as carried on outside the UK if a majority of the trustees were non-UK resident.

However, the professional trustee "let-out" did not apply for income tax purposes.

Income Tax

A trust was UK resident for income tax purposes if there was a sole trustee who was UK resident or if there was more than one trustee and all were UK resident.

If one or more trustees were UK resident and one or more were not (i.e. mixed residence trust) then the trust was UK resident if the settlor was domiciled or resident or ordinarily resident in the UK when the funds were provided.

Post 5 April 2007

The consequence of the changes introduced by FA 2006 is that the test for residence of trustees is now the same for income and capital gains taxes. Basically, the pre 6 April 2007 income tax rules now apply.

As indicated above, the trustees of a trust are treated as if they are a single person (distinct from the persons who are the trustees).

The trust will be treated as resident and ordinarily resident in the UK at any time if:

- all the trustees are resident in the UK; *or*
- at least one trustee is resident in the UK and at least one trustee is not resident in the UK and the settlor was resident *or* ordinarily resident *or* domiciled in the UK when the trust was made (if made in lifetime) or the date of death (if made on death).

Thus, a trust where all of the trustees are non-UK resident will be non-UK resident irrespective of the domicile and/or residence status of the settlor.

However, where the settlor is non-UK resident, not ordinary resident and non-UK domiciled the trust will be non-UK resident so long as at least one trustee is non-resident.

The professional trustee let-out referred to above has been abolished (regarded as State Aid under EU competition law) and the place of administration of the trust is now also irrelevant.

Example 16.1
Bertrand Dublin, a non-UK domiciled but UK resident individual, is keen to set up a trust (post 6 April 2007) outside the UK for family planning purposes.

He is a little wary of the trust comprising exclusively non-UK resident professional trustees and suggests that in addition his UK domiciled and UK resident brother or his non-UK domiciled but UK resident sister (or both) should also act as trustees.

If either Bertrand's brother and/or sister act as trustees the trust will be classified as UK resident.

A trust is UK resident or not for the whole of a tax year with respect to capital gains tax as ESC D2 (see Chapter 8) does not apply to trustees, only individuals. However, for income tax purposes the tax year may be split where the residence status of the trust changes during the tax year.

Given that the rule for income tax purposes remains unchanged it is with respect to capital gains tax that the impact of the changes introduced by FA 2006 were felt. Thus, it became likely that trusts which were non-UK resident for capital gains tax purposes pre 6 April 2007 would fall to be treated as UK resident effective 6 April 2007. In this event the re-exportation of the trust's UK residence would precipitate a capital gains tax charge on the part of the trustees. This occurs because there is a deemed disposal by the trustees of all trust assets at their market value at the date of export (and a deemed reacquisition at the same values).

The above situation would have arisen if, for example, pre 6 April 2007 the trust administration was carried on outside the UK, a majority of the trustees were non-resident and the settlor was resident in the UK but non-UK domiciled. Such a trust would be UK resident for income tax but non-UK resident for capital gains tax. However, on 6 April 2007 such a trust would, while remaining UK resident for income tax, become UK resident for capital gains tax.

It was therefore important if any UK tax charges were to be avoided (e.g. the exportation capital gains tax charge) that steps were taken pre 6 April 2007 to ensure the non-UK resident trust remained so under the new rules. In the above example, this required that all (not just a majority) the trustees were non-UK resident.

FA 2008 IMPACT

FA 2008 has had a significant impact on the income tax and capital gains tax treatment of UK resident trusts although it is primarily with respect to capital gains tax that the greatest changes have occurred.

The provisions of FA 2008 in this regard apply to any trust income which arises on or after 6 April 2008 and to any trust disposals, of either UK or non-UK situs assets, made on or after 6 April 2008.

Income Tax

With respect to the income tax treatment of UK resident trusts the changes introduced in FA 2008 are restricted to:

- changes in the rates of income tax applied to trust income (these changes also apply to the income of individuals and thus these changes are not restricted in their application just to trusts).

Capital Gains Tax

With respect to the capital gains tax treatment of UK resident trusts, however, the changes are much more significant. They are as follows:

- a change in the rate of capital gains tax applied to trust gains (this change also applies to the capital gains of individuals and thus this change is not restricted in their application just to trusts);
- the abolition of the indexation allowance and taper relief (this change also applies to the capital gains of individuals and thus this change is not restricted in their application just to trusts);
- the introduction of a new form of relief, namely, entrepreneur relief (this change also applies to the capital gains of individuals and thus this change is not restricted in their application just to trusts);
- abolition of the UK resident "settlor interested" trust provisions;

INCOME TAX

As the provisions of the FA 2008 only impact on the rates of income tax (and do not affect the principles of the income taxation of UK resident trusts) the comments below apply to UK resident trusts whether such trusts were set up before or after FA 2008.

The income tax consequences for the UK resident trust are the same whether the trust was/is set up by a UK domiciled and UK resident individual or a non-UK domiciled but UK resident individual. This is the position with respect to both UK and non-UK source income accruing to the trust.

It is worth noting that prior to changes made with respect to the definitions used to determine the residence of a trust, introduced in FA 2006 which became effective from 6 April 2007, a UK resident trust was in principle able to take advantage of the remittance basis with respect to relevant foreign income (e.g. dividends and interest arising outside the UK). This, however, is no longer the case for UK resident trusts receiving such income post 5 April 2007.

UK resident trustees are liable to self assessment in the same manner as individuals (albeit with their own designed Tax Return) and make payments on account in the same way. They are liable to income tax on worldwide trust income on the arising basis, i.e. whether such income is remitted to the UK or not.

However, there are differences between the income (and capital gains) tax treatment of individuals and of trusts:

- trustees are generally liable to income tax at the basic rate with respect to both savings and non-savings income (20% for tax year 2008/09) or, in the case of dividends, the dividend ordinary rate (10% for tax year 2008/09); for the tax year 2007/08 and earlier tax years rates of 10%, 20% and 22% applied to income as appropriate;
- the rates of 32.5% and 40% only apply to certain trusts;
- trustees were not entitled to the 10% starting rate band (applicable for tax years 2007/08 and earlier tax years);
- trustees are not entitled to the "new" 10% "starting rate for savings";
- trustees are not entitled to any personal allowances;
- trustees are entitled to 50% of the normal annual exemption applicable to individuals in respect of any liability to capital gains tax, i.e. for tax year 2008/09 (50% of £9600).

Discretionary (and Accumulation and Maintenance) Trusts

The trustees of a discretionary trust (or an accumulation and maintenance trust) are subject to income tax at the rate of 40% (the "trust rate" effective 6 April 2007; formerly referred to as the "rate applicable to trusts") on any trust income other than dividend income. Dividend income (whether UK source or not) is subject to income tax at 32.5% (the "dividend trust rate").

Thus, the dividend ordinary rate of 10% and the basic rate of 20% (referred to above) are inapplicable to the income of discretionary trusts.

However, effective 6 April 2006 a new "standard rate band" was introduced which applies only to the income of discretionary and accumulation and maintenance trusts. Pre FA 2008 the first £1000 of taxable income was subject to tax at the 10% (i.e. dividend ordinary rate), 20% (i.e. the lower rate) or 22% (i.e. basic rate) rate depending upon the type of the income. Post FA 2008, this first £1000 of taxable income is subject to tax at the 20% basic rate of tax on income other than dividend income. In the case of dividend income the 10% (i.e. dividend ordinary rate) rate applies.

Interest in Possession Trusts

The trustees of an interest in possession trust (see Chapter 14) are liable to income tax at varying rates depending upon the type of income. Thus, dividend income is subject to the dividend ordinary rate (i.e. 10%); savings and non-savings income is subject to the basic rate of 20% (pre FA 2008, i.e. tax years 2007/08 and earlier, the rate on dividend income was 10%; savings income 20%; and non-savings income 22%).

However, the interest in possession beneficiary is technically subject to income tax on the trust income as it arises, not the trustees. This apparent conflict is discussed below.

BENEFICIARIES

Discretionary Beneficiaries

Unlike a beneficiary with an interest in possession, a discretionary beneficiary has no right to the trust income. A discretionary beneficiary thus receives payments from the trust only as and when the trustees so decide by exercising their discretion.

The trustees may make payments to the beneficiary out of the income of the trust or out of the trust capital. Under the former option the beneficiary will receive income and be taxed accordingly (see below). In the latter case, generally, the receipt will be treated as capital and thus not subject to income tax. However, this may not always be so in which case the receipt will fall subject to income tax.

The remittance basis cannot apply to the trustees even with respect to non-UK source income.

UK Resident Beneficiary

Any payments made to the UK resident beneficiaries of a discretionary trust which are treated as income on the part of the beneficiary are received net of the income tax paid by the trustees on that income (it may be that if the payments by the trustees are payments of capital and are treated as capital in the hands of the beneficiary no income tax will be due thereon). The beneficiary is then liable to income tax on the grossed-up amount (basically, grossed up at the 40% rate applicable to discretionary trusts irrespective of whether the payment of income to the beneficiary is out of income of the trust which is dividend income that has been subject to income tax at 32.5%). If the beneficiary is a higher rate income taxpayer no further income tax liability arises. If the beneficiary is not a higher rate taxpayer then income tax will be reclaimable by the beneficiary from HMRC.

In the case of a discretionary trust it is clear that depending upon the tax position of the beneficiaries different income tax consequences may arise. Other things being equal, income tax is mitigated by the trustees making payments to those beneficiaries who are either not liable to income tax or are liable at the basic rate only. Repayments of income tax may then arise to the beneficiary.

Example 16.2
Henry Taxation set up a discretionary trust for his three adult children, Clarissa, Tig and Bro.

The trust's income for the tax year 2008/09 is £75 000 and the trustees liability is 40% thereof, i.e. £30 000.

The trustees pay (in the tax year 2008/09) the following income to each of the beneficiaries:

- £3000 to Clarissa (who is a non-taxpayer);
- £12 000 to Tig (who is a basic rate taxpayer);
- £24 000 to Bro (who is a higher rate taxpayer).

Each of the beneficiaries is in principle liable to income tax at their applicable marginal rate on the "grossed-up" amount received from the trust, i.e. £5000 re Clarissa; £20 000 re Tig and £40 000 re Bro.

Clarissa is a non-taxpayer and therefore has no liability on the income and thus may apply to HMRC for a refund of the £2000 tax paid by the trustees.

Tig is a basic rate taxpayer and therefore has a liability on the income of 20% of £20 000, i.e. £4000 and thus may apply to HMRC for a refund of the extra £4000 tax paid by the trustees.

Bro is a higher rate taxpayer and therefore has a liability on the income of 40% of £40 000, i.e. £16 000 which matches the income tax already paid by the trustees and thus no additional tax liability arises on the part of Bro, but neither is he entitled to any tax refund from HMRC.

Alternatively, the trustees might choose to accumulate all or part of the income of the trust. Where this occurs the income is in effect converted into capital. As and when such accumulations are paid out to a beneficiary no income tax consequences arise, i.e. the receipt by the beneficiary is "income tax free". However, the 40% income tax liability originally paid by the trustees on the income of the trust (which income is accumulated) is in essence "lost".

If the trust income arises outside the UK and remains outside the UK and is appointed out to a non-UK domiciled but UK resident beneficiary (with the income remaining outside the UK) no income tax liability arises at that time on the part of the beneficiary (as the remittance basis applies to the beneficiary). However, given the availability of a credit for the tax paid by the trustees on the income no additional income tax charge would arise even if the income was remitted to the UK by the beneficiary. For the beneficiary liable to income tax at the basic rate a reclaim would be possible from HMRC but only on remittance.

Non-UK Resident Beneficiary

Any payments made to non-UK resident beneficiaries of a discretionary trust which are treated as income on the part of the beneficiary will, generally speaking, qualify as "excluded income" on the part of the beneficiary and thus not be liable to UK income tax. This applies irrespective of the source of the underlying income arising to the trustees.

The above applies whether the non-UK resident beneficiary is UK or non-UK domiciled.

Interest in Possession Beneficiaries

UK Resident Beneficiary

A beneficiary of an interest in possession trust, as indicated above, is entitled to the income of the trust as it arises and is accordingly liable to income tax thereon (whether the trustees actually make a payment of that income to the beneficiary in that tax year or not).

The income tax treatment of the beneficiary, however, will depend upon the source of the income (i.e. UK or non-UK) and the domicile status of the beneficiary. For the UK domiciled beneficiary both UK and non-UK source income will be subject to income tax on the arising basis. However, for the non-UK domiciled individual the UK source income will be subject to income tax on the arising basis but the non-UK source income will be subject to income tax on the remittance basis.

Typically, in practice, the trustees will have already paid income tax on such income as it is the trustees who will in the first instance often have actually received the income and thus who are initially subject to tax thereon. As a consequence, the interest in possession beneficiary receives income from the trust net of the income tax liability of the trustees. The beneficiary is then liable to income tax on this net amount after it has been "grossed up" at the appropriate rate according to the type of income (i.e. 10% if paid out of dividend income or 20% otherwise).

Depending upon the beneficiary's own tax position the beneficiary will then be in a position to reclaim from HMRC some or all of the tax paid by the trustees (albeit no reclaim in respect of any dividend tax credit is possible) or the beneficiary may be liable to additional income tax thereon if the beneficiary is a higher rate taxpayer (i.e. 40% taxpayer).

Example 16.3

Jenny Chair is an interest in possession beneficiary of a trust set up by her great grandfather about five years ago. She is a higher rate taxpayer and is UK domiciled and UK resident.

The trust mainly generates interest and dividend income on its investments.

In the tax year 2008/09 the net dividend income amounted to £18 000 and the interest income (after tax had been deducted at source, at 20%, by the bank) amounted to £64 000.

The trustees' liability is 10% on the dividend income:

$$10\% \text{ on } [£18\,000 + £2000] = £20\,000$$

(this amount of liability is offset by the £2000 of dividend tax credit); thus no net tax due by the trustees.

and 20% on the interest income:

$$20\% \text{ on } [£64\,000 + £16\,000] = £16\,000$$

(this amount of liability is offset by the £16 000 of tax which the bank deducted before paying the interest); thus no net tax due by the trustees.

Jenny is liable at 32.5% on the "gross" dividend of £20 000 less the tax credit of £2000 producing a net income tax liability on the dividends of £4500 and liable at 40% on the "gross" bank interest of £80 000 less the credit for the tax deducted by the bank of £16 000 producing a net income tax liability of £16 000.

Example 16.4

Jonathan White set up an interest in possession trust in the tax year 2007/08 with his mother, Sophia Roma, as the life tenant remainder to their four children.

John is UK domiciled and UK resident. Claudia is non-UK domiciled but UK resident.

In the tax year 2008/09 the trust receives UK source income of £20 000 and non-UK source income of £40 000. The UK source income is credited directly to the UK bank account of the trustees and the non-UK source income is credited directly to the non-UK bank account of the trustees.

Sophia is liable to income tax on the UK source income on the arising basis but no income tax liability arises on her part on the non-UK source income unless it is remitted to the UK. If, unknowingly, the trustees had arranged for the non-UK source income to have been credited to their UK bank account a remittance of the income would have occurred and Sophia would be subject to income tax thereon (the fact that Sophia did not personally remit the income is irrelevant for this purpose).

Non-UK Resident Beneficiary

As the interest in possession beneficiary is entitled to the trust income as it arises then to the extent that the income arising to the trust is non-UK source no income tax charge arises thereon due to the non-UK resident status of the beneficiary. With respect to any UK source income the beneficiary is in principle liable to income tax thereon but often such income qualifies as "excluded income" (i.e. interest and dividends; not rental or trading income) and, as a consequence, the beneficiary is not liable to income tax on such income.

The above applies whether the non-UK resident beneficiary is UK or non-UK domiciled.

CAPITAL V. INCOME

In some cases "capital" receipts of the trust are deemed to be "income" in which case the normal income tax (i.e. not the capital gains tax) provisions would apply.

These provisions apply whether the trust is a discretionary, accumulation and maintenance or interest in possession trust. However, in the case of the interest in possession trust the interest in possession beneficiary is only entitled to the trust income (as defined for trust not tax law; the capital receipts would thus form part of the trust's capital not income) and thus such beneficiary would not be entitled to such capital receipts of the trust and, accordingly, would not be subject to income tax thereon (the trustees being so liable).

Perhaps the two most common examples where capital receipts are treated as income for income tax purposes are offshore income gains (e.g. gains arising on non-distributor fund disposals; see Chapter 18) and gains on life assurance policies (e.g. gains arising on offshore non-qualifying life policies; see Chapter 18).

CAPITAL GAINS TAX

As stated above, FA 2008 has affected quite significantly the capital gains tax treatment of UK resident trusts.

The provisions of FA 2008 apply to disposals by trustees of UK resident trusts on or after 6 April 2008.

Thus, the provisions of FA 2008 apply to both those trusts set up pre 6 April 2008 with respect to disposals by such trusts on or after 6 April 2008 and trusts set up on or after 6 April 2008.

Accordingly, the positions pre and post FA 2008 will be considered separately below.

Pre FA 2008

Unlike the position with respect to income tax, all types of UK resident trusts were liable to capital gains tax at the 40% rate on the disposal of trust assets.

Trustees, like individuals, were also entitled to indexation and taper relief.

Trustees, like individuals, were also entitled to an annual exemption but equal to 50% of that applicable to individuals (i.e. £4600 for tax year 2007/08 (£4800 for 2008/09)). Where the settlor of the trust had also created other trusts the annual exemption for each trust so created is pro-rated subject to a minimum annual exemption of 10% of the annual exemption applicable to individuals (i.e. 10% of £9600 for tax year 2008/09, namely, £960).

However, trustees of a UK resident trust are not able to take advantage of the remittance basis with respect to non-UK source capital gains.

Post FA 2008

For disposals by trustees of UK resident trusts on or after 6 April 2008 (whether such trusts were set up pre or post FA 2008) the rate of capital gains tax has been significantly reduced to 18% (from the previous 40% rate) in line with that applicable to individuals.

However, this rate reduction is not as attractive compared to the former 40% rate as it first appears. This is because for such disposals (i.e. those on or after 6 April 2008) neither an indexation allowance nor taper relief is available as both these reliefs have been abolished.

Having said this, a new relief, so-called "entrepreneur relief", has been introduced which applies to trust disposals on or after 6 April 2008 (see Chapter 8). Where this relief applies the rate of capital gains tax is reduced from 18% to an effective rate of 10%. Inter alia, for entrepreneur relief to apply to disposals of trust assets requires that a beneficiary of the trust has an interest in possession in the relevant assets which must also qualify as business assets (as defined for the new relief).

Entrepreneur relief thus cannot apply to sales of assets by the trustees of a discretionary trust.

However, trustees of a UK resident trust are not able to take advantage of the remittance basis with respect to non-UK source capital gains.

ANTI-AVOIDANCE PROVISIONS

The income and capital gains tax treatment set out above assumes that none of the various anti-avoidance provisions discussed below apply. Where such provisions do apply the income and capital gains tax treatment may be different from that set out above.

The provisions of FA 2008 have also impacted on some of these anti-avoidance provisions, namely, those affecting capital gains tax (the anti-avoidance provisions affecting income tax are not affected by FA 2008).

Although trusts are separately taxed, as outlined above, where any of the anti-avoidance provisions apply the settlor, rather than the trust, is liable to either income tax or capital gains tax on the trust's income or, capital gains even though the income/capital gains are, as a matter of fact, those of (i.e. belong to) the trust.

The purpose of these provisions (referred to as anti-avoidance provisions) is to seek to prevent the use of trusts to mitigate the tax liabilities of the individual.

It should be noted that anti-avoidance provisions (although slightly different) apply to both UK resident and non-UK resident trusts. Only those applicable to UK resident trusts are examined in this chapter.

It is therefore important when any trust is created and/or operating that the possible applicability of these anti-avoidance provisions is ascertained. They are extremely broad ranging and highly complex, in many cases overlapping.

INCOME TAX

The anti-avoidance provisions (none of which were affected by FA 2008) applying for income tax purposes apply to:

- "settlor interested" trusts;
- trusts for the minor children of the settlor;
- capital payments to the settlor.

The impact of each of these anti-avoidance provisions is that the income of the trust is deemed to be that of the settlor for the relevant tax year and not that of the trustees. Accordingly, it is the settlor who is then liable to income tax on the income.

However, the settlor has the right to recover from the trustees any income tax upon which the settlor is liable. Thus, where, for example, the settlor is a higher rate taxpayer and is thus liable on the trust income at the higher rate of income tax (i.e. 40%), the trust effectively bears this 40% charge.

The above right of recovery does not, however, apply where the charge arises due to capital payments to the settlor; in this case a credit for tax paid by the trustees is available but no repayment (see below).

In each of the above three cases it is a prerequisite for the provisions to apply that the settlor is alive in the relevant tax year.

Settlor Interested Trusts

If the income (or capital) of a trust may in any circumstances whatsoever be payable to or for the benefit of the settlor *or* spouse then the trust is settlor interested. In principle, any income of the trust is then treated as that of the settlor for income tax purposes. However, it is only income arising from trust property in which the settlor has an interest that is caught (i.e. if the settlor is unable to benefit from parts of the trust property then income arising therefrom cannot be taxed upon the settlor).

Where, for example, the settlor and/or spouse is/are beneficiaries of a discretionary trust (or may be added to the class of beneficiaries) the trust is treated as settlor interested. A revocable trust, which on revocation reverts to the settlor or spouse, is also caught by these provisions.

With respect to interest in possession trusts the trust may still be settlor interested. In principle, if the beneficiary with the interest in possession is not the settlor (or spouse) the trust may still be settlor interested if the settlor (or spouse) can benefit under the trust. Where the interest in possession beneficiary is the settlor (or spouse) the trust is not, however, settlor interested (see below).

These provisions only apply during the settlor's lifetime.

Example 16.5
Using the facts from Example 16.2 above, Henry Taxation set up a discretionary trust for his three adult children, Clarissa, Tig and Bro, but also included as a beneficiary his wife, Meridian.

The trust's income for the tax year 2008/09 is £75 000.

The trustees pay (in the tax year 2008/09) the following income to each of the beneficiaries:

- £3000 to Clarissa (who is a non-taxpayer);
- £12 000 to Tig (who is a basic rate taxpayer);
- £24 000 to Bro (who is a higher rate taxpayer).

As Henry's wife is within the class of beneficiaries the trust is "settlor interested". The trust income is thus treated as that of Henry even though he cannot personally benefit under the trust.

Assuming Henry is a higher rate taxpayer his income tax liability is 40% of £75 000, i.e. £30 000, which he is able to recover from the trustees.

The receipts by the three children are not then subject to income tax on their part.

The term "spouse" excludes:

- a spouse from whom the settlor is separated under a court order or separation agreement (or where the separation is likely to be permanent, separation of at least 12 months normally);
- any former spouse;
- the widow or widower of the settlor;
- an individual who the settlor might marry in the future but to whom the settlor is not currently married.

Discretionary Trust

The settlor interested discretionary trust causes the trust income to be treated as that of the settlor.

However, if the settlor is non-UK domiciled but UK resident and the trust income comprises non-UK source income the remittance basis will apply to such income. If the trustees should remit the income to the UK then at that time an income tax liability will be precipitated on the part of the settlor.

If, however, the trustees appoint trust income out to a beneficiary (whether UK or non-UK domiciled) outside the UK and the beneficiary then remits the income to the UK no income tax liability arises on the part of the settlor at that time as the income is that of the beneficiary at the point of remittance.

Interest in Possession Trust

In the event that the settlor is also the beneficiary with an interest in possession the "settlor interested" provisions do not apply. In this case, the settlor, as interest in possession beneficiary, is subject to income tax on the trust income as it arises in any event (see above). However, if the settlor/beneficiary is non-UK domiciled but UK resident and the income of the trust comprises non-UK source income the remittance basis will apply to this non-UK source income.

However, if the interest in possession beneficiary is not the settlor, the settlor interested provisions above still apply despite the fact that under the normal rules the trust income would for income tax purposes be treated as that of the interest in possession beneficiary (see above). The interest in possession beneficiary is thus not in this case subject to income tax on the income. If the income of the trust comprises non-UK source income the remittance basis will apply if the settlor is non-UK domiciled and the settlor will not be taxed until such income is remitted to the UK. In this case, however, if the interest in possession beneficiary is UK domiciled and UK resident and the settlor is non-UK domiciled but UK resident and the trust income comprises non-UK source income, the interest in possession beneficiary is subject to income tax on the arising basis (in effect, the settlor interested provisions in this case being overridden).

Example 16.6

Jonathan White set up an interest in possession trust in the tax year 2007/08 with his wife, Claudia Roma, as the life tenant remainder to their four children.

John is UK domiciled and UK resident. Claudia is non-UK domiciled but UK resident.

In the tax year 2008/09 the trust receives UK source income of £20 000 and non-UK source income of £40 000. The UK source income is credited directly to the UK bank account of the trustees and the non-UK source income is credited directly to the non-UK bank account of the trustees.

As the interest in possession beneficiary, Claudia is in principle liable to income tax thereon. However, the trust is "settlor interested" as John's wife can (and as interest in possession beneficiary does) benefit under the trust.

Thus John, as UK domiciled settlor, is liable to income tax on the trust income and Claudia is no longer subject to income tax thereon.

On these particular facts, one consequence of the trust qualifying as "settlor interested" is that the remittance basis is inapplicable to the trust's income as John is UK domiciled.

Thus, while the trustees of a UK resident trust are not entitled to the remittance basis with respect to non-UK source income (see above), if the trust income is treated as that of the settlor (under the settlor interested provisions) or that of the interest in possession beneficiary each of whom are non-UK domiciled but UK resident then the remittance basis in principle applies to such income.

Income of Trust Paid to or for Benefit of Unmarried Minor

Income of a trust which is paid out during the settlor's lifetime for the benefit of any unmarried minor children of the settlor is treated as that of the settlor (not applicable if the amount paid out in the tax year is £100 or less; if above this figure the whole amount, not just the excess over £100, is taxable on the settlor).

Note, however, these provisions do not apply if the settlor is not the parent of the child, for example, a grandparent. As a consequence, trusts set up by grandparents for the benefit of the grandchildren were very common as the income tax anti-avoidance provisions were not applicable but, more importantly, such trusts often qualified as accumulation and maintenance trusts and thus also had significant inheritance tax advantages (see Chapter 15); post FA 2006, however, while such trusts can in principle continue to be set up the previous inheritance tax advantages available pre 22 March 2006 are no longer available as the concept of the accumulation and maintenance trust for inheritance tax purposes has effectively been abolished, albeit subject to transitional provisions which applied until 5 April 2008 (see Chapter 15).

Child for this purpose includes stepchild, adopted child and illegitimate child who is under 18. Where the child is a so-called "vulnerable person" payments to such a child may not give rise to a charge on the settlor.

If the trust is revocable and the settlor (or spouse) could benefit on the revocation, the settlor interested provisions above would take precedence and apply to treat the trust income as that of the settlor (i.e. actual payments to the child would thus not be necessary to trigger the charge).

Bare Trusts for Unmarried Minors

Pre 9 March 1999 it was possible for a parent to utilise a bare trust on which to settle trust assets to avoid a charge arising on the parent settlor. In such cases the income of the trust assets belonged to the child and was accordingly subject to income tax on the part of the child, not the child's parent (thus possibly saving income tax due to the lower rates of income tax applying to the child's income compared to that of the parent) so long as the income was not paid out to the child (which was often the case as a child under 18 was/is not capable of providing the trustees with a valid receipt).

Such trusts continue to be effective today assuming that no additions to the trust have been made post 8 March 1999. Where additions have been made to such trusts it is still only the income from the added capital which is caught (i.e. is subject to income tax on the part of the settlor when paid out). Assuming the income from the pre 9 March 1999 capital is not paid out to the child this income will continue to be treated as the child's and not the settlor's.

However, for bare trusts set up in this manner on or after 9 March 1999 the income of such trusts is subject to income tax on the part of the parent settlor whether paid out or not.

Capital Payments to the Settlor

These provisions, to some degree, are now of less importance due to the fact that the "trust rate" (formerly known as the "rate applicable to trusts") is 40% which is the same as that applying to income of the higher rate taxpayer individual, i.e. the trustees of a discretionary trust are liable to income tax on trust income at 40% (32.5% on dividend income) and thus no income tax saving arises if the settlor's marginal rate of income tax is also 40%.

These provisions, in particular, "catch" loans to the settlor (or spouse) and repayments thereof.

Under these provisions the capital payment to the settlor (or spouse) is matched with undistributed income of the trust (i.e. income not otherwise taxed on the settlor) and this "matched" income is then subject to income tax on the part of the settlor.

CAPITAL GAINS TAX

Settlor Interested Trusts post FA 2008

Whereas the above anti-avoidance provisions on the treatment of trust income of UK resident trusts for income tax purposes continue to apply post FA 2008 in the same manner as pre FA 2008 this is not the case for capital gains tax purposes.

In short, the "settlor interested" anti-avoidance provisions applicable to the capital gains tax treatment of UK resident trusts have been abolished from 6 April 2008.

Such provisions operated in a very similar manner to those discussed above. Broadly, the capital gains of the trust would be subject to capital gains tax on part of the settlor where the trust was "settlor interested".

Such provisions are thus no longer relevant where a trust, whether already in being on 6 April 2008 or one set up thereafter, makes a disposal of trust assets on or after 6 April 2008.

The reason for the repeal of these anti-avoidance provisions is that for disposals pre FA 2008 the rate of capital gains tax was 40% if the disposal was made by the trustees of the trust which was also the applicable rate if the higher rate taxpayer had made the disposal. Thus, no avoidance of capital gains tax arose by the use of the UK resident trust. Similarly, for disposals on or after 6 April 2008 the rate of capital gains tax is the same (i.e. 18%) whether the sale is effected by a UK resident individual or a UK resident trust.

In essence, at its simplest, no capital gains tax is avoided by a UK resident individual transferring assets to a UK resident trust vis-à-vis any subsequent capital gains arising.

Thus, for all, UK resident trusts, capital gains tax arising on post 5 April 2008 trust asset disposals will be the liability of the trustees not the settlor (or indeed any other person).

With respect to disposals made before 6 April 2008 the settlor interested provisions applied.

Settlor Interested Trusts pre FA 2008

Chargeable gains accruing to a UK resident trust were, pre FA 2008, treated as those of the settlor if the trust was "settlor interested".

The definition of a "settlor interested" trust for capital gains tax purposes was different to the definition which applied (and still applies post FA 2008) for income tax purposes (see above).

A trust was deemed to be a settlor interested trust if the settlor or spouse could benefit from the trust in any circumstances whatsoever. However, this definition was widened by the provisions of FA 2006.

With effect from 6 April 2006 a settlor was deemed to have an interest in a trust if, in addition to the possible benefit from the trust by the settlor or spouse, any dependent children of the settlor could benefit. For this purpose, a dependent child of the settlor was an unmarried living child under age 18. Child included stepchild.

The above FA 2006 change applied to all trusts including those created prior to 6 April 2006.

Where the settlor interested provisions applied the settlor would be charged to capital gains tax on the trust gains and any such tax paid could be reclaimed from the trustees. Unlike the position for income tax (see above) *all* the trust gains were charged on the settlor even though the settlor may not have been able to benefit from parts of the trust fund. To this extent, the capital gains settlor interested provisions were more penal than those which applied for income tax purposes.

However, even where the settlor is non-UK domiciled but UK resident the remittance basis was inapplicable to capital gains arising on the disposal of non-UK situs assets

The rules applicable to ascertaining the amount of capital gains of the trust to be charged on the settlor were changed from 6 April 2003. For the tax year 2003/04 and later tax years the trust gains charged on the settlor were the trust gains after the offsetting of any trust capital losses and pre taper relief to which the trustees were eligible. The settlor's own surplus of capital losses (i.e. after offset against the settlor's own capital gains) could then be used to reduce the pre taper relief gains of the trust apportioned to the settlor after which such net gains could be reduced by the taper relief to which the trust would have been entitled.

A surplus of trust capital losses (i.e. the surplus after the offset of trust losses against trust gains) was not, however, available for use by the settlor for offset against the settlor's own capital gains.

UK RESIDENT TRUST FOR NON-UK DOMICILED BUT UK RESIDENT INDIVIDUALS

Income Tax

The remittance basis does not apply to non-UK source income of UK resident trusts. From this perspective it is therefore disadvantageous for a UK resident but non-UK domiciled individual to hold non-UK situs assets via a UK resident discretionary trust as the income from such assets, if held directly by the individual, in principle qualifies for remittance basis treatment. If the trust is settlor interested, however, remittance basis treatment will be in point as the trust income is deemed to be that of the settlor. This is also the case if the settlor has an interest in possession in the trust.

A UK resident discretionary trust is liable to an income tax charge of 40% on non-dividend income and 32.5% on dividend income. Thus, for the settlor who is non-UK domiciled but UK resident and who is subject to income tax at the basic rate of 20% (i.e. not a higher rate taxpayer) the discretionary trust (which is not settlor interested) is tax inefficient even though on appointments out of the trust the recipient beneficiary may be able to reclaim some part of this tax from HMRC (e.g. if the beneficiary is a nil rate or basic rate taxpayer). There is still a cash flow disadvantage.

On balance, there is no income tax advantage (and typically the reverse) for the non-UK domiciled individual in using UK resident trusts of any description.

The above applies to such trusts whether created on or after, or before, 6 April 2008.

Capital Gains Tax

The remittance basis does not apply to non-UK source capital gains of UK resident trusts. From this perspective it is therefore disadvantageous for a UK resident but non-UK domiciled individual to hold non-UK situs assets via a UK resident discretionary trust as the capital gains from such assets, if held directly by the individual, in principle qualify for remittance basis treatment.

If the trust is settlor interested, however, remittance basis treatment will be in point as the trust capital gains are deemed to be those of the settlor. However, FA 2008 with respect to disposals on or after 6 April 2008 has abolished the settlor interested rules for UK resident trusts. Thus, on or after 6 April 2008 no trust capital gains are imputed to the settlor.

The rate of capital gains tax (i.e. 18%) for disposals on or after 6 April 2008 is the same for trusts and individuals. However, the annual exemption for trusts is only one half of that applicable to individuals but in the case of the non-UK domiciled but UK resident individual (who claims remittance basis treatment) the entitlement to the annual exemption is withdrawn (see Chapter 23).

Pre FA 2008 (i.e. before abolition of the settlor interested rules) capital losses of the trust were "locked" into the trust and thus were not available for offset against the settlor's capital gains (i.e. even where the trust was settlor interested capital losses within the trust were not apportioned to the settlor; such losses remained within the trust for offset against trust capital gains only).

On balance, there is little capital gains tax advantage for the non-UK domiciled individual in using UK resident trusts of any description.

Inheritance Tax

If all the trust assets are non-UK situs and the settlor is non-UK domiciled at the time of creation of the trust the assets will qualify as excluded property for inheritance tax purposes. It is not necessary for excluded property treatment for the trust to be non-UK resident. However, this is almost universally a preferable option for the non-UK domiciled individual.

UK RESIDENT TRUST FOR UK DOMICILED AND UK RESIDENT INDIVIDUALS

Income Tax

A UK resident discretionary trust is liable to an income tax charge of 40% on non-dividend income and 32.5% on dividend income. Thus, for the settlor who is UK domiciled but UK resident and who is subject to income tax at the basic rate of

20% (i.e. not a higher rate taxpayer) the discretionary trust (which is not settlor interested) is tax inefficient even though on appointments out of the trust the recipient beneficiary may be able to reclaim some part of this tax from HMRC (e.g. if the beneficiary is a nil rate or basic rate taxpayer). There is still a cash flow disadvantage.

There is no income tax advantage (and typically the reverse) for the UK domiciled individual in using UK resident discretionary trusts.

The interest in possession trust may be less income tax disadvantageous as the trust's income is that of the beneficiary and thus subject to income tax on the beneficiary's part at the latter's rate of marginal income tax (which may be the 20% basic rate not the 40% rate).

The above applies to such trusts whether created on or after, or before, 6 April 2008.

Capital Gains Tax

The rate of capital gains tax (i.e. 18%) for disposals on or after 6 April 2008 is the same for trusts and individuals. However, the annual exemption for trusts is only one half of that applicable to individuals.

FA 2008 with respect to disposals on or after 6 April 2008 has abolished the settlor interested rules for UK resident trusts. Thus, on or after 6 April 2008 no trust capital gains are imputed to the settlor.

Pre FA 2008 (i.e. before abolition of the settlor interested rules) capital losses of the trust were "locked" into the trust and thus were not available for offset against the settlor's capital gains (i.e. even where the trust was settlor interested capital losses within the trust were not apportioned to the settlor; such losses remained within the trust for offset against trust capital gains only).

On balance, there is no capital gains tax advantage for the UK domiciled individual in using UK resident trusts of any description.

Inheritance Tax

Unlike the position for the non-UK domiciled individual, even if all the trust assets are non-UK situs as the settlor is UK domiciled the assets will not qualify as excluded property for inheritance tax purposes. The normal rules of inheritance tax thus apply.

However, the discretionary trust while possibly giving rise to a 20% charge on set-up (unless the NRB is available to the settlor) is only subsequently subject to ten yearly charges at the maximum rate of 6% which compares extremely favourably with the 40% rate applicable to individuals on death. Interest in possession trusts created in lifetime on or after 22 March 2006 are treated in the same manner (the position for such trusts created pre 22 March 2006 is different).

The NRB trust may be particularly attractive.

The UK resident trust may, however, offer non-tax advantages in particular in relation to their use to avoid probate and as substitute wills.

SUMMARY

Trustees of a UK resident trust are in principle liable to income tax on trust income and capital gains tax on trust capital gains. The trust in this regard is a distinct and separate person from either its settlor or its beneficiaries.

The rates of income tax on trust income vary according to whether the trust is a discretionary trust or an interest in possession trust. However, the rate of capital gains tax applicable to the trust is the same (i.e. 18% post FA 2008, 40% pre FA 2008) irrespective of the type of trust.

The settlor interested trust provisions applicable to income tax continue to apply in the same manner post FA 2008 as prior to FA 2008. FA 2008 has had no impact on these provisions.

The "settlor interested" trust provisions no longer apply to the capital gains of UK resident trusts following their abolition by FA 2008. Accordingly, all trust gains of a UK resident trust arising on or after 6 April 2008 will be subject to capital gains tax on the part of the trustees (not the settlor).

UK resident trusts are of limited value for the non-UK domiciled but UK resident individual.

UK resident trusts do, however, qualify for excluded property treatment for inheritance tax purposes. It is unlikely, however, that this would tip the balance in favour of a UK resident trust vis-à-vis the non-UK resident trust for the non-UK domiciled individual.

17

Non-UK Resident Trusts: Income and Capital Gains Taxation

BACKGROUND

The previous chapter looked at the income tax and capital gains tax position of UK resident trusts. This chapter will look at the corresponding tax position of the non-UK resident trust (other than the rules regarding trust residence; see the earlier Chapter 16 on UK resident trusts).

The same approach will be adopted as in the earlier chapter, i.e. the income tax and capital gains tax position of the non-UK resident trust will be addressed and then the implication of any anti-avoidance provisions will be examined thereafter.

It is important to bear in mind that, as in the earlier chapter, perhaps more than the other chapters in the book, this chapter will also contain many generalisations to which there may be many exceptions.

The taxation of a trust depends upon the following factors:

- residence of the trust (i.e. UK resident or non-UK resident);
- type of trust (e.g. discretionary versus interest in possession);
- residence status of the settlor;
- domicile status of the settlor;
- residence status of the beneficiaries;
- domicile status of the beneficiaries.

While the trust, as will be seen below, is a separate taxable entity from both the settlor and the beneficiaries certain anti-avoidance provisions may apply (see below) the consequences of which may be, for example, that it is the settlor and not the trust who is subject to tax on the trust's income and/or capital gains.

Strictly speaking, it is the trustees of the trust (not the trust, per se) who are liable to any income and/or capital gains tax charges. Trustees are treated as a single person or single body distinct from the persons who are in fact the trustees (companies and individuals may be trustees).

FA 2008 IMPACT

FA 2008 has had a significant impact on the capital gains tax treatment of non-UK resident trusts but a less significant impact on their income tax treatment.

The provisions of FA 2008 in this regard apply to any trust income which arises on or after 6 April 2008 and to any trust disposals, of either UK or non-UK situs assets on or after 6 April 2008. However, transitional provisions also apply with respect to the income and capital gains of the trust which arose prior to 6 April 2008.

Income Tax

With respect to the income tax treatment of non-UK resident trusts the changes introduced in FA 2008 are restricted to:

- changes in the rates of income tax applied to trust income (these changes also apply to the income of individuals and thus these changes are not restricted in their application just to trusts);
- amendments to the rules with respect to "remittances".

As will be seen below, non-UK resident trusts are liable to UK income tax only on UK source income. Thus, the above referred to rate changes are applicable only with respect to UK source income.

While remittance basis treatment for the income of the non-UK resident trust is irrelevant for the trust, per se, this is not the case for the settlor and/or beneficiaries who, if non-UK domiciled but UK resident, may be in a position to take advantage of this basis of treatment. This would arise where the settlor and/or the beneficiaries of the trust, who are non-UK domiciled but UK resident, either receive or are deemed to receive income and/or capital gains and/or some form of benefit from the trust.

Capital Gains Tax

With respect to the capital gains tax treatment of non-UK resident trusts the changes introduced by FA 2008 are much more significant. They are as follows:

- amendments to the offshore "capital payments" trust regime;
- amendments to the rules with respect to "remittances".

A number of FA 2008 changes referred to in the earlier chapter have no import for the non-UK resident trust. Thus, the abolition of indexation and taper relief has no impact as non-UK resident trusts were, and are not, liable to capital gains tax even on the disposal of UK situs assets (unless the non-UK resident trust was, or is, itself involved in the carrying on in the UK of a trade; generally speaking, this is unlikely because where a UK trade is carried on it is invariably the case for such trade to be carried on by a non-UK resident company whose shares are in turn owned by the trust. Thus, it is not the trust itself carrying on the trade).

Although the newly introduced entrepreneur relief for capital gains tax purposes (see Chapter 8) does in principle apply to both UK and non-UK resident trusts it is unlikely in practice that it will actually be in point for the non-UK resident trust.

Although the "settlor interested" provisions for UK resident trusts have been abolished with respect to capital gains tax (but not income tax) (see Chapter 16) this is not the case with respect to the equivalent provisions for non-UK resident trusts. These provisions have not been abolished or in fact even amended (see below).

Other things being equal, for the non-UK domiciled but UK resident individual, non-UK resident trusts are undoubtedly preferable and are more tax efficient than UK resident trusts. This, however, is unlikely to be the case for the UK domiciled and UK resident individual.

INCOME TAX

Discretionary Trusts

Non-UK resident discretionary (or accumulation and maintenance) trusts are liable to UK income tax on UK source income only. Any income arising outside the UK is not subject to UK income tax on the part of the trust.

Assuming the excluded income rules (see below) do not apply, the rate of income tax applicable to the UK source income is the trust rate (i.e. 40%) for all forms of UK source income other than UK source dividend income which is subject to income tax at the dividend trust rate (i.e. 32.5%).

The income tax liability of the trust with respect to dividend income is calculated as follows. The net dividend is "grossed up" to take into account the attaching tax credit and the gross amount is subject to income tax at 32.5% albeit with an offset for the 10% tax credit. This produces a net income tax liability of 22.5% for the trust of the "gross" dividend (or 25% of the "net" dividend).

With respect to UK source bank interest the bank will deduct income tax at source (i.e. at 20%) on crediting the interest to the bank account. The trust will have a liability at 40% (albeit with the 20% credit offset) producing a net liability of 20% of the gross interest.

UK source rental income is subject to income tax at 40%.

While HMRC may have difficulty in collecting the above income tax liabilities from non-UK resident trusts, nevertheless that does not, of course, remove the liabilities of the trustees.

It is because of the possible exposure to 40% and 32.5% income tax liabilities that, typically, the non-UK resident trust will interpose a non-UK resident company between it and the UK income/assets.

A non-UK resident company is not liable to higher rate tax (i.e. 40%). A rate of 20% (i.e. the basic rate for the tax year 2008/09; 22% for tax year 2007/08) applies to UK source rental income; no income tax is payable on any net UK source dividend received; and in the case of UK source bank interest the income constitutes "excluded income" (see below) and thus no income tax liability arises (other than that which may have been deducted at source; in the case of interest paid to companies, however, there is in any event no requirement on the part of the bank to deduct tax at source).

Thus, it is usually tax efficient for the trustees to interpose such a company where UK source income arises to the trust.

However, it may be the case that the UK source income arising to the trust qualifies as "excluded income" (i.e. broadly, dividend and interest income). Where this is the case any UK income tax charge is restricted to any UK income tax deducted at source. No withholding tax applies to dividend payments although 20% income tax at source may be deducted from bank interest. For the excluded income provisions to apply to the trust, however, the class of beneficiaries of the trust must not include any UK resident individuals; if such individuals are included then the UK source income referred to above no longer qualifies as excluded income and becomes taxable as normal (i.e. at 40% or 32.5%; see above). Where none of the beneficiaries is UK resident income will constitute excluded income and the trust may then arrange for any bank interest to be credited "gross" by the bank thus avoiding the normal 20% income tax deducted at source.

In practice excluded income treatment where the trust has been set up by the UK domiciled and UK resident individual is often unlikely to apply as, invariably, one or more of the beneficiaries is likely to be UK resident (one such individual being sufficient to preclude the application of excluded income treatment). However, if in fact none of the beneficiaries are UK resident excluded income treatment will apply.

The tax treatment of the beneficiaries of the discretionary trust is considered below.

Interest in Possession Trusts

Where the non-UK resident trust is an interest in possession trust the beneficiary with the interest in possession has the right to the trust income as it arises, whereas the beneficiary of a discretionary trust has no such right.

As a consequence, the UK domiciled and resident interest in possession beneficiary is liable to UK income tax on the non-UK resident trust's income whether the income arises in the UK or outside the UK. The rate of income tax applicable is dependent upon the tax position of the beneficiary.

Excluded income treatment referred to above has no application here as the beneficiary is UK resident and thus liable to income tax on all UK source income.

Example 17.1

Kenneth Cigar set up a non-UK resident trust in 2002 with his brother, Keith, as the interest in possession beneficiary. Keith is UK domiciled and UK resident and a higher rate taxpayer.

In the tax year 2007/08 the trust's income constituted UK source rental income and, after expenses, amounted to £60 000.

Keith is subject, for the tax year 2007/08, to income tax at 40% on the £60 000.

However, if the interest in possession beneficiary while UK resident is non-UK domiciled then the remittance basis will apply to the trust's non-UK source income but not to the trust's UK source income.

Example 17.2
Kenneth Cigar set up a non-UK resident trust in 2002 with his brother, Albert, as the interest in possession beneficiary. Albert is non-UK domiciled but UK resident individual and a higher rate taxpayer.

In the tax year 2007/08 the trust's income constituted UK source rental income and, after expenses, amounted to £60 000.

Albert, although non-UK domiciled, is subject, for the tax year 2007/08, to income tax at 40% on the £60 000.

Albert is entitled to the income as it arises as the rental income is UK source; the remittance basis is inapplicable.

However, had the rental income arisen from, say, a Spanish villa then as such income constitutes non-UK source Albert would only be subject to income tax thereon if and when the income was remitted to the UK.

In the case of the non-UK resident interest in possession beneficiary (irrespective of domicile status) UK income tax is chargeable on the UK source income of the trust. However, excluded income treatment would apply in this case and thus no income tax is chargeable on the UK source dividends and interest.

It should be noted that for the interest in possession beneficiary the source of the income is the underlying source of the income which accrues to the trust, not the trust itself. Whereas in the case of a beneficiary who receives income appointed out of a discretionary trust the source of the income on the part of the beneficiary is the trust itself, not the underlying source of the income to the trust (see below).

The above applies whether the trust is set up by a UK or non-UK domiciled individual.

BENEFICIARIES OF THE NON-UK RESIDENT DISCRETIONARY TRUST

Beneficiaries of a discretionary trust have no right to the income or capital of the trust and only benefit as and when the trustees exercise their discretion in the beneficiaries' favour.

Where a UK resident trust makes a distribution of income to a beneficiary a tax credit in respect of any tax paid by the trust is available to the beneficiary (see Chapter 16). No such tax credit, however, is in principle available to the beneficiary with respect to the tax borne by the trustees on a distribution by a non-UK resident trust (see below).

Thus where, for example, the non-UK resident trust receives UK source income subject to income tax at 40% or 32.5% (which is likely to be the case where one or more of the beneficiaries are UK resident; in which case the UK source income cannot qualify as "excluded income") and subsequently makes a distribution to the UK domiciled and UK resident beneficiary a further 40% income tax charge will arise on the distribution on the part of the beneficiary (assuming the beneficiary is a higher rate income tax payer) without any corresponding tax credit offset with respect to the tax already paid by the trustees.

This unfavourable result is, however, ameliorated by concession under which a tax credit (at 40%) is in fact made available to the UK resident beneficiary. The result for the resident beneficiary is thus the same as applies where distribution is made by a UK resident trust.

It must be noted, however, that no UK tax credit is available to the beneficiary where the income of the trust which is distributed to the beneficiary is non-UK source income as, of course, no UK tax will have been suffered by the trust on such income (the beneficiary also receives no tax credit for any foreign tax paid on the non-UK source income by the trustees).

For the non-UK domiciled but UK resident individual beneficiary who receives a distribution of trust income, an income tax liability will only arise if and when the beneficiary remits the income to the UK; otherwise no UK income tax liability arises on the part of the beneficiary (it needs to be appreciated that the payments of income from the trust constitute a new source of income for the beneficiary and, as the trust is not UK resident, the source is non-UK source in origin; this is the case even if the income paid to the beneficiaries which arises to the trust is itself UK source). Credit for any income tax paid by the trust on the UK source income will be available to the beneficiary when the income is remitted to the UK.

Example 17.3
Kenneth Cigar set up a non-UK resident discretionary trust in 2002 for his brother, Dutch, and two sisters, Mary and Jane.

Kenneth is UK domiciled, UK resident and a higher rate taxpayer. Dutch is non-UK domiciled but UK resident and Kenneth's two sisters are both UK domiciled and UK resident.

All of the trust's income constitutes UK source rental income.

The trustees in the tax year 2007/08 appoint out £36 000 to Dutch and £12 000 to each of the two sisters.

The two sisters will be liable to income tax at their respective marginal rates of income tax.

Dutch will be liable to income tax at his marginal rate of income tax but only as and when the income appointed to him is remitted to the UK. The reason for Dutch's differing treatment compared to that of Albert in Example 17.2 above is that the source of the income for Dutch is the trust (which is non-UK resident) not the UK source income itself. Whereas for Albert, as the interest in possession beneficiary, the source of the income is (in Example 17.2) the UK source rental income to which Albert is entitled.

ANTI-AVOIDANCE PROVISIONS

The anti-avoidance provisions with respect to non-UK resident trusts are much more extensive than those applying to UK resident trusts. In the case of UK resident trusts FA 2008 abolished the settlor interested rules for capital gains tax but left the equivalent rules for income tax intact.

With respect to non-UK resident trusts, however, FA 2008 has not affected the settlor interested provisions for either income tax or capital gains tax. Thus, the pre and post FA 2008 positions in this regard remain unchanged.

However, as will be seen below, for the non-UK resident trust additional anti-avoidance provisions may also be in point under which the settlor and beneficiaries may be exposed to tax on the income of the trust.

Settlor Interested Rules: Income Tax

For the non-UK resident trust if the settlor or spouse is able to benefit from the trust the income of the trust will be subject to income tax on the part of the settlor if the settlor is UK domiciled and UK resident. Where the settlor is non-UK domiciled but UK resident only UK source income will be subject to income tax on the settlor; non-UK source income is subject to income tax on the settlor only if remitted to the UK.

If the settlor is, however, non-UK domiciled but UK resident and the income of the settlor interested trust is non-UK source and thus the remittance basis applies, as indicated above, such income is then considered "relevant income" for section 731 purposes (see below) and is thus available for "matching" with benefits provided to beneficiaries of the non-UK resident trust in respect of which a tax charge may arise. Once the income of the trust is so "matched" it cannot then be taxed on the settlor under the settlor interested rules at a later date.

Example 17.4
Yaki Trinidad a non-UK domiciled but UK resident individual set up a non-UK resident discretionary trust some years ago for himself, his wife and their two non-UK domiciled but UK resident children, Yoki and Yuki, aged 25 and 27, respectively.

In the tax year 2008/09 the trust received £60 000 of income of which £20 000 derived from UK sources and £40 000 from non-UK sources.

The £20 000 will be attributed to Yaki and subject to income tax on his part for the tax year 2008/09. The £40 000 will also be attributed to Yaki but will only be subject to income tax on his part if he remits the money to the UK.

Had Yaki been UK domiciled the whole £60 000 would be attributed to him for the tax year 2008/09.

Where the trust income is or includes "offshore income gains" (i.e. gains arising on disposals of interests in offshore non-distributor funds) such offshore income gains cannot be treated as the settlor's income under the settlor interested provisions. However, offshore income gains may still be subject to income tax under sections 720 or 731 ITA 2007 (see below).

Sections 720 and 731 ITA 2007

Sections 720 and 731 have no application whatsoever to UK resident trusts. They are extremely complex. They are powerful anti-avoidance provisions which apply to non-resident trusts and companies.

Section 720 is very similar to the above settlor interested provisions. It is, generally speaking, broader than the settlor interested provisions and, for example, applies to income of a non-UK resident company whereas the settlor interested provisions only apply to non-UK resident trusts. The terminology used is also different. However, both sets of provisions may apply to the same set of circumstances. Where this occurs, in practice, the settlor interested provisions take precedence.

Section 720 applies where the transferor (or the transferor's spouse) is able to enjoy the income (including offshore income gains) of a non-UK resident person (e.g. trust and/or company) as a consequence of a transfer of assets abroad. Where it applies the income of the non-UK resident person is attributed to the transferor and the transferor is then liable to income tax on the income. Thus, section 720 applies where the individual sets up a non-UK resident trust (and/or a non-UK resident company) and the settlor/transferor (or spouse) is able to enjoy the income of the trust in some way or another. The section also applies to any benefit provided to the transferor (or spouse) out of the income.

Where the transferor/settlor is non-UK domiciled but UK resident only UK source income will be subject to income tax on the transferor/settlor; non-UK source income enjoyed outside the UK is subject to income tax on the transferor/settlor only if remitted to the UK. However, the non-UK source income which is unremitted falls to be available for "matching" under section 731 (see below) and thus may still precipitate tax liabilities.

Example 17.5
Using the facts of Example 17.4 above, under section 720 the exact same tax consequences apply.

However, section 720 only applies where the transferor (or spouse) can enjoy the income of the non-UK resident trust. It may be that although the transferor (or spouse) is not able to so benefit other individuals under the trust are able to enjoy the income or some form of benefit under the trust. Section 720 does not apply to such individuals. Nevertheless, such individuals receiving income and/or some form of benefit are subject to income tax on the income/benefit under a different section, namely, section 731.

Where the income of the non-UK resident person is appointed out to such an individual the latter is subject to income tax on the income. However, if the individual is non-UK domiciled but UK resident the income appointed out is subject to income tax only if remitted unless some part of the non-UK resident person's income arose from UK sources.

Example 17.6
Using the facts of Example 17.4 above. Assume in this case however that neither Yaki nor his spouse can benefit under the trust.

The trust is thus not settlor interested and indeed section 720 cannot apply. As a consequence no part of the £60 000 (£20 000 derived from UK sources and £40 000 from non-UK sources) of income for the tax year 2008/09 can be attributed to Yaki.

Just before the end of the tax year £15 000 was paid out to Yoki and £15 000 to Yuki; both payments were made to their respective bank accounts in Turks and Caicos.

Although Yoki and Yuki are non-UK domiciled under Section 731. Yoki and Yuki are subject to income tax on £10 000 each (i.e. 50% each of the £20 000 UK source income) with the balance of their £15 000 payment subject to income tax only when this balancing amount is remitted.

Where some form of benefit (as opposed to actual income) is provided to the individual out of the trust the charge to income tax is levied on the value of the benefit but only to the extent that "relevant income" which has arisen to the non-UK resident person is available to "match" the quantum of the benefit.

"Relevant income" is, broadly, income arising to the non-UK resident person in respect of which the individual may benefit.

As for section 720, the remittance basis applies where the individual in receipt of the benefit is non-UK domiciled. However, in this case if the benefit is provided outside the UK it may still be subject to income tax on the part of the non-UK domiciled but UK resident individual (without the benefit being remitted to the UK) if and to the extent that the non-UK resident person has UK source relevant income to match to the benefit and/or non-UK source income but only if remitted to the UK. A benefit received in the UK is matched to both UK and non-UK source relevant income of the person (irrespective of whether the non-UK source income is remitted to the UK).

Example 17.7
Nomura Leeds, a UK domiciled and UK resident individual, set up a non-UK resident trust for his three UK domiciled UK resident children, all aged over 18, Fuji, Nippon and Mazda. Neither Nomura nor his wife can benefit under the trust.

In the tax year 2008/09 the trust received income of £80 000 of which £15 000 arose in the UK and the balance of £65 000 arose outside the UK.

The trust owned a UK property in which for the whole of 2008/09 one of the children, Fuji, lived rent free although the child did pay all the house running costs. The trust also owned a non-UK property in which for the whole of 2008/09 one of the children, Mazda, lived rent free although the child did pay all the house running costs.

As the "benefit" provided under the trust to Fuji is enjoyed in the UK by Fuji, he is subject to income tax on the value of the benefit which is the amount of rent which should have been paid, say, £20 000.

The trust received £80 000 of income which qualifies as "relevant income".

Fuji thus has an income tax liability for 2008/09 on the £20 000 as both the UK and non-UK source income is available for aportionement as Fuji is UK domiciled.

Similarly, Mazda has an income tax liability for 2008/09 on £30 000 (assume this is the value of the benefit of the non-UK property) as both the UK and non-UK source income are available for apportionment as Mazda is UK domiciled.

Example 17.8
Nomura Tokyo, a non-UK domiciled but UK resident individual, set up a non-UK resident trust for his three non-UK domiciled UK resident children, all aged over

18, Fuji, Nippon and Mazda. Neither Nomura nor his wife can benefit under the trust.

In the tax year 2008/09 the trust received income of £80 000 of which £15 000 arose in the UK and the balance of £65 000 arose outside the UK.

The trust owned a UK property in which for the whole of 2008/09 one of the children, Fuji, lived rent free although the child did pay all the house running costs. The trust also owned a non-UK property in which for the whole of 2008/09 one of the children, Mazda, lived rent free although the child did pay all the house running costs.

The trust received £80 000 of income which qualifies as "relevant income".

The "benefit" provided under the trust is enjoyed in the UK by Fuji (say, value £20 000) but, for Mazda, the benefit (say, value £30 000) is enjoyed outside the UK.

All the £80 000 of trust income is available for apportionment.

An apportionment of the trust income thus becomes necessary.

Of the UK source income (£15 000) of the trust 2/5ths (£6000) is apportioned to Fuji and 3/5ths (£9000) is apportioned to Mazda (based on measure of benefits).

The non-UK source income (which is not remitted to the UK) is also apportionable to the benefit provided to Fuji and thus £14 000 of the £65 000 of non-UK source trust income is so apportioned (thus producing the £20 000 total for Fuji).

Fuji thus has an income tax liability for 2008/09 on the £20 000.

However, for Mazda of the £30 000 of benefit only £9000 is subject to income tax. The non-UK source income apportioned to Mazda of £21 000 is subject to income tax but only as and when it is remitted to the UK.

However, relevant income is only matched to UK resident individuals. The provision of a benefit to a non-UK resident individual is not subject to income tax and, as a consequence, no relevant income is matched with the benefit. The quantum of relevant income is thus not reduced and remains to be matched to UK resident individuals receiving benefits and thus creating possible income tax charges (so-called "washing out" is thus not possible; see below re matching for capital gains tax purposes where "washing out" is permitted).

Example 17.9
Nomura Tokyo, a non-UK domiciled but UK resident individual, set up a non-UK resident trust for his three non-UK domiciled children, all aged over 18, Fuji, Nippon and Mazda. Neither Nomura nor his wife can benefit under the trust.

Assume only Fuji is UK resident, i.e. Nippon and Mazda are non-UK resident.

The income of the trust is £80 000 (all UK source) for the tax year 2008/09 and nil for the tax year 2009/10.

The trust owned one property in the UK which Fuji occupied for 2009/10 only. The other two properties the trust owned were outside the UK and Nippon and Mazda each occupied one of these rent free for 2008/09 only.

Although in 2008/09 Nippon and Mazda enjoyed benefits under the trust no UK tax charges arise as both are non-UK resident while enjoying the benefits. Thus, none of the £80 000 relevant income is matched to their benefits.

In 2009/10 the £80 000 relevant income of 2008/09 which has not been previously matched is thus available to match with Fuji's benefit (Fuji being UK resident) and thus an income tax charge arises on his part on the benefit he receives, say, £20 000.

Example 17.10
Nomura Tokyo, a non-UK domiciled but UK resident individual, set up a non-UK resident trust for his three non-UK domiciled but UK resident children, all aged over 18, Fuji, Nippon and Mazda. Neither Nomura nor his wife can benefit under the trust.

The income of the trust is £80 000 (all UK source) for the tax year 2008/09 and nil for the tax year 2009/10.

The trust owned three properties in the UK one of which Fuji occupied rent free for 2009/10 only. The other two properties were each occupied by Nippon and Mazda rent free for 2008/09 only.

Nippon and Mazda are subject to income tax in 2008/09 on the benefit they receive from the trust. Assuming that each benefit was £40 000 each of them would be subject to income tax on £40 000 this amount being matched with the trust's £80 000 relevant income.

In 2009/10 Fuji's benefit (say, £20 000) is subject to an income tax charge. However, there is no relevant income of the trust to match the benefit and thus for 2009/10 no actual income tax charge arisies on Fuji.

If the trust income in 2010/11 is £20 000 (and assuming none of the children occupy any of the properties any longer) then Fuji will be subject to income tax on £20 000 for 2010/11.

Settlor Interested Rules: Capital Gains Tax

Section 86 TCGA 1992 is the relevant section here. The section has not been changed by FA 2008.

The key point to note is that the section only applies where the settlor is UK domiciled and UK resident; it is thus inapplicable where the settlor is non-UK domiciled irrespective of the non-UK domiciled's residence status. This is the position both pre and post FA 2008.

Although following FA 2008 a non-UK domiciled but UK resident individual may choose not to be taxed on the remittance basis (by simply not lodging a claim for remittance basis treatment; see Chapter 23) and would then be subject to tax on the arising basis, section 86 is still inapplicable as the individual is still non-UK domiciled.

A non-UK resident trust currently qualifies as "settlor interested" for capital gains tax purposes if the beneficiaries include any of the following:

- settlor;
- spouse of the settlor;
- children of settlor or spouse;
- children's spouses;

- grandchildren;
- grandchildren's spouses.

It should be noted that the definition of a settlor interested trust has changed over time. Thus, the extension of the definition to include grandchildren and/or their spouses was introduced in FA 1998 and applies only to trusts set up on or after 17 March 1998 (or trusts set up before this date if certain events occurred on or after 17 March 1998 such as the adding of further property to the trust).

This definition is much broader than that which was applicable for capital gains tax purposes in the case of the UK resident settlor interested trust (where the settlor or spouse (or minor unmarried children from 6 April 2006; see above) of the settlor may benefit under the trust).

Where section 86 applies the capital gains of the trust are apportioned to the UK domiciled and UK resident settlor who is then subject to capital gains tax thereon. Capital losses of the trust are not, however, apportioned to the settlor (although they are utilised within the trust to offset trust capital gains prior to apportionment).

It should also be noted that capital gains of the trust available for apportionment on the settlor include capital gains of a non-UK resident company, in which the non-UK resident trust is a greater than 10% shareholder. This assumes that the company would be a "close" company if it was UK resident.

One of the implications of the restriction of section 86 to UK domiciled settlors only is that the non-UK resident trust offers the non-UK domiciled settlor an effective tax planning vehicle with respect to investments in non-UK (or indeed UK) situs capital growth assets. In this case, neither the trust nor the settlor is exposed to any capital gains tax charge on trust asset disposals.

Example 17.11
Kitty Kenya is a non-UK domiciled but UK resident individual.

After arriving in the UK in 2003 she set up a trust in the Cayman Islands to which she transferred £500 000 of her offshore cash. The trust has been be used to invest in non-income producing capital growth shares. Kitty is a beneficiary under the trust.

In late 2008 the trust sold a significant part of its share portfolio realising £750 000 of capital gains.

As the trust is non-UK resident it is not subject to capital gains tax. In addition, the settlor interested rules (i.e. section 86) do not apply and thus none of the trust's capital gains are apportioned to Kitty.

If, however, Kitty had been UK domiciled the £75 000 of trust capital gains would be subject to capital gains tax on her part for the tax year 2008/09.

On the other hand, no capital gains tax liability is avoided where the non-UK resident trust is UK domiciled settlor interested (see Example 17.11 above). In view of the broad category of individuals which causes a non-UK resident trust to qualify as settlor interested (see above) the non-UK resident trust does not offer, from the capital gains tax perspective, any real opportunity to avoid capital gains tax for the UK domiciled individual unless the trust is not in fact settlor interested.

Section 86 does not apply to attribute "offshore income gains" (i.e. gains arising on the disposal of interests in offshore non-distributor funds) of the trust to the settlor.

Even though a capital gains tax liability is avoidable for the non-UK domiciled non-resident settlor interested trust (or the non-UK resident trust set up by a UK domiciled settlor which is not settlor interested) such a charge may arise where the trust makes "capital payments" to the beneficiaries under section 87 TCGA 1992 (see below).

Section 87 TCGA 1992 (Charge on Beneficiaries)

Section 87 applies where a beneficiary receives a "capital payment" or some other form of "benefit" from the non-UK resident trust. However, it can only apply if section 86 (see above) does not apply. Thus, section 87 will always apply if the settlor is non-UK domiciled but will not apply where the settlor is UK domiciled (unless in the latter case the trust is not settlor interested).

Example 17.12

Jake Window, a UK domiciled and UK resident individual, set up a non-UK resident trust two years ago for his two brothers and three sisters.

Neither he nor his wife can benefit under the trust.

The trust is not settlor interested for capital gains tax purposes and thus section 86 cannot apply to the trust capital gains but section 87 is in point.

FA 2008 has had a significant impact on section 87. Pre FA 2008 non-UK domiciled beneficiaries were not "caught" by the section whereas post FA 2008 such individuals are brought within the ambit of the section.

Thus, pre FA 2008 neither sections 86 nor 87 applied to the non-UK domiciled individual. As a consequence, a significant tax planning opportunity arose for such individuals resident in the UK. Where the non-UK resident trust made capital gains it could effect payments to the non-UK domiciled but UK resident beneficiaries in the UK without any capital gains tax charge arising either under section 86 or 87. This represented a major "loophole" for the non-UK domiciled individual.

Example 17.13

Placido Naples, a non-UK domiciled but non-UK resident individual, set up a non-UK resident trust in the tax year 2005/06 for his own benefit and that of his wife and four children all of whom are non-UK domiciled and UK resident.

In the tax years 2005/06 and 2006/07 the trust capital gains amounted to £60 000 and £40 000, respectively (i.e. in total £100 000). In 2007/08 the trust appointed out the whole of the trust monies of £500 000 to Placido, his wife and the children equally in the UK of which £100 000 comprised the aggregate trust capital gains.

None of the £100 000 of capital gains is subject to capital gains tax as in 2007/08 neither sections 86 nor 87 applied to non-UK domiciled individuals.

Example 17.14

Placido London, a UK domiciled and UK resident individual, set up a non-UK resident trust in the tax year 2005/06 for his own benefit and that of his wife and four children all of whom were UK domiciled and UK resident.

In the tax years 2005/06 and 2006/07 the trust capital gains amounted to £60 000 and £40 000, respectively (i.e. in total £100 000). In 2007/08 the trust appointed out the whole of the trust monies of £500 000 to Placido, his wife and the children equally in the UK of which £100 000 comprised the aggregate trust capital gains.

Section 86 applied to the trust capital gains for each tax year and thus Placido was subject to capital gains tax on £60 000 and £40 000 in each of 2005/06 and 2006/07.

Thus, the actual payments by the trust in 2007/08 precipitated no capital gains tax consequences for any of the recipients (otherwise double tax would arise).

However, post FA 2008 while the non-UK domiciled individual is still not within the ambit of section 86, section 87 now applies to such individual.

Although now within the ambit of section 87 the remittance basis still applies to the non-UK domiciled but UK resident individual in receipt of a capital payment *or* is some other form of benefit. This requires the appointment of trust monies in respect of trust capital gains to be made outside the UK. Similarly, any other form of benefit needs to be provided to the beneficiary outside the UK. Thus, if the provision of the benefit is in the UK a capital gains tax charge arises as the apportioned trust capital gains are treated (under the wider definition of remittance) as remitted to the UK.

It should be noted, however, that *any trust gains arising on UK situs assets are to be regarded as if they were gains arising on non-UK situs assets if the beneficiary concerned is non-UK domiciled and claims the remittance basis*. Thus, all section 87 trust capital gains are in principle eligible for remittance basis treatment (assuming the individual beneficiary is non-UK domiciled). A non-UK domiciled individual beneficiary who does not, however, claim the remittance basis will be taxed on the arising basis under section 87 in the same manner as a UK domiciled beneficiary.

A "capital payment" to a beneficiary is defined as any payment by the trust which is not subject to income tax on the part of the beneficiary *or* is a transfer of assets or some other form of benefit conferred on the beneficiary (e.g. permitting the beneficiary to occupy trust property "rent free"). If the beneficiary is non-UK resident any payment which is received otherwise than as income is a capital payment.

Under section 87, the capital gains of the trust are apportioned to beneficiaries who receive capital payments from the trust. If in the tax year the trust makes capital gains and makes capital payments to beneficiaries in that tax year, then the capital gains are apportioned to the beneficiaries up to the amount of the capital payments. The beneficiary is then liable to capital gains tax on the apportioned capital gains. If the capital gains of the trust for the tax year exceed the capital payments of that tax year then the excess may be carried back to the prior tax year and apportioned to capital payments made in that tax year which have not previously been matched and so on.

In the event that a surplus of capital gains still remains then such capital gains will be available to match against future capital payments made by the trust.

The capital gains of the trust available for matching with capital payments to beneficiaries includes capital gains which may have been apportioned to the trust from a non-UK resident company in which the trust is a greater than 10% shareholder.

Example 17.15

Luigi Lima, a non-UK domiciled but UK resident individual, set up a non-UK resident trust for himself, his UK domiciled wife and their non-UK domiciled but UK resident son aged 26.

In the tax year 2008/09 the trust capital gains amounted to £600 000 on sales proceeds of £900 000. No capital gains arose in 2009/10.

On the last day of the tax year 2008/09 the trust appointed out the sum of £300 000 to each of Luigi, his wife and their son. The monies were kept outside the UK.

Section 86, even post FA 2008, does not apply to non-UK domiciled settlors (i.e. Luigi). Thus, section 87 is in point.

Under section 87 each of the individuals has £200 000 of trust capital gains apportioned to them but only his UK domiciled wife has a capital gains tax charge for 2008/09.

If, however, in the following tax year 2009/10 Luigi remitted £200 000 out of his appointment of £300 000 to the UK, capital gains tax will arise on the £200 000 (under the new remittance rules the first part of the remittance in this case is the capital gain).

The trust may, however, make capital payments to beneficiaries prior to the trust having made any capital gains. In such cases any capital gains made by the trust at a later date are then, at that time, apportioned to the capital payments thus precipitating the capital gains tax charge at that time.

Example 17.16

Baz Desk, a UK domiciled but UK resident individual, set up a non-UK resident trust for his six UK domiciled and UK resident children, all aged over 18.

In 2008/09 capital payments were made equally to three of the children amounting to £150 000 in total but in 2008/09 the trust made no capital gains. In 2009/10 trust capital gains amounted to £275 000.

In the tax year 2008/09 there are no trust gains to apportion to the beneficiaries who received capital payments. No capital gains tax charge thus arises on their part in 2008/09.

However, in 2009/10 there are sufficient trust capital gains to apportion to the three beneficiaries. In 2009/10 each beneficiary is subject to capital gains tax on £50 000 of trust capital gains.

FA 2008 has, however, fundamentally altered the allocation process applying under section 87 to capital payments made to beneficiaries on or after 6 April 2008.

Pre FA 2008 the allocation was carried out on a so-called *FIFO* (i.e. "first in first out") basis. Post FA 2008 the allocation is to be carried out on a *LIFO* ("last in first out") basis. The new LIFO basis applies whether the settlor of the non-UK resident trust is UK or non-UK domiciled.

Thus, under the new rules, post FA 2008, later capital payments will now be matched with later trust gains (pre FA 2008 capital payments were matched with the first available trust capital gains). This new basis is to apply whether the beneficiaries receiving the capital payments are UK or non-UK domiciled and the new LIFO rule applies when matching any trust gains to capital payments where such payments are made on or after 6 April 2008.

Example 17.17
A non-UK resident trust has the following capital gains:

2008/09	£12 000
2009/10	£25 000
2010/11	£45 000
2011/12	£10 000

The trust is not settlor interested and none of the trust capital gains have been matched under section 87 with any capital payments as none have been made.

In 20012/13 a capital payment is made of £72 000.

Under section 87 (under the new LIFO matching rules) the £72 000 is matched as follows:

2011/12	£10 000
2010/11	£45 000
2009/10	£17 000

Thus, for the beneficiary concerned a capital gains tax liability arises on the full £72 000 capital payment in the tax year 2012/13.

Example 17.18
Capital payments under a non-UK resident trust have been made as follows:

2008/09	£12 000 beneficiary A
2009/10	£25 000 beneficiary B
2010/11	£45 000 beneficiary C
2011/12	£10 000 beneficiary D

The trust is not settlor interested and no trust capital gains have arisen over this period.
In 2012/13 the trust makes capital gains of £72 000.

Under section 87 (under the new LIFO matching rules) the £72 000 of capital gains are matched as follows to the capital payments:

2011/12 £10 000 beneficiary D
2010/11 £45 000 beneficiary C
2009/10 £17 000 beneficiary B

Thus, for each of beneficiaries D, C and B a capital gains tax liability arises on the above amounts of apportioned trust capital gains in the tax year 2012/13.

Beneficiary A has no capital gains tax liability as no trust capital gains have been apportioned at this point in time.

If the trust in 2013/14 makes capital gains of £20 000 of this amount £8 000 is apportioned to beneficiary B (to cover the shortfall against the £25 000 capital payment) and the remaining £12 000 of trust capital gains are apportioned to beneficiary A.

Thus, B and A each have capital gains tax liabilities for 2013/14.

Pre FA 2008, unmatched capital payments and unmatched capital gains were each separately aggregated over time and thus any distinction between payments/gains of one tax year compared to another was not relevant (except in the case of the "supplementary charge"; see below); in effect two "pools" were created, one comprising unmatched capital gains and one comprising unmatched capital payments.

The capital gains comprising the section 87 capital gains pool were, pre FA 2008, those capital gains after the offset of any trust capital losses, indexation and taper relief but before the trust annual exemption (the position post FA 2008 is slightly different primarily due to the abolition of the indexation allowance and taper relief; see below). Even though taper relief was abolished by FA 2008, pre FA 2008 trust gains remain as originally computed and thus no recomputation is necessary.

Post FA 2008, however, the above "pooling" will not apply. This is because under the new rules capital payments for a *particular* tax year are first matched with trust capital gains of the same tax year.

Under the FA 2008 LIFO matching rules the first step is to identify the trust gains and capital payments for the tax year concerned. If the former equal or exceed the latter then all capital payments are matched. Any surplus capital gains are carried back to the immediately preceding tax year and any unmatched capital payments for that year are matched. This process is repeated until either the surplus capital gains have been fully matched or there are no unmatched capital payments left in any earlier tax year (in which case the still remaining surplus capital gains are available for matching against future tax years' capital payments).

Where the latter (i.e. capital payment) exceed the former (i.e. trust gains) in the tax year concerned any surplus capital payments are carried back in the same manner as above (i.e. matching the surplus with earlier tax years' unmatched capital gains). To the extent that after carrying out the above a surplus of capital payments still remains, these are available to be matched against future tax years' capital gains.

Post FA 2008 the trust gains for any tax year which are to be matched are those trust gains less allowable capital losses (i.e. current tax year losses and unrelieved prior tax years' losses brought forward).

Transitional Provisions

Under the transitional provisions of FA 2008 no account is to be taken of:

- capital gains accruing in or before the tax year 1980/81;
- capital payments received before 10 March 1981;
- capital payments received on or between 10 March 1981 and 5 April 1984 where an element of the gain relates to a pre 6 April 1981 period.

No capital gains tax charge will arise on a non-UK domiciled beneficiary where a *capital payment received before 6 April 2008* is matched with capital gains of the tax year 2008/09 or later. Similarly, no capital gains tax charge will arise on a non-UK domiciled beneficiary where a *capital payment received in or after 2008/09* is matched with capital gains of 2007/08 or any earlier tax year. Both of these measures apply where the beneficiary is non-UK domiciled whether a claim to the remittance basis has been made or not. These provisions are designed to maintain the pre FA 2008 position for such individuals.

The effect of the above is to exempt the non-UK domiciled beneficiary where one of the matching events (i.e. receipt of a capital payment *or* the arising of a trust gain) took place before the tax year 2008/09 when the beneficiary would not, at that time, have been taxable under the then existing tax rules. Matching, however, is still carried out.

Example 17.19
Manuel Madrid, a non-UK domiciled but UK resident individual, is a beneficiary of a non-UK resident (non-settlor interested) trust.

In 2007/08 Manuel received a capital payment of £33 000. Pre FA 2008 section 87 did not apply to non-UK domiciled individuals.

In 2008/09 the trust had unmatched capital gains of £50 000. £33 000 of these trust gains are matched with the £33 000 capital payment but no capital gains tax charge arises.

Example 17.20
Manuel Madrid, a non-UK domiciled but UK resident individual, is a beneficiary of a non-UK resident (non-settlor interested) trust.

In 2008/09 Manuel received a capital payment of £33 000.

In 2007/08 the trust had unmatched capital gains of £50 000. £33 000 of these trust gains are matched with the £33 000 capital payment but no capital gains tax charge arises.

In addition, the trustees (not settlor or beneficiaries) of the non-UK resident trust (whether the settlor was UK domiciled or not) have an option under FA 2008 to "rebase" the trust assets to their market value as at 6 April 2008. The effect under such rebasing is that trust capital gains accruing but not realised prior to 6 April 2008 will not be chargeable on the part of the non-UK domiciled beneficiary (whether the remittance basis claim has been made or not) if matched to capital payments made on or after 6 April 2008. Under the LIFO basis of matching the post 5 April 2008 element of any trust gain will be matched prior to the pre 6 April 2008 element in respect of capital payments made on or after 6 April 2008.

The election is irrevocable and applies to all trust assets. It must be made on or before 31 January following the first tax year in which a capital payment is made to a UK resident beneficiary irrespective of the beneficiary's domicile status. Thus, although the rebasing only impacts upon the non-UK domiciled beneficiary's liability to capital gains tax the deadline for the election may be dictated by a capital payment to a UK domiciled beneficiary. Thus, where a capital payment is made in the tax year 2008/09, whether to a UK or non-UK domiciled beneficiary, the deadline for making the election is 31 January 2010.

In order to prevent manipulation of the new rules by non-UK domiciled beneficiaries any capital payments made between 12 March 2008 and 5 April 2008 are to be left out of account and thus not matchable with post 5 April gains. Without this provision a non-UK domiciled beneficiary could have engineered to have received a large capital payment between the above dates which would have then been matched with post 5 April 2008 trust gains but not then subject to capital gains tax (see above). In effect, the large capital payment in this case would be matched with post 5 April 2008 capital gains thus removing them from the possibility that they could otherwise be used to create a capital gains tax charge on post 5 April 2008 capital payments.

Pre FA 2008 where a capital payment was either in whole or in part matched to the section 87 capital gains pool a possible supplementary charge applied thus increasing the capital gains tax charge on the beneficiary from 40% (assuming a higher rate income taxpayer) to a maximum of 64%. This supplementary charge did not, however, apply where the trust made a capital payment which was matched with the section 87 pool trust gains of the tax year in which the payment was made or the capital gains of the immediately preceding tax year.

In effect this supplementary charge (which continues to apply post FA 2008) is an attempt to compensate HMRC for the delay in collecting any capital gains tax due to the time delay between the trust realising the capital gains and the beneficiaries subsequently receiving (e.g. three years later) the proceeds (as matched) in the form of capital payments.

Where it does apply the charge is levied at 10% per annum on the amount of the capital gains tax payable on the capital payment for the period ending with 1 December following the year of assessment in which the payment is made and beginning on the later of six years before this date or 1 December following the tax year in which the trust capital gain is matched with the capital payment.

For the higher rate taxpayer the maximum supplementary charge pre FA 2008 was 24% (i.e. six years at 10% of 40%) and the minimum was 8% (i.e. two years at 10% of 40%).

Example 17.21
Elisabeth Brow set up a non-UK resident discretionary trust in 2000. The trustees invested in various growth shares realising capital gains in the tax year 2001/02.

In the tax year 2003/04, on 1 May 2003 the trustees made a capital payment of £10 000 to one of the UK domiciled and UK resident beneficiaries who is a higher rate taxpayer.

The interest charged will be at the rate of 4% (i.e. 10% of 40%) for the period 1 December 2002 to 30 November 2004.

The additional charge will thus be 4% for two years, i.e. 8%, producing a capital gains tax charge of 48% on the payment of £10 000, i.e. £4800.

Had the trustees actually made the payment on or before 5 April 2003 no supplementary charge would have arisen.

The matching process pre FA 2008 involved matching capital payments with capital gains of the trust on a FIFO basis. If more than one capital payment was made in the same tax year the capital gains were allocated to the capital gains on a pro-rata basis.

The supplementary charge which pre FA 2008 did not apply to capital payments made to non-UK domiciled individuals (because the basic charge under section 87 was inapplicable) has been extended to include payments to such individuals (post FA 2008 the supplementary charge thus applies to both UK and non-UK domiciled individuals). For such individuals the charge is based upon the tax year in which the capital payment is made not the tax year in which it is remitted.

In view of the reduction in the capital gains tax rate under FA 2008 to a flat 18% (compared to a marginal rate of 40% pre FA 2008) the minimum and maximum supplementary charges are, post 6 April 2008, 3.6% and 10.8% (compared to 8% and 24%, respectively, pre FA 2008). Whether the change from FIFO to LIFO will create larger or smaller supplementary charges appears to depend upon the quantum of trust gains arising in each tax year and the manner and quantum in which capital payments are made to the beneficiaries.

"Washing out"

"Washing out" continues to be available as a capital gains tax mitigation technique post FA 2008.

The effect of matching capital payments made to non-UK domiciled individuals (whether UK resident or not) outside the UK or to non-UK resident UK domiciled individuals is that the quantum of capital gains available for matching are reduced without at the same time precipitating a capital gains tax charge on such beneficiaries.

Having then "washed out" the capital gains in this manner, either in whole or in part, capital payments may then subsequently (i.e. in the following tax year) be made to UK resident and UK (or non-UK) domiciled individual beneficiaries without any immediate capital gains tax charge arising (due to the lack of any gains with which to match the capital payment). In effect a deferral of the capital gains tax charges on such beneficiaries is obtained.

Example 17.22
Feliciano Portugal is a non-UK domiciled but UK resident individual and Fiona Birmingham, her sister, is a UK domiciled but UK resident individual.

Both individuals are beneficiaries of a non-UK resident trust set up by their uncle. The trust is not settlor interested.

The trust had monies of £500 000 and unmatched capital gains of £100 000 for 2008/09 and nil for 2009/10 with it being unlikely that the trust would make further capital gains for some years.

The trustees wished to make capital payments of £100 000 to each of Feliciano and Fiona. In 2008/09 such capital payments were made.

£50 000 of the trust capital gains were apportioned to each of the two sisters, Feliciano's payment is made outside the UK. Feliciano, non-UK domiciled, is not subject to capital gains tax on the apportioned trust capital gains until they are remitted. Fiona, however, UK domiciled, is subject to capital gains tax on the apportioned trust capital gains in 2008/09.

Fiona's capital gains tax liability above could have been avoided (or deferred) if the trustees had made a capital payment to Feliciano in 2008/09 of £100 000 and £100 000 to Fiona in 2009/10.

As above, Feliciano, non-UK domiciled, is not subject to capital gains tax on the apportioned trust capital gains (in this case £100 000 not £50 000) until they are remitted.

In 2009/10 there are no unmatched trust capital gains to match to Fiona's capital payment of £100 000 in 2009/10. Thus, Fiona has no capital gains tax liability in 2009/10. In due course trust capital gains may be made which may then be eligible to match to Fiona's capital payment but until then she has avoided a capital gains tax charge.

Offshore Income Gains

Both pre and post FA 2008 offshore income gains do not fall within the settlor interested provisions in relation to income tax. Similarly, section 86 which relates to settlor interested trusts for capital gains tax purposes is also inapplicable (as the offshore income gain is not subject to capital gains tax).

Offshore income gains are in reality "capital" although the legislation treats them as "income" and thus subject to income tax.

One distinction, pre FA 2008, between capital gains and offshore income gains of non-UK resident trusts was that section 87 did not apply to non-UK domiciled beneficiaries whereas the offshore income gain provisions did apply to such individual beneficiaries. Post FA 2008 section 87 now also applies to non-UK domiciled beneficiaries (see above).

The new capital payments regime applicable to capital gains of non-UK resident trusts also applies to offshore income gains of such trusts. In addition, both pre and post FA 2008 sections 720 and 731 (see above), also apply to offshore income gains of a non-UK resident trust and thus such income gains may be apportionable to the transferor/settlor of the trust or subject to the section 731 rules.

The position post FA 2008 is that offshore income gains for a tax year are first attributed to the transferor under section 720 assuming, of course, that the transferor is able to benefit under the trust. If this is not the case (i.e. the transferor cannot so benefit) then capital payments made to beneficiaries in the tax year are available to be matched against offshore income gains of the trust for that tax year (precipitating income tax liabilities). Where the offshore income gains exceed the capital payments for that tax year the excess is matched with capital payments of earlier tax years. Any still remaining unmatched offshore income gains are then treated as income for section 720 and 731 purposes. Thus, the offshore income gains at this point are no longer available for matching within the section 87 regime. Where the capital payments for the tax year exceed the offshore income gains for that tax year the excess is then matched with capital gains of the trust for that tax year, i.e. offshore income gains are matched to capital payments in priority to capital gains.

The inclusion of unmatched offshore income gains as income for section 720/731 purposes (as indicated above) means that such offshore income gains are then no longer available for matching to capital payments of later tax years.

Example 17.23
Harry Bushes is a UK domiciled and UK resident individual. He set up a non-UK resident trust for his nephews and nieces, Tom, Dick, Mary and Joan, all aged over 18, UK domiciled and UK resident.

Section 720 is inapplicable to the trust as neither Harry nor his spouse can benefit under the trust.

The trust has made offshore income gains as follows:

2008/09	£50 000
2009/10	£65 000
2010/11	£90 000

The trust has received no income.

The trust makes a capital payment to Mary of £75 000 in 2009/10 and £70 000 to Joan in 2010/11.

2009/10
The offshore income gain of £50 000 in 2008/09 was not matched as no capital payments were made in that tax year. Accordingly, the £50 000 is treated as income for section 731 purposes.

Mary is subject to income tax on the matched £50 000 under section 731 and on £25 000 of the £65 000 of offshore income gain.

The balance of the £40 000 (i.e. £65 000 less £25 000) falls to be treated as income under section 731.

2010/11

Joan is subject to income tax on the matched £40 000 of section 731 income and £30 000 of the £90 000 offshore income gains.

Example 17.24

Harry Bushes is a non-UK domiciled and UK resident individual. He set up a non-UK resident trust for his nephews and nieces, Tom, Dick, Mary and Joan, all aged over 18, non-UK domiciled and UK resident.

Section 720 is inapplicable to the trust as neither Harry nor his wife can benefit under the trust.

The trust has made offshore income gains, capital gains and has received income as follows:

	Income	Offshore income gains	Capital gains
2008/09	£10 000	£30 000	£15 000
2009/10	£25 000	£35 000	£30 000
2010/11	£35 000	£40 000	£50 000

The trust makes a capital payment in the UK to Mary of £125 000 in 2009/10 and £135 000 to Joan in 2010/11.

2009/10

The £30 000 offshore income gains for 2008/09, as they were not matched to a capital payment in that tax year, is treated as income and then aggregated with the £10 000 of income to produce £40 000 income carry forward. The £125 000 capital payment to Mary is matched with the £40 000 income carry forward; £25 000 income; £35 000 offshore income gains; £25 000 of the £30 000 capital gains (leaving £5000 capital gains unmatched for the tax year 2009/10).

2010/11

Joan's £130 000 capital payment is matched with the £35 000 income; £40 000 offshore income gains; £50 000 capital gains; £5000 capital gains from 2009/10; and £5000 capital gains from 2008/09.

The remittance basis applies to the non-UK domiciled individual with respect to offshore income gains.

Where the beneficiary is non-UK domiciled in addition to the above the following rules will apply:

- the rebasing election (see above) available to trusts will also apply to offshore income gains in the same manner as the election is to apply to ordinary capital gains;
- the matching of capital payments made before 6 April 2008 with post 6 April 2008 offshore income gains will not precipitate a tax charge and offshore income gains

accrued before this date (under rebasing) will similarly, if matched with post 6 April 2008 capital payments, not be subject to tax.

With respect to the offshore income gains such income gains are matched with capital payments made to a beneficiary irrespective of whether the beneficiary is UK resident or UK domiciled or not. It is therefore possible to "wash out" (i.e. reduce) any offshore income gains by simply making capital payments to non-UK residents (be they UK or non-UK domiciled).

INTERACTION OF THE VARIOUS APPORTIONMENT RULES WITH RESPECT TO "CAPITAL PAYMENTS"

Capital payments made by non-UK resident trusts to beneficiaries, whether UK or non-UK domiciled, are matched to three possible categories of income/gains.

The legislation lays down the order which applies.

Thus, a capital payment for a tax year is first matched to "relevant income" of the trust which comprises relevant income of that tax year plus relevant income from earlier tax years which has not been previously matched. It will also include offshore income gains of earlier tax years which have not been previously matched. Any part of the unmatched capital payment is then matched with the trust's offshore income gains for that tax year. Any still unmatched capital payment is then matched to the trust's capital gains of that tax year and earlier tax years (on a LIFO basis)

NON-UK RESIDENT TRUSTS FOR NON-UK DOMICILED BUT UK RESIDENT INDIVIDUALS

Income Tax

A non-UK resident discretionary trust is liable to an income tax charge of 40% on non-dividend UK source income and 32.5% on UK source dividend income. No such liabilities arise on non-UK source income. However, UK source income may qualify as excluded income for the trust thus precipitating no UK income tax liability thereon.

However, if the trust is settlor interested UK source income of the trust is subject to income tax on the part of the settlor although any non-UK source income of the trust is subject to income tax on the settlor on the remittance basis. This tax treatment also applies where the settlor possesses an interest in possession in the trust.

For the settlor who is non-UK domiciled but UK resident and who is subject to income tax at the basic rate of 20% (i.e. not a higher rate taxpayer) the discretionary trust, which is not settlor interested, may be (e.g. if excluded treatment is inapplicable) tax inefficient even though on appointments out of the trust the recipient beneficiary may be able to reclaim some part of this tax from HMRC (e.g. if the beneficiary is a nil rate or basic rate taxpayer). There is still a cash flow disadvantage.

Where the trust is not settlor interested the provision of any benefits by the trustees to non-UK domiciled but UK resident beneficiaries where such benefits are provided in the UK (e.g. rent-free house in the UK) is likely to precipitate an income tax charge on the beneficiary. This charge will be the value of the benefit (e.g. rent which should have been paid). For the income tax charge to apply the trust must have "relevant income" available for apportionment which comprises both UK and non-UK source income of the trust. If no such income is available the benefit is not tax free but the income tax charge on the beneficiary may be deferred until the trust has such income in the future (although, if the trust has any capital gains at that time, not otherwise apportioned, a capital gains tax charge arises on the apportioned capital gains equivalent to the value of the benefit).

The provision of benefits outside the UK to non-UK domiciled but UK resident beneficiaries precipitate an income tax charge on apportioned UK source income of the trust but only on non-UK source income of the trust to the extent remittance occurs.

For income tax purposes the non-UK resident trust set up by the non-UK domiciled settlor does not offer any particular income tax advantages (and may in limited circumstances be cash flow disadvantageous if UK source income is in point; see above). Having said this, such trust can be used where, for example, within the non-UK domiciled settlor's family some/all of the individuals are UK domiciled. In this case, gifts of non-UK situs assets from the non-UK domiciled individual to UK domiciled members of the family cause any income from such assets to then fall within an income tax charge on the arising basis (and indeed such assets will similarly fall within the capital gains tax provisions on the arising basis). By settling such assets into a non-UK resident trust for the benefit of such family members allows income of the trust and/or the assets to be appointed to the family members when necessary but in the meantime no UK income tax or capital gains tax charges arise. Thus, the trust offers tax flexibility.

On balance, there is no real downside for the non-UK domicile setting up non-UK resident trusts for income tax purposes. There may be distinct advantages.

It may make sense to split income producing assets into two categories, namely, UK situs assets and non-UK situs assets, and to settle each category into separate trusts. This may then permit benefits to be provided in the UK yet at the same time mitigating any consequent income tax charge on the part of the beneficiary.

The above discussion applies to such trusts whether created on or after, or before, 6 April 2008.

Capital Gains Tax

Neither UK nor non-UK source capital gains of non-UK resident trusts are subject to capital gains tax on the part of the trust. This is thus advantageous for the non-UK domiciled individual (even if the trust is settlor interested as the settlor interested provisions do not apply to non-UK domiciled settlors) with respect to UK situs assets in respect of which the individual is subject to capital gains tax.

Although the settlor interested provisions are not applicable to the non-UK domiciled settlor any benefits provided by the trustees to non-UK domiciled but UK resident beneficiaries where such benefits are provided in the UK (e.g. rent-free house in the UK) is likely to precipitate a capital gains tax charge on the beneficiary. This charge will be the value of the benefit (e.g. rent which should have been paid). For the capital gains tax charge to apply the trust must have trust capital gains available for apportionment which comprise both UK and non-UK source capital gains. If no such capital gains are available the benefit is not tax free but the capital gains tax charge on the beneficiary may be deferred until the trust has such capital gains in the future (although, if the trust has any relevant income at that time, not otherwise apportioned, an income tax charge arises on the apportioned capital gains).

The provision of benefits outside the UK to non-UK domiciled but UK resident beneficiaries does not precipitate a capital gains tax charge assuming no remittance of the benefit.

The non-UK resident trust can be used where, for example, within the non-UK domiciled settlor's family some/all of the individuals are UK domiciled. In this case, gifts of non-UK situs assets from the non-UK domiciled individual to UK domiciled members of the family cause the assets to then fall within the charge to capital gains tax on the arising basis. By settling such assets into a non-UK resident trust for the benefit of such family members allows the capital gains of the trust to be appointed to the family members when necessary but in the meantime no capital gains tax charges arise. Thus, the trust offers tax flexibility.

It may make sense for the non-UK domiciled but UK resident individual to create separate non-UK resident trusts in order to segregate capital growth assets from income producing assets. This allows a degree of tax mitigation by trying to ensure that payments to UK resident beneficiaries result in a matching of capital gains (or benefits which will cause matching of trust capital gains) and thus subject to capital gains tax at 18%. Income apportionment may be subject to income tax at 40% if the individual concerned is a higher rate taxpayer.

Inheritance Tax

If all the trust assets are non-UK situs and the settlor is non-UK domiciled at the time of creation of the trust the assets will qualify as excluded property for inheritance tax purposes. While it is not necessary for excluded property treatment for the trust to be non-UK resident it is almost universally a preferable option for the non-UK domiciled individual; primarily because of the advantages the non-UK resident trust offers with respect to income and capital gains tax.

NON-UK RESIDENT TRUSTS FOR UK DOMICILED AND UK RESIDENT INDIVIDUALS

Income Tax

A non-UK resident discretionary trust is liable to an income tax charge of 40% on non-dividend UK source income and 32.5% on UK source dividend income. No such liabilities arise on non-UK source income. However, UK source income may qualify as excluded income for the trust thus precipitating no UK income tax liability thereon.

If the trust is settlor interested UK and non-UK source income of the trust is subject to income tax on the part of the settlor. This tax treatment also applies where the settlor possesses an interest in possession in the trust.

For the settlor who is UK domiciled but UK resident and who is subject to income tax at the basic rate of 20% (i.e. not a higher rate taxpayer) the discretionary trust, which is not settlor interested, may be (for example, if excluded treatment is inapplicable) tax inefficient even though on appointments out of the trust the recipient beneficiary may be able to reclaim some part of this tax from HMRC (e.g. if the beneficiary is a nil rate or basic rate taxpayer). There is still a cash flow disadvantage.

Where the trust is not settlor interested the provision of any benefits by the trustees to UK domiciled and UK resident beneficiaries (and indeed non-UK domiciled but UK resident beneficiaries) where such benefits are provided in the UK (e.g. rent-free house in the UK) is likely to precipitate an income tax charge on the beneficiary. This charge will be the value of the benefit (e.g. rent which should have been paid). For the income tax charge to apply the trust must have "relevant income" available for apportionment which comprises both UK and non-UK source income of the trust. If no such income is available the benefit is not tax free but the income tax charge on the beneficiary may be deferred until the trust has such income in the future (although, if the trust has any capital gains at that time, not otherwise apportioned, a capital gains tax charge arises on the apportioned capital gains equivalent to the value of the benefit).

The provision of benefits outside the UK to UK domiciled and UK resident beneficiaries precipitate an income tax charge on apportioned UK and non-UK source income of the trust.

For income tax purposes the non-UK resident trust set up by the UK domiciled settlor does not offer any particular income tax advantages (and may in limited circumstances be cash flow disadvantageous if UK source income is in point; see above). Having said this, such trust can be used where, for example, within the UK domiciled settlor's family some/all of the individuals are non-UK domiciled. In this case, there appears to be two options. Gifts of non-UK situs assets from the UK domiciled individual to non-UK domiciled members of the family cause any income from such assets to then fall outside an income tax charge unless remitted (and indeed such assets will similarly fall outside the capital gains tax provisions subject to remittance). Alternatively, the assets may be settled on a non-UK resident trust for the benefit of such non-UK domiciled family members which allows income of the trust and/or the assets to be appointed to the family members when necessary but in the meantime no UK income tax or capital gains tax charges arise (assuming the trust is not settlor interested). However, a possible disadvantage of using the trust is that while the non-UK situs assets remain in the trust they do not constitute excluded property for inheritance tax purposes whereas the outright gift of such assets immediately results in them qualifying as excluded property.

The advantages and disadvantages of the non-UK resident trust for the UK domiciled settlor depend upon the surrounding circumstances. However, the applicability of the settlor interested provisions severely curtails their use.

The above suggestion (in the case of the non-UK domiciled settlor) of splitting income producing assets into two categories, namely, UK situs assets and non-UK situs assets, and settling each category into separate trusts would appear to be of no benefit for the UK domiciled.

The above discussion applies to such trusts whether created on or after, or before, 6 April 2008.

Capital Gains Tax

Neither UK nor non-UK source capital gains of non-UK resident trusts are subject to capital gains tax on the part of the trust. This is thus advantageous for the UK domiciled individual (assuming the trust is not settlor interested as the settlor interested provisions do apply to UK domiciled settlors) with respect to UK situs assets in respect of which the individual is subject to capital gains tax.

Where the settlor interested provisions are not applicable any benefits provided by the trustees to UK domiciled and UK resident (and indeed non-UK domiciled but UK resident) beneficiaries whether such benefits are provided in the UK (e.g. rent-free house in the UK) or outside is likely to precipitate a capital gains tax charge on the beneficiary (remittance basis for non-UK domiciled). This charge will be the value of the benefit (e.g. rent which should have been paid). For the capital gains tax charge to apply the trust must have trust capital gains available for apportionment which comprise both UK and non-UK source capital gains. If no such capital gains are available the benefit is not tax free but the capital gains tax charge on the beneficiary may be deferred until the trust has such capital gains in the future (although, if the trust has any relevant income at that time, not otherwise apportioned, an income tax charge arises on the apportioned capital gains).

The provision of benefits outside the UK to non-UK domiciled but UK resident beneficiaries does not precipitate a capital gains tax charge assuming no remittance of the benefit. However, for the UK domiciled and UK resident beneficiary such benefits do not escape the charge.

The non-UK resident trust can be used where, for example, within the UK domiciled settlor's family some/all of the individuals are non-UK domiciled. One option is for gifts of UK situs assets to be made from the UK domiciled individual to non-UK domiciled members of the family which causes the assets to then fall outside the charge to capital gains tax subject to remittance. Another option is to settle such assets into a non-UK resident trust for the benefit of such non-UK domiciled family members (or indeed UK domiciled members) which allows the capital gains of the trust to be appointed to the family members when necessary but in the meantime no capital gains tax charges arise (assuming the trust is not settlor interested).

The suggestion made above for the non-UK domiciled settlor concerning the creation of separate non-UK resident trusts in order to segregate capital growth assets from income producing assets may still apply for the UK domiciled settlor as this allows a degree of tax mitigation by trying to ensure that apportionment to UK resident beneficiaries are of capital gains (or benefits which will cause apportionment of trust capital gains) and thus subject to capital gains tax at 18%. Income apportionment may be subject to income tax at 40% if the individual concerned is a higer rate taxpayer.

Inheritance Tax

Excluded property is inapplicable to the UK domiciled settlor.

Excluded property treatment is only possible where such individual gifts non-UK situs assets (or UK situs assets if moveable) to a non-UK domiciled individual; trusts whether UK or non-UK resident for the UK domiciled settlor are of no help in this regard.

However, the discretionary trust while possibly giving rise to a 20% charge on set-up (unless the NRB is available to the settlor) is only subsequently subject to ten yearly charges at the maximum rate of 6% which compares extremely favourably with the 40% rate applicable to individuals on death (assuming settor cannot benefit). Interest in possession trusts created in lifetime on or after 22 March 2006 are treated in the same manner (the position for such trusts created pre 22 March 2006 is different).

The NRB trust may be particularly attractive.

SUMMARY

The tax provisions which apply to non-UK resident trusts are extremely complex. In part this is due to the overlap of the various applicable provisions.

Non-UK resident trusts are not liable to capital gains tax even on UK situs assets and only liable to income tax on UK source income. This means that UK domiciled and UK resident individuals could readily avoid income and capital gains tax by setting up non-UK resident trusts. As a consequence, anti-avoidance provisions seek to preclude this as an option.

The basic thrust of these anti-avoidance provisions is to charge the UK domiciled and UK resident settlor on the income and capital gains of the trust as if the income and capital gains had been made directly by the settlor; in effect looking through the trust. However, these provisions only apply if the trust is "settlor interested" which broadly means that the settlor or spouse (and in some cases other members of the family) can benefit under the terms of the trust deed. Where this is not the case then the setting up of such a trust would enable UK tax to be avoided.

The settlor interested provisions while applying to non-UK resident trusts for income tax purposes where the settlor is non-UK domiciled did not, pre FA 2008, apply for capital gains tax purposes. FA 2008 has not in fact changed this position. However, non-UK domiciled beneficiaries of the trust may, post FA 2008, now be subject to capital gains tax where trust gains or some form of benefit are paid out to such beneficiaries.

Generally speaking, non-UK domiciled but UK resident individuals are able to utilise the remittance basis as normal.

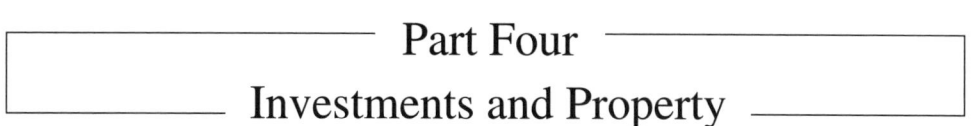

Part Four
Investments and Property

18
Investments

BACKGROUND

For the individual investor the range of possible investments continues to grow at a pace. This chapter is concerned with identifying the tax treatment of the more common investments. The tax treatment of products such as bond futures, interest rate swaps and index futures contracts are not addressed.

This chapter is also not concerned with issues such as asset allocation (broadly, the maximisation of investment returns by allocating investment capital among different types of asset for a given level of risk), valuation models and portfolio management.

The tax treatment of investments undertaken by individuals varies and will depend upon, inter alia, the nature of the investment (e.g. a capital growth investment versus an income producing investment); the domicile and residence status of the investor; whether the investment is a UK or non-UK situs investment; and whether or not anti-avoidance provisions (i.e. provisions which may reclassify an investment return from, say, capital to income for tax purposes) are in point.

For the individual investor some or all of the following tax-related factors will need to be taken into account when considering a particular investment:

- whether the return is subject to income or capital gains tax;
- whether inheritance tax is applicable on death and/or a lifetime gift;
- whether loss relief is available on a disposal;
- what constitutes a disposal for tax purposes;
- what restrictions (if any) apply where favoured tax status is granted;
- whether double tax issues arise;
- whether any tax exemptions are applicable;
- the timing of any tax liability;
- whether remittance basis treatment applies to returns from non-UK investments by non-UK domiciled but UK resident individuals.

The tax treatment of some of the more common types of investment will now be considered.

DEPOSIT-BASED INVESTMENTS

Such investments are offered by both banks and building societies. In return for placing money on deposit, interest is paid thereon. The level of interest will typically vary depending upon the amount of the deposit and the length of time the deposit is to be tied up. At the end of the period the deposit is simply repaid.

Such investments thus offer no capital growth potential.

The return of the original capital creates no tax liability (unless the deposit is in foreign currency and sterling has depreciated during the time of the deposit; see Chapters 6 and 8) but the interest credited is subject to income tax at the marginal rate of the investor in the tax year the interest is credited to the account (interest income for individuals is not taxed on the accruals basis).

In the case of deposits with UK-based banks or building societies, tax at source is withheld prior to crediting the interest at the rate of 20%. It is possible for the depositor to receive the interest "gross" (i.e. without the bank having withheld tax at source) if a certificate (Form R85; see Appendix 3) is completed confirming the depositor is not ordinarily resident in the UK.

Thus, for example, there are many English individuals who have left the UK and are now living in France or Spain but who still maintain interest bearing deposits with UK-based banks. Often such individuals are no longer ordinarily resident in the UK and thus by completion of Form R85 such individuals may have the interest credited without tax at source being deducted (such income will also qualify as excluded income and thus is not liable to income tax).

The 20% income tax withheld at source can be reclaimed if appropriate, i.e. if the depositor is, for example, UK resident and whose personal allowance is greater than the amount of interest credited (assuming no other income) or where the interest is the depositor's sole income and the new 10% starting rate for savings income (applicable in tax year 2008/09) is applicable.

Increasingly, interest bearing deposits are made by UK residents with "offshore" banks and building societies as no tax at source is withheld when the interest is credited thereon. Despite a common misconception such interest is still subject to income tax in the UK if the depositor is resident in the UK and must therefore be declared on the UK Tax Return (unless the individual is non-UK domiciled). However, effective 1 July 2005, the EU Savings Directive has resulted in many offshore banks now having to deduct income tax at source (as do UK-based banks) prior to crediting any interest. This deduction is referred to as a "retention" tax and prior to 30 June 2008 was at rate of 15%; effective 1 July 2008 the rate has increased to 20% (see Chapter 25). Not surprisingly, to avoid this retention tax, monies have moved to non-EU destinations such as Dubai, Hong Kong and Singapore.

MONEY MARKET ACCOUNTS

Money market accounts are available where the amount of the deposit is above a certain size. Such monies are typically invested for short terms (e.g. sometimes overnight).

The main difference between these accounts and the deposit accounts discussed above is that interest is always credited without deduction of tax at source for deposits of £50 000 or more.

Otherwise the tax consequences are the same.

FIXED INTEREST SECURITIES

"Gilts" are perhaps the best example of fixed interest securities. In effect subscriptions to gilts amount to investors granting loans to the government.

Such investments are issued by the government for a fixed term but the investor may sell the investment at any point prior to maturity. Where such a sale is effected a loss may arise, i.e. the original investment may be at risk (see below).

Interest is paid "gross" and the investor is liable to income tax at the marginal rate of the investor.

One advantage of gilts is that any capital gains arising on sale are not subject to capital gains tax; any capital losses arising are not allowable.

Certain gilts (see terms of their issue) constitute excluded property for inheritance tax purposes if the individual investor is non-UK domiciled and not ordinarily resident *or* is simply not ordinarily resident (the precise status depending upon the year of issue of the gilt; see Chapter 12).

The above applies whether the gilts are index linked or not.

Example 18.1

John and his wife Claire are UK domiciled, resident and ordinarily resident.

They emigrated from the UK on 3 March 2008 becoming non-UK resident and non-UK ordinary resident from 4 March 2008 (see Chapter 4).

They liquidated some of their investments on 23 May 2008 and reinvested the proceeds in a variety of post 1996 gilts.

In July John died.

Despite still being UK deemed domiciled under the three-year rule, as John was non-UK ordinary resident at the time of his death the gilts are not subject to inheritance tax as they qualified as excluded property.

SHARES (INCLUDING AIM SHARES)/OPTIONS

Ordinary Shares

Equity investments (e.g. ordinary shares; zero coupon preference shares) are either listed or unlisted on which, typically, dividends are paid.

Dividend income arising on UK equities is subject to income tax at a rate of 10% or 32.5% depending upon the investor's income tax position. However, any liability is reduced by a tax credit which attaches to a net dividend; this tax credit is equal to 1/9th of the net dividend.

Unlike the income tax withheld from interest credited to a bank/building society deposit account which is potentially reclaimable by the investor (see above) the tax credit attaching to a net dividend is not reclaimable.

Following FA 2008, dividends from equity investments in non-UK resident companies will now also give rise to a dividend tax credit of 1/9th of the "gross" dividend. The investor must own less than 10% in the non-UK resident company; however, effective

6 April 2009 those investors owning 10% or more will also become eligible for the tax credit. Typically, foreign source dividends will have suffered a local withholding tax (normally varying between rates of nil and 30%) with the investor receiving in cash form the original "gross" dividend less the withholding tax. This withholding tax is creditable against any UK income tax liability arising on the dividends.

Example 18.2

Fred Gutter, a higher rate taxpayer, owns foreign shares in ABC Ltd (less than 10%) and in the tax year 2008/09 received a cash dividend of £8100 after foreign local withholding tax at 10% had been applied.

For UK income tax purposes Fred's tax position 2008/09 is as follows:

Net dividend received	£8100
Plus local w/tax	£900
	£9000
Plus UK tax credit (1/9th)	£1000
Gross dividend	£10 000
UK income tax at 32.5%	£3250
Less tax credits	£1900
Net UK tax liability	£1350

The original "gross" foreign dividend was £9000 from which 10% (i.e. 900) withholding tax was levied resulting in Fred actually receiving £8100.

Fred's UK income tax liability is £1350 so that Fred's net cash receipt after all taxes is £6750.

Had Fred received the same cash dividend in the tax year 2007/08 his tax position would have been as follows:

Net dividend received	£8100
Plus local w/tax	£900
Gross dividend	£9000
UK income tax at 32.5%	£2925
Less tax credits	£900
Net UK tax liability	£2025

Fred's UK income tax liability is £2025 so that Fred's net cash receipt after all taxes is £6075 (compared to a net cash receipt in 2008/09 of £6750).

The granting of a UK tax credit on foreign dividend income has thus improved the attractiveness of equity investments in non-UK resident companies. However, no credit is available with respect to dividends from investments in offshore mutual funds.

Any gain arising on the sale of the equity investment is a capital gain and thus subject to capital gains tax. Entrepreneur relief may be in point.

Capital losses are allowable.

Zero Coupon Preference Shares

Zero coupon preference shares are shares issued by a split-level investment trust which offers a prearranged buy-back price at a prearranged date. No dividends are paid on the shares (hence the term "zero coupon").

Capital gains tax applies to any gain arising on a sale of the zero coupon shares. Capital losses are also available if losses arise on a sale.

Alternative Investment Market (AIM) Shares

Investment in AIM tends to be dominated by the EIS and VCT funds and institutional investors although individuals may also subscribe.

The tax treatment of dividends arising on AIM shares is exactly the same as described above with respect to an equity investment. Similarly, on a disposal capital gains tax may be payable.

Pre FA 2008 one of the key tax attractions of AIM (most but not all AIM companies) shares was that they would typically qualify for business asset taper relief which, after a holding period of two years, reduced any capital gain by 75%; a significant reduction producing an effective capital gains tax rate for the higher rate taxpayer of 10%. In addition, AIM shares would typically (as above but not all AIM companies) also qualify for business property relief at the 100% rate for inheritance tax purposes (whether on a lifetime gift or on death).

Post FA 2008, while the inheritance tax advantages referred to above remain untouched, taper relief for capital gains tax purposes has been abolished. The replacement entrepreneur relief is unlikely to apply for the passive investor as the requirements include not only a minimum 5% shareholding but also that the investor is a full time employee of the company. The 18% rate of capital gains tax will thus apply.

Other things being equal, the FA 2008 changes have made investment in AIM shares less attractive.

INDIVIDUAL SAVINGS ACCOUNTS (ISAs)

ISAs became available after 5 April 1999 and were a replacement for PEPs and TESSAs.

ISAs are available for subscription only by individuals over 18 who are UK resident *and* ordinarily resident (although post 5 April 2001 extended to 16 and 17 year olds re a cash mini-account or the cash component of a maxi-account subject to £3000 maximum; now post FA 2008 a "cash account" and a limit of £3600).

The key attributes of ISAs include:

- no statutory "lock-in" period;
- no minimum subscription;
- no minimum holding period;
- withdrawals without loss of tax relief.

Interest and dividends arising on the "cash account" and/or the "stocks and shares account" (see below) are not subject to income tax and any capital gains arising on the sale of shares in the stocks and shares account are not subject to capital gains tax (correspondingly, no losses are allowable for capital gains tax purposes).

Should an individual previously UK resident and ordinarily resident become non-UK resident any ISAs previously subscribed for may be retained (with the accompanying benefits) but no further subscriptions may be made until UK residency and ordinary residency is reacquired.

All subscriptions to an ISA must be made in cash (it is possible for certain employee acquired shares to be transferred to a stocks and shares component without tax effect) and must be made by individuals, i.e. subscriptions by trustees of a trust (whether UK resident or not) are not permitted.

Post FA 2008

ISAs are now to be available indefinitely.

The terms "maxi-account" and "mini-account" applicable pre FA 2008 are to be replaced with the terms "stocks and shares account" and "cash account".

Individuals are allowed to subscribe for two ISAs in a tax year: one "cash" ISA and one "stocks and shares" ISA. The maximum annual ISA investment allowance has increased to £7200 for the tax year 2008/09 (previously, £7000 for tax year 2007/08)

Up to £3600 per tax year can be invested in a cash ISA with one provider with the balance (i.e. £7200 less £3600) available for investment in the tax year in a stocks and shares ISA (whether with the same or another provider). Alternatively, the whole of the tax year allowance of £7200 may be invested in a stocks and shares ISA.

Transfers between accounts of the same type are permitted and transfers between cash ISAs and stocks and shares ISAs are also permitted.

Self-select ISAs

A self-select ISA enables an individual to pick the investments which will form part of the ISA. However, not all forms of investment are permitted. The investments which are eligible include:

- fixed interest investment listed on a stock exchange (including gilts);
- shares listed on a stock exchange in the UK or overseas;
- collective funds authorised by the FSA for distribution in the UK that invest in shares, fixed interest or commercial property; and
- investment in an REIT (i.e. a Real Estate Investment Trust).

Although shares listed on AIM cannot be included in an ISA, the ISA may comprise units in a fund that itself invests in AIM shares.

Pre April 2008

Maxi ISA

A maxi ISA allowed an individual to invest up to £7000 for the tax year 2007/08.

A maxi ISA was able to hold stocks and shares and cash. However, an individual could only take out one maxi ISA with one provider. It was not possible to take out a maxi ISA and a mini ISA in the same tax year.

A maximum of £7000 allowance may be invested into the stocks and shares component without penalty. A self-select ISA enabled an individual to pick his own investment funds.

However, it was possible to split the allowance between the two different components, investing a maximum of £3000 in cash and the rest (up to £4000) in stocks and shares.

Mini ISA

It was possible to invest £7000 for the tax year 2007/08 with two companies in up to two mini ISAs.

Each tax year one *cash* mini ISA up to £3000 and one *stocks and shares* mini ISA £4000 maximum could be opened.

It was not possible to hold a mini ISA and a maxi ISA in the same tax year.

Each mini ISA could be run by a different provider.

In a mini ISA only one component could be held.

PACKAGED/INSURANCE INVESTMENTS

Insurance serves a number of roles. It can, for example, provide financial support to the surviving spouse and family following the death of the "breadwinner"; provide funds to meet an inheritance tax liability whether on death or a lifetime gift due to the death of the donor; or be used as a so-called "tax wrapper" for tax planning purposes (e.g. the single premium bond; see below).

Term and Whole of Life Assurance Policies

Term Assurance

Term assurance is probably one of the cheapest forms of insurance. If the life assured survives the term of the policy no sum assured is payable. If, on the other hand, the life assured dies within the term of the policy the sum assured becomes payable. It is particularly ideal for a young married couple with young children; the policy is taken out by the breadwinner for say a 15- to 20-year term for low cost but maximum sum assured. In the event of the breadwinner's death the sum assured is payable to the surviving spouse to be used to provide financial support (e.g. funding of mortgage; school fees; etc.).

Typically, the policy should be written into trust so as to avoid an inheritance tax liability on the life assured's death.

Term assurance policies are also a useful method of funding the potential inheritance tax liability which may arise on the death of the donor within seven years of making a PET (see Chapter 9). The term of the policy should of course be seven years with the sum assured equal to the inheritance tax liability facing the donee. As the actual inheritance liability reduces due to taper relief over the seven-year period a decreasing term policy (matching the actual inheritance liability over the seven years) may be effected instead which will be cheaper.

Whole of Life Assurance

The whole of life policy is suitable to fund inheritance tax liabilities arising on the chargeable estate of the deceased. The use of a trust would be necessary to avoid the policy proceeds forming part of the chargeable estate of the deceased.

The other major advantage of the use of trusts for life policies is that the insurance company will pay out the proceeds to the trustees (or beneficiaries) on the production of the death certificate. Probate is not necessary.

Husband and Wife

In the case of a husband and wife, a joint whole of life policy may be appropriate with payment on either the death of the first to die or on the surviving spouse's death. The choice will depend upon the particular facts including which of the two deaths produces the greater inheritance tax liability.

Single Premium Bonds

For tax purposes a single premium bond (i.e. an investment bond or a unit-linked bond) is a non-qualifying single premium life policy. A single premium is normally paid at the commencement of the policy and a lump sum is paid out on maturity of the policy or in the event of the death of any lives assured.

It may be possible to make further premium payments under the policy often at irregular intervals. During the period of the policy it may be sold, assigned or surrendered prior to maturity. In addition, sums may be withdrawn under the policy (see below) and/or loans made under it.

Single premium bonds can be written by UK-based life offices or, more usually, by life offices outside the UK. Little mortality risk is in fact necessary for qualification as a life policy and many of these bonds are written outside the UK in jurisdictions where the policyholder need not have an insurable interest in the life assured (a requirement under UK law).

Single premium bonds are not chargeable assets for capital gains tax purposes and thus any gain arising is treated as income not capital gain. While pre FA 2008 the marginal rates of income and capital gains tax were the same (i.e. 40%), post FA 2008 the comparable rates are 40% and 18%, respectively. Other things being equal, this makes the single premium bond investment significantly less attractive post FA 2008.

The potential attractiveness of the single premium bond is that no tax liability arises unless or until the bond is cashed in (i.e. surrendered) *or* matures *or* the relevant life assured dies *or* it is assigned for money (an assignment for no consideration precipitates no tax charge). Thus, assuming none of these events occurs, the investment returns underlying the bond "roll up" tax free. The bond in this sense acts as a tax efficient "wrapper".

On encashment/surrender (or partial encashment/surrender) or maturity or death or assignment for money, a "chargeable event" for income tax purposes occurs. For a bond issued by a UK-based life office the gain is subject to the higher rate of income tax only (i.e. no charge to basic rate tax is levied). In the case of a bond issued by a non-UK life office the liability may be at (post FA 2008) a rate of 20% or 40% depending upon the tax position of the individual concerned. The reason for the different tax treatment is that a tax credit (20%) is available with respect to a UK-based life office issued policy which is not the case for a non-UK life office issued policy. Thus, in the former case a basic rate taxpayer is liable at 20% but has an offsetting tax credit of 20% in effect causing no tax liability to arise; a 40% taxpayer has a net liability of 40% less the tax credit of 20%, i.e. 20%.

In ascertaining the quantum of the gain slightly different rules apply depending upon the nature of the event which precipitates the charge.

Thus, where the chargeable event is death, the gain is measured against the surrender value, not the policy proceeds, and thus the difference between these two amounts is effectively received tax free (although any difference is likely to be small due to the low life assurance element of the contract). In the case of maturity or full surrender the gain is measured against the amount payable under the policy.

Example 18.3
Harry Brewin invested in an offshore single premium bond investing £250 000.
  After seven years Harry decided to surrender the policy receiving £400 000.
  The gain is [£400 000 − £250 000] = £150 000.
  As a higher rate taxpayer Harry's income tax charge is £60 000 (as a higher rate taxpayer no top-slicing relief (see below) is applicable).
  If the investor had been Harry Blaunt, a non-UK domiciled but UK resident individual, the income tax consequence would be the same as the remittance basis is inapplicable (see below).

Example 18.4
Using the facts from the above Example 18.3, seven years after taking out the policy Harry died. The policy proceeds on death amounted to £400 000 but the surrender value at that time was £350 000.
  The gain is [£350 000 − £250 000] = £100 000.
  As a higher rate taxpayer Harry's income tax charge is £40 000. Thus, the "extra" £50 000 of monies received are "tax free".

Top-slicing relief may apply to relieve any tax charge arising on a chargeable event. Top-slicing only applies to individuals (not trustees or executors). The effect of the relief is to reduce the amount of higher rate income tax charge (if any) on any gain. The relief is only applicable to individuals who, ignoring the gain on the policy, are not liable to higher rate income tax but who become liable to higher rate income tax when the "sliced gain" is added to the taxable income of the individual (the "sliced gain" is the gain arising on the chargeable event divided by the number of years between effecting the policy and the chargeable event). If the individual is a higher rate taxpayer before inclusion of any gain, top-slicing relief is inapplicable.

Example 18.5

Ben Trouble invested £75 000 in an offshore single premium bond.

After 10 years, in the tax year 2008/09, Ben surrendered the policy receiving £125 000.

Ignoring the gain arising on the policy Ben is not a higher rate taxpayer. His taxable income amounts to £34 000.

The "sliced gain" = [£125 000 − £75 000]/10 = £5000.

The inclusion of the sliced gain with Ben's other taxable income makes Ben a higher rate taxpayer and thus entitled to top-slicing relief. This involves the following calculations:

1. Income tax liability on £39 000 of taxable income, i.e. £8640.
2. Income tax liability ignoring the "sliced gain", i.e. £6800.
3. The income tax liability on the gain of £50 000 is thus [£8640 − £6800] × 10 = £1840 × 10 = £18 400.

Without the top-slicing relief the income tax liability on the gain would be 40% of [£84 000 − £34 800], i.e. £12 720.

Note:

(i) For the tax year 2008/09 the 40% rate applies on taxable income above £34 800.
(ii) Strictly speaking gains arising on chargeable events are entitled to the 10% "starting rate on savings income" applicable from 6 April 2008. However, this has been ignored in this example.

For the non-UK domiciled but UK resident individual the remittance basis does *not* apply to any gain arising outside the UK as a result of a chargeable event occurring. Thus, single premium bond investments by a non-UK domiciled but UK resident individual require careful thought (given that the remittance basis applies to virtually all other forms of non-UK investment). A chargeable event occurring while such individual is UK resident will thus precipitate an income tax charge on the arising basis.

It also needs to be noted that there is no automatic "tax-free" uplift on death as occurs with chargeable assets for capital gains tax purposes; as indicated above, single premium bonds are not chargeable assets for capital gains tax purposes. Thus, if the bond is held beneficially by the individual (or on trust created by the individual) on the individual's death a chargeable event occurs which results in the gain arising being treated as part of the deceased's (not the executor's income of the period of administration) income for the tax year of death.

Where the individual settles the bond on a UK resident trust any gain arising in the trust (e.g. on a surrender) will be subject to income tax on the part of the settlor assuming the latter is alive at this date. Otherwise, the trustees are liable to income tax at 40%. If the trust is a non-UK resident trust and the individual settlor is alive at the date of the chargeable event the individual is liable to income tax as the remittance basis is inapplicable. However, if the settlor is dead at the date of the chargeable event (e.g. chargeable event arises due to death of the life assured who is not the individual under the policy after the individual settlor has already died) and the policy is held in a non-UK resident trust created by the individual no income tax charge arises. However, if and when the non-UK resident trust appoints any of the income arising from the chargeable event out to a beneficiary an income tax charge arises at that time for that beneficiary; this applies even if the beneficiary is non-UK domiciled but UK resident as the remittance basis is inapplicable. A UK or non-UK domiciled but non-UK resident beneficiary, however, could enjoy the income outside the UK free of income tax.

As indicated above, an advantage of the offshore bond is that no income tax liability arises until a chargeable event occurs and in the meantime the income/gains underlying the bond accrue tax free. A second advantage is that the bond holder may effect tax deferred withdrawals of up to 5% each year of the amount of the one-off initial premium paid. Any such sum not withdrawn may be carried forward for withdrawal in future tax years. The maximum amount of such withdrawals in aggregate is the amount of the initial premium. Thus, if 5% is withdrawn each tax year, after 20 tax years no further withdrawals can be made without then precipitating a tax charge. Such withdrawals are not, as often thought, "tax free". They are treated as partial surrenders and are taken into account in determining any income tax liability on the occasion of a chargeable event.

Example 18.6
Mandy Purple invested £50 000 in an offshore single premium policy on 16 June 2006.

She withdrew £2500 in the years to 15 June 2007 and 2008, respectively. Neither withdrawal precipitates an income tax charge as Mandy is entitled to withdraw each year up to 5% of the initial premium, i.e. 5% of £50 000, namely, £2500 without precipitating an income tax charge.

Example 18.7
Using the facts in the above Example 18.6, in the year to 15 June 2009 Mandy withdraws a further £4000.

Mandy is entitled to withdraw 5% of the initial premium each year, i.e. 5% for the years ended 15 June 2007, 2008 and 2009, i.e. £7500 in total.

However, her actual withdrawals amount to £9000 in total.

A gain thus arises in the year ended 15 June 2009 of:

$$[£9000 - £7500] = £1500$$

Example 18.8
Continuing the facts from the above Example 18.7, after 10 years Mandy decides to surrender the policy receiving £80 000. No further withdrawals were made after the £7500 withdrawal in 2009.

The gain arising on surrender is:

$$[£80\,000 + £2500 + £2500 + £7500] - [£50\,000 + £1500] = £41\,000$$

As can be seen, the 5% withdrawals which are treated as partial surrenders are eventually brought into account on the policy's surrender, i.e. they are not, as commonly thought, "tax-free" withdrawals. In essence, they are a form of tax deferral.

For the non-UK domiciled but UK resident individual, however, care with respect to the 5% withdrawals is required. If such individual used non-UK source income or capital gains to fund the purchase of the bond, which if remitted to the UK would have fallen subject to income or capital gains tax, the 5% withdrawals will be treated as if the monies used to fund the purchase had been remitted to the UK; the result being that the 5% will fall to be subject to income tax or capital gains tax as appropriate and thus will not be tax deferred withdrawals as indicated above.

Example 18.9
Mandy Paris, a non-UK domiciled but UK resident individual, invested £50 000 in an offshore single premium policy on 16 June 2006.

She withdrew £2500 in the years to 15 June 2007 and 2008, respectively, bringing the monies into the UK.

Neither withdrawal, per se, precipitates an income tax charge as Mandy is entitled to withdraw each year up to 5% of the initial premium, i.e. 5% of £50 000, namely, £2500.

However, Mandy used her non-UK source earnings to fund the £50 000 purchase.

As a consequence, Mandy will be treated as if she had remitted part (i.e. £5000) of her offshore earnings in each of the two tax years when she effected the withdrawals thus giving rise to an income tax charge on the deemed remitted non-UK source earnings.

This is the position both pre and post FA 2008.

Following the FA 2008 changes as to what constitutes "remittances" (see Chapter 23) it has been suggested that if the non-UK domiciled but UK resident individual (having used non-UK source income or capital gains to effect the bond purchase) arranged for the 5% withdrawals to be paid outside the UK an income tax charge will still arise as the remittance basis is inapplicable to single premium bond investments. The contrary view is as follows.

The 5% withdrawals do not constitute "chargeable events" for the purposes of the legislation as they are merely "partial surrenders". Hence no immediate charge to tax arises (although such are taken into account eventually). However, as discussed above, it is possible to link the 5% withdrawals to the individual's non-UK source income/capital gains used to purchase the bond.

As the non-UK source income/capital gains used to effect the purchase is itself not subject to income tax (pre or post FB 2008) unless remitted (as now defined) it is difficult to see how the 5%, even if linked to such income/capital gains, can be subject to income tax if it is withdrawn outside the UK and retained outside the UK.

However, if the 5% is "brought" to the UK under the now broader definition of "remittance" then it would seem to be the case that 5% of the non-UK source income/capital gains used to fund the purchase would have itself been remitted to the UK and accordingly taxable.

In short, the remittance basis does not apply to chargeable events (i.e. arising basis applies). A "partial surrender" is not a chargeable event. The only difference between the pre and post FA 2008 position in this regard is that post FA 2008 the definition of "remittance" is much broader and thus may apply to a transaction which pre FA 2008 would not have been the case. However, even post FA 2008, under the transitional rules if the individual who purchased the bond made a gift of the 5% withdrawal outside the UK to a "relevant person" who then brings the 5% monies into the UK it will not give rise to a taxable remittance of the original income or capital gains of the individual used to effect the purchase of the bond (unless the individual benefits from the remittance). If, however, the bond is purchased out of post FA 2008 non-UK source income or capital gains the position is different (see Chapter 23).

In this case to avoid a taxable remittance where the 5% withdrawal is to be enjoyed by the individual in the UK the purchase of the offshore bond should be effected using non-UK source "pure" capital monies (see Chapter 23) or UK source taxed income/capital gains.

A possible course of action for the non-UK domiciled individual intending to acquire UK residency is for the policy to be surrendered prior to the acquisition of UK residency or, if surrendered shortly after arrival, significant non-resident relief should be available reducing any chargeable income gain arising.

As capital gains tax does not apply to gains on single premium bonds the temporary non-resident capital gains tax provisions do not apply to individuals disposing of them (e.g. surrender) while non-UK resident (i.e. the minimum five-year non-residence period is not necessary; see Chapter 8). However, FA 2008 has introduced an equivalent provision which is applicable to non-UK domiciled but UK resident individuals for income tax purposes (see Chapter 8). The new provision only applies to relevant foreign income (which includes income gains arising on bonds) which arose in the tax year of departure (prior to the departure date) or in earlier tax years. Thus if the non-UK domiciled but UK resident individual becomes non-UK resident, surrenders the offshore bond and then remits the proceeds to the UK while non-UK resident a deemed income tax charge on reacquiring UK residency should not apply; the income gain not having arisen before departure.

A typical use of the offshore single premium bond is for parents or grandparents to effect one or more bonds on the life or lives of the various children/grandchildren. The bonds could be settled on trust for the benefit of the children subject to attaining age 18 or 21. On attaining the relevant age the bond will pass to the beneficiary by way of assignment without tax charge (as no consideration passes). The beneficiary is then free to deal with the bond as appropriate. Should the bond be cashed in (i.e. surrendered) by the beneficiary an income tax charge will arise but at rates of income tax applicable to the beneficiary. Alternatively, the beneficiary could continue to hold the bond.

Offshore issued life policies (e.g. single premium bonds) are treated as debts for inheritance tax purposes and thus the location of the debtor determines its source (i.e. the residence of the life office). Thus, for the non-UK domiciled individual such bonds qualify as excluded property (see Chapters 6 and 12).

To prevent certain abuses which were prevalent with respect to the sale of offshore single premium bonds new measures were introduced (effective 22 March 2007, i.e. new policies made on or after this date and existing policies if further premiums on or after this date are paid in respect thereof). These new measures apply in connection with short- to medium-term life policies where a person invests premiums exceeding £100 000 per tax year. In calculating any gain arising on such policies the allowable amount of premium will be reduced by the amount of any commission rebated or any commission waived and reinvested in the policy.

VENTURE CAPITAL TRUSTS (VCTs) AND ENTERPRISE INVESTMENT SCHEMES (EISs)

VCTs and EISs are designed to attract new investment into the unquoted company market.

The approach of each varies slightly but each offers attractive (i.e. income and capital gains) tax reliefs to the individual investor.

Enterprise Investment Scheme

EISs involve the issue of ordinary shares to *individual* investors who subscribe for the shares on their own behalf; thus relief is not available for investment by or via trusts or companies (inter alia, the individual investor must be unconnected with the company; broadly, an individual who is an employee or paid director of the company *or* the individual plus associates possess more than 30% of the voting power of the company would be connected).

The individual need not, however, be UK resident and the company issuing the shares does not itself need to be UK resident.

Income Tax Relief

EIS income tax relief operates by way of a "tax reducer". In simple terms, an individual's income tax liability is calculated as normal for a particular tax year and any EIS income tax relief is then deducted directly therefrom.

FA 2008 refers to the income tax relief under EISs as relief at the "EIS rate". EIS relief is available at the lower of:

- 20% of the amount subscribed for the shares;
- the individual's income tax liability for the tax year of the investment *after* deducting any VCT relief.

Pre FA 2008 the maximum annual subscription was £400 000. FA 2008 has increased this figure to £500 000 (the increase requires EU confirmation that the proposals did not amount to State Aid).

Thus, if an individual subscribed for the full amount of £500 000 in the tax year 2008/09 the individual's income tax liability for that tax year (after VCT relief if any) would need to be at least £100 000 for full EIS relief (at least £40 000 2005/06 or £80 000 2006/07). Thus, an individual's income tax liability, after any VCT relief, needs to be quite significant.

A carry-back option exists under which a subscription undertaken in a particular tax year on or before 5 October in that tax year may receive tax relief in the immediately preceding tax year (subject to that earlier tax year's relief not exceeding the limit for relief for that tax year). Up to one half of the subscription in the tax year may be treated as if made in the immediately preceding tax year (subject to a maximum carry-back of £50 000).

Income tax relief requires that the shareholding is held for a minimum holding period of three years (shares issued after 5 April 2000). Any disposal within this period will result in the income tax relief already granted being withdrawn either in whole or in part (which depends upon whether the disposal is at arm's length or not).

Any dividends arising on the shares are subject to income tax in the normal manner.

Capital Gains Tax Relief

Any disposal of the shareholding is exempt from a charge to capital gains tax if the shares have been held for at least three years. Perhaps surprisingly, any capital losses arising on such a disposal are available for offset; indeed, a disposal precipitating a capital loss even within the three-year period is also an allowable capital loss. In calculating the amount of any allowable capital loss, account must be taken of any income tax relief which has not been withdrawn (in effect reducing the quantum of the capital loss).

Any capital loss may be offset against "income" of the tax year of sale and/or the preceding tax year; any remaining unrelieved loss is then eligible for capital gains offset.

Venture Capital Trust

Unlike the EIS which involves subscriptions for shares in individual unquoted companies, subscriptions to VCTs are subscriptions for shares in a listed company (i.e. the VCT) which in turn subscribes for shares in unquoted trading companies. Accordingly, the shares in the VCT must be listed in the Official List of the Stock Exchange.

As in the case of the EIS any subscriptions must be by individuals beneficially.

Income Tax Relief

VCT income tax relief operates by way of a "tax reducer". In simple terms, an individual's income tax liability is calculated as normal for a particular tax year and any VCTR income tax relief is deducted directly therefrom.

VCT relief is available as a tax reducer at the lower of:

- 30% of the amount subscribed for the shares (effective 6 April 2006; 40% of the amount invested subject to a maximum investment of £200 000 for the tax year 2006/2007);
- the individual's income tax liability for the tax year of the investment.

To qualify for income tax relief the shares must be held for a minimum holding period of five years where the shares are issued on or after 6 April 2006 (three years where shares were issued after 5 April 2000).

Any disposal within the five-year period will result in any income tax relief being withdrawn either in whole or part (depends if the disposal is arm's length or not).

Unlike the position with respect to EIS, dividend income arising on a subscription to a VCT is tax exempt (irrespective of any minimum holding period).

Capital Gains Tax Relief

Any gain arising on a disposal of the shareholding in the VCT is exempt from capital gains tax irrespective of the length of the ownership period prior to the disposal. Capital losses, however, are not allowable.

Chargeable Gains Deferment Possibilities (EIS only)

Where an individual has a crystallised capital gain on a disposal of any chargeable asset, the whole or part of the gain may be deferred (i.e. held over) by matching the gain against a subscription for qualifying shares in an EIS (effective 6 April 2004, any deferment is no longer possible if the investment is into a VCT (i.e. for shares issued on or after 6 April 2004)).

This deferral is possible even where the vendor invests in his own company (although EIS income tax relief would be prohibited as he would typically (together with associates) own $\geqslant 30\%$ and no capital gains tax relief would be available on an ultimate sale) assuming that the shares in his company are "qualifying shares" and his company is a "qualifying company".

The investment in the EIS must be made within one year before and three years after the chargeable event giving rise to the capital gain. There is no limit to the amount of chargeable gain which may be deferred (i.e. the £500 000 limit re income tax relief does not apply to the deferral).

The deferral operates by holding over the gain (i.e. not levying capital gains tax immediately) on the sale of the original asset until a disposal of the EIS shares occurs at which time the original gain held over will be subject to capital gains tax at that time and at the rates, etc. in force at that time. However, a disposal of the EIS shares to a spouse will not crystallise the held-over gain.

The held-over gain may also be crystallised if the shareholder becomes non-UK resident within three years of the issue of the EIS shares (unless the shareholder goes abroad under a full time contract of employment for up to three years and retains the EIS shares until his return to the UK).

Any gain deferred does not become chargeable on the death of the investor (in effect the gain held over is wiped out as normal).

It is also possible to defer gains arising on the sale of EIS shares into further EIS investments.

Although *trustees* are not eligible for EIS income or capital gains tax relief re EIS investments, trustees may still defer chargeable gains arising on trust asset sales by reinvesting in EIS investments.

COLLECTIVE INVESTMENTS

Collective/pooled investments are simply an aggregation of individual investment monies which are pooled in a single investment vehicle. The investment vehicle may be a unit trust or an open ended investment company (OEIC), commonly referred to as "authorised investment funds" or an investment trust. Such vehicles may be UK or non-UK resident.

With respect to UK resident unit trusts, investment trusts and OEICs there are no particular tax advantages for the UK resident individual investor. Any income (dividend or interest) arising on the investment is subject to income tax in the normal manner. Any disposal of the investment will also be subject to capital gains tax in the normal manner. Furthermore, none of the investments are likely to qualify for business property relief for inheritance tax purposes (see Chapter 10). However, for the non-UK domiciled individual investment in authorised unit trusts and UK OEICs, while UK situs, constitute excluded property (see Chapter 12).

OFFSHORE FUNDS

Special, unfavourable, tax treatment is accorded to investments in certain offshore funds. This unfavourable tax treatment is not applicable to all offshore funds but, where applicable, is designed to neutralise the tax benefits to UK residents who invest in offshore funds (which vehicles are outside the ambit of UK taxation); this tax benefit is due to the fact that advantage may be taken of a "tax-free roll-up" within the fund.

Offshore funds are in essence structured as non-UK resident open ended investment companies or non-UK resident unit trusts (and which would, if set up in the UK, constitute a collective investment scheme within section 235 Financial Services and Markets Act 2000).

As will be seen below under current law offshore funds are classified as distributing or non-distributing funds for tax purposes. FA 2008, however, has introduced amendments to the offshore funds legislation under which the "distributor" fund is to be reclassified as a "reporting" fund. Despite this change, however, in principle no changes are made to the manner of taxing individual investors.

The offshore fund provisions apply where an investor (individual or UK resident trust) disposes of a material interest in a *non-qualifying* offshore fund (often referred to as roll-up funds, e.g. hedge funds). A material interest is, broadly speaking, one in which the investor expects to realise the net asset value of his investment within seven years (i.e. his proportion of the market value of the fund).

All offshore funds are non-qualifying unless HMRC certifies that the fund is a *distributing* fund. To qualify as a distributing fund requires that the fund each year distributes at least 85% of its income for that year to its investors.

As indicated above, the FA 2008 changes replace the term "distributing" fund with the term "reporting" fund; in addition, a fund post FA 2008 will be classified as such once and for all (subject to satisfying ongoing basis various conditions) whereas pre FA 2008 the test was an annual test which thus needed to be satisfied every year; finally, whereas pre FA 2008 actual annual distributions needed to be made by the fund, post FA 2008 the fund will report income to investors who will be subject to tax thereon but actual distribution by the fund will no longer be necessary.

Tax Treatment

Distributor/Reporting Status Offshore Fund

The advantage for the investor in investing in a distributing/reporting fund is that on a disposal of the investment any gain is a capital gain and thus subject to capital gains tax. The remittance basis is thus applicable for the non-UK domiciled but UK resident individual.

Dividend income from such a fund is liable to normal income tax rates for the UK domiciled and resident individual (i.e. 10% or 32.5%) but for the non-UK domiciled but UK resident individual the rates applicable are 20%/40% (see Chapter 2).

FA 2008 has extended the dividend tax credit to investments in non-UK resident companies. However, dividends on investments in offshore funds do not qualify for the tax credit.

Other things being equal, this makes investments in offshore (distributor) funds less attractive than direct equity investments in non-UK resident companies.

Non-distributor Status Offshore Fund

In the case of a non-resident offshore non-distributor fund, broadly, any gain on a disposal by the investor in the fund is treated as an *offshore income gain* and charged to income tax not capital gains tax. Thus, for the higher rate taxpayer any such gain will be subject to income tax at 40% compared to a capital gains tax charge of 18% (post 6 April 2008) on any gain from a disposal of a distributor fund investment.

Pre FA 2008, while the marginal income and capital gains tax rates were the same at 40% in the case of a capital gain indexation and taper relief would apply; which would not have been the case with respect to a disposal of an investment in a non-distributor fund.

Despite an income tax liability arising on any gain on the disposal of the investment any loss arising is available for offset for capital gains tax purposes. However, pre FA 2008 such capital losses were not available for relief for the non-UK domiciled but UK resident individual. Post FA 2008 such losses are potentially usable against capital gains arising on other UK and non-UK situs assets (see Chapter 8).

On death, assets held by the deceased in a distributor fund are revalued at their then market value without a capital gains tax charge being deemed to have arisen (see Chapter 8). However, this does not apply with respect to an investment in a non-distributing offshore fund. In this case the death of the investor precipitates a deemed disposal and any gain arising is subject to income tax.

Pre FA 2008, if the investor in a non-distributor fund became non-UK resident in the tax year of disposal no income tax charge arose on any gain. The rule requiring non-UK residency for a minimum period of five tax years was not in point as this provision applied only for capital gains tax purposes (see Chapter 8). Although this capital gains tax provision has been broadened under FA 2008 it is still inapplicable to an offshore income gain.

However, FA 2008 introduced a brand new provision corresponding to the newly broadened capital gains tax provision but is of application for income tax purposes.

Under the new income tax rule an income tax charge may arise where a non-UK domiciled individual remits relevant foreign income (an offshore income gain, for remittance purposes, is categorised as "relevant foreign income") to the UK, while non-UK resident, *where such income arose either in the tax year of departure or in a prior tax year*. The remittance is, however, subject to income tax in the tax year of the reacquisition of UK residency (it is assumed above that the four out of seven tax year test is satisfied and the non-UK residency period is less than five complete tax years; see Chapter 4).

However, as can be seen, the new income tax provision only applies to relevant foreign income generated in the tax year of departure or a prior tax year. It would thus apply if the non-UK domiciled individual while UK resident disposed of the offshore non-distributor fund investment leaving the funds outside the UK, and then, on subsequently becoming non-UK resident, remitted the monies to the UK during this non-UK residence period.

If, however, the disposal took place after having acquired non-UK residency and the proceeds then remitted to the UK no income tax charge should arise on the reacquisition of UK residency.

Offshore fund investment via offshore (i.e. non-UK resident) trusts may also be useful for non-UK domiciled but UK resident individuals as, again, the remittance basis is applicable. The use of such trusts for the UK domiciled and UK resident individual is unlikely to be tax effective.

Irish Offshore Funds

Pre FA 2008 a non-UK domiciled but UK resident individual was subject to income tax on the *arising* not remittance basis with respect to Irish source income although for capital gains tax purposes the remittance basis applied.

Despite this, any gain on the disposal of an investment in a non-distributor Irish-based fund was still subject to tax on the remittance basis despite being treated as income.

Post FA 2008 there is no longer a distinction between Irish source income and income from other countries, i.e. the remittance basis applies (this change was implemented following a ruling by the EU that it was discriminatory).

One impact of this change is that for the non-UK domiciled but UK resident individual there is no (tax) distinction between investing in an Irish-based distributor fund versus a Luxembourg distributor fund. Pre FA 2008 the dividend income from the Irish fund would have been subject to income tax on the arising basis whereas the corresponding income from the Luxembourg fund would have been subject to income tax on the remittance basis; thus, favouring Luxembourg-based funds. This distinction has now disappeared.

Example 18.10
Brucella Lyons, a non-UK domiciled but UK resident individual, invested in the tax year 2006/07 in a distributor offshore fund based in Ireland.

Her investment was £40 000. In the tax year 2008/09 she sold the investment for £75 000 having received dividends of £2000 in each of the tax years 2006/07, 2007/08 and 2008/09.

As the fund is a distributor fund the gain on the sale of the investment is subject to capital gains tax but only if she remits the proceeds to the UK.

However, the dividend income is subject to income tax on the arising basis for the tax years 2006/07 and 2007/08 but, following FA 2008, the dividend income for 2008/09 is subject to income tax on the remittance basis.

STRUCTURED PRODUCTS

Structured products are typically described as products which offer a defined return over a defined period where the return is linked to defined underlying assets (e.g. FTSE 100; NASDAQ, etc.).

Normally, the capital investment is protected (e.g. 90% protected) with the return varying according to the performance of the underlying assets class(es) albeit often capped at a certain percentage (e.g. 25% cap on growth of, say, 175%).

The life of the product may vary although pre FA 2008 maximum taper relief for capital gains tax purposes required a life of 10 years (40% taper relief then applies giving an effective 24% capital gains tax rate).

The underlying structure typically consists of a zero coupon bond purchase with the discount element being used by the investor to invest in a call option. On maturity the investor receives the original principal and any return will depend upon the performance of the call option.

Any gains arising from the call option will be subject to capital gains tax treatment (see above); any losses ranking as capital losses.

One disadvantage of this type of product is the possible devaluation over time of the original principle and lack of regular income flow (available on a normal bond investment).

The product may be structured as a structured deposit account (or structured note). Here the return is potentially higher than on a conventional deposit as the return is linked to, for example, equity markets or foreign exchange markets.

As with the above option-based product, capital gains tax treatment applies to any gain arising on the structured deposit/note.

LIMITED PARTNERSHIPS

Private Equity Funds

Private equity funds (i.e. funds used for the purpose of raising funds for equity investment in unquoted companies) are often structured as limited partnerships in the UK (and elsewhere).

Such partnerships may be onshore or offshore (often in the Channel Islands).

The offshore structure is particularly valuable for the non-UK domiciled but UK resident individual as non-UK source income accruing to the partnership will only subject to UK income tax on the remittance basis.

Whether onshore or offshore the partnership for UK income and capital gains tax purposes is transparent, i.e. the partnership is not liable to tax; its income and gains flowing straight through to the partners. This is also the tax treatment in the USA but partnerships are not transparent for local tax purposes in, for example, France or Italy (or the Netherlands in certain cases).

In principle this transparency:

- avoids extra layers of possible taxation (possible applicable where companies are involved);
- enables the partner to offset, for example, capital losses arising in the fund against capital gains made elsewhere (or vice versa); and
- enables the partner to offset personal reliefs elsewhere against the share of the partnership's profit.

Property Funds

The limited partnership structure is also used to structure property funds.

As above, the partnership is basically transparent and thus the partnership's income and gains are directly attributable to the partners.

LIMITED LIABILITY PARTNERSHIPS (LLPs)

LLPs were introduced into the UK in 2000. They are treated as transparent for UK tax purposes but a body corporate for company law.

REAL ESTATE INVESTMENT TRUSTS (REITs)

REITs are a completely new vehicle in UK tax terms (the new rules apply to accounting periods beginning on or after 1 January 2007).

REITs are UK resident listed companies (not open ended) involved in the property rental business.

Under the tax rules such companies are exempt from corporation tax on such business income and on associated capital gains. A distribution of 90% of their tax exempt income (excludes capital gains) must be distributed to its shareholders.

Investors who receive dividends from the companies on their investment do so under a 20% income withholding tax and are then subject to income tax at their marginal rate (typically 40%) as if the investor had received property income and not a distribution. Thus, the normal tax credit which applies to corporate paid dividends does not apply.

The UK's rules are similar but not identical to the REIT rules in the USA.

SELF-INVESTED PERSONAL PENSIONS (SIPPs)

SIPPs are personal pensions under which the member can select how his contributions can be invested subject to certain restrictions.

SIPPs may be utilised by both self-employed and employees.

Investments available to a SIPP include:

- stocks and shares both in the UK and overseas;
- unit trusts, investment trusts and OEICs;
- deposit accounts;
- commercial property;
- residential property.

SUMMARY

For the individual investor it is important to identify the nature of any gain which may arise from the investment, i.e. is the gain to be taxed as an income gain, and thus subject to income tax, or capital gain, and thus subject to capital gain tax.

It is also particularly important for the non-UK domiciled but UK resident individual to ascertain if any gain and/or income arising from a non-UK situs investment is subject to remittance basis treatment.

The position with respect to the possible relief for any losses should also be ascertained. Following FA 2008 relief for capital losses arising to non-UK domiciled but UK resident individuals on non-UK situs investments are now available and can now be potentially offset against capital gains.

The extension of the tax credit to dividends received on equity investments in non-UK situs equities has enhanced the attractiveness of such investments; however, the extension does not apply to equity investments in offshore funds.

19
Main Residence or Home

BACKGROUND

For many individuals the family home or main residence constitutes their most valuable asset. It is an asset in respect of which any capital gain arising on a disposal is exempt from capital gains tax. There are, however, no corresponding tax reliefs/exemptions with respect to inheritance tax and any rental income which may arise from the letting out of the property is subject to income tax.

It is an asset that, for many, is held jointly whether by husband and wife, cohabitees, or just friends.

It is a UK situs asset for inheritance tax purposes (and also for capital gains tax purposes) and thus, as indicated above, falls subject to inheritance tax whether it is owned by UK or non-UK domiciled individuals (see Chapters 6 and 9). In view of the potential magnitude of any such charge attempts have been made and "schemes" have been developed (some no longer available) designed to enable the avoidance of an inheritance tax charge on death yet continued occupation of the property in lifetime.

The exemption for capital gains tax has eased planning for inheritance tax purposes as, typically, transfers of interests in the property between spouses may be effected without a capital gains tax charge arising.

Nevertheless, while in principle any gain arising on a disposal of the property is exempt from capital gains tax, the legislation is littered with caveats and thus not all disposals may necessarily be effected without a charge to capital gains tax arising. Where a capital gains tax charge does arise on some part of the capital gain the annual exemption (£9600 for the tax year 2008/09) is available to reduce the charge.

The conflict which typically arises between the mitigation of capital gains tax and the mitigation of inheritance tax is less acute with respect to the matrimonial home due to the general exemption from capital gains tax. However, having said this, it is not usually realistic to give the matrimonial home away in lifetime as the property will, of course, be required for living purposes. Any such gift followed by continued occupation will, generally speaking, fall foul of the gift with reservation rules (see Chapter 11).

This chapter will examine the key issues and impact of both these taxes on the individual's main home or residence including the tax position which arises on divorce.

Chapter 7 discussed the possible ownership structure of the main residence/home and that chapter should be read in conjunction with this chapter.

CAPITAL GAINS TAX

An overview of the key points applicable to the capital gains tax issues relating to the main residence/home are set out below before a more detailed consideration of some of the points is undertaken.

Overview

Terms used to describe the main home include "home", "residence" and "principle private residence". The capital gains tax statute actually refers to:

> a dwelling house... which is, or has at any time in his period of ownership been, his only or main residence....

The statute continues:

> No part of a gain... shall be a chargeable gain if the dwelling house... has been the individual's only or main residence throughout the period of ownership....

The reference to any "gain" not being a "chargeable gain" means that any such gain is exempt from capital gains tax.

The legislation also extends the exemption to capital gains attributable to surrounding land (e.g. gardens) of up to one half of a hectare. In certain cases this limit of one half a hectare may be increased depending upon the size and character of the dwelling-house.

Two or More Residences of the Individual

The use of the phrase "only or main residence" suggests that the individual may have more than one residence (which is in fact correct as will be seen below) and use of the term "individual" suggests that the exemption applies to individuals only (which is in fact incorrect).

Where the individual has two residences it may be possible to elect which of the two residences is to be treated as the main residence.

The capital gains tax exemption also in principle applies to disposals made by trustees and executors.

Non-UK Property

There is no geographical restriction contained within the legislation and therefore a residence outside the UK may qualify as the individual's only or main residence in the same manner as a residence within the UK. This may apply in the case of the non-UK domiciled but UK resident individual who may own at least two residences, one in the UK and one in the country of nationality. It may also apply to the UK domiciled and

Main Residence or Home 349

UK resident individual who has a residence in the UK and another residence outside the UK.

Example 19.1
Toby and Helen Blue own a detached property in Yorkshire where they, together with their three children, live for most of the time.

Three years ago they purchased an apartment in Marbella, Spain, which they tend to use for three months each summer.

Toby and Helen thus own two properties with the UK property likely to be their "main residence", i.e. on the sale of the Spanish property any capital gain will in principle be subject to capital gains tax.

It may be necessary for Toby and Helen to elect which of the two properties is to be treated as their main residence.

Example 19.2
Tobias and Maria Barcelona, who are non-UK domiciled but UK resident, own a detached property in Barcelona, Spain.

Three years ago they purchased an apartment in London where they currently spend most of their time.

Tobias and Maria thus own two properties.

It is, perhaps, less clear in this case which of the two properties is their main residence and thus on which property on sale a capital gains tax charge may arise.

However, an election may be made under which Tobias and Maria elect for their UK property to be their main residence thus avoiding a capital gains tax charge on sale. Any capital gain arising on the sale of their Spanish property will be not in any event be subject to capital gains tax so long as no remittance of the sale proceeds to the UK occurs.

Married Couple and Cohabitees

It is important to note that a married couple who are living together can only have one main residence (see below for the position where spouses are separated or divorced).

For cohabitees, on the other hand, each cohabitee may have a main residence (perhaps this is one of the few tax advantages available to cohabitees compared to married couples).

Total v. Partial Capital Gains Tax Exemption

For the capital gain arising on the disposal of the main residence to be completely exempt requires (as indicated above) that the property is the main residence throughout the whole period of ownership of the property. In the event that this is not the case (e.g. for part of the ownership period the individual perhaps lived elsewhere, e.g. abroad, in the meantime letting the property out) some part of the capital gain on disposal may fall subject to capital gains tax; typically, a time apportionment approach is adopted when computing any capital gain.

Example 19.3
Gregory Pick owned a UK property for 20 years following which the property was sold for £500 000 (purchase cost £100 000).

For five years of this 20-year ownership period Gregory went to live in his Florida villa letting out his UK property in the meantime.

On the sale of the UK property, of the 20-year period of ownership 15 years qualifies as Gregory's sole residence.

Exempt capital gain = 15/20ths of £400 000 = £300 000.
Taxable capital gain = 5/20ths of £400 000 = £100 000.

However, certain absences from the property may be deemed to be periods of occupation and thus no loss of the exemption for such a period would occur. Such an absence may be due, for example, to the individual being required by an employer to work elsewhere in the UK such that it is not possible during this period of working away to continue to live in the property.

In any event, if a property has at any point in time during ownership qualified as the sole or main residence the last three years of ownership are always regarded as periods of residence irrespective of any other circumstance (even if during this three-year period another residence is acquired and that other residence becomes the individual's main residence; see below). Thus, strictly speaking, in Example 19.3 above the respective fractions used should have been 18/20ths and 2/20ths.

Example 19.4
Norris Yellow purchased his home on 1 January 2000. He resided in the property until 31 December 2005.

On 1 January 2006 he moved into a new home, no longer residing in his former home.

On 31 December 2008 his former home was sold.

No capital gains tax arises on the capital gain on sale of the former home despite the fact that for the last three years Norris' former home did not strictly qualify as the sole or main residence of Norris.

This is because, irrespective of all circumstances, as Norris' former property had been his sole residence at some point in time the last three years of ownership are always treated as periods of occupation/residence. Thus, Norris is deemed to have resided in the property for the complete nine years of ownership.

It is also necessary if the capital gain on disposal of the main residence is to be completely exempt that the property is not either in whole or in part used exclusively for business purposes. If this is the case then an apportionment of the capital gain on disposal is necessary with that relating to the business element constituting a chargeable capital gain.

The letting out of the property will also impact upon the extent of any capital gains tax exemption on disposal although "letting relief" may apply to ameliorate the otherwise adverse impact of the lettings period.

Profit Motive

This issue is often overlooked.

If the individual acquires a residence for the purpose of disposing of it at a profit then the capital gains tax exemption will not apply. Thus, intention at the time of purchase is important.

RESIDENCE

It is perhaps this term which often generates much misunderstanding.

As indicated above, an exemption from capital gains tax on a disposal requires in the first instance that the owned property qualifies as a residence. Thus, no exemption applies where the owned property is not a residence of the individual.

A property in the ownership of the individual thus may not necessarily qualify as a residence and, correspondingly, a property not owned by the individual may be a residence of that individual (albeit the lack of ownership means that the property is, not that of the individual to dispose of).

Example 19.5
Thomas Golding lives in a rented flat in London and the house which he owns in the country has been let out almost continually from the date of purchase. When the house has not been let Thomas spends the odd night there.

Although Thomas does not own the flat it qualifies as a residence.

The house is arguably not a residence of Thomas and thus on sale it is likely that the exemption from capital gains tax will not apply to any capital gain.

It has been said that a residence, quite simply, is "a place where somebody lives". Accordingly, whether a property is a residence of the individual is a question of fact to be determined in the light of all the surrounding circumstances.

A property to qualify as the individual's residence must be occupied and must be occupied with some degree of permanence. It is not necessary for the individual to live in the property every day but some degree of permanence is required. If the individual purchases a property and never ever lives in it then almost certainly it will not qualify as a residence. Spending the odd night in the property may also fail to cause the property to qualify as a residence (as in Example 19.5 above).

DEEMED PERIODS OF RESIDENCE

Reference was made above to periods of ownership during which the property is not in fact the residence of the individual due to absence from the property but such periods of absence may still be nevertheless treated as periods of residence.

Periods of absence treated as periods of residence are:

- any period(s) of absence not exceeding three years;
- any period when the individual was employed abroad;
- any period, up to four years, where the individual was employed elsewhere in the UK.

For the above periods of absence to qualify as periods of residence the individual must in principle reside in the property both at some time before the period of absence and at some time after it.

Where any of the above periods are exceeded only the excess is no longer deemed to be a period of residence (i.e. the whole period is not so treated). In addition, the individual may qualify for each of the three periods of absence, i.e. the periods are additive.

It must not be forgotten that in addition to the above absence periods the last three years of ownership are always treated as periods of residence whatever the circumstances.

Example 19.6
Tommy Television purchased a property on 1 January 1990 moving in on that day.

Due to his occupation as a travel agent, Tommy often travelled. In particular, he worked abroad between 1 July 1995 and 30 June 2000 and between 1 August 2002 and 30 September 2004.

He was also required to work some 300 miles from his home for the period 1 May 2005 to 31 December 2006 and stayed in a local hotel for this period.

He sold the property on 15 August 2008.

The property was Tommy's sole residence and all the periods of absence qualify as periods of residence.

On sale the whole of the capital gain is exempt.

Lettings relief may also apply where during the period of absence the sole or main residence has been let out (see below).

Finally, if a property is purchased but due to work with respect to alterations occupation of the property is prevented, for a period of up to 12 months, then the first 12 months are nevertheless treated as a period of residence. This would also apply if occupation was prevented due to the property being built.

MORE THAN ONE RESIDENCE

The individual may own more than one property yet still only one of which qualifies as a residence.

Example 19.7
Barbara Tomkins owns a house in the country where she resides and which she regards as her home.

She also owns a flat in London which she permanently lets out.

Barbara owns two properties but only the house is a residence. On the sale of the house any capital gain will be exempt from capital gains tax but the exemption does not extend to the flat which is not a residence.

On the other hand, the individual may own two (or more) properties each of which qualifies as a residence.

Example 19.8
Barbara Tomkins owns a house in the country where she spends every weekend.

She also owns a flat in London where she stays during the working week as she works in London and it is not possible to travel each day from her country house to London.

Barbara owns two properties each of which qualify as a residence of hers.

Where the individual owns more than one property and each qualifies as a residence it is not possible for the exemption from capital gains tax to apply to capital gains made on the sale of each property. Only the capital gain arising from the disposal of the individual's *main* residence so qualifies. The capital gain arising on the sale of any other residence will be subject to capital gains tax as normal.

Electing Main Residence

A determination of which of more than one residence qualifies as the main residence may be made by the individual by way of a formal election. Where no such formal election is made by the individual the issue is to be determined on the facts.

Inter alia, factors which point to a property qualifying as a main residence include the address appearing on important documents such as driving licence and passport; the location of registration with doctors and dentists; address for voting purposes; possibly location of schools; and where the majority of the individual's personal possessions are kept.

To remove any doubt as to which property qualifies as the individual's main residence the best option is to simply elect; then there is no doubt.

To make the election it is important, however, to appreciate (as indicated above) that the properties in the first instance do each qualify as a residence.

Example 19.9
Using the facts from Example 19.7 above, Barbara Tomkins owns a house in the country where she resides and which she regards as her home.

She also owns a flat in London which she permanently lets out.

Barbara owns two properties but only the house qualifies as a residence and thus an election is not possible or indeed needed.

Example 19.10
Using the facts from Example 19.8 above, Barbara Tomkins owns a house in the country where she spends every weekend.

She also owns a flat in London where she stays during the working week as she works in London and it is not possible to travel each day from her country house to London.

Barbara owns two properties each of which qualify as a residence of hers.

Barbara would thus be advised to make a formal election to determine which of her two residences she wants to be treated as her main residence.

A formal election must be made in writing and must be made within two years of the acquisition of the second residence.

Example 19.11
Alistair Duckling purchased his country house 10 years ago.

On 1 January 2006 Alistair purchased a flat in London which he immediately let out on a two-year lease.

The acquisition of the flat in January 2006 has not given rise to Alistair having two residences (although he owns two properties) since he does not occupy the flat.

On 1 January 2008, following the termination of the lease, Alistair began to occupy the flat intending to do so most weekends.

It is arguable that effective 1 February 2008 Alistair now has two residences and it would be advisable that he lodges an election to determine which of the two residences is to be treated for capital gains tax purposes as his main residence.

The election would need to be made on or before 31 December 2010.

Should a formal election not be made, or is made out of time, then Alistair's main residence will be determined on the facts.

Planning and the Election

The election mechanism can be used as a tax planning device to mitigate capital gains tax liabilities on sales where more than one residence is owned. While an election may need to be made (as outlined above) such election can be varied at a later date. The later variation then takes effect from two years prior to the date of the variation.

Example 19.12
Simon Plus owns two properties, a house in the country and a flat in London. Both qualify as residences and Simon has made an election in favour of his country house (on which he anticipates will be the larger gain should a sale be effected).

On 1 August 2008 Simon sells his flat on which a capital gain will arise with no exemption. Simon therefore lodges a variation on, say, 10 August 2008 of his original election under which he elects for the flat to be his main residence. This variation is effective from two years earlier, i.e. 10 August 2006.

As the flat is now to be regarded as his main residence the last three years of ownership are also to be so treated. Thus, the capital gain attributable to the period 10 August 2005 to 10 August 2008 will be exempt (whereas without the variation no part of the capital gain on sale of the flat would be exempt).

Simon still owns the country house and so effects a second variation on 31 August 2008 restoring from two years earlier (i.e. 31 August 2006) the country house as his main residence.

Thus, only for the period 10 August 2006 to 31 August 2006 (some three weeks) is the country house, due to the two variations, not Simon's main residence, i.e. on an eventual sale of the country house three weeks' worth of capital gain will be subject to capital gains tax. This is the (small) "cost" of avoiding a capital gains tax liability on three years' worth of capital gain on the sale of the flat (and indeed such gain may fall within the annual exemption of that time).

MARRIED COUPLES

As indicated above, a married couple living together are permitted only one main residence. Where a married couple own more than one property each of which qualifies as a residence then, as above, a formal election is advisable. Any such election is required to be signed by both spouses.

It is not unusual for the spouses prior to marriage to each own their own property with each property qualifying as the residence of the respective spouse. On marriage, however, the couple are only permitted one residence. An election thus needs to be made (within two years of the date of marriage) if both properties are to be retained as residences. If one of them is to be sold within three years of the date of marriage then no election is strictly necessary as the capital gain arising on the sale will be exempt as the last three years of ownership is a deemed period of residence (whether or not this is in fact the position). Any sale after this period of three years will cause some element of any capital gain to be subject to capital gains tax.

The position on separation or divorce is somewhat complex. It should, however, be noted that despite the marital home qualifying as the main or sole residence of the married couple while they live together, for any spouse who leaves the home on separation or divorce a sale thereafter may precipitate capital gains tax consequences for such spouse.

This would occur if the former matrimonial home was sold more than three years after one of the spouses ceased to occupy the home as a residence. This would be so whether the sale of the departing spouse's, typically 50%, interest in the home was to a third party or to the spouse remaining in the home.

Such a sale within three years of departing the home would not, however, give rise to a capital gains tax charge as the last three years of ownership are always regarded as periods of residence.

Example 19.13
Ted and Mary have been married for 25 years and also owned their marital home for the same period, but on 1 May 2004 they separated and Ted moved into rented accommodation while Mary remained in the marital home. Ted and Mary owned the home as joint tenants (i.e. 50% each).

On 30 April 2008 the marital home was sold.

For Mary the whole of the capital gain arising on her 50% interest is exempt from capital gains tax as throughout the whole period of her ownership the home was her sole residence.

For Ted, however, of his 29 years of ownership the home was his residence for 25 years. In addition, the last three years of ownership are deemed to be periods of residency.

Thus, for Ted, the home was his sole residence for 28 years and as a consequence 1/29th of any capital gain arising on the sale of his interest will be subject to capital gains tax.

It therefore may be the case that for the spouse who moves out of the former marital home a sale after a further period of three years will be undesirable due to the precipitation of a capital gains tax charge. The longer the period after departure and before sale the greater the potential capital gains tax charge (assuming increases in property values). There is, however, an extra statutory concession (namely, ESC D6) under which, subject to satisfying certain conditions, a transfer by the spouse who left the matrimonial home will not precipitate a capital gains tax charge irrespective of when the transfer is effected. The concession only applies, however, in limited circumstances. It applies if:

- the transfer is from the spouse who left the marital home, to the spouse who remained in it, as part of the financial settlement following the separation/divorce;
- the marital home must have remained the sole or main residence of the spouse who remained in the home;
- the spouse who left the home must not have elected for some other property to be the spouse's sole or main residence.

If the spouses agree to a third party sale of the marital home the above concession will not apply; the spouse who previously occupied the home must therefore transfer their interest in it to the spouse who remained in the home if the concession is to apply.

In principle, wherever possible, the spouse who departs the former marital home should try and ensure any disposal of interest in the home should be effected within three years of leaving.

INTER-SPOUSE TRANSFERS

Transfers of property between spouses who are living together take place at no gain/no loss for capital gains tax purposes, i.e. the transferee spouse acquires the property at the original cost to the transferor spouse; not market value at the date of the transfer (see Chapter 8). This also applies to transfers between spouses in the tax year of separation up to the end of that tax year.

However, this is not so for transfers between spouses from the commencement of the tax year following the tax year of separation. In this case any transfer is treated like any other transfer (albeit the transfer is between connected persons and thus assumed to be at market value; see Chapter 8) and a capital gains tax charge may arise.

Where the transfer between spouses living together is of an interest in the sole or main residence of the transferor spouse, the transferee spouse is treated as "standing in the shoes of the transferor spouse". Thus, not only is the transferee spouse deemed to have acquired the property at the original cost to the transferor spouse but the transferee spouse is assumed to have owned the newly acquired interest from the date the transferor spouse acquired it. This has the effect that periods of residence by the transferor spouse are attributed to the transferee spouse.

This attribution occurs irrespective of the true position and even applies where at the date the transferor spouse acquired the property the transferee spouse and transferor spouse were not married. In effect a fiction is created for capital gains tax purposes on inter-spouse transfers of an interest in a sole or main residence.

The transfer from one spouse to the other may be effected by way of will on the death of the property owning spouse. The above consequences still apply. The only difference is that a lifetime transfer is deemed to take place at the original cost of the property to the transferor spouse, whereas, on death, the transferee spouse acquires the property at its probate, i.e. market value.

Example 19.14
Alice Spring acquired her house in September 1999 for £200 000 and married Jim Horse in July 2002 when the house was worth £250 000.

As a wedding present Alice transferred a 50% interest in the house to Jim.

In August 2008 they decided to downsize and sold the house for £650 000.

In July 2002 when Alice transferred 50% of her interest to Jim he is deemed to have acquired that interest for £100 000 (i.e. 50% of the original cost to Alice).

On the sale in August 2008 the capital gain each spouse made was £225 000 (i.e. £325 000 less £100 000).

As Alice had resided in the property since its purchase her capital gains is exempt from capital gains tax.

Jim is deemed to have acquired the 50% interest in September 1999 and Alice's period of residency from September 1999 to July 2002 is attributed to Jim. From July 2002 to August 2008 Jim continued to reside in the house. Thus, the whole of Jim's capital gain is also exempt from capital gains tax.

LETTINGS RELIEF

Lettings relief applies where the sole or main residence has during the period of ownership been let out either wholly or in part.

In essence, while the capital gain arising on the disposal of the sole or main residence which is attributable to the period of letting is subject to capital gains tax, lettings relief reduces the quantum of the gain which is taxable.

The reduction is the least of three amounts:

- £40 000;
- the capital gain attributable to the letting period;
- the amount of the capital gain which is exempt due to sole or main residence relief.

Example 19.15
Sonia Bird acquired her house 25 years ago and recently sold it making a capital gain of £275 000.

She occupied the house as her main residence for 15 years, letting it out for 10 years.

Capital gain		£275 000
Less:		
Exempt portion: 18*/25 of £275 000	(£198 000)	
		£77 000
Less:		
Lettings exemption		(£40 000)
(i.e. least of:		
(i) £40 000		
(ii) £110 000 (10/25 of £275 000)		
(iii) £198 000)		
Chargeable gain		£37 000

*includes last three years of ownership.

TRUSTS AND SOLE OR MAIN RESIDENCE

A residence comprised in a trust may on a disposal be exempt from capital gains tax, i.e. the exemption with respect to the sole or main residence is not restricted to direct ownership by individuals.

In order for the exemption from capital gains tax to apply to a capital gain on the disposal of the property by the trustees, one or more beneficiaries under the trust must satisfy the various conditions discussed above (e.g. the property must be the sole or main residence of the beneficiary) and be entitled to occupy the property under the terms of the trust.

Occupation under the terms of the trust by a beneficiary arises where the beneficiary has an interest in possession in the property or, if the trust is a discretionary trust, the trustees have power to permit the beneficiary to occupy the property (i.e. it is not necessary for the beneficiary to have a right to occupy under the trust).

It may be that more than one beneficiary has an interest in possession in the property but, for example, only one of the beneficiaries actually occupies the property as a sole or main residence. Nevertheless, on a disposal of the property, exemption from capital gains tax on the whole of the capital gain will apply to the trustees (even though, if there are four interest in possession beneficiaries, the beneficiary in occupation has an interest in only one quarter of the property).

The ability to utilise trusts to avoid capital gains tax charges arising on the sale of "second homes" (i.e. non-main residence properties) is no longer possible.

If, on or after 6 April 2006, the individual transfers a property into trust under which either the settlor or spouse or dependent child of the settlor may benefit then the trust qualifies as "settlor interested" (see Chapter 16). As a consequence, "hold-over relief" (see Chapter 8) is not available and a capital gains tax charge will arise at that time (assuming that the property, as is usually the case, was not the sole or main residence of the settlor). Transfers on or after 10 December 2003, but pre 6 April 2006, into trust under which the settlor or spouse (children of the spouse during this period did not cause a trust to be settlor interested) could benefit is also a transfer into a settlor interested trust and again hold-over relief is denied.

For "hold-over relief" to apply requires that the trust is not settlor interested (i.e. none of the above individuals must be able to benefit under the trust). Assuming that this is the case the property can be moved into trust without at that time precipitating a capital gains tax charge. However, even if a beneficiary under the trust occupies the property as outlined above and satisfies the conditions for main residence exemption, the exemption from capital gains tax on sale by the trustees is denied with respect to not only the held-over gain but also the gain which is attributable to the period since the trust acquired the property.

In short, hold-over relief *and* capital gains tax exemption on a trust sale of the property which is the main residence of a beneficiary is no longer possible post 10 December 2003 with respect to settlor interested trusts.

Exemption on a capital gain realised by the trustees is, however, possible but only where the settlor does not claim hold-over relief on the transfer of the property into trust (this requires that the trust is not settlor interested) which would thus at that time precipitate a capital gains tax charge.

DEATH AND SOLE OR MAIN RESIDENCE

The fact that the property of the deceased is the deceased's sole or main residence during lifetime does not mean that a disposal by the deceased's executors during the administration period will also be exempt from a capital gains tax charge.

Executors are liable to capital gains tax on capital gains arising on disposals of chargeable assets made during the administration period (any capital gain will be the difference between the probate value, i.e. market value at the date of death of the asset, and the disposal value).

However, in certain cases a disposal by executors of such a residence may be exempt. In order for the exemption to apply the following conditions need to be satisfied:

- immediately before and immediately after the death of the individual the property was the sole or main residence of one or more individuals;
- one of those individuals or two or more of those individuals have, under the will, an entitlement to at least 75% of the net proceeds of the disposal (broadly, sales proceeds less deductible expenditure).

Example 19.16

Eric Dunce is a widower and his two daughters, Louise and Clare, have lived with him following his wife's death in order to look after him. His son, Brian, does not live with them as he is married and lives with his wife in their own home.

His two daughters, following his death, continue to live in the property.

Under his will Eric leaves his property to each of his three children equally. At the date of Eric's death the property had a market value of £600 000.

Unbeknown to his children Eric had incurred substantial gambling debts. The executors decided to sell the property 12 months later for £675 000 and distributed the proceeds.

As Louise and Claire are only entitled to 2/3rds of the property sale proceeds (i.e. less than 75%) a capital gains tax charge arises on the £75 000 capital gain arising on the sale of the property.

Had Eric left the property to Louise and Claire only, and assuming that the executors sold the property (for whatever reason) then on sale the capital gain would have been exempt from capital gains tax.

A deed of variation under which Brian redirects his inheritance to his sisters, equally, would enable exempt capital gains tax treatment on a sale by the executors.

INHERITANCE TAX

The matrimonial home will often constitute the major asset of the individual's estate. As a consequence, a significant inheritance tax liability is likely to arise on the individual's death. In the early years of ownership of the property the potential inheritance tax liability may often be significantly reduced on death due to borrowings secured against the property (typically, by way of mortgage). As the individual gets older this borrowing tends to reduce until in later life the property may be debt free, thus increasing substantially the potential inheritance tax charge on death (not least also because of the rise in the property value).

In general, inheritance tax on the individual's death may, to a degree, be reduced by lifetime gifts (usually PETs). Unfortunately, very few individuals are able to gift, in this way, the matrimonial home.

Should a lifetime gift of the property be made (e.g. to the children or in trust) but the donor(s) continue to live in the property the gift is a gift with reservation (see Chapter 11) and on the death of the donor(s) the property simply still forms part of the donor(s)' estate; indeed it is the value of the property at the date of death (not the date of the gift) which is subject to inheritance tax.

Schemes were designed which enabled such gifting to occur while at the same time not constituting a gift with reservation. The donor(s) could thus gift the property yet still continue to live in it until death without the above adverse inheritance tax consequences arising. Following defeats in the courts concerning such schemes HMRC modified the provisions which dealt with gifts with reservation and later introduced the pre-owned asset legislation (see Chapter 11) specifically targeted at such schemes.

As a consequence, four schemes commonly known as Ingram, Eversdon, reversionary lease and home loan schemes are unlikely to be utilised in future.

It also seems highly likely that any future devised "schemes" will be "attacked" by HMRC, and the more "artificial" the scheme, the greater the risk of attack.

Very careful thought should therefore be given before any such scheme is embarked upon.

Nevertheless, some "safer" degrees of planning are available to mitigate the potential inheritance tax liability on the matrimonial home. Planning to mitigate inheritance tax on the matrimonial home may be divided into lifetime and death planning.

Lifetime Planning

It is not unusual later in life, particularly when the children have left home, for the parents to contemplate so-called "downsizing" which simply involves selling the home and purchasing a smaller home thus releasing surplus cash.

The whole or some element of the surplus cash can then be gifted to members of the family (constituting PETs) in the hope of surviving seven years thus avoiding inheritance tax thereon. On death the size of the death estate would have been reduced. Alternatively, the surplus cash could be invested in assets that on death will qualify for business property relief (see Chapter 10) at either 50% or 100%; for example, shares listed on AIM.

The options below do not necessarily resolve the inheritance tax exposure issue completely but do offer a possible reduction in the ultimate inheritance tax liability on death.

- shared home arrangements;
- cash gifts;
- sale;
- gift plus rent payable.

All these options are not necessarily applicable to all situations. The advantage of these options is that the existing legislation specifically provides that none of them are "caught" under either the gift with reservation or the pre-owned asset rules.

Joint Ownership Arrangements

Under this option the existing owner of the property (the donor) gifts a share of the property (to the donee) and both donor and donee both occupy the property thereafter. It may be that the gift is to more than one donee.

It is interesting to note that occupation does not appear to require "full time" occupation. Occupation from time to time may be acceptable.

It is important to note, however, that 100% of the property cannot be gifted under this option. Only a part of the property may be gifted and although there is some lack of clarity as to the maximum percentage of the property which may be so gifted (the legislation is silent) it is generally accepted that up to 50% is not problematic and even up to 80% may not be perceived as unacceptable.

It is necessary that following the gift the donor does not receive any benefit from the donee associated with the gift (whether directly or indirectly). This requires that the expenses of the property (i.e. heating, lighting, etc.) are paid by the donor and donee reflecting their respective usage (not reflecting their respective ownership percentages). Thus, if the donor has given 75% of the property to the donee this does not mean the expenses associated with the property need to be split 75/25. It is the respective usage of the facilities by the donor and donee which determine the payments by each. Assuming, the donor and donee live in the property which is their only property then, other things being equal, donor and donee should each contribute 50/50.

It may be, however, that with respect to non-recurrent expenditure (i.e. "one-off" capital expenditure) the respective contributions should in fact be in line with their respective ownership percentages. In the above example (i.e. gift of 75%), should the property subsequently need re-roofing it would seem that each should contribute 75/25 not 50/50.

The important point to note is that the donor must not receive any benefit from the donee either directly or indirectly. To avoid this risk the donor could simply pay more than the requisite percentage share, even perhaps by paying for all the "running costs", so as to reduce the risk that the gift with reservation rules will be invoked by HMRC.

This option may be suitable in a number of situations; following the death of one parent, should the surviving parent subsequently require help/support, then a gift of part of the property could be made to the child who moves in with the parent to effect the caring of the parent; the need for support/help by the parent is, of course, not a strict necessity. Another example where this option may be appropriate is where one or more of the children cannot afford to purchase their own home.

Cash Gift

This option is perhaps of less practical use than the option examined above.

Under this option the donor makes a gift of cash to the donee. The donee uses the cash to purchase a property in which the donor then resides.

The gift would not constitute a gift with reservation but in order for the gift not to be "caught" by the pre-owned asset legislation the donor must not occupy the property for seven years. Occupation within the seven-year period would cause the pre-owned asset legislation to apply; the consequence, in broad terms, would be that the donor will be assessed to income tax on a deemed market rental of the property (or the donor could elect to bring the property back into his estate for the purposes of inheritance tax (see Chapter 11)).

Perhaps a practical example of this option would be where an Englishman has lived and worked abroad for a number of years generating significant surplus cash. The individual knows that, say, on retirement in 10 years' time that he/she will return to live in the UK. Accordingly, the cash could be gifted to one of the children who purchase the UK property for occupation in due course by the parent but, in any event, not within seven years.

Sale

Under this option no gifts are involved; in fact quite the reverse.

The property is sold for a market value to, say, one of the children. The child purchaser then allows the vendor parent to live in the property (no rent need be charged). It must be noted that the whole of the owner's interest in the property must be sold (i.e. a part sale will not qualify under this option).

Either the purchase can be effected by cash or the purchase price may be left outstanding on loan account. In the latter case the loan must be on terms as would be agreed between third parties (thus, for example, it could not be "interest free"). However, it would not be acceptable for the vendor parent to make cash gifts to the child who has purchased the property in order to enable the latter to effect interest and/or capital repayments on any loan incurred to fund the original purchase cost.

The preferred option would be for cash to be used to effect the purchase as this would then allow the parent vendor to make gifts to family members (i.e. PETs) out of the cash thus reducing even further the size of the future death estate and hence the associated inheritance tax charge.

Gift plus Rent Payable

It was stated above that a gift of the property by the owner followed by continued residence constituted a gift with reservation. Thus, a simple gift by the parent to, say, the child and continued residence by the parent results in no inheritance tax saving.

However, if the occupant parent pays a market rent to the child in order to occupy the property then neither the gift with reservation nor the pre-owned asset legislation will apply.

Under this option the receipt of the rent will be subject to income tax, each tax year, at the donee's marginal tax rate, possibly 40%.

In essence there is a potential "trade-off", i.e. inheritance tax at 40% on the property on death is avoided by the donor but during the donor's lifetime an annual 40% income tax charge on the market rent from the property (broadly, say 5% of the property's market value) will arise on the part of the donee. The longer the donor survives the greater the income tax charge in aggregate.

General Comments

Three points are perhaps worth noting.

First, it is important to appreciate that in each of the above options where a gift is made from one individual to another individual it will constitute a PET whether or not it is treated as a gift with reservation. In the event of the death of the donor within seven years of the gift the PET will become chargeable.

Second, where the property is owned by, say, a child of the parent but the parents alone occupy the property, on any future sale of the property the child will be subject to capital gains tax on any capital gain. The exemption available with respect to ownership of a sole or main residence is inapplicable as the property is not the residence of the child (see above).

However, if the child and parent each have an interest in the property and both live in it then the exemption from capital gains tax will apply to each individual with respect to their respective interests on any sale.

Third, where a parent makes a gift either in whole or in part of their home to one or more of their children the parent loses control over the property. Should the child(ren) decide to sell the property against the wishes of the parent complications are likely to arise. The requirement to sell may be forced on the child following a "messy" divorce or perhaps a business bankruptcy or simply following a "fall-out" with the parent.

Thus, while some of the above options may offer effective inheritance tax planning, regard must be had to all the factors (i.e. non-tax as well as tax) before implementation of any of the above options. Indeed, this comment applies to all forms of tax planning discussed in this book.

As the saying goes "the tax tail should not be allowed to wag the dog".

Death Planning

For the individual who dies owning the whole or part of the matrimonial home such property will form part of the individual's death estate which in principle will be subject to inheritance tax. This liability may be avoided by the first spouse to die leaving their (typically, 50% interest in the property) interest to the surviving spouse.

While this avoids an inheritance tax charge on the first death it merely exacerbates the charge on the death of the surviving spouse and the NRB of the first spouse to die may have been wasted depending upon the size of the estate. It is because of this that elsewhere in the book (see Chapters 10 and 26) it is argued that equalisation of estates between spouses should be adopted to ensure that each spouse's NRB is fully utilised.

This was certainly the position before FA 2008 introduced the concept of the "transferable nil rate band" between spouses (applicable where one or both spouse deaths occur on or after 9 October 2007). As discussed elsewhere in the book (see Chapters 10 and 26) the introduction of the transferable NRB does mean that even where the first spouse to die does leave their interest in the matrimonial home to the surviving spouse the NRB will not in principle be wasted as it may be subsequently transferred and used against the estate of the surviving spouse.

Nevertheless, reliance upon this transferability in future to ensure efficient NRB utilisation by both spouses may not necessarily be the better option to pursue.

Before the introduction of the transferable NRB (*and* pre FA 2006), to ensure utilisation of the NRB of the first spouse to die the interest of the spouse, typically 50% in the matrimonial home, was left to the children absolutely or on trust (a discretionary trust). In either case, the NRB was thus utilised. The surviving spouse would remain in occupation of the whole house even though owning a part (typically 50%) of it. In such cases HMRC would often seek to argue that although the surviving spouse owned only, say, 50% of the property the spouse effectively had an interest in possession in the whole property. Thus, on death of the surviving spouse the whole of the property would fall within the spouse's estate and the effect of utilising the children or trust on the first death (in order to use the spouse's NRB) would be completely nullified (recall for trusts set up pre 22 March 2006, where a beneficiary had an interest in possession under a trust the trust property in which the interest subsisted was treated on the beneficiary's death as part of the death estate; see Chapter 15).

Following FA 2006, interests in possession under trusts created in lifetime on or after 22 March 2006 do not result in the trust assets in which the interest subsists forming part of the beneficiary's estate on death. However, in the case of trusts set up by will, an "immediate post death interest" (IPDI) may arise and in this case the assets in which the IPDI subsists will be included in the estate of the beneficiary entitled to the IPDI on the beneficiary's death (see Chapter 15).

It is therefore important to ensure that where on the death of the first spouse to die their interest in the matrimonial home is left on trust (e.g. discretionary trust) the surviving spouse cannot be regarded as acquiring an IPDI under the trust.

In order to try to remove any argument as to whether the surviving spouse does or does not possess an IPDI, so-called "debt" or "charge" schemes are sometimes used. Under the former, the surviving spouse agrees to pay to the trustees of the trust created under the will of the first spouse to die a sum equivalent to the NRB. In exchange, the deceased's remaining estate is left to the surviving spouse including the interest of the deceased spouse in the matrimonial home.

Under the latter, the executors effect a charge over the estate's interest in the matrimonial home (equivalent to the NRB) and then assent that interest to the surviving spouse (i.e. the surviving spouse acquires the deceased spouse's interest in the matrimonial home albeit subject to the charge).

SDLT (see Chapter 21) is an issue with respect to the former option and will generally be payable (as the surviving spouse effectively provides consideration by way of the debt given to the trustees in exchange for the interest in the matrimonial home). This does not arise under the "charge" option.

Where neither of these two options has been included in the will of the first spouse to die use of a deed of variation (see Chapter 26) may be considered.

SUMMARY

The individual's only or main residence will typically be a major valuable asset. On death a significant inheritance tax liability may arise thereon. Depending upon the circumstances options exist which, if implemented, may mitigate such an inheritance tax charge. Some of these options involve lifetime gifts while others involve arrangements effected on death.

The capital gains tax exemption applies to the capital gain on the sale of the main or sole residence. It is important, however, that the property owned does constitute a "residence". Owning a property but not living there would not constitute a "residence".

Ownership of two or more residences involves the need to formally elect the "main residence". In the absence of such a formal election the facts will determine the matter.

Divorce or separation may precipitate adverse capital gains tax consequences for the departing spouse. Other things being equal a sale of the matrimonial home within three years of the date the spouse departs is desirable.

20
Non-UK Domiciliaries and UK Homes

BACKGROUND

For most non-UK domiciled but UK resident individuals the purchase of a UK property in which to live invariably arises.

This chapter will examine some of the options available to such individuals.

The factors which need to be taken into account are basically two-fold:

- structuring/ownership of the property;
- financing the acquisition.

OWNERSHIP

The property may be owned in one of the following manners:

- by the individual;
- by a non-UK resident trust;
- by a non-UK registered company.

Individual

This is arguably the most straightforward of the options.

The individual simply purchases the property directly, i.e. no intermediate vehicles are used. One advantage of this route is that on any disposal no capital gains tax liability arises due to the main residence exemption (see Chapter 19).

If such individual also owns a property outside the UK which is also used as a residence then it may be necessary for an appropriate election to be made and notified to HMRC. Under the election the individual would simply elect that the UK property is to be regarded for capital gains tax purposes as the main residence. Any such election needs to be made within two years of the acquisition of the second residence (normally, the UK property, as typically the non-domiciled individual will prior to arriving in the UK already own another residence outside the UK; see Chapter 19).

However, a major problem of direct ownership is the risk of an inheritance tax charge arising on death. The property is a UK situs asset (see Chapter 6) and thus falls within the charge to inheritance tax. The charge will, however, only arise if the aggregate of the individual's UK situs assets exceed the NRB in the tax year of death (non-UK assets ranking as excluded property).

There are a number of ways in which such a risk may be removed or eliminated.

One option is to take out insurance to cover the potential liability.

A second option is for the house to be left by will to the surviving spouse. On death the inter-spouse exemption would apply. This option is perhaps the most practical if it is likely that the surviving spouse will leave the UK (possibly returning "home") and then sell the property relatively soon after leaving.

A third option is to finance the purchase of the property in part by way of a substantial mortgage as it is only the net equity which is liable to inheritance tax. Pre FA 2008 an offshore mortgage could be raised and non-UK source monies (which if remitted to the UK would be a taxable remittance) could be used to fund the interest (but not capital repayments) offshore without precipitating any remittance problems. However, post FA 2008, utilisation of such offshore monies whether to fund interest *or* capital repayments will be treated as remittances to the UK (subject to transitional provisions with respect to existing mortgages; see Chapter 23).

This third option is still, however, feasible if the individual has access to non-UK source monies to fund the interest and capital repayments where the funds so used would not in any event constitute remittances to the UK (e.g. if the monies represented inheritances, or gifts from others). UK taxed source monies (e.g. salary) could also be used.

A fourth option, although probably impractical, is for the house to be purchased by a number of members of the family (e.g. husband, wife, brother and sister) such that the aggregate of the NRBs equals or exceeds the value of the house, i.e. on the death of any individual member the value of their interest is within their NRB.

One final point to note: if a UK situs asset is immovable property, then probate will be needed following death before any title transfer may occur (see Chapter 26).

Non-UK Resident Trust

The fact that the trust is non-UK resident does not insulate the trust from charges to inheritance tax (see Chapters 9 and 15).

Where a non-UK resident discretionary trust is set up by the non-domiciled individual (whether UK resident or not) who is to reside in the house then the individual will be a beneficiary of the trust. As a result the trust is settlor interested and, inter alia, the gift with reservation rules will apply (see Chapter 11). The consequence is that on the individual's death the house will be regarded as forming part of the individual's estate and thus subject to inheritance tax.

In addition, the trust falls within the relevant property regime (see Chapter 15) and ten yearly (at 6%) and exit charges will apply to the trust property.

Where the trust is an interest in possession trust (see Chapter 15) set up in lifetime, on or after 22 March 2006, the above consequences still apply. However, if such a trust was created prior to this date while the ten yearly and exit charges will not apply to the trust, on the death of the individual possessing the interest in possession the value of the property will still form part of the death estate (see Chapter 15).

The points made above concerning mortgaging the property to reduce the inheritance tax exposure still apply. Funding the interest and capital repayments requires care if taxable remittances are not to arise.

An issue which arises under trust ownership, but is of no relevance where direct ownership of the property occurs, is the possible application of the various anti-avoidance provisions which may affect non-UK resident trusts (see Chapter 17). Although the non-UK domiciled individual is subject to remittance basis treatment with respect to non-UK source income and capital gains the individual is in fact enjoying the benefit of a trust asset in the UK, i.e. the house. Thus, the income and/or capital gains of the trust may be apportioned to the individual and a consequent tax charge will arise (the position pre FA 2008 in this regard was slightly more favourable). Assuming that the trust's sole asset is the UK house, and no income or capital gains arise to the trust, although the anti-avoidance provisions just referred to are in point, in practice no tax liabilities will arise on the part of the individual.

The trust, as a non-UK resident vehicle, is not subject to capital gains tax on the capital gain arising from trust asset disposals. Thus, a sale by the trust of the house will not precipitate a capital gains tax charge on the part of the trust (irrespective of the sole or main residence exemption). However, depending upon the beneficiaries of the trust under anti-avoidance provisions either the settlor interested provisions are in point with respect to the capital gain or such a gain would be "matched" (see Chapter 17) against the benefits the individual has received in the UK due to occupation of the house and a capital gains tax liability would arise on the part of the individual at that time (i.e. in the tax year in which the house was sold). The benefit the individual receives under the trust is probably equal to the rent which the trust could have obtained if the house had been let out to a third party. However, the taxability on the part of the individual presupposes that in the tax year of sale the individual is UK resident. Thus, a sale after the end of the tax year in which the individual became non-UK resident should avoid such a tax charge.

Where, however, the house has been the individual's sole or main residence no capital gain arises on a sale by the trust and the tax charge on the individual referred to in the immediately preceding paragraph should be avoided. An election may be necessary if the individual has two (or more) residences.

It is also worth noting that probate would not be necessary should the individual die, as ownership of the house does not change, i.e. it remains with the the trustees of the trust.

Non-UK Registered Company

Unlike the inheritance tax problem associated with direct, and non-UK resident trust, ownership of the UK property, ownership via a non-UK registered company instantly solves this problem. This is because the asset owned (whether by the individual or a trust) is not the UK property but the shares in the company which are non-UK situs for inheritance tax purposes (see Chapter 6).

As the company is non-UK resident it is not subject to capital gains tax on any sale of the house (whether it is the main residence of the individual or not).

Prima facie, this option would appear to be the "best" option. However, this is not in fact the case. The main reason why this is so is that where the individual owns the shares of the company directly HMRC are of the view that a "benefit in kind" arises on the part of the individual as the individual is regarded as being either an employee or director of the company or a "shadow director" thereof and as a consequence the property has been provided to the individual in this capacity.

The measure of the benefit is substantial. It is an annual benefit approximately equal to 5% of the property's market value. If the individual is a higher rate taxpayer then the annual income tax charge will equal 40% of this figure (e.g. if the market value of the property is £1 million the income tax charge will be 40% × 5% × £1 million, namely, £20 000 per annum).

There are various arguments against this stance by HMRC but it is well known that this is their view and will so argue where necessary.

In an attempt to ameliorate this potential charge, the shares of the non-UK registered company are often held by a non-UK resident trust. The logic for this structure is that the trust insulates the individual from the underlying company and thus prevents the benefit in kind charge from arising as the individual could no longer be said to be an employee, director or shadow director of the underlying company. This may or may not be the position.

The use of the trust, while attempting to solve one issue, does give rise to other issues already discussed above.

FINANCING THE ACQUISITION

The UK property may be purchased for cash or a mixture of cash and borrowing.

If the individual uses non-UK source income and/or capital gains to effect the purchase, in whole or in part, a remittance of the income or gains to the UK will have occurred and a tax charge will arise (assuming of course the non-UK monies constitute taxable income/gains). This may make the cost of the purchase somewhat prohibitive.

The use of non-UK source monies which if remitted will not be subject to tax (e.g. "pure" capital; see Chapter 23) or UK source taxed monies may be a "better" option.

Pre FA 2008, typically, non-UK source mortgages were utilised. This was highly tax efficient (see above and Chapter 23). Post FA 2008, this tax efficient option is no longer available with respect to "new" borrowings.

Tax efficient funding is, thus, post FA 2008, much more of a problem.

PRELIMINARY CONCLUSIONS

Not one of the above options appears to be clearly the "best" option for all non-UK domiciled individuals wishing to purchase UK property in which to live.

The choice of option will depend upon many factors including whether, for example, both spouses are non-UK domiciled or whether one of the spouses is UK domiciled.

In the latter case offshore trusts and companies may give rise to more problems than they solve.

The impact of the individual (or both spouses) becoming deemed UK domiciled for inheritance tax purposes also needs to be considered.

Perhaps the option to consider first is the simple one of the individual purchasing in their own (and/or the spouse's name) name; to consider then what the intention of each spouse is likely to be once the other spouse dies; and to ascertain finally the cost of effecting an appropriate insurance to cover any potential inheritance tax charge on death.

SUMMARY

Non-UK domiciliaries purchasing a UK home need to consider the twin issues of ownership structure and finance. While for such individuals non-UK resident trusts are an important vehicle in structuring ownership of UK situs assets, it may be that with respect to UK home ownership the use of such trusts may not be the "better" option.

Direct ownership by the non-UK domiciled individual may be the simplest and most inheritance tax and capital gains tax effective option. Any inheritance tax exposure may be "managed" and any capital gain arising on the sale of the property should not fall subject to capital gains tax.

21
Stamp Duty and Stamp Duty Land Tax

BACKGROUND

Tax planning for wealth management purposes typically involves transferring assets around family members and/or into/out of trusts. Such transfers involve consideration of the possible income, capital gains and/or inheritance tax consequences.

However, such transfers may give rise to "transfer taxes", in the UK referred to as stamp duty, stamp duty reserve tax (SDRT) and stamp duty land tax (SDLT).

While the rates (see below) are significantly below the corresponding rates applicable to income, capital gains and inheritance tax they are applicable to "gross" amounts of consideration which pass on a transaction. The implication of stamp duty and SDRT and, in particular SDLT, should not therefore be overlooked.

Stamp duty, SDRT and SDLT while generally leviable on lifetime transactions may also apply on the administration of the death estate following death.

STAMP DUTY/STAMP DUTY RESERVE TAX

Stamp duty was first levied under the Stamp Act 1694 and has been amended over the years by various Finance Acts until a major overhaul of the tax was implemented by the Finance Act 2003.

Under the reform, stamp duty was replaced by SDLT in connection with land transactions. In addition, stamp duty was abolished in connection with all documents and transfers other than transfers with respect to shares and marketable securities (indebtedness which is marketable).

In 1986 SDRT was introduced. SDRT is chargeable where there is an agreement to transfer shares or marketable securities.

Stamp duty and SDRT are taxes on documents (basically, no document no tax) whereas SDLT is a transaction-based tax, applicable whether or not a document exists in connection with the transaction.

SDRT is levied at the ad valorem rate of 0.5% of the amount or value of the consideration and is payable by the purchaser.

Stamp duty is levied either at the *ad valorem* rate of 0.5% of the amount or value of the consideration or at a fixed amount of £5 and in either case is payable by the purchaser.

SDRT, as indicated above, is levied on agreements (e.g. contracts) for the sale of shares whereas stamp duty is levied on an actual transfer of the shares. Where payment of the stamp duty is made this cancels any charge to SDLT, i.e. in this case stamp duty takes priority.

STAMP DUTY LAND TAX

SDLT is a tax on land and applies from 1 December 2003. It replaced the former stamp duty which applied to land.

SDLT applies to transactions relating to freeholds, leaseholds and options over UK situated land. Where the land is UK situated SDLT applies, despite some views to the contrary, irrespective of whether the parties to the transaction and/or the instrument relating to the land are within the UK.

For a charge to SDLT to arise there must be consideration.

A typical land transaction giving rise to a potential charge to SDLT is the straightforward sale for consideration of a freehold interest in land. The payment of SDLT is the responsibility of the purchaser (as is the reporting of the transaction) and payment of any SDLT due must be made within 30 days of the transaction.

The consideration does not need to be monetary; consideration in "money's worth" is also subject to SDLT with the amount determined by market value.

SDLT applies whether the consideration is provided by the party to the transaction or by a "connected person" (broadly, a person is connected with an individual if that person is the individual's spouse, sister, brother, ancestor or lineal descendant; in addition, trustees of a settlement of which the individual is a settlor are connected).

The rates of SDLT vary according to whether the land is residential or non-residential and according to the amount of the consideration. A 0% rate applies to residential land where the consideration is £125 000 or below (a temporary measure has been introduced under which the acquisition of residential property worth not more than £175 000 between 3 September 2008 and 2 September 2009 will be exempt from SDLT) and a 4% rate applies where the consideration exceeds £500 000 (1% applies where the consideration is $>$£125 000 but $\leqslant$£250 000; 3% applies where the consideration is $>$£250 000 but $\leqslant$£500 000). The rate applicable applies to the whole consideration, not just the excess. Thus, for example, a consideration of £1 million is subject to SDLT of 4% of £1 million, i.e. £40 000, not 4% of [£1 million less £500 000].

The appropriate rate is levied on the consideration with no discount applicable should the consideration be deferred.

MATRIMONIAL HOME

As indicated at the beginning of the chapter, inter-spouse transfers are often utilised as part of family tax planning. Whereas with respect to income, capital gains and inheritance tax inter-spouse transfers can usually be effected without precipitating a tax charge no such exemption applies in respect of SDLT.

As a consequence, the possible SDLT consequences should not be overlooked where land transfers between spouses are contemplated.

It might be thought that an outright gift of land from one spouse to another should not precipitate an SDLT charge. While this is in principle correct, it is not necessarily so where any indebtedness attaches to the land.

A classic example of this would be where the individual has purchased a UK house utilising a mortgage. The individual subsequently marries and agrees with the new spouse to transfer, say, 50% of the property to the new spouse for no consideration, i.e. a gift is made. While the recipient spouse has provided no explicit consideration to the transferor spouse, an assumption of 50% of the mortgage debt has occurred which is regarded as consideration and SDLT is thus in principle payable by the recipient spouse. If, however, only a 25% interest in the house is transferred then SDLT is levied on only 25% of the mortgage.

The amount of the mortgage taken into account is the amount outstanding at the date of the transaction not the original amount of the borrowing.

The result is the same even if the house is remortgaged at the time of the gift, i.e. even though, prima facie, the recipient spouse is not assuming any liability of the transferor spouse a SDLT charge arises.

Purchase of House plus Chattels

Often a purchase of a residential property may include a sum which represents chattels to be included in the sale. Chattels are not land and therefore not subject to SDLT. However, any attempt to allocate a disproportionate amount of the consideration to the chattels will fail as provisions exist under which only a reasonable proportion of the aggregate consideration may be so allocated.

No Consideration

If no consideration is provided (including no assumption of any debt) in respect of a land transaction no SDLT is payable.

There are no "arm's length"-type provisions (with one exception; see below) which impute a market value consideration. Thus, an outright gift of land (assuming the land is unencumbered) will not give rise to an SDLT charge.

However, where the transfer of the land is by the individual to a "connected company" the land will be treated as having been transferred for a consideration equal to the market value of the land at the date of the transfer. This rule applies irrespective of the actual consideration paid. For this purpose an individual is connected to a company if the individual "controls" (broadly, owns more than 50% of the voting or share capital) the company.

Such a transaction might arise where, for example, a non-UK domiciled but UK resident individual owns UK land which it was desired to remove from the potential inheritance tax charge on death. The land is UK situs and thus falls within the charge to inheritance tax. However, if the individual sets up a non-UK registered company and then transferred the land to the company the asset now owned by the individual would be non-UK situs (i.e. the shares in the non-UK registered company; see Chapter 6). Typically, the land would be gifted.

However, even though no consideration passes, in this case, the anti-avoidance provision referred to above applies and market value would be imputed with SDLT being levied thereon. The transfer designed to reduce inheritance tax would thus be at an SDLT cost; it would thus be a matter of comparison of the two costs to ascertain if the transfer is worthwhile.

The capital gains tax consequences of the transfer also need to be identified.

LINKED TRANSACTIONS

The basic thrust of the "linked transaction" provisions is to prevent one potentially large transaction (subject to SDLT at, say, 4%) being broken down into smaller transactions (each subject to SDLT at, say, 1% or even 0%). It achieves this objective by treating the various separate transactions as if they were a single transaction, i.e. the separate considerations are simply aggregated into one sum.

Broadly, a linked transaction is a transaction or series of transactions between the same vendor and purchaser. Thus, if one purchaser effected a purchase of land from a number of unrelated vendors such transactions are not linked transactions; similarly, a sale of land by one vendor to a number of unrelated purchasers does not constitute linked transactions.

An example of a linked transaction is where an attempt is made to split a purchase of a residential property into two separate purchases; a purchase of the house and a separate purchase of the surrounding land/garden. Even if one of the purchases is by one spouse and the other purchase is effected by the other spouse the transactions would be linked. SDLT is then payable on the aggregate consideration, not on the two separate considerations.

MATRIMONIAL BREAKDOWN

As indicated elsewhere (see Chapter 19) in the case of matrimonial breakdown transfers of land (usually, the ex-matrimonial home) from one spouse to the other spouse may remain exempt from a charge to capital gains tax even though for the transferor spouse the ex-matrimonial home is no longer that spouse's main residence (see Chapter 8).

SDLT exemptions may also apply to such transfers.

Thus, where an interest in the ex-matrimonial home is transferred in pursuance of an order of the court on the granting of a divorce decree or judicial separation (an order of the court pursuant to which the parties to the marriage no longer have to cohabit) no SDLT is charged. Similarly, no SDLT is charged if the transfer is in pursuance of an agreement between the parties made in contemplation of the divorce or judicial separation.

TRUSTS

It is possible for SDLT to apply with respect to land transactions involving trusts.

A purchase of land by trustees of the trust would, in the normal manner, give rise to an SDLT charge on the part of the purchasing trustees. However, SDLT may also be leviable:

- where beneficiaries deal with their interests under the trust; or
- where appointments of trust land are made by the trustees.

Interest of Beneficiaries

An individual with an interest in possession in land owned by trustees constitutes a chargeable interest. If the interest in possession beneficiary assigns or releases their interest with respect to the land SDLT is leviable (the assignment or surrender must be done for consideration for the SDLT charge to arise).

Similar SDLT consequences may also arise with respect to interests of the remainderman; consideration again being necessary.

However, the above does not apply to the interests of beneficiaries under discretionary trusts. The reason is because a discretionary beneficiary (unlike an interest in possession beneficiary) merely has a "hope" that the trustees may exercise their discretion in the beneficiary's favour and nothing else (see Chapter 14).

Appointments

Generally speaking, on the exercise by trustees of a power of appointment (i.e. a right given to the trustees under the trust deed to appoint trust property to one or more beneficiaries) no SDLT charge arises as the exercise is normally effected without any form of consideration passing. However, as indicated above, should land be appointed to a beneficiary subject to a mortgage then SDLT will be in point.

Non-UK Resident Trusts

Non-UK resident trusts are not outside the scope of SDLT. Thus, for example, a disposal, whether by way of assignment or surrender, by the interest in possession beneficiary of their interest in UK situated land for consideration precipitates an SDLT charge. It should also be noted that such a charge applies irrespective of the residence (or domicile) status of the beneficiary concerned.

The point was made in Chapter 22 that trustees of non-UK resident trusts generally do not invest in UK situs assets directly, but via non-UK resident companies whose shares are in turn owned by the trust. This potentially removes the trust from any inheritance tax exposure; reduces any income tax charge on UK source income; and enables any possible capital gains tax consequences to be avoided (re a UK business) by effecting a sale of the company shares rather than the underlying UK business. The use of such a company may also remove any possible SDLT charge as the interest of the trustees is in the company shares not the underlying UK land.

Bare Trusts

A bare trust is basically a trust where the trustees hold the trust property on trust for one or more beneficiaries absolutely (see Chapter 14). Effectively, the trustees are nominees and have no duties to perform apart from doing as instructed by the beneficiaries.

Thus, perhaps it is not surprising that for SDLT purposes it is the beneficial owners (i.e. the beneficiaries) who are liable for any SDLT on any land transfer; in effect the bare trust is treated as if it simply did not exist.

DEATH

On the death of the individual the deceased's assets vest in the executors (see Chapter 26). However, no SDLT arises on the vesting of land (e.g. the deceased's matrimonial home) in the executors even if the land is subject to a mortgage at the time of the testator's death (i.e. there is an assumption of the mortgage by the executors).

Any assent or appropriation by the executors to a beneficiary under the will does not precipitate any SDLT charge (assuming, as will invariably be the case, that no consideration is provided). This applies even if the land appropriated is subject to a mortgage (even though as was seen above re inter-spouse transfers the assumption of a debt attached to land by a purchaser is regarded as consideration). In this case even though the beneficiary receives the land subject to the mortgage the transaction is regarded as exempt for SDLT purposes.

Instruments of Variation

Commonly referred to as deeds of variation, instruments of variation executed within two years of death of the deceased permit a degree of inheritance tax-free reorganisation of the deceased's estate (see Chapter 26).

Such variations do not precipitate charges to SDLT. However, there is a possible trap.

When the land, the subject of the variation, is appointed out to the "new" or "replacement" beneficiary no SDLT arises (assuming no consideration) but if the land appointed is subject to mortgage, the assumption of the debt by the "new" beneficiary is treated as consideration and SDLT is in point.

LIFE POLICIES

No stamp duty is leviable on life policies or on their assignment or any declarations of trust thereof.

SUMMARY

Stamp duty, SDRT and, in particular, SDLT are commonly overlooked when wealth planning for the individual is undertaken. Given the value of UK land and buildings, SDLT at a maximum rate of 4% thereof is likely to represent a significant cost to the purchaser/transferee.

Often, inter-spouse transfers and/or transfers to other members of the family and/or transfers into and out of trusts involve the assumption by the transferee of borrowings attached to property. SDLT, in such cases, is in principle payable.

The SDLT legislation contains anti-avoidance provisions designed to prevent attempts to reduce the charge by "artificial" means. Such provisions apply to "linked transactions" and transfers to companies.

22
Non-UK Resident Taxation

BACKGROUND

This chapter looks at the tax treatment of non-UK resident persons (i.e. individuals, trusts and companies) who are not resident in the UK.

UK tax becomes relevant to such persons where the person:

- is entitled to income from UK sources;
- makes a disposal of UK situs business assets;
- dies owning UK situs assets;
- makes a gift of a UK situs asset;
- is the recipient of a UK situs asset gift.

Apart from any of the above the non-UK resident person is not exposed to UK tax.

Even where any of the above is in point, the terms of a double tax agreement may override the ability of the UK to levy the tax charge (see Chapter 25).

Non-UK residents are in principle not exposed to UK taxes on non-UK source income or capital gains. However, inheritance tax may be in point for the non-UK resident individual who is UK or non-UK domiciled on UK situs assets or the non-UK resident trust in respect of which the settlor was UK domiciled at the date of creation of the trust. (Although not addressed in this chapter, but addressed elsewhere in the book, it is important to note the possible application of various UK anti-avoidance provisions which, while not levying tax on the non-UK resident person directly, may impute the person's income and/or capital gains arising from/on non-UK source assets to a UK resident individual thus precipitating a tax charge thereon (see Chapter 17).)

Any UK tax charge may in principle apply to non-UK resident individuals, trusts and companies. It applies in the same manner to non-UK resident individuals irrespective of domicile status. The remittance basis applies only to non-UK source income and capital gains of the non-UK domiciled but UK resident individual and is thus of no relevance to the non-UK resident person.

GENERAL RULES

Income Tax

In principle a non-UK resident individual is exposed to income tax on UK source income at the rates applicable to the UK resident individual, i.e. 20%/40% for the tax year 2008/09. However, with certain exceptions, the non-UK resident individual is not entitled to any of the normal personal allowances. Those individuals who are so entitled include residents of the Channel Islands and Isle of Man; those previously UK resident and who reside outside the UK for health reasons or the health reasons of a member of the family who resides with the individual; EEA nationals and Commonwealth citizens; and those currently employed in the service of the Crown or have been so employed in the past.

Non-UK resident discretionary trusts are liable to income tax on UK source income at the rate applicable to trusts, i.e. 40% or 32.5% in respect of UK source dividend income.

Non-UK resident companies are liable to income tax at the basic rate only (i.e. 20% for the tax year 2008/09; for earlier tax years such companies were liable to the then basic rate (22%) on non-savings income and 20% on savings income). The 40% charge applicable to individuals does not apply.

However, where the non-UK resident company carries on a part of its trade within the UK through a UK permanent establishment it is liable to corporation tax on its trading profit attributable to the UK activity at corporation tax rates not income tax rates (see below).

Capital Gains Tax

Non-UK resident persons are not within the charge to capital gains tax on UK situs assets unless the person is carrying on a trade, or part of a trade, within the UK. In this case capital gains tax is chargeable on a disposal of the UK situs assets used for the purposes of the trade.

Inheritance Tax

Inheritance tax is levied according to the domicile status of the individual, not the individual's residence status (see Chapter 9). Thus, non-UK residence does not, per se, remove an inheritance tax charge on UK (or indeed non-UK) situs assets unless such assets qualify as excluded property (e.g. UK authorised unit trusts; see Chapter 12).

Inheritance tax is thus leviable on UK situs assets on death and on the making of lifetime transfers whether the individual is UK or non-UK domiciled (subject to the excluded property point made above).

Non-UK resident trusts are within the inheritance tax charge on UK situs assets.

TYPES OF UK SOURCE INCOME

As indicated above non-UK resident persons are liable to income tax on UK source income. Such income includes trading income, property income, employment income, interest and dividends.

Trading Income

All non-UK resident persons are subject to tax on trading profits attributable to the UK trading activity. Non-UK resident individuals and trusts are subject to income tax thereon. Non-UK resident companies are in principle subject to corporation tax thereon if the trading is carried on through a UK permanent establishment (where the trading activity in the UK is carried on without the existence of any UK permanent establishment the trading profits are subject to income, not corporation, tax).

The rate applicable for the non-UK resident individual is 20% or 40% depending upon the level of UK source taxable income and for the non-UK resident discretionary trust is 40% irrespective of income levels.

The rate applicable for the non-UK resident company is 20% (income tax) assuming no UK permanent establishment and 21% or 28% (corporation tax) otherwise.

Property Income

All non-UK resident persons are subject to income tax on UK source rental income.

For the individual the rate is 20% or 40% depending upon the level of UK source taxable income; 40% for the non-UK resident trust; and 20% for the non-UK resident company.

The payment of rent directly to a non-UK resident person requires the tenant to deduct income tax at source at the basic rate (20%) from the gross rents and account to HMRC for the tax so deducted. Where the tenant pays the rent to a UK letting agent the rent is paid gross and it is then the responsibility of the letting agent to deduct income tax at source and account to HMRC for the tax so deducted (in this case, however, the tax deducted is from gross rents less deductible expenses, e.g. interest on borrowings used to purchase the property).

It is, however, possible for the non-UK resident person to obtain the agreement of the Financial Intermediaries and Claims Office (FICO) under which no requirement to deduct income tax at the basic rate (20%) at source is necessary. The non-UK resident person, where such agreement is obtained, then makes an annual return of the gross income less deductible expenses (e.g. interest on borrowings used to purchase the property) under the normal self assessment procedure.

Employment Income

A non-UK resident individual is liable to income tax on earnings related to UK source duties. This applies irrespective of the residence status of the employer with whom the contract of employment subsists.

Savings Income: Interest and Dividends

Interest (e.g. interest arising on bank or building society deposits) and dividends (e.g. dividends from UK resident companies) constitute UK source income and thus in principle non-UK resident persons are subject to income tax thereon at rates indicated above. However, with respect to "excluded income" (i.e. interest and dividends) such income tax liability is restricted to the amount of any income tax actually deducted at source.

Interest

Interest credited to UK bank and building society deposit accounts is credited after income tax at source has been deducted (at 20%). This tax deduction at source does not apply where the non-UK resident person is a company or trust (but in the latter case only if all beneficiaries are non-UK resident). Where the non-UK resident person is an individual, tax at source is not deducted where the individual makes a declaration (on Form R85; see Appendix 3) to the bank or building society that the individual is non-UK resident.

Thus, excluded income treatment (i.e. no income tax liability) with respect to interest will not apply to non-UK resident trusts if at least one of the beneficiaries is UK resident. In this case, interest will not be credited gross by the bank or building society and the trust, if discretionary, will also have an additional income tax liability on the interest of 20% (i.e. 40% rate applicable to trusts less 20% tax already deducted).

Where the non-UK trust is an interest in possession trust excluded income treatment will apply to the interest in possession beneficiary in respect of the UK source interest arising to the trust if the beneficiary is non-UK resident.

In short, non-UK resident individuals, certain trusts and companies are not subject to income tax on UK source interest.

Dividends

Unlike interest, dividends are not subject to the tax deducted at source mechanism. On the payment of a dividend by a UK resident company to a UK resident shareholder a tax credit is granted to the recipient shareholder. This tax credit equals one ninth of the net dividend. The tax credit is not, however, granted to non-UK resident shareholders except where the shareholder is an individual who is in one of the categories of non-UK resident who is entitled to the personal allowances (see above).

Non-UK resident companies have no further income tax liability on the net dividend. However, non-UK resident individuals and non-UK resident discretionary trusts are each liable to income tax at 32.5% on the grossed-up equivalent of the dividend less a deemed tax credit equal to 10% of the grossed-up dividend, i.e. 25% of the net dividend received.

As the dividend income qualifies as excluded income for the individual, in fact no income tax liability arises on the net dividend. Similarly, for the discretionary trust no income tax liability arises on the net dividend assuming none of the beneficiaries are UK resident (otherwise the above 25% liability arises).

SOME POINTS TO NOTE

Perhaps the major exposure to any UK tax on the part of the non-UK resident is inheritance tax which applies only to UK situs assets for the non-UK domiciled.

Such exposure, as discussed elsewhere in the book (see Chapters 9 and 20), may be eliminated or reduced by, for example, moving the situs of the asset outside the UK (e.g. by transferring the asset to a non-UK registered company); insuring against the liability; creating a borrowing against the asset; or, in the event of death, leaving the asset to the surviving spouse.

Capital gains tax is not a problem unless the non-UK resident is carrying on a trade within the UK. To mitigate the capital gains tax exposure on any sale of UK situs assets associated with the trade, a non-UK resident company could be used to conduct the trade and in the event of any sale the shares in the non-UK resident company could be sold instead of the company's underlying trade.

Income tax arises on UK source income unless such income qualifies as excluded income. For non-UK resident discretionary trusts excluded income treatment is only available if all the beneficiaries are non-UK resident. It may be preferable in this latter case for the trust to utilise an underlying company to undertake any UK investment. This not only increases the possibility of excluded income treatment but also for non-excluded income (e.g. rental income) the rate of income tax on the part of the company is restricted to the basic rate (20%) as compared to the rate applicable to trusts (40%). Such a structure would also insulate the discretionary trust against charges to inheritance tax on its assets which would be non-UK situs (i.e. shares in the non-UK resident company) and not UK situs assets (i.e. the UK situs assets being held by the company) assuming the trust is created by the non-UK domiciled settlor.

Non-UK resident discretionary trusts created by non-UK domiciled settlors (who are also non-UK resident) owning non-UK situs assets and receiving no UK source income are outside all UK taxes. However, where any of the beneficiaries are UK resident, income distributed to such individuals or benefits provided out of the trust to such individuals may create UK income and/or capital gains tax liabilities for the beneficiaries (see Chapter 17).

A non-UK resident trust may be used as a substitute will and probate is avoided.

As commented above, the terms of an appropriate double tax agreement may reduce any UK income, capital gains and/or inheritance tax exposures and should always be checked to ascertain their implication.

SUMMARY

Non-UK resident persons (i.e. individuals, trust and companies) are in principle exposed to UK taxes but only with respect to UK situs assets and income.

Inheritance tax probably offers the greatest exposure of the three taxes (i.e. income, capital gains and inheritance tax). Capital gains tax is not in principle a problematic tax for the non-UK resident.

The concept of excluded income is important for income tax purposes as it removes any UK income tax charge even if the income concerned is UK source.

UK tax mitigation can in general be achieved by the utilisation of offshore companies and/or trusts.

23
Accessing Offshore Monies: The Non-UK Domiciled Perspective

BACKGROUND

This chapter has no relevance to the UK domiciled, resident *and* ordinarily resident individual as the "remittance" basis has no application to such individual (see Chapter 2). However, it should be noted that a UK domiciled and UK resident individual who is *not* ordinarily resident in the UK is able to utilise the remittance basis in the same manner as a non-UK domiciled but UK resident individual.

The comments in this chapter are therefore addressed to the non-UK domiciled but UK resident individual (and the UK domiciled and UK resident but non-ordinarily resident individual).

Unless otherwise so specified, in this chapter, the term "individual" will be used to refer to a "non-UK domiciled but UK resident individual" and references to "income" or "gains" are references to "non-UK source income" and "non-UK situs gains", respectively.

Invariably the bulk of such individual's wealth is likely to reside outside the UK. The issue for many such individuals is how to access such wealth for enjoyment in the UK in a tax effective manner.

To the extent that the individual enjoys such wealth completely outside the UK no UK tax issues arise. It is possible, however, that UK tax issues will arise where enjoyment in its broadest sense is in the UK even though any payments in connection therewith are effected completely outside the UK.

Perhaps the classic example of this would be where the individual borrows monies from a non-UK-based bank to effect the purchase of UK residential property. The individual's income and/or capital gains are then used to service the loan, i.e. make interest payments and principal repayments outside the UK.

In such a case tax may be charged on what might be termed a "deemed" remittance to the UK by the individual of the income or capital gains used to make the interest payments and/or capital repayments to the bank (see below).

Similarly, the use in the UK of offshore issued credit cards may also precipitate unintended tax consequences.

Before FA 2008 the options available to the individual to "enjoy" the fruits of the income and gains tax free in the UK were much greater. FA 2008 has, however, severely tightened up the position post 6 April 2008 although transitional provisions to some degree ameliorate the transition from the pre to the post FA 2008 position. In addition, the new provisions introduce the concept of "exempt property", a concept unknown pre FA 2008 (see below).

This tightening up has taken the form of extending the definition of what constitutes a "remittance" and the closing of perceived loopholes (e.g. source cessation).

In addition, FA 2008 has changed the mechanics (but not the principles) which affect the ability of a non-UK domiciled but UK resident individual to utilise the remittance basis treatment with respect to non-UK source income and capital gains.

Before examining the FA 2008 rules affecting what constitutes a "remittance" and identifying the perceived loopholes now closed the changed mechanics applicable to the non-UK domiciled but UK resident individual will be considered.

This chapter will concentrate on the position for the individual post FA 2008 but where necessary the pre FA 2008 position will be addressed.

Broadly, the provisions of FA 2008 are effective from 6 April 2008.

Appendix 6 contains flowcharts relevant to this chapter.

CATEGORIES OF NON-UK DOMICILED INDIVIDUAL

The basic thrust of the provisions in this area is, in principle, two-fold:

- the introduction of the need for certain non-UK domiciled but UK resident individuals to make a claim for remittance basis treatment for a tax year;
- the introduction of a new annual tax charge referred to as the "remittance basis charge" of £30 000.

The original proposal was that a "charge" of £30 000 would be levied on non-UK domiciled but UK resident individuals who wanted to utilise the remittance basis of taxation for a particular tax year. The charge would be levied for each tax year the individual wished to utilise the remittance basis. Under this original proposal the £30 000 was an additional charge over and above any income and/or capital gains tax charge which would have arisen on any remittance to the UK. Thus, even if the individual had remitted all non-UK source income and capital gains to the UK arising in the tax year the £30 000 charge would have applied in addition to the normal tax charges.

The original proposal, however, was not implemented. The £30 000 figure is now an additional "tax" charge not a pure charge. Thus, if for example, the non-UK domiciled but UK resident individual remits, for example, all non-UK source income and capital gains arising in the tax year 2008/09 to the UK in, say, the tax year 2008/09 the £30 000 payable for 2008/09 would be deemed to have been paid on some part of the remitted income and/or capital gains. In this case the £30 000 will not be a charge over and above the tax liability arising on the remitted income and/or capital gains but a part of it. That part of any such remittance in respect of which the £30 000 tax will be deemed to have already been paid is referred to as the "nominated amount" (see below).

The £30 000 applies in full if the non-UK domiciled individual is UK resident in a tax year even if residency is only for part of the tax year, i.e. there is no facility for an apportionment of the £30 000.

The claim for remittance basis treatment is an annual claim and needs to be lodged within five (reduced to four under FA 2008 subject to a date to be appointed) years of 31 January following the tax year concerned. It may be made for some tax years but not for others. Where a claim is not made for a particular tax year the non-UK domiciled but UK resident is subject to income and capital gains tax for that year on the same basis as a UK domiciled, resident and ordinarily resident individual, i.e. the arising basis.

However, not all non-UK domiciled but UK resident individuals are required to claim the remittance basis for a tax year (yet may still be taxed as if such a claim had in fact been made) and not all non-UK domiciled individuals will be liable to the £30 000 tax charge.

Unless the non-UK domiciled but UK resident individual falls into one of the categories below (i.e. (a), (b) or (c)) a claim for remittance basis treatment *must* be lodged. Those individuals where a claim must be lodged may be categorised into the following three categories:

1. aged 18 or over in the relevant tax year *and* has been UK resident in at least seven out of the nine tax years immediately preceding the relevant tax year; or
2. irrespective of age has not been UK resident in at least seven out of the nine tax years immediately preceding the relevant tax year; or
3. under age 18 in the relevant tax year *and* has been UK resident in at least seven out of the nine tax years immediately preceding the relevant tax year.

In the examples immediately below it is assumed that none of the individuals are able to satisfy (a), (b) or (c) set out below.

Example 23.1
Bertram Munich is non-UK domiciled but UK resident and aged 50.
Bert has resided continuously in the UK for the last 15 tax years.
For the tax year 2008/09 Bert will need to lodge a claim for remittance basis treatment.

Example 23.2
Jose Madrid is non-UK domiciled but UK resident and aged 50.
Jose has resided continuously in the UK for the last seven tax years prior to 2008/09.
For the tax year 2008/09 Jose will need to lodge a claim for remittance basis treatment.

Example 23.3
Jose Estepona is non-UK domiciled but UK resident and aged 50.
Jose has resided continuously in the UK for the last five tax years prior to 2008/09.
For the tax year 2008/09 Jose will need to lodge a claim for remittance basis treatment.

Example 23.4
Bert Frankfurt is non-UK domiciled but UK resident and aged 50.
Bert has resided continuously in the UK for the last six tax years prior to 2008/09.

For the tax year 2008/09 Jose will need to lodge a claim for remittance basis treatment.

Example 23.5
Yashimoto Tokyo is non-UK domiciled but UK resident and aged 17.

Yashimoto has resided continuously in the UK for the last three tax years prior to 2008/09.

For the tax year 2008/09 Yashimoto will need to lodge a claim for remittance basis treatment.

Example 23.6
Milano Milan is non-UK domiciled but UK resident and aged 17.

Milano has resided continuously in the UK for the last seven tax years prior to 2008/09.

For the tax year 2008/09 Milano will need to lodge a claim for remittance basis treatment.

For the individual who is non-UK domiciled but UK resident, satisfaction of any one of the following three categories (i.e. (a), (b) and/or (c)) means that no formal claim for remittance basis treatment is required as such treatment will apply automatically:

(a) those individuals whose "unremitted foreign income and gains" (basically foreign income and capital gains arising in the relevant tax year less the amount of such income and/or gains which are remitted to the UK in that tax year) for the relevant tax year is less than £2000;
(b) those individuals who have no UK source income or gains, who have been UK resident in not more than six out of the nine tax years immediately preceding the relevant tax year and who have remitted no income or gains to the UK in the relevant tax year;
(c) those individuals who have no UK source income or gains, who are under 18 throughout the relevant tax year and who have remitted no income or gains to the UK in the relevant tax year.

Example 23.7
Bertram Munich is non-UK domiciled but UK resident and aged 50.

Bert has resided continuously in the UK for the last 15 tax years.

For the tax year 2008/09 Bert's non-UK source income amounted to £65 000 of which £64 000 was remitted to the UK in 2008/09.

For the tax year 2008/09 Bert falls into (a) above and thus will not need to lodge a claim for remittance basis treatment.

Example 23.8
Jose Madrid is non-UK domiciled but UK resident and aged 50.

Jose has resided continuously in the UK for the last seven tax years prior to 2008/09.

For the tax year 2008/09 Jose's non-UK source income amounted to £65 000 of which £56 000 was remitted to the UK in 2008/09.

For the tax year 2008/09 Jose will need to lodge a claim for remittance basis treatment as he does not fall into (a), (b) or (c) above.

Example 23.9
Jose Estepona is non-UK domiciled but UK resident and aged 50.

Jose has resided continuously in the UK for the last five tax years prior to 2008/09.

Jose has no UK source income or gains for 2008/09 and has not remitted any of his non-UK source income or gains to the UK.

For the tax year 2008/09 Jose will not need to lodge a claim for remittance basis treatment as Jose falls into (b) above (and indeed (a)).

Example 23.10
Bert Frankfurt is non-UK domiciled but UK resident and aged 50.

Bert has resided continuously in the UK for the last seven tax years prior to 2008/09.

Bert has no UK source income or gains for 2008/09 and has not remitted any of his non-UK source income or gains to the UK.

For the tax year 2008/09 Bert will need to lodge a claim for remittance basis treatment as he does not fall into (a), (b) or (c).

Example 23.11
Yashimoto Tokyo is non-UK domiciled but UK resident and aged 17.

Yashimoto has resided continuously in the UK for the last three tax years prior to 2008/09.

Yashimoto has no UK source income or gains for 2008/09 and has not remitted any of his non-UK source income or gains to the UK.

For the tax year 2008/09 Yashimoto will not need to lodge a claim for remittance basis treatment as he falls into both (b) and (c) above (and indeed (a)).

Example 23.12
Milano Milan is non-UK domiciled but UK resident and aged 17.

Milano has resided continuously in the UK for the last seven tax years prior to 2008/09.

Milano has no UK source income or gains for 2008/09 and has not remitted any of his non-UK source income or gains to the UK.

For the tax year 2008/09 Milano will not need to lodge a claim for remittance basis treatment as he falls into (c) above (and indeed (a)).

Consequences of A Claim

Where it is necessary for the non-UK domiciled but UK resident individual to claim remittance basis treatment such a claim will be made as part of the individual's self assessment Tax Return.

One of the consequences of the making of such a claim is the loss of entitlement to personal allowances *and* the capital gains tax annual exemption.

For the non-UK domiciled but UK resident individual falling within category (1) above (i.e. aged 18 or over in the tax year *and* UK resident for at least seven out of the immediately preceding nine tax years), two additional consequences follow:

- a requirement to pay £30 000 for the relevant tax year;
- a requirement to "nominate" foreign income and/or foreign chargeable gains of the relevant tax year.

The above two requirements thus only apply to those individuals who are required to claim remittance basis treatment *and* who are aged 18 or over in the relevant tax year *and* who satisfy the minimum seven out of nine tax year test.

Thus, these two additional consequences do *not* apply to those individuals within categories (2) or (3) above, i.e. those individuals who are required to lodge a claim for remittance basis treatment but who, irrespective of age, have not been resident in the UK for at least the preceding seven out of nine tax years *or* are under age 18 but have been resident in the UK for at least seven out of the immediately preceding nine tax years (or, of course, to those individuals within (a), (b) or (c) where no claim is in any event needed).

Example 23.13
Using the facts of each of Examples 23.1 to 23.12 above the following individuals would need to pay the £30 000 for the tax year 2008/09 if a claim to remittance basis treatment was made (and required to be made):

Example 23.1 Bertram Munich
Example 23.2 Jose Madrid

These are the only two non-UK domiciled but UK resident individuals who are aged 18 or over *and* who have resided in the UK for at least seven out of the immediately preceding nine tax years.

Example 23.14
Claire Texas is a non-UK domiciled but UK resident individual aged 22.
Claire has been resident in the UK for six tax years out of the preceding nine tax years prior to the tax year 2008/09.
Claire is not required to pay the £30 000 if she claims remittance basis treatment for the tax year 2008/09.
However, for the tax year 2009/10 Claire will have been UK resident for seven out of the immediately preceding nine tax years and thus if she claims remittance basis treatment for the tax year 2009/10 she will be required to pay the £30 000.

It is important to appreciate that the individual, when forming a view as to whether a claim for remittance basis treatment should be made (in particular if this means the £30 000 charge has to be paid) needs to take account of any non-UK source income and/or capital gains which would be imputed to the individual under the various anti-avoidance provisions (see Chapter 17) with respect to non-UK resident trusts (and companies) should no claim be lodged.

Example 23.15

Dominic Barcelona, a non-UK domiciled but UK resident individual, will need to pay the £30 000 charge for the tax year 2008/09 should he decide to elect for remittance basis treatment.

Some years ago he set up a non-UK resident trust under which he may benefit. The annual income of the trust is usually around £200 000.

This income is imputed to Dominic but where remittance basis treatment applies no income tax charge arises so long as the monies remain outside the UK.

If, however, he does not elect for remittance basis treatment this trust income will be imputed to him without him having the benefit of remittance basis treatment. A 40% income tax charge (i.e. £80 000) will thus arise.

£30 000 Charge

The £30 000 is to be paid through the self assessment system. Where the £30 000 is paid from a non-UK source *directly* to HMRC by cheque or electronic transfer the £30 000 will itself not be treated as a remittance. Thus, no tax liability will arise thereon. Any cheque needs to be drawn on a non-UK bank account and any electronic transfer should not be made via a UK bank account.

Where the transfer is via a UK bank account prior to onward transmission to HMRC then the £30 000 will be treated as a remittance and potentially taxable depending upon the source of the funds utilised.

The £30 000 applies if the non-UK domiciled individual is UK resident in a tax year even if residency is for only part of the tax year, i.e. there is no facility for an apportionment of the £30 000.

Nomination

As part of the claim for remittance basis treatment the non-UK domiciled individual falling within category (1) above is required to "nominate" either foreign income and/or foreign chargeable gains of the relevant tax year. The nominated amount will relate to one of three categories of non-UK source income/gains, namely, relevant foreign income, employment income and capital gains.

The amount of income and/or capital gains nominated is subject to tax on the arising basis. The amount nominated cannot be such as to precipitate a tax charge thereon in excess of £30 000 (thus it is not possible for the individual to nominate "too much" income/gains). Where the actual nominated amount gives rise to a tax charge of less than £30 000 the individual is treated as if in fact they had also in addition nominated enough extra income (not capital gains) so as to, in total, give rise to the £30 000 charge. In this case the nominated amount is actually made up of the actual amount nominated plus an amount of income deemed to have been nominated. This distinction is important.

The income which is deemed to have been nominated is not, however, subject to the ordering rules which are discussed below (i.e. where income and/or capital gains which have actually been nominated are in whole or in part remitted to the UK at a time when any non-UK source income/gains (non-nominated) have not been remitted, ordering rules apply to determine what income/gains are deemed to have been remitted). In addition, when this deemed nominated amount of income is remitted to the UK a tax charge arises thereon and no part of the £30 000 can be regarded as having already been paid in respect thereof. Double tax therefore appears to apply to this deemed income should it ever be remitted to the UK.

Assuming the individual nominates the requisite amount (i.e. no deemed nominated amount is necessary) the individual's tax position is relevant. Thus, for example, in the case of a higher rate income tax payer in the relevant tax year the maximum nominated amount of foreign income would be £75 000 (i.e. £30 000/0.4), i.e. a rate of 40% on £75 000 produces £30 000.

If in the relevant tax year the individual is a basic rate (i.e. 20%) taxpayer then the maximum nominated amount of foreign income would be £150 000 (i.e. £30 000/0.2).

Where the nominated amount comprises exclusively foreign chargeable gains the applicable rate will be the new rate of 18%. Thus, the maximum nominated amount will be £166 667 (i.e. £30 000/0.18). This will apply irrespective of the rate of income tax applicable to the individual as the rate of capital gains tax is no longer linked to the individual's applicable rate of income tax (as was the case prior to 6 April 2008).

Now it may be that the individual decides to nominate an amount in respect of which the tax liability of the individual is less than the required £30 000 in the hope of reducing the amount needed to be paid to still secure remittance basis treatment. However, in this case, the actual nominated amount (which may comprise income and/or capital gains) is increased by an amount of deemed income (not capital gains) so as to produce the £30 000 charge in total. This deeming applies even if in fact the individual has insufficient income to be so deemed nominated. The deemed amount of tax will thus be income tax.

The effect is that £30 000 will always be payable. It will thus not be possible to reduce this figure by nominating a smaller amount.

Example 23.16
Henri Nice is a non-UK domiciled but UK resident individual and has been resident in the UK for the last 15 tax years. He is aged 46.

He is a higher rate taxpayer.

Prior to the tax year 2008/09 Henri had never received any non-UK source income or gains. However, in the tax year 2008/09 he anticipates receiving one of the following amounts of non-UK source income:

(a) £45 000
(b) £75 000
(c) £180 000

Henri is proposing to claim remittance basis treatment for 2008/09 as he does not wish to remit any income to the UK.

(a)
Henri decides to nominate the £45 000. However, as this produces only £18 000 (i.e. 40% of £45 000) income tax a further £30 000 of income is deemed to have been nominated. This then produces the £30 000 charge. It would thus not make sense for Henri to make a remittance claim should (a) occur as the cost to him will be £30 000. Without the claim a liability of only £18 000 arises thus saving Henri £12 000.

(b)
It would not matter under this option whether a claim for remittance basis treatment was made or not. In either case the income tax charge is £30 000.

(c)
By nominating £75 000 of income precipitates the £30 000 tax charge. However, by claiming remittance basis treatment an income tax charge of £72 000 (i.e. 40% of £180 000) is avoided, producing a net tax saving of £42 000.

As nominated income/capital gain may be remitted without precipitating an additional tax charge, as tax will already have been paid thereon (i.e. the £30 000), it might therefore be thought that the "best" strategy for the non-UK domiciled but UK resident individual claiming the remittance basis would be to always remit to the UK the nominated amount (as the tax thereon will already have been paid in any event, i.e. the £30 000).

Unfortunately, under the rules, where any part of the actual (not deemed) nominated income or capital gains, whether for the current tax year or any previous tax year (beginning with the tax year 2008/09), is remitted to the UK but the individual has other non-UK source income and/or capital gains (not nominated) whether arising in the tax year or any previous tax year (beginning with the tax year 2008/09) which have not in their entirety been remitted to the UK, then effectively the quantum of nominated amount remitted is treated as a remittance out of the latter (i.e. the non-nominated amount) and thus subject to tax (the £30 000 not being deemed to apply to this substituted amount).

The aggregate actual nominated amount thus remains intact (i.e. none of it is assumed to have been remitted to the UK) and an amount of the non-nominated income or gains is substituted thus precipitating a tax charge thereon (i.e. the individual will have paid £30 000 plus the tax charge arising on the remittance).

The implication of these rules is that until the individual's entire non-UK source income and capital gains (other than the actual nominated amounts) arising since 6 April 2008 have been remitted to the UK it is not possible for the individual to access the "tax-free" actual nominated amounts for each tax year.

The effective substitution of non-nominated income/capital gain for remittances of actual nominated income/capital gain is carried out by applying a sequence of rules to the various categories of non-UK source income/capital gains (which are in fact the same categories as used when determining remittance from "mixed funds"; see below) for the relevant tax year. Where insufficient non-nominated income/capital gains arise in the relevant tax year for matching, the whole process is repeated for the immediately preceding tax year and so on until a full matching has occurred.

The categories utilised for matching and the order of the matching is as follows:

- relevant foreign earnings;
- foreign specific employment income;
- relevant foreign income;
- foreign chargeable gains;
- relevant foreign earnings subject to foreign tax;
- foreign specific employment income subject to foreign tax;
- relevant foreign income subject to foreign tax;
- foreign chargeable gains subject to foreign tax.

"Relevant foreign earnings" refers to earnings of the non-UK domiciled but UK resident individual from a non-UK resident employer in respect of duties all of which are performed outside the UK; the remittance basis applies to such income.

"Foreign specific employment income" refers to, inter alia, termination payments and share-related income.

"Relevant foreign income" refers to, inter alia, foreign source interest and dividends and also includes foreign source pension income.

"Foreign chargeable gains" refers to chargeable gains arising on the disposal of assets situated outside the UK.

Even where remittances have actually been made from the non-nominated categories of non-UK source income and gains (as well as remittances having been made from the nominated amount) the above rules will also determine and then substitute the deemed remittances resulting from the application of these rules for any actual remittances (in other words, the actual remittances in a sense are deemed not to have occurred and in their place are substituted the remittances of the categories of income produced by the above rules).

Where, however, the individual does *not* remit to the UK any part of the actual nominated amount in a tax year (i.e. does not remit any part of earlier tax years' nominated amounts or that amount for the tax year concerned) then there is no requirement for the above rules to be applied to determine which foreign source income and/or capital gains have been remitted to the UK. The amounts actually remitted will simply be identified with their specific source and subject to tax as normal.

Example 23.17
Felix Stuttgart is a non-UK domiciled but UK resident individual and should he wish to utilise the remittance basis a claim will need to be lodged. Felix is a higher rate taxpayer.

In the tax year 2008/09 Felix receives the following income and capital gains:

£100 000 of foreign bank interest
£200 000 of relevant foreign earnings

£300 000 of foreign capital gains
£150 000 of foreign capital gains subject to foreign tax

Each of the above amounts have been credited to separate accounts (i.e. no mixed funds).

Unless Felix lodges a claim for remittance basis treatment all the above income/capital gains will fall subject to tax on the arising basis. A claim therefore needs to be lodged.

He nominates £75 000 of his "relevant foreign earnings" but intends to remit none of this amount. As a consequence his income tax liability will be based upon the actual categories of income/gains remitted.

He wants to know his tax position should any of the following occur:

(a) a remittance of £50 000 of the bank interest;
(b) a remittance of the £150 000 of the foreign capital gains subject to foreign tax;
(c) a remittance of £50 000 of the foreign capital gains.

(a)
The remittance gives rise to an income tax liability of £20 000 (i.e. 40% of £50 000) giving rise to an aggregate tax liability of £50 000 due to the need to pay in addition the £30 000 (i.e. 40% on the nominated £75 000 taxed on the arising basis).

(b)
The remittance gives rise to an income tax liability of £27 000 (i.e. 18% of £150 000) giving rise to an aggregate tax liability of £57 000 (less credit for the foreign tax paid) due to the need to pay in addition the £30 000 (i.e. 40% on the nominated £75 000 taxed on the arising basis).

(c)
The remittance gives rise to a capital gains tax liability of £9000 (i.e. 18% of £50 000) giving rise to an aggregate tax liability of £39 000 due to the need to pay in addition the £30 000 (i.e. 40% on the nominated £75 000 taxed on the arising basis).

Example 23.18
Felix Stuttgart is a non-UK domiciled but UK resident individual and should he wish to utilise the remittance basis a claim will need to be lodged. Felix is a higher rate taxpayer.

In the tax year 2008/09 Felix receives the following income and capital gains:

£100 000 of foreign bank interest
£200 000 of relevant foreign earnings
£300 000 of foreign capital gains
£150 000 of foreign capital gains subject to foreign tax

Unless Felix lodges a claim for remittance basis treatment all the above income/capital gains will fall subject to tax on the arising basis. A claim therefore needs to be lodged.

He nominates £75 000 of his "relevant foreign earnings" and remits £25 000 thereof.

He wants to know his tax position should any of the following occur:

(a) a remittance of £50 000 of the bank interest;
(b) a remittance of the £150 000 of the foreign capital gains subject to foreign tax;
(c) a remittance of £50 000 of the foreign capital gains.

As Felix has remitted some of his actual nominated amount and has not remitted all his non-nominated income/gains then it is necessary to "match" the remittances in the order set out below:

- relevant foreign earnings;
- foreign specific employment income;
- relevant foreign income;
- foreign chargeable gains;
- relevant foreign earnings subject to foreign tax;
- foreign specific employment income subject to foreign tax;
- relevant foreign income subject to foreign tax;
- foreign chargeable gains subject to foreign tax.

(a)
The remittance of £25 000 of relevant foreign earnings plus the remittance of £50 000 of bank interest amounts to £75 000. This £75 000 is deemed to have been remitted out of the £200 000 of relevant foreign earnings precipitating an income tax liability of £30 000 (i.e. 40% of £75 000) plus the £30 000 charge producing an aggregate tax liability of £60 000.

(b)
The remittance of £150 000 of foreign capital gains subject to foreign tax plus the remittance of £25 000 of relevant foreign earnings gives rise to a remittance of £175 000. This £175 000 is deemed to have been remitted out of the £200 000 of relevant foreign earnings precipitating an income tax liability of £70 000 (i.e. 40% of £175 000) plus the £30 000 charge producing an aggregate tax liability of £100 000.

(c)
The remittance of £50 000 of foreign capital gains plus the remittance of £25 000 of relevant foreign earnings gives rise to a remittance of £75 000. This £75 000 is deemed to have been remitted out of the £200 000 of relevant foreign earnings precipitating an income tax liability of £30 000 (i.e. 40% of £75 000) plus the £30 000 charge producing an aggregate tax liability of £60 000.

It will be noted that under (c) although Felix remitted £50 000 of foreign capital gains (which should precipitate a capital gains tax liability based on 18%) the application of the "matching" rules results in this amount being deemed to be a remittance out of "relevant foreign earnings" on which the liability is to income tax at 40%.

In addition, under all of the above, although Felix actually remitted £25 000 from his nominated amount of £75 000 this is substituted as a remittance from "relevant foreign earnings" thus leaving intact £75 000 of unremitted nominated income (the £25 000 of nominated income not having been regarded as remitted to the UK).

Thus, no part of any of the remittances under (a), (b) or (c) was remitted "tax free" despite the £30 000 charge having been paid.

Where no Claim is Necessary

For the three categories of non-UK domiciled but UK resident individual where no claim for remittance basis treatment is necessary (i.e. (a), (b) and (c) above) none of the above discussion relating to the £30 000 or the need to nominate income/gains applies.

Even without the claim, for those individuals in categories (a), (b) or (c) above, the remittance basis will automatically apply to non-UK source income and capital gains for those individuals.

It should also be noted that no loss of entitlement to, inter alia, personal allowances or the capital gains tax annual exemption arises for those individuals falling within (a), (b) or (c).

REMITTANCES TO THE UK

As seen in Chapter 2 the individual is subject to income and capital gains taxes on income and capital gains only as and when any part (or the whole) of the income and/or gains are "remitted" to the UK. It is thus necessary to be able to identify when such remittances occur and, if so, the quantification of the remittance.

FA 2008 has had a significant impact on this area. In particular, the pre FA 2008 definition of "remittance" has been significantly widened so as to catch remittances not previously caught. The new definitions and conditions apply to:

- "relevant foreign earnings" charged on the remittance basis;
- "relevant foreign income" (RFI) charged on the remittance basis;
- "foreign chargeable gains" charged on the remittance basis;
- "offshore income gains" (treated for remittance purposes as relevant foreign income).
- various anti-avoidance provisions (e.g. section 87 TCGA 1992).

Unless the context otherwise requires the terms "income" and "gains" refer to all of the above categories.

Despite the "new" rules becoming effective with effect from 6 April 2008 there is a degree of retrospection to the "new" rules and thus it is not safe to assume that all pre 6 April 2008 income and gains of the individual can be remitted tax free under the "old" rules.

In very broad terms, post FA 2008, the income or gains of the individual may be regarded as having been remitted to the UK (and thus taxable) where the individual or a so-called "relevant person" effects the remittance to the UK whether for the benefit in the UK of the individual or a relevant person and whether or not the remittance takes the form of the actual (in whole or in part) non-UK source income or gains or some other form of property which represents that income or gains.

Thus, inter alia, the new FA 2008 provisions catch (i.e. tax):

- the bringing into the UK of a car purchased outside the UK by the individual out of the income or gains;
- the bringing into the UK of a car purchased outside the UK by the individual out of the income or gains but gifted to the individual's wife prior to bringing the car into the UK;
- the gifting of the income or gains to the individual's wife who then brings the monies into the UK.

It should, however, be noted that even pre FA 2008 where the individual utilised either foreign source earnings and/or foreign source capital gains (i.e. not relevant foreign income) to purchase an asset outside the UK which was then brought into the UK by the individual (the bringing into the UK of an asset by someone other than the individual following a gift from the latter was not taxable), a taxable remittance of the foreign source earnings/capital gains arose.

The ability of the individual to bring an asset into the UK without precipitating a tax charge was restricted to the use of relevant foreign income to effect the purchase; however, a subsequent sale of the asset, purchased out of relevant foreign income, while the asset was in the UK gave rise at that point to a remittance of the relevant foreign income used to effect the purchase.

Example 23.19

Chuck Toronto, a non-UK domiciled but UK resident individual, had generated non-UK source income and capital gains by 5 April 2006 as follows:

Foreign source employment income	£250 000
Relevant foreign income	£150 000
Foreign capital gains	£125 000

Each of these three amounts had been credited to three separate non-UK bank accounts BC1, BC2 and BC3, respectively.

Chuck very much wanted to purchase a very valuable vase (£125 000) he had seen in China while on holiday for display in his UK home. He accordingly purchased the vase in August 2007 and brought it into the UK the following month.

If he purchased the vase using monies from accounts BC1 or BC3 then a taxable remittance of the monies in BC1 or BC2 as appropriate would be deemed to have occurred.

However, the utilisation of the monies in BC2 would not have resulted in a taxable remittance (although a subsequent sale while the vase was in the UK would at that time constitute a taxable remittance).

FA 2008 now seeks to remove the distinction for tax purposes between the remittance treatment of "relevant foreign income" on the one hand and "foreign employment income" and "foreign capital gains" on the other when such monies have been used to purchase assets out of the UK which have then been brought into the UK. At the same time, FA 2008 has also significantly broadened what constitutes a "remittance".

Under FA 2008 it is thus now not only the remittance of *money* which gives rise to a taxable remittance to the UK but also a remittance of *property other than money* (e.g. pottery; cars; antiques; etc.) if such property is derived directly or indirectly from the income or gains.

However, FA 2008 does provide for:

- a degree of transitional relief, i.e. a remittance of the income or gains which have arisen pre FA 2008 may be remitted post FA 2008 but subject to the pre FA 2008 rules. This relief is not, however, available in all cases (e.g. source cessation). This form of transitional relief is normally referred to as "grandfathering" (see below);
- certain otherwise taxable remittances to be classified as exempt property (a new concept introduced by FA 2008) and thus not subject to tax on remittance (see below).

ALIENATION OF INCOME AND GAINS AND ASSET PURCHASE

"Alienation" refers to the transfer (typically by gift) of the income or gains (or an asset purchased therefrom) from the individual to another person (e.g. the spouse) who then brings the money (or asset) into the UK. The FA 2008 provisions in principle treat such a remittance as taxable.

"Asset purchase" refers to the purchase of an asset (e.g. a painting) by the individual out of the UK utilising the income or gains followed by the subsequent bringing into the UK of the asset either by the individual or a person to whom the asset has been gifted. The FA 2008 provisions in principle treat such a remittance as taxable.

Under FA 2008, an individual's income or gains are "remitted to the UK" if one of three sets of conditions are satisfied.

The first set of conditions is the "catch all" category and seeks to treat as a remittance a broad range of activities ("Conditions A/B"); the second set of conditions is more specific and seeks to treat as a remittance property which has been given to one of a specified class of person ("Condition C"); and the third set of conditions seeks to treat as a remittance gifts to "third parties" involving a "connected operation" ("Condition D").

Conditions A/B

The first set of conditions provides that a "remittance to the UK" is where:

> money or other property is brought to, or received or used in, the UK by or for the benefit of a "relevant person" and the property *is* the income or gains *or* the

property is property of the "relevant person" that has been derived wholly or in part from the income or gains.

Condition C

The second set of conditions provides that a "remittance to the UK" is where:

"qualifying property" of a "gift recipient" is brought to, or received or used in, the UK, and is "enjoyed" by a "relevant person".

Condition D

The third set of conditions provides that a "remittance to the UK" is where:

property of a person other than a "relevant person" (excluding that referred to in Condition C) is brought to, or received or used in, the UK, and is "enjoyed" by a "relevant person" in circumstances where there is a "connected operation".

Extensions of the Definition of "Remittance to the UK" for Each of Conditions A/B, C and D

FA 2008 extends each of the above:

1. to cover the position where the property/money is used outside the UK but in connection with a "relevant debt" (broadly, a debt somehow or other related to the property/money);
2. to cover the use of the property/money as consideration for the provision of services in the UK.

For simplicity of explanation the main consideration below is restricted to examining the implication of Conditions A/B, C and D above ignoring the extensions of the legislation as indicated under (1) and (2) above. A brief look at the implications of (1) and (2) is then taken at the end of this section (just prior to a consideration of "exempt property").

For the purposes of Conditions A/B, C and D a "relevant person" is defined as:

- the individual;
- the individual's spouse;
- the child or grandchild of the individual or spouse if the child is under 18;
- a close company (i.e. broadly a company under the "control" of five or fewer shareholders whether the company is UK resident or not) in which a person above is a shareholder;
- the trustees of a trust where any of the above individuals is a beneficiary (thus being the settlor does not, per se, cause the trustees to be a relevant person);
- cohabitees living together as husband and wife.

Example 23.20
Albert and Claudia have been married for 20 years.
They have a son, Tom, aged 27, and a daughter, Fiona, aged 31, who has married Brian aged 35.
Brian and Fiona have three children, Matthew (10), Karen (15) and Nicholas (19).
Under FA 2008 relevant persons of Albert are Claudia; Matthew and Karen.

This definition encompasses quite a wide range of individuals (including trustees) although it excludes, for example, children/grandchildren aged 18 or over, brothers, sisters, nephews, nieces, parents and grandparents irrespective of age. The definition, extremely unusually, extends to cohabitees but only where the cohabitees are living together as husband and wife. Thus, two people (e.g. two friends) simply living under the same roof but not as husband and wife would not constitute "relevant persons".

It should be noted that the term "relevant person" includes the individual concerned and is thus not, as might be expected, a reference to persons related to the individual but excluding the individual. Thus, in Example 23.20 above "relevant persons" are Albert, Claudia, Matthew and Karen.

CONDITIONS A/B

Under these Conditions, for a remittance to the UK of the income or gains to arise does not literally require the remittance of the monies. Thus, for example, if the individual concerned utilised the monies to purchase an asset outside the UK (e.g. an antique painting) and then imported the asset into the UK, this will be sufficient to trigger a remittance of the monies as the asset has in essence been derived from these monies.

The quantum of the remittance is the amount of income/gains used to purchase the asset. Thus, for example, where an asset is purchased outside the UK with the individual's income/gains but brought into the UK at a later date when its value has diminished, the remittance will still be a remittance of the amount of income/gains used to effect the purchase not the equivalent of the current market value of the asset at the date it is remitted (i.e. brought in) to the UK.

These Conditions also apply where the benefit of the remittance is for someone who is treated as a "relevant person" (e.g. the benefit is not for the individual) irrespective of who actually effects the remittance (i.e. the individual or a relevant person other than the individual) whether of money or property. Thus, the individual may gift the income/gains outside the UK to a relevant person who then brings the income/gains into the UK; or the individual may purchase an asset outside the UK which is gifted to the relevant person outside the UK who then brings the asset into the UK; or, alternatively, the individual may purchase an asset outside the UK which is brought into the UK and then is gifted to the relevant person. In all these cases a remittance to the UK will have occurred on the part of the individual with respect to the income or gains and thus a charge to tax will have been precipitated on the individual.

In short, even though the individual does not enjoy in the UK the benefits of the income/gains and/or any asset purchased out of the monies but a relevant person does (e.g. his spouse; his young son) then a taxable remittance on the part of the individual arises.

Example 23.21

income & dividends

Chiquita Sweden, a non-UK domiciled but UK resident individual, has RFI for the tax year 2008/09 of £275 000. This money has been credited to a newly opened bank account in Bermuda. No interest has been credited to the account.

Chiquita uses the income in 2008/09 as follows:

NB

(a) she remits £75 000 directly to her UK bank account;
(b) she transfers £25 000 from the Bermuda account to her husband's bank account in Stockholm of which he then remits £15 000 to the UK;
(c) while she and her daughter are in New York she draws a cheque on the Bermuda account to pay for a pair of shoes she bought for her daughter as a birthday present; the cost of the shoes was £2500. Her daughter (age 12) wears the shoes when she returns with her mum to the UK;
(d) while she and her daughter are in New York Chiquita purchases a set of golf clubs for £10 000 for her son (age 22) which she gives to him on her return to the UK;
(e) she transfers £7500 to her best friend's New York bank account who immediately transfers it to her UK bank account.

The tax position of each of the above transactions on the part of Chiquita is as follows:

(a) £75 000 taxable. She has simply remitted RFI to the UK.
(b) £15 000 taxable. The transfer to her husband's account of £25 000 gives rise at that point to no tax charge. However, the subsequent transfer by her husband of £15 000 to the UK is a transfer by (and in fact for the benefit of) a relevant person.
(c) <u>Not taxable</u>. Property (i.e. the shoes) derives from the RFI and this property has been brought to the UK by a relevant person. Prima facie, a taxable remittance has occurred. However, "<u>the shoes</u>" qualify as "<u>exempt property</u>" (see below) and thus the RFI has not been remitted.
(d) Taxable. Property (i.e. the golf clubs) derives from the RFI and this property has been brought to the UK by a relevant person (i.e. Chiquita) albeit not for the benefit of a relevant person (i.e. the son). Nevertheless the bringing to the UK by a relevant person precipitates a taxable remittance.
(e) Not taxable. The transfer to her best friend's account of £7500 gives rise at that point to no tax charge. The subsequent transfer by her friend of the £7500 to the UK is not a transfer by (or in fact for the benefit of) a relevant person.

CONDITION C

The second set of conditions provides that a "remittance to the UK" is where:

> "qualifying property" of a "gift recipient" is brought to, or received or used in, the UK, and is "enjoyed" by a "relevant person".

For Condition C therefore to apply there must be both "qualifying property" and a "gift recipient" with "enjoyment" being that of a "relevant person". Effectively, this Condition is designed to prevent the individual gifting property or money to someone, subsequent to which, the property or money is brought into the UK but is then enjoyed by a relevant person (which includes the individual).

If, however, the relevant person provides full consideration for the enjoyment or, if the property or money is enjoyed to the virtual exclusion of all relevant persons, such enjoyment is to be disregarded (i.e. no remittance will have been deemed to have occurred in these circumstances).

For this purpose a "gift recipient" is a person other than a relevant person to whom the individual makes a gift (i.e. for no, or below market value, consideration) of money or property that is income/gains of the individual or derives from the income/gains of the individual. Thus, a gift to an individual who does not fall within the definition of "relevant person" (see above) would constitute a "gift recipient".

Whether the gift is to a relevant person or not is determined at the time of the gift.

Should the recipient subsequently become a relevant person, at that time the person ceases to be a "gift recipient" (e.g. recipient subsequently becomes the spouse of the individual or a cohabitee of the individual then living as husband and wife). In such cases Condition C will thereafter have no relevance in the determination of whether a remittance to the UK occurs. It will become necessary to consider Conditions A/B.

"Qualifying property", inter alia, refers to property that the individual gave to the gift recipient or anything that derives from that property. Qualifying property would thus, for example, include an asset which had been purchased by the gift recipient from a gift of income/gains by the individual (i.e. the asset would derive from the income/gains).

Condition C, unlike Conditions A/B, has no relevance to direct remittances to the UK by the individual. The individual is required, for Condition C to operate, to have made a gift to a non-relevant person of property or money.

As indicated above when considering Conditions A/B, the term "relevant person" is arguably somewhat limited. Condition C is thus designed to "catch" gifts to persons other than to relevant persons, for example gifts to brothers, sisters, etc. subsequent to which a relevant person enjoys in the UK the property or money gifted.

CONDITION D

The third set of conditions provides that a "remittance to the UK" is where:

> property of a person other than a relevant person (excluding "qualifying property" of a "gift recipient", i.e. Condition C) is brought to, or received or used in, the UK, and is "enjoyed" by a "relevant person" in circumstances where there is a "connected operation".

The term "connected operation" in relation to property means an operation which is effected with reference to a "qualifying disposition". A "qualifying disposition" is a disposition made by a relevant person (including the individual) to or for the benefit of a person who is a not a relevant person. Where, however, this disposition is made for full consideration it is not a qualifying disposition.

In essence, this Condition is designed to prevent the enjoyment in the UK of property or money by a relevant person (which includes the individual) as a consequence of a gift from a relevant person (not the individual) to a non-relevant person (a so-called "connected operation").

Condition D is designed to "catch" where the individual may have made a gift to a relevant person who then in turn gifts the property received from the individual to a non-relevant person who brings the gift into the UK for the benefit of a relevant person (including the individual).

If, however, the relevant person provides full consideration for the enjoyment or if the property or money is enjoyed to the virtual exclusion of all relevant persons such enjoyment is to be disregarded (i.e. no remittance will have been deemed to have occurred in these circumstances).

TRANSITIONAL PROVISIONS (PRE 6 APRIL 2008 INCOME/GAINS)

As indicated above, FA 2008 provides for certain transitional reliefs to apply. These transitional provisions relate to income and capital gains which arose pre 6 April 2008. However, it is necessary to consider the position separately for RFI and non-RFI (i.e. income other than interest and dividends which would thus include, for example, employment income and capital gains).

These transitional provisions apply to each of the above Conditions A/B, C and D.

Income or Gains (Other than RFI) Arising pre 6 April 2008

The newly introduced concept of "relevant person" is not applicable with respect to such non-RFI and capital gains. The pre 6 April 2008 tax position is maintained.

Thus, a taxable remittance only occurs if the remittance of the non-RFI or the capital gains (or property derived therefrom) is effected by, or for the benefit of, the individual.

RFI: interest, dividends, non UK Trading Income, non UK Property Income

For example, it is open to the individual *on or after 6 April 2008* to effect any of the following such that a taxable remittance to the UK will not occur:

(a) the individual uses the non-RFI/gains to purchase an asset outside the UK, transfers it to any person while the asset is out of the UK who then brings the asset into the UK;
(b) the individual simply transfers outside the UK the non-RFI/gains to a any person who then brings the monies into the UK.

It is important, however, to avoid a taxable remittance in (a) and (b) above that the individual cannot, and does not in fact at some point in the future, benefit from the bringing into the UK by the person of the non-RFI/gains or asset; otherwise a remittance by the individual will have occurred. For example, if the individual transferred cash to his spouse's non-UK situs bank account and the spouse then brought the monies into the joint bank account in the UK a taxable remittance will have occurred.

The remittance to the UK of the non-RFI/gains by the individual will, however, constitute a taxable remittance as will the purchase of assets by the individual outside the UK using the non-RFI/gains followed by a remittance of the assets to the UK by the individual.

In (a) and (b) above it does not matter at what point in time the person (not the individual) brings the non-RFI/gains or assets into the UK as no remittance will arise at that time.

Thus, where the individual on or after 6 April 2008 still has pre 6 April 2008 non-RFI and/or gains outside the UK, the only manner in which a tax-free remittance to the UK is possible, on or after 6 April 2008, is if a gift is made to another person (either of the money or property first purchased out of the money) who then remits the money (or property) to the UK; the individual must not, however, be in a position to enjoy the remittance personally.

RFI Arising pre 6 April 2008

The transitional provisions with respect to RFI (which includes mainly interest and dividends; RFI, however, also includes non-UK source trading income and non-UK source property income) are more complex than those applying to non-RFI and capital gains discussed above. This is because the provisions which applied pre FA 2008 in determining when remittances of RFI occurred were different to those which applied to non-RFI/gains.

The transitional provisions in principle seek to retain the pre FA 2008 tax treatment for pre 6 April 2008 RFI while at the same time introducing the "new" provisions which apply to RFI arising on or after 6 April 2008.

With respect to RFI which arose pre 6 April 2008, FA 2008 provides a general rule to determine when a taxable remittance from such income arises. This general rule is subject to (i.e. overridden by) two specific situations either of which, if satisfied, result in no taxable remittance of RFI.

None of these transitional provisions, however, affect the pre 6 April 2008 tax position, per se, i.e. the transitional provisions are not retrospective.

The two specific situations referred to above are as follows:

(a) if, before 6 April 2008, property (including money) consisting of or deriving from an individual's relevant foreign income is brought to or received or used in the UK by or for the benefit of a relevant person treat the relevant foreign income as not remitted to the UK on or after that date (*if it otherwise would be regarded as so remitted*).

(b) if before 12 March 2008, property (other than money) consisting of or deriving from an individual's relevant foreign income was acquired by a relevant person, treat the relevant foreign income as not remitted to the UK on or after 6 April 2008 (*if it otherwise would be regarded as so remitted*).

[handwritten margin note: Tight timeframe of history → now]

Considering the situation described in (b) first:

[handwritten note: All CC purchases before this date were ok]

Pre 12 March 2008 Condition

This deals with the position where assets (not money) have been acquired by a relevant person before 12 March 2008.

Where this is the case such assets can be brought to the UK at any point in time on or after 6 April 2008 without precipitating a taxable remittance of the RFI used to effect the purchase. It does not matter who remits the asset nor for whose benefit.

Thus, any of the following if effected on or after 6 April 2008 will not give rise to a taxable remittance of the RFI used to effect the asset purchase:

(i) remittance of the asset by the individual who owns the asset;
(ii) remittance of the asset by the relevant person (not the individual) who owns the asset;
(iii) remittance of the asset following a gift of the asset, at any time, by the relevant person who owns the asset;
(iv) remittance of monies arising from sale of the asset outside the UK (or where the sale is effected in the UK).

There is no applicable time limit within which the asset must be brought to the UK and/or when it needs to be sold to avoid taxable remittance treatment.

Furthermore, it does not matter whether a relevant person (including the individual) or another person is involved in (i) to (iv).

Considering the situation described in (a) above:

Pre 6 April 2008 Condition

This deals with the position where assets or the RFI itself is brought to the UK on or before 6 April 2008 by or for the benefit of a relevant person. However, as (b) above specifically refers to assets acquired by relevant persons pre 12 March 2008 then (a) has no application to such assets.

Thus, (a) refers to:

(i) assets acquired by relevant persons on or after 12 March 2008 and brought to the UK pre 6 April 2008;
(ii) RFI which arose at any time pre 6 April 2008 if it was brought to the UK by a relevant person pre 6 April 2008.

Under (i) above no remittance of the RFI used to purchase the assets occurs whether the relevant person is the individual or not.

Under (ii) above no remittance of the RFI occurs only if its remittance to the UK is not by (or for the benefit of) the individual; a remittance of the RFI by the individual precipitates a remittance of the RFI at that time. Thus, (ii) presupposes that the individual has gifted the RFI to the relevant person prior to remittance.

Unlike (b) above, (a) refers to not only assets but the RFI itself (i.e. money). However, unlike (b), for (a) to apply the assets or RFI need to have been brought to the UK on or before 6 April 2008 (i.e. a time limit is imposed). If, however, the assets or RFI are not brought to the UK within this time limit, see below.

Assuming the conditions in (a) above are satisfied with respect to the property (including money) then any of the following if subsequently effected (with respect to the property including money) on or after 6 April 2008 whether within the UK or not will not give rise to a taxable remittance of the RFI at that time:

(i) asset gifted by the relevant person to another person;
(ii) asset gifted by the relevant person to another person who then sells the asset;
(iii) asset sold by the relevant person;
(iv) RFI (which has been remitted to the UK pre 6 April 2008 by a relevant person other than the individual; see above) gifted by the relevant person to another person;
(v) RFI (which has been remitted to the UK pre 6 April 2008 by a relevant person other than the individual; see above) gifted by the relevant person to another person who purchases an asset;
(vi) RFI (which has been remitted to the UK pre 6 April 2008 by a relevant person other than the individual; see above) used to purchase an asset.

There is no applicable time limit within which any of (i) to (vi) above needs to be carried out (assuming the asset or RFI was brought to the UK pre 6 April 2008).

Furthermore, it does not matter whether the relevant person (including the individual) or another person is involved in (i) to (vi). For example, under (iv) above the gift of the RFI by the individual to the relevant person pre 6 April 2008 who then remitted the RFI to the UK pre 6 April 2008 may, on or after 6 April 2008, gift the RFI "back to" the individual (whose RFI it originally was) whether, within or outside the UK, without the individual then subject to tax on the RFI. This does presuppose that there was no collusion/agreement between the two individuals that this was to occur (i.e. there was no agreement pre 6 April 2008 by which the individual agreed to gift the RFI to the relevant person conditional on the latter then post 5 April 2008 re-gifting the RFI back to the individual).

General Transitional Rule

The general transitional rule deals with the position re pre 6 April 2008 RFI which is not dealt with under either of the above specific conditions (a) and (b) above.

Thus, the general rule applies to:

- assets acquired [not money] on or after 6 April 2008;
- assets acquired on or after 12 March and pre 6 April 2008 but not brought to the UK on or before 6 April 2008;
- RFI not brought to the UK on or before 6 April 2008.

Under the general rule a taxable remittance of pre 6 April 2008 RFI only occurs on or after 6 April 2008 if the RFI and/or assets derived therefrom (falling within any of the above categories to which the rule applies) are remitted to the UK for the benefit of the individual. If a relevant person (not including the individual) brings the RFI or assets to the UK no taxable remittance of the RFI occurs assuming that the individual does not enjoy the remittance by the relevant person.

Thus, under the general rule, any of the following if effected on or after 6 April 2008 will not give rise to a taxable remittance of the RFI:

- assets acquired on or after 6 April 2008 by the individual but gifted to any person who brings the asset to the UK (not for the individual's benefit);
- assets acquired on or after 12 March and pre 6 April 2008 by the individual but not brought to the UK on or before 6 April 2008 which are then gifted by the individual to any person who brings the asset to the UK on or after 6 April 2008 (not for the individual's benefit);
- RFI not brought to the UK on or before 6 April 2008 but which is gifted by the individual to any person who brings the RFI to the UK on or after 6 April 2008 (not for the individual's benefit).

Some observations:

- the purchase by the individual of an asset outside the UK out of pre 6 April 2008 RFI on or after 12 March but not brought to the UK pre 6 April 2008 cannot now be brought to the UK without precipitating a taxable remittance for the benefit of the individual; it could, however, be given to another person for them to remit assuming the individual doesn't enjoy it; whereas if the asset had been purchased outside the UK by the individual pre 12 March 2008 it could on or after be brought to the UK by the individual without precipitating a taxable remittance;

- pre 6 April 2008 RFI not brought to the UK pre 6 April 2008 can be remitted without precipitating a taxable remittance if gifted by the individual to any person prior to remittance (and the individual doesn't enjoy it);
- pre 6 April 2008 RFI not brought to the UK pre 6 April 2008 can be used to effect an asset purchase and remitted to the UK without precipitating a taxable remittance if the asset is purchased by the individual and gifted by the individual to any person prior to remittance (and the individual doesn't enjoy it) *or* the RFI is given by the individual to any person who effects the purchase of the asset and brings it to the UK;
- pre 6 April 2008 RFI brought to the UK pre 6 April 2008 by a relevant person (other than the individual) after the individual gifted the RFI to the relevant person can then be used on or after 6 April 2008 for the benefit of the individual tax free (in essence a gift can be made back to the individual).

"RELEVANT DEBT" AND "UK SERVICES"

The discussion above concerning "remittances" and "alienation" concentrated on the position with respect to remittances of income and gains and on property derived therefrom. However, Conditions A/B (and Conditions C and D) have a much wider application.

Conditions A/B also provide that a "remittance to the UK" occurs in two further situations, namely, where:

(a) a service is provided in the UK to or for the benefit of a "relevant person" and the consideration for the service *is* the income or gains *or* the consideration is consideration given by a "relevant person" that derives from the income or gains; *or*

(b) a service is provided in the UK to or for the benefit of a "relevant person" and the income or gains are used outside the UK in respect of a "relevant debt" or anything deriving from the income or gains is used outside the UK in respect of a "relevant debt".

The term "relevant person" as above means:

- the individual;
- the individual's spouse;
- the child or grandchild of the individual or spouse if the child is under 18;
- a close company (i.e. broadly a company under the "control" of five or fewer shareholders whether the company is UK resident or not) in which a person above is a shareholder;
- the trustees of a trust where any of the above individuals is a beneficiary (thus being the settlor does not, per se, cause the trustees to be a relevant person);
- cohabitees living together as husband and wife.

The term "relevant debt" means, inter alia, a debt (broadly, the obligation to pay a sum of money owed and includes a debt for interest on money lent) that relates to:

- money or other property which is brought to, received or used in, the UK by or for the benefit of a relevant person; or
- a service which is provided in the UK to or for the benefit of a relevant person.

Pre FA 2008 if the individual received some sort of service supplied in the UK (e.g. advice from a firm of lawyers) and paid the fees utilising income or gains, no remittance arose. It was important, however, that the payment was made outside the UK (i.e. payment needed to be made into the non-UK bank account of the firm of lawyers, not their UK bank account which would have precipitated a taxable remittance). This continues post FA 2008 to be possible but only if the service provided relates wholly or mainly to property situated outside the UK *and* the whole of the consideration is given by way of payment(s) to bank accounts held outside the UK by (or on behalf of) the person who provided the service. This continued possibility would appear to apply to, for example, a UK law firm acting with respect to the purchase/sale of overseas real estate; the acquisition/sale of shares in a foreign registered company; investment advice provided by a UK investment firm with respect to an overseas investment portfolio of an individual or trust; accountancy advice in connection with the completion of UK and non-UK tax returns.

The important point to note is that the UK service provided must be made in connection with property more than 50% of which is non-UK property (thus, accountancy advice with respect to UK or non-UK tax returns which primarily relate to UK property would not qualify).

Similarly, if a borrowing is incurred outside the UK to pay for a service provided to a relevant person in the UK the utilisation of income or gains to repay the borrowing and/or any interest levied will precipitate a remittance of the income or gains (under (b) above) unless the exception (i.e. the service relates primarily to non-UK property) referred to above applies.

It may be that payment for the service provided to a relevant person in the UK is by way of the use of an overseas issued credit card. It would seem that the individual whose credit card is used has created a "relevant debt". If the income or gains of the individual are used to discharge the debt due to the credit card company, albeit outside the UK, a remittance of the income or gains will arise (under (b) above) unless the exception referred to above applies.

Whether property is situated within or outside the UK for the purposes of the provision of services within the UK exception is determined by the rules applicable for capital gains tax purposes (see Chapter 6).

In fact, the issue of "relevant debt" has application not only in the case of the provision of a *service* in the UK to a relevant person but also to:

> money or *other property* brought to, or received or used in, the UK by or for the benefit of a "relevant person".

Thus, the use of an overseas issued credit card *or* an overseas borrowing in connection with the purchase of *goods outside* the UK which are subsequently brought into the UK, by or for the benefit of a related person, gives rise to a related debt. The use of income or gains outside the UK to discharge either of these two forms of indebtedness will precipitate a remittance of the income or gains.

Similarly, the use of an overseas issued credit card *or* an overseas borrowing in connection with the purchase of *goods in* the UK (i.e. not just *services*) by or for the benefit of a related person gives rise to a related debt. The use of income or gains outside the UK to discharge either of these two forms of indebtedness will precipitate a remittance of the income or gains.

EXEMPT PROPERTY

Under FA 2008 certain types of property which are brought to, received or used in the UK by or for the benefit of a relevant person (including the individual) are not treated as remitted to the UK and thus precipitate no tax charge.

Such property comprises:

- clothing, footwear, jewellery and watches that derive from relevant foreign income and if they meet the "personal use rule";
- property of any description that derives from relevant foreign income if the "notional amount" remitted is below £1000;
- property that derives from relevant foreign income and meets either the "temporary importation rule" or "the repair rule";
- property that meets the "public access rule" which derives from income or gains (i.e. not just relevant foreign income).

"Property", however, does not include "money" for exempt property purposes (although elsewhere the term "property" includes "money").

Clothing, etc. and the "Personal Use Rule"

The personal use rule applies where the clothing, etc. is the property of a relevant person and is for the personal use of the individual, the individual's spouse, or children or grandchildren under age 18.

To qualify the property must be derived from RFI.

There is no monetary limit as to the amount of relevant foreign income which may be utilised in purchasing the items.

Example 23.22
Steven Alberta, a non-UK domiciled but UK resident individual, used RFI which arose in the tax year 2008/09 to purchase for his wife, Henrietta, a gold watch worth £300 000.

The watch was purchased in Geneva and his wife imported the watch to the UK on her return.

No remittance of the £300 000 of RFI is deemed to have occurred.

Similarly, if the RFI had arisen in the tax year 2007/08 and the purchase had been effected in 2008/09 no remittance would be deemed to have occurred.

Under either option the watch qualifies as exempt property.

Example 23.23

Steven Alberta, a non-UK domiciled but UK resident individual, used RFI which arose in the tax year 2008/09 to purchase for himself an antique painting whilst in Geneva.

Steven imported the painting into the UK on his return.

A remittance of the £300 000 of RFI is deemed to have occurred as the transitional provisions are not in point and the painting is not exempt property.

Property Below £1000 Rule

Any property involving a "notional remitted amount" of below £1000 constitutes exempt property.

The property must be derived from RFI.

The "notional amount remitted" is the amount of income which would normally be regarded as having been remitted in relation to the property. This would be the quantum of the RFI used to effect the original purchase of the goods.

Temporary Importation Rule

Property imported into the UK for 275 days or less in aggregate constitutes exempt property. The 275 days is not a limit applied per tax year but refers to the aggregate permitted days over its useful life.

Property imported for part of a day counts towards the 275 day limit.

Where property imported meets any of the other four rules the time during which it meets any of these rules will not be taken into account in ascertaining whether the temporary importation rule is met.

To qualify the property must be derived from RFI.

Example 23.24

Ronaldo Milan, a non-UK domiciled but UK resident individual, purchased a Ferrari in Italy out of RFI which arose in 2008/09.

He imported the car into the UK in June 2008 where he used it until the end of December. He then exported the car back to Italy.

As the conditions of the temporary importation rule are satisfied the Ferrari would qualify as exempt property and no remittance of the RFI arises.

Repair Rule

Property brought to the UK for repair constitutes exempt property.

"Repair" extends to actual repair work and also storage both pre and post repair; it also extends to transit between a place outside the UK to the premises where the repairs are to be carried out and/or stored by the repairer pre and post repair.

To qualify the property must be derived from RFI.

Prima facie, however, the use of income/gains to pay for the repairs does give rise to a remittance of the income/gains whether the payment is effected within or outside the UK.

Property and Public Access Rule

Property utilised for public display/access broadly encompasses property which comprises works of art, collector's pieces and antiques which is available for public access at an approved establishment (e.g. museum, gallery) up to a period of two years from the time of importation.

Pre FA 2008 such property, if purchased outside the UK using foreign source earnings and/or foreign capital gains and if brought into the UK would constitute a taxable remittance. Where, however, the purchase had been effected using relevant foreign income no taxable remittance arose.

Post FA 2008, however, whether such property is purchased out of any of the above categories of income or gains (i.e. not just RFI) it will now qualify as exempt property and as a consequence no taxable remittance will occur.

Exempt to non-Exempt Property

In the event that exempt property ceases to be exempt for whatever reason it is treated as remitted to the UK at that time.

This will occur if the property (or part of it) is sold or otherwise converted into money (i.e. converted into money otherwise than from a direct sale for cash) while it is in the UK or if it fails to meet (having previously satisfied) any of the four rules (i.e. public access; personal use; repair, or temporary importation).

"Money" includes bills of exchange, traveller's cheques and debt instruments.

Thus, the sale of the property after it is removed outside the UK will not precipitate a taxable remittance (assuming the sale proceeds are not then brought back to the UK).

Example 23.25
Basil Amsterdam, a non-UK domiciled but UK resident individual, imported a Dutch masterpiece on 1 May 2008 which he then immediately loaned to the British Museum. The painting had been purchased out of Basil's non-UK source capital gains.

On 31 December 2008 the painting was returned to Basil who then kept it in his UK family home.

The painting had hung in the British Museum for 245 days.

On 31 January 2009 the painting would have been in the UK for 276 days and thus on this date it no longer qualified as exempt property.

A remittance of the capital gains used to effect the purchase will thus be deemed to have occurred on 31 January 2009.

OFFSHORE INCOME GAINS

Chapter 18 considers offshore mutual fund investments in relation to which for tax purposes the concept of the "offshore income gain" arises.

To an extent the "offshore income gain" is somewhat contradictory. The typical offshore mutual fund is structured in either corporate or trust form. The investor thus invests in shares of the mutual fund in corporate form and in units of the mutual fund in trust form.

The sale of either shares or units is the sale of a capital asset, in normal parlance, and any gain arising thereon a capital gain.

However, in certain cases (i.e. where the fund is a so-called "non-distributor" fund; see Chapter 18) although the gain is a capital gain it is treated as an "income gain" and subject to income, not capital gains, tax.

The amendments introduced by FA 2008 to the remittance rules refers to income and capital gains. The concept of the offshore "income gain" would not appear to sit comfortably under the new FA 2008 provisions. Accordingly, FA 2008 makes specific provision to deal with the position on remittance and offshore income gains.

It provides that in determining the extent and amount of any remittance in relation to an offshore income gain such an income gain is to be treated as RFI and all the provisions applicable to remittances of RFI (see above) are to be regarded as applicable to an offshore income gain.

As there are transitional provisions applicable to RFI (see above) such provisions will also be applicable to the offshore income gain.

The provision which applies where a non-UK situs asset is disposed of at less than market value (e.g. is gifted into an offshore trust; see below under "Gifts of assets precipitating foreign chargeable gains") while of application only in connection with capital gains tax is in essence duplicated and applicable to the offshore income gain. Thus, where the individual disposes of the investment (i.e. shares or units) in the fund for less than market value (e.g. a gift into trust) the asset disposed of (i.e. shares or units) is treated as deriving from the income gain.

The effect is that where the asset (i.e. shares or units) is subsequently brought into the UK a remittance of the offshore income gain (deemed to have arisen at the time of the disposal) will be deemed to have been itself remitted to the UK and thus taxable.

MIXED FUNDS

Under FA 2008 the term "mixed fund" refers to:

> money or other property which, immediately before the transfer, contains or derives from more than one kind of income and capital *or* income and capital for more than one tax year.

The income and capital referred to above is:

- (1) employment income subject to UK income tax;
- (2) relevant foreign earnings;
- (3) foreign specific employment income;
- (4) relevant foreign income;
- (5) foreign chargeable gains;
- (6) employment income subject to foreign tax;
- (7) relevant foreign income subject to foreign tax;
- (8) foreign chargeable gains subject to foreign tax;
- (9) income and capital not in any of the above. *eg GIFT*

Examples of the last category, "income and capital not in any of the above", would be gifts received; inheritances; gambling winnings; UK source income/gains (other than employment income).

Interestingly, the term "mixed fund" refers to "property" (although this term includes "money") as well as "money" and thus, for example, an asset purchased by the individual using a mixture of, say, relevant foreign income and foreign chargeable gains would be considered a mixed fund.

Mixed funds in practice are extremely common.

It is by no means unusual for the individual to have one or more offshore bank accounts into which may flow various categories of income and gains. Thus, for example, the same bank account may be used by the individual to receive offshore dividend income, gains from the disposal of offshore assets and offshore employment or self-employed income. It may also be the case that surplus UK source monies are also remitted to one or more such accounts.

Inevitably, the monies in such accounts will generate interest which will often be credited directly to these accounts.

Where the individual, for example, remits monies from such an account directly to the UK the issue arises as to the nature of the remittance e.g. is it a remittance of the dividend income, gains or interest or some pro rata remittance from all three. Pre FA 2008, there was no clear statutory tax provisions which dealt with this matter and it was usually advisable to maintain separate accounts containing monies from different sources. This enabled the identification of a source of monies remitted to the UK and hence its taxability.

Pre FA 2008, separate offshore accounts might have consisted of:

- "capital" account (containing gifts received; inheritances; surplus UK source originated monies);
- "capital gains" tax account (containing offshore realised capital gains);
- "RFI" account (containing offshore generated interest and dividend income);
- non-UK source employment income.

Pre FA 2008 HMRC laid down its own rules which were applied in practice to cover remittances from mixed accounts. These rules were as follows:

(i) Arising Basis and Remittance Basis Mixed Income

Where an account contains income taxed on the arising basis and income taxed on the remittance basis any remittance is deemed to be out of the taxed arising basis income first; the balance only then coming out of the other income.

(ii) Income and Capital Gains Taxable on Remittance

Remittance is deemed to be out of income first then capital.

(iii) Tax-free Capital and Remittance of Taxable Income

The remittance out of an account containing capital (i.e. not taxable if remitted, e.g. a gift) and income which if remitted is taxable is viewed as generally constituting a remittance of the taxable income first.

(iv) Tax-free Capital and Taxable Chargeable Gains

The remittance out of an account containing capital (i.e. not taxable if remitted) and capital part of which is a capital gain should be a remittance out of the tax-free capital first.

FA 2008 now provides statutory authority for determining the nature of a remittance from a mixed fund. Under the new rules a series of steps are employed which broadly involve attributing to the remittance income and gains from each of the above nine categories in turn, commencing with employment income first, until the remittance has been matched in its entirety. The determination is made at the date of the remittance, i.e. the amounts in the various categories are determined immediately before the remittance. Thus, for subsequent remittances in the same tax year the quantum of each (or some) of the categories will have been depleted by the "matching" to earlier remittances.

If in the event there is insufficient income or gains arising in the tax year of the remittance to match to the remittance then it becomes necessary to repeat the whole process matching the immediately prior tax year's income and gains using the same procedure. This process is repeated until a full matching has occurred.

These new FA 2008 provisions do not, however, apply to the individual's income or gains for the tax year 2007/08 or earlier tax years. In such cases the pre FA 2008 rules will apply.

It may be that transfers are effected outside the UK which do not constitute remittances to the UK. For example, transfers may simply be made outside the UK from, or into, a mixed account. Such transfers are referred to as "offshore transfers". In such cases a transfer into a mixed account is treated as a transfer of the category of income comprising the transfer. A transfer out of a mixed account is treated as containing the appropriate proportion of each kind of income/capital in the mixed fund immediately before the transfer. The appropriate proportion is the market value/amount of the transfer divided by the market value of the mixed fund immediately before the transfer.

However, the transfer out of the mixed fund is not treated as an "offshore transfer" if by the end of the tax year in which the transfer is made (or in the forseeable future) it is (or will be) treated as a remittance to the UK. In this case the normal rules set out above to determine the categories of the remittance apply (i.e. the remittance to the UK is determined as if the offshore transfers had not been effected).

These rules are designed to prevent manipulation of the income/gains to reduce the quantum of taxable remittances.

Example 23.26
Safira Iran, a non-UK domiciled but UK resident individual, opened a new Swiss bank account (SB1) on 6 April 2008.
In the tax year 2008/09 Safira received into the account:
- £150 000 as a gift from her mother
- £60 000 dividend income on overseas shareholdings
- £30 000 sale proceeds arising from sales of some of her overseas shareholdings (in respect of which chargeable gains amounted to £10 000).

Safira intends to remit £60 000 to the UK in the tax year 2009/10 from SB1.

Prior to the remittance Safira intends to open a second bank account in Switzerland (SB2) and then intends to transfer £60 000 from SB1 to SB2. The £60 000 in SB2 is then to be remitted to the UK.

Safira believes that by effecting the above the tax liability in the UK will be reduced as the £60 000 remittance from SB2 will comprise £15 000 of dividend income; £7500 of sale proceeds (of which £2500 represents chargeable gain); and £37 500 of "tax free" capital (the remittance from SB1 to SB2 comprising [£60 000/£240 000]ths of each of the components comprising the £240 000 in SB1).

In other words Safira believes that the bulk of the remittance from SB2 will be deemed to be that arising from the gift from her mother and thus precipitating no tax charge.

However, the remittance to the UK from SB2 causes the "offshore transfer" from SB1 to SB2 to effectively be ignored and the £60 000 remittance will be assumed to have come from SB1 prior to the transfer of monies to SB2.

The £60 000 from SB1 will be deemed to comprise £60 000 of dividend income (i.e. RFI) and accordingly taxable as such.

Anti-avoidance arrangements also exist to prevent arrangements or schemes designed to mitigate the quantum of taxable remittances to the UK out of a mixed fund.

Where a pre FA 2008 mixed fund is further "mixed" by the addition of monies arising on or after 6 April 2008 the position appears unclear as to how any matching should be carried out. Prima facie, the new rules would apply to the income/gains added on or after 6 April 2008 (at this point ignoring the pre 6 April 2008 income/gains in the mixed account) and the pre FA 2008 rules then applying to the remaining elements of the mixed fund once the post 5 April 2008 income/gains have been deemed to have been remitted. *post FA 08 funds remitted first.*

SEGREGATION OF INCOME AND CAPITAL GAINS

Mixed accounts, both pre and post FA 2008, are generally to be avoided. The reason is that the individual has no control over the category of income/gains to be remitted to the UK. Thus, for example, a remittance from an account comprising relevant foreign income and capital gains will precipitate in the first instance a remittance of relevant foreign income (subject to income tax at the marginal rate of 40%) as opposed to capital gain (subject to capital gains tax at the rate of 18%). If each category of income/gains had been credited to two separate accounts then a direct remittance from the capital gains account would have been possible.

Arguably, post FA 2008, in view of the introduction of the statutory rules governing the order of remittances from mixed accounts, the introduction of the concept of the nominated amount and the possible need to avoid the remittance of this amount (whether in whole or in part) it is now more important than ever to segregate the various sources of income/gains.

The start point is to segregate pre and post FA 2008 income/gains. Thus, ideally, all accounts as at 5 April 2008 should have been frozen, i.e. no additions of any sort to be made to any of these accounts arising from post 5 April 2008 income/gains. Where this was not done and post 5 April 2008 income/gains have been added to these accounts it may still be appropriate to consider freezing the accounts as soon as possible. This presupposes that the pre 6 April 2008 rules are more likely to produce a more favourable tax consequence than those applying post 5 April 2008 and that the post 5 April 2008 rules will apply to the whole of the mixed account (which as indicated above should not, prima facie, in fact be the case).

New accounts should then be created to match the individual's particular income/gains position. The starting point is to adopt the nine categories referred to above, i.e. create a separate account for each category.

This would then enable the individual to remit from whichever specific category produced the most tax efficient result.

Example 23.27
Ethelred Norway, a non-UK domiciled but UK resident individual, credited the following amounts of income/gains, which arose in the period 6 April 2008 to 31 August 2008, to his sole bank account in the Bahamas:

Non-UK source employment income	£225 000
Non-UK source bank interest	£100 000
Non-UK source capital gains (on sale proceeds of £1 million)	£225 000
Gifts from his father	£225 000

The employment income was in respect of non-UK duties under a contract of employment with a Cayman Island company.

To pay for his daughter's lavish wedding in the UK on 1 October 2008 he remitted £225 000 to the UK but then found himself remitting a further £100 000 two weeks later. None of this represented his nominated amount for 2008/09.

Ethelred is a higher rate taxpayer.

Ethelred has precipitated an income tax liability of:

40% of £225 000 (of employment income)
40% of £100 000 (of bank interest)

Aggregate income tax charge £130 000

Example 23.28

Egbert Norway, a friend of Ethelred of Example 23.27, a non-UK domiciled but UK resident individual, credited the following amounts of income/gains, which arose in the period 6 April 2008 to 31 August 2008, to four separate bank accounts in the Bahamas:

B1. Non-UK source employment income	£225 000
B2. Non-UK source bank interest	£100 000
B3. Non-UK source capital gains (on sale proceeds of £1 million)	£225 000
B4. Gifts from his father	£225 000

The employment income was in respect of non-UK duties under a contract of employment with a Cayman Island company.

To pay for his son's lavish wedding in the UK on 1 October 2008 he remitted £225 000 from B4 to the UK but then found himself remitting a further £100 000 from B3 two weeks later. None of this represented his nominated amount for 2008/09.

Egbert is a higher rate taxpayer.

Egbert has precipitated an income tax liability of:

0% of £225 000 (of gifts from his father)
18% of £100 000 (of capital gains; under the new FA 2008 rules the capital gains element of the sale proceeds is deemed to be remitted prior to the then capital element)

> Aggregate income tax charge   £18 000

Egbert, faced with the identical situation to Ethelred of Example 23.27 above, has managed to save £112 000 in UK tax.

If, for example, the non-UK source capital gains are actually comprised of capital gains of £375 000 (on sale proceeds of £750 000) and capital losses of £150 000 (on sale proceeds of £250 000) Egbert's above tax position could have been improved even further.

Had Egbert utilised two separate accounts for the sale proceeds, one in respect of capital gains and one in respect of capital losses then he could have remitted the balancing £100 000 required in the UK from the capital loss proceeds account of £250 000. His aggregate income tax liability would then have been reduced from £18 000 to nil.

While in principle non-UK source capital losses are available for offset against capital gains (see Chapter 8) there is no requirement for the gains to be remitted in order for the losses to be utilised. However, it would be of benefit to be able to remit sales proceeds from disposals which give rise to capital losses rather than from disposals which precipitated capital gains. Unfortunately, where the proceeds are mixed any remittance would be of the net capital gain element in the first instance. Thus, separation of capital losses from capital gains is likely to be tax efficient.

It may also be advantageous to create an additional "nominated amount" account into which is credited nominated amounts each tax year. This will then ensure that it can be demonstrated that remittance from nominated amounts has not occurred and thus this will avoid the need for the "matching" process outlined above where remittances to the UK comprise both nominated amounts and non-nominated amounts. It should also as a result simplify any record keeping.

GIFTS OF ASSETS PRECIPITATING FOREIGN CHARGEABLE GAINS

Chapter 8 states that a capital gain (or of course capital loss) may arise on the disposal of chargeable assets (i.e. assets which are not exempt) and with it a capital gains tax charge.

The disposal by the individual of a non-UK situs asset also precipitates a potential capital gains tax charge. However, as the disposal is of a non-UK situs asset no capital gains tax charge arises until a remittance of the gain to the UK occurs.

Where the individual gifts the non-UK situs asset it is deemed to have been disposed of at its then market value which, if in excess of original cost, precipitates a capital gain. However, no monies are received by the individual as, of course, the disposal is by way of gift. Thus, there is nothing which the individual can remit to the UK and therefore no capital gains tax charge can arise.

This was the position pre FA 2008.

Examples of such gifts would be a simple gift by the individual to another individual (e.g. brother, sister, son, daughter) or perhaps, much more likely, a gift into an offshore trust.

FA 2008 now imposes a potential capital gains tax charge in such circumstances and does so by treating the asset disposed of as deriving from the chargeable gain. What this means is that should the asset (or property derived therefrom) subsequently be remitted to the UK a capital gains tax charge will arise on the individual at that time with respect to the chargeable gain which arose on the original gift of the asset.

However, the new provisions of FA 2008 do not apply where the gift was made in the tax year 2007/08 or earlier tax years if the remittance of the asset gifted is made on or after 6 April 2008 and the individual does not benefit.

This would mean that, for example, if the individual pre 6 April 20008 transferred (i.e. gifted) an asset into an offshore trust and on or after 6 April 2008 the trust appointed the asset out to someone in the UK (other than the individual) no taxable remittance on the part of the individual would arise. On the other hand, the appointment out to the individual in the UK would cause the gain deemed to have been made on the transfer of the asset into the trust to have been remitted with the consequent capital gains tax liability.

The above would still apply if, for example, the trust had sold the asset and then appointed the cash to the individual.

CESSATION OF SOURCE R.I.P.

Pre FA 2008, a cardinal rule with respect to the taxation of income was that the source of the income had to exist in the tax year in which the income was remitted to the UK.

If the source did not so exist then the income was not subject to income tax in the tax year of remittance.

Thus a common ploy was for the individual to close the source of the income in one tax year and then remit the income which had arisen from that source in the following (or a later) tax year without precipitating a charge to income tax. For example, a non-UK bank account ("Account 1") in which money had been credited would give rise to interest which would then be credited to Account 2. Account 1, when appropriate, would be closed down in a tax year and the interest would be remitted from Account 2 in the following tax year without precipitating a charge to income tax.

Another example might be the remittance of dividends, credited to a non-UK bank account, in a tax year following the tax year in which the shares which had given rise to the dividends had been sold or simply transferred to the spouse.

The source cessation principle did not, however, apply to capital gains or employment income.

FA 2008 has introduced provisions designed to prevent this type of planning.

Accordingly, relevant foreign income which is remitted to the UK by the individual is subject to income tax in the tax year of remittance whether or not the source of the income exists in the tax year of remittance.

There are no transitional provisions and thus relevant foreign income remitted to the UK by the individual in the tax year 2008/09 will be automatically subject to income tax in that tax year irrespective of the tax year in which the source of the income ceased.

Thus, the last occasion where the principle of source cessation could be used tax effectively was where the source ceased in the tax year 2006/07 (or earlier) and the income attributable thereto was remitted on or before 5 April 2008.

Where the source ceased pre 6 April 2007 but the relevant foreign income remained outside the UK as at 5 April 2008 the relevant foreign income can thus no longer be brought into the UK without a tax charge by the individual. However, the individual could gift the relevant foreign income to another person (even a relevant person) who could then remit the income without tax charge (assuming the individual cannot benefit therefrom).

Where relevant foreign income, following source cessation, has not been remitted to the UK pre 6 April 2008 unfavourable and unforeseen consequences may arise. Thus, for example, where the relevant foreign income is used to purchase an offshore bond (see Chapter 18) in 2008/09 (or later tax years) and the permitted 5% withdrawals are remitted to the UK, such withdrawals will be regarded as remittances of the relevant foreign income used to effect the purchase and will thus fall to be subject to income tax (as would the relevant foreign income had it simply been remitted).

The position is, however, different where the relevant foreign income has been remitted to the UK pre 6 April 2008 after having successfully closed the appropriate source in an earlier tax year. Assume, as above, that the remitted relevant foreign income is used to purchase an offshore bond and the 5% withdrawals are remitted to the UK. In this case the 5% withdrawals will not constitute a taxable remittance (see the discussion above under "RFI arising pre 6 April 2008" re RFI brought to the UK pre 6 April 2008).

Whilst the purchase of offshore bonds is used above to illustrate the possible unfavourable tax consequences which may arise when the unremitted relevant foreign income is utilised post source cessation, any utilisation for whatever purposes needs to be carefully considered.

OFFSHORE MORTGAGES

The position with respect to the offshore borrowings has changed following the FA 2008 albeit transitional provisions provide a degree of "grandfathering".

An offshore borrowing is a borrowing from a non-UK source incurred for the purpose of enabling the individual to acquire an interest in UK residential property.

Pre FA 2008 the individual was able to use relevant foreign income to fund part of an offshore borrowing used to buy (and typically secured on) UK situs property (e.g.

a residential home typically) without precipitating a taxable remittance. The relevant foreign income could be used outside the UK to fund any interest charges but not any capital repayments.

The use of such income to fund capital repayments would give rise to a taxable remittance of the income so used to the UK. This would not be the case if the income was used to fund interest payments. The capital repayments would thus normally be made when the individual no longer resided in the UK; or out of previously taxed income (e.g. UK source income or indeed capital gains); or out of gifts or inheritances received outside the UK. Any capital repayments effected after the death of the borrower do not, in any event, constitute a remittance.

As the above was perceived as a loophole, under the FA 2008 provisions if relevant foreign income is used on or after 6 April 2008 to fund interest and/or capital repayments (even outside the UK) such income will be regarded as having been remitted to the UK and thus taxable.

However, transitional provisions protect the pre FA 2008 position under certain circumstances.

Grandfathering Provisions

Under these provisions the use of relevant foreign income to fund payments of interest outside the UK will continue to be treated as not giving rise to a remittance of such income to the UK where such payments are made before *6 April 2028.*

For the grandfathering provisions to apply:

- the loan must have been made to the individual prior to 12 March 2008;
- the *sole* purpose of the loan must have been the acquisition of a residential property in the UK;
- on or before 5 April 2008 the money had to be received in the UK; used to acquire the property; and repayment of the debt had to be secured on the property.

A failure to satisfy any of these conditions would preclude these transitional provisions from applying.

It is important, however, that on or after 12 March 2008 (note, not on or after 6 April 2008) none of the terms of the loan are varied; the debt does not cease to be secured on the property; no other debt is secured on the property; and the individual's interest in the property does not cease. Should any of these conditions be breached then any interest paid on or after 12 March 2008 will constitute a remittance to the UK.

However, remortgaging of the property is acceptable but only if the remortgage was completed before 6 April 2008 and the above conditions are also satisfied.

The term "residential property" is that used for stamp duty land tax purposes. It includes a building used or suitable for use as a dwelling and extends to a building that is in the process of being constructed or adapted as use as a dwelling together with the surrounding gardens.

The impact of FA 2008 provisions is to cause a remittance to occur where relevant foreign income is used outside the UK to fund either interest or capital repayments if the foreign loan is made on or after 12 March 2008.

Loans Secured on Property: IHT Impact

UK residential property is UK situs and thus falls within a potential inheritance tax charge whether owned by the UK domiciled or non-UK domiciled individual.

Any such potential liability may be mitigated by charging debt against the property (e.g. a mortgage; see Chapter 20). This occurs because in determining the value of an individual's estate for inheritance tax purposes on death, any liabilities of the individual are taken into account, i.e. liabilities are deducted from assets to arrive at the net chargeable estate. This rule applies even though the borrowing may be from a connected person (e.g. borrowing from a trust which the individual has set up).

It is important, however, that the foreign loan is specifically charged against the particular UK property. Any such loan which is not secured against UK property is deductible from non-UK (i.e. excluded) property and thus totally inheritance tax ineffective.

Often the loan to value of an offshore mortgage is lower than for an onshore mortgage and an offshore bank may suggest a charge not only over the UK property but, for example, also over an overseas share portfolio. This has the consequence of an apportionment of the charge and reduced inheritance tax effectiveness.

Loans Secured on Property: Capital Gains Tax Impact

Any loss which may arise on the repayment of a foreign currency denominated loan (when measured in sterling terms) is not an allowable capital loss (as it arises on a liability not an asset). Thus, correspondingly any gain made is not taxable.

TEMPORARY NON-UK RESIDENTS

Income Tax

Pre FA 2008 the individual was able to lose UK residence status and during the tax years of non-residence remit to the UK relevant foreign income which had arisen prior to acquiring non-UK residency (i.e. income which had arisen during a period of UK residency) without an income tax charge arising on such income.

On return to the UK the individual would then be able to enjoy the remitted income in the UK tax free.

FA 2008 has introduced completely new provisions (compare the corresponding capital gains tax provisions, see below) designed to prevent this perceived loophole.

Accordingly, subject to the satisfaction of certain conditions, any such remittance will be treated as a remittance in the tax year of the reacquisition of residency.

The conditions are as follows:

- the individual is resident in the UK in at least four out of the seven tax years prior to the tax year of departure;
- the number of complete tax years of non-UK residence between the tax year of departure and the tax year of return is less than five.

To avoid the new FA 2008 provisions (assuming UK residency for the four out of seven tax year condition) requires that the individual becomes non-UK resident for at least five complete tax years before returning to the UK. In this event, relevant foreign income can continue to be remitted to the UK during the period of non-residency without precipitating a tax charge.

The relevant foreign income to which the provisions apply include that for the tax year of departure and any earlier tax years and extends to relevant foreign income which arose in the tax year 2007/08 and earlier tax years (assuming that in respect of 2007/08 and any earlier tax year a claim under the "old" provisions had been made for the individual to be taxed on the relevant foreign income for the tax year concerned on the remittance basis).

In short, no transitional provisions apply. Thus, pre 6 April 2008 relevant foreign income remitted to the UK post 5 April 2008 while the individual is non-UK resident will be taxed in the tax year of return to the UK (unless, of course, the above five tax year period of absence condition is satisfied).

However, remittances occurring in the tax year 2007/08 and earlier tax years are not affected by the new provisions.

Example 23.29
Billy Florida Snr, a non-UK domiciled but UK resident individual, has been UK resident for the last 10 tax years prior to the tax year 2008/09.

During this period he has generated relevant foreign income of £175 000 which has been credited to his bank account in Dubai.

He leaves the UK on 6 June 2008, losing his UK residency status, intending to return to the UK on 6 April 2014. In the tax year 2010/11 he intends to remit the whole £175 000 to his bank account in the UK so as to enjoy the monies in the UK on his return.

Assuming that he fulfils his plans then no income tax will arise on the remittance as he will have remained non-UK resident for at least five complete tax years, namely, 2009/10, 2010/11, 2011/12, 2012/13 and 2013/14.

Example 23.30
Billy Florida Snr's son, Billy Florida Jnr, is in exactly the same position (see Example 23.29 above) and leaves with his dad on 6 June 2008.

On 6 April 2013 Billy Florida Jnr reacquires UK residency as he is unable to remain outside the UK any longer due to family issues.

Income tax will arise on the remittance of £175 000 made in the tax year 2010/11 while non-UK resident as he has not satisfied the five tax year condition. The liability will arise in the tax year of return, i.e. 2013/14.

However, remittances of relevant foreign income which arose on or after 6 April 2009 (i.e. during the period of non-UK residency) will not be subject to income tax as such income had not arisen in tax years prior to his departure or in the tax year of departure.

Capital Gains Tax

The FA 2008 provisions just discussed with respect to temporary non-UK resident individuals and income tax discussed above are a completely new set of provisions.

Similar provisions with respect to capital gains tax, however, already existed pre FA 2008 (see Chapter 8). However, these capital gains tax provisions did not catch the capital gains made by the non-UK domiciled individual on the disposal of non-UK situs assets while non-UK resident (with respect to assets owned prior to acquiring non-residency) even where such gains were (while the individual was still non-UK resident) remitted to the UK. Capital gains arising on non-UK situs assets realised when the individual was UK resident but remitted during the period of non-UK residency were similarly not subject to capital gains tax.

FA 2008 has now extended these provisions to deal with this loophole.

In effect, post FA 2008, the provisions which deal with income and capital gains tax are effectively identical.

Gains now made by the individual on assets owned prior to departure while non-UK resident on non-UK situs assets which are remitted to the UK during a period of non-residency, where this period is less than five complete tax years, will be treated as remitted in the tax year of return and taxed accordingly (assuming that the four out of previous seven tax year condition is satisfied; see above and Chapter 8). Similarly, gains made on non-UK situs assets prior to departure (i.e. whilst UK resident) but remitted whilst non-UK resident are now also subject to capital gains tax in the tax year of return.

No transitional provisions apply. Thus, pre 6 April 2008 capital gains on non-UK situs assets remitted to the UK post 5 April 2008 while the individual is non-UK resident will be taxed in the tax year of return to the UK (unless, of course, the above five tax year period of absence condition is satisfied).

However, remittances occurring in the tax year 2007/08 and earlier tax years are not affected by the new provisions.

Example 23.31
Billy Florida Snr, a non-UK domiciled but UK resident individual, has been UK resident for the last 10 tax years prior to the tax year 2008/09. During this period he has generated foreign chargeable gains of £175 000 which has been credited to his bank account in Dubai.

He leaves the UK on 6 June 2008, losing his UK residency status, intending to return to the UK on 6 April 2014. In the tax year 2010/11 he intends to remit the whole £175 000 to his bank account in the UK so as to enjoy the monies in the UK on his return.

Assuming that he fulfils his plans then no capital gains tax will arise on the remittance as he will have remained non-UK resident for at least five complete tax years, namely, 2009/10, 2010/11, 2011/12, 2012/13 and 2013/14.

Example 23.32
Billy Florida Snr's son, Billy Florida Jnr, is in exactly the same position (see Example 23.31 above) and leaves with his dad on 6 June 2008.

On 6 April 2013 Billy Florida Jnr reacquires UK residency as he is unable to remain outside the UK any longer due to family issues.

Capital gains tax will arise on the remittance of the £175 000 of gains made in the tax year 2010/11 while non-UK resident as he has not satisfied the five tax year condition. The liability will arise in the tax year of return, i.e. 2013/14.

In addition, as Billy Jnr is not non-UK resident for five complete tax years any capital gains remitted to the UK arising on the disposal of non-UK assets (owned prior to departure) and sold whilst non-UK resident will be subject to capital gains tax in the tax year of return i.e. 2013/14.

However, remittances of capital gains which arose on disposal of assets acquired on or after 6 June 2008 (i.e. when non-UK resident) will not be subject to capital gains tax.

It should also be noted that, both pre and post FA 2008, capital gains tax will be charged in the tax year of return of the individual on capital gains arising on the disposal of UK situs assets while the individual is non-UK resident (assuming, inter alia, the period of non-UK residency is less than five complete tax years).

SUMMARY

FA 2008 has dramatically changed the rules which apply to the taxation of non-UK source income and capital gains of the non-UK domiciled but UK resident individual. In particular, the definition of "remittance" has been significantly widened to encompass the newly created concept of "relevant persons".

As a consequence, a number of options available to the non-UK domiciled individual to enjoy tax effectively the fruits of their offshore income and capital gains in the UK pre 2008 are no longer possible. In particular, tax efficient alienation of income/gains is now much more difficult.

The new rules apply not only to the income and capital gains of the individual but also to such income and gains of offshore trusts of which the individual (and/or family members) may be the settlor and/or beneficiary.

The new rules in principle apply with respect to income and capital gains arising on or after 6 April 2008. However, these rules in certain instances apply to income and capital gains which arose before this date although transitional provisions are also applicable.

FA 2008 has also introduced the requirement for certain non-UK domiciled individuals to lodge a claim for each tax year in respect of which remittance basis treatment is to apply. However, this need for a claim is not applicable to all non-UK domiciled individuals.

An annual £30 000 tax charge is now payable by certain non-UK domiciled individuals which represents a real additional tax burden.

New statutory rules (to replace the historic HMRC unofficial rules) have been introduced to identify the order in which monies are remitted from a mixed account. Accordingly, segregation of accounts is paramount if UK tax is to be minimised on remittances to the UK.

The concept of source cessation has been abolished which has wider ramifications than is at first sight thought.

24
The Offshore Dimension

BACKGROUND

For the high net worth individual mitigation of tax is clearly a high priority. However, as observed elsewhere in this book, sometimes the mitigation of one tax may exacerbate another; this will often be the case with respect to capital gains and inheritance taxes. The statement also begs the question as to over what time period should taxes be mitigated. Saving tax today may increase tax in the future or vice versa.

Tax mitigation techniques vary in form and substance and it must be observed that what may be an acceptable tax mitigation practice in one jurisdiction may not be so in another. In the UK there is a very important distinction between tax "avoidance" and tax "evasion"; the former is perfectly legal whereas the latter is not.

What is clear, however, is that it is not necessary for the individual to restrict tax planning to within the borders of the country in which the individual is resident. Thus, for the UK resident individual investor, options include offshore cash deposits with banks located elsewhere in the world, including locations such as Guernsey, Isle of Man, Jersey or the Bahamas; offshore fund investments in funds located in the Cayman Islands, Ireland or Luxembourg; equity investments on overseas stock exchanges such as that in Singapore; real estate investments in Italy, Spain or the USA and offshore bonds issued out of Gibraltar or the Isle of Man.

For the non-UK domiciled but UK resident individual non-UK situs investments are critical in tax mitigation planning and even for the UK domiciled and UK resident individual non-UK situs investments can also be tax efficient. For the UK domiciled but UK resident individual the strategy may simply be restricted to tax deferral rather than outright tax avoidance which, for such individuals, is very difficult. Nevertheless, UK domiciled individuals should not overlook non-UK investments.

Structuring of the holding of the investments is just as important as the underlying investments. Use of offshore companies and/or trusts is often vital to achieving overall tax efficiency. Invariably, such vehicles are located neither in the country of residence of the individual investor nor in the country of the investment itself but in a suitable intermediate offshore financial centre (OFC).

The OFC will typically not create any extra layer of tax but may enable the return from the underlying investments (be that income and/or capital growth) to be "warehoused" outside of the high tax territories' jurisdiction pending timely repatriation and/or reinvestment. In addition, the OFC may offer the individual strong bank secrecy laws, protection of assets from third party challenges and vehicles with attributes unavailable elsewhere.

A simple example is where a non-UK resident investor wishes to invest in income producing UK real estate. By utilising a company located in an OFC (e.g. British Virgin Islands) not only is there a degree of protection from UK tax authorities as to the ownership of the company but the UK income tax liability on the UK source rental income is restricted to a rate of 20% (for the tax year 2008/09) as compared to 40% where the individual invests directly. Such a company also offers protection from inheritance tax where the individual is non-UK domiciled. For the UK resident individual such intermediate companies may offer similar advantages vis-à-vis the country of the ultimate investment.

Trusts add yet another dimension to tax planning for the individual and the combination of trusts and companies located in various OFCs often offer formidable tax efficient structures.

The term "offshore financial centre" is now in wide use in the financial/tax world. Formerly, such OFCs were simply described as "tax havens". The change of terminology came about partially due to the term "tax haven" being increasingly perceived as referring to something negative and illegal and a view by the countries to which the label was normally attached that the local incentives offered were not exclusively tax related and thus the term "tax havens" was misleading.

THE OFFSHORE FINANCIAL CENTRE

There are almost as many definitions of the term "offshore financial centre" as there are OFCs themselves. Typically, these definitions are not definitions as such but merely a list of attributes that appear to be common to such centres. The IMF in early 2007 defined the OFC as:

> a country or jurisdiction that provides financial services to non-residents on a scale that is incommensurate with the size and the financing of its domestic economy.

The OECD has described the term "tax haven" (not in fact using the increasingly accepted term "offshore financial centre") as a jurisdiction which has:

- no or very low tax on financial income;
- no effective exchange of information;
- a lack of transparency;
- a lack of the need for any entity (e.g. company; trust) to have a local substantive presence.

Depending upon the definition of the term OFC there are probably approaching one hundred centres dotted around the world. These centres can be conveniently categorised, geographically, into those located in one of the following broad areas, namely, the Caribbean; Europe; the Indian Ocean; and Australasia.

Caribbean located territories would include: Antigua, Aruba, Bahamas, Belize, Bermuda (although, of course, not technically in the Caribbean), British Virgin Islands, Cayman Islands, Netherlands Antilles, Nevis and Turks and Caicos and Panama.

European located territories would include: Andorra, Cyprus, Gibraltar, Guernsey, Isle of Man, Jersey, Liberia, Liechtenstein, Luxembourg, Madeira, Malta, Monaco, San Marino and Switzerland.

Indian Ocean located territories would include: Mauritius and the Seychelles.

Australasian located territories would include: Cook Islands, Hong Kong, Marshall Islands, Nauru, New Hebrides, Singapore and Vanuatu.

As can be seen, many of these offshore financial centres are British Crown Dependencies or former British colonies and, to a degree, their respective success has to a great extent arguably derived from this fact although it may be counter-argued that this historic link militates against their use due to the continued direct and indirect influence the UK often has over their affairs.

The use by individuals of such centres as part of wealth planning will be, without question, perceived by the "high tax" countries of the world as "suspect" whether or not this is in fact the case. This view, however, is perfectly understandable given that, almost without exception, every such centre has been shown to have been used for illegal purposes be it tax evasion, money laundering and/or terrorist financing.

There are countless documented examples where this has been shown to be the situation. Such use has not been restricted to the very rich and corrupt political leaders (typically dictators). Every day "normal" individuals have also been caught using such centres for illegal, typically, tax evasion (not avoidance) purposes. As recently as 2007/08, in the UK, HMRC obtained information from a number of British-based banks which confirmed that many UK resident individuals have deposited monies in offshore bank accounts and then failed to declare the interest income earned thereon; often for many years.

In a not disimilar exercise a number of years ago it is alleged that the Internal Revenue Service (i.e. the USA equivalent of the UK HMRC) forced Mastercard to supply records of nearly two million transactions relating to accounts held by Americans in Antigua, the Bahamas and the Cayman Islands and similar account information was apparently sought from both Visa and American Express.

Fortunately, for the individuals involved in the recent HMRC onslaught, on 17 April 2007 HMRC offered an olive branch in the nature of what the press referred to as an "amnesty" but is more accurately described as "an offshore disclosure facility" (ODF).

Broadly, under the ODF individuals with undeclared offshore bank accounts were invited to make a voluntary disclosure of the monies involved and make appropriate payment of tax due (over up to a 20-year period) plus interest and penalties within a defined time period (roughly six months) of the announcement of the ODF. In return for such voluntary disclosure, the "penalty" for failing to disclose the taxable income was reduced to 10% of any tax which had been underpaid which compares to a worst case scenario under normal circumstances of a 100% penalty and/or criminal prosecution.

Strictly speaking, the ODF extended to any offshore irregularity not just undeclared interest on offshore bank accounts (and a parallel procedure was introduced relating to onshore irregularities).

Other countries including, for example, Australia, Ireland and Italy have adopted similar approaches with, it would seem, remarkable success in terms of tax collected and/or capital repatriated.

However, such stances by the tax authorities should not by any means be taken as a green light to attempt tax evasion by "hiding" monies in these OFCs believing that the "upside" is never getting caught and saving tax and the "downside" is simply paying basically the tax that was due in the first instance plus, arguably, not unreasonable penalties.

It should not be forgotten that in most of the high tax jurisdictions tax evasion is a criminal offence and imprisonment may beckon.

Underpinning the attraction of the world's OFCs (in addition to zero or very low rates of tax) are invariably two critical factors. Strong bank secrecy laws combined with a very strong reluctance (indeed, in many cases blunt refusal) to exchange information with other (in particular the high tax countries) jurisdictions about the financial affairs of local companies, trusts and individuals.

It is these two factors, perhaps more so than the reduced tax rates, which the high tax jurisdictions (e.g. Australia, Canada, Germany, the UK and USA) find unacceptable. As a consequence, significant activity has taken place over the last 10 to 15 years by such countries and in particular by a number of international organisations designed to encourage (by agreement and discussion and a touch of "economic pressure") the OFCs to become more "open" and willing to exchange information with other jurisdictions; in the jargon, to become more transparent.

Various degrees of success in this area have been achieved.

In the UK two major initiatives in this area resulted in the production of two separate reports. The first, published in 1998, was headed "Review of Financial Regulation in the Crown Dependencies" (namely, Guernsey, Isle of Man and Jersey) and the second, published two years later, headed "Review of Financial Regulation in Anguilla, Bermuda, British Virgin Islands, Cayman Islands, Montserrat and Turks and Caicos".

As recently as April 2008 the Treasury Committee announced yet another initiative which is designed to "undertake an inquiry into Offshore Financial Centres, as part of its ongoing work into Financial Stability and Transparency".

Perhaps the initiative that really started serious international global cooperation to combat the use of OFCs for tax evasion, fraud, etc. was that launched in 1996 by the OECD into what was referred to as "harmful tax practices" which led to the production of the "Harmful Tax Competition: An Emerging Global Issue" report in 1998. Other reports from the OECD then followed, in essence providing updates on subsequent work being undertaken designed to tackle and eliminate "harmful tax practices" (interestingly, "harmful tax practices" were found to exist not only in OFCs but also in member countries of the OECD). "Harmful tax practices" are described as "preferential tax regimes in the OECD member countries" and "those occurring in the form of tax havens". Thus, by definition, OFCs/tax havens are according to the OECD "harmful".

The objectives of the 1998 report were as follows:

- to identify and eliminate harmful tax practices of preferential tax regimes in OECD countries;
- to identify "tax havens" and seek their commitments to the principles of transparency and effective exchange of information;
- to encourage other non-OECD economies to associate themselves with the harmful tax practices work.

The report produced a list of 35 tax havens referred to as "uncooperative". These included: Bahamas, Barbados, British Virgin Islands, Gibraltar, Guernsey, Isle of Man, Montserrat, Netherlands Antilles, Nevis, Panama, Turks and Caicos, and Vanuatu. To be removed from this list required the OFC to enter into a commitment to eliminate its harmful tax practices (within a predefined time frame) which included a willingness to exchange information with, primarily, the high tax countries of the world (including access to banking information).

As at today's date (i.e. mid 2008) only three OFCs continue to be listed as "uncooperative", namely, Andorra, Liechtenstein and Monaco. Interestingly, in 2008 Liechtenstein has found itself at the centre of a scandal in Germany in which many German residents have apparently been involved in tax evasion activities utilising facilities in Liechtenstein. It is alleged that the use of Liechtenstein was due to its secrecy rules and its failure to cooperate with other countries on tax matters.

In 2007 the OECD released yet another report, "Tax Co-operation Towards a Level Playing Field – 2007 Assessment by the Global Forum on Taxation", which indicates that a number or jurisdictions' standards required by the OECD still fall short. The 2007 report states that significant restrictions on access to bank information for tax purposes remain in three OECD countries (Austria, Luxembourg and Switzerland) and in a number of OFCs including Cyprus, Liechtenstein, Panama and Singapore. The 2007 report also states that despite commitments being entered into by tax havens to implement effective exchange of information arrangements a number have failed to do so.

Thus, while Andorra, Liechtenstein and Monaco officially remain on the "uncooperative" list, in fact many OFCs are in reality also failing to respond to be as "cooperative" as they indicated to the OECD in written formal "commitment letters" issued some years ago.

However, a number of OFCs have in fact entered into some form of exchange of information agreement with various countries. These agreements are often referred to as "Tax Information Exchange Agreements" (TIEAs) and are based on a Model Agreement produced by the OECD in 2002. In the case of the UK an agreement was signed with Bermuda in 2007 and the Isle of Man in 2008 and discussions continue with Anguilla, British Virgin Islands and Cayman Islands.

Other TIEAs which have been entered into by various OFCs include agreements between Guernsey and the Netherlands; Isle of Man and Ireland; Jersey and the Netherlands; Antigua and Australia; Aruba and the USA; British Virgin Island and the USA; and Cayman Islands and the USA.

Despite the views expressed by, inter alia, the OECD and the various high tax territories as to a lack of transparency in the OFCs, when used "properly", OFCs offer the individual a powerful option not only to mitigate tax on income and assets both in lifetime and on death but also to achieve other objectives. Such objectives might include using the OFCs' facilities for asset protection; probate mitigation; and forced heirship avoidance.

Whatever the reason for use of the OFC, almost without exception, the vehicles that will be involved are the company and/or trust. However, in some instances the individual will simply utilise the services of banks located in the OFC without the need for companies and/or trusts. As observed above, albeit for tax evasion purposes, it would seem that many UK resident individuals simply opened bank accounts with offshore banks which involved for many neither company nor trust.

As will be seen below, the OFCs have proved themselves to be extremely inventive in respect of both the company and the trust adapting where necessary the "normal" company laws and trust laws found in the high tax countries to make both vehicles "more attractive" from various perspectives.

OFFSHORE FINANCIAL CENTRE VEHICLES

Companies

OFCs have created basically two generic types of locally incorporated company, namely, the "international business company" (IBC) and the "exempt company". In the Caribbean the former tends to have been adopted whereas in Europe the latter is more prevalent although they are basically the same.

The common characteristics of both types of company are that they are not permitted to do business within the location of incorporation (i.e. within the OFC itself) and they must be owned (i.e. share ownership) by non-local residents. The benefits typically include no local (or minimal) tax on profits; freedom of repatriation of profits; minimum (if any) local disclosure requirements (e.g. no need to file detailed or sometimes, any, accounts, etc.); flexibility with respect to the location of the "books" of the company (i.e. possibility of maintaining books in another location); and often no or minimal requirements with respect to the holding of company meetings (e.g. annual general meeting).

Historically, many OFCs permitted companies to issue bearer shares (some still do, e.g. Panama) but slowly, due to pressures from, inter alia, various international organisations, bearer share companies are now unavailable in many OFCs, i.e. all shares issued are in registered form as applies in most high tax territories (e.g. the UK). The logic in seeking to preclude bearer share company formations is that the identity of the shareholders may be more readily ascertained.

However, this assumption of shareholder identity is perhaps more illusory than real. First, not all OFCs require the true identity of the beneficial shareholders when the company is set up. Second, even where the OFC requires the identity of the true beneficial owners on set-up, the company is usually permitted the simple expedient of using local nominee arrangements, i.e. in the local register of shareholders the names shown are simply nominees who hold the shares for the ultimate beneficial owners whose identity to third parties (e.g. foreign tax authorities) remain hidden. While the authorities of the OFC may, as indicated above, demand to know the true beneficial shareholders invariably the local authorities will refuse to disclose such details to third party enquirers (e.g. the tax authorities of the high tax jurisdictions). This lack of transparency is precisely what the OECD, etc. are trying to stamp out by encouraging the OFCs to enter into TIEAs (see above) with other countries.

Where any form of local filing by the company is required with the local Registrar of Companies invariably the information filed is extremely limited. It may simply constitute, for example, the company's registered office address; the address and name of the locally registered agent (on whom "service" may be served); and a register of shareholders. In some OFCs such information is available for public inspection; in other OFCs this is not possible; and in some OFCs the company's permission is needed in any event to inspect any documents so filed.

The permitted activities these types of company may undertake are virtually unlimited. Thus, the individual could make use of, say, an IBC to hold real estate (including the matrimonial home); to hold portfolio investments; to trade; or to act as agent/broker in international transactions of whatever type. It is also possible for such companies to engage in activities which involve banking and/or insurance but, generally speaking, in many OFCs such companies are more tightly supervised and controlled although this is not true in all cases.

Thus, the IBC offers the individual the opportunity to operate in a tax-free environment without restriction, with minimal supervision and no real disclosure with respect to either its activities or its shareholders.

Trusts

Trusts, as legal entities, are very different from companies but are an inevitable part of any wealth planning structure. Trusts, while offering possible tax attractions, can also be used for other purposes (see below).

Very few OFCs have any registration requirements with respect to trusts. The formation of a trust in an OFC can thus be carried out in complete secrecy (typically, using a local law firm). There is, generally speaking, no "Registrar of Trusts" equivalent of the "Registrar of Companies". Trust deeds are thus not lodged with any local authority.

The trust is a creature of equity and over many years equitable doctrines have evolved into a bundle of rules which apply to trusts. Three such rules are the rule against perpetuities; the rule against accumulations; and the rule prohibiting purpose trusts other than those with charitable objectives.

Under the first rule a trust is not permitted to continue forever but has a life which is limited (charitable trusts are different). Under common law the maximum perpetuity period is a life in being (i.e. a life in being at the date of creation of the trust) plus 21 years but under the Perpetuities and Accumulations Act 1964 the maximum period is 80 years.

Under the second rule income of a trust may be accumulated within the trust for one of six possible accumulation periods of which, in practice, the main one used is the 21 years from the date of creation of the settlement period (this is because the accumulation periods permitted in excess of this 21 years tend to give rise to uncertainty and the others are for periods of less than this).

It is often felt that these restrictions are, in the modern age, inappropriate. As a consequence, a number of OFCs have modified both rules although the particular modifications vary albeit only in detail.

For example, some OFCs have simply abolished the rule against perpetuities while other OFCs have increased the normal maximum period referred to above (e.g. the Bahamas Perpetuities (Amendment) Act 2004 increased the period of a perpetuity from 80 to 150 years; in the British Virgin Islands the maximum perpetuity period is 100 years; the maximum perpetuity for Guernsey trusts until recently was 100 years, now unlimited for new trusts (see below); and in Barbados, the rule against perpetuities does not apply).

With respect to the accumulation rule similar modifications have been made by various OFCs. For example, in Barbados accumulation of income is permitted for up to 100 years whereas in Guernsey following the Trusts (Guernsey) Law 2007 (which came into force on 17 March 2008) the accumulation period for new trusts is unlimited.

These modifications make the OFC trust significantly more attractive and flexible than its onshore counterpart (although modifications to the UK law on trusts in this regard have been suggested in a 2002 paper by the Law Commission entitled "The Rules against Perpetuities and Excessive Accumulations").

With respect to the last rule, namely, purpose trusts, the common law requires that the beneficiaries of a trust are identifiable and thus a trust set up for a specific purpose (other than charitable) is prohibited due to the lack of identifiable beneficiaries. Many OFCs have introduced specific legislation to recognise purpose trusts (not just those with charitable purposes).

For example, purpose trusts may be set up in the Bahamas, Belize, Bermuda and the Isle of Man under their respective legislation which to a degree are not all that dissimilar. However, in 1997 the Cayman Islands introduced its own legislation in this regard, namely, the Special Trusts (Alternative Regime) Law 1997 which gave rise to the so-called STAR trust. The STAR trust may be set up for persons or purposes or both and the persons may be of any number and the purposes may be of any number whether charitable or non-charitable.

Irrespective of the OFC, typically, the purposes must be lawful and not contrary to public policy.

The role of "protector" is another innovation of OFCs in relation to trusts.

A protector is in a sense an intermediary between the settlor and the trustees. Unlike the trust itself, the protector is not a creature of equity. The protector is a role created under the trust deed (i.e. the written instrument creating the trust and setting out the terms of the trust) and/or by legislation. The role of the protector may vary extending from a role which is primary reactive to a positive proactive role. The former role might be one where the protector is merely required to respond to trustee requests for help and/or guidance about trust matters. The latter role might be one where the consent of the protector is required before the trustees may carry out certain actions or take certain decsisions and one where the protector also has powers including the power to dismiss and appoint trustees and even to change the governing law of the trust.

The rationale behind the concept of protector is an attempt to offer the settlor some comfort about the manner and way in which the trust will be operated both during the lifetime of the settlor and in particular following the death of the settlor. A trust created in an OFC will invariably require the appointment of local trustees who typically will be unknown to the settlor (and beneficiaries). Such trustees will thus not really understand the mentality of the settlor or what is in the settlor's mind about how in practice the trust should function. The protector is thus the person who is to bridge this gap and is in a position to do so because the protector will almost without exception be a "family friend" who has a good knowledge about the settlor, his family and what the settlor is really trying to achieve.

It is important, however, that the settlor does not use the protector in such a manner that causes the trust to be "controlled" by the settlor with the consequence of the trust being treated as a "sham". Where this can be established (e.g. by the tax authorities of the country in which the settlor is resident) the trust is likely to be ignored for tax purposes thus defeating any tax adavantages that were intended by its use. Similarly, if the settlor had set up the trust in order to circumnavigate the forced heirship rules applicable to the settlor's estate on death proof that the trust is a sham would, of course, defeat the settlor's objective in this regard.

In fact the whole point of the protector role is to allow the settlor to be distanced from the trust so as not to be seen as controlling it, whether directly or indirectly, while at the same time offering the settlor some comfort that his views and/or wishes are not totally disregarded by the trustees. It is in this precise context that the "letter of wishes" (sometimes also referred to as a "memorandum of wishes") emerged.

The letter of wishes is literally a letter from the settlor to the trustees expressing the settlor's wishes with respect to certain aspects of the trust. It is not intended to be binding upon the trustees or be treated as part of the formal trust deed. The trustees can if they so choose ignore its content but not surprisingly, in practice, they will where possible take serious cognisance of its content.

By combining the appointment of a protector with the letter of wishes the settlor is typically well placed to convey to the trustees the factors the settlor would like the trustees to note and be aware of and, at the same time, enable their actions to be monitored by the protector and in the ultimate cause their dismissal if appropriate.

OFFSHORE FINANCIAL CENTRE USES

Tax Planning

The trust, as has been noted elsewhere in the book, may offer the individual various tax planning options. For example, the non-UK domiciled but UK resident individual can insulate non-UK situs assets from liabilities to inheritance tax by the utilisation of a non-UK resident trust and such a trust may also offer significant income and capital gains tax advantages (see Chapter 17).

For the UK domiciled and UK resident individual non-UK resident trusts offer no inheritance tax advantages but depending upon circumstances may, albeit somewhat limited, offer some income and capital gains tax advantages.

Almost without exception the tax advantages accrue due to locating the trust's residence outside the UK and invariably in the OFC (i.e. there is little point in a UK resident locating a trust's residence in another high tax jurisdiction) where, inter alia, local taxes thereon are nil, i.e. the income and capital gains of the trust are not subject to local taxes; no inheritance and/or death taxes apply in any form; and appointments out of the trust are not subject to tax.

Probate Mitigation/Will Substitute

UK probate is required with respect to UK situs assets, following death, before any distribution of such assets to beneficiaries under the deceased's will can be effected (see Chapter 26). This applies to UK situs assets irrespective of the residence and/or domicile status of the testator. The need for probate is driven by the requirement to transfer ownership of assets of the testator to the beneficiaries identified in the testator's will. Such transfer cannot be satisfactorily executed without probate having been obtained by the executors of the will.

Probate can only be granted after various forms; etc. have been completed and any inheritance tax arising on death discharged; all this takes time and cost. In the meantime the beneficiaries under the will are denied access to the deceased's assets (e.g. bank accounts).

Trusts avoid the need for probate because when the individual who set up the trust (i.e. the settlor) dies (or indeed if a beneficiary of the trust dies) assets held by the trust continue to be held by the trust and no change in asset ownership occurs. Strictly speaking, an "onshore" (i.e. UK) trust also produces the same advantage but at a possible ongoing tax cost as the trust is itself a taxable entity. In addition, as an onshore trust flexibility is much reduced by comparison to its offshore brethren. This loss of flexibility is due to the typically more onerous requirements applicable to trusts governed by UK laws be they those specifically applicable to trusts (e.g. the rules against perpetuities and purpose trusts; see above) or those appertaining to wider issues such as forced heirship or creditor protection (see below).

The offshore trust not only permits the avoidance of probate on death but it may also act as a substitute will. While it is unlikely that the whole of the individual's worldwide assets will necessarily be placed in one or more offshore trusts a significant portion of such assets may be so settled. The use of the trust in this manner has a number of advantages including the fact that the terms of trust are confidential (the will becomes a public document following death); the trustees under a discretionary trust may take into account changes in legislation and the fortunes of the beneficiaries even after the settlor has died (whereas once the testator dies the will is "set in stone"); and the trust assets may be located in a number of different jurisdictions yet administered by the same trustees (probate may be required in all countries in which the deceased owned assets making the probate process not only time consuming but very expensive).

Asset Protection

All trusts offer "asset protection". The term "asset protection trust" (APT) is a generic term and is commonly used to refer to trusts which are specifically set up to protect the assets of the settlor from third party claims. Such third parties typically include creditors, those claiming under forced heirship rules and disgruntled ex-spouses. However, such third parties may also extend to governments seeking to expropriate the individual's assets.

Although the concept of asset protection from third parties underpins the APT the treatment of APTs in the OFCs often varies according to whether the trust is designed specifically to protect against creditors versus other third parties (e.g. forced heirship claims). In addition, OFCs vary in the extent to which foreign creditor judgements may be enforced locally in the OFC.

The effectiveness of the APT against creditors varies according to the particular circumstances of the individual. Many onshore jurisdictions (of which the UK is one) have specific legislation designed to prevent individuals from defrauding creditors and thus simply settling assets in an APT in an OFC may not fully protect the individual's assets as intended; although an APT offshore is, other things being equal, likely to offer in practice greater protection than an APT onshore.

Issues of forced heirship are increasingly common and again many OFCs have introduced legislation designed to defeat such claims. Such legislation will typically ensure that despite the legal regime applying in the settlor's home jurisdiction trusts created in the OFC by the individual will be regarded as valid and foreign forced heirship judgements will not be recognised and/or enforced in the OFC.

CHOOSING AN OFFSHORE FINANCIAL CENTRE

It is clear from the above discussion that there is arguably no one "best" OFC for all purposes.

Some OFCs are particularly appropriate for certain types of planning while not appropriate for others. The APT, for example, is not a vehicle available in all OFCs and, where it is available, the degree of protection offered by an APT in one OFC may differ markedly from an APT in another. Filing requirements for the IBC differ among the various OFCs offering this type of company.

However, there are certain minimum requirements for any OFC to meet if it is to be considered for use in any planning exercise.

These minimum requirements include political stability; financial stability; judicial stability; and a highly proficient and highly regarded professional infrastructure. While not necessarily a minimum requirement for all individuals, from the UK perspective a legal system based on common law and English as the main "professional" language would seem highly desirable attributes. The requirement for local legal and other documents to be constantly translated from, say, Portuguese (in the case of Madeira) to English, only adds to time, cost and the possibility of confusion.

A less stringent requirement but, again, possibly desirable are OFCs located in the same time zone as the individual, although with relatively instantaneous communication by phone, fax, email, etc. this, today, perhaps seems less necessary.

Once an OFC qualifies under the above minimum requirements the choice may be then narrowed by investigating the reputation, laws and attitude of the OFC with respect to the particular planning purpose in mind. In addition, the strength of local bank secrecy laws should be examined and whether the OFC is a party to any agreements under which information may be exchanged (e.g. under TIEAs and/or exchange of information provisions contained within double tax agreements) with other countries should also be checked. Other things being equal an APT, for example, located in an OFC with strong bank secrecy laws and which is not a party to any exchange information agreements is likely to be more robust to external "attack" than might otherwise be the case.

Similarly, the use of a trust to avoid "forced heirship" issues is likely to be more robust from external "attack" where the OFC is not a party to any information exchange agreements, where bank secrecy is strongest and where specific local legislation exists to deal with such issues.

Where the individual requires what might be termed a conventional trust for general family planning purposes local trust legislation may differ between OFCs and it is important that whatever the precise nature of the local law that, under UK law, the trust would be recognised as a properly constituted trust. Thus, for example, where local trust law permits the settlor extremely wide powers to "control" the trust (which may be acceptable under the OFC's local law, i.e. the trust would still be recognised as a separate entity) it may be that under UK law the trust would be regarded as transparent and, inter alia, tax ineffective.

Even for the conventional trust the issues of information exchange agreements and bank secrecy mentioned above, while possibly of slightly less importance, are still factors to take into account.

With respect to companies the differences between the local laws of various OFCs is perhaps less significant. Broadly, whether the OFC has adopted IBC legislation or exempt company legislation the "bottom line" is usually that no local taxes of any kind are levied. Technically, under some OFCs the exemption from all taxes is for a defined time period (i.e. not indefinite) but such periods are usually for many years in the future. Nevertheless, this is probably worth checking.

The main differences, generally speaking, relate to non-tax factors; issues to be examined include requirements as to company/shareholder meetings in terms of number per annum, location and whether meetings need to be held physically or whether they can be effected by telephone; minimum requirements as to the number of directors, nationality or residence requirements; the possibility of nominee arrangements; disclosure requirements relating to names and/or addresses of directors or the need for company accounts to be filed; and the position with respect to public access of filed information.

The twin issues referred to above of information exchange agreements and bank secrecy are again also relevant.

Of extreme importance in the final analysis is the individual's own perception of the OFC. The individual must feel comfortable with any choice made.

UK TAX AND INFORMATION DISCLOSURE REQUIREMENTS

Settlors who set up trusts in OFCs must appreciate that once the trust is operational the trustees' responsibilities are to the beneficiaries (of which, of course, the settlor may be one) and not to the settlor.

Thus, for example, it may be the case that the UK resident settlor has a capital gains tax liability arising from capital gains made by the offshore trust which for UK tax purposes are attributed to the settlor (due to the settlor's spouse being a beneficiary) (see Chapter 17). Under UK law specific provisions provide in such cases for the settlor to recover any such capital gains tax charge from the trustees. The trustees, however, owe no fiduciary duty to the settlor and any reimbursement may be regarded by the beneficiaries as a breach of trust. Any attempt at enforcement for such recovery on the part of the settlor in the OFC may well be given short shrift.

Non-UK resident trustees are liable to UK income tax on UK source income at the 40% rate if the trust is discretionary (assuming the income is not "excluded income"; see Chapter 22). However, in view of collection and enforcement difficulties on the part of HMRC the trustees may simply refuse to file appropriate tax returns and/or discharge the liability. Should, on the other hand, the trustees discharge the liability again as above they may be held to be in breach of trust. However, for the settlor of such a trust residing in the UK such a position is not particularly satisfactory.

The inclusion of clauses in the trust deed enabling trustees to discharge tax liabilities arising under other jurisdictions may not in fact solve the problem.

To some extent the above discussion presupposes that HMRC know about the trust in the OFC and, inter alia, who set it up (i.e. the identity of the settlor). It is possible, although generally speaking highly unlikely, that the authorities of the location in which the trust has been set up may have conveyed information to HMRC voluntarily or on request under the terms of a relevant double tax agreement. The UK is a party to double tax agreements with the following OFCs: Antigua; Barbados; Belize; Cyprus; Fiji; Grenada; Guernsey; Isle of Man; Jersey; Malta; Mauritius; Montserrat; St Kitts and Trinidad and Tobago.

As the UK is currently only a party to two TIEAs (namely, that with Bermuda and the Isle of Man) which have both only in fact very recently been signed, information under this route affects of course only Bermuda and the Isle of Man.

In fact the only information that at the time of set up of the trust needs to be notified to HMRC relates to any person who in the course of their trade or profession (other than a barrister) has been concerned with the making of the trust and has reason to believe that the settlor is domiciled in the UK. Such a person is required within three months of making the trust to inform HMRC of the names and addresses of the settlor and the trustees.

This requirement is laid down in the inheritance tax legislation. It applies only to inter vivos trusts not those created by will. Penalties are leviable for failure to notify as required.

It should also be noted that where the individual settles property on trust (whether UK resident of not) which constitutes for inheritance tax purposes a chargeable lifetime transfer (see Chapter 9) an account on Form IHT 100 may need to be lodged depending upon the amount of the transfer (see Chapter 13). Following the inheritance tax changes introduced in FA 2006 under which all transfers into trusts are chargeable lifetime transfers (i.e. not potentially exempt transfers; see Chapter 15) the requirement to file a Form IHT 100 is now more likely than pre FA 2006.

Of course it should not be forgotten that the individual is in any event liable to disclose income/capital gains as appropriate on the personal Tax Return, where necessary, which will alert HMRC to the trust's existence.

All other information concerning the trust requires HMRC to specifically request it under various of the UK's tax provisions. This will involve asking the individual to supply it as a direct request made to the offshore trustees will almost certainly prove unfruitful.

TAX EXPOSURE OF TRUST SETTLOR

There is no general UK tax rule under which the settlor is liable for taxes not discharged by trustees of non-UK resident trusts.

In the case of UK source income the trustees are liable to income tax as appropriate. A failure to discharge such liabilities does not, however, cause the settlor to become liable thereon.

As non-UK resident, the trustees have no exposure to capital gains tax (except on the disposal of UK situs business assets).

With respect to inheritance tax the position is slightly different to that for income and capital gains tax. The non-UK resident trust is still within the ambit of the tax (see Chapter 15). Thus, for example, a UK domiciled individual possessing a pre 22 March 2006 interest in possession is within the charge to inheritance tax on death with respect to the assets (wherever located) of the trust in which the interest subsists. For the non-UK domiciled individual, possessing a similar interest, the inheritance tax charge is only applicable if on death the interest subsisted in UK situs property. Where the trust is discretionary, the trustees are within the charge to inheritance tax with respect to the ten yearly and exit charges (see Chapter 15). However, under certain circumstances the settlor and/or beneficiaries in effect have a possible secondary liability in respect of these charges.

RELOCATION TO AN OFC

Perhaps the ultimate tax efficient plan is to relocate to an OFC and become a resident there. While local residents are subject to local tax in some OFCs this is not usually the position. Indeed, even where local tax is levied it is invariably at rates significantly lower than in the high tax countries and often only on income and possibly capital gains but not on death or gifts.

Relocating, however, is, of course, a very serious option with all that it entails but is an option often pursued by the extremely wealthy. It is by no means uncommon for "pop stars", tennis players, golfers and formula one grand prix drivers to leave their original countries of residence (where taxes are relatively speaking "high") and relocate to a country with a more favourable tax climate.

In many cases, however, the relocations in such cases are not to the conventional OFCs (e.g. Bermuda, the Bahamas, Turks and Caicos) but to countries not normally categorised as OFCs but which nevertheless offer favourable tax status to high net worth individuals; countries such as Monaco and Switzerland are two notable destinations. For the UK individual Guernsey, Isle of Man and Jersey, while not "tax-free" jurisdictions, are also popular options but countries as far a field as Belize and the Seychelles have also found favour with some high profile individuals.

The choice will depend upon many factors (e.g. language, geographical location, political stability, accessability) although, probably almost without exception, low taxes are a prerequisite to any move.

Even if such a move is made it should be noted that the country from which the departure has been made may continue (albeit for a limited time period) to impose its own taxes. This is primarily in the area of inheritance/death taxes where so-called "trailing taxes" may apply (see Chapter 2). The UK, for example, as highlighted elsewhere in the book (Chapter 9) levies inheritance tax on worldwide assets for three years following loss of UK domicile status and, of course, the USA still levies the whole gamut of its taxes on those individuals who, despite having left the USA, retain their USA citizenship.

Relocation to an OFC does not mean that the individual's assets are now simply owned directly in the individual's own name. Many of the issues discussed still apply although perhaps with less need to mitigate tax. Issues such as APTs, probate and information disclosure all need to be addressed. Residency in the British Virgin Islands, for example, does not mean that all trusts should thus be set up in, and governed by the laws of, the British Virgin Islands. Indeed, it could be argued that "offshore" structures become even more important as the OFC of the individual's residency may become politically unstable, more amenable to supplying information to the tax authorities and/or may change its local laws in an unfavourable manner.

SUMMARY

Mitigation of UK taxes may be achieved by a variety of means. OFCs offer the individual one option to achieve such mitigation.

OFCs may also be utilised for non-tax reasons including the avoidance of forced heirship laws, creditor protection and general family planning.

OFCs offer vehicles tailored to achieving efficient family asset structuring. The two main vehicles are those available elsewhere, namely companies and trusts, but the attributes of both these vehicles have been amended within the various OFCs to increase their flexibility. Examples are the IBC and exempt company and APTs.

The choice of a suitable OFC depends upon a number of factors. No one OFC is likely to be the "best" OFC for all purposes.

Relocation to an OFC may be the answer for some individuals but even in this case many of the issues discussed are still relevant.

In view of the attractive financial and non-financial benefits of OFCs high tax jurisdictions and a number of international bodies take a jaundiced view of them and any individual using them is likely to face close scrutiny from their home tax authority.

25
International Taxation

BACKGROUND

As indicated elsewhere the main thrust of this book has been a detailed consideration of the various UK tax issues which impact upon both UK and non-UK domiciled individuals vis-à-vis their wealth. However, as also pointed out elsewhere in the book, the non-UK tax issues should not be overlooked.

Where the non-UK domiciled (or indeed UK domiciled) individual dies owning assets in various countries it is highly likely that more than one country's tax regime will impact upon the deceased's estate. Thus, the possibility of double (if not triple, etc.) taxation is extremely likely and, unchecked, would present material problems for the deceased's heirs.

This chapter examines the issue of double taxation and the manner in which the UK seeks to relieve its ramifications.

DOUBLE TAXATION

Double taxation arises where two (or more) different taxing jurisdictions seek to tax the same taxpayer and/or the same income/asset.

This double taxation may take the form of two charges to income tax on the same income; two charges to capital gains tax on the same capital gains; or two charges to taxation on the same lifetime gifts and/or death estate.

Unchecked, international activities would be severely curtailed.

In the UK, the provision is made which is designed to alleviate the double taxation of UK resident taxpayers (referred to as unilateral relief, i.e. relief proffered by the UK tax authorities irrespective of the stance taken by other countries). The basic approach adopted is to allow a credit for any overseas taxes levied on non-UK source of income/asset by way of the offset against the corresponding UK tax on that income/asset; in essence for every £1 of overseas tax paid this reduces the UK liability by £1.

Alternatively, double tax relief may also be available under one of the double tax agreements to which the UK is a party. However, with respect to inheritance tax there are only ten such agreements (see below).

Nevertheless, as indicated above, even if there is no applicable double tax agreement the UK's unilateral provisions may be applied to allow relief to be obtained.

DOUBLE TAX AGREEMENTS

While the provisions of a double tax agreement deal with double taxation issues such agreements are in fact of much wider application.

A double tax agreement is a bilateral agreement (i.e. an agreement between two countries) whose principal objectives are:

- the prevention of tax avoidance/evasion; and
- the prevention of double taxation.

The UK's double tax agreements fall into two categories. One category of double tax agreement deals with income and capital gains taxes and the other category deals with inheritance tax.

While it is a basic rule of international law that the terms of an international agreement (such as a double tax agreement dealing with taxation) override domestic law, the provisions of a domestic law passed after the conclusion of an international agreement may override the provisions of the latter where it is clearly intended to so do. Generally speaking, however, this is not the case.

It is widely accepted that a double tax agreement while offering relief from double tax cannot impose a tax liability which is not imposed under domestic law.

Income and Capital Gains Tax Agreements

The UK is a party to over 100 double tax agreements which deal with income and capital gains tax issues. The form of all these agreements generally follows the structure laid down by the OECD in their so-called Model Convention "OECD Model Tax Convention on Income and Capital". The current Model Convention is that of 1977 but since that date it has undergone a number of revisions.

The Model Convention consists of a number of "Articles", each Article dealing with a specific tax issue. The basic philosophy underlying all double tax agreements is that the country in which the individual is resident has the primary right to tax the individual and that it is this country that is then obliged to grant any double tax relief.

Thus, for example, a UK domiciled and UK resident individual is liable to UK income and capital gains tax on worldwide income/gains but any overseas (i.e. non-UK) tax which the individual suffers is to be allowed by the UK to offset the individual's UK tax liability (i.e. reduce the UK liability).

However, the country which is a party to the double tax agreement but in which the individual does not reside may still levy its own taxes on income/gains which arise within its borders. Normally, however, the rates of tax so charged are reduced (sometimes in fact to nil) under the agreement as compared to that country's domestic rates which would normally apply in the absence of such an agreement.

In effect, the two countries party to a double tax agreement are mutually agreeing to each tax their own residents but not the residents of the other country except to the extent that income and/or capital gains arise in their country. In this latter case the parties to the agreement are then agreeing to reduce their normal domestic levels of tax which would normally apply to income/gains arising to a non-resident.

For example, under the double tax agreement between the UK and the USA a UK resident individual may receive dividends arising on USA equities (i.e. US source income). The UK will levy UK income tax on this income as it is income of a UK resident. The USA, however, levies a dividend withholding tax (basically cash at source is deducted from the dividend payment and kept by the USA tax authorities) under their domestic law at the rate of 30%. Under the UK/USA double tax agreement this 30% rate is reduced to 15% where paid to a UK resident individual.

When computing the individual's UK income tax liability relief for this 15% rate of withholding tax will be granted (i.e. the USA tax so deducted will be used to reduce the UK tax charge). The effect of this "credit mechanism" is that the individual pays the higher of the two countries' tax charges.

As a quid pro quo in the above scenario the UK in principle reduces the level of its domestic dividend withholding tax on UK source dividends paid to USA residents (in fact this is not necessary as the UK does not levy a dividend withholding tax but, if it did, this is what would have happened).

Thus, the idea behind the concept of the double tax agreement is that both countries party to the agreement agree to tax each other's residents in a similar and less penal manner to encourage activity between the two countries (e.g. investment and trade).

As a general rule, domestic withholding taxes are often levied on the investment income of non-residents. The rate of these withholding taxes is typically reduced from their normal domestic levels and in many cases to zero in order to attract foreign investment. Capital gains of non-residents may also simply not be taxed at all (as applies in the UK).

In some cases, irrespective of the existence of a double tax agreement, countries offer tax attractive environments to encourage foreign investment. Both the Republic of Ireland and Luxembourg, for example, have managed to attract significant numbers of offshore mutual funds to their shores by offering a tax attractive environment for the fund itself (e.g. low or no taxes) plus zero withholding taxes on interest and dividend payments made by the funds to their non-resident investors. In addition, the countries do not levy capital gains tax on the disposal by the investor of their investment in the funds.

However, not all double tax agreements are literally identical and as a consequence, a practice of so-called "treaty shopping" began under which individuals resident in one country (X) would seek to invest in another country (Y) but via a third country (Z). The reason for so doing was because the terms of the double tax agreement between Y and Z were more favourable than those in the agreement between X and Z.

Thus, for example, the withholding tax on dividends on USA equities from the USA to a resident of the Netherlands under the USA/Netherlands double tax agreement is nil. The rate applicable on such dividends to a UK resident individual is 15%. If a UK resident individual thus set up a Dutch resident company to receive USA source dividends the USA withholding tax would be reduced from 15% to nil and this income could then in principle be extracted from the Netherlands company in the form of dividends under a zero Dutch withholding tax under the UK/Netherlands double tax agreement.

Many double tax agreements now contain anti-avoidance provisions designed to prevent this form of tax planning.

In order to try to prevent tax avoidance/evasion each double tax agreement also contains provisions in one of its Articles permitting each country to exchange information with the other. Thus, for example, a UK resident investing in real estate in France or Spain may find that the investment is reported to the UK tax authorities either automatically or possibly if and when the UK tax authorities request such information.

It is possible for an individual to be dually resident, i.e. the individual is, for example, resident in the UK under UK law but, say, resident in Italy under Italian domestic law. Such individual is thus exposed to UK and Italian tax on income/gains. Typically, in such cases the relevant double tax agreement (in this example the UK/Italy agreement) will resolve such dual residence by applying a series of so-called "tie-breaker" tests (e.g. resolving dual residence in favour of the country in which the individual has a permanent home; if there are such homes in each country then residence will be where economic ties, etc. are closest) laid out in the agreement thus resulting in single residency (e.g. in the UK in this example). The individual will thus in principle in this example be subject to UK tax on worldwide income/gains as a resident thereof but only subject to Italian tax on Italian source income/gains.

As is clear throughout the book the non-UK domiciled but UK resident individual is subject to UK taxes in a different manner to the UK domiciled and resident individual. The remittance basis applies to non-UK source income and capital gains. However, under a number of the UK's double tax agreements where such an individual receives income from sources within the other country the reduced rates of withholding tax applicable under the agreement in that other country will only apply if the income is remitted (and thus subject to tax) to the UK by the individual. A failure to remit in such circumstances will mean that the normally higher domestic rates of withholding tax will apply in the other country (e.g. UK/Cyprus double tax agreement; Article 6).

Inheritance Tax Agreements

The UK is a party to ten double tax agreements which address inheritance tax; significantly less than the number of such agreements dealing with income and capital gains tax.

The agreements are with:

- France
- India
- Ireland
- Italy
- the Netherlands

- South Africa
- Sweden
- Switzerland
- Pakistan
- the USA.

These 10 agreements can be conveniently divided into those agreements which were entered into *after* capital transfer tax (now inheritance tax) was introduced, namely:

- Ireland
- the Netherlands
- South Africa
- Sweden
- Switzerland
- the USA.

and those agreements which were in existence previously which dealt with the then tax of estate duty (inheritance tax ultimately replaced estate duty):

- France
- India
- Italy
- Pakistan.

Of the above agreements the most recently concluded is that with the Netherlands in 1980 and the oldest is that concluded with India in 1956.

Each of the six agreements listed above are similar in content and principle but different from the remaining four agreements.

PRE 1975 AGREEMENTS

The four agreements above which were concluded during the estate duty (between 1945 and 1968) era only apply on the death of an individual and not to lifetime gifts. Furthermore, these four agreements each disapply the UK's domestic rules for inheritance tax purposes relating to the concept of "deemed UK domiciled" (because under estate duty no similar rule existed). Thus, in considering the terms of these agreements deemed UK domicile is effectively ignored.

Although concluded during the estate duty era the agreements now apply to inheritance tax although their content remains unchanged.

Despite the continued existence and current applicability of all four agreements, both India and Pakistan have abolished death duties (India in 1985 and Pakistan in 1979). Thus, today, the main effect of the agreements with India and Pakistan is to restrict the application on death of the deemed UK domicile rules; potentially of major significance in practice given the probable large numbers of Indian/Pakistan nationals who have resided in the UK for at least 17 tax years out of the last 20 tax years (thus, under UK domestic law would be regarded as having become deemed UK domiciled; see Chapter 9).

The basic (although not identical) approach of each of the four agreements is to deny the UK the right to levy UK inheritance tax on death if the individual is domiciled in the other territory. The determination of the individual's domicile status, however, is under the respective domestic laws of each country. Thus, a determination as to whether, for example, an individual is domiciled in India is determined not under UK rules but those of India. The rules determining domicile under Indian law, or indeed the other three countries, may depend upon an individual's nationality or habitual residence and have nothing whatsoever to do with the approach adopted in the UK.

In fact none of these agreements completely precludes the UK from charging inheritance tax on death. What each agreement does is to restrict the UK's rights in this regard where the individual under the terms of the double tax agreement is regarded as domiciled in the other country. Thus, for example, in the case of the UK/Pakistan agreement, UK inheritance tax is only leviable on a Pakistani domiciled individual if the property is UK situs. Non-UK situs property, whether in Pakistan or outside of both the UK and Pakistan, may only be subject to Pakistan death taxes (in fact now abolished).

A further complication is that the rules determining situs of assets laid down in the agreement may not be entirely in accord with those under UK domestic law as outlined in Chapter 6 (and it is the rules in the agreement that prevail). In the agreement with France, for example, monies payable under a life policy are deemed to be situated at the place where the deceased individual was domiciled at the time of death, whereas under UK domestic law such a policy is regarded as a debt and thus located where the debtor company (i.e. the life insurance company issuing the policy) is resident.

POST 1975 AGREEMENTS

These agreements are significantly different from those discussed above. They have each been entered into after estate duty was abolished in the UK in 1975.

These agreements, unlike the four agreements referred to above, apply to lifetime gifts as well as the death estate and the deemed UK domiciled rules are not disapplied. They are therefore of wider application than the pre 1975 agreements.

To a degree they are each similar in content as they are each based on the OECD Model "OECD Estate, Inheritance and Gift Model Convention" of 1966 which is now replaced by a revised and updated Model of 1982.

The basic approach adopted by this Model Agreement is to grant primary taxing rights to the country in which the individual is domiciled. The other country may levy its own tax on such individuals but typically only with respect to property sited in that country and even then such taxing rights may not extend to literally all property sited therein (e.g. shares of companies registered in that country may fall outside that country's right to tax). Real estate, however, is an exception as the country in which such real estate is situated always has the primary taxing rights (similarly, the country in which business property is situated typically will have primary taxing rights).

The major problem in practice (as also applies to the pre 1975 agreements) is the determination of the individual's domicile status. As mentioned above, each country applies its own domestic laws to determine the domicile status of the individual. These respective tests are likely to differ. Thus, the UK will apply the rules described in Chapter 3 of this book. The other country's rules are likely to be very different and may, for example, be based on the individual's nationality, ordinary residence or basic residence status.

In France, for example, an individual's domicile status is determined where that individual is "principally established", whereas in Italy it is where the individual's "real home" is located, neither of which tests are identical to the rules applicable in the UK.

In view of the disparate tests applied in determining domicile status dual domicile may arise, i.e. each country under its own domestic rules classifies the individual as domiciled in their country. Each of the agreements thus applies a so-called "tie-breaker" test to resolve this issue. Usually, this tie-breaker test involves a number of sequential tests and normally follows the following format: the individual is domiciled in the country where a permanent home is available to the individual; if the individual has permanent homes in each country then domicile is the country where that individual's personal and economic ties are closer; failing this the individual's domicile status is the country of which he is a national. If the domicile status of the individual can still not be determined then the two countries have to resolve the issue by mutual agreement (a potentially long and drawn-out process).

The issue of "treaty shopping" discussed above in connection with the income/capital gains tax double tax agreements is not addressed in any of the inheritance tax agreements but arguably treaty shopping in this context is somewhat difficult to implement.

The UK/Switzerland agreement is a little different from the other post 1975 agreements. First, although the current agreement applies to deaths on or after 6 March 1995, unlike the other agreements post 1975 the agreement with Switzerland only applies to death and not lifetime gifts (although it does, prima facie, apply to gifts with reservation).

Second, primary taxing rights are granted to the country in which the individual is domiciled (if necessary using the tie-breaker tests) but this only extends to third country property, i.e. with respect to property situated outside both the UK and Switzerland only the country where the individual is domiciled may tax such property. If, however, the individual is domiciled in the UK under UK law and in Switzerland under Swiss law (irrespective of the conclusion applying the tie-breaker tests) the country in which the property is situated (i.e. the UK or Switzerland) has sole taxing rights.

Third, a specific provision applies to certain inter-spouse transfers. In principle under this provision a better (i.e. more favourable) UK inheritance tax position arises where the transfer is from a Swiss domiciled individual, who is deemed UK domiciled, to a non-UK domiciled individual on the death of the former.

The agreement between the UK and France does not extend to Northern Ireland and only applies on death. In line with the Model Agreement the country with primary taxing rights is the country in which the individual is domiciled (if necessary applying the tie-breaker tests). The other country is not then permitted to levy its tax on property situated outside its own country.

What becomes clear is that each of the ten agreements to which the UK is a party each have their own particular Articles which may not be in line with the Model Agreement. To generalise about any of these agreements is thus extremely dangerous. The only safe way to proceed is to read the particular agreement which may apply in the circumstances.

It is, however, probably fair to say that as an agreement cannot levy tax (which is not levied under domestic law) the terms of any particular agreement are likely to be to the individual's benefit as its terms may restrict taxation to just one of the countries. This may not only reduce the problem of double taxation arising but, equally importantly, may reduce the overall tax burden.

EUROPEAN UNION/COMMUNITY

The European Union was formally the European Economic Community when it was founded in 1957. The UK became a party to the European Community on 1 Janury 1973. The primary organs of the EU are the Council, Commission, Paliament, the Court of Justice and the Court of Auditors.

EC law takes priority over national law and the main source of EC law is the EC Treaty. Legislation may take different forms including regulations, directives and opinions.

In 1998 the UK by way of the Human Rights Act 1998 introduced the provisions of the European Convention of Human Rights and Freedoms (ECHR) into UK domestic law. The ECHR is not a creature of the EU/EC but of the Council of Europe in Strasbourg, an institution entirely separate from any organs of the EU/EC. The European Court of Human Rights was also created.

The legislation of the EC, the decisions of the Court of Justice and the decisions of the European Court of Human Rights have each impacted on the UK's domestic tax laws (and others) in significant ways.

One of the recent initiatives of the EU which affects the savings of individuals is the EU Savings Directive.

EU SAVINGS DIRECTIVE

Background

The EU Savings Directive has as its objective the prevention of tax evasion on savings income by providing for the automatic exchange of information between Member

States of the EU on cross-border savings income payments made to beneficial owners who are *EU resident individuals* However, three Member States are to apply a withholding tax on the cross-border savings income payments made by these States as opposed to supplying information to other Member States. The three States are Austria, Belgium and Luxembourg.

While the Directive applies to Member States of the EU its effect is extended to dependent and associated territories of both the UK and the Netherlands and certain countries who are neither Member States nor dependent or associated territories (see below).

The Directive took effect on 1 July 2005 and relates to relevant payments on or thereafter.

Savings Income

The term "savings income" is perhaps misleading. The Directive only applies to payments of *interest* (thus, is inapplicable to dividends, rents, insurance benefits, pension benefits and any other form of savings income).

"Interest" only

The Directive, as indicated above, applies only to "interest" payments which include interest typically paid/credited to a bank account and interest relating to debt claims of every kind whether secured or not. Any interest which is accrued or capitalised is also covered.

Interest payments made by some (but not all) mutual funds are also covered including mutual funds which are UCITS (i.e. undertakings for collective investment in transferable securities) within Directive 85/611/EEC.

Interest arising on domestic and international bonds (or other negotiable securities) issued prior to 1 March 2001 is not subject to the Directive; such instruments are not regarded as debt claims within the Directive. This, however, is a transitional provision applying until 31 December 2010.

Information Exchange

Under the provisions of the Directive where a paying agent (broadly, the person responsible for making the actual payment of the interest to the recipient) makes a payment of interest to an individual resident in another Member State details of the individual will be conveyed by the paying agent to the tax authority in which the paying agent is resident. The latter tax authority will then pass this information to the tax authority in which the individual is resident.

The details which will be collected and passed on include the identity of the individual and their residence status; the account number of the individual giving rise to the interest or details of the debt claim giving rise to the interest if there is no account.

The provision of this exchange is automatic and is to be provided no less than once a year and within six months of the end of it.

Withholding Tax

However, as indicated above three Member States, namely, Austria, Belgium and Luxembourg, are to levy a withholding tax rather than supplying information about the individual concerned.

This "opt out" is to apply for a transitional period only. However, the transitional period ends only when Switzerland, Liechtenstein, San Marino, Monaco, Andorra and the USA agree to the provision of information exchange in accordance with the Directive (these territories, the USA excepted, currently agreeing only to the levying of the withholding tax). It may be some time before this occurs.

The amount of the withholding tax is set at 15% for the first three years (i.e. 1 July 2005 to 30 June 2008); 20% for the subsequent three years; and 35% thereafter. These withholding taxes are in addition to any other form of withholding tax that each of these countries already levies under their own domestic law and thus, in aggregate, such withholding taxes could represent serious adverse cash flow to the individual.

Where the withholding tax under the Directive is levied it is to be creditable against any tax liability arising on the part of the individual entitled to it and to the extent it exceeds the individual's liability it is to be repaid to the individual by the tax authority of the country in which the individual is resident. It may be that under the normal domestic law of the country in which the interest arises a local domestic withholding tax is also levied; the tax levied under the Directive would in such cases be in addition to this local domestic withholding tax. The local withholding tax is to be credited before the withholding tax under the Directive.

Withholding Tax v. Information Supply

Despite this approach adopted by these three countries it is possible for the individual to opt for no withholding under the Directive to be applied. For a UK resident either the individual may simply instruct the paying agent to supply the information as above to the relevant tax authority *or* the individual may obtain from HMRC (the local tax office who has the individual's details and to which a Tax Return is normally made) a certificate detailing, inter alia, the individual's name, address and tax identification number which can then be submitted by the individual to the paying agent requesting non-deduction of the withholding tax levied under the Directive. Any such certificate is valid for up to three years and will generally be issued by HMRC within two months of the individual making the request.

Non-Member States and TIEAs

In addition to Austria, Belgium and Luxembourg the following territories have opted for the levying of a withholding tax as opposed to the supply of information. These territories are: Andorra, British Virgin Islands, Gibraltar, Guernsey, Isle of Man, Jersey, Liechtenstein, Monaco, Netherlands Antilles, San Marino, Switzerland and Turks and Caicos Islands.

In the case of British Virgin Islands, Gibraltar, Guernsey, Isle of Man, Jersey, Netherlands Antilles and Turks and Caicos Islands separate bilateral agreements are entered into between each of these territories and the various Member States.

In the case of the Cayman Islands, Montserrat, Aruba and Anguilla each of these territories have agreed to the supply of information, ab initio, rather than adopting the withholding tax approach.

There are no agreements between the Bahamas and Member States.

The agreements between the UK and these various dependent and associated territories in relation to the Savings Directive are referred to as "TIEAs", i.e. Tax Information Exchange Agreements. The UK has also entered into other ITEAs which are not related to the Savings Directive.

Interestingly, the TIEAs entered into by the UK in connection with the Savings Directive and the above territories are not all identical. They are divided into those which are reciprocal and those which are not. The former comprises the agreements with Aruba, British Virgin Island, Gibraltar, Guernsey, Isle of Man, Jersey, Montserrat and Netherlands Antilles and the latter those agreements with Anguilla, Cayman Islands and Turks and Caicos.

The procedures referred to above for the UK resident to avoid the levying of the withholding tax levied by a Member State also apply to interest paid by paying agents in each of these territories listed above in the same manner.

It is, however, for the country which has opted for the withholding tax option to determine whether it will permit the individual to choose for information to be supplied instead.

With respect to payments of interest by UK paying agents information will be supplied by HMRC where the individual is resident in one of the other Member States or resident in any of the following territories: Aruba, British Virgin Islands, Gibraltar, Guernsey, Isle of Man, Jersey, Montserrat and Netherlands Antilles.

Switzerland and the USA

It will be noted that Switzerland is listed as a territory which is to levy a withholding tax on interest payments made by its paying agents. Switzerland is not, of course, in the EU but the EU felt that without Switzerland's involvement the objective of the Directive would be seriously undermined. The EU would also like the USA to agree to the adoption of similar procedures but so far the USA have not agreed to do so.

Savings Directive and Directive 77/799/EEC

It may be noted that Directive 77/799/EEC of 19 December 1977 which concerns mutual assistance in the collection of direct and indirect (e.g. VAT) taxes of Member States also allows for information to be exchanged among Member States. Such information would extend to interest payments. However, there are certain restrictions in the 1977 Directive and it is specifically provided in the Savings Directive that such restrictions should not be allowed to preclude information provision under the Savings Directive. Despite this Directive being introduced some 30 years ago the UK only signed it in early 2007 becoming, at that time, the 15th country to so sign.

Implications of the Savings Directive

First and foremost the Directive only applies to *interest* payments made to *individual* beneficial owners who are *EU resident*. The UK also applies the Directive to individuals who are resident in Aruba, British Virgin Islands, Gibraltar, Guernsey, Isle of Man, Jersey, Montserrat and Netherlands Antilles.

The nationality of the individual is irrelevant; if the individual is EU resident the Directive applies. On the other hand, an EU national who is resident outside the EU (and outside the above territories) receiving EU source interest will fall outside the the Directive.

However, given the voluminous information which is being conveyed automatically under the Directive among the various Member States there is no guarantee that, by accident or otherwise, information will not be disclosed to the tax authorities of the individual's country of residence in circumstances where the Directive does not in fact apply. In such circumstances the "damage" will be done irrespective of any remedy (if any).

For those individuals with monies deposited in Austria, Belgium or Luxembourg (and in those offshore territories levying the withholding tax) who, for whatever reason, may not wish the tax authority of their country of residence to know of the deposit will suffer relatively penal rates of withholding tax, now 20%, increased from 15% post 30 June 2008. The next proposed increase will be effective 1 July 2014 and the rate then applicable will be 35%. Even if the withholding tax is completely offsettable against the individual's county of residence tax liability the withholding tax amount represents serious adverse cash flow.

The Directive is inapplicable where the beneficial recipient of the interest is not an individual, e.g. a company. The company may be owned itself by the individual or a trust set up by the individual. Where the monies belong to the trustees of the trust (i.e. not the underlying company) the Directive's applicability seems unclear although the UK conventional discretionary trust should not be "caught". The position with respect to the interest in possession trust is less clear although there appears to be stronger grounds for an argument that the Directive does apply in this case.

In principle, the Directive applies to both the UK and non-UK domiciled but UK resident individual as there is no specific reference in the Directive to individuals who are non-UK domiciled. However, non-UK domiciled but UK resident individuals are subject to UK income tax only on remittances to the UK. Typically, non-UK source interest may not be remitted to the UK. In this regard HMRC have commented as follows:

> The Directive makes no mention of domicile or remittance. If you are resident in the UK and you receive savings income from a territory covered by the Directive (or a related agreement) then the details of the payment should be reported to the UK, or it should be subject to withholding tax. You may apply for a certificate from HMRC for the income to be paid gross. Alternatively, if tax is withheld, you may claim credit for the tax on your Self Assessment return.

This seems relatively straightforward. However, interestingly, interest paid by paying agents in Guernsey, Jersey or the Isle of Man (each of which territories levy the withholding tax) to non-UK domiciled but UK resident individuals may be paid without the withholding tax (and of course without any information being supplied to HMRC). This applies even where the individual "self-certifies" as to his entitlement to the remittance basis treatment, i.e. there is no strict requirement for HMRC to have provided the certificate as would normally apply.

This stance adopted by each of these three territories appears to operate in practice although as to its correctness under the terms of the Directive this may be open to challenge.

Following FA 2008 presumably this approach may need to be reviewed. A non-UK domiciled but UK resident individual may be entitled to remittance basis treatment without a claim or may require a claim to be lodged (see Chapter 23) or may be subject to tax on the arising basis. Where tax on the arising basis is applicable presumably each of these three territories would be required under the Directive to withhold tax. It would seem that the paying agents will need to be informed of the non-UK domiciled's individual's tax position which may now vary on a tax year by tax year basis. As a claim for the remittance basis treatment may in any event not need to be lodged for up to five (possibly four; see FA 2008) years after the relevant tax year this would only appear to complicate matters even further.

The obvious manner of mitigating the impact of the Directive is for monies to be no longer deposited in countries affected by the Directive. Such countries would include financial centres such as Dubai, Hong Kong and Singapore.

The inapplicability of the Directive to interest beneficially belonging to companies and/or certain trusts offers the EU resident individual the option to still maintain monies within the EU and/or the other territories mentioned above. For the non-UK or UK domiciled but UK resident individual, however, care needs to be exercised to ensure that while a Savings Directive "problem" is resolved bigger adverse UK income tax consequences do not follow (see Chapter 17).

Alternatives to the use of offshore companies and/or trusts include the utilisation of insurance- and/or pension-based products as neither fall within the Savings Directive definition of savings income. Non-qualifying offshore life policies (often referred to as investment bonds or single premium offshore bonds) in this regard offer the individual the possibility of making cash deposits and/or investing in, say, domestic or international bonds without the Directive being in point. The reason is that the individual is investing in a life policy not in the investments underlying the policy (see Chapter 18).

In March 2008 the European Council reiterated its intention to broaden the network of savings tax agreements and the EU Council requested the Commission to start exploratory talks with Hong Kong, Macao and Singapore. Later, in mid-2008, in a review of the Directive since its implementation the Commission identified a number of areas for further investigation and clarification. These areas included the possible expansion of the definition of beneficial owner to include interest payments to all legal persons; a widening of what constitutes a debt claim; and whether the Savings Directive is in fact the appropriate vehicle to apply to, inter alia, dividends, capital gains and "out payments" from those life insurance contracts and pension schemes where the mortality or longevity risk covered is not merely ancillary.

It seems inevitable that the current restriction of the Savings Directive to "interest" only payments to individuals will be broadened to encompass interest payments to other persons (e.g. trusts; companies; foundations) and/or other types of savings income (e.g. dividends). This seems a logical extension of the Directive's provisions. Within what time frame any such extensions will apply is difficult to predict.

Extension of the Directive's ambit to include other countries seems less likely in the short term. The USA seems reluctant to commit and Switzerland will not agree without a fight.

Human Rights

The Human Rights Act 1998 basically provided for the incorporation into UK law of the European Convention for the Protection of Human Rights effective October 2000.

One example of its possible application is a determination as to whether the inter-spouse exemption for inheritance tax purposes can be restricted to just married couples (or registered civil partnerships), i.e. whether it is a breach of human rights to deny the exemption to cohabitees and/or siblings who live together (see Article 14 "Prohibition of Discrimination" ECHR).

In *Holland (Exec.) v. IRC (2003)* the Special Commissioners held that the inheritance tax inter-spouse exemption referred to spouses who were legally married. It thus did not apply to an elderly couple (two sisters) who had lived together for 31 years. The Commissioners further held that this did not constitute discrimination against unmarried couples.

In late April 2008, the European Court of Human Rights in deciding the appeal lodged by the two sisters in the above case held that to deny the inter-spouse exemption for inheritance tax to the two sisters was not a breach of their human rights. No further appeals are possible.

It is highly likely that the European Courts (not just the European Court of Human Rights) will increasingly be called upon to ascertain whether a number of the UK's domestic tax provisions are in some way discriminatory.

SUMMARY

Any wealth planning advice needs to take into account the international, not just domestic, tax implications. To solve a *UK* inheritance tax issue for the individual but in so doing precipitating a "bigger" problem elsewhere is unsatisfactory.

Double tax agreements, of which there are two types, generally speaking alleviate the tax burden. Unfortunately, the UK is a party to only ten such agreements that deal with inheritance tax and, of those, four are from the era of estate duty and are inapplicable to lifetime gifts (only applying on death).

Unlike the income/capital gains double tax agreements the content of each inheritance agreement may be different in its implications.

It is likely to be the case that a double tax agreement will alleviate a tax liability of an individual. However, it is important that the terms of any particular agreement are read as generalisations may be misleading.

The EU is increasingly encroaching on UK tax domestic law and cannot be ignored.

The EU Savings Directive is one example.

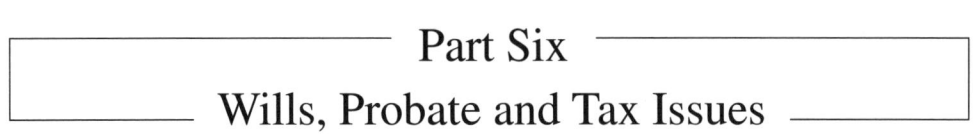

Part Six
Wills, Probate and Tax Issues

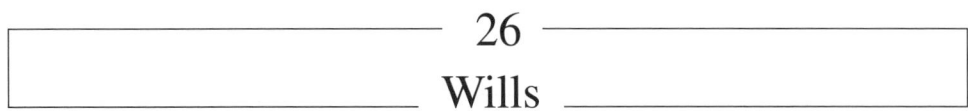

26
Wills

This chapter addresses the position where the governing law of the will is that of England/Wales. The position in Scotland or Northern Ireland may be different.

BACKGROUND

The will enables the individual on death to distribute the estate (i.e. assets owned at death less liabilities) among various heirs as desired by the testator. Where no valid will has been executed by the individual the law dictates how, on death, the individual's estate is to be divided among certain classes of beneficiary; in this case the individual is said to have died intestate.

The will is of relevance to both UK and non-UK domiciled individuals (in the case of the latter where UK situs assets are owned directly by the individual).

The will is also an important tax planning vehicle, particularly with respect to inheritance tax.

REQUIREMENTS FOR VALID WILL

Many wills are often found, usually by the courts, to be invalid. Such findings typically occur only when the testator has died and thus it is no longer possible to ask the testator what his/her intentions were when preparing the will. It is therefore important to ensure that all formalities are correctly followed.

The Trustee Act 2000 defines a will as:

> a document by which a person (called the testator) appoints executors to administer his estate after his death and directs the manner in which it is to be distributed to the beneficiaries he specifies.

A will to be valid needs to be in writing and executed in accordance with certain statutory formalities (see Wills Act 1837 as amended).

A will written entirely in the handwriting of the testator is referred to as a holograph will and is acceptable (i.e. the will does not need, for example, to be typewritten or printed) so long as it conforms to the normal statutory requirements.

A codicil is a document which adds to, varies or revokes the provisions of a will previously made; more than one codicil may be made in relation to the same will. The same statutory provisions apply to codicils as apply to wills.

A will is a confidential document only falling in the public domain on death (this compares with a trust which can often be used as a substitute will which remains permanently confidential).

A will has no effect whatsoever until the death of the testator and thus prior thereto may be varied and/or revoked (revocation remains possible even if the will is expressed to be irrevocable). As a consequence, any gifts made by the testator under the will have no effect prior to the testator's death and thus the testator is still free to deal with his property during his lifetime as however he pleases.

Once a will is executed, if unchanged thereafter, the dispositions made thereunder will operate on the testator's death.

Any person is free to make a will subject only to legal capacity. Such capacity is determined by the law of the domicile of the testator at the time of making the will. Minors (i.e. persons under age 18; applicable to wills executed on or after 1 January 1970; before that date the requisite age was 21) lack capacity to make a will. Similarly, persons of unsound mind do not possess the requisite capacity. It is at the time of making the will that the person's capacity is tested.

Following the execution of a valid will subsequent incapacity (e.g. becoming insane) does not revoke or otherwise invalidate the earlier executed will.

Not all property of a testator can be disposed of by will as the law may dictate how such assets are to pass on death. Perhaps the classic example are assets held by the deceased under a joint tenancy of which the most common is likely to be the matrimonial home. Assets held under a joint tenancy pass by survivorship automatically on death, i.e. the deceased's interest in the property passes to the surviving joint tenant(s) automatically (this may not prove the most tax effective manner in which to own property; see below).

Property may also pass under a "donatio mortis causa" which seems to fall somewhere between a lifetime gift and a gift on death by will (although it is included as part of the deceased's estate for inheritance tax purposes; see Chapter 9). Such a gift is made in lifetime but is conditional on death and must be made in contemplation of death in the near future. The gift which is the subject of the donatio mortis causa passes (effectively retroactively) to the recipient on the death of the donor, never in fact vesting in the executors. In the event that the donor does not in fact die the gift is revoked. A donatio mortis causa cannot be revoked by will.

TYPES OF WILL

Wills may be joint wills, mutual wills or international wills.

A joint will is simply a will which purports to dispose of the property of two or more testators. Mutual wills involve normally two (but can be more) testators each executing their own will but with each will containing provisions under which each confers on the other reciprocal benefits.

As a general rule, both forms of will should be avoided in particular due to a loss of flexibility to which they give rise.

An international will is one drawn up in accordance with the provisions of the Convention Providing a Uniform Law on the Form of an International Will. The concept underlying such a will is that it is to be regarded as valid and thus should be recognised in the various countries who have ratified the Convention and who have also where necessary incorporated the Convention into its own domestic law (as the UK has already done). Theoretically, where a testator owns assets in the various countries who are signatories to the Convention it should in principle only be necessary to execute the one international will.

MARRIAGE

Marriage (or remarriage) automatically revokes a will (unless the will was made in contemplation of a specific marriage) but divorce does not.

SEPARATION/DIVORCE

In the case of divorce the testator's former spouse is assumed to have died on the date on which the marriage was dissolved or annulled and thus the spouse does not inherit any gifts made under the will and is also prohibited from acting as executor/trustee (applicable where the testator dies on or after 1 January 1996).

A decree of judicial separation has no such effect on the will which remains unaffected. Separating spouses should thus review their wills as soon as possible after separation.

As testamentary gifts to the divorced spouse lapse they will fall into residue unless an alternative gift is made in the will to cover such circumstances. Where the spouse is given a life interest in possession in a trust created under the will, the effect of the lapse is an acceleration of the remainder interests.

REVOCATION

A will may be revoked prior to death by the execution of a later will or codicil or by destroying the will whether by tearing it up, burning it or otherwise destroying it with the intention of its revocation. A will which is simply lost is not necessarily revoked although there will be a presumption (albeit a rebuttable presumption) to this effect.

It is not uncommon for the individual who possesses overseas assets (e.g. a property in Spain) to execute more than one will each typically dealing with assets in a particular country. Where, for example, the English will is intentionally revoked (or indeed where one or more of the overseas wills are revoked) the issue as to whether the other wills will also automatically be revoked arises. Care is thus required when intentionally revoking any will. It needs to be borne in mind that any decision as to the extent (if any) of revocation may not lie exclusively with the UK courts.

INTESTACY

The obvious intention of a will is for the testator to make dispositions of his property on death according to his own wishes rather than such dispositions being made in an alternative manner which would be the case on intestacy. Total intestacy occurs where the person makes no effective disposition of any of his property over which he had the capacity to dispose of by will; a partial intestacy occurs where the person makes dispositions by will but some dispositions fail for one reason or another while others are effectively disposed of by the will.

In either case the law lays down rules which dictate the extent to which certain beneficiaries (typically, the surviving spouse and/or children) may benefit.

Thus, the consequence of the individual dying intestate is that it is the law not the individual which decides who and the extent to which any person should benefit. Inter alia, this may of course produce a less than satisfactory tax position for all concerned.

TYPES OF GIFT

A *specific gift* is property owned at the date of death which can be separately and specifically identified within the testator's property at the date of death (other than cash). Although slightly old fashioned a specific gift of property is referred to as a legacy whereas a specific gift of real property is referred to as a devise.

A *general* gift is an item of property not distinguishable from property of a similar type and is paid out of the deceased's general estate.

A *pecuniary* gift is a gift of an amount of money.

A *residuary* gift is a gift of the property of the deceased not otherwise disposed of in the will.

Failure of Gift

A disposition under a will may fail for a number of reasons in which case the issue arises as to what then happens to the gift. The failure of the disposition may be due to:

- the beneficiary of the gift no longer being alive at the date of the testator's death (i.e. predeceases the testator);
- the effect of divorce;
- the attestation of the will by the beneficiary or spouse;
- subsequent revocation by codicil;
- disclaimer; → beneficiary refuses gift
- uncertainty.

Where a disposition under a will fails it will fall into residue and if the residuary gift itself also fails the property is regarded as not having been disposed of and the gift will then pass under the rules applicable to intestacy. This could readily be avoided by the testator including a substitutional gift in the will (i.e. a gift to another person in the event the initial gift fails).

Where a substitutional gift has not been made the consequences may be somewhat dramatic. For example, the testator in his will (among other things) left the residue of his estate to his favourite charity and had left his very valuable collection of stamps (worth £1 million) to his son. The son died before the testator and no substitutional gift had been made in the father's will and the testator did not revise his will in the light of his son's death. The effect would be that the testator's stamp collection would fall into residue and the charity would inherit.

The classification of the gift under a will is also important. One reason is that the doctrine of ademption only applies to specific gifts. Ademption refers to the failure of a specific gift due to the fact that at the date of death the property no longer forms part of the deceased's estate. This would occur, for example, if the deceased had prior to death sold the property or it had been destroyed. The beneficiary due to receive the gift will simply inherit nothing unless a substitutional gift has been made.

Ademption does not, however, apply to general gifts.

The death of the beneficiary prior to the testator's death will cause the gift to fail unless the will provides for someone else to take the gift.

A disclaimer is made where a beneficiary under the will simply does not wish to receive their inheritance. The disclaimant cannot redirect the inheritance to another person of their choice and so the gift will fall into residue unless the will contains a substitutional gift in relation thereto. A disclaimer cannot be made prior to the death of the testator. In other words, a beneficiary knowing about a prospective entitlement under a will cannot disclaim it during the testator's lifetime.

The uncertainty principle applies if either the gift or the beneficiary cannot be identified with certainty. In this case the gift fails and falls into residue subject to a substitutional gift having been made in the will in relation thereto. Examples of gifts which may be void for uncertainty include gifts which are to be applied in perpetuity for purposes which are not in law charitable gifts. Gifts for the maintenance of animals may or may not be regarded as charitable gifts; those not regarded as charitable must be subject to the perpetuity rule and thus restricted in time within the rule. A gift for the benefit of a particular animal (e.g. the family pet) is valid, but not a charitable gift, and thus subject to the perpetuity rule; on the other hand, a gift for the welfare of animals in general is likely to be charitable.

SURVIVORSHIP CLAUSE

Testator's can include a so-called survivorship clause in the will. Under such a clause the beneficiary only takes under the will if the beneficiary survives for the stated period after the testator's death. Failure to survive the requisite period causes the gift to pass as provided in the will. A typical survivorship period is 28 days but may be as long as desired (note, however, a period beyond six months may cause adverse inheritance tax consequences; see below).

The logic of such a clause is that had the testator known prior to death that the particular beneficiary named in the will would only survive for a few days after the testator's death, the testator may have left the gift to some other person. Without the survivorship clause, in effect, it is the survivor who controls the ultimate long-term destination of the gift, not the original testator.

It is, however, arguable that if this is really a concern of the testator a survivorship period of only, say, 28 days does not in reality solve the concern. To this extent it might be argued that a 28-day period survival condition achieves nothing. Nevertheless, 28 days does tend to be the period adopted in many wills. This is probably because any longer period (e.g. six months) does mean that the intended beneficiary is unable to access the gift left in the will (until expiry of the six months) which may, depending upon the circumstances, cause the beneficiary some hardship.

It does therefore appear that the utilisation of a survivorship clause involves a balancing act on the part of the testator between not wanting the inheritance to pass too soon after death yet at the same time not wanting to inflict undue hardship on the intended beneficiary.

This issue may be particularly important in second marriages where there are children from the former marriages. Spouses will often be together and travel together and the probability of both spouses dying in the same accident where it is uncertain which spouse survived the other is perhaps higher than normal. Where this occurs, under the Law of Property Act 1925 (although it must be noted not for inheritance tax purposes) the law deems the older of the two to have died first. Without a survivorship clause, the younger of the two will inherit as appropriate from the elder under the elder's will with the elder's property so inherited then passing under the younger's will. This may not have been what the elder would have wanted to have happened if he had known that his spouse was not going to survive him for a decent period of time. If it is the elder (say, husband) who has children from his former marriage then while he was, for example, prepared to leave 50% of his estate to his wife and 50% to his children (from the former marriage) on the basis that his wife would need financial support following his death, had he known she was to die at the same time as him or within a short time thereafter he may have preferred to have left his estate 100% to his children.

To some extent the answer in the above scenario is for the testator to leave the surviving spouse an immediate post death interest (see Chapter 15) in a trust set up under the will with the capital of the trust going to the children from the former marriage on the surviving spouse's death. Thus, the surviving spouse receives the income of the trust for the rest of her life (and thus is in principle provided for) with the capital of the trust safe (i.e. surviving spouse cannot access it) for the children.

On the other hand, in the case of spouses where it is their first marriage it may be preferable not to include a survivorship clause.

Even where a survivorship clause is to be included in the will it may be appropriate to specifically preclude its use where both spouses die in circumstances where it is not possible to ascertain who died first. The reason is that a possible inheritance tax advantage can be obtained by so doing. For inheritance tax purposes (unlike the position outlined above with respect to the passing of property title) where two spouses die in circumstances where it is not possible to determine who died first, it is assumed that they both died at the same time.

Example 26.1

Jackie and her husband Michael have two children. Jackie and Michael work together and often, as a consequence, travel together on business. Neither has been married before.

They have each made a will leaving their respective estate to each other with substitution gifts to their children in equal shares. They have been advised that, for inheritance tax purposes, given the likelihood of both dying in the same crash that no survivorship period in the wills should apply in such circumstances.

Their aggregate estate amounts to £2 million. Jackie's estate is £800 000 and Michael's £1.2 million.

Neither has made any lifetime gifts.

In May 2008 both Jackie and Michael are killed in a plane crash and it is not possible to determine which of the two died first. Michael was aged 52 and Jackie 48.

As the elder of the two under LPA 1925 Michael is assumed to have died first and, as a consequence, his estate passes in its entirety to his wife Jackie (as she is in effect deemed to have survived him). Jackie's estate, which now includes that of Michael, passes to the children as Michael (having been deemed to have died first cannot take under Jackie's will).

However, for inheritance tax purposes, both are assumed to have died at the same time. This means that although as a matter of the law of property Michael's estate passes to Jackie, for inheritance tax purposes she cannot be treated as inheriting Michael's estate as she did not for this purpose survive him. Thus, Jackie's estate for inheritance tax comprises only her own estate (i.e. £800 000). Michael's estate (i.e. £1.2 million) is thus not included as part of Jackie's estate for inheritance tax purposes but does pass to the children under her will because under LPA 1925 she does actually inherit Michael's estate.

Thus, a 40% charge (above the nil rate band) is levied on Jackie's £800 000 but no charge is levied on Michael's £1.2 million as it passed to Jackie as an inter-spouse transfer and then to the children. Total inheritance tax charge £320 000 (ignoring the nil rate band).

If, however, the survivorship clause in the wills had applied, even on simultaneous death, then Jackie would not inherit Michael's estate as she would not have survived the, say, 28-day survivorship period. The children would thus inherit from Michael (under substitutional gifts) and inheritance tax would be chargeable thereon (i.e. 40% × £1.2 million).

Similarly, under Jackie's will, the children would inherit and again inheritance tax would be chargeable thereon (i.e. 40% × £800 000). Total inheritance tax charge £800 000 (ignoring the nil rate band).

It should be noted that the provisions of LPA 1925 apply to all persons not just spouses. The rule does not, however, apply where the elder person dies intestate. Quick succession relief may also be in point where two deaths occur within a short period of time (see Chapter 10).

WITNESSING THE WILL

Another often overlooked issue is the need to ensure that any beneficiary under the will (or indeed the spouse) does not witness the will. Where a beneficiary or the spouse does in fact witness the will, while also being a beneficiary, the gift fails. The validity of the will is unaffected. The matter is determined at the time of execution of the will; thus, for example, if a witness to the will subsequently married a beneficiary under the will this would not cause the gift to fail.

The above applies only to beneficial gifts and thus, for example, does not extend to invalidate a gift made to a person who is to hold the property on trust for others. Witness by the trustee or spouse would not be a problem in this regard.

If ignoring the attestation by the witness (or spouse of the witness) who is also a beneficiary still causes the will to be valid then the gift will not fail (so-called "superfluous attestation").

CAPACITY TO INHERIT

Broadly speaking, any person has the capacity to inherit a gift under a will. Incapacity is usually in relation to the then inability to provide the executors with a satisfactory form of discharge. Thus, in the case of gifts to minors such gifts are valid but minors are unable to give a valid receipt until full age (i.e. age 18) unless the will specifically provides for such discharge (which might well apply to small gifts to the minor). However, a parent with parental responsibility for the minor can now give a valid receipt for the gift to the minor under the will.

Mental incapacity of a beneficiary does not preclude inheriting under a will. However, such an individual is not able to give a valid receipt. Normally, the attorney acting (or receiver) would give the valid receipt.

In general, a person who has unlawfully killed another is unable to profit in consequence of that killing as a matter of public policy (although there are exceptions).

UK "FORCED HEIRSHIP"

In England and Wales a testator is in principle free to distribute his estate in whatever manner is felt appropriate. This was certainly the position until the Inheritance (Family Provision) Act of 1938 now replaced by the Inheritance (Provision for Family and Dependants) Act 1975 as amended.

The 1975 Act provides for certain persons to claim where the person believes that adequate provision has not been made under the will. The possible claimants are a spouse, former spouse, a child (not necessarily a minor) of the testator and any other person who immediately before the death of the testator was being maintained by the testator either wholly or partially.

With respect to deaths on or after 1 January 1996 the possible claimants were extended to include a cohabitee where such cohabitee lived with the testator as husband and wife for at least two years preceding the testator's death.

For a former spouse to be in a position to lodge a claim he/she must not have remarried (a claim could not be lodged where a remarriage has occurred even if the marriage subsequently terminates, e.g. through divorce).

The 1975 Act only applies to those dying domiciled within England and Wales and any claim needs to be lodged within six months of the date of the grant of probate (not date of death). Otherwise the beneficiary may have to resort to, inter alia, blocking the grant of probate or challenging the validity of the will.

It is for this reason that a number of court cases on domicile arise due to the lodgement of claims under the 1975 Act (see Chapter 3).

FOREIGN ASPECTS

Foreign issues associated with wills may arise in a number of different ways.

For example, an English domiciled person may make a will under English law but which purports also to deal with assets located outside the UK; alternatively, a person with a foreign domicile (as determined under English law) may leave a will (or its equivalent) which deals with UK situs assets. It may be that an English domiciled person may leave assets to persons resident outside the UK who may or may not also be domiciled in England; alternatively, a foreign domiciled person may leave assets to persons resident and/or domiciled in England.

In all of the above cases a foreign dimension is introduced and conflict, ambiguity and interpretational issues will invariably abound. This is particularly so given the different legal systems of countries around the world including those of the common law, civil law and Shari'a law.

The two major issues relate to the identification of the individual who is to be responsible for administering the deceased's estate and the determination of the succession to the deceased's estate. Not surprisingly, it is often the case that a clash of the various applicable laws arises.

Such clashes may include issues such as whether the individual executing the will has so-called "capacity" to so do; whether the will has been validly executed (which under English law raises issues of "formal" and "material" validity); whether the laws prohibit the leaving of assets by the testator in the manner prescribed in the will (i.e. issues of succession, e.g. whether rules of so-called "forced heirship" are in point); whether marriage and/or divorce and/or separation has any impact on the will; whether there are definitional differences (e.g. definition of "child" and whether, for example, it extends to an illegitimate child; the position of cohabitees); where more than will has been executed; etc.

It may therefore be hardly surprising that in such cases the potential for conflict among beneficiaries is extremely high and resolution both time consuming and costly and not always resolved to the satisfaction of all those involved.

Succession

For present purposes perhaps the key issue relates to succession matters, namely, what is the basic position under English law applicable to succession where foreign elements are involved; do foreign laws impact on this; is it necessary or advisable for a person in such circumstances (i.e. where foreign elements are involved) to execute more than one will; and what are the tax (both UK and overseas) issues involved.

The discussion below is based on the English conflict of law rules.

At the heart of a consideration of the above issues is the need for a classification of assets. Under English conflict of law rules it is the law of the country where the asset is situated (i.e. the lex situs) which determines whether the asset is to be considered *immovable* or *movable* (note under English *domestic* law the normal distinction is between personalty and realty). The distinction is not, it is to be noted, the same as a distinction between tangibles and intangibles. Tangibles may be movable (e.g. a painting) or immovable (e.g. land). Intangibles (e.g. debts; shares; goodwill) which cannot of course be touched and thus cannot be moved are nevertheless treated for conflict of law purposes as movables.

The situs of an asset is determined as follows:

- *land* is situated where it lies;
- *chooses in action* (e.g. debts; shares in companies; interests under trusts) are situated in the country where they are properly recoverable or can be enforced;
- *chattels* (e.g. a painting; race horse; furniture) are situated in the country where the chattel is physically located at any given time.

The High Court has jurisdiction to determine the success to property of any person if there is a properly constituted representative of the estate before the court. In effect, such a person is someone who has obtained an English grant of probate.

The courts of a foreign country have jurisdiction to determine the succession to all movables wherever situated of a testator who dies domiciled (as determined under England's conflict of law rules) in that country and to all property which is situated in that country.

The following issues are relevant:

- capacity
- formal validity
- material validity
- construction
- revocation.

Capacity

The law of the country in which the deceased is domiciled at the time of his death determines whether the testator had personal capacity to make a will dealing with movables. This will, for example, cover issues such as whether a particular individual (e.g. a minor; a married woman) can validly make a will.

This rule does not, however, govern the position as to the material validity of the will which deals with issues such as whether a testator is permitted to, for example, leave nothing to his children or spouse.

Although there appears to be no rule which specifies which law governs capacity to make a will of immovables it is generally felt that it is the lex situs (i.e. the law of the place where the property is situated) which would be held to govern the position.

Formal Validity

Generally speaking, under England's conflict of law rules it would be difficult for a will to be formally invalid.

Inter alia, a will is treated as validly executed if its execution conforms to the internal law in force in the territory where it is executed *or* where the testator is domiciled (*or* had his habitual residence *or* is a national thereof).

Material Validity

The material validity of a will of *movables* is governed by the testator's domicile at the time of death (not the date of the making of the will as applied in determining capacity; see above).

Material validity refers to fundamental issues such as, for example, whether the testator has unrestricted freedom to distribute his estate by will and whether an attestation by a person precludes that person from inheriting under the will.

The material validity of a will of *immovables* is governed by the lex situs (i.e. the law of the place where the property is situated).

Again, as indicated above, the relevant law will govern, for example, the extent to which the individual has freedom to distribute his estate. This is in practice likely to be a very important matter for many English persons as many such persons own real estate (i.e. immovables) in countries outside the UK (for example, in particular, France, Italy and Spain).

Construction

The interpretation of a will of movables is governed by the law intended by the testator which in turn is normally accepted as being the law of the testator's domicile at the date the will is made (this rule also probably applies to immovables although it may well be that the law of the lex situs should apply).

This issue may be extremely important.

Interpretation includes issues as to the definitions of words used in the will. For example, it may be necessary to ascertain the identity of the heirs of a particular person where that person's domicile status is different from that of the testator. In such a case is it the law of domicile of the testator which should be applied not the law of domicile of the person whose heirs it is to be determined.

Revocation

There appears to be no general rule which applies in all circumstances to determine whether a will has been revoked.

This issue is particularly important given the common practice of an individual executing more than one will where each will only deals with property in a particular country. It may, however, also be the case that subsequent wills are executed dealing with exactly the same property but each will doing so in a different and conflicting manner (e.g. the same piece of property is left to a different person in different wills).

In the latter situation given in the immediately preceding paragraph, as the matter appears to be one of construction then it would seem that it is the law of the testator's domicile at the time of making the later will which should govern the position.

In the former situation the position would appear to be a little different. Although more than one will may have been executed at different times each will deals with separate property in different countries. In such situations it would seem that none of the wills, even if executed later in time, should revoke an earlier will unless it does so explicitly which would seem in practice prima facie unlikely, because the whole raison d'être is for each will to deal with separate parts of the testator's estate located in different countries.

As indicated above, marriage automatically revokes any will made by any party to the marriage. This applies under English law but does not necessarily apply elsewhere; in fact the English rule tends to be the exception rather than the rule. Under the legal systems of many civil law jurisdictions (e.g. those of mainland Europe) such a rule of revocation does not exist. Indeed, Scottish law does not cause marriage to automatically revoke a will.

Any determination as to the revocation of a will by marriage depends upon the law of the testator's domicile immediately after the marriage.

It is to be noted that for marriages pre 1 January 1974 on marriage a woman automatically acquired (as domicile of dependence) that of her husband. This therefore inevitably may impact on possible revocation of any will which she may have made prior to the marriage. For example, if a Scottish lady made a will before the above date and married an Englishman before the above date she will just after marriage have acquired an English domicile; thus, on the marriage her previously executed will will be revoked. On the other hand, if an English lady made a will before the above date and married a Scotsman before the above date she will just after marriage have acquired a Scottish domicile; thus, on the marriage her previously executed will is not revoked.

MISCELLANEOUS MATTERS

Under English law property owned by a woman prior to marriage and property acquired by her after marriage belongs to her in her own right; the husband has no interest therein (this was not always the situation). This, however, is not necessarily the position elsewhere, in particular in those countries with a civil law system.

The concept of "community property", unknown under English law, is found in many other countries including Belgium, France, Germany and Spain in mainland Europe; South Africa; and many (e.g. California, Nevada, Texas and Washington) but not all States in the USA. The basic essence of the concept is that property within the marriage is jointly owned by both spouses. There are, however, different degrees.

Under some systems property owned at the time of marriage by the spouses and property acquired while married represent community property; under others only property acquired while married forms community property; and in others only chattels owned at the time of marriage or acquired during the marriage form community property (land being excluded). Still, under other systems property is not held jointly during marriage but in the event of death, for example, the surviving spouse is by law entitled to a percentage of the combined estates.

However, virtually all countries under which the concept of community property operates allow spouses to "contract out" of the system.

In the absence of a contract the requisite rights of either spouse in each other's movable property are determined by the law of the "matrimonial domicile" which is the country where both parties are domiciled if they are domiciled in the same country. If not, then the applicable law is that of the country with which the parties to the marriage have the closest connection.

With respect to immovables, in the absence of a contract, prima facie, it is the lex situs rules which would govern the position.

"Forced Heirship"

This is the term frequently applied by common law jurisdictions (England being one) to the rules applicable in many civil law jurisdictions under which a testator is not free to dispose of his estate in any manner he may choose; basically, the law lays down certain restrictions on the distribution of his estate on death.

Technically, the jurisdictions require that a "legal reserve" or "portio legitima" or "reserved share" apply to a proportion of the deceased's estate. Normally, this legal reserve is exercised in favour of children but also sometimes in favour of surviving spouses.

Such a legal reserve may apply in addition to any community property rules.

Thus, an important issue is the extent to which a particular country's legal reserve rules apply to "foreigners" who own property (be it movable or immovable) in that country. The position in fact varies from country to country. For example, in France the lex situs (the law of the place where the property is situated) rule applies with respect to immovables.

PROBATE

The will sets down the testator's wishes with respect to the distribution of property owned at death among the various beneficiaries. The will may also contain the wishes of the testator with respect to the disposal of the body.

Perhaps surprisingly, any such expressed wish concerning disposal of the body cannot be legally enforced (although in practice the wishes of the testator tend to be honoured). The reason for this is that there is no "property" in a body and thus it does not form part of the individual's estate and cannot pass by way of will (or intestacy). The deceased (believe it or not!) is, therefore, not in a position to decide what should happen on death.

However, a direction in the testator's will with respect to the donation of body parts (e.g. for research) are enforceable pursuant to specific statutory provision.

The primary duty to dispose of the deceased's body (and indeed the ashes following cremation) lies with the executors of the will.

The testator's wishes concerning the distribution of the estate on death are carried into effect by the executors appointed in the will but, before doing so, the executors need to be able to prove to their "right" to so do. This is done by applying for and being granted probate.

The death of the individual must be registered, often at the Registrar of Births, Deaths and Marriages. It must be registered within five days of the death with the registrar for the area in which the death occurred.

Following registration the death certificate is issued, the original being retained by the registrar, with certified copies issued as appropriate. Registration requires production of a certificate of death signed by a doctor.

The right to a grant of probate rests with the executor named under the will. It is under the will that the executor has authority to act and under which the executor's title to the deceased's assets derives; such title takes effect on the testator's death (whether probate has or has not been obtained). It is the grant of probate, however, which in practical terms provides the evidence to (e.g. banks) that the executor has the requisite authority to deal with the deceased's assets.

The application for probate may be made at any time after the testator's death but no such grant will be issued within seven days of the death.

The primary duty of the executors is to the beneficiaries and is to administer the estate properly which involves, inter alia, the collection of all the deceased's assets and the discharge of the debts of the deceased. The powers of the executors, as indicated above, derive from the will but also extensive powers derive from statute, e.g. Administration of Estates Act 1925.

Inheritance Tax

Before a grant of probate can be issued the inheritance tax position arising on the deceased's estate must be addressed. An inheritance tax *account* must be submitted to

HMRC (on the appropriate forms, e.g. Form IHT200 "Inheritance Tax Account" plus the various "D" forms) and any inheritance tax liability which arises must be paid. On receipt of the completed forms and payment HMRC will issue a stamped Form D18 (or stamped Form D19 where no actual tax is payable) to the executor which confirms receipt of payment.

The executor then submits Form D18/19 together with the application for probate to the probate registry. No application for probate will be considered unless and until the deceased's inheritance tax liability (if any) has been discharged.

It may be, however, that the deceased's estate qualifies as an "excepted estate". Where this is so then it is not necessary for any forms in connection with the inheritance tax position of the deceased's estate to be submitted to HMRC. In such cases the requisite form (i.e. Form IHT205 "Return of Estate Information") is completed (i.e. a return of information but not an account in the Form IHT200 sense above) which is then despatched with the probate application directly to the probate registry (not to HMRC).

On issue of the grant of probate the registry will send the completed Form IHT205 to HMRC who have thirty five days (from the date of the grant) to request the executors to complete an inheritance tax account (i.e. Form IHT200, etc.). If no such request is received the executors are deemed to have received a clearance from HMRC.

Excepted Estates

An "excepted estate" (for deaths on or after 1 January 2006) is, very broadly, an estate where the deceased is UK domiciled at the time of death and the aggregate gross value of the estate does not exceed the NRB (see Chapter 13) applicable at the time of death (£312 000 for deaths on or after 6 April 2008).

For the individual who has never been domiciled in the UK (or deemed UK domiciled; see Chapters 3 and 9) the estate will, very broadly, qualify as "excepted" if the value of the estate situated within the UK is wholly attributable to cash or quoted shares the gross value of which does not exceed £150 000.

Once the inheritance tax position has been satisfactorily resolved and a grant of probate issued the executors are then in a position to administer the deceased's estate. This will involve, inter alia, collecting all the assets together owned by the deceased at the date of death and discharging any liabilities. Distributions can then be made as required under the will to the various beneficiaries.

Assets not Requiring Probate

Probate is not necessarily required in respect of all the deceased's assets and thus the executors may gain access to these assets before probate is granted. This is possible because such assets either do not form part of the deceased's estate for probate purposes or do form part of the estate for probate purposes but in respect of which the production of probate is not required for the assets to be realised.

It is to be appreciated that even though assets may not require probate for title to pass to the beneficiaries under the will, the deceased's interest in any such assets does still form part of the deceased's estate for inheritance tax purposes.

Such assets where probate is not required include:

- assets held as beneficial joint tenants (see Chapter 7);
- death benefits paid under life policies written in trust (see Chapter 18);
- death benefits paid under pension schemes;
- chattels (i.e. tangible movable property);
- bare trusts.

Jointly Held Assets

Assets held as beneficial joint tenants means that on the death of one owner their share passes automatically by survivorship to the surviving joint owner. In other words, the deceased's interest cannot, and does not, pass by will.

Typically, this form of ownership will apply to bank accounts held by spouses and may also apply to the matrimonial home (see Chapter 19).

Production of the death certificate is sufficient evidence should this be necessary.

If property (e.g. the matrimonial home) is held as beneficial tenants in common, however, the above does not apply. In this case the deceased's interest would pass under the will.

Life Policies

Any amount paid out on death will if the policy has been written in trust be payable to the trustees (not the executors qua their executor capacity) on production of the death certificate.

If, however, the deceased had title to the life policy which has not been written in trust then probate will be required.

Pension Death Benefits

It is quite common under company pension schemes for death benefit payments to be made, as a matter of law, at the discretion of the pension trustees. The payment is usually paid to the individual who the deceased former employee nominated while a member of the scheme (typically the surviving spouse).

The discretion element is sufficient for the death benefit not to form part of the deceased's estate.

Again, as above, production of the death certificate is sufficient to obtain payment.

Personal pension schemes and retirement annuity contracts may be a little different and unless the benefit has been written into trust probate will invariably be required.

Chattels

Title to chattels (e.g. jewellery; paintings; pens; etc.) may pass by simple delivery and thus without the need for probate.

Bare Trusts

The deceased's beneficial interest in the asset held by a third party does form part of the deceased's estate for probate purposes. However, the legal title to the asset is held by the "trustee" of the bare trust, not the deceased, and accordingly probate is not required.

Small Payments

With respect to small sums of money (i.e. less than £5000) it may be possible to access such monies without the need for probate depending upon the attitude of the holder of the asset (i.e. not possible to demand payment).

Usually banks/building societies will release small sums of money on deposit without the need for probate; an indemnity or release may be required by the bank/building society.

GENERAL TAX ISSUES

Inheritance Tax

The major tax which impacts upon the death of an individual is inheritance tax. A potential 40% charge may arise on the entire deceased's net (i.e. after deduction for any liabilities) estate; a significant proportion of the net estate. The inheritance tax charged is generally payable out of the estate (i.e. is treated as a testamentary expense payable out of residue; see Chapter 9) although the testator may state in the will that some or all of the gifts must bear their own inheritance tax.

Capital Gains Tax

On death there is no deemed disposal by the deceased of assets beneficially owned at death for capital gains tax purposes; thus no capital gains tax liability arises on death. In fact, all the assets owned beneficially by the deceased on death are deemed to have been acquired by the executors at their market value at the date of death (referred to as probate value). On appointment out to the beneficiaries the latter are assumed to have also acquired the assets transferred to them at their market value at the date of death, i.e. the executors in transferring assets to those beneficiaries who inherit under the will do not make a disposal for capital gains tax purposes. As a consequence, any accrued capital gain on each asset owned at death is thus wiped out.

Income Tax

Death precipitates no income tax consequences.

Any tax planning for death thus needs to concentrate primarily on inheritance tax issues.

Inheritance Tax Planning: Some Thoughts

Whether lifetime gifting is preferable to gifting by will is an important issue and one not readily and easily resolvable. From the tax perspective there is often a clash between mitigating inheritance tax and mitigating capital gains tax. From the capital gains tax perspective simply making no lifetime gifts and passing all assets owned by will is most tax efficient (due to the so-called tax uplift on assets owned on death; see above). Such a strategy, however, clashes with the strategy for inheritance tax mitigation which, at its simplest, involves making lifetime gifts (hopefully surviving seven years thereafter) and leaving no assets on death to be left by will.

In practice, for most individuals, the answers lie somewhere in between.

On balance, and as a generalisation, it is inheritance tax that is likely to produce the higher liability. This is because inheritance tax is a flat 40% rate tax applicable to the value of the transfer (i.e. gift) whereas capital gain tax is levied only on any gain (i.e. sales proceeds less original cost) at a maximum rate of 18% (post FA 2008; pre FA 2008 rates of capital gains tax were 10%, 20% and 40%; see Chapter 2).

It might be deduced from the above that perhaps the potentially most tax efficient strategy (both with respect to capital gains and inheritance tax) is to operate on the principle that lifetime gifting should be adopted unless there are reasons for not so doing; such reasons may be tax related or non-tax related. This then minimises the amount of the death estate and thus the inheritance tax liability while at the same time precipitating, relatively speaking, lower capital gains tax charges by comparison. This simple strategy does, however, ignore the time value of money as lifetime gifting will, other things being equal, bring forward any tax charge (be it capital gains or inheritance tax).

Maximum use should be made of any reliefs and exemptions under both taxes. Thus, for spouses it is important that each spouse is able to take advantage of any such reliefs and exemptions available to each spouse. This would suggest that there should be a degree of "estate equalisation" between spouses, i.e. each spouse should have sufficient assets to ensure full use of the reliefs and exemptions.

For example, the annual capital gains tax exemption (£9600 for tax year 2008/09; see Chapter 8) should be fully utilised by each spouse every tax year whenever possible; inter alia, the NRB (£312 000 for tax year 2008/09) for inheritance tax should be fully utilised by each spouse during their lifetime; and the annual exemption (£3000 per annum) for lifetime gifts for inheritance tax purposes should also be utilised each tax year by each spouse.

However, the need for such estate equalisation has perhaps been reduced to a degree as a consequence of two recent developments. First is the introduction effective for deaths on or after 9 October 2007 (see Chapter 9) of the "transferable NRB" between spouses for inheritance tax purposes; second, is the removal of the linking of the rate of capital gains tax to the individual's applicable marginal rate of income tax coupled with the reduction in the capital gains tax rate to 18% (for disposals on or after 6 April 2008 under FA 2008) from a marginal rate of 40% (pre 6 April 2008).

The transferable NRB between spouses for inheritance tax means that should the first of the spouses to die fail to utilise their NRB (typically, by simply leaving their whole estate on death to the surviving spouse; inter-spouse transfers being exempt from inheritance tax whether in lifetime or on death) then the percentage of the NRB not utilised (in this example 100%) is effectively transferred for utilisation by the surviving spouse (thus in the above case doubling it). Pre 9 October 2007, however, if a spouse failed to utilise their NRB then it was simply lost (at a cost of 40% of the NRB, e.g. 40% of £300 000 of tax year 2007/08).

Having said this, the transferability of the NRB does not help mitigate inheritance tax with respect to the utilisation of lifetime reliefs and exemptions. If one spouse owns all the assets then the spouse owning no assets is clearly unable to take advantage of the lifetime reliefs and exemptions each tax year unless transfers are made from the other spouse specifically for these purposes which in any event may not always work (e.g. assets qualifying for BPR (see Chapter 10) on the part of one spouse cannot simply be transferred just prior to the recipient spouse making a lifetime gift thereof. In such a case BPR on the gift by the recipient spouse would be lost as the holding period of qualification, i.e. two years, would not have been satisfied).

With respect to capital gains tax (pre FA 2008) the rate of capital gains tax applicable to an individual was linked to their marginal rate of income tax. In the case of spouses it is often the case that one spouse, for example, is a higher rate income tax payer (i.e. 40%) whereas the other spouse either is not liable to income tax or, perhaps, is liable at the basic rate (22% pre FA 2008). It was thus common practice to try to ensure the lower rate taxpaying spouse effected the disposals precipitating the capital gains tax liabilities. Post FA 2008 as the capital gains tax rate applicable to either spouse is a flat 18%, irrespective of the rate payable on income for income tax purposes, such a strategy of "estate equalisation" is less important (subject to trying to ensure each spouse is able to use their annual exemption).

It should also be noted that the transferability of the NRB for inheritance tax purposes is restricted to transfers between spouses (i.e. persons married albeit not necessarily living together; see Chapter 9). It thus does not apply to cohabitees (even if living as husband and wife); single individuals; or divorcees. Thus, in the case of cohabitees living as husband and wife, for example, "estate equalisation" for inheritance tax purposes still has a significant role to play.

While the introduction of the transferable NRB for inheritance tax is a positive step (i.e. is beneficial rather than detrimental) it is not necessarily the answer to all inheritance tax will planning.

First, it is important to appreciate that any planning based upon its utilisation in the future (i.e. on the death of the surviving spouse) does implicitly presuppose that the law in this regard will not change for the worse.

Second, at present, the NRB is linked to inflation but again there is no guarantee that this will necessarily continue in the future (in which case it may be that in "real" terms the future value of the NRB is much less than anticipated thus producing a greater "real" inheritance tax liability; in turn suggesting that not utilising the full NRB on the death of the first spouse to die (because it was transferred to the surviving spouse) was not perhaps the better decision.

Third, the simple strategy of the first spouse to die leaving all their estate to the surviving spouse (on the grounds that the survivor will be able to utilise the first spouse's NRB on death as well as their own) may be less inheritance tax efficient than the utilisation of an NRB discretionary trust (NRB discretionary trusts were used before the introduction of the transferable nil rate band to secure its utilisation on the death of the first spouse; see below). This is likely to be the case where, in particular, the assets left by the first spouse increase in value significantly after the spouse's death (and in any event increase at a rate greater than the increase in the NRB over the same time period). This is because the rates of inheritance tax payable by the trust will be lower than those applicable on the death of the surviving spouse and thus the quantum of inheritance tax payable will also be less.

Nevertheless, despite whatever strategy is followed it is highly likely that on death the deceased's estate may still be substantial and thus a tax efficient will becomes paramount.

Following the changes introduced in FA 2006 in connection with the inheritance tax treatment of trusts (see Chapter 15) the need for a tax efficient will is arguably even greater than before. This is because, other things being equal, the creation of lifetime trusts has been made less attractive (due to the fact that transfers into basically all trusts, post 21 March 2006, are chargeable lifetime transfers not potentially exempt transfers thus precipitating inheritance tax charges at that time). Will trusts (i.e. trusts set up under a will) now thus take on a more significant role than pre FA 2006.

For the testator writing a will there are two basic options with respect to how assets could be left to the beneficiaries. One option is to leave the assets directly to the beneficiaries absolutely; the other is to leave the assets in trust for the beneficiaries; or, of course, a combination of the two.

Each may precipitate different tax (i.e. income, capital gains and inheritance) consequences.

A choice between the two options will be affected by both tax and non-tax factors. In the case of minors (i.e. children below age 18; particularly likely to be applicable to grandchildren) trusts are likely to be the better option and where one or both of the spouses have children from former marriages again trusts may be the better option.

In essence the trust is likely to be the better option where some flexibility for the future is required and/or where some form of protection of assets is needed.

Minors are not in a position to manage their own affairs and it is difficult to know what the future holds for them. Leaving assets in trust permits the trustees flexibility to take into account changes which may have occurred whether with respect to the lives of the children concerned and/or changes generally in the fiscal climate between the time of the death of the testator and the later time.

With respect to second marriages (where children exist from former marriages) the use of trusts can offer a convenient solution to competing demands. The first spouse to die will, generally speaking, want to provide the surviving spouse with financial support for the rest of their life but at the same time will also want any assets to be left (either in whole or in part) to their children from the former marriage without any risk of the surviving spouse squandering the assets prior to death. Trusts can allow these twin objectives to be met (e.g. using an immediate post death interest trust for the surviving spouse; see above).

Post FA 2006 the three main categories of trust which may be set up by will are the discretionary trust; the IPDI (i.e. immediate post death interest) trust; and the 18 to 25 trust (also known as a section 71D trust).

The technical aspects of each of these trusts are discussed in Chapter 15.

Where, however, none of the above issues are in point leaving the assets to the beneficiaries absolutely (i.e. no trust involved) may be the simpler and the preferred option.

As is evident from the above discussion no one will is likely to suit all.

MARRIED COUPLES

One general approach is for the residue of the testator's estate to pass to a will trust under which the surviving spouse has an IPDI (no inheritance tax charge arises as this transfer is an inter-spouse transfer) with the trust assets thereafter being held on discretionary trust for the family when the surviving spouse dies.

The testator's NRB can then be fully utilised by gifts to non-exempt beneficiaries (e.g. brothers, sisters, children, etc.) absolutely (i.e. not in trust).

One advantage of using a trust under which an IPDI for the surviving spouse arises is that a degree of flexibility is retained. For example, if following the death of the testator it would have been preferable for the surviving spouse to have inherited absolutely (rather than acquiring an IPDI), the trustees are able to appoint assets out of the trust to the spouse without precipitating an inheritance tax charge. If the appointment is made within two years of death no capital gains tax charge arises. If the appointment is effected prior to completion of the administration of the testator's estate a capital gains tax liability arises.

An alternative to the absolute gifts above is the use of the NRB discretionary trust. This alternative may be more appropriate if, for example, flexibility needs to be retained so as to ensure that the surviving spouse could access the funds in the trust if necessary (i.e. absolute gifts once made to others would preclude their availability to the surviving spouse).

However, to avoid possible adverse inheritance tax consequences either (but not both) a NRB discretionary trust or an IPDI trust (followed by discretionary trusts) for the surviving spouse may be used.

Cohabitees

For inheritance tax purposes cohabitees are not treated as married couples and they are thus more akin to two separate individuals for tax purposes.

However, almost certainly, on the death of one cohabitee the deceased cohabitee would no doubt have wished to make some provision for the other cohabitee.

No inter-spouse exemption is applicable on transfers between cohabitees.

One option is for an NRB discretionary trust to be set up under the will with the residue given absolutely to the surviving cohabitee or, somewhat simpler, a straightforward discretionary trust of the whole estate.

As indicated above, trustees may make appointments out of the trust within two years of death without precipitating any adverse inheritance or capital gains tax consequences.

Single Persons

Possibly the best (i.e. greatest flexibility and tax efficient) option is a discretionary trust of the residuary estate coupled with specific absolute gifts to selected individuals.

Charitable Giving

Gifts to charities are exempt and thus if a testator leaves an amount to charity by will no inheritance tax will arise thereon.

Having said this, complications can arise for estates for inheritance tax purposes where both exempt (e.g. gifts to charity) and non-exempt (gifts to brothers, sisters and children) gifts are made out of residue of the testator's estate.

In particular it is perhaps worth noting that gifts by way of will (or in fact in lifetime) to foreign charities are not exempt (a foreign charity is not subject to the jurisdiction of the UK courts which is a requirement for charitable status) and thus such gifts will be subject to inheritance tax as part of the deceased's estate.

Believe it or not charities can become extremely aggressive in seeking to ensure that any property left by will is actually received by them and this can cause problems. As testamentary expenses (e.g. executor's fees/expenses) are paid out of residue (thus reducing the amount left to the residuary beneficiaries) if the testator has left a part of the residue to a charity (which is quite common) the latter may seek to challenge the level of these charges. To avoid this type of problem it may be preferable for the testator to leave the charity a fixed amount of money which is thus not payable out of residue.

Foreign Aspects

Transfers from UK domiciled to non-UK domiciled spouses can be problematic for inheritance tax purposes. The reason is that transfers from the UK to the non-UK domiciled spouse are not exempt without limit (see Chapter 9). On death (assuming no chargeable gifts have been made during the seven years prior to death) the UK domiciled spouse is able to leave the surviving non-UK domiciled spouse up to £367 000 without precipitating a charge to inheritance tax (i.e. £55 000 exemption plus £312 000 subject to inheritance tax at 0% for 2008/09 tax year); over and above this amount inheritance tax at 40% will be payable.

The UK domiciled spouse has basically two options on death, namely, to leave the non-UK domiciled spouse assets absolutely or on trust. Under the former option the non-UK domiciled spouse is then free to possibly rearrange the assets so acquired so that in future they will qualify as excluded property (see Chapter 12) thus falling outside the ambit of inheritance tax.

For example, in the case of chattels these may simply be removed outside the UK thus constituting non-UK situs assets (see Chapter 6). In the case of UK registered shares these could be transferred to a non-UK registered and non-UK resident company whose shares are in turn owned by a non-UK resident trust (the transfer may precipitate capital gains tax consequences although unlikely if effected soon after their inheritance). UK real estate could similarly be transferred to such a company (again, possibly precipitating capital gains tax and SDLT (see Chapters 8 and 21)).

Under the latter option (i.e. use of a non-UK resident will trust) the property within the trust will not rank as excluded property (as this requires a non-UK domiciled settlor; see Chapter 12) but perhaps greater flexibility is obtained. Thus, for example, the trust could simply continue in existence or, within the two-year period following death (see below), appointments out of the trust could be made whether to the surviving non-UK domiciled spouse and/or other beneficiaries (e.g. the non-UK domiciled children) although any inheritance tax charges may be precipitated.

As the trust property can never rank as excluded property (see above) perhaps the discretionary will trust should be viewed as a vehicle which permits two years of extra consideration, following the death of the UK domiciled spouse, during which to decide the "best" way forward but with the intention of the trust terminating within the two-year period. This option may be particularly useful where the surviving spouse's non-UK domicile status at the date of execution of the will by the UK domiciled spouse is reasonably clear, but which status may have become less clear at the date of the UK domiciled's death (e.g. the surviving spouse may have acquired a UK domicile of choice at this time or perhaps become deemed UK domiciled; see Chapter 9).

For the non-UK domiciled spouse the choice of how to leave assets to the surviving UK domiciled spouse may be a little clearer. This is because non-UK situs property settled into trust by a non-UK domiciled testator is excluded property and remains so, i.e. does not subsequently fall within the death estate of the surviving UK domiciled spouse. The trust should, however, preferably be discretionary in nature. If the will trust provides the surviving UK domiciled spouse with an interest in possession, this will constitute an IPDI (see Chapter 15) and on the UK domiciled surviving spouse's death the trust property will therefore no longer constitute excluded property.

The above has addressed only the UK tax implications for the non-UK domiciled individual. Inevitably, however, overseas tax issues may be just as, if not more, important for such individual (particularly for the USA citizen subject to all USA taxes irrespective of residence status). Inter alia, it is thus important to ascertain the domestic tax position in any other relevant country including whether a double tax agreement may be in point.

The existence of any such double tax agreement is likely to affect the overall inheritance tax exposure of the non-UK domiciled individual; this may restrict any inheritance tax charge to UK situs assets only even if the individual is deemed UK domiciled.

Chapter 25 looks in a little more detail at the implications of some of these double taxation agreements.

Remember, also that for the non-UK domiciled individual issues other than UK inheritance tax will invariably be in point (e.g. forced heirship rules; community property rules; the tax system applicable to the individual's nationality or residence, etc.; see above) and may be in fact more important.

Solving a UK tax issue but creating a bigger non-UK tax issue is probably not wise!

POST DEATH ISSUES

Deeds of Variation and Discretionary Will Trusts

On the testator's death one of the responsibilities of the executors is to ascertain the amount of inheritance tax liability on the death estate of the deceased. Such tax is to be paid prior to the obtaining of probate (see above).

However, matters may not always be so simple and following death it may be possible, broadly speaking, to change the dispositions made under the will, one consequence of which may be a change to the inheritance tax due on the estate.

Any such changes are regarded as post death planning and the two main options available are, namely, deeds of variation and/or two-year discretionary will trusts. A deadline of two years after death applies to both options and various conditions need to be satisfied for them to apply. They are, however, extremely valuable options and should not be overlooked. Each will now be considered in turn.

Deeds of Variation

Strictly speaking the reference should be to "*instruments* of variation" not "*deeds* of variation" although in practice variations of the sort described below are usually effected by way of deed. Both terms will be used interchangeably below.

Instruments of variation are a post death planning option (the other is the two-year discretionary will trust; see below) which are treated favourably for inheritance tax purposes. They create a fictional tax world which in reality does not exist (see below).

While they are commonly used where a will is in point, a deed of variation is of equal application under the intestacy rules or with respect to property passing by survivorship under beneficial joint tenancies.

The deed of variation does not, as many appear to believe, actually vary the will itself but only the effects of the will. The beneficiary who benefited under the will, X, effects a disposition of the inheritance by way of deed to someone else, Y.

Having said this, it is also important to appreciate that it is not the property comprised in the gift under the will which is redirected but the gift under the will. Thus, for example, it may be that X has received the gift under the will (e.g. a painting) and sold it prior to the execution of the deed of variation. In this case the sale proceeds from the sale of the gift would be that which is then redirected to Y.

Interestingly, Y does not need to be an existing beneficiary under the will in order to benefit from the variation.

The disposition under the deed takes place at the date of the variation. It is for X to dictate the terms under which the disposition occurs (normally as an outright gift).

The instrument of variation must be executed in writing within two years of the testator's death; the date of the grant of probate is irrelevant. As consideration for the variation is not permitted it is usual to effect the variation by deed so as to ensure its enforceability.

The parties to the deed must be all the beneficiaries who originally benefited under the will and whose benefit is being varied, i.e. the variation must be signed by those beneficiaries whose interests are adversely affected. Those beneficiaries under the will whose interests are not affected are not required to sign the variation. The executors are not required to sign the variation unless the effect of the variation is to increase the amount of inheritance tax on the deceased's estate although it is good practice for them to sign.

Problems do arise where beneficiaries who are affected by the variation include minors (or unborn beneficiaries) as minors cannot be parties to a deed of variation without the court's consent. This is a requirement even if the effect of the variation is to cause the minors' interests under the will to be improved in the sense that the minors will be "better off". Seeking the court's approval will inevitably eat into the two-year deadline for execution of the deed and it is necessary for the court order to be made within the two-year period.

Where a beneficiary under the will has died, subsequent to the testator, the executors of the will of the deceased beneficiary are able to be parties to a variation of the testator's will, in effect being allowed to stand in the shoes of the deceased beneficiary.

It is important to appreciate that what is happening in the "real world" when a deed of variation is executed is that X is in fact actually making a gift of the property inherited under the will. The testator's will is not, as indicated above, itself changed or varied as this cannot be done.

However, for inheritance tax purposes the variation effected by X is treated as if it had been made by the deceased and thus X is not treated as if he had made a transfer of value/gift (which in the real world he has, as indicated above). This avoids an inheritance tax charge that would otherwise arise on the transfer of value/gift. It is also to be noted that X cannot be regarded as making a gift with reservation (see Chapter 11) on effecting the variation and the pre-owned asset legislation (see Chapter 11) is similarly inapplicable.

Any reliefs and exemptions that may be in point will apply (e.g. gift under testator's will was to brother and thus subject to inheritance tax as part of the deceased's death estate; deed of variation executed and gift to brother redirected to testator's spouse. The inter-spouse exemption would then apply.)

For the above inheritance tax consequences to occur it is necessary that the variation contains a statement to the effect that section 142(1) IHTA 1984 is intended to apply to the variation. This means that the variation is read back into the will as at the date of death. It is, in a sense, as if the terms of the variation were substituted in the testator's original will and that the gifts under the original will to X are replaced with gifts to Y as if the testator had so provided (pre 1 August 2002 variations required a formal election to be lodged with HMRC; this is no longer required for variations made on or after this date).

The execution of the deed of variation does not need to be executed before the deceased's estate has been administered. Whether the administration of the estate has been completed or not and irrespective of whether the gift under the will has taken effect (i.e. the property comprised in the gift has already been distributed to the original beneficiary) a deed of variation can still be satisfactorily implemented.

Often the deed of variation will be executed once probate has been obtained. However, if the effect of the variation is to decrease the amount of inheritance tax liability on the deceased's estate then it would be sensible to effect the deed prior to the obtaining of the grant of probate; otherwise inheritance tax would be payable and any reduction due to the deed would involve a reclaim.

It may be thought that as deeds of variation (more than one deed in respect of the same estate may be executed but not in connection with the same gift) can be used, in simple terms, to change a will that it is not strictly necessary to be too careful when drafting a will. This is, however, misguided. As remarked above, where minors are involved (which may be so in many cases) permission from the courts is necessary which takes time and money and the courts may in the event not agree to the variation. Furthermore, agreement of *all* affected beneficiaries is needed. Should only one beneficiary not agree to the variation then it cannot proceed. This risk is, generally speaking, a very real risk.

Careful drafting of the will thus needs to be effected, ab initio, and reliance should not be placed upon the use of deeds of variation to "put right" issues in the original will following the testator's death.

Subject to the above, there is little doubt that deeds of variation do offer a number of options following the testator's death perhaps either to make the will more inheritance tax efficient and/or permit a different (possibly fairer) distribution of the deceased's assets.

One common use of the variation is where the whole of the estate of the first spouse to die is simply left to the surviving spouse. The NRB of the first spouse to die is in this case wasted. The variation may be used to redirect the equivalent of the NRB of the first spouse to die to the couple's children (whether absolutely or in trust) thus utilising the NRB. Otherwise the estate of the second spouse to die would have been inflated with only one NRB (i.e. that of the surviving spouse) available.

Following FA 2008 and the transferability of the NRB between spouses arguably there is less need to effect a variation in the above scenario. However, it may still be sensible where, for example, certain assets of the first spouse to die are likely to experience substantial growth as deferral of a future inheritance tax charge could be achieved by the children inheriting (as the transferable NRB will not necessarily be sufficient to compensate for the growth in assets left to the surviving spouse).

Another use of the variation might be where the surviving spouse's estate on death is below the then NRB whereas the estate of the first spouse to die was in excess of the nil rate band. Assuming that the deaths were within two years of each other a variation in the distribution of the estate of the first spouse to die by a rerouting of a proportion of the estate to that of the surviving spouse would reduce the aggregate inheritance tax liability of both spouses (the deaths would need to be within two years of each other, otherwise the deadline two-year period to vary the first spouse's estate would have expired).

As well as the guiding principle that full use must be made of the NRB on death, it is equally important that full use of any available reliefs/exemptions should be made. A relief of immense importance is business property relief ("BPR"; see Chapter 10) which may (depending upon the type of business asset) be 100%.

If the spouses do not wish to lose control over the property a simple transfer of the property on death to the surviving spouse would enable this to occur and would not precipitate any inheritance tax charge due to the inter-spouse exemption. However, the 100% BPR would be "wasted". One option may therefore be for the first spouse to die to leave the property subject to BPR not to the surviving spouse but chargeable beneficiaries (e.g. preferably non-minor children; a will trust under which no IPDI for the surviving spouse is created).

Due to the 100% BPR no inheritance tax liability will arise on the gift of the business property. Property of the testator's estate which does not qualify for any form of relief is left to the surviving spouse (an inter-spouse transfer and thus no charge to inheritance tax).

In due course the surviving spouse could purchase the business property back from the beneficiaries who had inherited it on the death of the first spouse to die (effectively substituting, say, cash/borrowing, which would be subject to inheritance tax on death for fully relievable business property). Assuming the surviving spouse in due course satisfies the conditions for BPR (see Chapter 10) on death (or lifetime gift) no inheritance tax charge will arise. Indeed, if the transfer is on death the values of the business property will be revalued for capital gains tax purposes to their then market values. It needs, however, to be borne in mind that the sale by the beneficiaries to the surviving spouse will, inter alia, constitute disposals for capital gains tax purposes. Whether the above is thus viable requires looking at the overall tax position of all parties to ascertain if on balance the option makes sense.

Yet another consideration and possible use of the variation relates to charitable giving. Where the testator's will does not provide for any dispositions to charity (or an insufficient amount is left to charity as perceived by the beneficiaries under the will) a variation can be used to redirect monies to the charity. By so doing the amount of inheritance tax on the deceased's estate on death will be reduced as the disposition to the original beneficiary (chargeable; unless to the surviving spouse) would be replaced by a disposition to a non-chargeable beneficiary, i.e. the charity. For the original beneficiary to take under the will and then to effect the gift to charity is inheritance tax inefficient; hence the need for the variation.

While it is the case that variations are often used to mitigate inheritance tax arising from dispositions made under a will, this does not always need to be the case. A variation can be very useful where for one reason or another the beneficiaries feel that perhaps a different distribution of the testator's assets would have been more appropriate. This may be the case where, for example, the testator disinherited one of the children but the surviving siblings and the surviving spouse do not agree with the disinheritance; the variation would allow inheritance (and capital gains) tax efficient redirecting of some of the dispositions under the will. It may be that between the date of drawing up the will and the date of death the circumstances of one or more beneficiaries has changed and thus the original dispositions under the will may no longer be viewed by the beneficiaries as perhaps appropriate; the variation again would permit suitable and tax efficient reorganisation.

Capital Gains Tax

The execution of a deed of variation may, as with inheritance tax, have a backdating effect for capital gains tax purposes in a similar manner as applies for inheritance tax.

Broadly, the effect is that X (the beneficiary of the variation) is deemed to have acquired the property under the will of the testator at the date of death and the market value at that time (i.e. date of death). Thus, there is no disposal (and thus no potential capital gains tax charge) deemed to have been made to X by the beneficiary executing the variation.

All the conditions applicable to the execution of a deed of variation discussed above continue to apply.

There is no need for two separate deeds of variation, one for each of the two taxes; one deed for both taxes is sufficient.

Discretionary Will Trusts

Discretionary will trusts are another post death planning option.

Subject to satisfying certain conditions no inheritance tax charge arises on the termination of the discretionary trust or on the distribution of property from the trust (charges would normally arise on such occasions as the trust is a relevant property trust; see Chapter 15). The inheritance tax consequences are those which would apply if the testator's will had provided for the appointments (i.e. there is in effect, as with the instruments of variation, a "reading back" into the will; see above).

It is important that outright appointments from the trust are not effected within three months of the testator's death if the above favourable treatment is to apply (however, for appointments on or after 22 March 2006 the appointment of an IPDI (see Chapter 15) within three months does not give rise to inheritance tax problems).

One of the main conditions is that the distributions and/or the trust termination must occur within two years of the testator's death (subject to the three months point made in the above paragraph).

Perhaps the main advantage of the two-year will trust is that it allows factors to be taken into account at the date of death of the testator which may be different from those which subsisted at the time the will was drawn up. These factors may, for example, be changes in legislation and/or changes in the circumstances of the beneficiaries. It is, however, the trustees not the testator who will thus determine the distributions from the trust among the class of beneficiaries following the testator's death. It is therefore not unusual for the testator to have provided the trustees with a so-called "letter of wishes". This letter, while not binding upon the trustees, would contain the preferences and/or wishes of the testator vis-à-vis distributions and is something which the trustees would typically heed when making their decisions.

It may be, for example, that on the death of the testator it is unclear whether certain property owned at the date of death qualifies for BPR (see above). The use of the will trust provides the trustees with a "window" of two years to ascertain the position in this regard. If, for example, it is found that no BPR applies (or the matter is still unresolved two years after the testator's death) the trustees could simply appoint the property to the surviving spouse. Because of the reading back the inheritance by the surviving spouse of the property is deemed to have been gifted by the deceased under the will, i.e. the inter-spouse exemption thus applies and no inheritance tax on death arises with respect to the property. If, on the other hand, it is found that BPR does apply at the date of the testator's death the trustees could appoint the property to, say, the children of the testator which, again under the reading back, would precipitate no inheritance tax charge due to 100% (or possibly 50%) BPR.

There is no requirement for the trust to terminate within the two-year period after death. Where, however, the trust continues beyond this two-year period the relevant property regime will then apply to the trust (i.e. inheritance tax charges on appointments out of the trust thereafter; see Chapter 15) with the 10-year charge and any exit charges measured from the time of death.

Capital Gains Tax

Unlike the position with respect to instruments of variation (see above) there is no reading back for capital gains tax purposes. However, where the deceased's estate has not been fully administered, in practice, the appointment of property to a beneficiary will be regarded as the beneficiary having acquired the property at its probate value (i.e. no disposal for capital gains tax purposes will be deemed to have occurred).

INTESTACY

Dying without a will is referred to as dying intestate. In such circumstances English law provides how the potential beneficiaries are each to benefit. The extent of any particular beneficiary's entitlement varies according to the extent to which (and the number of) the deceased's relatives survived the deceased and the size of the estate.

Thus, for example, if the deceased died leaving a surviving spouse and surviving issue (i.e. children) and the estate (i.e. net after deduction for liabilities) was £125 000 or below then all of the estate goes to the surviving spouse. In the same circumstances but where the deceased's estate is in excess of £125 000 then the spouse takes all the personal chattels of the deceased plus a statutory legacy of £125 000 plus a life interest in half of the remainder of the estate (with a reversion to the issue on death). The issue take the other half of the remainder but absolutely.

Where the deceased leaves a surviving spouse but no issue and the estate is £200 000 or below the surviving spouse takes all. If the estate is in excess of £200 000 the surviving spouse takes all the personal chattels of the deceased plus a statutory legacy of £200 000 plus one half of the remainder absolutely. The other half of the reminder is left to the deceased's parents (if alive), alternatively to the deceased's brothers and sisters equally (or the children equally if that brother or sister has died).

The failure to make a will results in a total intestacy. A total intestacy also arises where the will is invalid or where the will fails to dispose of any of the property. A partial intestacy may arise where even though a will has been made it deals only with a part of the estate or the residuary gift fails either in whole or in part.

In principle the consequences are the same whether the deceased dies totally or partially intestate.

The key point to note is that the deceased has no control over the destination of the estate on death in the case of the total intestacy and also loses some control where a partial intestacy occurs. Thus, simply making a will may not be sufficient. The will must be both valid and must dispose in an effective and proper manner of the entire estate of the deceased (which may require substitute gifts to be made, e.g. to cover the position should the beneficiary die before the testator).

SOME POINTS TO NOTE

- Wills can be changed by executing subsequent codicils prior to death.
- Wills are of no import whatsoever until death occurs.

- Probate is almost without exception always necessary although, for example, this is not the case with respect to jointly held assets which pass automatically by survivorship.
- Where *non-UK domiciled beneficiaries* are included in any will of a *UK domiciled testator*, outright gifts (rather than settling on trust; offshore assets settled on trust can never be excluded property if settlor UK domiciled) may enable the beneficiary to ensure excluded property treatment in the future (e.g. moving the asset situs outside UK).
- Where the *testator is non-UK domiciled* and the will includes *UK domiciled beneficiaries* non-UK assets may be better settled on offshore trust, thus becoming excluded property for inheritance tax purposes (remember £55 000 exemption limit for transfers from a non-UK domiciled spouse to a UK domiciled spouse).
- Gifts to UK charities are exempt from inheritance tax (as are gifts to bodies of national importance, e.g. museums).
- A survivorship clause:

  – prevents the double inheritance tax charge if the beneficiary dies shortly after testator (although quick succession relief may apply);
  – avoids property passing under the will of the second (i.e. younger) to die (i.e. if death within the survivorship period occurs the will should provide for a substitute beneficiary/legatee);
  – for spouses should be made inapplicable where deaths occurs in circumstances such that it is not possible to determine who died first.

- The will should state whether gifts under the will are to be "inheritance tax free" or not.

SUMMARY

In English law the concept of the will permits the individual to freely dispose of the individual's estate on death. In principle, subject to the IPFDA 1975, English law does not have forced heirship rules. Forced heirship rules are, however, very common in civil law jurisdictions.

The non-UK domiciled individual owning UK situs assets may also need a UK will to deal with such assets.

As a general rule, a will should be executed under the law of the territory in which the individual owns real estate (i.e. immovables) irrespective of whether a will has been executed under the country's laws of the individual's domicile or nationality.

Care is needed to ensure that a will is not accidentally or unknowingly revoked which may happen if more than one will is executed. Marriage automatically revokes an English will and divorce, while not revoking a will, impacts on the former spouse as beneficiary.

The will has an important role to play with respect to tax planning, particularly with respect to inheritance tax. The use of the so-called NRB discretionary will trust, certainly pre FA 2008 (i.e. before the introduction of the transferable NRB) was an important tax planning vehicle and indeed is still likely to remain so even post FA 2008.

Post death tax planning may also be important in mitigating inheritance tax on death and the role of the deed of variation and discretionary will trust in particular can be crucial.

Appendix 1
Income Tax Pro Forma Personal Tax Computation

	NSI	SI	DIVS

Profits of an unincorporated trade
Employment income
Property business profit

Savings income (e.g. interest from: bank and building society deposit amounts)
Dividends on shares
Less: Tax reliefs
Statutory total income (STI)
Less: Personal allowance
Taxable income
Tax thereon @ appropriate rates
Less: Tax reducers
Sub-total
Add back: Basic tax retained on payments

Income tax liability

Less: Tax collected at source on income
    (e.g. dividends; bank interest; other taxed income)

Income tax payable

Notes
1. NSI = Non-savings income; SI = Savings income; DIVS = Dividend income.
2. Note difference between "Income tax liability" and "Income tax payable".
3. The "Income tax payable" figure may need to be paid by two payments on account under the self assessment system on 31 January within the tax year and 31 July following the tax year. Any balancing tax due is paid on 31 January following the tax year.
4. Offset Tax reliefs and Personal allowance against NSI first, then SI and then DIVS.

Appendix 2A
Capital Gains Tax Pro Forma Tax Computation (post FA 2008)

BASIC COMPUTATIONAL PRO FORMA LAYOUT FOR SALE OF SINGLE ASSET

Disposal proceeds
Less: Incidental disposal costs

Less: Allowable expenditure

Chargeable gain

Less: Annual exemption

Capital gain subject to tax

Notes
1. Offset current year losses before losses brought forward.
2. No carry-back of losses except in year of death; then carry-back for previous three tax years permitted.

Appendix 2B
Capital Gains Tax Pro Forma Tax Computation (pre FA 2008)

BASIC COMPUTATIONAL PRO FORMA LAYOUT FOR SALE OF SINGLE ASSET

Disposal proceeds
Less: Incidental disposal costs

Less: Allowable expenditure

Unindexed gain
Less: Indexation allowance

Chargeable indexed gain

Less: Taper relief

Post TR indexed gain

Less: Annual exemption

Capital gain subject to tax

Notes
1. Indexation factor is applied to each element of allowable expenditure separately other than "incidental costs of disposal" and represents an additional deduction due to inflation.
2. Taper relief, on the other hand, simply reduces the "net chargeable gains" (i.e. after current and carried forward losses) according to the prescribed table figure once indexation relief has been obtained.
3. Offset current year losses before losses brought forward.
4. No carry-back of losses except in year of death; then carry-back for previous three tax years permitted.

Appendix 3
HMRC Forms

The forms included in this appendix are crown copyright material reproduced with the permission of the Controller of HMSO and the Queen's Printer of Scotland. Parliamentary copyright material is reproduced with the permission of the Controller of Her Majesty's Stationery Office on behalf of Parliament.

A companion website to the book contains additional material and will also include quarterly updates. Go to www.wiley.com/go/wealth management planning.

Appendix 3 503

Leaving the United Kingdom

Tax reference

National Insurance number

Please use these references if you write or call. It will help to avoid delay.

Issued by

Telephone

Income Tax claim when you have left *or are about to leave* the UK

To claim tax relief, or repayment of UK income tax, please
- answer all the questions in order, passing over those questions where you are directed to another section
- complete Section 6 *if appropriate*, and Section 7 in all cases, making sure that you sign and date the sections
- take a copy of the completed form *in case we need to refer you to it*, and return the original to the above office.

Section 1 Residence details	Complete ALL parts of this Section

What is your nationality?

On what grounds do you claim this nationality?

Which country are you going to?
Give your address abroad if you know it

When did you leave, *or* when are you leaving, the UK? *Enter Day, Month, Year*   /   /

How long were you living in the UK before the date you left *or date you intend to leave*?

Do you intend to live outside the UK permanently?   Yes ✓ No

- If 'No', do you intend to live outside the UK for a full tax year starting on 6 April after your departure?   Yes ✓ No

  – if also 'No' to the above, when do you expect to return to the UK?   /   /

Will you be visiting the UK while you are living abroad?   Yes ✓ No

- If 'Yes', what periods do you expect to spend in the UK over the next 3 years?

Are you leaving the UK to work?   Yes ✓ No
- If 'Yes' go to **Section 2**
- If 'No' give your reason for leaving the UK in the box, and go to **Section 3**.

P85   HMRC 03/06

Section 2 Employment details
Complete ALL parts IF you are leaving the UK to work

What type of job is it?

- Enter your employer's name and address

  Postcode

  – enter the name of your **department** if you are employed by the UK Government.

Will you be working full-time? Yes ✓ / No

Do you have a separate contract for your work abroad? Yes ✓ / No
- If 'Yes' how long is the contract for?

Will any of your work be carried out in the UK? Yes ✓ / No
- If 'Yes' give details of the work you will be doing in the UK.

Is your work abroad done on a days on/days off rota? Yes ✓ / No
- If 'Yes' give details, including where you expect to spend the days off. *Enter the name of the town or city, and country.*

In what currency will you be paid for your work abroad? Country Currency

Where will you receive your earnings? Country where (Bank) Account held Currency

If any part of your pay is to be paid through an office or agent in the UK, give the full name and address of the payer.
Name
Address
Postcode

Section 3 Accommodation details
Complete ALL parts unless you are directed to another Section

Will you, or your spouse or civil partner, have any accommodation in the UK while you are away? Yes ✓ / No
- If 'No' go to **Section 4**
- If 'Yes'
  – give details of the kind of accommodation it is *for example house, flat, etc.,* and
  – enter its address.

  Description
  Address
  Postcode

If you left the United Kingdom **after 5 April 2000**, go to **Section 4**.

Do you own or have you ever owned the accommodation described above? Yes ✓ / No
- If 'No' go to **Section 4**
- If 'Yes' please tick one box to show whether the property is solely owned ☐ or jointly owned ☐

Do you intend to return to the property as your sole or main residence within four years of the date of your departure? Yes ✓ / No

Section 4 Further property details *Complete ALL parts unless you are directed to another Section*

Will you be receiving rents, premiums, or other income from any property in the UK? Yes ☐ No ☐
- If 'No' go to **Section 5**
- If 'Yes' please tick one box to show whether the property is solely owned ☐ or jointly owned ☐

How much income from letting will you receive each year? *Give an **estimate** if you do not know the precise amount.*

In the year of your departure £ _____   In the following year £ _____

Will you be receiving the income direct *either into your UK bank account or overseas*? Yes ☐ No ☐

- If 'Yes' give details of the person who will be paying you.
  - Name _____
  - Address _____
  - Postcode _____

Will you be receiving the income through an agent who manages the property for you? Yes ☐ No ☐

- If 'Yes' give details of the agent *or if the agent lives **outside the UK** details of the payer.*
  - Agent/Payer _____
  - Address _____
  - Postcode _____

Date agent began managing the property __ / __ / __

Section 5 Other details *Answer ALL the questions in this Section*

Will you have any other source of income in the United Kingdom after you have left? Yes ☐ No ☐

- If 'Yes' give details

Do you have life insurance policies that were taken out before 14 March 1984? Yes ☐ No ☐
Any entitlement to pay premiums net of tax relief may be affected when you move abroad.

- If 'Yes' give details of the policy, **and** all premiums you will continue to pay **after** leaving the UK

Name of the insurer	Policy number	Premiums payable in the year to 5.4.
		£
		£
		£

- Did you notify your insurance companies of your date of departure from the UK? Yes ☐ No ☐

Do you have a personal pension? Yes ☐ No ☐

- If 'Yes' give details of all contributions you will continue to pay **after** leaving the UK

Name of personal pension scheme	Contract number	Contributions payable in the year to 5.4.
		£
		£
		£

- Did you notify your personal pension provider of your date of departure from the UK? Yes ☐ No ☐

Section 6 Repayment claim and payment authority   *Complete unless directed to Section 7*

If you are being sent abroad by your present employer, any repayment of tax you are due will be dealt with through your employer's HM Revenue & Customs office, go to **Section 7**.

**I claim repayment of tax that I may be entitled to for the year ending on 5 April   ,
and enclose Parts 2 and 3 of my** *P45 Details of employee leaving work.*

Please enter your address in the box below.
Any repayment will be made direct to you at that address unless you tell us otherwise.

If you want your repayment made to a nominee, complete the remaining boxes in this Section *as well.*

Your address		Name of nominee	
		Address	
	Postcode		Postcode

Enter the account details where the nominee is a bank or building society

| Branch Sort Code | — — | Account number | |

I authorise repayment to be made to the person, bank or building society shown above.

| Signature | | Date | / / |

Section 7 Declaration   *You can be prosecuted if you give false information*

The information I have given on this form is correct and complete to the best of my knowledge and belief.

| Signature | | Date | / / |
| Print your full name | | | |

Please enter here a telephone number *including dialling code* at which we can contact you with any questions.

Notes

The HMRC website contains information on residence and tax issues that you may find helpful: www.hmrc.gov.uk/cnr

If you are leaving the UK to work abroad, and you or your employer require advice about your **National Insurance liability** contact: *Centre for Non-Residents, Employers Team, Benton Park View, Newcastle Upon Tyne, NE98 1ZZ.*

For use in HM Revenue & Customs office

			Date	Initials
	Personal pensions	Notice to S/M	/ /	
		Notice to S/A	/ /	
	Life Assurance *Paragraph 14*	Notice to P.H.	/ /	
		Notice to L.O.	/ /	

Appendix 3   507

 **HM Revenue & Customs**

Arrival in the United Kingdom

Please use these if you write or call. It will help to avoid delay.

Tax reference

National Insurance number

Issued by

As you have come to the United Kingdom (UK) for the first time, or after a period of absence, we need some information from you. **It is important that you complete this form** so that we can make sure you pay the right amount of tax.

Please print your full name

Please show your National Insurance number, if you know it, unless it is already shown in the above reference.

The HMRC website contains information on residence, ordinary residence and domicile that you may find helpful: www.hmrc.gov.uk/cnr

A Residence and Ordinary Residence

Please answer all of the following questions

1   When did you arrive in the UK?

    /   /

2   a. Why have you come to the UK, for example, employment?

    b. Do you intend to stay permanently in the UK?

    Yes No
    ✓ ☐ ☐

    c. If you answer 'No' to question 2b

    • how long do you intend staying, for example less than 2 years, 2 to 3 years, 3 years or more?

• how much time in each year of your stay here do you intend spending outside the UK?

3   If you visited the UK during the 5 years before the date of arrival, approximately how many complete days did you spend in the UK

    a. in each year ending on 5 April?

    b. for the tax year of arrival, in the period between 6 April and the date you entered at 1?

P86

HMRC 04/06

4   a. Have you, your spouse or your civil partner had any accommodation of any description for your use in the UK from the date you arrived in the UK?

Yes No
 ✓   ☐

b. If you answer 'Yes' to question 4a
- what is the address?

Address _____

Postcode _____

- in what capacity have you occupied the accommodation, for example, owner, tenant, employer provided?

[   ]

- if owned, on what date was the accommodation purchased?

[/ /]

c. if it is rented
- what is the period of the tenancy agreement?

[   ]

- what was the date of the agreement?

[/ /]

If you have held accommodation at more than one address, please give the details for each, on a separate sheet or in the Additional Information box on page 4.

B Income Tax Allowances and Liabilities

5   a. What is your nationality?

[   ]

b. On what grounds do you claim this nationality?

[   ]

c. In which country were you resident before your arrival in the UK?

[   ]

d. Have you retained a residential property in that country?

Yes No
 ✓   ☐

6   a. What is your date of birth?

[/ /]

b. If you have a spouse or civil partner
- what is his or her date of birth?

[/ /]

- on what date did you marry or form a civil partnership?

[/ /]

7   a. Where and for whom did you work during the five years before your arrival in the UK?

[   ]

b. When did each employment begin and end? Continue in the 'Additional Information' box on page 4 if necessary

[   ]

c. Were any duties of these employments performed in the UK?

Yes No
 ✓   ☐

If 'Yes' please give details on page 4 in 'Additional Information'

d. Has the most recent of these employments continued (on leave or otherwise) since you arrived in the UK?

Yes ✓ No ☐

e. If you answer 'Yes' when is this employment likely to end?

[   ]

f. If you answer 'No' and you are in employment, what is the name and address of your employer in the UK?

Name/Address _____
_____
_____

Postcode _____

C Relevance of Domicile

Domicile is a concept of general law. It is different from residence and ordinary residence.

It is only necessary to consider your domicile if this is immediately relevant to deciding your liability to UK Income Tax and Capital Gains Tax.

Answer all of the following questions unless otherwise directed.

8   Will you have income from employment:

   - where the employer is not resident in the UK, **and**
   - all duties of the employment will be carried out abroad, **and**
   - you do not expect to remit all the income to the UK?

Yes ✓ No ☐

9   a. Are you (or will you be) making a claim for UK tax relief for contributions to a non-UK pension scheme or retirement benefit plan which are incurred out of remuneration you receive from an employer who is not resident in the UK?

Yes ✓ No ☐

b. If you answer 'Yes' what is the name of the pension scheme or retirement benefit plan.

[   ]

c. Date joined

[/   /]

10 a. Do you have income arising abroad (other than from the Republic of Ireland) or gains on assets situated outside the UK which will not be wholly paid to the UK?

Yes ✓ No ☐

b. If you answer 'Yes' please state the main source of income (for example, pension, bank interest, royalties, dividends) or capital gains, and the country in which it arises.

[   ]

11 Have your costs, or those of your family, in travelling between the country in which you normally live and the UK, been borne or reimbursed by your employer?

Yes ✓ No ☐

If you answer 'No' to ALL questions 8 to 11 domicile is not immediately relevant in deciding your liability to UK Income and Capital Gains Tax. You should go to Part E.

12 Do you claim to be **not** domiciled in the UK?

Yes ✓ No ☐

If you answer 'No' go to Part E, if 'Yes' continue with the questions below

13 a. Were you born outside the UK?

Yes ✓ No ☐

b. If you answer 'Yes' in which country were you born?

[   ]

14 Have you come to the UK for the sole purpose of employment (including self-employment)?

Yes ✓ No ☐

If you answer 'Yes' to both questions 13a and 14 please go to Part D.

If you answer 'No' to either questions 13a or 14 please ask your HM Revenue & Customs office for form DOM 1 and go to Part E.

D Domicile Information

Complete this Part only if you have answered 'Yes' to any of questions 8 to 11.

15 Where was your father domiciled at the date of your birth (in the case of a country with a federal system, please show the particular state or province)?

16 Where do you consider you are domiciled and on what grounds (in the case of a country with a federal system, please show the particular state or province)?

17 a. What are your intentions for the future?

b. If you do not intend to stay permanently in the UK, when and in what circumstances do you envisage that your residence will cease?

Present address

Address

Postcode

If appropriate, please print the full name and address of your present employer

Name

Address

Postcode

Additional Information

E Declaration

I declare that

- I will notify the HM Revenue & Customs without delay if there is a change in my circumstances or intentions which would affect any of the answers given

- the information I have given in this form is correct and complete to the best of my knowledge and belief.

Signature

Date

/   /

Please return this form to the HM Revenue & Customs Office that sent it to you.

Appendix 3   511

Inland Revenue

Reference

District date stamp

INCOME AND CHARGEABLE GAINS - DOMICILE

A. Relevance of Domicile

It is only necessary for the Inland Revenue to consider your domicile if it is immediately relevant in deciding your liability to United Kingdom income tax and capital gains tax. It will only be relevant for those purposes if you have answered 'Yes' to any of the questions (I to 4) below. Please answer each question by entering a tick in the appropriate box.

1. a. Do you have any income arising abroad or gains on assets situated outside the United Kingdom which will not be wholly remitted to the United Kingdom?   Yes ☐   No ☐

    b. If you answer 'Yes' to question 1a, please state the main source of income (for example pension, bank interest, royalties, dividends) or capital gains. _____

2. a. Are you (or will you be) making a claim for United Kingdom tax relief in respect of contributions to a non-United Kingdom pension scheme or retirement benefit plan which are incurred out of remuneration you receive from an employer who is not resident in the United Kingdom?   Yes ☐   No ☐

    b. If you answer 'Yes' to question 2a, please state the name of the pension scheme or retirement benefit plan. _____

3. Have your costs, or those of your family, in travelling between the country in which you normally live and the United Kingdom been borne or reimbursed by your employer?   Yes ☐   No ☐

4. Will you have income from an employment
    - where the employer is not resident in the United Kingdom, **and**
    - all the duties of the employment will be carried out abroad, **and**
    - you do not expect to remit all the income to the United Kingdom?   Yes ☐   No ☐

If you have answered 'Yes' to any of the questions 1 to 4 go to *Part B*, otherwise sign and date the statement below and return this form to me.

Signature _____   Date _____

DOM 1   CCO 6/94

B. Domicile Information

Please answer the following if you completed any 'Yes' box in Section A.

5. In which country were you born? _____

6. What is your date of birth? _____

7. Where was your father domiciled at the date of your birth (in the case of a country with a federal system, show the particular state or province)? _____

8. What changes, if any, took place in your father's domicile during your minority? _____

9. If your father is dead, what was his full name and the date and place of his death? _____

10. Where do you consider you are domiciled (in the case of a country with a federal system, show the particular state or province)? _____

11. On what grounds do you consider yourself to be domiciled there? _____

12. Have you retained accommodation for your use in that territory? ☐ Yes ☐ No
    If 'Yes'
    a. what is the address? _____

    b. what is the nature of the accommodation? _____

    c. is it kept available for your occupation? ☐ Yes ☐ No

13. What are your business, personal, social or other connections with that territory? _____

14. a. Are you married? ☐ Yes ☐ No

    b. If you answer 'Yes" to question 14a

       1. on what date were you married? _____

       2. in which country were you married? _____

       3. in which country do your husband/wife and children now live? _____

15. What periods have you spent in the United Kingdom during each of the past 10 years? *(Please attach a separate sheet if necessary)*

16. a. Do you have accommodation of any description for your use in the United Kingdom?   Yes ☐   No ☐

    b. If you answer 'Yes" to question 16a

       1. what is the address?

       2. in what capacity do you occupy the accommodation (for example owner, tenant, employer provided)?

17. a. If you were born abroad, what was your reason for coming to the United Kingdom, for example business, employment or education of children?

    b. As appropriate

       1. what is the nature of the business or employment?

       2. what is the position you hold?

       3. what are the dates of birth of your children?

18. If you were born in the United Kingdom

    a. why did you leave the United Kingdom?

    b. in what year did you leave?

19. a. What are your intentions for the future?

    b. If you do not intend to stay permanently in the United Kingdom, when and in what circumstances do you envisage that your residence here will cease?

If you are a widow or divorced woman whose marriage was before 1 January 1974 answer the questions in *Part C*. In all other cases please complete the declaration in *Part D*.

C. Supplementary Information

20. What is your former husband's full name? _____

21. In which country was he born? _____

22. On what date was he born? _____

23. As applicable

    a. when and where did he die? _____

    b. when and where were you divorced? _____

24. In which country, state or province was his father domiciled at the time of your former husband's birth? _____

25. What, if any, changes took place in the father's domicile during your former husband's minority? _____

Please now complete the declaration below.

D. Declaration

I declare that

- I will notify the United Kingdom Inland Revenue without delay if there is a change of circumstances or intentions which would affect any of the answers given
- the information I have given in this form is correct and complete to the best of my knowledge and belief.

Signature _____ Date _____

I suggest that you keep a copy of this completed form

Joint property and income

Reference

Please use these if you write or call. It will help to avoid delay.

National Insurance number

Issued by

Notice of declaration of beneficial interests in joint property and income

If you and your husband or wife or civil partner live together, we normally treat income from property held in joint names as if it belonged to the two of you in equal shares. Each of you is taxed on half the income. This rule applies even if you own the property in unequal shares.

However, if you hold property jointly and

- you actually own the property in unequal shares, and
- you are entitled to the income arising in proportion to those shares, and
- you want to be taxed on the actual basis

you may make a declaration on this form, and we will tax the income on the 'actual basis'. Before you fill in this form, please read the notes below.

Income

You cannot make a declaration

- unless the property and income are actually held by you in unequal shares. You cannot simply choose to have the income taxed on an unequal basis because you think it would be to your advantage

- about income that is earned income (or, like furnished holiday lettings, treated as earned income)
- about income from a trade or profession that you and your husband or wife or civil partner carry on in partnership
- from 6 April 2004, about income arising from shares held in a close company (broadly, a company controlled by no more than five people)
- about income which for tax purposes is treated as the income of a third party, even if the income arises from property held in the joint names of you and your husband or wife or civil partner.

Property

For the purposes of this declaration, property includes land and buildings and investments of any kind.

Bank and Building Society accounts

You cannot make a declaration about investments in which you and your husband or wife or civil partner invest as 'joint beneficial owners'. In such accounts each owner is equally entitled to the whole account, and any income from it is paid to both parties jointly.

All bank/building society accounts are held on this basis.

If you have changed your investments from the 'joint beneficial owners' basis to some other basis, for example by way of a deed, please attach evidence.

Beneficial interest

You may not be familiar with the meaning of beneficial interest in property and income. You should seek professional advice if you are in any doubt about

- your beneficial interest in property held in joint names
- your beneficial interest in income from such property
- whether you should complete this form and sign the declaration.

Although we can explain the practical effects of completing this form, we cannot help you to determine beneficial interests.

If the address shown above is wrong please correct it in the box below.

Address

Postcode

For official use only

Date received

Declaration accepted

Initials

Date stamp

HMRC 02/06

Declaration by husband and wife or civil partners — You may be prosecuted if you make a false statement

Your declaration must reflect the facts about your shares in each property and the income from it.

List each item of property separately, even if you share them all in the same proportions. For example, if you jointly hold shares in several companies you must make a separate entry for each company.

If you need to make more than five entries you should ask me for extra forms. Both of you must sign and date every form that you fill in.

Description of joint property	Beneficial interest in the property itself		Beneficial interest in any income arising	
	% share		% share	
	spouse A/civil partner A		spouse A/civil partner A	
	spouse B/civil partner B		spouse B/civil partner B	
	% share		% share	
	spouse A/civil partner A		spouse A/civil partner A	
	spouse B/civil partner B		spouse B/civil partner B	
	% share		% share	
	spouse A/civil partner A		spouse A/civil partner A	
	spouse B/civil partner B		spouse B/civil partner B	
	% share		% share	
	spouse A/civil partner A		spouse A/civil partner A	
	spouse B/civil partner B		spouse B/civil partner B	
	% share		% share	
	spouse A/civil partner A		spouse A/civil partner A	
	spouse B/civil partner B		spouse B/civil partner B	

We declare that the details above correctly state our beneficial interests in the property described, and the income arising from it, and that the property is held in our joint names.

	spouse A/civil partner A	spouse B/civil partner B
Full name		
Signature		
Date	/ /	/ /

Please also give the following details if you know them

Tax reference		
National Insurance no.		

You may wish to keep a copy of this declaration for your records.

To give me notice of this declaration you must return it to me within 60 days of the date you both sign and date it.

Your declaration will then be effective from the date you signed the form. You cannot make a back-dated declaration.

Your declaration will remain in force until (but only until) your interests in the property or income change, or you stop living together as a married couple or civil partners. **If your circumstances change you must tell me immediately.** Return this completed form, and any extra forms, to the office address shown overleaf.

Appendix 4
EU Savings Directive International Issues for UK Investors* The European Directive on the Taxation of Savings

INTRODUCTION

1. Finance Act 2003 introduced legislation to enable the Treasury to make regulations for a scheme to collect information about overseas residents. These regulations implement most of the European Directive on taxation of savings ("the Directive"). The Directive is intended to counter tax evasion on savings income by providing for automatic exchange of information between Member States on cross-border savings income payments made to EU resident individuals.

2. Three Member States – Austria, Belgium and Luxembourg – will, as an alternative to exchanging information from the outset, apply a withholding tax during a transitional period. In addition to Member States, certain UK and Netherlands dependent and associated territories and certain third countries will be either exchanging information or imposing a withholding tax.

3. The Directive takes effect from 1 July 2005.

[. . .]

WHAT THE DIRECTIVE SAYS ABOUT EXCHANGE OF INFORMATION

5. Any relevant payee who receives savings income from a paying agent established in another Member State may have details about them collected and verified by that paying agent. The paying agent will then report that information and information about the savings income payment to its own tax authority, who will pass it on to the tax authority of the country or territory in which the individual is resident (according to the Directive rules). This will help tax authorities ensure that the correct amount of tax is paid on the savings income.

---

* Information extracted form HMRC website.

WHAT THE DIRECTIVE SAYS ABOUT WITHHOLDING TAX

6. For a transitional period, Austria, Belgium and Luxembourg will withhold tax from savings income payments instead of exchanging information. Some of the other participating countries and territories may also decide to withhold tax initially rather than exchange information. The tax withheld under this system will be in addition to any tax withheld under the territory's domestic legislation.

7. However, investors who receive savings income from a paying agent in a withholding country may elect not to have tax withheld or, if withholding tax is charged, they will be able to avoid double taxation, as set out below.

HOW TO OPT NOT TO HAVE TAX WITHHELD

8. Withholding countries will enable investors to request that tax is not withheld by implementing at least one of two procedures. Individual investors who are tax resident in the UK will be able to make use of these procedures to receive their overseas savings income without deduction of the withholding tax.

Procedure 1

9. The individual may authorise the paying agent to report details of the savings income payment to its tax authority, who will supply it to HMRC. The individual will have to follow whatever procedures are prescribed for this purpose by the territory where the paying agent is established.

Procedure 2

10. The individual can ask HMRC for a certificate showing:

- His name, address, and a tax identification number (or, if he does not have one, his date/place of birth);
- The name and address of the paying agent;
- The account number in question or some other means of identifying the security; and
- The period (up to three years) for which the certificate is valid.

11. The individual will need to provide information about the paying agent and the source of the savings income to HMRC so that the certificate can be drawn up. The individual then presents the completed certificate to the paying agent, and requests them not to withhold tax from the savings income.

12. Guidance is available on how to apply for a certificate. HMRC will issue a certificate within two months of receiving the request. It will be valid for up to three years.

HOW TO ELIMINATE DOUBLE TAXATION

13. In order to make sure that investors are not taxed more than once on the same savings income, investors who have tax withheld under the new scheme rules may claim credit for the tax withheld from their tax authority.

14. These rules are in addition to the normal rules on double taxation, which will continue to apply in the normal way to any tax withheld in the territory where the original payer of the income is established.

15. Once the Directive takes effect investors may find that two amounts of foreign tax have been withheld from the gross amount of the savings income:

- Tax withheld, as now, in the territory where the original payer of the income is resident under that territory's domestic law; and
- Tax withheld by a paying agent (known in the legislation as "special withholding tax") as part of the new scheme in those countries and territories that opt to withhold tax rather than exchange information.

16. The UK will ensure the elimination of any double taxation that may occur as a result of the imposition of withholding tax as follows:

- As now, any tax withheld in the territory where the original payer of the income is resident under its domestic law will be credited first against the UK tax payable on the savings income, provided that credit is allowable under UK law or under the UK's DTA with that territory. It will remain the case that such tax cannot be repaid if it exceeds the UK tax liability on that income;
- The special withholding tax will be credited against the remaining UK Income or Capital Gains tax liability;
- Any special withholding tax remaining after the UK Income and Capital Gains tax liability will be repaid to the investor by HMRC.

17. The Government envisages that investors will be able to reclaim the tax withheld under the Directive either through their tax return or by submitting a claim to HMRC. Self assessment returns for 2005–06 will be amended to allow this withholding tax to be set off against income tax and capital gains tax, and any repayment claimed.

18. The Government has included legislation in Finance Act 2004 to complete the implementation of the Savings Directive. The legislation:

- allows the crediting of tax withheld by the paying agent under the new scheme prescribe the order of relief where credit is allowable for special withholding tax against an individual's UK Income or Capital Gains tax liability.
- authorises the repayment of any excess special withholding tax credit remaining after exhausting an individual's UK Income or Capital Gains tax liability.
- provides for the certificate outlined above.

Appendix 5
Domicile of Choice and the Robert Gaines-Cooper Case: A Note

The decision of the UK Special Commissioners of Income Tax handed down on 31 October 2006 in respect of the affairs of Robert Gaines-Cooper regarding his domicile status seemed unsurprising. Now the Court of Appeal in October 2008 (as did the High Court in 2007) has confirmed the decision of the Special Commissioners. This article looks at the original Commissioners findings.

In short, Mr Gaines-Cooper, currently aged 69, possessed an English domicile of origin but had tried to argue that for the period 1992/93 to 2003/04 he had in fact acquired a domicile of choice in the Seychelles. The Commissioners disagreed holding that he had never abandoned his domicile of origin and thus remained for this period English domiciled, i.e. a Seychelles domicile of choice had never been acquired.

While appreciating that hindsight is a wonderful thing, given the extent of Mr Gaines-Cooper's UK links during the above period it does seem unlikely that he would have been able to successfully argue that he had acquired a Seychelles domicile of choice. To have planned his UK tax affairs, if in fact he did, on the basis of having lost his English domicile of origin would seem to have been a high risk strategy.

As every UK tax advisor is aware, losing a UK domicile of origin is probably one of the most difficult things for a client to achieve, albeit not impossible. Perhaps the most recent "success" in this regard is the case of *Morgan v. Cilento (2004)* (see below) not apparently discussed in the Gaines-Cooper case.

Prima face, Mr Gaines-Cooper appeared to do "all the right things". He bought a house in the Seychelles; he expressed the wish that his ashes be scattered there; he married a Seychellois woman; and in his wills he stated that he lived there and his domicile status was that of the Seychelles.

Unfortunately this, according to the Commissioners, was not enough to have resulted in a domicile of choice in the Seychelles having been acquired.

Without doubt the strong connections Mr Gaines-Cooper retained with the UK were fatal. Perhaps of decisive impact was the acquisition and retention of significant properties in the UK in which he and his family lived albeit that for certain periods the properties were rented out to third parties. In this regard the Commissioners said that:

> We regard as significant the fact that nearly all of the Appellant's connections with the UK were located in a comparatively small area of the contiguous counties of Berkshire and Oxfordshire... born there... went to school... mother lived

there ... married twice ... purchased two houses ... business offices ... attended Royal Ascot ... son went to school ... We also regard the 1999 will ... to be of significance. It was prepared by English solicitors; it is to be construed and take effect according to English law; and the ... guardians of [the son] live in the UK ... retained his British citizenship and did not apply for citizenship in the Seychelles ....

It might, in any event, be thought that it is in fact impossible to acquire a domicile of choice outside the UK if a UK property is retained. This, however, is not so:

> loss of domicile of origin ... is not inconsistent with retention of a place of residence in that country if the chief residence has been established elsewhere. (*Plummer v. IRC [1987]*)

Acquisition of a non-UK domicile of choice requires both residence in the overseas country *and* an intention of permanent or indefinite residence; one without the other is insufficient. "Residence" for this purpose means:

> physical presence in [a] country as an inhabitant of it [as opposed to someone who is in a country as a traveller or casually]. (*IRC v. Duchess of Portland [1982]*)

Where two residences occur it seems that it then becomes necessary to determine which of them is the person's "chief residence" (unfortunately a term not defined in the judgements in which the term appears; *Udny v. Udny [1869]*).

In the current case the Commissioners not only felt that Mr Gaines-Cooper's chief residence remained that of the UK and not the Seychelles but in any event he also lacked the "intention" to reside in the Seychelles indefinitely. He thus failed to satisfy either of the two legs of the test.

While not referred to in their decision it is perhaps interesting to note that the Commissioners did comment on Mr Gaines-Cooper's evidence given over four and a half days of the 10-day hearing:

> ... the Appellant did his best to be truthful and honest but ... he made mistakes ... much of the oral evidence of the Appellant was digressive and discursive and unsupported by any documents ... the Appellant also seemed to confuse one of his business ventures with another ... *For these reasons we approach the oral evidence of the Appellant with some caution* .... (italics added)

A number of other high ranking witnesses from the Seychelles were also called to give evidence on Mr Gaines-Cooper's behalf all of whom:

> spoke very highly of the help given by the Appellant to charities and good causes in the Seychelles.

However, the Commissioners appeared to give short, but polite, shrift to their evidence simply stating that:

> ... [their evidence was] of relevance to the Appellant's attachment to the Seychelles rather than establishing the place of his principal attachment.

It is interesting to contrast this case with that of *Morgan v. Cilento [2004]* decided by the High Court. The *Morgan* case was one relating to a claim made by a Ms Minutolo who had had a relationship with Mr Shaffer during the latter part of his life and sought to claim under the Inheritance (Provision for Family and Dependants) Act 1975 (which required for it to be viable that Mr Shaffer had died domiciled in England).

Mr Anthony Shaffer, the playwright, possessed an English domicile of origin. He died aged 75 in late 2001 in England having spent a significant amount of time in Australia. However, he was held to have acquired a domicile of choice in Queensland, Australia. In his findings the judge stated that the facts which were of weight included:

- marriage to an Australian citizen and matrimonial home in Queensland;
- the bulk of his personal possessions were in Queensland;
- he had sold most of his UK assets;
- he had no home in the UK;
- his bank account and credit card were Australian;
- he exercised the right to vote in Queensland;
- majority of his time spent in Australia;
- will made in Queensland;
- he never stopped talking of Queensland as his home.

The contrast between the two cases could not perhaps be much greater and the different decisions are not perhaps surprising. Arguably, the affairs of Mr Shaffer were far less complex than those of Mr Gains-Cooper and certainly the "UK taint" significantly less in Mr Shaffer's situation albeit that he died in the UK.

So, has the *Gaines-Cooper* case added anything material to the issues associated with domicile determination for UK tax purposes?

Probably not.

What it does do is to reinforce the fact that the loss of a UK domicile of origin requires, for all intents and purposes, a severing of virtually all UK ties, in particular, including the sale of all UK properties which might be used as residences and the sale of significant UK-based businesses. Perhaps to a lesser extent wills should be drawn up under the law of country of the hopeful domicile of choice (i.e. not be subject to UK law) by local lawyers and acquisition of local citizenship must be helpful.

However, as always, each decision turns on its own particular facts and the respective weights to attach to each fact (as is evident from a study of past decisions where the same facts have often nevertheless produced different decisions). Furthermore, decisions of a lower court are often overturned on appeal (see *IRC v. Bullock [1976]*; *Winans v. AG [1904]*; *Aguilian & Anr v. Cyganik [2006]*) making the whole area of tax planning based on domicile status a very tricky and risky business indeed in particular when it is also appreciated that the burden of proof alleging the acquisition of a domicile of choice falls fairly and squarely on the client (as applied to Mr Gaines-Cooper).

The bottom line is to advise clients that any tax planning based on a loss of a UK domicile of origin is likely to be vigorously fought (often after their deaths as in the *Morgan v. Cilento* case) either by HMRC and/or disgruntled ex-spouses/mistresses and simply buying a foreign grave plot and making a foreign will just simply doesn't work (if it ever did)!!

Appendix 6
Domicile Flowcharts

Appendix 6 525

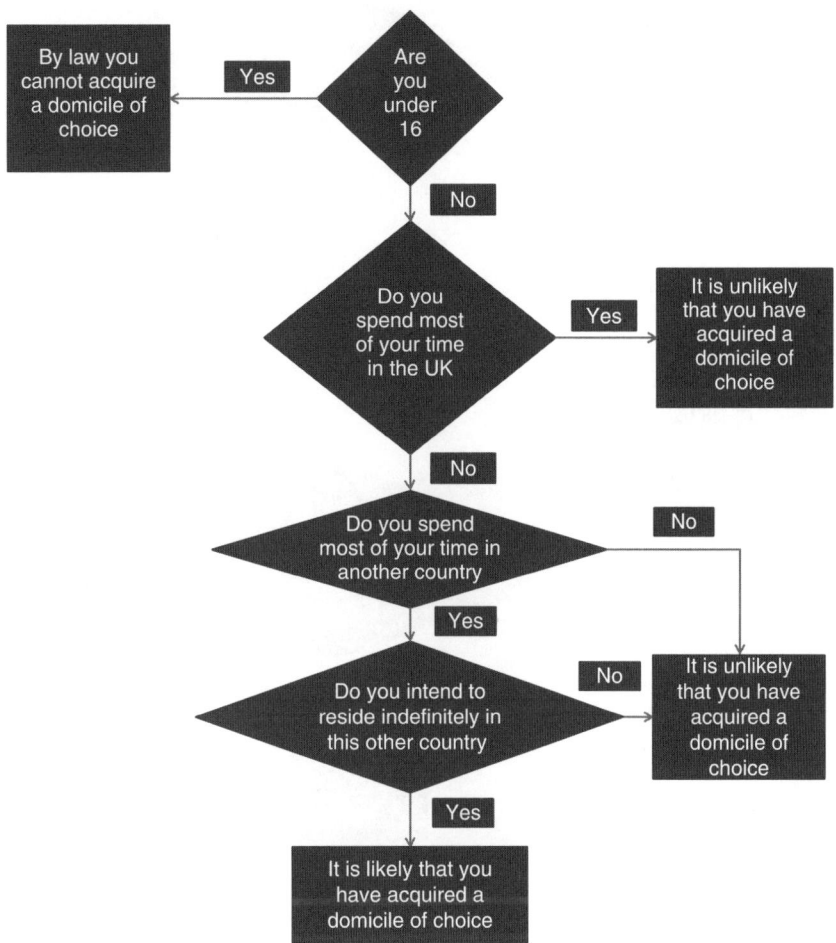

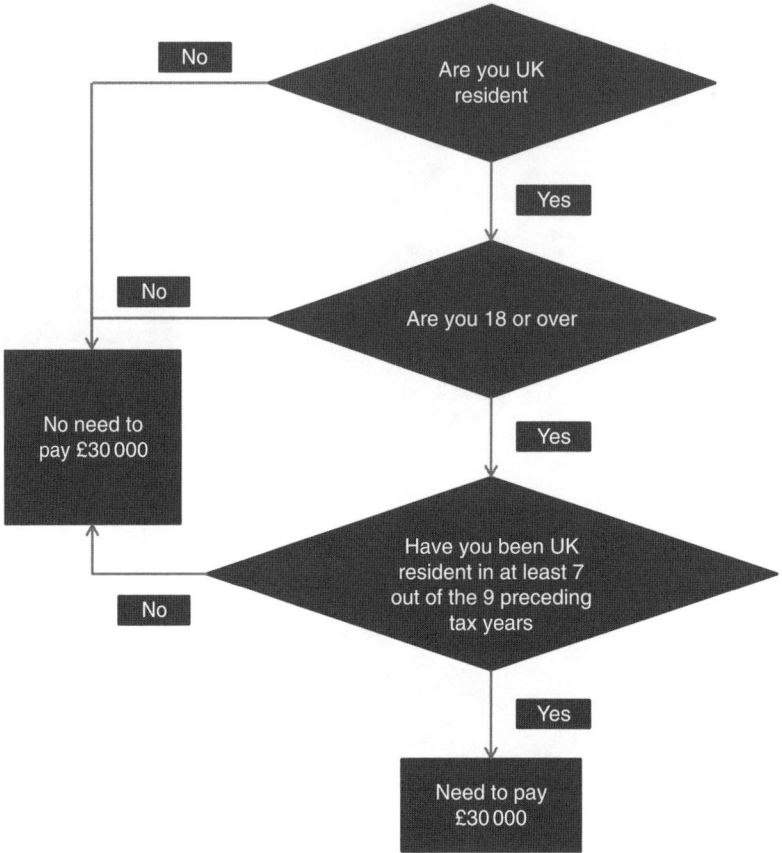

Appendix 6

ASCERTAINING WHEN NON-UK DOMICILED INDIVIDUAL NEEDS TO MAKE A CLAIM FOR REMITTANCE BASIS TREATMENT

EXAMPLE OF REMITTANCES TO UK USING OVERSEAS BORROWING (NON-REAL ESTATE)

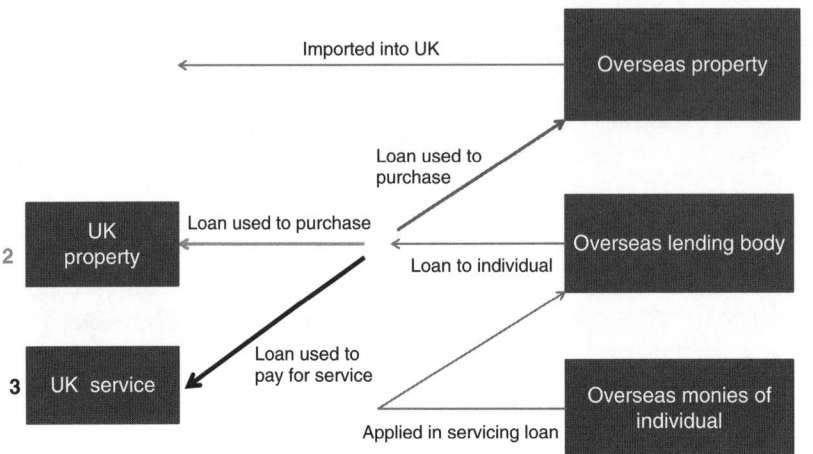

Appendix 7
Sample Model Will

THIS IS THE LAST WILL and TESTAMENT of [ME]

1 I HEREBY REVOKE all previous wills and testamentary dispositions made by me and DECLARE that this Will deals with all my property real and personal [*except my real estate situate in France/Spain/Portugal*][1]

2 I APPOINT my wife[2] [*Winifrid*] (*"Winifrid"*) and [*A N Other*] of [*address*] to be the Executors of this my Will (hereinafter called "my Executors" which expression shall include any executor or executors for the time being hereof)

3 I APPOINT [*Winifrid and T2 and T3/Offshore Trustee Company Ltd whose registered office is at...*] or the successor company to that company to be the Trustees of the trusts established by this my Will and any Codicil to it AND I DECLARE that the expression "my Trustees" means the trustees hereof for the time being

4 I GIVE the following pecuniary legacies

4.1 to my godson Frederick the sum of £5,000 (five thousand pounds)

4.2 etc etc

5 I GIVE the following

5.1 my diamond solitaire engagement ring to my daughter Eloise

5.2 my largest diamond tiara to my god-daughter Princess Zoe

5.3 etc etc (not that the testator in this model is a cross-dresser)

6 IN this my Will and in the Schedule hereto "Fund" means such sum as is equal to the amount which is the upper limit at the date of my death of the first nil-rate portion of value referred to in Section 7(3) of the Inheritance Tax Act 1984 in accordance with Section 8 of that Act but reduced by the aggregate of the values transferred by previous chargeable transfers made by me in the period of seven years ending with the date of my death and the value of any legacies in this Will or any Codicil hereto to the extent

---

[1] Real estate owned outside the UK should be subject to a separate will made in the jurisdiction where the property is situated.
[2] This model is drafted for a testator. Where a testatrix uses this model, appropriate changes will need to be made.

that they are not exempt from inheritance tax and the terms "values transferred" and "chargeable transfers" have the same meanings as in the Inheritance Tax Act 1984 and references to any statute shall mean such statute modified or re-enacted from time to time and words and phrases defined in the Schedule hereto shall have the same meaning as in this my Will

7   IF my wife [*Winifrid*] shall survive me by thirty days at least[3] then I GIVE the Fund free of inheritance tax and all other duties payable on or in respect of my death to my Trustees to hold upon trust with and subject to the powers and provisions set out in the Schedule which forms part of this my Will and my Executors may require my Trustees to accept in satisfaction of all or part of the Fund a binding promise of payment whether secured or unsecured made personally by my wife [*Winifrid*] or by my Executors which debt shall be payable on demand and my Trustees shall accept such as the whole or as part (as the case may be) of the Fund

8   I BEQUEATH AND DEVISE all the residue of my real and personal property wheresoever and whatsoever to which this Will applies ("my Residuary Estate") to my Executors to hold UPON TRUST to sell call in and convert the same into money (with power to postpone such sale calling in and conversion for so long as my Executors think fit without being responsible for any consequent loss and with power to distribute assets in specie) and to hold the same together with any ready money belonging to me at the date of my death to pay thereout my just debts and my funeral and testamentary expenses and any inheritance tax or other taxes arising on or by reason of my death and to pay or transfer the balance of my Residuary Estate to my Trustees TO HOLD upon trust for my wife [*Winifrid*] for life if she shall have survived me by thirty days at least (except that such conditional survivorship shall not apply where our deaths are simultaneous or our deaths occur in circumstances rendering it uncertain which one of us survived the other) and subject thereto and if she shall not so survive me (or otherwise as aforesaid and in any event after her death) UPON THE TRUSTS specified in the Schedule hereto which forms part of this my Will

9   MY TRUSTEES may in their discretion from time to time pay to [*Winifrid*] free of the trusts hereof the whole or any part or parts of the capital of my Residuary Estate

10   THE POWER of appointing and removing Trustees in respect of the trust of my Residuary Estate shall be vested in the person or persons for the time being who may be the Appointor in accordance with the Schedule to this my Will

11   SUBJECT always to the life interest of my wife [*Winifrid*] given by clause 8 above in dealing with my Residuary Estate my Trustees shall in addition have all

---

[3] A conditional survivorship clause is advisable, in order to keep average rates of IHT as low as possible between partners. Without the conditional survivorship clause, it if the wife were to die immediately after husband, the advantage of owning assets between them in approximately equal shares will be lost, so that distributions from will trusts will attract higher rates of IHT.

the powers and discretions set out in the Schedule to this my Will (including without limitation and without the need to obtain the consent of any person[4] the power of appointment given to then by paragraph 5 of that Schedule)

12   I DECLARE that the receipt of the parent or guardian of any infant beneficiary hereunder and the receipt of the secretary or other proper officer of any charity or other organisation taking benefit hereunder shall be a full discharge to my Executors and Trustees in respect of the same

13   I DECLARE that all income of my estate shall be treated as arising at the time of its receipt by my Executors and shall not be apportioned to any other time or period under the Apportionment Acts 1834 and 1870 and I hereby exclude for the purposes of this my Will the rules of equitable apportionment and any other technical rules of administration

14   MY EXECUTORS and MY TRUSTEES shall have power at any time to exercise the power of appropriation conferred upon personal representatives by Section 41 of the Administration of Estates Act 1925 and to exercise such power without the consent of any person whose consent could or might but for this present provision be or have been made requisite

15   Any of my Executors and any of my Trustees who is engaged in any profession or business shall be entitled to charge and be paid all usual reasonable professional and other charges for work or business done or transacted by him or his firm in connection with acting as an Executor hereof including acts which Executors or Trustees not being engaged in any profession or business could do personally[5]

16   SUBJECT TO paragraph 15 of the Schedule hereto this Will shall be construed in accordance with the laws of England

Schedule

1   Name

This Trust shall be known as **The #### Will Trust** or by such other name as the Trustees shall from time to time determine.

2   Definitions

In this Trust where the context admits—

2.1 The following expressions mean and include the following—

---

[4] Avoiding the need to obtain the consent of the surviving partner before making a capital advance within Trustee Act 1925 s 32(1), and avoiding the 50% advancement restriction in that section.
[5] The all-important clause to any professional will draftsman. Absent this clause no executor can charge fees for acting. *Re Barber* (1886) 34 Ch D 77; *Dale v IRC* [1954] AC 11,27.

Expression	Meaning
"Appointor"	Winifrid during her lifetime unless and until and for such period as she is incapable of managing her own affairs by reason of mental or physical incapacity (such mental incapacity to be certified to the Trustees by a medical practitioner of at least 5 years standing and so certified at intervals of not longer than 12 months during such period of incapacity and such physical incapacity to be evidenced conclusively by Winifrid in the opinion of my Trustees being unable to sign a document or to give an oral or demonstrative instruction to another person to sign a document on her behalf) and during such period of Winifrid's incapacity and in any event after her death my Trustees.
"Beneficiaries"	The persons specified in the Appendix hereto (and "Beneficiary" shall include any one or more of the Beneficiaries).
"Trustees"	The Trustees for the time being of this Trust (and "Trustee" shall include any one or more of the Trustees).
"Trust Fund"	(1) For the purposes of Clause 6 of the Will, the Fund, and the purposes of Clause 8 of the Will, my Residuary Estate; and in either case; (2) all other (if any) money investments and other property which may in future be paid or transferred to or under the control of the Trustees by any person to be held on these trusts and which shall be accepted by the Trustees as an addition to the Trust Fund; (3) all other accretions to the Trust Fund by way of accumulation of income or otherwise; and (4) all money investments or other property for the time being representing all or any part of the above.
"Trust Period"	The period ending eighty years after the date of my death or such shorter period as the Trustees shall in their absolute discretion in writing decide and that period shall be the perpetuity period applicable hereto.
"Will"	The Will of [ME] to which this is the Schedule.

2.2 References to the singular shall include the plural and vice versa.

2.3 References to any gender shall include the other genders.

2.4 References to statutory provisions shall include statutory modifications and re-enactments of such provisions.

2.5 References to a particular power or discretion vested in the Trustees shall be construed without prejudice to the generality of any other powers or discretions.

2.6 Clause descriptions are included for reference only and shall not affect the interpretation of this Trust.

2.7 Words and phrases defined in the Will shall have the same meaning in this Schedule.

3 Trust for sale

The Trustees shall hold the Trust Fund upon trust in their absolute discretion either to retain the Trust Fund in its existing state or to sell call in or convert into money the whole or any part or parts of the Trust Fund (but with power to postpone such sale calling in and conversion) and in their absolute discretion to invest or apply the net proceeds of such sale calling in or conversion in any manner authorised by this Trust or by law with power at any time or times to vary or transpose any such investments or application for others so authorised.

4 Trusts of added property

The Trustees may at any time during the Trust Period accept such additional property of whatever kind (including property of an onerous kind the acceptance of which the Trustees consider to be beneficial) as may be paid or transferred to them upon these trusts by any person in whatever manner.

5 Power of appointment over capital and income

5.1 The Trustees shall hold the capital and income of the Trust Fund upon trust for all or such one or more of the Beneficiaries at such ages or times in such shares and upon such trusts (whether created by the Trustees or not) for the benefit of all or any one or more of the Beneficiaries as the Trustees may in their absolute discretion decide at any time to times during the Trust Period to appoint and in making any such appointment the Trustees shall have powers as full as those which they could possess if they were the absolute beneficial owners of the Trust Fund including the power (in their absolute discretion subject to paragraph 8 hereof) to extend restrict amend vary or release all or any of the powers of administration or investment hereunder or (with the written consent of the Appointor) at any time(s) to add to the class of Beneficiaries hereunder and provided always that if the terms of any revocable appointment have not been revoked before the end of the Trust Period such appointment shall at that time become irrevocable.

5.2 In addition the Trustees may from time to time pay or transfer the whole or any part or parts of the capital or income of the Trust Fund to the Trustees for the time being of any other trust wheresoever established to existing and whether governed by the same proper law as this Trust or by the law of any other state or territory under which any one or more of the Beneficiaries is or are interested notwithstanding that such other trust may also contain trusts powers and provisions (discretionary or otherwise) in favour of some other person or persons or objects if the Trustees shall in their absolute discretion consider such payment to be for the benefit of such one or more of the Beneficiaries.

5.3 The receipt of the parent or guardian of any infant to whom assets may be appointed and the receipt of the secretary or other property officer of any charitable or other organisation to which assets may be appointed will be a conclusive and complete discharge to the Trustees.

6 Power to accumulate income

In default of and subject to any appointment made under the provisions of the preceding paragraph 5 during the Trust Period the Trustees shall pay or apply the income of the Trust Fund to or for the maintenance and support or otherwise for the benefit of all or any one or more of the Beneficiaries as the Trustees may in their absolute discretion think fit but during the period of twenty-one (21) years from the date of my death the Trustees may if they in their absolute discretion think fit accumulate such income or any part of it by way of compound interest by investing the same and its resulting income in any way hereby authorised and if they do so they shall hold such accumulations as part of the capital of the Trust Fund but may nonetheless in any future year during the Trust Period apply them or any part of them as if they were income arising in that year.

7 Ultimate default trusts

Subject as above the Trustees shall hold the Trust Fund and its income for the Beneficiaries described in paragraph 3 of the Appendix hereto living at the end of the Trust Period if more than one in equal shares absolutely.

8 Power to vary

The power to extend restrict amend vary or release any powers of administration or investment hereof or to add to or restrict in any way the class of Beneficiaries hereunder may be validly exercised by the Trustees only if prior to implementing any such act the Trustees shall have been advised in writing by a lawyer qualified for at least ten years in the jurisdiction to which the Trust Fund is then subject that it would be expedient for the purposes of the management and administration of the Trust Fund to act in the manner specified in such written advice and provided that acting in such manner will not be in breach of any relevant law against perpetuities.

9 Power to invest

The Trustees in their absolute discretion may retain any investments in which the Trust Fund is invested from time to time and may invest monies as is without restriction they were the absolute beneficial owners thereof and in particular they may purchase or lend at interest upon the security of any property real or personal of whatever nature and wheresoever situate in such manner as the Trustees think fit whether or not producing income or involving liabilities or not including in particular (but without prejudice to the generality of the foregoing) insurance policies on the life of any Beneficiary or other person shares stocks and land including any house or flat and its contents as a residence for any Beneficiary on whatever terms the Trustees in their discretion think appropriate and may vary or switch any such investment in all cases without being liable for loss and in all respects as if they were absolutely beneficially entitled and not subject to any restriction as to taking advice or otherwise in relation to investment.

10 Power to borrow and insure

In addition to their statutory powers the Trustees shall have the following powers—

10.1 to borrow money with or without giving security and on such terms as they think fit for any purpose (including investment);

10.2 to insure as they think fit any property which may form part of the Trust Fund, the cost of such insurance to be paid out of the income or capital of the Trust Fund as the Trustees shall think fit.

11 Liability for loss

In the professed execution of the trusts and powers hereof no trustee being an individual shall be liable for any loss to the trust fund or for breach of trust arising by reason of any improper investments made in good faith or for the negligence or fraud of any agent employed by him or by any other trustee hereof although the employment of such agent was not strictly necessary or expedient or by reason of any mistake or omission or commission made or suffered to be made in good faith by any trustee hereof or by reason of any other matter or thing except wilful and individual fraud of which he was personally conscious on the part of the trustee sought to be made so liable or gross negligence and no trustee shall be bound to take proceedings against a co-trustee or past trustee or his personal representatives for any breach or alleged breach of trust committed or suffered by such co-trustee or past trustee.

12 Appointment and removal of trustees

12.1 The power of appointing new and additional Trustees hereof shall be vested in the Appointor for the time being hereof and subject thereto in the Trustees for the time being.

12.2 The Appointor shall be entitled to remove Trustees (provided at all times that there remains a minimum of one Trustee acting) upon giving not less than 21 days written notice to the Trustees and by executing a Deed removing the Trustee. Any such removed Trustee shall do all that is necessary to effect the transfer of the Trust Fund to the remaining or newly appointed Trustee(s) and if such actions have not been completed within 30 days of the date of the Deed removing any Trustee from office the then Trustees for the time being hereof are hereby empowered in the name of the removed Trustee to do all acts and things necessary to effect the transfer of the Trust Fund into the name of the Trustees.

13 Indemnity to retiring trustees

13.1 Subject to paragraph 13.2 below any person ceasing to be a trustee of this Trust shall be entitled to an indemnity from the Trustees to the extent permitted by law from and against all and any actions proceedings or defaults accounts costs claims and demands including without prejudice to the generality of the foregoing any liability incurred or which may have been incurred whether of a fiscal nature or not and whether enforceable or not and arising in any part of the world.

13.2 No indemnity given pursuant to paragraph 13.1 above shall extend to provide indemnity to any person who has acted at any time as a Trustee of this Trust in respect of any act or omission of fraud or willful or gross negligence by such person.

14 Trustee charges

Any Trustee for the time being of this Trust being engaged in any profession or business shall be entitled to charge and be paid all usual reasonable professional and other charges for work or business done or transacted by him or his firm in connection with the trusts hereof including acts which a Trustee not being engaged in any profession or business could do personally and any corporate trustee hereof for the time being shall be entitled to charge in accordance with its published scale of fees for the time being in force PROVIDED THAT during the lifetime of the Appointor no fees shall be paid to any Trustee unless the amount of such fees are approved in writing by the Appointor.

15 Proper law

This Trust is subject to the law of England and Wales but the Trustees may in their discretion from time to time by Deed declare that this Trust shall thenceforth be subject to the laws of any other jurisdiction.

Appendix

The Beneficiaries

1 My wife Winifrid.

2 My children A (born on ####)[6] B (born on ###) and C (born on ###)

---

[6] Appropriate only if children are infants when the Will is signed.

3 The issue of the Beneficiaries names or described in paragraph 2 above born before the end of the Trust Period.

4 Any person added to the class of Beneficiaries by exercise of the power conferred by paragraph 5.1 of this Trust.

IN WITNESS whereof I have signed my name this day of Two thousand and [###]

SIGNED by the above-named)

[*testator*])

and for his last Will in the presence of)

us both being present at the)

same time who at his request)

and in his presence and in the)

presence of each other have)

hereunto subscribed our names as)

witnesses:)

Witness Signature ....

Full Name ....

Address ....

....

Occupation ....

Witness Signature ....

Full Name ....

Address ....

....

Occupation ....

Bibliography

PART ONE: THE BUILDING BLOCKS

Chiltern (2008), *Chiltern's Yellow Tax Guide 2008–09*. LexisNexis Tolley, London.

Collins, Lawrence (2006), *Dicey, Morris & Collins: The Conflict of Laws Volumes 1 and 2*, 14th edition. Thomson Sweet & Maxwell, London.

Davis, Denzil (2006), *Booth: Residence, Domicle and UK Taxation*, 10th edition. Tottel Publishing, Haywards Heath.

Finney, Malcolm (2004), *UK Taxation for Students: A Simplified Approach*, 3rd edition. Spiramus, London.

Howarth, Peter (2001), *Tax Investigations*, 2nd edition. LexisNexis Tolley, London.

Jones, Sue, Waterworth, Michael (2007), *Tolley's Taxwise II 2007–08*. LexisNexis Tolley, London.

Kessler, James (2007), *Drafting Trusts and Will Trusts: A Modern Approach*, 8th edition. Thomson Sweet & Maxwell, London.

Kessler, James (2008), *Taxation of Foreign Domiciliaries Volumes One and Two*, 7th edition. Key Haven Publications PLC, Oxford.

Lee, Natalie (2008), *Revenue Law – Principles and Practice*, 26th edition. Tottel Publishing, Haywards Heath.

McKie, Simon, McKie, Sharon (2006), *Tolley's Estate Planning 2006–07*. LexisNexis Tolley, London.

Rayney, Peter (2007), *Tax Planning for Family and Owner-managed Companies 2006/07*. Tottel Publishing, Haywards Heath.

Reader, Michael (2004), *Dealing with Revenue Enquires*. LexisNexis Tolley, London.

Smailes, David, Flint, Andrew (2008), *Tolley's Income Tax 2008–09*. LexisNexis Tolley, London.

Tiley, John, Collinson, David (2006), *Tilley and Collinson UK Tax Guide 2006–07*, 24th edition. LexisNexis Butterworths, London.

PART TWO: THE MAJOR TAXES

Chamberlain, Emma, Whitehouse, Chris (2005), *Pre-owned Assets and Tax Planning Strategies*, 2nd edition. Thomson Sweet & Maxwell, London.

Gaudern, Emma, Biggs, A.K. (2007), *Probate and the Administration of Estates: The Law and Practice*, 2nd edition. Callow Publishing, London.

Golding, Jon (2008), *Tolley's Inheritance Tax 2008–09*, LexisNexis Tolley, London.

McLaughlin, Mark, Harris, Toby, Wunschmann-Lyall, Iris (2008), *Inheritance Tax 2008/09*, Tottel Publishing, Haywards Heath.

Walton, Kevin, Flint, Andrew (2008), *Tolley's Capital Gains Tax 2008–09,* LexisNexis Tolley, London.
Waterworth, Michael, Dew, Richard (2007), *Tolley's Inheritance Tax Planning 2007–08,* LexisNexis Tolley, London.

PART THREE: TRUSTS

Burn, E.H. (2002), *Maudsley & Burn's Trusts & Trustees Cases & Materials,* 6th edition. LexisNexis Butterworths, London.
Cassell, Elizabeth (2002), *Equity and Trusts (150 Leading Cases),* 2nd edition. Old Bailey Press, London.
Chamberlain, Emma, Whitehouse, Chris (2007), *Trust Taxation Planning After the Finance Act 2006.* Thomson Sweet & Maxwell, London.
Eastaway, Nigel, Richards, Ian, Garlick, David (2005), *Tottel's Tax Advisers' Guide to Trusts,* 3rd edition. Tottel Publishing, Haywards Heath.
Edwards, Richard (2005), *Trusts and Equity,* 7th edition. Pearson Longman, Essex.
Halliwell, Margaret (2003), *Equity and Trusts (Textbook),* 4th edition. Old Bailey Press, London.
Hutton, Matthew (2006), *Tolley's UK Taxation of Trusts,* 16th edition. LexisNexis Tolley, London.
Martin, Jill E. (2005), *Hanbury & Martin Modern Equity,* 17th edition. Thomson Sweet & Maxwell, London.
Martin, Elizabeth A., Law, Jonathan (2006), *Oxford Dictionary of Law,* 6th edition. Oxford University Press, Oxford.
McClean, David, Beevers, Kisch (2006), *The Conflict of Laws,* 6th edition. Thomson Sweet & Maxwell, London.

PART FOUR: INVESTMENTS AND PROPERTY

Bray, Judith (2007), *Unlocking Land Law,* 2nd edition. Hodder Arnold, London.
Chisholm, Andrew (2002), *An Introduction to Capital Markets.* John Wiley & Sons, Ltd, Chichester.
Davis, Colin (2004), *Tax on Property 2004–05.* Wolters Kluwer (UK) Ltd, Surrey.
Ellinger, E.P., Lomnicka, E., Hooley, R.J.A. (2006), *Ellinger's Modern Banking Law,* 4th edition. Oxford University Press, Oxford.
Finney, Malcolm, Dixon, John (1996), *International Tax Planning,* 3rd edition. Tolley's, Surrey.
Gray, Kevin (1987), *Elements of Land Law.* Butterworths, London.
Maude, David (2006), *Global Private Banking and Wealth Managements: The New Realities.* John Wiley & Sons, Ltd, Chichester.
Newcombe, Stephen (2003), *Tolley's Taxation of Collective Investment.* LexisNexis Tolley, London.
Vass, Jane (2005), *Daily Mail Savings & Investments Guide.* Profile Books, London.
Williams, David (2006), *CGT & The Private Residence,* 4th edition. Wolters Kluwer (UK) Ltd, Surrey.

PART FIVE: THE INTERNATIONAL DIMENSION

Capgemini, Merrill Lynch (2007), *Annual World Wealth Report.* Capgemini, London/New York.
Clarke, Giles (2008), *Offshore Tax Planning,* 15th edition. LexisNexis Tolley, London.
Isenbergh, Joseph (2000), *International Taxation.* Foundation Press, New York.
Kochan, Nick (2005), *The Washing Machine.* Thomson, Ohio.
McDaniel, Paul, Ault, Hugh J., Repetti, James R. (2005), *Introduction to United States International Taxation,* 5th edition. Kluwer Law International, The Hague.
Morris-Cotterill, Nigel (1999), *How Not to be a Money Launderer,* 2nd edition. Silkscreen Publications, Essex.
Rohatgi, Roy (2002), *Basic International Taxation.* Kluwer Law International, The Hague.
Scott, Hal (2004), *International Finance: Law and Regulation.* Thomson Sweet & Maxwell, London.
Shelton, Ned (2004), *Interpretation and Application of Tax Treaties.* LexisNexis Tolley, London.
Spitz, Barry (2001), *Offshore Strategies.* LexisNexis Tolley, London.
Tolley (2000), *Tax Havens,* 3rd edition. Butterworths Tolley, Surrey.

PART SIX: WILLS AND SUCCESSION PLANNING

Arthur, Stephen, Jarman, Chris, Thurston, John (2007), *Tax-efficient Will Drafting,* 1st edition. LexisNexis Tolley, London.
Barlow, J.S., King, A.G., King, L.C. (2008), *Wills, Administration and Taxation: A Practical Guide,* 9th edition. Thomson Sweet & Maxwell, London.
Biggs, A.K. (2006), *A Practitioner's Guide to Wills,* 3rd edition. Callow Publishing, London.
Carlisle, Kate (2004), *The Sunday Times Working and Living Italy.* Cadogan Guides, London.
Cousal, Helen, King, Lesley (2008), *Private Client: Wills, Trusts and Estate Planning 2008.* College of Law Publishing, Guildford.
Endicott, David, Jones, Andrew (2007), *Brighouse's Precedents of Wills,* 14th edition. Thomson Sweet & Maxwell, London.
Garb, Louis (2004), *International Succession.* Kluwer Law International, The Hague.
Goodman, Dawn, Hall, Brendan, Hewitt, Paul, Mason, Henrietta (2008), *Probate Disputes and Remedies,* 2nd edition. Jordans, Bristol.
Kerridge, Roger, Brierley, A.H.R. (2002), *Parry and Clark: The Law of Succession,* 11th edition. Sweet & Maxwell, London.
King, Lesley (2006), *A Practitioner's Guide to Wills,* 2nd edition. Callow Publishing, London.
Rovati, Veena, Kanda (2002), *Succession: The Law of Wills and Estates (Revision Workbook),* 3rd edition. Old Bailey Press, London.
Sherrin, C.H., Barlow, R.F.D., Wallington, R.A. (2002), *Williams on Wills Volumes 1 and 2,* 8th edition. Butterworths, London.
Thurston, John (2007), *A Practitioner's Guide to Powers of Attorney,* 6th edition. Tottel Publishing, Haywards Heath.

Index

A& M *see* accumulation and maintenance trusts (A& M)
accessing offshore monies: non-UK domiciled perspective
   alienation of income and gains and asset purchase, 403–5
   background, 389–90
   categories of non-UK domiciled individual, 390–401
   cessation of source, 425–6
   condition C, 407
   condition D, 408
   conditions A/B, 405–6
   exempt property, 415–18
   gifts of assets precipitating foreign chargeable gains, 424–5
   mixed funds, 419–22
   offshore income gains, 418
   offshore mortgages, 426–8
   "relevant debt" and "UK services", 413–15
   remittances to UK, 401–3
   segregation of income and capital gains, 422–4
   temporary non-UK residents, 428–31
   transitional provisions (pre 6 April 2008 income/gains), 408–13
accumulation and maintenance trusts (A& M), 268
Act (1975), 474
Ademption, 471
Administration of Estates Act 1925, 480
after capital transfer tax, 453
agricultural property relief (APR), 221–2
   and death within seven years of a transfer, 222
   ownership requirements, 222
AIM *see* Alternative Investment Market (AIM)
alienation, 398, 403
alienation of income and gains and asset purchase, 403–5
   condition C, 404
   condition D, 404
   conditions A/B, 403–4
   extensions of "remittance to the UK" for conditions A/B, C and D, 404–5
Alternative Investment Market (AIM), 327
annual exemption, 200–1

anti-avoidance provisions, non-UK resident trusts, 296
   offshore income gains, 311–14
   settlor interested rules, capital gains tax, 301–11
   settlor interested rules, income tax, 297–301
APR *see* agricultural property relief (APR)
APT *see* asset protection trust (APT)
Arctic Systems case, 120
asset protection trust (APT), 443
asset purchase, 403, 406, 413
asset situs, capital gains tax
   bearer shares, 104
   debts, 105
   life policies, 109
   real estate, 104
   shares, 104
   tangible property, 104
   units of unit trusts, 109
asset situs, inheritance tax
   bank accounts, 102–3
   bearer shares, 102
   intangible property, 102
   life policies, 104
   nominees, 103
   ordinary debts, 102
   registered shares, 102
   speciality debt, 102
   unit trusts, 103
assets not requiring probate, 481–2
authorised investment funds, 339
authorised unit trusts (AUTs), 100, 236, 242, 339
AUTs *see* authorised unit trusts (AUTs)
averaging, computational rules (arrivals), 86

bank accounts, 102–3
"banking," indexation allowance/taper relief, 150–2
bare trusts, 483
bearer shares, 104
beneficial ownership, 111–13
beneficiaries, UK resident trusts, 276–9
   discretionary, 276–7
bottom line (choosing), company legislation, 444
   see also offshore financial centre (OFC)

BPR *see* business property relief (BPR)
breach of trust, 256, 445
business, 211
business asset, 136–8
business assets, gifts of assets (not
    inter-spouse), 142
business property relief (BPR), 211
    businesses not qualifying, 212–13
    death within seven years of transfer, 217–19
    inter-spouse transfers, 216–17
    order of transfers, 219–20
    ownership requirements, 214–17
    pro-rata BPR, 213–14
    relevant business property, 211–12
businesses not qualifying for BPR, 212–13
buy to let, 149

capacity to inherit, 474
"capital" account, 419–22
capital gains and segregation of income, 422–4
capital gains tax
    account, 420
    annual exemption, 17, 129, 280, 288, 289
    asset situs *see* asset situs, capital gains tax
    "banking" the indexation allowance/taper
        relief, 150–2
    basics, 126–7
    bearer shares, 104
    business assets, 136–8, 142
    capital losses, 152
    claim for, and amount of, relief, 164–5
    debts, 105
    effect of gift relief, 142–4
    entrepreneur relief, 162–3
    indexation allowance, 132–4
    inter-spouse transfers, 127–9
    leaving/arriving in UK, 167–8
    life policies, 109
    married couple and cohabitees, 349–51
    new 18% rate, abolition of indexation
        allowance and taper relief, 144–9
    non-resident recipient, 139
    non-spouse joint ownership, 118
    non-UK domiciled and UK resident individual
        capital loss utilisation, 154–62
    non-UK property, 348–9
    non-UK situs assets, 144
    offshore companies, 165–7
    overview, 348
    payment of tax, 130
    post FA 2008, 280–1
    pre FA 2008 reliefs, 131
    precipitation of immediate inheritance tax
        charge, 139–42
    profit motive, 351

    real estate, 104
    relevant business assets, 164
    settlor interested trusts post FA 2008, 286
    settlor interested trusts pre FA 2008, 286–7
    shares, 104
    spouse joint ownership, 118
    tangible property, 104
    taper relief, 134–5
    tax calculation, 129
    total v. partial capital gains tax exemption,
        349–51
    two or more residences of individual, 348
    UK domiciled and UK resident individual
        capital loss utilisation, 152–4
    units of unit trusts, 109
    year of death, 130–1
capital gains tax statute *see* principle private
    residence
capital losses, 152
    claim for, and amount of, relief, 164–5
    connected person capital losses, 154
    entrepreneur relief, 162–3
    non-UK domiciled and UK resident individual
        capital loss utilisation, 154–62
    relevant business assets, 164
    UK domiciled and UK resident individual
        capital loss utilisation, 152–4
capital payment, 304
capital v. income distinction, 5
    UK Taxation, 14–15
cash account, 328
cash gift, 362–3
categories of non-UK domiciled individual,
        390–401
    £30 000 charge, 395
    consequences of claim, 393–5
    nomination, 395–401
    where no claim is necessary, 401
categories of trusts, 257
cessation of source, 425–6
Channel Islands and Isle of Man, 238–9
chargeable event, 331
chargeable gains deferment possibilities (for EIS
    only), 338–9
chargeable lifetime transfer (CLT), 172–3,
    176–7, 179–82
charitable giving, 488
chattels, 483
choice, domicile of, 35
    age requirement, 38
    basic requirements, 38–51
    misleading nature of word "choice", 36–8
    special categories of individual and, 67–9
    UK domiciled individuals failing to acquire
        non-UK, 55–8

CLT *see* chargeable lifetime transfer (CLT)
codicil, 468
cohabitees, 488
collective/pooled investments, 339
"community property," concept of, 479
concession, 77
concession D2, 78
connected operation, 408
co-ownership, 228–9

death and sole or main residence, 359–60
death estate, 182, 249–51
    assets, 182–8
    clearance certificate, 251
    "D" forms, 251
    transferable NRB, 251
death planning, 364–5
    see also inheritance tax
death within seven years of transfer
    and BPR, 217–19
debts, 105
decree of judicial separation, effect on will, 469
deeds of variation, 490–4
    and discretionary will trusts, 490
"deemed" remittance, 389
dependence, domicile of, 30–5
    children and, 31–2
    married women and, 32–5
deposit-based investments, 323–4
devise, 470
discretionary beneficiaries, 276–7
    non-UK resident beneficiary, 277
    UK resident beneficiary, 276–7
discretionary trusts, 221, 261–5, 262–3
    exit charge before first 10-year charge, 262–3
    income tax, 293–5
    settled business property, 221
    ten-year charge, 263–5
discretionary v. interest in possession trust, 268–9
    post FA 2006, 269
    pre FA 2006, 268–9
discretionary will trusts, 495
disposal(s), 126, 127–8
"distributing" fund, 340
doctrine of ademption, 471
domicile, 21, 22, 23
    abandonment of domicile of choice, 65–7
    categories of, 25–51
    concept of private international law not taxation, 21–3
    deemed UK domicile, 69–73
    English/Welsh, Scottish or Northern Irish, 23–4
    factors considered change of domicile, 36
    importance of, 24–5
    non-UK domiciled individuals spending significant time in UK, 51–5
    and residence rulings, 95, 96–8
    special categories of individual and domicile of choice, 67–9
    tax return, 93–4
    UK domiciled individuals acquiring non-UK domiciles of choice, 58–65
    UK domiciled individuals failing to acquire non-UK domiciles of choice, 55–8
domiciled individual, 11–12
"donatio mortis causa", 468
double tax agreements, 450
    income and capital gains tax agreements, 450–2
    inheritance tax agreements, 452–3
double taxation, 449
"downsizing", 361
dual resident, 76

ECHR *see* European Convention of Human Rights and Freedoms (ECHR)
EISs *see* enterprise investment schemes (EISs)
employees owning shares in employer company, 149
employment income, 385
enterprise investment schemes (EISs), 336–9
    capital gains tax relief, 337
    income tax relief, 337
entrepreneur relief, 162–3
    disposal of whole or part of a business, 162–3
    disposal qualifying as "associated" disposal, 163
equitable interests, 113–14
equity, trust, 257
ESC A11, 77
ESC D2, 77
estate tax, 4
EU resident individuals, 457
EU savings directive, 456–63
    implications of savings directive, 460–2
    information exchange, 457–8
    non-member states and TIEAs, 459
    savings directive and directive 77/799/EEC, 460
    savings income, 457
    Switzerland and USA, 459
    withholding tax v. information supply, 458
European Convention of Human Rights and Freedoms (ECHR), 456
European union/community, 456
excepted asset, 211, 213
excepted estates, 481
"excluded income", 386

excluded income treatment, 294, 386
  see also UK source income, types of
excluded property, inheritance tax, 233
  AUT and OEIC, 236
  authorised unit trusts and OEICs, 242
  Channel Islands and the Isle of Man, 238–9
  excluded property and non-UK domiciled, 233–5
  "excluded property trusts" and FA 2006, 244–5
  foreign currency UK bank accounts, 238, 242
  and gifts with reservation, 243–4
  mixing UK situs and non-UK situs property in trust, 242–3
  non-settled property, 233
  non-UK situs property, 235–6
  settled property, 233, 239–41
  UK government securities and gilts, 242
  UK government securities or gilts, 236–7
  UK situs assets, 236
  UK situs trust assets, 241–2
excluded property and non-UK domiciled, 233–5
excluded property trusts, 234, 245
  and FA 2006, 244–5
exempt property, 415–18
  clothing and "Personal Use Rule", 415–16
  exempt to non-exempt property, 417–18
  property and public access, 417
  property below £1000, 415–16
  repair rule, 417
  temporary importation rule, 416
"exempt property", 406
  concept of, 390
exempt transfers, 199–200
  death only, 203
  lifetime only, 200–3
  lifetime or on death exemptions, 203–9

FA 2008, 125, 126, 140, 152
  "banking" the indexation allowance/taper relief, 150–2
  new 18% rate; abolition of indexation allowance and taper relief, 144–9
FA 2008 impact, 273–4
  capital gains tax, 274, 292–3
  income tax, 274, 292
  on non-UK resident trusts, capital gains tax, 292–3
FA 2008 provisions catch, 402
FICO see Financial Intermediaries and Claims Office (FICO)
Financial Intermediaries and Claims Office (FICO), 385
financing acquisition, Non-UK domiciliaries and UK homes, 370
fixed intentioned short-term visitors, 85

fixed interest securities, 325
  "gilts", 325
forced heirship, 479
  see also offshore financial centre (OFC)
  issues, choosing, 443
foreign aspects, wills
  "capacity", 475, 477
  construction, 477–8
  English domiciled person, 475
  "forced heirship", 475
  formal validity, 477
  material validity, 477
  revocation, 478
  succession, 476
Foreign chargeable gains, 398, 401
Foreign specific employment income, 398
Form IHT 200 "Inheritance Tax Account", 481
Form IHT 205 "Return of Estate Information", 281
free estate, 182
freely chosen, 67

"gift recipient", 407
gifts, 172, 470
  of assets precipitating foreign chargeable gains, 424–5
  classification, under a will, 471
  in contemplation of marriage, 202–3
  failure of gift, reasons, 470–1
  for family maintenance, 203
  general, 470
  plus rent payable, 363
  reasons for failure, 470–1
  relief, 139
  with reservation, 183, 243–4
gifts of assets (not inter-spouse), 138–9, 138–44
  business assets, 142
  effect of gift relief, 142–4
  non-resident recipient, 139
  non-UK situs assets, 144
  precipitation of immediate inheritance tax charge, 139–42
gifts with reservation (GWR), 225–31
"grandfathering", 403, 426
grossing up, 174
GWR see gifts with reservation (GWR)
GWR, inheritance tax, 225–31, 228
  co-ownership, 228–9
  full consideration, 228
  inter-spouse gifts, 228
  pre-owned assets, 229–31
  trusts, 229

Hearsay, 46
Her Majesty's Revenue and Customs (HMRC), 13–14
higher rate taxpayer, business/non business asset
　indexation allowance and taper relief, 146–7, 148–9
　no indexation allowance but taper relief, 146, 147–8
HMRC see Her Majesty's Revenue and Customs (HMRC)
"hold-over relief", 359
holograph, 467
human rights, 462–3
Human Rights Act 1998, 456
hypothetical transfer, 262–3

IBC see international business company (IBC)
IHT return, 95
immediate inheritance tax charge, 139–42
immediate post death interest (IPDI), 141, 244, 261, 265, 266–7, 266–7, 365, 472, 487
immovable or movable asset, 476
income and capital gains tax, 5
　agreements, 450–2
　citizenship test, 6–7
　residency, 6
　source basis, 7–8
　tax returns, 19
　territorial basis, 6
　timing of tax payments, 20
　worldwide basis, 6
"income gain", 418
income or gains (other than RFI) arising pre 6 April 2008, 408–9
income source, 99
　AUT, 100
　dividends, 100
　interest, 101
　mutual (offshore) funds, 101
　rental income, 99–100
　UAUTS, 100–1
income tax, 15–17, 77–8, 80–1, 116–17
　general rules, 383–4
　non-spouse joint ownership, 117
　spouse joint ownership, 116–17
income tax, anti-avoidance provisions, 281–5
　bare trusts for unmarried minors, 285
　capital payments to the settlor, 285
　discretionary trust, 283–4
　income of trust paid to or for benefit of unmarried minor, 284–5
　settlor interested trusts, 282–3
income tax, non-UK resident trusts, 293–5
　discretionary trusts, 293–4
　possession trusts, interest in, 294–5

income/capital gains tax treatment of individuals/trusts, differences, 275
index factor, 132
indexation allowance, 132–4
indexed gain, 132
"individual", 348
individual ownership, 367–8
individual savings accounts (ISAS), 327–9
　post FA 2008/Self-select ISAs, 328
　pre April 2008/Maxi/Mini ISA, 329
information exchange, 457–8
inheritance, 474
Inheritance (Provision for Family and Dependants) Act 1975, 22, 54, 60, 474, 543
inheritance tax, 4, 8–9, 115, 169–70, 199, 360–6, 384
　agreements, 452–3
　agricultural property relief (APR), 221–2
　annual exemption, 200, 202
　APR and death within seven years of a transfer, 222
　bank accounts, 102–3
　bearer shares, 102
　BPR see business property relief (BPR)
　CLTs and PETs, 179
　CLTs only, 177–9
　death estate, assets, 182–8
　death planning, 364–5
　discretionary trusts, 221
　exempt transfers, 199–200
　intangible property, 102
　inter-spouse exemption, 115, 269, 493
　life policies, 104
　lifetime, 177
　lifetime gifts, CLT, 172–3
　lifetime planning, 361–4
　nominees, 103
　NRB, see nil rate band discretionary trust
　ordinary debts, 102
　payment and bearing of inheritance tax on death, 182–96
　persons responsible for payment of CLTs, 179–82
　persons responsible for payment of PETs, 182
　PET, 173
　planning considerations, 197
　post/pre 22 March 2006 created interest in possession trust, 220–1
　quantum of transfer of value, 173–5
　quick succession relief, 222–3
　rates of, 171
　rates of tax (2008/09), 18
　registered shares, 102
　reliefs, 210–11
　settled business property, 220

inheritance tax (*Continued*)
  speciality debt, 102
  taper relief, CLT, 176–7
  taper relief PET, 175–6
  tax returns, 19
  territorial, deemed UK domicile, 170–1
  territorial, domicile, 170
  timing of tax payments, 20
  trailing tax imposition, 9
  trusts, 221
  unit trusts, 103
  variation *see* post death issues, deeds of variation
  will planning, 486
inheritance tax, asset situs *see* asset situs, inheritance tax
inheritance tax: trusts, 261
  accumulation and maintenance trusts (A& M), 265–8
  background, 261
  discretionary trusts, 261–5
  discretionary v. interest in possession trust, 268–9
  "excluded property" trusts and domicile, 270
  interest in possession trusts, 265–8
"Inheritance Tax Account" (Form IHT 200), 481
inheritance tax administration, 247
  clearance certificate, 251
  "D" forms, 251
  death estate, 249–51
  death estate, clearance certificate, 251
  death estate, transferable NRB, 251
  lifetime transfers, 247
  obtaining information, 252
inheritance tax administration, penalties, 252
  non-UK resident trusts, 252
"*instruments* of variation", 490
interest in possession trusts, 265–8
  post FA 2006, 265–6
  pre FA 2006, 265
  transitional interest, TSI, 265
international business company (IBC), 438
international taxation
  double tax agreements, 450
  double taxation, 449
  EU savings directive, 453–63
  European union/community, 456
  post 1975 agreements, 454–6
  pre 1975 agreements, 453–4
international will, 468
Interpretation Act 1978, 23
inter-spouse gifts, 228
inter-spouse transfers, 127–9, 203–4, 203–9, 356–7
  NRB, 204–9

intestacy, 470, 496
investments
  background, 323
  collective investments, 339
  deposit-based investments, 323–4
  fixed interest securities, 325
  individual savings accounts (ISAS), 327–9
  limited liability partnerships (LLPS), 344
  limited partnerships, 343–4
  money market accounts, 324
  offshore funds, 339–42
  packaged/insurance investments, 329–36
  real estate investment trusts (REITS), 344
  self-invested personal pensions (SIPPS), 344
  shares (including aim shares)/options, 325–7
  structured products, 342–3
  venture capital trusts (VCTs) and enterprise investment schemes (EISs), 336–9
IPDI *see* immediate post death interest (IPDI)
ISAS *see* individual savings accounts (ISAS)
ISAs, key attributes of, 327–8

joint ownership arrangements, 361–2
joint tenancy
  beneficial ownership, 111–13
  capital gains tax, 118
  income tax, 116–17
  inheritance tax, 115
  land, equitable interests/legal title, 111–14
  non-UK domiciled individual, 118–19
  spouses, 119–20
  tax issues, 114–15
  tenancy in common, 113, 114
joint tenants, 111, 112
joint will, 468
jointly held assets, 482

lack of definitions and IR20, 75–6
land
  equitable interests, 113–14
  legal title, 113
Law of Property Act 1925, 472
leaving/arriving in UK, 167–8
legacy, 470
legal capacity to make will, 468
"legal reserve", 479
legal title, 113
"letter of wishes", 495
lettings relief, 357–8
life policies, 109, 482
lifetime gifts
  chargeable lifetime transfer (CLT), 172–3
  potentially exempt transfer (PET), 173
  quantum of transfer of value, 173–5
lifetime or on death exemptions, 203–9

lifetime planning
  see also inheritance tax
  cash gift, 362–3
  comments, 364
  gift plus rent payable, 363
  joint ownership arrangements, 361–2
  sale, 363
lifetime transfers, 247
  CLT, 247
  excepted settlements, 248–9
  excepted transfers, 248
  PET, 247
limited liability partnerships (LLPS), 344
limited partnerships, 343–4
  private equity funds, 343
  property funds, 344
LLPS see limited liability partnerships (LLPS)
long-term visitors, 86–7

main residence or home, 347–66
  capital gains tax, 348–51
  death and sole or main residence, 359–60
  deemed periods of residence, 351–2
  inheritance tax, 360–6
  inter-spouse transfers, 356–7
  lettings relief, 357–8
  married couples, 355–6
  more than one residence, 352–5
  residence, 351
  trusts and sole or main residence, 358–9
marriage and will, 469
married couples, 355–6
  charitable giving, 488
  cohabitees, 488
  foreign aspects, 489–90
  single persons, 488
"matrimonial domicile", 479
matrimonial home
  house plus chattels, purchase of, 375
  no consideration, 375–6
Maxi ISA, 329
mental incapacity, 474
mixed funds, 397, 419–22
  arising basis and remittance basis mixed income, 420
  income and capital gains taxable on remittance, 420
  tax-free capital and remittance of taxable income, 420
  tax-free capital and taxable chargeable gains, 420–2
mixing UK situs and non-UK situs property in trust, 242–3
money market accounts, 324

nil rate band discretionary trust, 197, 207, 264, 486, 487–488
"nominated amount", 390, 424
"non-distributor", 418
non-domiciled individual, 12
non-qualifying offshore fund, 340
non-resident recipient, gifts of assets (not inter-spouse), 139
non-settled property, 233
non-spouse joint ownership, 118
non-trading company, 136
non-UK domiciled and UK resident individual capital loss utilisation, 154–62
non-UK domiciled individual, 118–19
non-UK domiciled individual, categories of, 390–401
Non-UK domiciliaries and UK homes, 367–71
  background, 367
  financing acquisition, 370
  ownership, 367–70
  preliminary conclusions, 370–1
non-UK registered company, ownership, 369–70
non-UK resident taxation
  background, 383
  general rules, 383–4
  points to note, 387
  relevance to persons, 383
non-UK resident trust, ownership, 368–9
non-UK resident trusts, income and capital gains taxation
  anti-avoidance provisions, 296–314
  background, 291
  beneficiaries of non-UK resident discretionary trust, 295–6
  FA 2008 impact, 291–3
  income tax, 293–5
  non-UK resident trusts for non-UK domiciled but UK resident individuals, 314–16
  non-UK resident trusts for UK domiciled and UK resident individuals, 316–19
non-UK resident trusts for UK domiciled and UK resident individuals, 316–19
  capital gains tax, 318–19
  income tax, 316–18
  inheritance tax, 319
non-UK situs assets, gifts of assets (not inter-spouse), 144
non-UK situs property, 235–6
  minimum length of time to hold assets, 236
normal expenditure out of income, 201–2
"notional amount", 415

ODF see offshore disclosure facility (ODF)
"OECD Estate, Inheritance and Gift Model Convention", 454

"OECD Model Tax Convention on Income and Capital", 450
OEIC *see* open ended investment companies (OEIC)
OFC *see* offshore financial centre (OFC)
OFC relocation
 "trailing taxes", 447
offshore companies, 165–7
offshore dimension
 see also offshore financial centre
 choosing centre, 443–5
 financial centre, 434–8
 financial centre uses, 442–3
 financial centre vehicles, 438–41
 relocation, 447–8
 tax exposure of trust settlor, 446–7
 UK tax and information disclosure requirements, 445–6
offshore disclosure facility (ODF), 435
offshore financial centre, 434
 companies, 438–9
 trusts, 439–41
 vehicles, 438–41
offshore financial centre (OFC), 433, 434–8
 asset protection, 443
 choosing, 443–5
 choosing bottom line, company legislation, 444
 choosing "forced heirship" issues, 443
 "Harmful Tax Competition: An Emerging Global Issue", 436
 "Harmful tax practices", 436
 offshore disclosure facility (ODF), 435
 probate mitigation/will substitute, 442–3
 relocation to OFC, 447–8
 "Review of Financial Regulation in the Crown Dependencies", 436
 Tax Co-operation Towards a Level Playing Field – 2007 Assessment, 437
 "tax haven", 434
 Tax Information Exchange Agreements (TIEAs), 437
 tax planning, 442
 "uncooperative", tax havens, 437
Offshore fund investment, 342
offshore funds, 339–42
 Irish offshore funds, 342
 tax treatment, 340–2
offshore income gains, 418
offshore issued life policies, 336
offshore mortgages, 426–8
 grandfathering provisions, 427–8
 loans secured on property: capital gains tax/IHT impact, 428

offshore transfers, 421
open ended investment companies (OEIC), 236, 339
order of transfers and BPR, 219–20
"ordinary residence", 75
origin, domicile of, 26–30
 adoption, 29–30
 father dead at date of birth, 27
 legitimate v. illegitimate child, 26–7
 legitimation, 27–8
 loss of, 28
 parents married but separated, 27
 resurrection of, 28–9
ownership
 individual, 367–8
 non-UK registered company, 369–70
 non-UK resident trust, 368–9
ownership requirements for BPR, 214–17

packaged/insurance investments, 329–36
 single premium bonds, 330–6
 term and whole of life assurance policies, 329–30
 whole of life assurance, 330
"partial surrenders", 334, 335
payment and bearing of inheritance tax on death, 182–96
payment of tax, 130
pecuniary gift, 470
pension death benefits, 482
personal company, 142
"personal use rule", 415
persons responsible for payment of inheritance tax, 179
 CLTs, 179–82
 PETs, 182
PET *see* potentially exempt transfer (PET)
"portio legitima", 479
possession beneficiaries, interest in, 278–9
 non-UK resident beneficiary, 279
 UK resident beneficiary, 278–9
post 1975 agreements, 454–6
post death issues
 capital gains tax, 494, 495
 deeds of variation, 490–4
 deeds of variation and discretionary will trusts, 490
 discretionary will trusts, 495
post FA 2008, 129, 166–7, 328
 see also FA 2008
potentially exempt transfer (PET), 173, 179
pre 1975 agreements, 453–4
pre FA 2008, 128, 129, 131, 144, 166
 see also FA 2008
 business asset, 136–8

indexation allowance, 132–4
   taper relief, 134–5
principle private residence, 348
probate, 479
   assets not requiring probate, 481–2
   bare trusts, 483
   chattels, 483
   excepted estates, 481
   Form IHT 205, 481
   "Inheritance Tax Account", 481
   jointly held assets, 482
   life policies, 482
   pension death benefits, 482
   small payments, 483
property income, 385
pro-rata BPR, 213–14
"public access rule", 415

QSR *see* quick succession relief (QSR)
qualifying company, 136, 338
qualifying disposition, 408
qualifying property, 407
"qualifying shares", 338
quantum of transfer of value, 173–5
quick succession relief (QSR), 222–3

rates of tax (2008/09), UK Taxation, 15–18
   capital gains tax, 17–18
   income tax, 15–17
   inheritance tax, 18
real estate, 104
real estate investment trusts (REITS), 344
REITS *see* real estate investment trusts (REITS)
relevant business assets, 164
relevant business property, 211
   and BPR, 211–12
relevant debt, 414
   and "UK services", 413–15
relevant foreign earnings, 398, 400
relevant foreign income, 341
relevant person, 335, 401–2, 404
relevant property regime, 261
reliefs, inheritance tax, 210–11
remittance, 389
   basis charge, 390
remittances to UK, 401–3
repair rule, 415
"reporting" fund, 340
"reserved share", 479
residence, 75, 351
   deemed periods of, 351–2
   more than one *see* residence, more than one
   only or main, 348

residence, more than one
   electing main residence, 353–4
   planning and election, 354–5
residence and ordinary residence
   background, 75
   dual residence, 76
   lack of definitions and IR20, 75–6
   residence rules and IR20, 81–90
   split tax years, 76–9
   temporary non-UK residence, 79–81
residence rules and IR20, 81–90
   arriving and departing UK, 82–7
   183-day rule, 81–2
   departing from UK, 88–90
   long-term visitors, 83, 86
   short absences, 81
   short-term visitors, 83–6
   three-year rule/permanent rule, 83, 86
   working abroad, 87
residential property, 427
"Residents and non-residents, Liability to tax in UK", 75
residuary gift, 470
"retention", 324
retention tax, 324
"Return of Estate Information" (Form IHT 205), 481
reversionary interest, 234
"RFI" account, 420
RFI arising pre 6 April 2008, 409–13
   general transitional rule, 412–13
   Pre 6 April 2008 Condition, 410–12
   Pre 12 March 2008 Condition, 410
   some observations, 412–13
rolled over, 142
rules, non-UK resident taxation
   capital gains tax, 382, 384
   income tax, 383–4
   inheritance tax, 384

savings directive
   and directive 77/799/EEC, 460
   implications, 460–3
savings income, 457
   interest and dividends, 385–6
"second homes", 359
segregation of income and capital gains, 422–4
self-invested personal pensions (SIPPS), 344
Self-select ISAs, 328
separation/divorce and will, 469
settled business property, 220
   discretionary trusts, 221
   post 22 March 2006 created interest in possession trust, 220–1

settled property, 233, 239–41
　authorised unit trusts and OEICs, 242
　foreign currency UK bank accounts, 242
　UK government securities and gilts, 242
　UK situs trust assets, 241–2
"settlor interested", 359
settlor interested trusts, capital gains tax
　post FA 2008, 286
　pre FA 2008, 286–7
seven-year cumulation period
　CLTs and PETs, 179
　CLTs only, 177–9
　lifetime, 177
share sales, 136
shares, 104
shares (including aim shares)/options, 325–7
　Alternative Investment Market (AIM) shares, 327
　ordinary shares, 325–6
　zero coupon preference shares, 327
short-term visitors, 83
single persons, 488
single premium bonds, 330–6
SIPPS *see* self-invested personal pensions (SIPPS)
situs of asset, 476
"sliced gain", 332
small payments, 483
sole trader, 149
specific gift, 470
split tax years, 76–9
　capital gains tax, 78–9
　concession, 77
　concession D2, 78
　ESC A11, 77
　ESC D2, 77
　income tax, 77–8
spouse joint ownership, 118
spouses, 119–20, 283
stamp duty land tax (SDLT), 365, 373
stamp duty/stamp duty land tax, 373
　background, 373
　death, instruments of variation, 378
　life policies, 378
　linked transactions, 376
　matrimonial breakdown, 376
　matrimonial home, 374–6
　stamp duty/stamp duty reserve tax, 373–4
"stocks and shares account", 328
structured products, 342–3
substitutional gift in will, 470–1
"superfluous attestation", 474
survivorship clause, 471–3
Switzerland and USA, 459

tangible property, 104
taper relief, 136
　CLT, 176–7
　PET, 175–6
tax "avoidance", 433
tax calculation, 129
　annual exemption, 129
tax efficient "wrapper", 331
tax "evasion", 433
tax exposure of trust settlor, 446–7
tax haven, 434
Tax Information Exchange Agreements (TIEAs), 437
tax issues, general
　capital gains tax, 483
　"estate equalisation", 484–5
　income tax, 484
　inheritance tax planning, 484–7
tax of estate duty, 453
tax returns, 19, 91–2
　claim for remittance basis to apply, 94
　domicile, 93–4
　income and capital gains tax, 19
　inheritance tax, 19
tax systems and bases of taxation, 3–4
　capital v. income distinction, 5
　categories of tax, 4
　worldwide v. territorial tax systems, 5–9
tax treatment
　distributor/reporting status offshore fund, 340
　Irish offshore funds, 342
　non-distributor status offshore fund, 340–2
"tax wrapper", 329
"tax-free roll-up", 340
temporary non-UK residence
　capital gains tax, 79–80
　income tax, 80–1
temporary non-UK residents, 428–31
　capital gains tax, 430–1
　income tax, 428–30
term and whole of life assurance policies, 329
term assurance, 329–30
territorial, inheritance tax
　deemed UK domicile, 170–1
　inheritance tax, domicile, 170
testator a survivorship period, 472
TIEAs *see* Tax Information Exchange Agreements (TIEAs)
TIEAs and non-member states, 459
"tie-breaker" tests, 452
top-slicing relief, 332
total intestacy, 496
trading company, 136, 163
trading income, 385
trailing tax, 9

"transferable nil rate band", 364
transitional interest (TSI), 265, 267–8, 267–8
transitional provisions (pre 6 April 2008 income/gains)
 income or gains (other than RFI) arising pre 6 April 2008, 408–9
 RFI arising pre 6 April 2008, 409–13
"treaty shopping", 451
trust income, 279
trusts
 background, 255
 breach of trust, 256, 445
 categories, 257
 classification, 258–9
 definition, 255
 equity, 257
 uses, 257–8
trusts, stamp duty/stamp duty land tax, 377–8
 appointments, 377
 bare trusts, 378
 interest of beneficiaries, 377
 non-UK resident trusts, 377–8
trusts and sole or main residence
 "second homes", 359

UAUTS *see* unauthorised unit trusts (UAUTS)
UCITS *see* undertakings for collective investment in transferable securities (UCITS)
"UK domicile," 24
UK domicile, deemed, 69–73, 170–1
 17 out of 20 tax year rule, 70
 15 tax years plus two-day trap, 70–1
 dealing with deemed UK domicile status, 71–3
 three-year rule, 69–70
UK domiciled and UK resident individual capital loss utilisation, 152–4
 connected person capital losses, 154
UK "forced heirship", 474–5
UK government securities
 and gilts, 242
 or gilts, 236–7
UK inheritance tax, 454
UK resident trust for non-UK domiciled but UK resident individuals, 287–8
 capital gains tax, 288
 income tax, 287–8
 inheritance tax, 288
UK resident trust for UK domiciled and UK resident individuals, 288–9
 capital gains tax, 289
 income tax, 288–9
 inheritance tax, 289
UK resident trusts, income/capital gains taxation, 271

 anti-avoidance provisions, 281
 background, 271
 beneficiaries, 276–9
 capital gains tax, 280–1, 286–7
 capital v. income, 279–80
 FA 2008 impact, 273–4
 income tax, 274–6, 281–5, 288–9
 UK resident trust for non-UK domiciled but UK resident individuals, 287–8
 UK resident trust for UK domiciled and UK resident individuals, 288–9
 UK resident v. non-UK resident trusts, 272–3
UK resident v. non-UK resident trusts, 272
 post 5 April 2007, 272–3
 pre 6 April 2007, 272
UK situs assets, 236
 AUT and OEIC, 236
 foreign currency UK bank accounts, 238
 UK government securities or gilts, 236–7
UK source income, types of, 384–6
 employment income, 385
 property income, 385
 savings income, interest and dividends, 385–6
 trading income, 385
UK tax and information disclosure requirements, 445–6
UK taxation
 allowances, 18–19
 capital v. income distinction, 14–15
 domicile, residence and ordinary residence, 11–13
 persons other than individuals, 13
 rates of tax (2008/09), 15–18
 tax returns, 19
 timing of tax payments, 20
UK taxes and law, 13
 and HMRC, 13–14
unauthorised unit trusts (UAUTS), 100–1
uncertainty principle, 471
unclear intentioned short term visitors, 83–5
undertakings for collective investment in transferable securities (UCITS), 457
units of unit trusts, 109
USA and Switzerland, 459
uses of trusts, 257–8
utilisable capital losses, 157–8

variations, *see* deeds of variation and post death issues
VCTs *see* venture capital trusts (VCTs)
VCTs and EISs, 336–9
 chargeable gains deferment possibilities (EIS only), 338–9

VCTs and EISs (*Continued*)
  enterprise investment schemes (EISs), 336–9
  venture capital trust, 336–9
venture capital trusts (VCTs), 336–9
  capital gains tax relief, 338
  income tax relief, 338

wills
  background, 467
  capacity to inherit, 474
  defined by Trustee Act 2000, 467
  foreign aspects, 475–8
  general tax issues, 483–7
  intestacy, 470, 496
  marriage, 469
  married couples, 487–90
  miscellaneous matters, 479
  post death issues, 490–6
  probate, 480–3
  requirements for valid will, 467–8
  revocation, 469
  separation/divorce, 469
  some points to note, 496–7
  survivorship clause, 471–3
  types of gift, 470–1
  types of will, 468–9
  UK "forced heirship", 474–5
  witnessing the will, 474
withholding tax v. information supply, 458
witnessing the will, 474
worldwide v. territorial tax systems
  income and capital gains taxes, 5–8
  inheritance tax, 8–9

year of death, 130–1

zero coupon, 327

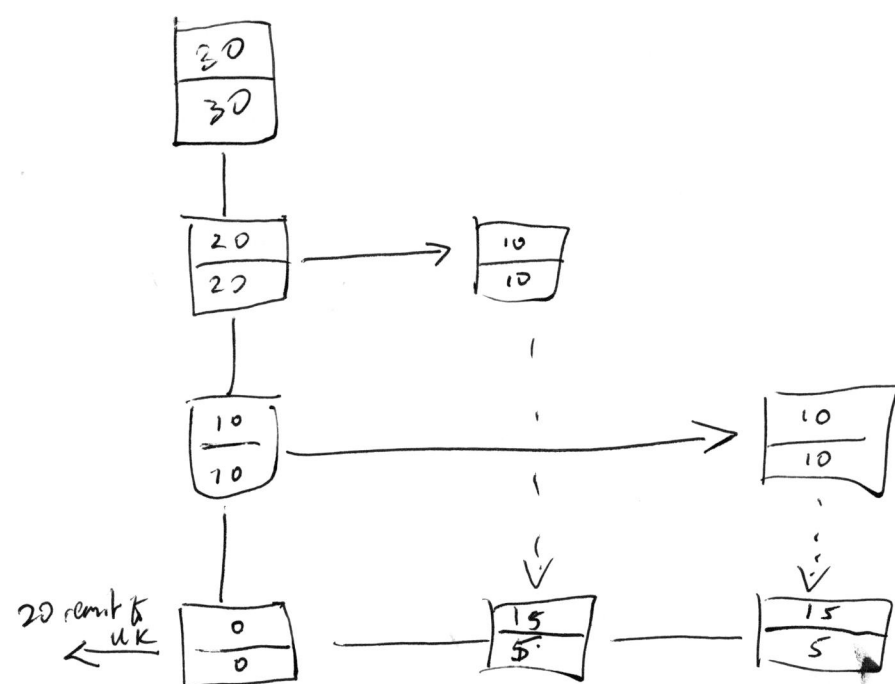

20 remit to
uk

Taxable Event Diagram

Capital Loss Pool
- F/Y 08/9
- F/Y 09/10
- F/Y 10/11

Taxable Event → Capital Loss Pool: *Increase or no change*

Taxable Event → Offshore Asset 1 (Sold): *Decrease Holding*

Taxable Event → Offshore Asset 2 (Bought): *Increase Holding*

Offshore Asset 1 → Offshore Asset 2: *Transfer between Components change. Depends if remitted within tax year*

Components can change value

Components — each component is broken down by tax year

1. UK emp Income
2. Foreign Earnings
3. " Emp Income
4. RFI
5. For Ch Gains
6. ① subj to For Tax
7. ② subj " " "
8. ⑤ " " " "
9. Clean Capital

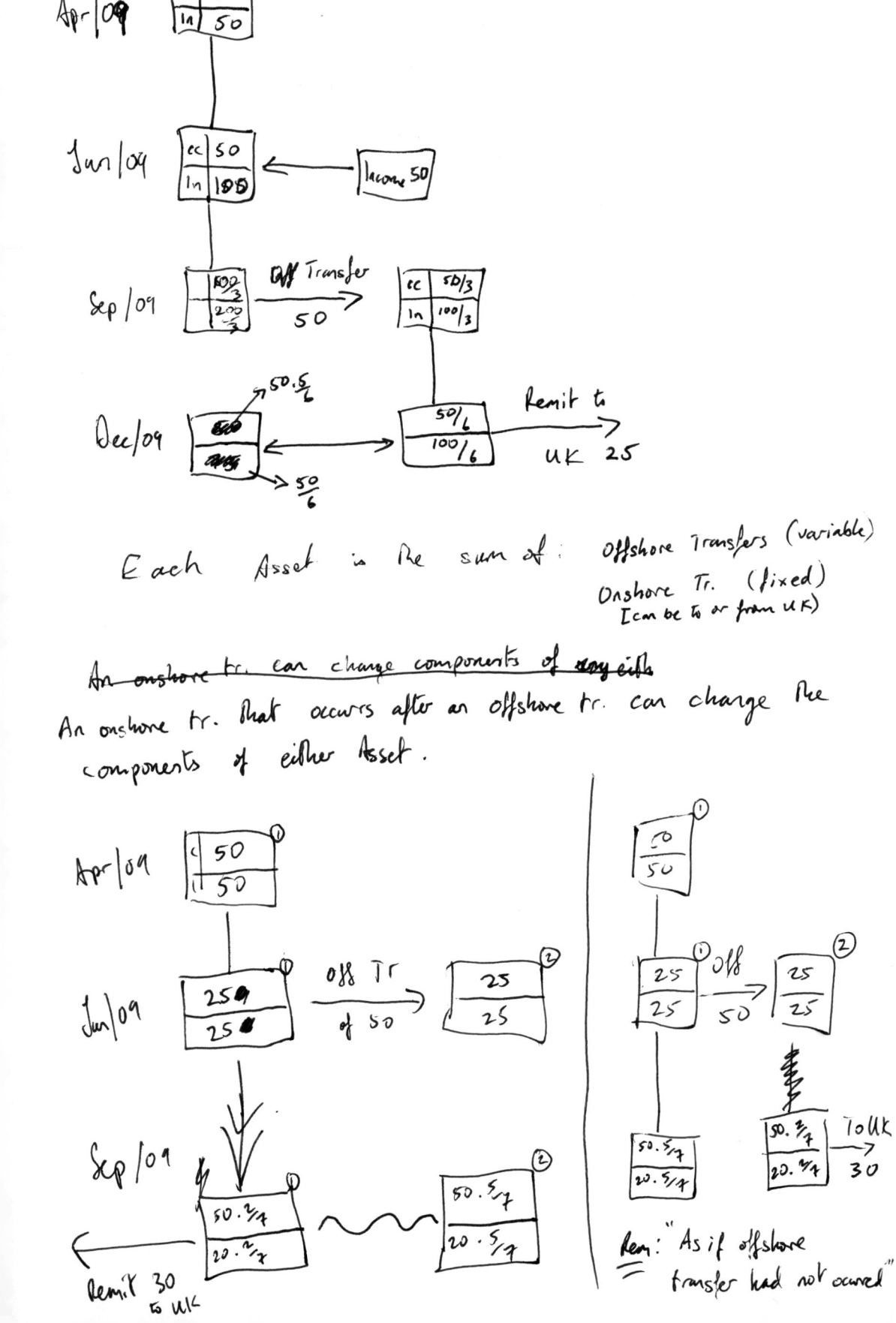

Do I have a fixed intention of establishing a permanent residence in the UK

(non - UK Domicile)

Against | For

Against
- M Sq house purchased as family home
- Will prepared by UK lawyers under UK law
- Living in UK since '00
- Remained in UK after last job
- Main Bank a/c by Barclays
- Member of golf clubs
- No home outside UK
- Apparently happy in UK

For
- Bank a/c in Ireland, UK
- Family in Ireland
- Irish passport: will never give up
- Told parents no intention of returning to Ireland
- ~~Remained in UK after last job~~
- No UK passport applied for or acquired
- Selina dislikes Ireland - damp & cold so can't live there

To Do

- ? Where buried
- Give a specific contingency that would result in leaving the UK
- ? Vote in Ireland elections ?
- Read Irish newspapers ?
- Buy flat in Ireland
- email Clo w/ dates
- Settle offshore assets before 17/20 rule ?
- Get P86 & DOM1 copies
- Get offshore a/c for Selina
- Check salient pts w/ lawyers